60th VOLUME

1992-1993

Higley Commentary

International Uniform Sunday School Series

Editor
Wesley C. Reagan

Y0-BGT-940

Writers
Gordon Talbot, PhD
Ronald O. Durham, PhD
Rod Kennedy, PhD
Harold Straughn
Bill Love, PhD

Illustrator
Leslie W. Smith

THE HIGLEY DIFFERENCE

TOP MANUFACTURED QUALITY:
High rated paper opacity eliminates "see through"
Durable stitched binding: "Perfect Bound"
Long lasting water-proof Kivar cover
Genuine embossed Gold lettering
Easy focus bold type highlights

FEATURES:
Lesson Introduction
Teacher's Target Objective
Teacher's Outline
Daily Bible Readings
Verse by Verse exposition
The Evangelistic Emphasis
Memory Selection
Daily Applications
Superintendent's Sermonette
Seed Thoughts (Questions & Answers)

THE MOST AFFORDABLE COMPREHENSIVE SUNDAY SCHOOL COMMENTARY AVAILABLE..

Higley Publishing Corporation
Post Office Box 5398
Jacksonville, FL 32247-5398

FORWARD

Most who teach or otherwise participate in a regular Sunday School Class have neither the resources nor the time to explore dozens of references on the text of the day. It is the intent of the Higley Commentary to bring you the most usable of those resources in a fraction of the time.

Without exception, our writers are devout believers in the Scriptures. With reverence they have studied the texts. They have sifted out the most reliable, insightful, and helpful material. Their writing skills have put this rich resource into a form that can be quickly accessed by busy Sunday School teachers and students.

The result of this effort is a single volume, modest in price, which provides a highly distilled treasure of Biblical knowledge on every text that will be studied for a year.

When the year of study is completed, this volume will occupy a proud place in your own library providing you resource material for years to come.

Welcome to the family of those who have discovered The Higley Commentary. It has been a growing group now for sixty years.

♦♦♦♦♦♦

Lessons and/or Readings based on International Sunday School Lessons. The International Bible Lessons for Christian Training, copyright © 1989 by the Committee on the Uniform Series.

Copyright © 1992
Higley Publishing Corporation
ISBN 0-9614116-3-5 (Kivar)
ISBN 0-9614116-4-3 (Hardcover)
ISBN 0-9614116-5-1 (Adult Bible class)

PREFACE - Higley Commentary...

From the time the apostle Paul charged Timothy to entrust what he had been taught to reliable men who would also be qualified to teach others (II Timothy 2:2) men and women have heard that charge and responded to it.

This book is intended to equip those who would lead adult Sunday School classes, and to provide a rich resource of basic material for their study. It offers more than "Pablum," or milk for the immature. There is the taste, even the feast of strong meat contained in this volume.

Writers of this commentary have no hidden agenda. Here you will find scholarship with honesty and openness. As basic a tool as a crescent wrench, this volume presents material that is both adjustable and versatile. It leaves room for personal input by the teacher, drawing from personal experiences and values.

What an encouragement this book of rich resources will be to teachers of adult classes. In my own four decades of Bible class teaching, adequate study preparation and effective presentation have always been dependent on the special aids available. Teachers using this commentary will find that it meets that criterion in a very fine way, as it is both interesting and helpful.

Sunday school is a powerful force for good in this age, and teachers of adults are on the cutting edge. If you have a passion to become more effective as a class leader, this book will be your friend.

> Dale Graham,
> Teacher of Adults for
> more than Forty Years

FALL QUARTER

God Chooses and Relates to a People (Lessons 1-4)
The People Choose a Monarchy (Lessons 5-8)
The Prophets' Roles in a Divided Kingdom (Lessons 9-13)

September 6	God's Call and Promise to Abram Genesis 11:31—12:9	1
September 13	God's Call to Moses Exodus 3:1-7, 10-14	11
September 20	God's Choice of Joshua to Succeed Moses Joshua 1:1-11	21
September 27	God's Provision of Leadership Through Deborah Judges 4:4-10, 14-16	31
October 4	Samuel, the Last Judge I Samuel 7:15—8:9, 19-22	41
October 11	David: King Over All the People I Samuel 16:1, 6, 7, 11-13; II Samuel 5:1-5	51
October 18	Solomon: Wise King I Kings 2:1-4; 3:5-12	61
October 25	Josiah: King of Reforms II Chronicles 34:2, 8, 14b-16a, 19, 21, 30-32	71
November 1	Elijah: Prophet of Courage I Kings 18:17-18, 20-24, 36-39	81
November 8	Amos: Prophet of Justice Amos 2:6-12; 3:2	91
November 15	Hosea: Prophet of God's Love Hosea 3:1-5	101
November 22	Micah: Prophet of Righteousness Micah 6:1-8	111
November 29	Jeremiah: Persistent Prophet Jeremiah 1:9-10; 20:7-11	121

WINTER QUARTER
Coming of the Good News (Lessons 1-4)
Living the Good News (Lesson 5-9)
Sharing the Good News (Lesson 10-13)

December 6	God's Purpose Through Love Hebrews 1:1-4; Ephesians 1:3-14	131
December 13	God's Promise to Zechariah Luke 1:5-17	141
December 20	God's Promise to the Gentiles Luke 2:1-7, 22-32	151
December 27	Jesus Filled with the Spirit Matthew 3:16—4:11	161
January 3	The Coming of the Holy Spirit Acts 2:1-7, 12-17a	171
January 10	A Call to Holy Living I Peter 1:13-25	181
January 17	The Church is for All People Acts 11:1-18	191
January 24	Learning God's Wisdom I Corinthians 1:18-31	201
January 31	One Body in Christ Ephesians 4:1-16	211
February 7	Commissioned to Witness Luke 24:36-53	221
February 14	Proclaim the Gospel Romans 10:5-17	231
February 21	Serve and Honor Romans 15:1-13	241
February 28	Teach the Truth II Timothy 2:14-26	251

SPRING QUARTER
John: The Word Became Flesh (Lessons 1-4)
John: The Great Love (Lessons 5-8)
John: Believe in Jesus (Lessons 9-13)

March 7	In Him Was Life John 1:1-18	261
March 14	Rebirth into Eternal Life John 3:1-17	271
March 21	Light of the World John 9:1-12, 35-41	281
March 28	Coming to Life John 11:1-4, 21-37, 38-44	291
April 4	Do As I Have Done John 13:1-16	301
April 11	I Have Seen the Lord (Easter) John 20:1-16	311
April 18	To Love is to Serve John 21:12-22	321
April 25	The Bread of Life John 6:35-51	331
May 2	The Witness of John the Baptist John 1:19-34	341
May 9	We Have Found Him John 1:35-40	351
May 16	Can This Be the Christ? John 4:7-15, 20-26	361
May 23	Confronting the Galilean John 7:37-52	371
May 30	The Promise of the Spirit John 14:15-27	381

SUMMER QUARTER
Joy in Serving Christ (Lessons 1-4)
Christ Above All (Lessons 5-8)
Newness Through Christ (Lessons 9-13)

June 6	A Worthy Life .... 391 Philippians 1:3-14, 27-30
June 13	Christ, Our Model .... 401 Philippians 2:1-16
June 20	Keep on Keeping On .... 411 Philippians 3:1-16
June 27	Rejoice in the Lord .... 421 Philippians 4:4-20
July 4	The Pre-eminent Christ .... 431 Colossians 1:3-5a, 11-23
July 11	The Sufficient Christ .... 441 Colossians 2:5-19
July 18	Life in Christ .... 451 Colossians 3:1-17
July 25	Christ Unites .... 461 Philemon 4-21
August 1	New Life .... 471 Ephesians 2:1-10; 3:14-19
August 8	New Fellowship .... 481 Ephesians 2:11-22
August 15	New Behavior .... 491 Ephesians 5:1-20
August 22	New Family Order .... 501 Ephesians 5:21-6:4
August 29	New Strength .... 511 Ephesians 6:10-20

HOW TO USE SEED THOUGHTS

The Seed Thought feature, with its ten questions at the end of each lesson, is designed to stimulate class participation. Use the questions where they best apply in the course of developing the lesson. The suggested answers are really just starters and can be enlarged on as needed.

The duplicate questions on the outside portion of the page can be cut out and given to selected students the week before. The names of the students to whom questions have been assigned can be written on the teachers half of the Seed Thoughts page.

♦♦♦

Also available from your Christian Bookstore:

CROSS and CARD

The cross in your pocket or handbag helps to remind you daily that Jesus Christ, the Son of God, died for you.

Invaluable as a conversation opener, its impact is long-lasting when given as a gift to a friend.

The reverse side of the card contains "Footprints" poem.

A perfect way to share your Christian experience with others.

ISBN 0-9614116-2-7
Price $1.00 + Shipping

Higley Publishing Corporation
P.O. Box 5398
Jacksonville, FL 32247-5398
904-396-1918

♦♦♦

September 6, 1992

God's Call and Promise to Abram

Genesis 11
31 And Te´-rah took Abram his son, and Lot the son of Ha´-ran his son's son, and Sa´-rai his daughter in law, his son Abram's wife; and they went forth with them from Ur of the Chal´-dees, to go into the land of Canaan; and they came unto Ha´-ran, and dwelt there.
32 And the days of Te´-rah were two hundred and five years: and Te´-rah died in Ha´-ran.

Genesis 12
NOW the LORD had said unto Abram, Get thee out of thy country, and from thy kindred, and from thy father's house, unto a land that I will shew thee:
2 And I will make of thee a great nation, and I will bless thee, and make thy name great; and thou shalt be a blessing:
3 And I will bless them that bless thee, and curse him that curseth thee: and in thee shall all families of the earth be blessed.
4 So Abram departed, as the LORD had spoken unto him; and Lot went with him: and Abram was seventy and five years old when he departed out of Ha´-ran.
5 And Abram took Sa´-rai his wife, and Lot his brother's son, and all their substance that they had gathered, and the souls that they had gotten in Ha´-ran; and they went forth to go into the land of Canaan; and into the land of Canaan they came.
6 And Abram passed through the land unto the place of Si´-chem, unto the plain of Mo´-reh. And the Ca´-naan-ite *was* then in the land. 7 And the LORD appeared unto Abram, and said, Unto thy seed will I give this land: and there builded he an altar unto the LORD, who appeared unto him.
8 And he removed from thence unto a mountain on the east of Beth´-el, and pitched his tent, having Beth´-el on the west, and Ha´-i on the east: and there he builded an altar unto the LORD, and called upon the name of the LORD.
9 And Abram journeyed, going on still toward the south.

◀ **Memory Selection**
Genesis 12:1-2

◀ **Devotional Reading**
Genesis 13:14-18

◀ **Background Scripture**
Genesis 11:27-12:9

◀ **Printed Scripture**
Genesis 11:31-12:9

GOD'S CALL AND PROMISE TO ABRAM

Teacher's Target

There is within us a two-fold desire when it comes to activities. We like the security and familiarity of routines in life, but we also like the excitement and challenge of doing new and adventurous things. We feel good about it if we can keep them in balance. It is even better if we can trust the Lord to keep them in balance for us. Knowing and doing His will, whether in the routine or adventurous activities of life should be all-important to us.

Help your students to study God's call to Abram and absorb the importance of receiving and keeping a divine covenant. God wanted Abram to uproot himself from his home country and seek out a new country. This involved leaving some relatives behind. It involved a long journey into possibly hazardous territory. It involved the prospect of family development in a foreign culture and location. The challenge was great, but the potential rewards were also great.

Lesson Introduction

Dr. J. Barton Payne listed eight divine covenants: (l) Edenic, (2) Noachian, (3) Abrahamic, (4) Sinaitic, (3) Levitical, (6) Davidic, (7) new covenant in Christ, and (8) future covenant of peace (*Zondervan Pictorial Bible Dictionary*, p. 186). It is the third one on which our study is centered. It is one of the three covenants given to ancient patriarchs (Adam, Noah, Abram) long before the nation of Israel was formed. God dealt with Abram as an individual, but He also dealt through him with all who would live righteously.

"Abraham believed God, and it was accounted to him for righteousness. Know ye therefore that they which are of faith, the same are the children of Abraham" (Gal. 3:6-7). Jews, physical descendants of Abraham, can claim the literal promises of the covenant. Believing Jews and Gentiles can claim the spiritual promises of the covenant. It is in Christ that all families of the earth may be blessed (Gen. 12:3; Gal. 3:8).

Teaching Outline

I. Caravan: Gen. 11:31-32
   A. Terah's move: 31
   B. Terah's death: 32
II. Covenant: Gen. 12:1-3
   A. Place: 1
   B. Promises: 2-3
III. Canaan: Gen. 12:4-9
   A. Journey I:4-7
   B. Journey II:8
   C. Journey III:9

Daily Bible Readings

Mon. God's Faithfulness to Abraham *Gen. 12:10-20*
Tue. God Blesses Abraham's Descendants - *Gen. 14:14-18*
Wed. God Promises Abraham a Son *Gen. 15:1-6*
Thu. God Promises to Deliver Abraham's People - *Gen. 15:12-16a*
Fri. God's Relationship with Abraham *Gen. 17:1-8*
Sat. Abraham's Relationship with God - *Gen. 17:9-14*
Sun. God's Relationship with Abraham's Family - *Gen. 17:13-21*

September 6, 1992

VERSE BY VERSE

I. Caravan: Gen. 11:31-32

A. Terah's move: 31

31. And Terah took Abram his son, and Lot the son of Haran his son's son, and Sarai his daughter in law, his son Abram's wife; and they went forth with them from Ur of the Chaldees, to go into the land of Canaan; and they came unto Haran, and dwelt there.

Terah lived in the ancient Mesopotamian city of Ur belonging to the Chaldeans. It was probably a port on the Persian Gulf at that time some two millenia before Christ. Sediment coming down from the Tigris and Euphrates Rivers built up a delta and pushed the shoreline further south in later centuries. Ur was a pagan city with many evil influences, and this may explain why God wanted Terah and his family to leave it.

Terah had three sons—Abram, Nahor, and Haran. Abram was married to Sarai, and they had no children. Nahor was married to Milcah. Haran had already died (Gen. 11:26-30). Terah took Abram and Sarai, as well as Lot, his orphaned grandson, with him and journeyed some 550 miles to the northwest at the other end of Mesopotamia. The place they settled was named Haran. It was here that the family was able to develop according to divine principles apart from the corrupting influences of Ur.

B. Terah's death: 32

32. And the days of Terah were two hundred and five years: and Terah died in Haran.

Abram was seventy-five years old when Terah died (Gen. 12:4). That means that Terah had been one hundred and thirty years old when Abram was born. Some have criticized Abram for staying too long in Haran, but family ties in those days were very strong He might better be commended for remaining in Haran until his father died.

II. Covenant: Gen. 12:1-3

A. Place: 1

1. Now the Lord had said unto Abram, Get thee out of thy country, and from thy kindred, and from thy father's house, unto a land that I will shew thee:

Although Genesis 11:31 states that Terah's family went from Ur of the Chaldees to go into the land of Canaan, its members did not necessarily know that Canaan was their destination. God told Abram to get out of his country (Mesopotamia), out of his kindred and out of his father's house. God told him to go unto a land which He would show him, but no name was given. Had he stayed in Haran, as Terah's oldest son, he would have become patriarch of the clan. God wanted him to leave this responsibility behind in order to become father of the Hebrews (those who crossed over the Fertile Crescent to Canaan).

Abram had to exercise great faith in leaving the familiar behind and moving out into the unknown. "By faith Abraham, when he was called to go out into a place which he should after receive for an inheritance, obeyed: and he went out, not knowing whither he went"

(Heb. 11:8). No holy Scriptures had yet been given to strengthen him such as believers in later centuries enjoyed. God spoke, and Abram obeyed.

B. Promises: 2-3

2. And I will make of thee a great nation, and I will bless thee, and make thy name great; and thou shalt be a blessing:

The elements of the Abrahamic Covenant are given in verses 2, 3, and 7. Verses 2 and 3 deal with people, while verse 7 deals with the land of Canaan. These elements are very important in understanding Jews today and the nation of Israel, for they provide the divine foundation for Jewish claims to that part of the Middle East. God said that He would make of Abram a great nation, referring to the Israelites his descendants through God-given Isaac. It would take another quarter of a century for Isaac to be born to aged Abraham and Sarah. In the meantime, Abram would sire Ishmael through Hagar, Sarai's handmaid. After Sarah's death, he would marry Keturah and have six sons through her. It was no wonder that God changed his name from Abram (high father) to Abraham (father of many nations) (Gen. 17:4-5). In spite of the animosities between Jews, Christians, and Moslems, all three honor Abraham.

God said that He would bless Abram, and, by implication, his descendants through Isaac. History has shown this to be true. Jews have contributed more to world progress in many fields than their numbers would suggest.

3. And I will bless them that bless thee, and curse him that curseth thee: and in thee shall all families of the earth be blessed.

God told Abram that people who treated him and his descendants well would be divinely blessed. Those who cursed and persecuted them would be divinely punished. History has shown this to be true. Judaism presents to the world what is known as "the religion of humanity," referring to the sharing of Jewish knowledge and skills with Gentiles. It is in this sense that Abram's descendants have blessed all the families of the world. However, Christians see in the latter part of Genesis 12:3 a veiled reference to Jesus Christ. It is through Him and His sacrificial atonement for sin that all families of the earth may be blessed. It is in His coming kingdom that all who belong to Him will find eternal peace and rest. It is as the Descendant of Abram that Jesus will bless all Jews and Gentiles who accept Him as Savior.

III. Canaan: Gen. 12:4-9

A. Journey I: 4-7

4. So Abram departed, as the Lord had spoken unto him; and Lot went with him: and Abram was seventy and five years old when he departed out of Haran.

Abram formed up a caravan which would move westward and southward over what remained of the Fertile Crescent, avoiding the Arabian Desert to the south. His nephew, Lot, went with him, although they were later to separate after settling in the land of Canaan. A caravan of people and animals provided a traveling group with mutual companionship and protection against marauders they might meet along the way. We do not know how the caravan received direction, but it would be natural for it to move along where there was sufficient foraging for the herds of animals in it. The Lord also had His ways of guiding the caravan to move toward the place of His choice. Men lived longer in those times. Terah had died at the age of two hundred and five years (Gen. 11:32). Abram was to live to be one hundred and seventy-five years old (Gen. 25:7). He had the greater part of his life still ahead of him.

5. And Abram took Sarai his wife, and Lot his brother's son, and all their substance that they had gathered, and the souls that they had gotten in Haran; and they went forth to go into the land of Canaan; and into the land of Canaan they came.

In obedience to God's command, Abram set out for Canaan. His wife and nephew accompanied him, along with all their portable goods, family members, and servants acquired over recent decades in Haran. The trip was apparently made without incidents caused by hostile men or wild animals. After traveling some 350-400 miles, they came to the land of Canaan along the eastern shore of the Great (Mediterranean) Sea. This was the place where God intended His people to dwell. They were deported only when they failed to obey and serve Him.

6. And Abram passed through the land unto the place of Sichem, unto the plain of Moreh. And the Canaanite was then in the land.

Sichem (Shechem) was located in the center of Canaan between Mounts Ebal and Gerizim about forty miles north of what would later be called Jerusalem. A grove of oak trees in the plain of Moreh may have provided a good camping spot. We are told that Canaanites dwelled in the land, but they were probably nomadic and not a threat to Abram.

7. And the Lord appeared unto Abram, and said, Unto thy seed will I give this land: and there builded he an altar unto the Lord, who appeared unto him.

This is a very important verse, because it gives God's promise that to Abram and his descendants through Isaac the land of Canaan would belong. It was in appreciation of this promise that Abram constructed a crude stone altar and no doubt offered up an animal sacrifice to the Lord. Keep this covenant promise in mind as current headlines proclaim the various opinions as to who has the right to occupy Palestine. If the Jews manage to control the land, it is hoped that those who are displaced will be adequately cared for, too.

B. Journey II: 8

8. And he removed from thence unto a mountain on the east of Bethel, and pitched his tent, having Bethel on the west, and Hai on the east: and there he builded an altar unto the Lord, and called upon the name of the Lord.

The place called Bethel (house of God) here was originally called Luz but renamed by Jacob (Gen. 28:19). Hai was later shortened to Ai by the time Joshua and the Israelites conquered it (Josh. 8:28). It was between Luz and Hai that Abram built another stone altar, no doubt offered up an animal sacrifice, and called upon the name of the Lord in prayer. He was evidently seeking guidance as to where he should go next in his exploration of Canaan. We are told that he later built an altar unto the Lord in the plain of Mamre in Hebron (Gen. 13:18).

C. Journey III: 9

9. And Abram journeyed, going on still toward the south.

There may be special significance in the fact that Abram continued traveling toward the south. It was in that direction that the pagan land of Egypt lay, and he was tempted to go down there. His reason for going was to find food while there was a famine in Canaan. The Lord could have sustained him and his people in Canaan, but Abram probably saw no harm in seeking food in Egypt. It was there that he got into trouble with the pharaoh over Sarai, but the Lord brought him back to Canaan safely (Gen. 12:10—13:1).

Abram's great contribution to us was his example of great faith. More space is alloted to him in the eleventh chapter of Hebrews than to any other hero of faith. You might want to close your lesson by reading Hebrews 11:8-19. Pray that you and your students will learn to emulate him.

GOD'S CALL AND PROMISE TO ABRAM

Evangelistic Emphasis

The story of Abraham is a story of promise and faithfulness. Not only does God call Abram, but he provides promises and power for Abram. Though there are often broken promises in the relationships between people, God always keeps the faith. He keeps His promises. God's "I will" always becomes "I have." In short, God's word can be counted on at all times.

All of us are called by God. It is essential that we grasp the nature of God's call. What, however, do we mean by a call from God? The call of God is wrapped up in the promises of God and the response of persons. Specifically Abram was called to go to a new land, but beyond that, Abram was called to be a blessing to the world. The call of God then is an invitation to accept responsibility for the well-being of the world, to be responsible for the world receiving the message of salvation, and to participate in God's world mission.

Imagine the confidence and courage that accrues to Christians who witness, conscious of their calling to be a blessing to the world. The evangelistic message of the church should never take a back seat to any other ministry. There are no negative connotations in a ministry intended to bless an entire world. Everyone who accepts God's call as witness to the gospel can rest assured they are sharing God's blessing with others. There is no higher calling.

Abram's acceptance of God's call was an act of faith, but Abram received unexpected blessings in return. He was blessed by God with a new home to replace the one he left. He was given a new family and a new name and a new status. He was blessed in order to be a blessing. But at the front end all Abram had to go on was the word from God. And guess what? That's all we have now. If that was enough for Abram then it should be enough to keep us witnessing for Jesus.

Memory Selection

"Go from your country and your kindred and your father's house to the land that I will show you. And I will make of you a great nation, and I will bless you, and make your name great, so that you will be a blessing."—*Genesis 12:1-2*

Go is always a big word in God's plans. God never calls people to a static, status quo relationship. The life of faith as a journey is one of the oldest of religious metaphors.

Thus God called Abram to leave behind all his cherished possessions to go toward an unseen, uncertain future. All Abram had to go on was word from God. Yet that is the essence of faith - going on word from God.

God still calls his people to go toward the promises of a better life. There is a leaving - a forsaking - a letting go. Then there is a moving forward to gain the blessing of The Lord. We never know until we go. Abram in Haran would have lived out an unimaginative life. He would have never known if God's word was true or if God's promises were true. Only as he went forth from Haran in faith did Abram possess the potential to become the father of faith. Thus faith begins with one step forward - in this case, a single act of obedience. Abram is potential - all the potential in the world. He is a man poised on the edge of promise. Abram had that extra dimension of faith that allowed him to move forward without knowing where he would end up. That is faith!

September 6, 1992

Weekday Problems

Betty listened intently to her pastor's sermon about the call of God. She knew she was a Christian, but did not understand how she could be called to any special mission. She was not at all like Abram. God had never called her to go on a dangerous journey.

Still Betty was disturbed by all the talk about God calling everyone. She had always thought that only preachers and missionaries were called. Why, she couldn't even teach a Sunday School class.

All Betty could do was cook and serve. Every time her church had a fellowship dinner, wedding reception, party, or banquet she did all the planning, promoting, cooking and cleaning. No one else in the whole city could handle a banquet for 100 people like Betty. As she listened to the sermon, however, she still did not feel called by God.

Betty tends to think of the call of God as the exclusive property of preachers. Only ministers get "called"; at least, that is what she has always thought. She needs a more imaginative understanding of God's call. The air is full of calls. Betty needs help finding the courage, the imagination, and the grace to say, "Here Am I. Send me."

*What is Betty missing with her narrow understanding of the call of God?
*Would she be helped by understanding that God's call is often related to our gifts and abilities?

Superintendent's Sermonette

Throughout history, most people have tended to do whatever their parents did. Economic and sociological factors have made it difficult for individuals to break out of a proscribed way of life and try something new. In modern times, by contrast, individuals have been able to move upward without as many entrenched limitations as before. However, upward mobility has brought with it the traumatic effects of frequent changes and frightening challenges. We can become disoriented if things change too fast. We need to move ahead but do it with careful planning and deliberation whenever possible.

Abram (later called Abraham) was faced with a divine order to make a great change halfway through his life. At the age of seventy-five years God called him to leave Mesopotamia and move to a land which would be pointed out to him. He needed faith to pull up stakes and head for a new life in a new place, but he trusted God and went.

Here is the secret for making changes in a smooth and confident manner. We should seek to know the will of God by studying His Word, praying for guidance, and consulting with God's people. Once we know what He wants us to do, let us move forward into whatever changes He has for us. His blessing will reward our obedience.

GOD'S CALL AND PROMISE TO ABRAM

This Lesson In Your Life

In the San Andres Mountains of New Mexico, in 1934, they buried Eugene Manlove Rhodes, the classic teller of western stories. On his tombstone, they carved the name of his best-loved novel *Paso Por Aqui*, the date, and his name. "Paso aqui" means "passed through here." When some conquistador, trapper, or prospector came through the pass which opens the old western route to Colorado, Wyoming, and Utah, he would cut his name on Inscription Rock with the words "paso por aqui."

"Paso por aqui" describes the feeling one gets from reading the story of Abram's call to follow God to a new land. Abram, like all of us, was passing through. But on the way through he was apprehended by the voice of the calling God. The 12th chapter of Genesis is a key chapter in the stories of God's people. These verses depict Abram as a man of faith and courage. He stands as the beginning, the source of our own faith journey.

To be called is to be invited. God is the inviting God. All of us are passing through but not everyone grasps the wonderful news that God invites all persons on a journey of faith. This invitation is to a new future. In New Testament language it is an invitation to a new birth and a living hope.

The invitation is to the adventure of our lives. While God's call to adventure is exacting, hard, and challenging, it is never boring. There are risks involved in any adventure. But the courage to accept God's adventure in faith is a crucial virtue. Not everyone is willing to give a positive response because to respond to God is to be responsible - response-able, able to respond to God's invitation.

We have no way of knowing how Abram would have turned out if he had refused God's call. There is an interesting piece of family history, however, that offers a partial clue. Terah, Abram's father, originally started for Canaan; but when he came to Haran, he settled there, and Terah died in Haran. Perhaps here is a significant warning and lesson for us. When God calls and gets no response, God moves on and calls other persons. In our lives this means that staying as we are and where we are may cause us to miss out on the future God has planned. Unless we respond to God's invitation we will never reach the land of promise. Of course, we can say "No" to God. We can stay put. We can say nothing, do nothing, never join that faithful band of exiles - the called, the chosen, the few, the joyful. If we do, we'll never know where faith would have carried us.

To be called also means to sever ties with the past. God's direct call is for Abram to go forth from his old home to a new land. The divine call includes a command to abandon all human ties and pull up all roots. God's people are to be aliens, strangers, and sojourners, never settlers in the land. Abram is simply to leave everything behind to follow God.

To be called does not mean to be abandoned by God and left to our own futile plans and devices. God promises to be with Abram. The promise includes the forming of a great nation, the blessing of Abram, and a great name for Abram. God never deserts his chosen ones. Along with the call comes the presence, the power, and the promise of God. Although we can not see or predict or control the future, we can have the faith that God never forsakes his called ones.

To be called is to stand on the edge of potential and promise. Only those who have eyes ever see the potential involved in following God. What a life we will have; a life of hope, of grace and peace, of salvation, of love, and of joy. What an adventure it will be to follow God to the land of promise. We will be able to inscribe our names on the places we pass through.

Seed Thoughts

1. **What motivated Abram's father, Terah, to leave home?**
   He wanted to go to Canaan. Perhaps the original call of God went to Terah, but he settled in Haran.

2. **In what ways are people today like Terah?**
   We are often settlers in the sense that we stop short of our potential? We make a good beginning but a less-than-satisfactory ending.

3. **What particular outstanding qualities did Abram possess that caused *God* to call him?**
   The Scripture does not list any such qualities. All the initiative rests with God.

4. **What does God ask Abram to give up in his quest for the land of Canaan?**
   The Lord commands Abram to leave his land, his kinfolk, and his father's house.

5. **What does God promise Abram in return?**
   When Abram leaves his country, God promises to make of Abram a great nation. When Abram leaves his family, God promises to give him a family without number. When Abram leaves his home, God promises to give him a greater home.

(PLEASE TURN PAGE)

---

1. What motivated Abram's father, Terah, to leave home?

2. In what ways are people today like Terah?

3. What particular outstanding qualities did Abram possess that caused *God* to call him?

4. What does God ask Abram to give up in his quest for the land of Canaan?

5. What does God promise Abram in return?

6. What comparisons can we draw between the attempt by men to *build* the Tower of Babel and God's promises to Abram?

7. What was Abram's first act upon entering the land of Canaan?

8. What is the significance of the plain of Moreh?

9. Where does Abram first settle in the land of Canaan?

10. What do we learn about *God's* missionary purpose from the story of Abram?

He wanted to go to Canaan. Perhaps the original call of God went to Terah, but he settled in Haran.

We are often settlers in the sense that we stop short of our potential? We make a good beginning but a less-than-satisfactory ending.

The Scripture does not list any such qualities. All the initiative rests with God.

The Lord commands Abram to leave his land, his kinfolk, and his father's house.

When Abram leaves his country, God promises to make of Abram a great nation. When Abram leaves his family, God promises to give him a family without number. When Abram leaves his home, God promises to give him a greater home.

Everything men tried to grasp for themselves: a city, a reputation, a name, and a country, God promised to give Abram.

Abram built an altar to the Lord, and worshiped God.

The oak of Moreh was located here, just outside the city of Shechem. It was considered a sacred tree. (See also Genesis 35:4; Deut. 11:30; Joshua 24:6; Judges 9:37).

He pitched his tent in the hill country around Bethel, with Bethel on the west and Ai on the east.

In Genesis 12:3, God promises Abram that all families of the earth will be blessed through Abram's faithfulness.

(SEED THOUGHTS--Cont'd)

6. **What comparisons can we draw between the attempt by men to *build* the Tower of Babel and God's promises to Abram?**
Everything men tried to grasp for themselves: a city, a reputation, a name, and a country, God promised to give Abram.

7. **What was Abram's first act upon entering the land of Canaan?**
Abram built an altar to the Lord, and worshiped God.

8. **What is the significance of the plain of Moreh?**
The oak of Moreh was located here, just outside the city of Shechem. It was considered a sacred tree. (See also Genesis 35:4; Deut. 11:30; Joshua 24:6; Judges 9:37).

9. **Where does Abram first settle in the land of Canaan?**
He pitched his tent in the hill country around Bethel, with Bethel on the west and Ai on the east.

10. **What do we learn about *God's* missionary purpose from the story of Abram?**
In Genesis 12:3, God promises Abram that all families of the earth will be blessed through Abram's faithfulness.

September 13, 1992

God's Call To Moses

Exodus 3

NOW Moses kept the flock of Je'-thro his father in law, the priest of Mid'-i-an: and he led the flock to the backside of the desert, and came to the mountain of God, *even* to Ho'reb.

2 And the angel of the LORD appeared unto him in a flame of fire out of the midst of a bush: and he looked and behold, the bush a burned with fire, and the bush was not consumed.

3 And Moses said, I will now turn aside, and see this great sight, why the bush is not burnt.

4 And when the LORD saw that he turned aside to see, God called unto him out of the midst of the bush, and said, Moses, Moses. And he said Here am I.

5 And he said, Draw not nigh hither: put off thy shoes from off thy feet, for the place whereon thou standest is holy ground.

6 Moreover he said, I am the God of thy father, the God of Abraham the God of Isaac, and the God of Jacob. And Moses hid his face; for he was afraid to look upon God.

7 And the LORD said, I have surely seen the affliction of my people which are in Egypt, and have heard their cry by reason of their taskmasters; for I know their sorrows;

10 Come now therefore, and I will send thee unto Pharaoh, that thou mayest bring forth my people the children of Israel out of Egypt.

11 And Moses said unto God, Who am I, that I should go unto Pharaoh and that I should bring forth the children of Israel out of Egypt?

12 And he said, Certainly I will be with thee; and this shall be a token unto thee that I have sent thee: When thou hast brought forth the people out of Egypt, ye shall serve God upon this mountain.

13 And Moses said unto God, Behold, when I come unto the children of Israel, and shall say unto them, The God of your fathers hath sent me unto you and they shall say to me, What is his name? what shall I say unto them?

14 And God said unto Moses, I AM THAT I AM: and he said, Thus shalt thou say unto the children of Israel, I AM hath sent me unto you.

◀ **Memory Selection**
Exodus 3:10

◀ **Devotional Reading**
Exodus 4:10-16

◀ **Background Scripture**
Exodus 3:1-4:17

◀ **Printed Scripture**
Exodus 3:1-7, 10-14

GOD'S CALL TO MOSES

Teacher's Target

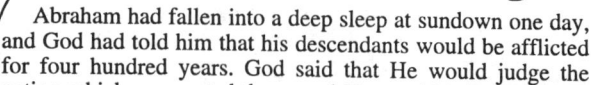

Abraham had fallen into a deep sleep at sundown one day, and God had told him that his descendants would be afflicted for four hundred years. God said that He would judge the nation which persecuted them, and He would bring His people out of bondage with great substance (Gen. 15:12-14). The children of Israel became a multitude in Egypt after Jacob went down there to live (Gen. 46:1-3; Exod. 1:7). The king (pharaoh) of Egypt made them slaves, but God raised up Moses to deliver them.
Help your students to realize that it is an honor and a privilege to serve the Lord. If we have reservations regarding our qualifications for leadership, we must learn to trust God's jugdement. He will not give us a task to do without providing what is needed for us to do it. Moses objected to God's choice of him to lead Israel out of bondage but God overcame each objection. We would be wise to offer no objections if God calls us to go on a mission for Him.

Lesson Introduction

The king of Egypt ordered Hebrew midwives to slay all sons born to Israelite mothers. Since these women feared God, they refused to do as the king said (Exod. 1:15-22). One Hebrew mother named Jochebed, wife of a Levite named Amram, decided to save her son from death by hiding him in a small ark floating among the reeds alongside the river. Her daughter Miriam watched over him from the shoreline. When the king's daughter came there to bathe and learned of the ark and the baby in it, she adopted him and named him Moses because he had been drawn out of the water (Exod. 2:1-10).

Moses had a royal upbringing, but when he was grown he took the side of his Hebrew brethren and slew an Egyptian. Because of this he had to flee and ended up in Midian tending sheep for a priest named Reuel (Jethro). He married Zipporah, the priest's daughter, and had two sons by her (Exod. 2:11-22; 18:1-4; Acts 7:29), In the meantime, God heard the cries of the Israelites for deliverance, and He acknowledged them (Exod. 2:23-25).

Teaching Outline

I. Presence: Exod. 3:1-7
  A. God's mountain: 1
  B. God's bush: 2-3
  C. God's voice: 4-7
II. Promise: Exod. 3:10-12
  A. Protest: 10-11
  B. Prediction: 12
III. Primacy: Exod. 3:13-14
  A. Protest: 13
  B. Proclamation: 14

Daily Bible Readings

Mon. God Promises to Rescue the Israelites—*Exod. 3:15-22*
Tue. Moses Responds Reluctantly to God's Call—*Exod. 4:1-9*
Wed. God Recommends Aaron to Speak for Moses—*Exod. 4:10-17*
Thu. Moses Accepts God's Call *Exod 4:18-24*
Fri. Aaron Supports God's Call to Moses—*Exod. 4:27-31*
Sat. Pharaoh's Heart Is Hardened against Israel—*Exod. 5:1-9*
Sun. God Reminds the Israelites of Their Covenant—*Exod. 6:1-9*

September 13, 1992

VERSE BY VERSE

I. Presence: Exod. 3:1-7

A. God's mountain: I

1. **Now Moses kept the flock of Jethro his father in law, the priest of Midian: and he led the flock to the backside of the desert, and came to the mountain of God, even to Horeb.**
The priest of Midian was called Reuel, and that may have been his personal name (Exod. 2:18). He was referred to as Jethro in other places (Exod. 3:1; 4:18; 18:1-12), and that may have been his title. We will refer to him as Jethro. It was kind of him to employ Moses as a shepherd, but this was a far different life from what Moses had pursued when he was a prince in Egypt. He had plenty of time to meditate on his past, present, and future. His situation must have appeared quite bleak, but he adjusted to the quiet life and probably thought it would never change. One day, however, he came to Horeb, the mountain of God on the backside of the desert, and there he was to have a life-changing encounter with God. This was the mountain we normally call Sinai. The life of Moses can be divided in three parts - a prince in Egypt (forty years), a shepherd in Midian (forty years), and the leader of Israel (forty years).

B. God's bush: 2-3

2. **And the angel of the Lord appeared unto him in a flame of fire out of the midst of a bush: and he looked, and, behold, the bush burned with fire, and the bush was not consumed.**
The presence of God was in the bush and had the appearance of a bright angel. The bush itself was burning but was not consumed by the fire. This unusual sight drew the attention of Moses and stirred his curiosity. Anything out of the ordinary would tend to have this effect in a place as desolate as that.

3. **And Moses said, I will now turn aside, and see this great sight, why the bush is not burnt.**
Moses may have seen fire in the desert caused by rare bolts of lightning or other natural phenomena, but he could not understand how something combustible could keep burning without being consumed. He decided to turn aside and investigate this great sight. God used this means to rivet Moses' attention on Himself. It has also been suggested that the burning bush symbolized the perpetual persecution of the Israelites by the Egyptians and their need for deliverance.

C. God's voice: 4-7

4. **And when the Lord saw that he turned aside to see, God called unto him out of the midst of the bush, and said, Moses, Moses. And he said, Here am I.**
The sight of the bush which burned but was not consumed was great. The sound of God's voice calling to Moses out of the bush was great. Moses was so astonished that all he could do was to acknowledge that he was there and ready to listen. It appears that he began to advance toward the bush.

5. **And he said, Draw not nigh hither: put off thy shoes from off thy feet, for the place whereon thou standest is holy ground.**
God stopped Moses so that He might tell him to slip off his sandals before walking onto sacred soil. There was

13

nothing inherently holy about the desert sand surrounding the burning bush. It was holy simply because the presence of God Almighty was there. Removing footwear was a sign of reverence for deity, and this practice is still followed in some parts of the world. Humility and obedience contribute to reverence.

6. Moreover he said, I am the God of thy father, the God of Abraham, the God of Isaac, and the God of Jacob. And Moses hid his face; for he was afraid to look upon God.

The Lord identified himself as the God of Jochebed, the Levite father of Moses, and as the God of Moses' famous ancestors, Abraham, Isaac, and Jacob. In other words, He was the covenant-keeping God of Israel. Believing what he was told, Moses hid his face, probably by covering it with his hands. He was afraid to look upon God Himself. Was this a legitimate fear? We know that God is a Spirit and is therefore invisible (John 4:24). However, we also know that His glory can be seen, and Stephen the martyr had that experience (Acts 7:55).

Digressing briefly, we read in Exodus 33:18-23 that Moses later placed himself in a cleft of a rock and watched the back of God as He passed by. This was evidently a theophany (visible appearance of God). Although these things are hard to explain, we know that angels, who are spirits, made visible appearances to men in various biblical settings.

7. And the Lord said, I have surely seen the affliction of my people which are in Egypt, and have heard their cry by reason of their sorrows; for I know their sorrows;

Verse 8 goes on to complete the thought by recording that God said, "I am come down to deliver them out of the hand of the Egyptians, and to bring them up out of that land unto a good land and a large, unto a land flowing with milk and honey." After four centuries of persecution in a foreign land, Israel was to be delivered and go home to Canaan, the land promised to Abraham, Isaac, and Jacob and their descendants. God was presented here as One Who was aware of the suffering of His people on the earth and ready to improve their situation. Let us take comfort in the fact that He still displays this awareness and compassion toward us.

II. Promise: Exod. 3:10-12

A. Protest: 10-11

10. Come now therefore, and I will send thee unto Pharaoh, that thou mayest bring forth my people the children of Israel out of Egypt.

Moses must have been rejoicing in the prospect of deliverance for his Hebrew brethren in Egypt. He may even have wondered whom God would use and the methods He would use to do this. He was not ready for God to point him out as His chosen instrument for effecting Israel's deliverance. He must have been terrified at the thought of going to deal with the pharaoh in Egypt. He must have considered the possibility that he would be executed if he made an appearance there. His mind raced in an attempt to find plausible excuses for refusing to implement God's plan.

11. And Moses said unto God, Who am I, that I should go unto Pharaoh, and that I should bring forth the children of Israel out of Egypt?

Moses saw things from his human perspective, not from God's divine perspective. He could not imagine why the Lord would choose him. He was now eighty years old. He had been away from the royal court in Egypt for forty years. He had adjusted to the quiet life of a shepherd in a desolate area. He had a wife and child. He was satisfied and complacent. He did not want to try something preposterous and fail at it. He wanted to maintain the *status quo*. Does any of this sound familiar as far as our own lives are concerned? We like a bold idea, but we want someone else to implement it.

B. Prediction: 12

12. And he said, Certainly I will be with thee; and this shall be a token unto thee, that I have sent thee: When thou hast brought forth the people out of Egypt, ye shall serve God upon this mountain.

In answer to Moses' objection that he was not the man for the job to be done, God told him that He would be with him in delivering the Israelites from Egypt. Knowing the end from the beginning, God stated that Moses would one day stand with his countrymen and worship at this same mountain. It was a faith-building prediction designed to help Moses trust in the Lord and not in himself. He could hardly call God a liar, but he was not yet resigned to doing what God proposed.

III. Primacy: Exod. 3:13-14

A. Protest: 13

13. **And Moses said unto God, Behold, when I come unto the children of Israel, and shall say unto them, The God of your fathers hath sent me unto you, and they shall say to me, What is his name? what shall I say unto them?**

Moses was worried about the Israelites' view of God. They had been immersed in a pagan culture for four centuries. They had wondered if God was concerned about them after allowing them to be bound in slavery all this time. They had no written Scriptures to guide them. Moses said that they would want to know the name of the God Who claimed He would deliver them. Implied in this would be their concern as to whether this God had the power to do what He promised He would do.

B. Proclamation: 14

14. **And God said unto Moses, I AM THAT I AM: and he said, Thus shalt thou say unto the children of Israel, I AM hath sent me unto you.**

This is a difficult verse to explain. God said that His name was inherently connected with His actions. He was the sovereign God of the universe, capable of implementing all that He proposed to do. Other versions render God's description of Himself as "I AM WHAT I AM" or "I WILL BE WHAT I WILL BE." The word for I AM here is similar to the Hebrew name *Yahweh* or *Jehovah*. This was the eternal name of God to be used throughout the generations.

Note that God repeated what He had said in Exodus 3:6 in Exodus 3:15 about Him being the God of Abraham, Isaac, and Jacob. In Exodus 3:15 he said, "This is my name for ever, and this is my memorial unto all generations."

The Lord then told Moses to go to the elders of Israel and tell them that the God of their fathers had seen what was done to them in Egypt. He was to tell them that God would deliver them from bondage. They would believe Moses and accompany him when he went to see the pharaoh. They would request permission to go three days' journey into the wilderness to sacrifice to their God, but the king would refuse to give it. God would then devastate the land of Egypt. When the king let the Israelites go, the Egyptians would give them many precious things, such as jewels and raiment (Exod. 3:16-22), Thus would be fulfilled God's prediction to Abraham found in Genesis 15:14.

All of this must have sounded wonderful to Moses, but he still was reluctant to assume leadership of the exodus. Exodus 4:1-18 tells us that God had to overcome two objections made by Moses. The first had to do with his supposed belief that the Israelites would not believe him when he told them that Jehovah had appeared to him. The Lord gave Moses three signs to use in convincing them. One was the changing of his staff to a serpent and back again. The second was putting his hand into his robe to make it leprous and once again to make it whole. The third was pouring water from the river on dry land and it becoming blood.

The second objection Moses had was his lack of eloquence. He claimed to be slow of speech and therefore unsuitable to carry on negotiations with the elders of Israel and the pharaoh of Egypt. God said that He would be with him to overcome this, but Moses still resisted going. The Lord became angry with Moses and told him to get his brother, Aaron the Levite, to be his spokesman, In fact, Aaron was already on his way to meet Moses. Moses then returned to Jethro and received his permission to go to Egypt to visit his brethren. We know that Moses' acceptance of God's call eventually resulted in the exodus of Israel from Egyptian bondage.

GOD'S CALL TO MOSES

Evangelistic Emphasis

Make no mistake. Moses is not some super-hero, some legendary good guy of the Bible smiting Egyptians. Moses is not the main character. Remember that the fingerprints of God are all over the events surrounding the birth and life of Moses. (The story "does not tell of a Great Man who rallied a slave community. . .This is precisely not the thrust of the biblical narrative. It tells the story of the Great God who redeemed a motley crew of slaves from Egypt.") The truth is anybody could have been Moses. For 40 years God had looked and called and anyone could have been the one. Yes, we can respect Moses, but when we read the story remember *the Great God* not *the Great Man*.

For you see, God takes the initiative. God calls. Otherwise Moses would still be in Midian, a stranger living out what the poet called the "butt-ends of his days and ways" as nobody in particular. God has been calling people for a long time. I'm afraid the call of God has been cut off, as if only preachers get called. We live in a world where a lot of folks ignore the call of God. Maybe you've made your peace with the world as it is and with yourselves as you are. Well, your peace treaty is declared null and void. God calls people and God is calling you. Doctors, lawyers, teachers, mechanics, moms, dads, you and me. Let's face facts: God loves the world and calls us to love the world. When the cry of pain goes up in the world, God calls some of his people to do something: give, help, serve, care, listen - God is calling us in love.

Guess what? The call of God reached to Midian - all the way to Moses in a burning bush. A voice from within the bush got Moses' attention. Well, no wonder God set the bush on fire. Getting our attention may be the hardest part. In a hectic world where people are inattentive to mystery and to religion, we have to do something to underline the importance of God. Grabbing at people's attention has become the challenge of our society.

Memory Selection

Come, I will send you to Pharoah that you may bring forth my people out of Egypt.
Exodus 3:10

The story of the Old Testament is centered around the will and purpose of a commanding God. God is always commanding people to come and go. Each command, however, is part of a larger purpose of freedom for all persons. This time God sends Moses into the land of Egypt to confront Pharoah. The story surprises at every turn.

That God would choose Moses to go to Pharoah is surprising on two counts. First, we are surprised that God sent a man like Moses. We know that Moses killed a man back in Egypt. Yet God called Moses and not only called him but gave him the single most significant mission in the storied history of the Jews.

Yet is it so surprising? Are we not aware that God has his standards and we have ours? Paul Tournier, in his writings, often speaks of the great reversal. He means that God turns our code of human values upside down and chooses people we would never dream of nominating.

So Moses is chosen along with Matthew the taxgatherer and Saul the persecutor. God is full of surprises.

16

September 13, 1992

Weekday Problems

Linda, a thirty-eight year old housewife, seemed depressed as she drank coffee with her best friend, Julie. "What's giving you the blues?" Julie asked.

"I am so confused about everything," Linda said. "I am so bored and I feel like such a nobody. Most women have careers. All I ever do is cook, wash, and take care of kids." Having confessed to a lack of self-esteem, Linda now felt guilty about what she had said about being a wife and a mother. Yet her self-image *was* a zero on a scale of one to ten.

"You should talk to your minister," implored Julie. "I'm sure he can be of some help."

Linda was not too sure that the preacher could do anything to help her feel better about her marriage or her life. Still later that day she went to see her pastor. With prayerful, positive reinforcement he helped Linda discover her own personal worth in the eyes of God. She realized for the first time that God had not judged her as unworthy. She also understood that being a wife and a mother was just as much a calling as being a lawyer or a corporate executive. Slowly the layers of defensiveness and shyness and inferiority began to be peeled away. She had so despised herself and so denigrated her role in life that she lacked the confidence to accept God's claim on her life.

*There is no question that God affirms human worth, but how can we communicate well-being to persons in a society that is so status-conscious?

*What affirmations can you think of that could help a person to overcome his own self-rejection?

*What biblical principles might help other women like Linda accept God's will for their important roles?

♦♦♦♦♦♦

Superintendent's Sermonette

Someone once said that when God calls you to a task He doesn't force you to go; He just makes you *willing* to go. God's dealing with Moses seemed to illustrate this. Born a Hebrew, but raised as the adopted son of the princess of Egypt, Moses slew an Egyptian whom he discovered beating a Hebrew. Fearing for his life if this were reported, Moses fled to Midian in the Sinai Peninsula. He met Jethro, the priest of Midian, and married his daughter, Zipporah. For forty years he was a shepherd tending sheep in the wilderness. When God called to him from the burning bush near Mount Horeb (Sinai), Moses was not ready to lead the Israelites out of Egypt.

Whether it is out of a feeling of personal inadequacy or humility, we may sometimes act the way that Moses did. We find excuses to keep from doing the will of God. He then has to strengthen our confidence, teach us to trust in His wisdom and power, and let go of our objections. This may be a long and painful process, or it may take place quickly. The important thing is that we yield to His sovereign right to do with us whatever He desires. The first step of faith is the hardest, but it leads to a steady walk with God.

This Lesson In Your Life

The most famous of all statues of Moses was chiseled out of stone by Michelangelo. Moses is shown as a man of strong physique and large stature. In his right hand he holds the tablets of The Ten Commandments. He is a man of active contemplation and awareness. The statue projects an image of a powerful man. What can we make of the lesson of Moses?

This story teaches us that back of all our stories is the hand of God. While we have all the respect in the world for Moses, the key focus is the power and purposes of God. Was it not God who delivered the baby Moses from almost certain death in the Nile River? How the Hebrew slaves must have laughed when Moses' own mother was put in charge of raising Moses as the son of Pharoah's daughter. Is it any surprise that Moses always knew that he was one of God's children? The unfolding events in the life of Moses often show the invisible leading of God.

Do you ever wonder what it all adds up to? Who am I? Why am I here? Responding to God means responding also to one another. One another involves much more than the other members of our family, or a tight little group of friends. We of this earth are all one family: God's family, on the face of the earth. "Inasmuch as you have done it unto one of the least of these my brothers," Jesus says, "You have done it unto me." Let me say straight out: THE CALL OF GOD IS THE CRY OF THE OPPRESSED CHILDREN OF THE WORLD.

God is always interested in the poor. So every time we hear the pain and cry of the needy, at that very moment you can be sure God is calling us.

Don't forget that Moses had insulated himself to get away from the cry of pain. (i.e., the call of God). "Moses, Moses," God called. Until that moment, Moses had been a spectator. He had tried once to take up the struggle of his people but his plan backfired. So he left the town of Midian, married, had a son, went into business with his father-in-law, and settled down. Suddenly, in the midst of all that security, he hears, "Moses, Moses . . ." Midian had not been far enough away. God had followed Moses to Midian and now was calling him right back into the thick of everything he had tried so hard to get away from for so long. We understand, don't we? We're always trying to protect ourselves from the fires of pain and fear, the sights of violence and poverty, the smells of the ill-clad and ill-fed. We know how Moses felt.

Remember Moses was not happy with his call, "Not me Lord," He said. Far from packing his bags for Egypt, he resisted with all his might. The cry of pain was met by the cry of protest; "You better get yourself another man. Get your dirty work done another way." The cry of protest sounds so familiar. It has been rehearsed for centuries. Jeremiah, and Saul and Simon Peter and enough professing Christians to create a veritable cacophony of protest like thousands of blue jays all squawking at one time: "Not me Lord." "Not me Lord."

Without pushing our religious guilt buttons for all the excuses we use to resist the call of God, here is why we must accept God's call. To the cry of protest God responded with the cry of presence: "I will be with you." There is a life-time of promise and hope and fulfillment in that cry. To live on the edge of creativity, to take risks, to undertake impossible missions all in the presence of and under the care of God.

Seed Thoughts

1. What are the biblical names for the mountain of God?
Horeb and Sinai are the names given to the mountain where God's presence and power was manifested to the Israelites. Before this mountain Israel camped when God bound her to Himself in covenant.

2. In what way did God attract the attention of Moses?
The angel of the Lord spoke to Moses from a burning bush. The significance of the account is Moses' recognition of the presence of God.

3. Why was Moses working for his father-in-law, Jethro?
When Moses identified himself as brother to the Hebrew slaves, he tried to assume a position of leadership. The aborted attempt ended when Moses killed an Egyptian and had to flee for his life.

4. Should God's servant ever question God's call?
Yes. The struggle to understand and respond to God's call is part of the remarkable honesty of Scripture from Adam to Jesus.

5. Why was Moses afraid?
He knew that Pharoah wanted him dead. He also remembered that the Hebrews had already rejected his leadership once. In addition, Moses lacked the courage to go back to Egypt.

(PLEASE TURN PAGE)

---

1. What are the biblical names for the mountain of God?

2. In what way did God attract the attention of Moses?

3. Why was Moses working for his father-in-law, Jethro?

4. Should God's servant ever question God's call?

5. Why was Moses afraid?

6. What did God promise to do for Moses?

7. What excuses did Moses give for not accepting God's call?

8. What signs did Moses receive from God and what was their significance?

9. What did God want Moses to do?

10. What might have happened to Moses if he had rejected the call of God?

Horeb and Sinai are the names given to the mountain where God's presence and power was manifested to the Israelites. Before this mountain Israel camped when God bound her to Himself in covenant.

The angel of the Lord spoke to Moses from a burning bush. The significance of the account is Moses' recognition of the presence of God.

When Moses identified himself as brother to the Hebrew slaves, he tried to assume a position of leadership. The aborted attempt ended when Moses killed an Egyptian and had to flee for his life.

Yes. The struggle to understand and respond to God's call is part of the remarkable honesty of Scripture from Adam to Jesus.

He knew that Pharoah wanted him dead. He also remembered that the Hebrews had already rejected his leadership once. In addition, Moses lacked the courage to go back to Egypt.

God promised to be with him and to give him the words to speak. God also promised to give Moses the necessary power to carry out the mission.

When Moses first heard the call of God he was not happy. Instead he complained that nobody would know who he was. Also he fretted that the Hebrews would not know that God had sent him. Moses figured no one would believe him. Besides all that, Moses claimed he was not an eloquent speaker.

The two signs Moses received were the rod which became a serpent and the Leprous hand.

God wanted Moses to accept leadership responsibility. Moses was to go down to Egypt and demand freedom for the Israelites. He was to confront the Pharoah himself.

Moses would probably have remained in Midian. He would have lived out his days in obscurity. He would never have known the adventure of following God.

(SEED THOUGHTS--Cont'd)

6. What did God promise to do for Moses?

God promised to be with him and to give him the words to speak. God also promised to give Moses the necessary power to carry out the mission.

7. What excuses did Moses give for not accepting God's call?

When Moses first heard the call of God he was not happy. Instead he complained that nobody would know who he was. Also he fretted that the Hebrews would not know that God had sent him. Moses figured no one would believe him. Besides all that, Moses claimed he was not an eloquent speaker.

8. What signs did Moses receive from God and what was their significance?

The two signs Moses received were the rod which became a serpent and the Leprous hand.

9. What did God want Moses to do?

God wanted Moses to accept leadership responsibility. Moses was to go down to Egypt and demand freedom for the Israelites. He was to confront the Pharoah himself.

10. What might have happened to Moses if he had rejected the call of God?

Moses would probably have remained in Midian. He would have lived out his days in obscurity. He would never have known the adventure of following God.

September 20, 1992

God's Choice of Joshua to Succeed Moses

Joshua 1
1 NOW after the death of Moses the servant of the LORD it came to pass, that the LORD spake unto Joshua the son of Nun, Moses' minister, saying,
2 Moses my servant is dead; now therefore arise, go over this Jordan, thou, and all this people, unto the land which I do give to them, *even* to the children of Israel.
3 Every place that the sole of your foot shall tread upon, that have I given unto you, as I said unto Moses.
4 From the wilderness and this Leb'-anon even unto the great river, the river Eu-phra'tes, all the land of the Hit'-tites, and unto the great sea toward the going down of the sun, shall be your coast.
5 There shall not any man be able to stand before thee all the days of thy life: as I was with Moses, so I will be with thee: I will not fail thee, nor forsake thee.
6 Be strong and of a good courage: for unto this people shalt thou divide for an inheritance the land, which I sware unto their fathers to give them.

7 Only be thou strong and very courageous, that thou mayest observe to do according to all the law, which Moses my servant commanded thee: turn not from it *to* the right hand or *to* the left, that thou mayest prosper whithersoever thou goest.
8 This book of the law shall not depart out of thy mouth; but thou shalt meditate therein day and night, that thou mayest observe to do according to all that is written therein: for then thou shalt make thy way prosperous, and then thou shalt have good success.
9 Have not I commanded thee? Be strong and of a good courage; be not afraid, neither be thou dismayed: for the LORD thy God is with thee whithersoever thou goest.
10 Then Joshua commanded the officers of the people, saying,
11 Pass through the host, and command the people, saying, Prepare you victuals; for within three days ye shall pass over this Jordan, to go in to possess the land, which the LORD your God giveth you to possess it.

◀ **Memory Selection**
Joshua 1:9

◀ **Devotional Reading**
Joshua 3:1-7

◀ **Background Scripture**
Joshua 1

◀ **Printed Scripture**
Joshua 1:1-11

21

GOD'S CHOICE OF JOSHUA

Teacher's Target

The passing of Moses from the leadership of Israel left a tremendous gap, but God had another man lined up to fill it. Joshua had been one of the twelve spies sent into Canaan many years before (Num. 13:8). Only he and Caleb had advised the Israelites to go in and take the land with God's help (Num. 14:6-9). They survived the forty years of wilderness wanderings and were on hand when the next generation was ready to take Canaan. Joshua was trained for leadership by serving with Moses.

Help your students to trust God to provide individuals to lead His people in every generation, including their own. As they walk with God and follow His orders, they will themselves be used of Him in leading others. In the meantime, they need to absorb all they can from others so that they will be qualified to lead. Education through the local church, correspondence courses, and various types of schools is available and ought to be utilized.

Lesson Introduction

An athletic team going into a game often has its confidence strengthened by a pep talk from the coach. A military platoon going into a battle may have a similar experience with its officer. When it came time for Israel to enter Canaan, God Himself appeared to Joshua. He announced that Moses was gone and it was Joshua's job to lead the people across the Jordan River and take the land promised to them. The heathen had polluted the land with their sins for four hundred years. God wanted His people to reclaim it and make it their own.

The Lord used strong but simple words with Joshua. He told him that every place the sole of his foot trod would be given to him. He said that no enemy would be able to stand against him. He was to be strong, courageous, and obedient to the law of God. The Lord's presence would be with him wherever he went. We may face different kinds of enemies today, but the Lord works in and through us in the same way. Divine inspiration should produce human action on our part, and when it does, God is glorified.

Teaching Outline

I. Ground: Josh. 1:1-7
   A. Commission: 1-4
   B. Companion: 5
   C. Courage: 6-7
II. Guide: Josh. 1:8-9
   A. Law: 8
   B. Lord: 9
III. Gift: Josh. 1:10-11
   A. Preparation: 10-11a
   B. Possession: 11b

Daily Bible Readings

Mon. Joshua Succeeds Moses—*Josh. 1:12-18*
Tue. Rahab Protects Joshua's Messengers—*Josh. 2:1-14*
Wed. The Israelites Follow the Ark of the Covenant—*Josh. 3:1-6*
Thu. God Promises to Be with Joshua—*Josh. 3:7-13*
Fri. Joshua Makes a Memorial of Twelve Stones—*Josh. 4:1-7*
Sat. Joshua Meets a Man of God near Jericho—*Josh. 5:10-15*
Sun. Joshua's Army Brings down the Wall of Jericho—*Josh. 6:15-21*

September 20, 1992

VERSE BY VERSE

I. Ground: Josh. 1:1-7

A. Commission: 1-4

1. **Now after the death of Moses the servant of the Lord it came to pass, that the Lord spake unto Joshua the son of Nun, Moses' minister, saying,**

Moses had looked forward to entering Canaan, but it was not to be. When the Israelites had feared dying of thirst at Rephidim, God had told Moses to strike a rock with his staff so that water could flow out of it (Exod. 17:1-7). When Moses later struck a rock for this purpose, rather than just speaking to it, God disapproved and told him he would not be allowed to take Israel into Canaan (Num. 20:7-13). The rock, symbol of Christ, was not to be stricken twice, for He was scheduled to die only once. God did let Moses view Canaan from Mount Nebo (Pisgah) before He took him away (Deut. 3:23-27; 34:1-7). Moses did appear with Elijah at the transfiguration of Jesus before Peter, James, and John many centuries later (Matt. 17:1-13).

With Moses out of the picture, the Lord turned to Joshua, his minister (assistant). All we know about Nun (Non), Joshua's father, was that he came from the tribe of Ephraim (1 Chron. 7:20-27). The original name of Joshua was Oshea (deliverer), but it was changed to Joshua (Jehoshua) (God's salvation). Both Moses and Eleazer the priest had taken part in the elevation of Joshua to his position of leadership (Num. 27:15-23).

2. **Moses my servant is dead; now therefore arise, go over this Jordan, thou, and all this people, unto the land which I do give to them, even to the children of Israel.**

Joshua must surely have known that he was to be the leader of Israel in Moses' place, but this describes how God made it very clear by coming directly to him with a commission. Having come up through Moab, the Israelites were on the eastern side of the Jordan River looking westward to the promised land. God declared that this was their land, and He was going to give it to them. They were to displace the pagan tribes which had inhabited it for the five hundred years which had passed since the land had been promised to Abraham and his descendants (Gen. 12:7).

3. **Every place that the sole of your foot shall tread upon, that have I given unto you, as I said unto Moses.**

4. **From the wilderness and this Lebanon even unto the great river, the river Euphrates, all the land of the Hittites, and even unto the great sea toward the going down of the sun, shall be your coast.**

This repeated what Moses had earlier told the Israelites. "Then will the Lord drive out all these nations from before you, and ye shall possess greater nations and mightier than yourselves. Every place whereon the soles of your feet shall tread shall be yours: from the wilderness and Lebanon, from the river, the river Euphrates, even unto the uttermost sea shall your coast be" (Deut. 11:23-24). Leadership had changed from Moses to Joshua, but the divine promise remained the same.

The Israelites were expected to keep God's ways and to occupy the land offered to them. The coasts of the occupied land were actually boundaries, even if they were not on any shoreline. The wilderness mentioned here was the Desert of Sin (Zin) in the southeastern part of Palestine. Lebanon was the range of mountains in the north, particularly Mount Hermon. The Euphrates River lay far to the northeast in ancient Mesopotamia. The great sea toward the west was the Mediterranean Sea. Hittites were descendants of Noah through Ham through Canaan's second son, Heth (I Chron. 1:13). They were spread over a wide area, including the southern part of Canaan. As the dominant people in that region, they would have to be defeated in order for the Israelites to occupy Canaan. Subsequent history indicates that Israel did not control all of the area described here until the reigns of King David and King Solomon.

B. Companion: 5

5. **There shall not any man be able to stand before thee all the days of thy life: as I was with Moses, so I will be with thee: I will not fail thee, nor forsake thee.**

The Lord encouraged Joshua's resolve by promising to be his constant Companion throughout the campaign to take the land of Canaan. He had been with Moses as Joshua knew well, and He would be with him, too. He would not fail him in any way. He would not abandon him. Further study in the book of Joshua proves that God kept His promise. Sometimes sin resulted in setbacks but God never forsook his people. One example of this was the defeat of Israel in its first attempt to take Ai. Achan's sin had to be dealt with before God gave Israel victory (Josh. 7).

6. **Be strong and of good courage: for unto this people shalt thou divide for an inheritance the land, which I sware unto their fathers to give them.**

Long months of battle and travel stretched out fore Israel, but Joshua could face them with confidence backed by divine inspiration. Reference to dividing the land was a sure sign of coming victory. When things became exhausting and difficult, the Israelites could claim God's promise of triumph.

7. **Only be thou strong and very courageous, that thou mayest observe to do according to all the law, which Moses my servant commanded thee: turn not from it to the right hand or to the left, that thou mayest prosper whithersoever thou goest.**

God impressed on Joshua the fact that victory could be expected only if he and his people observed the law of God in all things. They dared not turn away from it to the right hand or to the left hand. Victory depended on adherence to the will of the Lord. If this were neglected, the basis for courage would vanish and be replaced by desperation.

II. Guide: Josh. 1:6-9

A. Law: 8

8. **This book of the law shall not depart out of thy mouth; but thou shalt meditate therein day and night, that thou mayest observe to do according to all that is written therein: for then thou shalt make thy way prosperous, and then thou shalt have good success.**

The written guide for Joshua and the Israelites to follow was the law of God as given to them by Moses. This was composed in its larger sense of the Pentateuch, the first five books of the Bible. It was composed in its more restricted sense of the ten commandments and the Levitical Code allied with them. The original meaning for the Hebrew word for meditate was "to recite in an undertone." It suggests that God's people were expected to memorize and repeat His regulations from morning until night so that they became an integral part of their thinking and acting. They could not hope for things to go well for them unless they were governed by divine directives, and this had to include *all* of the directives, not merely those that they chose to select. We do well today to follow the *whole* counsel of God.

9. **Have not I commanded thee? Be strong and of a good courage: be not afraid, neither be thou dismayed: for the Lord thy God is with thee whithersoever thou goest.**

Note the similarity of this verse to preceding verse 7. God was not merely suggesting Joshua be strong and courageous. He was *commanding* him to have these traits. There was no reason for him to be afraid or dismayed because of the great challenge facing him. God had promised to go with him wherever he went, and that was supposed to be sufficient to strengthen his faith and produce good results in the campaign to oust the pagans due for divine retribution in Canaan.

Note the similarity of this verse to the great commission given by Jesus to His followers just before He ascended to heaven. They were told to make spiritual conquests and to take courage from the fact that He would be with them by His Holy Spirit. "Go ye therefore, and teach all nations, baptizing them in the name of the Father, and of the Son, and of the Holy Ghost: teaching them to observe all things whatsoever I have commanded you: and, lo, I am with you alway, even unto the end of the world. (Matt. 28:19-20). That applies to us today.

III. Gift: Josh. 1:10-11

A. Preparation: 10-11a

10. Then Joshua commanded the officers of the people, saying,

11a. Pass through the host, and command the people, saying, Prepare your victuals; ...

God had commanded Joshua, and now it was Joshua's turn to command the officers of the people. These were the *shot'rim* (or *shoterim*), meaning scribes or overseers who passed along administrative commands to the common people (Deut. 20:5). They were to make a thorough passage throughout Israel and make sure that everyone was aware of Joshua's order.

The people were told to spend the next three days gathering and preparing various kinds of food to sustain them when they marched into Canaan. The manna which they had gathered and eaten in the wilderness would soon be gone. Look ahead to Joshua 5:11-12: "And they did eat of the old corn of the land on the morrow after the passover, unleavened cakes, and parched corn in the selfsame day. And the manna ceased on the morrow after they had eaten of the old corn of the land; neither had the children of Israel manna any more; but they did eat of the fruit of the land of Canaan that year."

B. Possession: 11b

11b. ... for within three days ye shall pass over this Jordan, to go in to possess the land, which the Lord your God giveth you to possess it.

One of the primary characteristics of a leader should be to inspire his people to face challenges. God had inspired Joshua, and now it was time for Joshua to inspire the Israelites. He began well by stating firmly that within three days they were going to begin the march which would take them across the Jordan River. This required faith on his part, because this was flood season for the river. Something unusual would have to happen in order for the Israelites to get by this barrier.

Before the crossing took place, there were a couple of things Joshua had to do. He called the leaders of the Reubenites, Gadites, and half the tribe of Manasseh together and told them that they could leave their wives and children on the eastern side of the Jordan, but the men would have to go with their brethren to conquer the western side of the river. This they agreed to do (Joshua 1: 12-18). The other thing he did was to send two spies to look at Jericho and report back on conditions there. When the king of Jericho heard about them and demanded that Rahab produce them, she hid them until they could escape. They promised her that she and her loved ones would not be killed when the Israelites attacked. Crossing back over the river, they reported to Joshua and expressed their opinion that the Lord would deliver the people of Jericho into their hands (Josh. 2). This report confirmed to Joshua that God's promise to him would be fulfilled as the campaign began.

Evangelistic Emphasis

God's choice of Joshua to succeed Moses goes back to Joshua's faithfulness forty years earlier. Joshua was one of the two men who believed Israel could conquer the land of Canaan. Joshua heard God's promise that He would give the land to the Israelites. The others, with hard hearts and inattentive spirits, did not trust God's work. There is quite a contrast between the faithfulness of Joshua and the unfaithfulness of the people. Joshua believed without seeing; the people believed only what they saw. Joshua took God at his word; the people were afraid God's word would prove untrue.

Faithfulness is an important part of the evangelistic message. God needs persons who are dependable. He often chooses those who have proven themselves in other circumstances. God is always looking for and expecting faith. It is the prerequisite of salvation and service. Faith means to take God at His word. There are special promises and blessings attached to faith. God promises to be with us. God gives forgiveness of sins, the presence of His Spirit, and the expectation of heaven to those who have faith.

All of us, at times, are called upon to stretch our faith, to move forward in bold and unexpected ways. We do not, however, walk alone: "For the Lord your God is with you wherever you go." When God asks us to take on new tasks that threaten our security or new responsibilities that appear beyond our strength, He provides the courage and the encouragement we need. He is pleased with us when we go forth in faith to do His will.

God, knowing that the people would need a strong leader, chose Joshua, because Joshua had proven himself as a man of God. When others lacked faith, Joshua stepped forward and took a stand. Now, he was being given an even greater work to do. As Jesus put it, those faithful in the small things are given even greater work to accomplish.

Memory Selection

Be strong and of good courage; be not frightened, neither be dismayed: for the Lord your God is with you wherever you go.
Joshua 1:9

One of the root metaphors of the Bible is LIFE IS A BATTLE. The whole Bible supports the image of an intense struggle, a real fight, a difficult testing. From the Israelites poised on the edge of Canaan to the Christian soldier of Ephesians wearing the whole armour of God, the man of God faces wars within and battles without. The story of Joshua revolves around a battle to conquer the promised land. Thus the words of God to Joshua are words of encouragement and assurance, words intended to put confidence in God's warriors.

How important it is to remember that we too face a difficult fight in our Christian experience. No wonder the imperative "Be strong and of good courage" is frequently repeated in Joshua. We need steel and determination in our Christian lives. Like Joshua we face a powerful, pernicious, persistent enemy. Listen, we need the strength of the Lord.

God speaks to all of us: "Be not frightened, neither be dismayed." These notes of encouragement are sounded because God knows how easy it is for us to be overwhelmed.

September 20, 1992

Weekday Problems

Bill was happy with his career as a social worker. He enjoyed helping people with their problems. He was well known and a faithful member of the church in his community. The needs and problems he handled every day were the kind that were solved by filling out a form or referring folks to higher authorities. He had the normal ups and downs of any other social work professional, but, all in all, he was content with his life.

Then his pastor asked Bill to assume responsibility for the youth group. The small town where Bill lived had lots of churches, but for some reason none had a youth ministry. Now Bill's pastor wanted to assume that task. The young people faced a multitude of problems from peer pressure, drugs, alcohol and pornography. No doubt starting and maintaining a youth group would be a formidable challenge.

Bill was not sure he had enough time to give to such a bold project. He was not even sure if he could say yes and make that commitment.

*On what basis should Bill decide whether to take the volunteer youth position?
*How does God's promise to Joshua fit with Bill's opportunity?
*In what ways would Bill be fighting the good fight of the Christian by helping the youth?

Superintendent's Sermonette

Only God knows the end from the beginning in any given situation. If He withholds information regarding what is to happen, He may do it for a variety of reasons. He does not want us to become paralyzed by fear which would seize and master us if we knew the hard things awaiting us. He does not want us to feel defeated before we begin to wrestle with great challenges. He does want us to exercise faith in Him and to believe that He will help us face whatever lies ahead, depending on His unlimited power and wisdom.

Joshua had come out of Egypt in the exodus. He had been sent to spy out the land of Canaan and had returned to advise Israel to enter and conquer it with God's help. That first generation had failed to trust the Lord and had wandered for forty years in the wilderness until most died. Joshua and Caleb, however, were on hand when it came time for the second generation to enter the promised land. They were equal to the task because they had faith in Jehovah.

We live in perilous times, and we do not know all the challenges facing us, but we can meet them in the same way that Joshua did. Let us trust God and His Word, and let us do all that we can to get others to join us in living faithfully for Him.

27

GOD'S CHOICE OF JOSHUA TO SUCCEED MOSES

This Lesson In Your Life

In Robert Frost's poem, "The Death of the Hired Man," there are those haunting words: "Poor Silas, so concerned for other folk, and nothing to look backward to with pride, and nothing to look forward to with hope, so now and never any different." How tragic to be caught in the end with nothing in the past and nothing in the future. For Israel, that transitional time between the death of Moses and the ascension of Joshua provided time for contemplation of the past and the future.

Life in an in-between moment offers an opportunity to REMEMBER. One of the most important of human activities is remembering. God often insists that his people remember and never forget Him. Memory enables a people to know whose they are and who they are. Memory keeps alive mission for the people of God. If a person loses his memory, the resulting amnesia takes away not only the past but all his ties to life and kin. Well, God's people can not afford amnesia.

Therefore the death of Moses was a time to remember. The people could look back with pride, a legitimate pride, to the great faithfulness of Moses. Even more importantly they could remember how God had been with Moses. As they looked back they somehow tried to find evidence that gave them the hope to look forward. What a blessing to be able to look forward by looking backward. Here is how it works. The people remembered the crossing of the Red Sea. That would give them confidence for crossing the Jordan in the near future. The people remembered that God had been with Moses. Now they could know God would also be with Joshua.

This lesson reminds us that God's missionary purpose for all people to be saved must continue in spite of the death of Moses. Moses had died. Without so much as a pause to mourn, the writer of Joshua moves on to the call Joshua. Joshua was commanded to complete the work of Moses. God had already taken care of all the arrangements. Therefore the history as God's people continued as God appointed a successor to Moses.

The unbroken line of succession from Moses to Joshua is a reminder that God always has someone waiting in the wings. No one is indispensable. We are all part of an ongoing tradition. Each person plays his or her part in God's overarching missionary goal. As the writer of Hebrews reminds us we are surrounded by a great host of God's people who have already completed their segment of the journey. There is never a place for arrogance among the people of God.

We can take heart from this episode because God is always out in front of His people. While we may not have the exact announcement of God in our choices of leaders, we have the assurance that God will be with us and guide us in our decisions. Therefore we always look to the future, safe in the assurance that the key to success lies with God, not with one particular leader.

Transition periods are often difficult. National consulting firms now work full-time to help fathers pass their businesses on to their offspring. Churches often experience difficulty when one generation of leaders grows older, and younger Christians begin to assume responsibility. A long-term, beloved pastor is difficult to follow. Sometimes the next pastor is unable to meet expectations.

The in-between time also affords us an opportunity for renewal. We look back with pride on previous accomplishments but we also look forward with expectation to future successes, a time of remembering and a time of renewing. We have the privilege of thanking God for the strong effective leadership of the past, as well as giving our support and loyalty to the new leader or leaders.

Seed Thoughts

1. What event in Joshua's earlier life gave evidence of his potential for leadership?
He was one of the two spies sent into the land of Canaan who returned with a positive report that the land could be conquered with faith in God

2. The Lord promised Joshua success upon the meeting of what essential condition?
Joshua was expected to meditate upon the Law, observe the Law, and live by every word of the Law.

3. What was Joshua's first command upon assuming the leadership of the people of Israel?
The people were commanded to prepare food for a journey because in three days Joshua expected to cross over the Jordan.

4. What parallels can we draw from the experiences of Moses and Joshua?
The Lord spoke to and called both men. Both men received the promise of the land of Canaan. Moses led the Israelites across the Red sea and Joshua led them across the Jordan.

5. What symbol of the religion of Israel led the procession on the crossing of the Jordan?
The ark of the covenant, symbolizing the real presence of God, went before the people.

(PLEASE TURN PAGE)

---

1. What event in Joshua's earlier life gave evidence of his potential for leadership?

2. The Lord promised Joshua success upon the meeting of what essential condition?

3. What was Joshua's first command upon assuming the leadership of the people of Israel?

4. What parallels can we draw from the experiences of Moses and Joshua?

5. What symbol of the religion of Israel led the procession on the crossing of the Jordan?

6. What is the biblical significance of the ark of the covenant?

7. Who were the permanent bearers of the ark?

8. What did Joshua command the bearers of the ark to do?

9. What was to be the evidence that God was with the Israelites?

10. What divine sign would occur in the crossing of the Jordan that parallels the sign given in the crossing of the Red Sea?

(SEED THOUGHTS--Cont'd)

He was one of the two spies sent into the land of Canaan who returned with a positive report that the land could be conquered with faith in God

Joshua was expected to meditate upon the Law, observe the Law, and live by every word of the Law.

The people were commanded to prepare food for a journey because in three days Joshua expected to cross over the Jordan.

The Lord spoke to and called both men. Both men received the promise of the land of Canaan. Moses led the Israelites across the Red sea and Joshua led them across the Jordan.

The ark of the covenant, symbolizing the real presence of God, went before the people.

The ark was seen as the presence of God, as a symbol of power in war, as a container of the two tablets of the ten commandments, and as the earthly throne of God.

The Levite priests were responsible for carrying the ark.

After entering the Jordan River they were to stand still.

The Lord would drive out all the residents of Canaan. This included the Canaanites, the Hittites, the Hivites, the Perizzites, the Girgashites, the Amorites, and the Jebusites.

Both in the crossing of the Red Sea and the crossing of the Jordan, the waters were parted and the people walked over on dry ground.

6. What is the biblical significance of the ark of the covenant?
The ark was seen as the presence of God, as a symbol of power in war, as a container of the two tablets of the ten commandments, and as the earthly throne of God.

7. Who were the permanent bearers of the ark?
The Levite priests were responsible for carrying the ark.

8. What did Joshua command the bearers of the ark to do?
After entering the Jordan River they were to stand still.

9. What was to be the evidence that God was with the Israelites?
The Lord would drive out all the residents of Canaan. This included the Canaanites, the Hittites, the Hivites, the Perizzites, the Girgashites, the Amorites, and the Jebusites.

10. What divine sign would occur in the crossing of the Jordan that parallels the sign given in the crossing of the Red Sea?
Both in the crossing of the Red Sea and the crossing of the Jordan, the waters were parted and the people walked over on dry ground.

September 27, 1992

God's Provision of Leadership Through Deborah

Judges 4

4 And Deborah a Prophetess, the wife of Lap´-i-doth, she judged Israel at that time.
5 And she dwelt under the palm tree of Deb´o-rah between Ra´-mah and Beth´-el in mount E´-phra-im; and the children of Israel came up to her for judgment.
6 And she sent and called Ba´-rak the son of A-bin´-o-am out of Ke´ deshnaph´-ta-li, and said unto him, Hath not the LORD God of Israel commanded, *saying*, Go and draw toward mount Ta´bor, and take with thee ten thousand men of the children of Naph´-ta-li and of the children of Zeb´-u-lun?
7 And I will draw unto thee to the river Ki´-shon, Sis´-e-ra, the captain of Ja´-bin's army, with his chariots and his multitude; and I will deliver him into thine hand.
8 And Ba´-rak said unto her, If thou wilt go with me, then I will go: but if thou wilt not go with me, *then* I will not go.
9 And she said, I will surely go with thee: notwithstanding the journey that thou takest shall not be for thine honour; for the LORD shall sell Sis´-e-ra into the hand of a woman. And Deborah arose, and went with Ba´-rak to Ke´-desh.
10 And Ba´-rak called Zeb´-u-lun and Naph´-ta-Ii to Ke´-desh; and he went up with ten thousand men at his feet: arid Deb´o-rah went up with him.

14 And Deb´-o-rah said unto Ba´-rak, Up; for this is the day in which the LORD hath delivered Sis´-e-ra into thine hand: is not the LORD gone out before thee? So Ba´-rak went down from mount Ta´-bor, and ten thousand men after him.
15 And the LORD discomfited Sis´-e-ra, and all his chariots, and all his host, with the edge of the sword before Ba´-rak; so that Sis´-e-ra lighted down off his chariot, and fled away on his feet.
16 But Ba´rak pursued after the chariots, and after the host unto Ha-ro´-sheth of the Gentiles: and all the host of Sis´-e-ra fell upon the edge of the sword; and there was not a man left.

◆◆◆◆◆◆

◀ **Memory Selection**
Judges 4:6

◀ **Devotional Reading**
Judges 6:11-16

◀ **Background Scripture**
Judges 4-5

◀ **Printed Scripture**
Judges 4:4-10, 14-16

Teacher's Target

We all have heard the statement, "Behind every good man there is a woman...pushing!" This has often been true, whether that woman was a mother, wife, sister, daughter, or friend. Courage is not limited to men, and history has much to back up the fact that women have sometimes had more courage than men. Such was the case with Deborah and Barak. Deborah was in tune with God, and she was used by Him to motivate Barak when it came time to confront the pagan Canaanites.

Help your students to see how the God-given role of a woman can be used to support that of a man, even if the two are not related to one another. God's work will be done when each individual, regardless of gender, does what he or she is supposed to do. Emphasize the fact that courage can be stimulated by a good example and by persistence. Let us accept what God says and then persuade others to accept it and act upon it.

Lesson Introduction

The Canaanites, under King Jabin and General Sisera, had oppressed Israel for two decades. They plundered farms, restricted movement, and disarmed the Israelites. This was but one of many times that the heathen persecuted God's people, who had brought trouble on themselves by sinning. When the Israelites repented and called for God's help, He raised up judges (actually military deliverers) to release them from foreign domination. We find thirteen described in the book of Judges, if we count Deborah and Barak as one and if we include Abimelech, whom some consider an outlaw. The best known were Gideon, Samson, and Jephthah.

The thing that makes this lesson unique is the presentation of Deborah as a judge and prophetess in her own right plus her influence on Barak. Israel's victory over the Canaanites could be attributed to her at least as much as to Barak and his soldiers. If she had not obeyed God, Israel would not have experienced divine deliverance.

Teaching Outline

I. Advice: Judg. 4:4-5
   A. Prophetess: 4
   B. Popularity: 5
II. Argument: Judg. 4:6-10
   A. Command: 6-7
   B. Condition: 8
   C. Compliance: 9-10
III. Action: Judg. 4:14-16
   A. Challenge: 14a
   B. Conquest: 14b-16

Daily Bible Readings

Mon. Deborah and Barak Sing Praises to God - *Judg. 5:1-5*
Tue. Deborah's Rise to Leadership *Judg. 5:6-10*
Wed. Victory for Deborah and Barak *Judg. 5:11-15a*
Thu. Disunity among the Israelites *Judg. 5:15b-23*
Fri. The Enemy Is Defeated *Judg. 5:24-51*
Sat. God Calls Gideon to Lead the Israelites - *Judg. 6:11-17*
Sun. God Assures Gideon of Israel's Deliverance - *Judg. 7:36-40*

VERSE BY VERSE

Deborah

I. Advice: Judg. 4:4-5

A. Prophetess: 4

4. And Deborah, a prophetess, the wife of Lapidoth, she judged Israel at that time.

The period between theocracy (rule by God) and monarchy (rule by kings) was noted for anarchy. "In those days there was no king in Israel: every man did that which was right in his own eyes" (Judg. 21:25). Confusion prevailed, and foreign incursions took place. God repeatedly raised up judges (actually military deliverers) to help the Israelites throw off their oppressors as the cycle moved from sin to servitude to salvation.

Deborah was already a prophetess in Israel. She was the wife of Lapidoth, about whom nothing more is recorded. Deborah evidently had special wisdom from the Lord. People recognized this and came to depend on her for settling disputes.

B. Popularity: 5

5. And she dwelt under the palm tree of Deborah between Ramah and Bethel in mount Ephraim: and the children of Israel came up to her for judgment.

Lapidoth and Deborah lived between the towns of Ramah and Bethel. Ramah belonged to the tribe of Benjamin north of Jerusalem. Bethel belonged to the tribe of Ephraim and was located about five miles north of Ramah. The term "mount Ephraim" could mean "the hill country of Ephraim." The dwelling under the palm tree mentioned here may have referred to the home of Lapidoth and Deborah or to the place where she received people who came to her for decisions to settle disputes. It was because of her reputation as a wise and spiritual woman that Barak was later influenced by her.

II. Argument: Judg. 4:6-10

A. Command: 6-7

6. And she sent and called Barak the son of Abinoam out of Kedesh-naphtali, and said unto him, Hath not the Lord God of Israel commanded, saying, Go and draw toward mount Tabor, and take with thee ten thousand men of the children of Naphtali and of the children of Zebulum?

We do not know if Deborah's information came to her directly from the Lord or from some other source, but she felt compelled to act upon it. She sent word to Barak, son of Abinoam, at Kedeshnaphtali about eighteen miles north of the Sea of Galilee. This town had been taken by Joshua in his campaign to conquer northern Canaan (Josh. 12:7, 22). It later became part of the inheritance of the tribe of Naphtali (Josh. 19:32, 37). It was designated as one of the cities of refuge for individuals to go to until trials could be held for them (Josh. 20:1-7; 21:32).

Deborah reminded Barak that the

Lord God of Israel had commanded him to go to the Mount Tabor region and take an army of ten thousand men from among the tribes of Naphtali and Zebulun. Her question obviously carried with it a note of reproof for having failed to obey the Lord.

7. And I will draw unto thee to the river Kishon Sisera, the captain of Jabin's army, with his chariots and his multitude; and I will deliver him into thine hand.

The Lord had made the purpose for raising the army clear to Barak, and that is what must have scared him into doing nothing. God had said that He would draw Sisera, here called "the captain of Jabin's army," along with his chariots and his multitude of soldiers, to the Kishon River. This river rose from streams on Mount Tabor and Mount Gilboa and then flowed westward through the Plain of Esdraelon (Valley of Jezreel) to the Mediterranean at the Bay of Acre north of Mount Carmel. It could normally be crossed at certain fords, but in flood season it was impassable. This was the divinely-chosen place for Israel to gain a victory over the Canaanites.

B. Condition: 8

6. And Barak said unto her, If thou wilt go with me, then I will go: but if thou wilt not go with me, then I will not go.

We are not told why God chose Barak to lead His troops into battle. Barak must have had some measure of faith in Jehovah to be honored in this way, but he was reluctant to move out on God's promise. Barak, knowing of Deborah's reputation, decided that he would do as God commanded, provided she went with him. If she refused to go, he would not go, either. At this point, the nine hundred chariots and massive forces of Sisera were more intimidating to him than God's command. He felt that Deborah's presence was absolutely necessary for victory to take place. Perhaps he was convinced that her presence would inspire the men from Naphtali and Zebulun to fight triumphantly. Barak could have trusted the Lord on his own, but he deliberately called on Deborah to share her faith with him. He made this a condition for doing what God had told him to do.

C. Compliance: 9-10

9. And she said, I will surely go with thee: notwithstanding the journey that thou takest shall not be for thine honour; for the Lord shall sell Sisera into the hand of a woman. And Deborah arose, and went with Barak to Kedesh.

Realizing that Barak would not follow the divine order unless she accompanied him, Deborah agreed to go. However, she foretold the fact that this campaign would not add to Barak's stature as far as taking the Canaanite army leader was concerned With this prediction made. Deborah joined Barak in going north to raise the army of ten thousand from the tribes of Naphtali and Zebulun.

10. And Barak called Zebulun and Naphtali to Kedesh; and he went up with ten thousand men at his feet: and Deborah went up with him.

Once in Kedesh, Barak issued the call to arms in Naphtali and Zebulun, We do not know how the ten thousand men managed to find weapons to take with them, but they must have found arms of some type. Deborah was apparently helpful in recruiting them, and she proceeded to march with them to battle. She no doubt represented God and His promise of victory to them.

Judges 4:11-13 is not in our printed text, but you would do well to summarize it. Heber the Kenite, belonging to the descendants of Hobab (actually the son of Reuel or Jethro and thus the brother-in-law of Moses - Num. 10:29-32), had separated himself from the Kenites and had pitched his tent in the plain of Zaanaim near Kedesh. He informed Sisera that Barak was marching toward Mount Tabor with an army of ten thousand, Hearing this, Sisera assembled his troops and their chariots and headed from Harosheth (near Mount Carmel) to the Kishon River (near Mount Tabor). The stage was being set for the military confrontation.

III. Action: Judg. 4:14-16

A. Challenge: 14a

14a. And Deborah said unto Barak, Up; for this is the day in which the Lord hath delivered Sisera into thine hand: is not the Lord gone out before thee?

It was one thing to recruit an army and march to the scene of battle. It was something else again to initiate conflict. Barak was evidently squeamish about it, and Deborah had to issue a challenge which he could not ignore. She boldly told him to get up and get moving. She prophesied that this was the day in which the Lord was going to deliver Sisera and his hosts into the hand of the reluctant warrior.

B. Conquest: 14b-16

14b. So Barak went down from mount Tabor, and ten thousand men after him.

Fortified by Deborah's promise that God was moving out onto the battlefield ahead of him, and perhaps stung by her challenge, Barak moved ahead. He led his men into battle, rather than directing them from behind the lines. This put him into the hottest place with all of its attendant perils.

15a. And the Lord discomfited Sisera, and all his chariots, and all his host, with the edge of the sword before Barak;...

True to His word, the Lord was really the One leading the Israelites into battle. It would appear that He did most of the work, for He discomfitted (confused, terrorized) the Canaanite charioteers and foot-soldiers. Judges 5:21 records that some Canaanites were overwhelmed by the Kishon River and swept away in it. It was because the Lord used great fear and the forces of nature that the enemies of Israel were defeated. He deserved credit for what took place before the Israelites concentrated on a mopping-up operation.

15b. ...so that Sisera lighted down off his chariot, and fled away on his feet.

Let us skip ahead to verses 17-22 to conclude what happened to Sisera. Fleeing from the scene of battle Sisera came to the tent of Jael, wife of Heber the Kenite. She went out to invite him to come into the tent. He was exhausted and thirsty, and she gave him milk to drink and then covered him so that he could rest. He told her to stand in the door of the tent and tell anyone who asked that there was no man there. Jael took a tent spike and a hammer and drove it into Sisera's head while he slept pinning him to the ground and killing him. When Barak and his men came by, Jael revealed what she had done.

16. But Barak pursued after the chariots, and after the host, unto Harosheth of the Gentiles: and all the host of Sisera fell upon the edge of the sword; and there was not a man left.

Having explained how Sisera died, although there are more details about it in Judges 5:25-29, we now return to a description of how his army fared. Barak and his men pursued after the charioteers and foot-soldiers relentlessly as far as Harosheth near Mount Carmel at the western end of the Plain of Esdraelon. This bordered on Phoenicia, a Gentile nation. The search by the Israelites was so thorough that not one Canaanite warrior escaped the edge of the sword. It was a stunning victory for the nation of Israel. Judges 4:23-24 concludes the event by stating that God subdued Jabin the king of Canaan- allowing the Israelites to destroy him. This gave God the credit for the victory.

Looking back over the text, we note that this whole event hinged on the determined faith and action of Deborah. She was the one who was in touch with God. She was the one who challenged Barak. She was the one who went with him to give support in recruiting ten thousand men and taking them to battle. It is important that we who belong to God be serious about doing what He expects us to do. As our text today illustrates, the fate of a nation may depend on our faithfulness.

Evangelistic Emphasis

Evangelism can take many forms. There are many ways to invite people into a saving relationship with Jesus Christ. One important way is to encourage people to turn to Jesus Christ. Encouragement is a major factor in many experiences of life. One such experience is that of Deborah and Barak. Without Deborah's encouragement, Barak would never have gone into battle and gained the great victory for God's people.

When we attempt to lead others to Jesus Christ, we can remember the exploits of Deborah. She used her candid boldness to help Barak know that the Lord would be with him. People will be impressed and moved by our honesty and forthrightness. If a person knows that we are sincere, that we really believe what we are saying, he will be more likely to respond. Always encourage others to investigate the invitation of Jesus to salvation.

Encouragement may be the greatest gift we can give to others. For example, my wife once told one of her students, "Lawrence you are good with math. You can be a banker." The next day Lawrence told Johnelle, "My mother says you're crazy. I can't be a banker." Four months later, the class was doing an exercise called "My Good Friend Award." Lawrence read his to the class: "I give this good friend award to Mrs. Kennedy, because she loves me and wants me to be a banker." People never forget words of encouragement.

◆◆◆◆◆◆

Memory Selection

"(Deborah) sent and summoned Barak . . . and said to him, "The Lord the God of Israel, commands you, 'Go, gather your men at Mount Tabor.'"
Judges 4:6.

No explanation is given for Deborah being judge over Israel. The presence of a woman as spiritual leader in the ancient Hebrew culture is cause for at least some musing. Perhaps it is important to remember that God's ways are not always our ways. The fact that he used Deborah to put courage into Barak is a lesson in God's surprising ways. Without Deborah's charismatic, forceful insistence, Barak would have never gone into battle.

The confidence and boldness of Deborah was used by God to encourage Barak and his soldiers. God also has plans for other persons that will never unfold unless they are encouraged by other Christians. Deborah had the fate of an entire nation in her hands. She used all her God-given powers to persuade Barak into action. We are able to instill the same courage into modern-day Baraks, men who have great ability but lack initiative and courage. Remember that we are to always proclaim the message of God through convincing, rebuking and encouraging (2 Timothy 4:3). Encouragement is a major ministry of Christians in our day. From Deborah of the Old Testament to Barnabas of the New Testament, we see women and men putting new spirit into others. Remember that Barnabas means "son of encouragement," and use Barnabas as a New Testament parallel to the story of Deborah.

September 27, 1992

Weekday Problems

Jackson is president of the major bank in town. He has been a member of the church all his life. His family is the most prominent in the whole county. They also are the richest people in the church. Jackson, however, has never given much to the support of the church.

Now the church is in the middle of a $1 million capitol improvement campaign for a new sanctuary. In order for the campaign to succeed, the church needs a $100,000 contribution from Jackson. The problem is that no one seems to have the courage to ask Jackson for the money. He certainly can afford to make the gift. If he does give the money, the whole church will be encouraged and the campaign will succeed.

Bill, a local mechanic, does not make much money. He is not a member of a prominent family. However, he gives 10% of every dollar he makes to the church. For him, a $1,000 contribution would be a much greater sacrifice than Jackson giving $100,000. Bill has felt the leadership of the Holy Spirit to do two things: 1) pledge to give $1,000 to the church and 2) ask Jackson for the $100,000 contribution.

*Should Bill ask Jackson for such a large contribution? (Remember the principle of sacrificial giving.)

*Will Bill's example and encouragement be the primary factors in his favor when he approaches Jackson.

*Is it possible that we have not because we do not encourage others to join us in sacrificing for the work of the Lord?

♦♦♦♦♦♦

Superintendent's Sermonette

It is fairly easy for us to look back on historical figures and realize that God used them to implement His sovereign will in various circumstances. It is more difficult for us to look at our own lives and see how God might be using us to carry out His will, We pass through our daily routines and our times of crisis and perhaps think that we are merely drifting along with the tide of events. We listen and look at the media and wonder if we have any effect on the fast-paced happenings surrounding us both here at home and worldwide.

Barak may have felt that way in his time. Israel was ground under the heel of the pagan Canaanites led by King Jabin and Sisera, his military commander. There seemed nothing could be done, but God had a plan, and He fully intended to carry it out in this situation. The surprising factor was that He used Deborah, a prophetess and judge, to galvanize Barak and ten thousand recruits from Naphtali and Zebulun into action, The nine hundred chariots and huge army of Jabin and Sisera were decimated, and Israel was given an astounding victory. Let us never underestimate what God can do through individuals who are trusting in Him and ready to go into action for Him, We, like Deborah, can make a difference.

GOD'S PROVISION OF LEADERSHIP THROUGH DEBORAH

This Lesson In Your Life

When the church is not seduced by the sensual power of her culture, we are able to see clearly the illusions undergirding that culture. One of those illusions is that progress is the epitomy of the American way of life. Now, there can be no doubt that our civilization has made progress. More progress has been made in the past twenty-five years that all the preceeding centuries of human civilization. Our progress, however, has been in the material realm. There is little evidence that the basic nature of humanity has progressed, in short, we are still sinners.

In fact, our inability to progress is a recurring theme in the Old Testament Book of Judges. In unrelenting repetition, the writer shows how each generation passes through the same five stages: 1) the people worship the Lord and obey his commandments; 2) they reject the Lord and serve idols and provoke the Lord to anger; 3) the people are captured and enslaved to their enemies; 4) the people cry to the Lord and repent of their disobedience; 5) the Lord delivers his people. Thirteen times the cycle repeats itself as though human nature is incapable of change.

The story of Deborah plays a variation on the theme of man's wickedness. "And the children of Israel again did evil in the sight of the Lord..." (Judges 4:1).

Will we ever learn? No. That is the truth which the author of Judges presents through his series of everchanging events. The people did evil in the sight of the Lord. The story reads like the headlines of our daily paper. Obviously we have not progressed beyond that.

Another illusion of progress is that we can take care of ourselves. God is not needed and can therefore be consigned to the trash heap of history. We often take the attitude that history began yesterday and that all that went before is insignificant and unimportant. All around us there is evidence that people believe they are making it just fine without God's help. Our football stadiums are full, but our sanctuaries for worship are half empty. We scrimp and save and sacrifice to find money for missions, yet in 1985 advertisers spend $175 million on television spots for pet products. Priorities are skewed in the wrong direction by people who have forgotten the Lord. The illusion of progress gives way to the illusion of independence. Too many have wandered away from home, away from the presence of God.

When people fall for the illusion of progress, an illusion fed by the sense of independence, they no longer hear the voice of God calling them back. Yet the Lord still calls. Listen to the words of Jeremiah: "Thus saith the Lord, stand ye in the ways, and see, and ask for the old paths, where is the good way, and walk therein, and ye shall find rest for your souls. But they said, we will not walk therein." (Jeremiah 6:16) There are some ancient paths hammered out by experience. The experience is that of men who try to teach us that we are never independent. For all our supposed progress we are never in a position to live without the help of God.

The most important lesson about our illusions is that God has a way of puncturing our grand ideas of progress and independence. "And the Lord sold them into the hand of Jabin ... And the children of Israel cried unto the Lord ..." (Judges 4:21, 3a). That is one of the harsh lessons of the Bible and especially of the Hebrew scriptures. The wrath of God is poured out upon the disobedient. The means by which the people of Deborah lived, the illusions of their time, became ends which they did not expect, the judgment of God. While we may choose our means, we are not free to dictate our ends.

Seed Thoughts

1. The writer of the book of Judges repeats thirteen times a vicious cycle of conduct by the Israelites. What were the five stages of that cycle?
1) The people obeyed the Lord; 2) they did evil in the sight of the Lord; 3) the Lord delivered them over to an enemy; 4) the people cried out to the Lord for help; 5) the Lord saved them.

2. Who was the king of Canaan, during the judgeship of Deborah, who enslaved the Israelites?
The king of Canaan was Jabin. There are two kings named Jabin in the Old Testament. The Jabin in the book of Judges was a Canaanite king of Hazar.

3. What significance can we give to a woman being judge over Israel?
God's call was not limited only to men in the Bible. The presence of Deborah as judge may seem surprising to us, but nothing special is made of it by the writer of Judges.

4. Where was Deborah's seat of judgment located?
Deborah sat under the palm of Deborah between Ramah and Bethel in the hill country of Ephraim.

5. Whose aid did Deborah enlist for the battle against Jabin?
She instructed Barak, son of Abinoam from Kedesh in Naphtali, to gather an army.

(PLEASE TURN PAGE)

---

1. The writer of the book of Judges repeats thirteen times a vicious cycle of conduct by the Israelites. What were the five stages of that cycle?

2. Who was the king of Canaan, during the judgeship of Deborah, who enslaved the Israelites?

3. What significance can we give to a woman being judge over Israel?

4. Where was Deborah's seat of judgment located?

5. Whose aid did Deborah enlist for the battle against Jabin?

6. What was Deborah's military strategy?

7. What happened to Sisera, the commander of Jabin's army?

8. In Deborah's song to what did she attribute her victory?

9. What did Deborah imagine Sisera's mother was doing while she waited for her son return from battle?

10. What happened to King Jabin of Razar?

(SEED THOUGHTS--Cont'd)

1) The people obeyed the Lord; 2) they did evil in the sight of the Lord; 3) the Lord delivered them over to an enemy; 4) the people cried out to the Lord for help; 5) the Lord saved them.

The king of Canaan was Jabin. There are two kings named Jabin in the Old Testament. The Jabin in the book of Judges was a Canaanite king of Hazar.

God's call was not limited only to men in the Bible. The presence of Deborah as judge may seem surprising to us, but nothing special is made of it by the writer of Judges.

Deborah sat under the palm of Deborah between Ramah and Bethel in the hill country of Ephraim.

She instructed Barak, son of Abinoam from Kedesh in Naphtali, to gather an army.

She positioned her troops on Mount Tabor. Then she enticed Sisera and his chariots to move in on Barak. On ground not suited for chariots, Barak's troops defeated the Canaanites.

Sisera left his chariot and fled on foot to the tent of Jael, wife of Heber. Jael, under pretense of helping Sisera, killed him while he was asleep.

The Lord sent a sudden downpour that made it impossible for chariots to maneuver.

Sisera's mother looked out the window and wondered what was taking so long. She decided the troops were dividing the spoils.

The Israelite army attacked with increasing fierceness until they destroyed King Jabin.

6. **What was Deborah's military strategy?**
She positioned her troops on Mount Tabor. Then she enticed Sisera and his chariots to move in on Barak. On ground not suited for chariots, Barak's troops defeated the Canaanites.

7. **What happened to Sisera, the commander of Jabin's army?**
Sisera left his chariot and fled on foot to the tent of Jael, wife of Heber. Jael, under pretense of helping Sisera, killed him while he was asleep.

8. **In Deborah's song to what did she attribute her victory?**
The Lord sent a sudden downpour that made it impossible for chariots to maneuver.

9. **What did Deborah imagine Sisera's mother was doing while she waited for her son return from battle?**
Sisera's mother looked out the window and wondered what was taking so long. She decided the troops were dividing the spoils.

10. **What happened to King Jabin of Razar?**
The Israelite army attacked with increasing fierceness until they destroyed King Jabin.

October 4, 1992

Samuel, the Last Judge

I Samuel 7
15 And Samuel judged Israel all the days of his life.
16 And he went from year to year in circuit to Beth´-el, and Gil´-gal, and Miz´-peh, and judged Israel in all those places.
17 And his return was to Ra´-mah; for there was his house; and there he judged Israel; and there he built an altar unto the LORD.

I Samuel 8
AND it came to pass, when Samuel was old, that he made his sons judges over Israel.
2 Now the name of his firstborn was Jo´el; and the name of his second, A-bi´-ah: *they* were judges in De´-er-she´-ba.
3 And his sons walked not in his ways, but turned aside after lucre, and took bribes, and perverted judgment.
4 Then all the elders of Israel gathered themselves together, and came to Samuel unto Ra´-mah,
5 And said unto him, Behold, thou art old, and thy sons walk not in thy ways: now make us a king to judge us like all the nations.
6 But the thing displeased Samuel, when they said, Give us a king to judge us. And Samuel prayed unto the LORD.
7 And the LORD said unto Samuel, Hearken unto the voice of the people in all that they say unto thee: for they have not rejected thee, but they have rejected me, that I should not reign over them.
8 According to all the works which they have done since the day that I brought them up out of Egypt even unto this day, wherewith they have forsaken me, and served other gods, so do they also unto thee.
9 Now therefore hearken unto their voice: howbeit yet protest solemnly unto them, and shew them the manner of the king that shall reign over them.
19 Nevertheless the people refused to obey the voice of Samuel; and they said, Nay; but we will have a king over us;
20 That we also may be like all the nations; and that our king may judge us, and go out before us and fight our battles.
21 And Samuel heard all the words of the people, and he rehearsed them in the ears of the LORD.
22 And the LORD said to Samuel, Hearken unto their voice, and make them a king. And Samuel said unto the men of Israel, Go ye every man unto his city.

◆◆◆◆◆◆

◀ **Memory Selection**
I Samuel 8:7

◀ **Devotional Reading**
I Samuel 8:10-18

◀ **Background Scripture**
I Samuel 7:15-8:22

◀ **Printed Scripture**
I Samuel 7:15-8:9, 19-22

SAMUEL, THE LAST JUDGE

Teacher's Target

Primitive tribes had their chiefs and shamans (medicine men) to govern them. Autocratic monarchs (kings and queens) and priests ruled over nations both small and large. Israel was chosen by God to be a theocracy where He served as the heavenly King and was assisted by human seers, prophets, priests, and judges. Samuel was a transitional figure between the judges (military deliverers) described in the book of Judges and the kings who were to follow. He served primarily as a religious leader and a judge settling disputes.

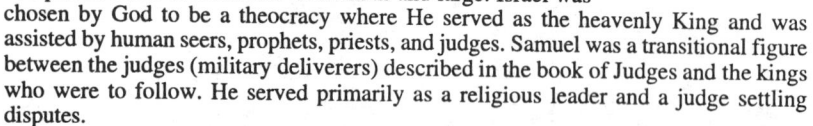

Help your students to see that God allowed the Israelites to have a king, even though this was not His first choice for them. He had to persuade Samuel to yield to the Israelites' demand for a king so that they could be like the other nations. They were to be warned about what this would mean to them. Through it all, God wanted to remain their heavenly king, and He reserved the right to lift up or put down any earthly king.

Lesson Introduction

Elkanah and Hannah were a couple in Israel who had no children until God sent them a little boy named Samuel. His mother dedicated him to the Lord's work, and he went to live with the aged priest named Eli. "And Samuel grew, and the Lord was with him, and did let none of his words fall to the ground. And all Israel from Dan even to Beersheba knew that Samuel was established to be a prophet of the Lord" (I Sam. 3:19-20).

Samuel lived in Ramah, but he traveled a circuit from there to Bethel, Gilgal, and Mizpah in order to serve as a judge in people's disputes. When he placed his sons, Joel and Abiah, as judges in Beersheba, they failed miserably. The elders of Israel demanded that they were removed and that a king be anointed to rule over the nation. Samuel was displeased, but he complied with God's command that the people's wish be granted. Let us learn from this incident that it is always best to yield to God's will regardless of personal feelings.

Teaching Outline

I. Circuit: I Sam. 7:15-17
   A. Vocation: 15
   B. Visits: 16-17
II. Complaint: I Sam. 8:1-6
   A. Delegation: 1-2
   B. Disaster: 3
   C. Demand: 4-5
   D. Displeasure: 6
III. Compliance: I Sam. 8:7-9, 19-22
   A. Instructions: 7-9
   B. Insistence: 19-20
   C. Instructions: 21-22

Daily Bible Readings

Mon. Samuel Prays to the Lord for Israel - *I Sam. 7:1-6*
Tue. Israel Triumphs over the Philistines - *I Sam. 7:7-14*
Wed. Saul Searches for a Man of God - *I Sam. 9:5-10*
Thu. Saul Meets Samuel *I Sam. 9:15-21*
Fri. Saul is Anointed by Samuel *I Sam. 10:1-7*
Sat. Saul Becomes a Prophet *I Sam. 10:9-16*
Sun. Saul Is Made King of Israel *I Sam. 10:17-27*

October 4, 1992

VERSE BY VERSE

I. Circuit: I Sam. 7:15-17

A. Vocation: 15

15. And Samuel judged Israel all the days of his life.

It was obvious that Samuel had unusual wisdom, as described in I Samuel 3:19: "The Lord was with him, and did let none of his words fall to the ground." "People listened carefully to his advice" (Living Bible). It was natural for him to become an arbitrator in people's disputes, and the Lord used him in this way. It became his vocation.

B. Visits: 16-17

16. And he went from year to year in circuit to Bethel, and Gilgal, and Mizpeh, and judged Israel in all those places.

Bethel, originally called Luz, was twelve miles north of Jerusalem and west of Ai. Gilgal was ten miles from the Jordan River toward Jericho. Mizpeh may have been to the northeast across the Jordan River, but it may have been in the territory of Benjamin west of the Jordan River. Samuel journeyed to these towns each year in order to listen to disputes and render judgments on them. His decisions were evidently well received by the people.

17. And his return was to Ramah: there was his house; and there he judged Israel; and there he built an altar unto the Lord.

Ramah was Samuel's hometown (I Sam. 1:19; 2:11). It was located within the territory of Benjamin, north of Jerusalem. It was to be his final resting place (I Sam. 25:1; 28:3). Ramah was the center of his activities during his lifetime. Three things are mentioned here about it. His house was there. He performed his ministry as a judge when he was there. He built an altar unto the Lord there. Deuteronomy 12:5 and 13 indicated that sacrifices of worship were to be made only in the place of God's choosing and not just anywhere an individual chose. However, God apparently approved of Samuel building an altar and offering sacrifices at Ramah, perhaps because of the upheavals in Israel at the time.

II. Complaint: I Sam. 8:1-6

A. Delegation: 1-2

1. And it came to pass, when Samuel was old, that he made his sons judges over Israel.

Although the text refers to Samuel as becoming old, he may have been only in his early fifties. Life expectancy was limited at that time. Personal health problems could have aged him prematurely. It appears that he sought to shift at least part of his responsibility for judging onto his two sons. He may have consulted with elders in various parts of the country to see if they would be willing to accept this arrangement, or he may have taken this action arbitrarily.

2. Now the name of his firstborn was Joel; and the name of his second, Abiah: they were judges in Beersheba.

These young men must have had distinct advantages growing up in Samuel's home, and they may have done well enough to be acceptable as judges by the elders in the southern region of the nation around Beersheba. Many who have started well have been known to misuse their skills and resources. Joel and Abiah probably began their magisterial duties in this outlying location in a state of optimism and hope for future enlarged opportunity. As things turned out, it would have been better if they had never settled there. This incident illustrates the fact that righteousness does not necessarily derive from having Godly parents.

B. Disaster: 3

3. And his sons walked not in his

ways, but turned aside after lucre, and took bribes, and perverted judgment.

What began with great promise eventually degenerated into a sordid example of perverted justice. Joel and Abiah took bribes in order to render judgments favoring their benefactors. They were diverted from the path of righteousness by the lure of lucre (financial gain in money or goods). Honest people in Beersheba could not get the justice which they deserved and wanted, and those guilty of injustice were sons of the highly-respected and righteous spiritual leader of the nation who acted as God's representative in Israel. Samuel had seen what had happened in the household of Eli the priest, for his two sons had perverted their roles and been immoral (I Sam. 2:22). God had denounced Eli for allowing his sons to be evil and restraining them not (I Sam. 3:13). Some would say that Samuel made the same mistake, but we do not know if he was aware of what his own sons had been doing in Beersheba until their evil was reported to him. Nothing is said here about God denouncing Samuel for any laxity.

C. Demand: 4-5

4. Then all the elders of Israel gathered themselves together, and came to Samuel unto Ramah,

It seems that considerable negotiation must have taken place behind the scenes as the situation in Beersheba deteriorated. Elders from the various tribes of Israel got together and discussed what could be done about this problem. Those outside of the Beersheba area did not want Joel or Abiah shifted to their own areas. It was decided that they would approach Samuel together and make a proposal to him which could affect all of them.

5. And said unto him, Behold, thou art old, and thy sons walk not in thy ways: now make us a king to judge us like all the nations.

The elders who came to Samuel felt that they had a reasonable and logical suggestion. They mentioned that Samuel was old, and, by implication, would soon be passing off the scene. They did not want his wicked sons to try to move into the vacuum which would be created. They wanted Samuel to find and anoint some individual to serve as their king and thus make Israel similar to surrounding nations. This was the basic thought for changing from a theocracy (rule by God) to a monarchy (rule by man). It was to have repercussions which would last for centuries in Israel's development as a nation.

D. Displeasure: 6

6. But the thing displeased Samuel when they said, Give us a king to judge us. And Samuel prayed unto the Lord.

Samuel was unhappy with the elders' demand for an earthly king, and there may have been various reasons for this. He may have felt let down that his work as judge was considered inadequate. He no doubt was grieved over the failure of his sons in Beersheba. He may have thought that God would punish Israel for displacing Him as King and asking for an earthly king. He was probably irked by the statement that the elders wanted Israel to have a king so that it could be like the pagan nations surrounding it. When he saw that the elders were adamant about their decision, he went in prayer to the Lord about the matter. He wanted no part of such a maneuver unless God approved of it. He probably was unprepared for what the Lord said.

III. Compliance: I Sam. 8:7-9, 19-22

A. Instructions: 7-9

7. And the Lord said unto Samuel, Hearken unto the voice of the people in all that they say unto thee: for they have not rejected thee, but they have rejected me, that I should not reign over them.

It may have come as a shock to Samuel, but God told him to comply with the demand of the elders of Israel. The Lord wanted His righteous servant to realize that the request for an earthly king did not indicate a rejection of Samuel and of his good service to the nation. It indicated a rejection of God Himself as Israel's heavenly King. The Israelites knew that they could not manipulate Jehovah, but they had hopes of manipulating any earthly king set up to rule over them. What was happening here was a matter of control and a shifting of it from a supernatural to a natural level.

8. According to all the works which they have done since the day that I brought them up out of Egypt even unto this day, wherewith they have forsaken me, and served other gods, so do they also unto thee.

God helped Samuel to realize that Israel had a long record of unfaithfulness. From the time of the exodus from Egypt to the time of Samuel, the Israelites had indulged in idolatry. God helped Samuel to realize that he was so closely allied to Himself that the people were involving him in their shift away from God's leadership to that of human leadership. It was as Jesus later said, "The servant is not greater than his lord" (John 13:16). Samuel would still have a place of spiritual service, but he would have to suffer the bad effects of the new system of leadership in Israel.

9. Now therefore hearken unto their voice: howbeit yet protest solemnly unto them, and shew them the manner of the king that shall reign over them.

For the second time God told Samuel to hearken unto the demand of the elders. However, Samuel was to warn them of what that king would require of them when he was placed in power over them. Samuel proceeded to reveal the harsh demands which Israel's first king would impose on them. He would draft young men into his service as personal guards, soldiers, farmers, and weapons makers. He would make young women serve him as confectionaries, cooks, and bakers. He would take the best fields, vineyards, and olive groves and give them to his staff members. He would take a tenth of their seeds, grapes, and sheep. When they cried out because of his demands, God would not hear and respond to their complaints (I Sam. 8:10-18), As he mentioned these things, Samuel may have hoped that the elders would change their minds, but he was to be disappointed in that.

B. Insistence: 19-20

19. Nevertheless the people refused to obey the voice of Samuel; and they said, Nay; but we will have a king over us;

20. That we also may be like all the nations; and that our king may judge us, and go out before us, and fight our battles.

The warnings by Samuel did nothing to change the minds of the elders of Israel. They still wanted an earthly king to reign over them. They were prepared to give up their unique position as a people ruled over by God the heavenly King and to trust their future to an earthly king out of their own ranks. They wanted such a man to judge them and settle disputes. They wanted him to lead them into battle against their enemies.

C. Instructions: 21-22

21. And Samuel heard all the words of the people, and he rehearsed them in the ears of the Lord.

Disappointed that he could not deter the elders from their intention, Samuel once again turned to the Lord and repeated what the people had said. He still seemed to need confirmation that God really wanted him to comply with their demand.

22. And the Lord said to Samuel, Hearken unto their voice, and make them a king. And Samuel said unto the men of Israel, Go ye every man unto his city.

Samuel obeyed God's instructions and dismissed the assembly of elders so that they could go home. The Lord had made provision for Israel to have a king at the time the law was given. Deuteronomy 17:14-20 describes this. The king was to be chosen by God and had to be an Israelite. He was to live modestly and be subservient to God and His holy law. Then he could expect a long life.

It was unfortunate that Saul, who became Israel's first king, failed to meet these qualifications after being in office a few years. With only a few exceptions, the kings of Israel and Judah who followed him were similar. God proved Himself to be the heavenly King by lifting up or putting down any earthly monarch He chose.

SAMUEL, THE LAST JUDGE

Evangelistic Emphasis

Our text today contains a note of sadness and pain. God's people had rejected the rule of kingship of The Lord. Such a decison had within it dramatic consequences. There is no way to avoid the connection between God as king over Israel and God as Lord of our lives. The very thrust of the gospel always forces us to make a decision. We choose, without coercion, whether or not God will be king.

We also have here a story of the gracious God. Never does God burglarize the human heart. When we reject God, God respects the rejection. This does not imply, however, that God gives up on us. On the contrary, God finds other ways to make His appeal to us. God respects and often works within human limitations to achieve divine goals. Here we see a broken-hearted God who, in spite of rejection, is for His people, not against them. He is out to win them over, not to destroy them.

The choice is ours. There is no more significant choice with eternal consequences than whether or not God will rule in our lives. As we have already noted, God, from His side, continues to work with us, to win us over. We are thus faced with the decision of destiny. Will God rule or will we reject the Lordship of God over our lives?

♦♦♦♦♦♦

Memory Selection

"The Lord said to Samuel, 'Hearken to the voice of the people in all that they say to you; for they have not rejected you, but they have rejected me from being king over them.'" - *I Samuel 8:7*

Why did the people insist on having a king? God had been their king for all these years. What had happened that convinced the people of Israel that they needed a new, human king?

Perhaps they were unduly influenced by the nations around them. Despite repeated warnings, God's people always face the temptation of conformity to the world. St. Paul urges Christians, "And be not conformed to this world: but be ye transformed by the renewing of your mind . . ." (Romans 12:2a)

Perhaps the people of Israel needed concrete, actual leadership. After all, they had never seen God. Their faith may not have been stong enough to sustain the rule of God. A monarchy, on the other hand, was a government they could see. If security was a prime need for Israel, no wonder they demanded a king.

God, on His part, took a benevolent position. The insistence that the people be allowed a king should not be interpreted as God's abdication of the throne. Even when Israel coronated her own king, God remained the selection committee and the giver of the blessing. The people were still expected to do the will of God.

While God points to the people's rejection of divine rule, there was no intention on God's part to dispossess His people. God still guided and directed His chosen ones. We do not know all the pain God felt by this rejection, but we are comforted that God went back to work for His people.

October 4, 1992

Weekday Problems

Jim is a prominent member of his local church. He gives a tithe of all he makes to the Lord. He teaches Sunday School and attends all services regularly. For as long as he can remember, he has supported and loved all the pastors of his church.

In the last six months, however, the church has changed pastors. Jim had a very close and personal friendship with the previous pastor, a relationship of over 10 years. Now Jim is having a hard time relating to the new pastor's style of leadership.

When he listens to the new pastor he hears a man who is aggressive and bold. The pastor has very definite ideas about changing the ministry of the church. Any other time, Jim would probably embrace these new ideas. At the moment, though, he is experiencing the grief of his former pastor's leaving. He is not able to be as objective as usual.

*What should Jim do while he works through his personal grief?
*Is there one and only one style of pastoral leadership?
*In what ways can you work with a pastor whose leadership style makes you uncomfortable?
*How can you help members of the church understand that the ministry of the church is of greater significance than the person serving as pastor?

◆◆◆◆◆◆

Superintendent's Sermonette

As we grow older and reflect on our lives, we may wonder if we have accomplished anything truly significant. Looking back over the years, we will think of things which amounted to little or nothing, but we may also conclude that there were things which helped others and added to God's glory. This type of reflection can be helpful, if it causes us to choose our priorities for the future carefully. We can be more effective for the Lord and His work as we yield ourselves and whatever resources we have to Him. However, we must expect setbacks as well as strides forward.

Samuel must have reflected on his long life of service for the Lord at a time when Israel bordered on anarchy. He consistently traveled around a circuit to judge the people at Ramah, Bethel, Gilgal, and Mizpeh. When he grew old, he sent his two sons, Joel and Abiah, down to Beersheba to serve as judges. The results were disasterous in their case, for they accepted bribes to pervert justices When the elders of Israel demanded a king to judge them, Samuel was distressed, but God told him to grant their request. If Samuel had to take the bad with the good, we should be ready to do the same. The important thing is that we keep in God's will and obey Him.

SAMUEL, THE LAST JUDGE

This Lesson In Your Life

My father-in-law practices his memory. Each morning as he walks through the cemetery on his two-mile journey, he recites all the states of the United States and their capitals and all the presidents of the United States, from Washington to Bush. He says he is keeping alive his memory. What a unique picture; here is a man working on his memory in the cemetery. Too soon we stop doing our memory work; we lose the habit of remembering, especially when it comes to the mighty acts of God. That is what happened to the Israelites in the latter years of Samuel. They suffered from a severe case of spiritual amnesia. As a result, they demanded an earthly king in place of the rule of God. What could lead the people of God to such a decision?

First of all, the people of God underestimated the goodness of God. In the rush of euphoria that followed the desire to be like all other nations, Israel simply forgot all that God had done for them. Was it not the goodness of God that brought them forth from the slave pits of Egypt? Was it not the goodness of God that had given them the land of Canaan for an everlasting possession? Was it not the goodness of God that had delivered them time and again from countless enemies? Of course! Yet when a people stop doing their memory work, the first casualty is forgetting God's goodness.

When people no longer remember to pray, "Thank you God for all that has been," they are suffering from amnesia. They are only a short stop from deciding to take credit for all the providential guidance of God. Such a people will believe in their own natural goodness. Such is the peril of a short memory.

Second, cut off from their memory of God's goodness, the people of Israel, overestimated the value of an earthly king. Cut off from their deep spiritual connections to the God of Abraham, Isaac, and Jacob, the people idealized a monarchy like that of other nations. Without benefit of memory, the Israelites no longer knew their own faith stories. For too long they had bowed at the altars of strange gods. No longer did they hear repeated the ancient stories of God's delivering power. They no longer possessed a vision of God parting the waters of the Red Sea, of God bringing Israel over Jordan on dry ground, or of the Lord defeating their enemies with His strong right hand. All they could see was the present. The past no longer possessed any sacred meaning. Now they wanted a king to judge them and fight their battles for them. Idealization of a not-yet-future blinded the Israelites to the realities of having an earthly king. They could see only the possible benefits and none of the real problems.

A third consequence of a bad memory was the caricaturing of the past. Instead of looking back and understanding their dependency upon the God who brought them the good old days, the people of Israel caricatured the past as the "bad old days." Filtering every experience of the past through the lens of lust for a king, all of the gracious acts of God were blotted out, and only the bad times and dark days were allowed as evidence. The people were unable and unwilling to hear the good news that the same God who brought them the good old days would bring them some good new days. In their haste to have their own way, the people simply ignored all that had been good about the past.

Once freed from a memory of God's goodness, the Israelites were free to idealize the future with an earthly king, and to caricature the past with God as the "bad old days." With these blinders in place, the people bought hook, line, and sinker the illusion that they would be better off living as other nations. Gone from their memory banks were the constant warnings against assimilating with the culture of pagan nations. Gone were the constant pleadings, be a holy and separate people. Without a memory, Israel felt free to jettison her faith in God, and go her own way.

Seed Thoughts

1. In what places did Samuel carry out his responsibility to judge Israel?
Samuel judged Israel from his home in Ramah as well as from three other cities on his circuit: Bethel, Gilgal, and Mizpeh.

2. When Samuel could no longer serve as judge, whom did he he appoint to serve in his place?
Samuel appointed his own sons, Joel and Abiah, to serve as judges.

3. What kind of judges did Joel and Abiah make, and how did their work compare to Samuel's?
Joel and Abiah were lacking in integrity. They served themselves and not others. In contrast, Samuel was a righteous man who served the people.

4. Why did the elders of Israel request Samuel to give them a king?
The people of Israel wanted to be like the other nations, and immoral behavior of Samuel's sons gave them the excuse they needed.

5. What was Samuel's response to the request for a king?
Samuel was angry with the people. To his credit, however, he prayed to God before making any decision.

(PLEASE TURN PAGE)

---

1. In what places did Samuel carry out his responsibility to judge Israel?

2. When Samuel could no longer serve as judge, whom did he he appoint to serve in his place?

3. What kind of judges did Joel and Abiah make, and how did their work compare to Samuel's?

4. Why did the elders of Israel request Samuel to give them a king?

5. What was Samuel's response to the request for a king?

6. How did Samuel describe what would happen to Israel under a king?

7. How did the people respond to Samuel's protest against a king?

8. Should the people of God be concerned about conformity with the world?

9. What should be the Christian's relationship with earthly rulers and officials?

10. What did the Lord decide to do about the request for a king?

(SEED THOUGHTS--Cont'd)

Samuel judged Israel from his home in Ramah as well as from three other cities on his circuit: Bethel, Gilgal, and Mizpeh.

Samuel appointed his own sons, Joel and Abiah, to serve as judges.

Joel and Abiah were lacking in integrity. They served themselves and not others. In contrast, Samuel was a righteous man who served the people.

The people of Israel wanted to be like the other nations, and immoral behavior of Samuel's sons gave them the excuse they needed.

Samuel was angry with the people. To his credit, however, he prayed to God before making any decision.

Samuel painted a harsh picture of how a king would control their lives. He would be abusive, exploitative, and unfair.

The people refused to obey the voice of Samuel. They rejected the rule of God by insisting upon a man for a king.

Unlike the Isrealites lusting for a king, God's people should never be conformed to the world.

We have a responsibility to be good citizens, but God's will and God's rule is more important.

The lord told Samuel to grant the request of the people and give them a king.

6. How did Samuel describe what would happen to Israel under a king?
Samuel painted a harsh picture of how a king would control their lives. He would be abusive, exploitative, and unfair.

7. How did the people respond to Samuel's protest against a king?
The people refused to obey the voice of Samuel. They rejected the rule of God by insisting upon a man for a king.

8. Should the people of God be concerned about conformity with the world?
Unlike the Isrealites lusting for a king, God's people should never be conformed to the world.

9. What should be the Christian's relationship with earthly rulers and officials?
We have a responsibility to be good citizens, but God's will and God's rule is more important.

10. What did the Lord decide to do about the request for a king?
The lord told Samuel to grant the request of the people and give them a king.

October 11, 1992

David: King Over All the People

I Samuel 16

1 AND the LORD said unto Samuel, How long wilt thou mourn for Saul, seeing I rejected him from reigning over Israel? fill thine horn with oil, and go, I will send thee to Jesse the Beth´-lehem-ite: for I have provided me a king among his sons.

6 And it came to pass, when they were come that he looked on E-li´-ab and said, Surely the LORD's anointed is before him.

7 But the LORD said unto Samuel Look not on his countenance, or on the height of his stature; because I have refused him: for the LORD seeth not as man seeth; for man looketh on the outward appearance, but the LORD looketh on the heart.

11 And Samuel said unto Jesse, Are here all *thy* children? And he said, There remaineth yet the youngest, and, behold, he keepeth the sheep. And Samuel said unto Jesse, Send and fetch him: for we will not sit down till he come hither.

12 And he sent and brought him in. Now he was ruddy and withal of a beautiful countenance and goodly to look to. And the LORD said Arise, anoint him: for this is he.

13 Then Samuel took the horn of oil, and anointed him in the midst of his brethren: and the Spirit of the LORD came upon David from that day forward. So Samuel rose up, and went to Ra´mah.

II Samuel 5

1 THEN came all the tribes of Israel to David unto He´-bron, and spake, saying, Behold, we are thy bone and thy flesh.

2 Also in time past, when Saul was king over us, thou wast he that leddest out and broughtest in Israel: and the LORD said to thee, Thou shalt feed my people Israel, and thou shalt be a Captain over Israel.

3. So all the elders of Israel came to the King to He´-bron; and king David made a league with them in He´-bron before the Lord: and they anointed David king over Israel.

4. David was thirty years old when he began to reign, and he reigned forty years.

5. In He´-bron he reigned over Judah seven years and six months: and in Jerusalem he reigned thirty and three years over all Israel and Judah.

◆◆◆◆◆◆

◀ **Memory Selection**
I Samuel 16:13

◀ **Devotional Reading**
I Samuel 16:1-13

◀ **Background Scripture**
I Samuel 16:1-13

◀ **Printed Scripture**
I Samuel 16:1,6-7,11-13;
II Samuel 5:1-5

DAVID: KING OVER ALL THE PEOPLE

Teacher's Target

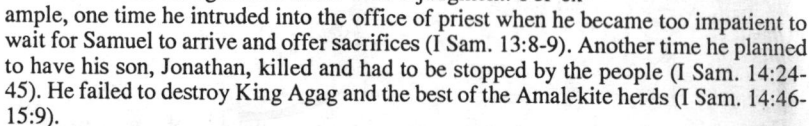

Samuel was permitted by God to anoint Israel's first two kings, Saul and David. Saul had started out well, but he made mistakes which brought him under God's judgment. For example, one time he intruded into the office of priest when he became too impatient to wait for Samuel to arrive and offer sacrifices (I Sam. 13:8-9). Another time he planned to have his son, Jonathan, killed and had to be stopped by the people (I Sam. 14:24-45). He failed to destroy King Agag and the best of the Amalekite herds (I Sam. 14:46-15:9).

Help your students to see that God always has a replacement for a wayward ruler. David had to wait for a long time and suffer much from Saul before the Lord removed the king and put David in his place. David was not perfect in his actions, but he was commended for having a perfect heart attitude toward the Lord. Here was the kind of individual whom God chose to use in His service, and He wants to find the same kind today.

Lesson Introduction

God told Samuel to stop mourning the death of Saul and to go and anoint a son of Jesse to be the next king. Samuel was amazed when seven sons of Jesse were paraded before him and were rejected by the Lord. As with most people, Samuel had been looking at outward appearances, whereas God had been looking at hearts. David, the youngest, had been out tending his father's sheep. He was summoned to come before Samuel, and the Lord made it clear that here was His choice for king. Samuel anointed David with oil, and then God anointed him with His Spirit.

David actually ruled over Judah, the southern kingdom, for seven years before he was invited to rule over Israel, the northern kingdom, as well. The elders of Israel anointed him to be their king, and he ruled over them for thirty-three years. It was under David and his son, Solomon, that the combined monarchy reached its highest development and covered its greatest amount of territory.

Teaching Outline

I. Appearance: I Sam. 16:1, 6-7
 A. Rejection: 1a
 B. Revelation: 1b
 C. Refusal: 6-7a
 D. Reason: 7b
II. Anointing I: I Sam. 16:11-13
 A. Summons: 11
 B. Selection: 12-13a
 C. Spirit: 13b
III. Anointing II: II Sam. 5:1-5
 A. Request: 1-2
 B. Reigns: 3-5

Daily Bible Readings

Mon. David Is Called to Serve Saul
I Sam. 16:14-23
Tue. David Is Anointed King of Judah
II Sam. 2:1-7
Wed. David Captures Jerusalem
II Sam. 5:6-10
Thu. David Defeats the Philistines
II Sam. 5:17-21
Fri. David Restores the Ark of God
II Sam. 6:1-5
Sat. Nathan Tells David to Build God's House - *II Sam. 7:4-17*
Sun. David Makes a Covenant with God - *II Sam. 7:18-29*

October 11, 1992

VERSE BY VERSE

I. Appearance: I Sam. 16:1, 6-7

A. Rejection: 1a

1a. And the Lord said unto Samuel, How long wilt thou mourn for Saul, seeing I have rejected him from reigning over Israel?

Saul was to remain as king for some time to come, but God had already rejected him and was planning to take him out of the position. This caused Samuel to be depressed and to mourn for Saul, and the Lord had to stir him up and move him in a different direction. Human emotion had to be overcome and yield to God's sovereign purpose in this situation. The Lord's decision and plan had to be implemented, and the sooner Samuel would accept that, the better off he would be.

B. Revelation: 1b

1b. ...fill thine horn with oil, and go, I will send thee to Jesse the Bethlehemite: for I have provided me a king among his sons.

Jesse lived in Bethlehem a few miles south of what would later become the Jewish capital and Judaism's most sacred city. God was setting the scene for the coming dynasty of David. God did not tell Samuel the name of the son whom He had chosen, preferring to keep that secret for a while longer.

God's order upset Samuel, because he was afraid that Saul would hear about it and kill him. The Lord told Samuel to take a heifer with him and invite Jesse and his sons to a sacrifice. It was during that event that God would show Samuel what to do about the anointing of the next king. The elders of Bethlehem were fearful of Samuel's coming, but they allowed the sacrifice to take place (I Sam. 16:2-5).

C. Refusal: 6-7a

6. And it came to pass, when they were come, that he looked on Eliab, and said, Surely the Lord's anointed is before him.

7a. But the Lord said unto Samuel, Look not on his countenance, or on the height of his stature; because I have refused him:...

Samuel had originally been impressed by the great height of Saul: "He was higher than any of the people from his shoulders and upward. And Samuel said to all the people, See ye him whom the Lord hath chosen, that there is none like him among all the people?" (I Sam. 10:23-24). Samuel evidently fell into the same state of mind when he saw Eliab, figuring that his handsome face and tall stature made him the logical choice for being the next king. The Lord rebuked Samuel for this, and it must have been embarrassing to him. He had to learn not to run ahead of the Lord.

D. Reason: 7b

7b. ...for the Lord seeth not as man seeth; for man looketh on the outward appearance, but the Lord looketh on the heart.

God provided the reason for His refusal of Eliab by stating a general principle. Divine sight is not concerned as much with outward appearance as it is with the condition of a person's heart. In other words, inner attitudes are what determine God's acceptance or refusal of an individual for a specific place of service. We should examine our own thinking along this line. Are we prone to make judgments on individuals on the basis of outward appearance rather than inner attitudes? If we want to think God's thoughts after Him, we have to see others through His eyes.

Jesse had seven of his sons pass before Samuel, including Eliab, Abinadab, and Shammah, and Samuel had to turn them down. He told Jesse that the Lord had not chosen any of them. It was now time for Jesse to be embarrassed.

II. Anointing I: I Sam. 16:11-13

A. Summons: 11

11. And Samuel said unto Jesse, Are here all thy children? And he said, There remaineth yet the youngest, and, behold, he keepeth the sheep. And Samuel said unto Jesse, Send and fetch him: for we will not sit down till he come hither.

Samuel could think of only one way to get out of his predicament. God had definitely said that he had a future king among the sons of Jesse (vs. 1). There had to be another son somewhere, and he asked Jesse about it. Jesse replied that only the youngest remained, and he was out tending sheep. It had not occurred to him that David might be the candidate for kingship. Samuel grasped it as a real possibility and ordered him to be summoned. He said that those assembled would not sit down to eat until the youngest son had arrived.

B. Selection: 12-13a

12. And he sent, and brought him in. Now he was ruddy, and withal of a beautiful countenance, and goodly to look to. And the Lord said, Arise, anoint him: for this is he.
13a. Then Samuel took the horn of oil, and anointed him in the midst of his brethren:...

When David arrived, Jesse presented him to Samuel. Commentators estimate that David was anywhere from ten to fifteen years old at this time. In describing him as ruddy, this may have meant that he was endowed with red hair and/or a reddish, fair, healthy complexion.

He had a handsome face, and his eyes seemed to be beautiful, pleasant, and sparkling. The Lord immediately indicated to Samuel that David was the one to be anointed, and Samuel complied. This was done in the midst of his brothers, and they must have been as surprised as any others. We wonder if they may also have been somewhat envious of him, much as Joseph's half-brothers had been many years before. God had spoken, and it was now clear that David was outstanding in both outward appearance and in his inner attitude.

C. Spirit: 13b

13b. ...and the Spirit of the Lord came upon David from that day forward. So Samuel rose up, and went to Ramah.

The Holy Spirit of the Lord took hold of David from that time onward to control him and lead him. When Samuel was convinced that the right choice had been confirmed to him, he was ready to leave Bethlehem and return to his home in Ramah. David was left to mature and become ready to become king. Note that, even as the Spirit of God came upon David, it was withdrawn from King Saul. The Lord allowed an evil spirit to come and trouble Saul because he had opened himself to this (I Sam. 16:14). Saul's path led downhill from this point onward.

In the remainder of the book of I Samuel the record is given regarding Saul, as well as a description of what happened to David until Saul's death. This included David's ministry to Saul in music, the slaying of Goliath the Philistine giant, the love covenant set up between David and Jonathan, Saul's son, Saul's attempts to have David killed, and David's wanderings with his small army of men. David spared Saul's life twice.

III. Anointing II: II Sam. 5:1-5

A. Request: 1-2

1. Then came all the tribes of Israel to David unto Hebron, and spake, saying, Behold, we are thy bone and thy flesh.

In I Samuel 31 and the opening chapters of II Samuel we learn details of the death of Saul and his sons, Jonathan, Abinadab, and Melchishua. After David mourned their passing, he was received as the king of Judah and made his capital at Hebron. Abner, captain of Saul's army, broke away and made Ishbosheth (another son of Saul) king over Israel. Civil war erupted and persisted for awhile. Abner defected to David but was murdered by Joab at Hebron. Ishbosheth was murdered, as well. Israel was now leaderless. Elders from the tribes of Israel came down to Hebron to approach David. They said that they were of his bone and flesh, meaning that both they and he were Israelites. Perhaps they were thinking of the requirement by God that a king over Israel should not be a foreigner but a brother (Deut. 17:15).

2. Also in time past, when Saul was king over us, thou wast he that leddest out and broughtest in Israel: and the Lord said to thee, Thou shalt feed my people Israel, and thou shalt be a captain over Israel.

The elders' second reason for David assuming leadership over Israel was that he had a good record of military campaigning. Even when Saul was king, David had been the hero who led the troops out to battle and returned in victory. The people of those times liked their leader to do this, whereas today our leaders remain far behind the front lines.

The elders' third reason for David assuming leadership over Israel was that he had been told by God to serve as a shepherd to His people. They then repeated their suggestion that he should be their captain (military leader). David had been raised as a shepherd, and these arguments must have had a strong impact on him. What he had done in feeding and protecting sheep was now to be done for the people of the nation of Israel, meaning the combined kingdoms of Judah in the south and Israel in the north. The ideal of having all twelve tribes together again could thus be realized.

B. Reigns: 3-5

3. So all the elders of Israel came to the king to Hebron; and king David made a league with them in Hebron before the Lord: and they anointed David king over Israel.

When Samuel had anointed Saul as the first king over Israel, he had written details down in a book (probably a scroll) and had laid it up before the Lord (I Sam. 10:25). Despite all of the disruption caused by Saul's sins and civil war, this document may have survived and served as a guide for rejoining the tribes of Israel as one nation under a king. In making a league with the elders at Hebron, David probably drew up a similar document.

4. David was thirty years old when he began to reign, and he reigned forty years.

David had a long reign of forty years altogether and ushered in the golden age for Israel, laying a foundation on which Solomon built.

5. In Hebron he reigned over Judah seven years and six months: and in Jerusalem he reigned thirty and three years over all Israel and Judah.

Hebron had served as David's capital over the southern tribes of Judah. After the combination with the northern tribes of Israel was made, David launched a campaign against the Jebusites so that he could take Jerusalem and make it his new capital. These pagans had insulted David by saying that even their blind and lame people would be able to keep his soldiers out. After he took the city, he greatly enlarged it. King Hiram of Tyre sent materials and craftsmen to build David a house. David rightly concluded that the Lord had established him as king over Israel and had exalted the kingdom for Israel's sake (II Sam. 5:6-12).

Evangelistic Emphasis

There may not be a more essential principle of evangelism than remembering that The Lord looks on the heart. The choice of David to be king, when he was not even in the royal line-up, is a reminder that no one should ever be excluded from our witness. Outward appearance, community reputation, or obvious sinfulness are not causes for refusing to tell someone the good news of Jesus Christ.

Our responsibility is to share the good news with everyone. God will take care of the person's heart. That means that we never "save" anyone. God does the choosing and the saving. Just think of the people that would be left out if the entrance into God's kingdom depended upon outward appearances like resumés, reputation, status, or good looks. Thank goodness, God looks on the heart.

A final consideration is that an act of worship precedes God's choice of David as king. Doesn't a biblical evangelism depend upon the priority of previous prayer and worship? The Lord needs to purify our hearts before we go forth as evangelists.

If someone feels unworthy of being a Christian, we need to go over this verse about God looking on the heart with such a person. Feelings of inferiority can become a stumbling block for both the witnessing Christian and the non-Christian.

◆◆◆◆◆◆

Memory Selection

The Lord said to Samuel, "Hearken to the voice of the people in all that they say to you; for they have not rejected you, but they have rejected one from being king over them."—*I Samuel 16:13*

Samuel seems to have accepted the blame, taken the personal responsibility, for the disobedience of the Israelites. The words of the Lord can thus be intended to encourage Samuel. We can understand. It is never easy to accept rejection.

But how easy it is to become despondent. When people reject the message of the Lord, refuse the Gospel, who doesn't feel personally responsible? Perhaps that happens in our churches and to us Christians. We speak the Word of God and no one listens. We witness to our lost friends and they refuse our invitation to accept Christ. We feel rejected. Then we no longer speak. Instead of continuing to tell others, we turn off and no longer say anything.

But take a look at the words of the Lord. He refuses to allow Samuel to wallow in self-pity and defeat. He reminds Samuel that the rejection goes far deeper. These people have rejected God. Samuel is the spokesman but God is their Savior. They have turned away from the ways of the Lord.

What then are we to do? Our task is to speak the word, to spread the Gospel, and to proclaim Christ. The rest then is up to God. We live to preach the Good News. God does all the rest.

October 11, 1992

Weekday Problems

Paul has been working for a major oil company for five years. He was an honor student in college, but he has always been shy and withdrawn. He is a modest man of Christian humility.

Already he has been passed over for promotion twice. His supervisor has not given him satisfactory evaluations because he thinks Paul should be more aggressive. The supervisor also detests Paul's Christian commitment. While other young men are pushing hard for promotion and going out with the bosses on drinking parties, Paul refuses to do so. He simply will not conform to such wordly standards. So men and women with lesser experience and lesser skills receive promotions that should have gone to quiet, hardworking Paul.

Paul could ask for a transfer to another city where his company has offices. He is reluctant, however, to make such a request. In his local church, Paul is a Sunday School teacher. During the last year, the class has been growing and a number of young adults have made professions of faith. Paul believes he is where the Lord wants him to be.

*What steps can Paul take to overcome his shy, introverted personality?

*What does Paul need to do about his relationship with his boss? Since conformity is out of the question, what positive steps can be suggested?

*How can Paul reconcile his Christian commitment and his professional goals?

♦♦♦♦♦♦

Superintendent's Sermonette

People today put too much emphasis on outward appearances. They spend billions of dollars on fancy clothes, cosmetics, automobiles, boats, planes, houses, and vacations. They want to impress others by showing their material acquisitions. They have been told by the media that success in life is described in terms of possessions, power, and prestige. Only a small minority seem to aspire to moral and spiritual improvement as defined by God and His Word. The physical and the material drive most people.

In our lesson today we meet this same type of thinking when it came time for Samuel to anoint a replacement for King Saul. Seven of the sons of Jesse were assembled at Bethlehem to be considered by Samuel, but not one of them was acceptable to God. It was not until the youngest son, David, was brought in from tending his father's sheep that the proper selection was made and confirmed by Samuel's anointing of him with oil and God's anointing of him by His Holy Spirit.

How is it with us? Are we trying to gain worldly approval by cultivating our outward appearances, or are we seeking to grow morally and spiritually so that God can approve of us and use us in His service? Let us take time to look inward and upward.

DAVID: KING OVER ALL THE PEOPLE

This Lesson In Your Life

In the Bible there is a paradoxical inversion of values. Our lesson contains an explanation for this phenomenon. The Lord said to Samuel, "Look not on his countenance, or on the height of his stature; . . . for the Lord seeth not as man seeth; for man looketh on the outward appearance, but the Lord looketh on the heart" (I Samuel 16:7). We see this reversal of values throughout the Bible in God's line-up of unexpected servants. There's Moses who murdered an Egyptian. There's Gideon, a humble man, who declared that he was the least man in the weakest clan of Israel. There's Jeremiah, a timid man called by God to the dangerous task of prophet. There's David, a young, ignored member of Jesse's family. What can we make of this inversion of values?

There may not be a more contemporary statement in the Bible than "man looketh on the outward appearance." Isn't that the way we live? Would we need so much Madison Avenue hype if there were not widespread anxiety about looking great? A modern ad trumpets "You never get a second chance to make a first impression." All the emphasis is on looking good. The superficial externals become the goal of such possession-crazed living. Status symbols! Brand names! There is so much posturing and pretending. It is an implicit admission that too many lives are built on a fragile foundation of external securities. By paying excessive attention to the externals, the appearance, the form, we buy into the illusion of people who have it made. There's a bumper sticker that expresses a fitting epitaph for our stressed-out-on-externals society: "HE WHO HAS THE MOST TOYS WHEN HE DIES, WINS."

God, however, warns us not to emphasize the externals. There is much more to life than what we see. The internal experience of the heart is more important than the external joy rides of status. Reality supercedes appearances. Content and character are more essential than form. When God goes looking for good and faithful servants, He does not check the ten best dressed list. Nor does He turn to *Fortune* magazine's list of the world's richest persons. He doesn't even bother to find out if they've been on the cover of *Newsweek*, *Vanity Fair*, or *People*. No, the Lord looks within. He checks the heart; "He looketh on the heart." And herein lies the reversal or values. For example, Jesse figured Samuel would anoint anybody but David. David was not even invited for an interview, but David was God's man. There may not be any clearer indication that God's ways are not our ways, God's thoughts are not our thoughts, and God's values are not our values.

Now, if the Bible is right in claiming that God uses a different measuring rod, we need a whole new perspective for life. We need to work for a kingdom where worries about fads and fashions are secondary considerations. Attention should be given to the building of inner character not outward conceit. In a world of inverted values, the weak, the timid, the insignificant, the unknown people are brought to center stage. There indeed is a reversal - a whole new way of determning worth and value. For in God's kingdom the last are first, the losers are the winners, and servants are the ones with the highest status. Recall St. Paul's words to the effect that God has called the foolish, the weak, the base, and the things that are not.

Perhaps we need to do some evaluating of our values. How do we stack up against God's value system? What are our priorities? How do we spend our time? How do we spend our money? Is righteousness more important to us than riches? Does character and integrity supersede clout and status? If the answer to these questions leaves us uncomfortable, then we need an inversion of our values.

Seed Thoughts

1. Why was the prophet Samuel mourning over Saul for such an extended time?
Samuel loved Saul and was heartbroken over Saul's disobedience of God's Word. As spokesman for God, it was Samuel's responsibility to tell Saul that there was going to be a new king in Israel.

2. What is the significance of the oil with which Samuel filled his horn?
The oil was used for anointing. The custom appears throughout the biblical period, and was used for anointing priests, prophets, and kings.

3. In what senses can Christians determine that their leaders are anointed today?
When leaders demonstrate the gifts of the Spirit through proclamation, administration, and service, Christians can feel confident that such leaders are anointed of God.

4. Which one of Jesse's sons did Samuel think would be God's choice for king?
Samuel thought that Eliab, the oldest son of Jesse, was the logical choice. Samuel, however, was to be surprised.

5. How many of Jesse's sons passed by Samuel, and what is the significance of that number?
Seven of Jesse's sons passed before Samuel. The number seven is the complete number. In this case, Jesse seems to believe that he has done all he can do.

(PLEASE TURN PAGE)

---

1. Why was the prophet Samuel mourning over Saul for such an extended time?

2. What is the significance of the oil with which Samuel filled his horn?

3. In what senses can Christians determine that their leaders are anointed today?

4. Which one of Jesse's sons did Samuel think would be God's choice for king?

5. How many of Jesse's sons passed by Samuel, and what is the significance of that number?

6. What was David doing when Samuel called for him?

7. In verse 7, the Lord tells Samuel not to look on the outward appearance, but in verse 12, the writer notes that David was a handsome young man. Explain the difference between these two accounts.

8. How can we know that we are guided by the Lord in our choice of leaders?

9. Which of Jesse's sons are named in the account as prospects for king?

10. How did Samuel consecrate David as king?

Samuel loved Saul and was heartbroken over Saul's disobedience of God's Word. As spokesman for God, it was Samuel's responsibility to tell Saul that there was going to be a new king in Israel.

The oil was used for anointing. The custom appears throughout the biblical period, and was used for anointing priests, prophets, and kings.

When leaders demonstrate the gifts of the Spirit through proclamation, administration, and service, Christians can feel confident that such leaders are anointed of God.

Samuel thought that Eliab, the oldest son of Jesse, was the logical choice. Samuel, however, was to be surprised.

Seven of Jesse's sons passed before Samuel. The number seven is the complete number. In this case, Jesse seems to believe that he has done all he can do.

David was keeping the sheep. He was the youngest son of Jesse. No one thought David had a chance to be anointed, so he was sent to look after the sheep.

The Lord does look on the heart. In the world, the outward appearance often counts most. In God's world, the pure heart is essential.

We pray and seek God's will.

Eliab, Abinadab, and Shammah are the three named.

Samuel anointed David's head and the Spirit of the Lord came upon David.

(SEED THOUGHTS--Cont'd)

6. What was David doing when Samuel called for him?
David was keeping the sheep. He was the youngest son of Jesse. No one thought David had a chance to be anointed, so he was sent to look after the sheep.

7. In verse 7, the Lord tells Samuel not to look on the outward appearance, but in verse 12, the writer notes that David was a handsome young man. Explain the difference between these two accounts.
The Lord does look on the heart. In the world, the outward appearance often counts most. In God's world, the pure heart is essential.

8. How can we know that we are guided by the Lord in our choice of leaders?
We pray and seek God's will.

9. Which of Jesse's sons are named in the account as prospects for king?
Eliab, Abinadab, and Shammah are the three named.

10. How did Samuel consecrate David as king?
Samuel anointed David's head and the Spirit of the Lord came upon David.

October 18, 1992

Solomon: Wise King

I Kings 2
1 NOW the days of David drew nigh that he should die; and he charged Solomon his son saying
2 I go the way of all the earth: be thou strong therefore, and shew thyself a man;
3 And keep the charge of the LORD thy God, to walk in his ways, to keep his statutes, and his commandments and his judgments, and his testimonies, as it is written in the law of Moses, that thou mayest prosper in all that thou doest, and whithersoever thou turnest thyself:
4 That the Lord may continue his word which he spake concerning me, saying, If thy children take heed to their way, to walk before me in truth with all their heart and with all their soul, there shall not fail thee (said he) a man on the throne of Israel.

I Kings 3
5 In Gib´-e-on the LORD appeared to Solomon in a dream by night: and God said, Ask what I shall give thee.
6 And Solomon said, Thou hast shewed unto thy servant David my father great mercy, according as he walked before thee in truth, and in righteousness, and in uprightness of heart with thee; and thou hast kept for him this great kindness, that thou hast given him a son to sit on his throne, as it is this day.
7 And now, O LORD my God, thou hast made thy servant king instead of David my father: and I am but a little child: I know not how to go out or come in.
8 And thy servant is in the midst of thy people which thou hast chosen, a great people, that cannot be numbered nor counted for multitude.
9 Give therefore thy servant an understanding heart to judge thy people, that I may discern between good and bad: for who is able to judge this thy so great a people?
10 And the speech pleased the LORD, that Solomon had asked this thing.
11 And God said unto him, Because thou hast asked this thing, and hast not asked for thyself long life; neither hast asked riches for thyself, nor hast asked the life of thine enemies; but hast asked for thyself understanding to discern judgment;
12 Behold, I have done according to thy words: lo, I have given thee a wise and an understanding heart.

◆◆◆◆◆◆

◀ **Memory Selection**
I Kings 3:9

◀ **Devotional Reading**
I Kings 1:15-30

◀ **Background Scripture**
I Kings: 1:28-37; 2:1-4; 3:5-12

◀ **Printed Scripture**
I Kings 2:1-4; 3:5-12

SOLOMON: WISE KING

Teacher's Target

God had given David a covenant in which he promised continuation of the royal dynasty through one of his sons (II Sam. 7:11-16). Absalom tried to seize the throne but failed (II Sam. 15, 18). Adonijah tried to do it but also failed (I Kings 1: 1-38). Solomon was God's choice to become king, and Adonijah had to submit to him (I Kings 1:39-53). Once this was settled, David advised Solomon to be strong and walk in God's ways. He did, and he was off to a great start (I Kings 2:1-12). It was at Gibeon that the Lord made Solomon three great promises and a conditional one (I Kings 3:5-14).

Help your students to perceive a place of leadership is an opportunity for service to Him through wise administration for people. Too many worldly leaders have clawed their way to the top for selfish reasons, and God has had to remove them. Those whom He blesses are the ones who seek His wisdom and do their best to help others live in peace and prosperity. Let us pray that our leaders today will be of the latter type.

Lesson Introduction

Sometimes a son will pattern himself closely after his father. Other times he will be quite different. David was a warrior, expanding his kingdom and safeguarding it through military means. Solomon was a man of peace, and he expanded the borders of Israel through diplomacy. David stockpiled materials to be used in building the first temple. Solomon saw that it was erected and dedicated. David made mistakes, but he was a man after God's Own heart. Solomon started off with a good relationship to God, but he was drawn off into pagan affairs by his foreign wives.

This lesson shows the connection between Solomon's good initial intentions and his outstanding reign over forty years. God gave him a wise and understanding heart, and it was this which made him successful. It was unfortunate that he later moved away from God and His ways. God let him die in peace, but upheaval followed and the kingdom was split asunder in subsequent years.

Teaching Outline

I. Charge: I Kings 2:1-4
   A. Challenge: 1-3
   B. Continuance: 4
II. Choice: I Kings 3:5-9
   A. Revelation: 5
   B. Review: 6-8
   C. Request: 9
III. Consent: I Kings 3:10-12a
   A. Pleasure: 10-11
   B. Provision: 12a

Daily Bible Readings

Mon. Solomon Receives His Inheritance - *I Kings 1:28-37*
Tue. Solomon Is Anointed King *I Kings 1:41-48*
Wed. Solomon Settles a Dispute between Two Women *I Kings 3:16-27*
Thu. God Gives Solomon Great Wisdom - *I Kings 4:29-34*
Fri. Solomon Makes a Covenant to Build God's House - *I Kings 6:1-5*
Sat. God Promises to Help Solomon Build the House - *I Kings 6:1-13*
Sun. Solomon Consecrates God's House - *I Kings 8:1-13*

October 18, 1992

VERSE BY VERSE

I. Charge: I Kings 2:1-4

A. Challenge: 1-3

1. Now the days of David drew nigh that he should die; and he charged Solomon his son, saying,
2a. I go the way of all the earth:...

In our last lesson we learned that David reigned over Judah and Israel for a total of forty years. "And he died in a good old age, full of days, riches, and honour: and Solomon his son reigned in his stead" (I Chron. 29:28). He evidently had had a premonition of his coming death. He realized that he was "going where every man on earth must some day go" (I Kings 2:2, Living Bible). He was resigned to the fact that the inevitable must happen and did not resist it. His main concern at that point was to challenge his son, Solomon, to carry on the kingdom in a proper manner.

2b....be thou strong therefore, and shew thyself a man;

David's challenge was presented in three parts. The first was that Solomon strive to be strong and manly. This apparently referred to strength of character and the courage resulting from it. We know nothing of Solomon's physical condition, but we know that he became an extremely wise and able leader. His strength of character was obviously greater in the earlier part of his reign when he walked with the Lord in close fellowship.

3a. And keep the charge of the Lord thy God, to walk in his ways, to keep his statutes, and his commandments, and his judgments, and his testimonies, as it is written in the law of Moses,...

The second part of David's challenge to Solomon was that he keep the charge of the Lord, which was more important than any earthly charge. David referred specifically to the divine law of God as it was given to Israel through Moses. That law told him how to walk in God's ways. The terms "statutes," "commandments," "judgments," and "testimonies" appear to be synonymous and referred to the instructions in His law. They included the famous ten commandments, plus all of the directives found in the Levitical Code. They provided the guidelines needed by all Israelites from the king on down to the lowliest peasant.

3b....that thou mayest prosper in all that thou doest, and whithersoever thou turnest thyself:

David told Solomon that walking according to the law of God would cause him to prosper (succeed, do wisely) in all things in whatever direction he moved. The wording here suggested that God had a master plan for Solomon's life and would keep him on it as long as he made no detours outside of His will. It was a marvelous promise, and it can be appropriated by all servants of the Lord in all generations, including our own.

B. Continuance: 4

4. That the Lord may continue his word which he spake concerning me, saying, If thy children take heed to their way, to walk before me in truth with all their heart and with all their soul, there shall not fail thee (said he) a man on the throne of Israel.

63

The Davidic covenant given by God, as recorded in II Samuel 7:11-16, made it clear that God would establish a royal dynasty for David and his descendants in Israel. David said that the Lord would continue this promise if those descendants were careful to walk in obedience before Him in truth with all their heart and soul. Solomon was to be the first. It was unfortunate that he and Rehoboam were to drift away from Jehovah in later years. However, although the historical line seemed to be broken, it became apparent again when Jesus Christ came to claim the throne of David.

The third part of David's challenge to Solomon was that he deal appropriately with David's enemies and friends (Joab, the sons of Barzillai, Shimei), and this is found in I Kings 2:5-9.

We find that Solomon sat upon the throne of his father, David, and his kingdom was greatly established (I Kings 2:12). What happened in this early part of his reign was evidently a trial run, and Solomon did well. Now the Lord was ready to confer great blessings on him.

II. Choice: I Kings 3:5-9

A. Revelation: 5

5. **In Gibeon the Lord appeared to Solomon in a dream by night: and God said, Ask what I shall give thee.**

Gibeon, located about ten miles northwest of Jerusalem, had a rich history. The tabernacle used in the wilderness by the Israelites was pitched at Gibeon and became the primary place of worship. Solomon offered up a thousand sacrificial animals there upon the altar (I Kings 3:4). His heart must have been right before God, because the Lord was pleased enough to offer to fulfill Solomon's greatest wish. He spoke to him in a dream at night, a normal type of revelation in ancient times.

B. Review: 6-8

6a. **And Solomon said, Thou hast shewed unto thy servant David my father great mercy, according as he walked before thee in truth, and in righteousness, and in uprightness of heart with thee;...**

We do not know how long it took Solomon to come up with a response to the Lord's offer, but he was adroit enough to review the situation involving his father and himself. God did not need a history lesson from Solomon, but He allowed him to put his feelings into words. Solomon began by recalling God's mercy to his father, and he made the connection with the fact that divine blessing flowed to David because of his close walk with the Lord in truth and righteousness.

6b. **...and thou hast kept for him this great kindness, that thou hast given him a son to sit on his throne, as it is this day.**

Note that the term "great mercy" found in the earlier part of the verse is now transposed to "great kindness" as Solomon praised God for fulfilling His promise to put a son of David on the throne at that time. Despite futile attempts by Absalom and Adonijah to capture the throne, God had prevailed and placed Solomon on it, instead. It was not simply that God wanted *a* son of David on the throne; He wanted a *particular* one there.

7. **And now, O Lord my God, thou hast made thy servant king instead of David my father: and I am but a little child: I know not how to go out or come in.**

Solomon was probably in his early twenties at this time. He did not refer to himself as a literal child but as a young man lacking the maturity and experience which his father had possessed. He mentioned the fact that he did not know how to go out or come in. This terminology was used to describe military activity, with a leader going out with his men to battle and coming back in victory. Solomon was not a warrior, as David had been. Whatever he did would have to be done by means of wisdom and diplomacy.

8. **And thy servant is in the midst of thy people which thou hast chosen, a great people, that cannot be numbered nor counted for multitude.**

As with all new, young rulers, Solomon must have felt the burden of being responsible for leading the chosen people of God. They had to be preserved as a divine witness to the pagan world. Although it may have been hyperbole, he claimed that he could not know how many were in Israel because of their great number. Perhaps he felt that not even a census could keep up with the expanding population. Thus ended his quick review, and now he was ready to make his request.

C. Request: 9

9. **Give therefore thy servant an understanding heart to judge thy people, that I may discern between good and bad: for who is able to judge this thy so great a people?**
Solomon later wrote, "The fear of the Lord is the beginning of knowledge" (Prov. 1:7). In making his request here, Solomon showed reverence and humility to the Lord. Even before he was endowed with special wisdom to rule Israel, he was intelligent enough to realize that God was the true Source of all knowledge. He wanted an understanding heart for ruling God's people. He had a personal conscience which helped him know right from wrong. Now he wanted a mind which could make proper decisions when judging disputes among the people. He wanted to be able to discern who was right and who was wrong among complainants who would stand before him.

III. Consent: Kings 3:10-12a

A. Pleasure: 10-11

10. **And the speech pleased the Lord, that Solomon had asked this thing.**
God had emotions, and what Solomon said brought pleasure and satisfaction to the heart of God. He was glad that Solomon had asked for something with which he could better serve Him and His people. It showed that Solomon had his heart in the right place, rather than on acquiring material things or great prestige. We might examine our own prayer requests to see if they are pleasing to the Lord.

11. **And God said unto him, Because thou hast asked this thing, and hast not asked for thyself long life; neither hast asked riches for thyself, nor hast asked the life of thine enemies; but hast asked for thyself understanding to discern judgment;**
Here was God's own list of things which Solomon might have requested, if his heart had not been right before God. They included a long life, riches, and the deaths of his enemies. God was pleased that Solomon set aside such personal requests as these and asked instead for wisdom in ruling over Israel.

B. Provision: 12a

12a. **Behold, I have done according to thy words: lo, I have given thee a wise and an understanding heart;**
In the latter part of this verse, God went on to say that Solomon would be unique. None was like him before he ruled, and none would be like him after he finished ruling.

In verses 13 and 14, God is described as giving Solomon two additional promises and one conditional one. He told Solomon that he had given him riches, meaning that he and his kingdom would prosper greatly in the years to come. He told Solomon that He had given him honor, meaning that his fame would spread throughout Israel and far beyond to foreign nations. He concluded by saying that no other kings would equal him all of his days.

The conditional promise that God made to Solomon was that of a long life. However, Solomon would have to walk in God's ways and be guided by His divine law, just as David had been guided by it. It is interesting to note that God allowed Solomon to finish his long reign in peace, even after he had sinned by promoting his pagan wives' idolatry, but He did it for David's sake (I Kings 11:1-13).

Looking back over the life of Solomon, we are reminded of the fact that there are various kinds of wisdom. He obviously was a brilliant man when it came to administration and diplomacy, but he was deficient in emotional knowledge, for he allowed his pagan wives to lead him astray. We need to ask the Lord to give us wisdom for all aspects of our lives - physical, material, mental, emotional, social, and spiritual.

SOLOMON: WISE KING

Evangelistic Emphasis

Solomon, when offered whatever he wanted from God, asked for an understanding heart. Here is a man standing on the threshold of greatness. All of his dreams are about to come true. He has stumbled upon a power greater than Aladdin's lamp. God, not some fictional genie, offers Solomon the desires of his heart. Solomon could ask for power, wealth, or status. Instead he asks for wisdom.

The request for wisdom should always precede our attempts at evangelism. Our evangelistic methods, at their worst, overemphasise emotional responses. There is, however, a corrective, an opposite polarity - the wisdom of God. Those who tell the Good News need to follow the example of Solomon and ask for wisdom.

To understand others means to identify with them in their lostness and alienation. It means to stand where they stand. Bill Moyers recently said that he belonged to the largest tribe in the world, the tribe of the wounded. Such a stance always precludes a spirit of judgmentalism. Understanding like that will give us the heart of an evangelist and save us from a mean spirit. Let others be the severe critics while we tell of Jesus the mighty to save. Let others put people down while we lift them up with words of empathy and understanding.

♦♦♦♦♦♦

Memory Selection

Give thy servant (Solomon) therefore an understanding mind to govern the people, that I may discern between good and evil; for who is able to govern this thy great people?—*I Kings 3:9*

Prayer for self is not usually considered to be a proper exercise of spiritual discipline. Prayer is not generally an act of selfishness. Prayer is an act of empathy; prayer is asking for others rather than self. Yet Solomon asks for something for himself.

Solomon's prayer is an act of self-expression. He expresses his feelings and desires to God. To his credit, Solomon is very specific. He does not pray in vague, pious generalities; he prays for an understanding heart to judge his people properly. There is often too much pious, religious language in prayer. We need specificity. Tell God the truth. Express your deepest desires. As Luther advised, "Never lie to God."

Sometimes it *is* proper to ask God for something for yourself. There is a definite humility in Solomon's request. He recognizes the job of king is too large for him. God will always hear the pleading of one who desperately wants to be of greater service to the kingdom.

Human beings often pray only to service their own desire for success. Solomon, on the other hand asks for a gift he can use to help others. Did not St. Paul encourage us to ask earnestly for the greater gifts? Through humility and a desire for the well-being for others, Solomon's prayer blocks out typical human requests based on greed, the desire to dominate, and the needs of a selfish ego. Here then is a model prayer of self-expression, here is a model for our own praying.

October 18, 1992

Weekday Problems

Jim is a bright young man with a degree in electrical engineering. He has already received a promotion with a major company. The future looks promising. He is a young executive on the fast track with unlimited potential.

There is, however, one major problem. Jim's immaturity blinds him to his need for patience and advice. Without doubt he has great skills and intellectual powers. Yet he lacks experience and wisdom. He does everything full speed, confident of his own abilities, and he never asks anyone for help. As a consequence, Jim forms no personal relationships. He has no sense of ethical responsibility. His goal is to get to the top as fast as possible.

When he considers the people ahead of him on the corporate ladder, he feels only contempt. His immediate supervisor is a commited Christian. He gently tries to help Jim gain a more compassionate perspective on life. Jim is not interested. He does, however, begin to wonder about the quiet confidence with which his supervisor lives.

Jim notices that his supervisor has a certain contentment and satisfaction level. Jim wonders how this can be when the fire that burns within him leaves him constantly unsatisfied and anxious for the future.

*What is Jim's most challenging problem?
*What else can Jim's supervisor do to help Jim change his selfish, immature lifestyle?
*In what ways could a Christian outlook make a difference in Jim's life?

♦♦♦♦♦♦

Superintendent's Sermonette

The basic meaning of the term "administer" is to serve others or minister to them. An administrator is someone who manages the affairs of others, and he will either do it well or badly, depending on his abilities, attitudes, or acceptability. History offers many illustrations of leaders who used positions of trust for their own personal aggrandizement and profit. It also offers examples of selfless leaders who served their people well and were revered because of it.

There is nothing intrinsically wrong with material possessions, power, or prestige. God can use them for His Own glory, and He can lend them to human leaders to use for His glory. What concerns Him most is the condition of those leaders' hearts. He questioned Solomon at Gibeon and discovered that the thing Solomon wanted most was wisdom for governing Israel. God gave him that, plus riches, honor, and a conditional promise of long life.

What should be our goal if God places us in any position of leadership? Let us seek His wisdom so that we may serve Him and others well. If we do that, He will supply us with whatever we need for getting the job done, and He will give us satisfaction for serving Him acceptably.

67

SOLOMON: WISE KING

This Lesson In Your Life

Oscar Wilde once wrote, "In this world there are only two tragedies. One is not getting what one wants, and the other is getting it." He was telling us that wealth and success are not all they appear to be. It is, in other words, possible to pay too high a price for success. We may make the mistake of sacrificing too much on the altar of success. For all our hard work and achievement we will get success, but that does not equate with satisfaction or joy or well-being.

Solomon must have learned at an early age something you and I might not know. Money and success will not satisfy the yearning of the human heart. Equipped with a realistic understanding of life, Solomon asked God to give him wisdom. Somehow the very act of asking for wisdom indicates that Solomon was already well on his way to being wise. Only the wise are ever able to see that having everything you ever wanted will not be enough. Human beings are made for God. Anything less leads to a poor quality of life.

There is room for plenty of introspection on our part. Although we recognize the validity of Solomon's request, we tend not to act in the same way. We continue to go hard after the visible trinkets of success. Our ambition is often not tempered with integrity and understanding. Solomon can thus serve as a model for us. His request for wisdom is, after all, a request for integrity and understanding. A person of wisdom has integrity. He is able to see clearly, to discern rightly, and to decide justly. The gift of integrity is certainly needed. Look at our world.

We live in a world of falsehood, pretense, and lies. A person's word is of no value. Contracts have to be signed. A promise and a handshake no longer have meaning. In a society where words are used deceitfully we have to be on guard. We are not sure who to believe. The advertisers have to be curbed by the FDA or they will make untrue claims. The sponsors will, after all, sell all they can. Witnesses have to swear on a Bible that they will tell the truth before testifying in court. In a world of secular falsity we have to do something to underscore the truth. Solomon's honesty seems out of place.

What is the answer when all the rules and contracts and oath-swearing cannot enforce the telling of the truth. The answer for us is a world full of persons like Solomon, a person of integrity. The word "integrity" comes from a math term, "integer." It means a whole number. A person of integrity is a whole person. He is the same person under all circumstances and conditions. He always tells the truth. He can be trusted to act in consistent ways. Wisdom is then integrity, but, it is also understanding. Perhaps Solomon's request can help us achieve understanding. In our culture, especially, we need to perceive the emptiness of wealth and success. Neither of these idols of materialism can guarantee happiness. Neither can prevent disease and death. Neither can provide significance and well-meaning.

The integrity and understanding that wisdom produces does, on the other hand, have numerous advantages. Wise people know the value of intimate and lasting relationships. They love people and use things rather than using people and loving things. They understand themselves and thus do not think more highly of themselves than they should. In addition wise persons enjoy their work without allowing it to consume them. Most of all, wise persons build their lives on a meaningful relationship with God.

Seed Thoughts

1. The struggle over the person to succeed David brought together what two unexpected persons as allies?
It is surprising to see Nathan, the prophet who denounced David and Bathseba's sin, on Bathsheba's side.

2. Does God work out His will in spite of the political intrigue of humans?
Yes. God works behind the scene to bring good out of evil. The very human account of the struggle for the kingship in no way detracts from the providence of God.

3. Who were the primary candidates to replace David as King?
Adonijah, because he was David's oldest living son, and Solomon. Chileab seems to have died young.

4. Who were the major allies of Adonijah?
All of David's children, except Solomon; Abiathar, the priest; and Joab, the general of the army.

5. Who favored Solomon as the best candidate to succeed David as king?
Bathsheba, Nathan, Zadok, Beniaiah, and David's bodyguards were all on Solomon's side.

(PLEASE TURN PAGE)

---

1. The struggle over the person to succeed David brought together what two unexpected persons as allies?

2. Does God work out His will in spite of the political intrigue of humans?

3. Who were the primary candidates to replace David as King?

4. Who were the major allies of Adonijah?

5. Who favored Solomon as the best candidate to succeed David as king?

6. How did David make known his decision concerning the next king of Israel?

7. What was the significance of Adonijah grasping the horns of the altar?

8. What were David's instructions to Solomon?

9. Where did Solomon make his famous request to the Lord for Wisdom?

10. The Lord was pleased because Solomon asked for wisdom instead of what other possibilities?

It is surprising to see Nathan, the prophet who denounced David and Bathseba's sin, on Bathsheba's side.

Yes. God works behind the scene to bring good out of evil. The very human account of the struggle for the kingship in no way detracts from the providence of God.

Adonijah, because he was David's oldest living son, and Solomon. Chileab seems to have died young.

All of David's children, except Solomon; Abiathar, the priest; and Joab, the general of the army.

Bathsheba, Nathan, Zadok, Beniaiah, and David's bodyguards were all on Solomon's side.

David announced that Solomon was the new king. He had Solomon ride on the king's mule to the spring at Gihon. There Zadok the priest and Nathan the prophet anointed Solomon as king.

When Adonijah heard that Solomon was king, he was afraid for his life. He took refuge before the altar. A person touching the altar was not supposed to be killed.

David's charge to Solomon is similiar to the one given to Joshua earlier. Solomon was to be strong and courageous. Most of all he was to obey the law of God.

At Gibeon the Lord came to Solomon in a vision and told Solomon to ask for whatever he wanted.

Solomon could have asked for a long life, riches, or the death of his enemies.

(SEED THOUGHTS--Cont'd)

6. How did David make known his decision concerning the next king of Israel?
David announced that Solomon was the new king. He had Solomon ride on the king's mule to the spring at Gihon. There Zadok the priest and Nathan the prophet anointed Solomon as king.

7. What was the significance of Adonijah grasping the horns of the altar?
When Adonijah heard that Solomon was king, he was afraid for his life. He took refuge before the altar. A person touching the altar was not supposed to be killed.

8. What were David's instructions to Solomon?
David's charge to Solomon is similiar to the one given to Joshua earlier. Solomon was to be strong and courageous. Most of all he was to obey the law of God.

9. Where did Solomon make his famous request to the Lord for Wisdom?
At Gibeon the Lord came to Solomon in a vision and told Solomon to ask for whatever he wanted.

10. The Lord was pleased because Solomon asked for wisdom instead of what other possibilities?
Solomon could have asked for a long life, riches, or the death of his enemies.

October 25, 1992

Josiah: King of Reforms

II Chronicles 34

2 And he did that which was right in the sight of the LORD, and walked in the ways of David his father, and declined neither to the right hand, nor to the left

8 Now in the eighteenth year of his reign, when he had purged the land, and the house, he sent Sha´-phan the son of Az-a-li´-ah, and Ma-a-se´-iah the governor of the city, and Jo´ah the son of Jo´-a-has the recorder, to repair the house of the LORD his God.

14b Hil-ki´-ah the priest found a book of the law of the LORD given by Moses. **15** And Hil-ki´-ah answered and said to Sha´phan the scribe, I have found the book of the law in the house of the LORD. And Hil-ki´-ah delivered the book to Sha´-phan.
16 And Sha´phan carried the book to the king,

19 And it came to pass, when the king had heard the words of the law, that he rent his clothes.

21 Go, enquire of the LORD for me, and for them that are left in Israel and in Judah, concerning the words of the book that is found: for great is the wrath of the LORD that is poured out upon us, because our fathers have not kept the word of the LORD, to do after all that is written in this book.

30 And the king went up into the house of the LORD, and all the men of Judah, and the inhabitants of Jerusalem, and the priests, and the Levites, and all the people, great and small: and he read in their ears all the words of the book of the covenant that was found in the house of the LORD.
31 And the king stood in his place, and made a covenant before the LORD, to walk after the LORD, and to keep his commandments, and his testimonies, and his statutes, with all his heart, and with all his soul, to perform the words of the covenant which are written in this book.
32 And he caused all that were present in Jerusalem and Benjamin to stand to it. And the inhabitants of Jerusalem did according to the covenant of God, the God of their fathers.

◆◆◆◆◆◆

◀ **Memory Selection**
II Chronicles 34:33

◀ **Devotional Reading**
II Chronicles 34:9-13 19, 21, 30-32

◀ **Background Scripture**
II Chronicles 34

◀ **Printed Scripture**
II Chronicles 34:2,8, 14b-16a, 19-32

JOSIAH: KING OF REFORMS

Teacher's Target

The combined kingdom of Judah and Israel over which David and Solomon reigned was split in two after Solomon died. Rehoboam, Solomon's son, alienated the northern tribes, and they withdrew under Jeroboam I and reformed Israel. A man of God prophesied that "a child shall be born unto the house of David, Josiah by name" (I Kings 13:2). Many years went by, but Josiah finally appeared and became the sixteenth king of Judah. He was eight years old when he began his thirty-one-year reign (II Chron. 34:1), and he was a reformer.

Help your students to see that God does not permanently leave people in the degraded state of sin which they deserve. He always brings someone along who points the way to righteousness and helps people rise to the challenge. Josiah was a bright light in a generally dark succession of sinful monarchs in ancient Judah. His life shows that someone good can come out of a bad situation. What he did in his generation should be our goal today.

Lesson Introduction

Every now and then someone may say to you, "I have just read a book which you must read, too," Their enthusiasm may motivate you to do that, and you could be equally impressed or, on the other hand, wonder why that person became excited about it in the first place. There is one book which has managed to stir people in every generation since it first began to be written and was finished some fifteen centuries later, and that is the Holy Bible. It has been the blueprint for the construction of countless lives.

In this lesson's texts we study about the impact made by a portion of God's Word on the ancient kingdom of Judah. Because of the neglect of the kings and priests, a copy of the law of Moses had been buried in the debris of the temple. Josiah ordered the temple to be repaired, and, in the process, a scroll of the law was found and presented to him. This led to the reforms which he instituted, and it will do the same whenever it is sincerely believed and implemented.

Teaching Outline

I. Determination: II Chron. 34:2
II. Discovery: II Chron. 34:8, 14b-16a
   A. Repair: 8
   B. Referral: 14b-16a
III. Distress: II Chron. 34:19, 21
   A. Clothes: 19
   B. Concern: 21
IV. Declaration: II Chron. 34:30-32
   A. Convocation: 30
   B. Covenant: 31-32

Daily Bible Readings

Mon. Josiah Destroys Graven Images in Judah and Jerusalem
II Chron. 34:3-7
Tue. The Lord's House Is Rebuilt
II Chron. 34:9-13
Wed. King Josiah Repents
II Chron. 34:17-21
Thu. The People of Judah Are Forgiven - *II Chron. 34:22-28*
Fri. Israel Renews the Covenant with the Lord - *II Chron. 34:29-34*
Sat. Israel Prepares for the Passover
II Chron. 35:1-6
Sun. King Josiah Dies
II Chron. 35:20-27

October 25, 1992

VERSE BY VERSE

I. Determination: II Chron. 34:2

2. And he did that which was right in the sight of the Lord, and walked in the ways of David his father, and declined neither to the right hand, nor to the left.

Similar words had been written about Hezekiah, the thirteenth king of Judah - "He did that which was right in the sight of the Lord, according to all that David his father [ancestor] had done (II Chron. 29:2), Hezekiah and Josiah were exceptions to the normal succession of sinful kings in Judah. Josiah's development was apparently a gradual one. When he was sixteen, he began to seek after God. When he was twenty, he began to purge Judah and Jerusalem from the high places of idolatry. When he was twenty-six, he made plans to repair the house of the Lord (II Chron. 34:3-8).

Although Josiah did not have a copy of the law of God to guide him at first, he apparently had principles of righteous conduct bequeathed to him from the time of David. He was meticulous in not deviating from them. He walked squarely in the middle of the path they laid out for him, detouring neither to the right or the left. Living up to the light he had, he was given more light.

II. Discovery: II Chron. 34:8, 14b-16a

A. Repair: 8

8. Now in the eighteenth year of his reign, when he had purged the land, and the house, he sent Shaphan the son of Azaliah, and Maaseiah the governor of the city, and Joah the son of Joahaz the recorder, to repair the house of the Lord his God.

When Josiah was twenty-six years of age, he had completed the task of purging Judah of idolatry, including all aspects of it found in the temple. He then commissioned three men to head up the massive task of repairing the dilapidated building. Shaphan the scribe was a faithful servant of Josiah, and three of his sons (Ahikim, Gemariah, and Elasah) followed in his footsteps, his fourth son Jaazaniah being the exception. Maaseiah was the governor (mayor) of Jerusalem. Joah was the son of the recorder (treasurer) of Jerusalem and perhaps in line to succeed his father in that office.

Levites had been collecting money with which to repair the temple, and these three men brought it to Hilkiah, the high priest. It was given to various tradesmen to pay for supplies and labor in repairing the structure (II Chron. 34:9-10).

B. Referral: 14b-16a

14b. Hilkiah the priest found a book of the law of the Lord given by Moses.

The scroll which Hilkiah discovered during repair work on the temple was probably the official copy of the Pentateuch usually kept by the ark (Deut. 31:25-26). It had evidently been misplaced during the previous years of neglect. Its importance was immediately recognized by true men of God.

15. And Hilkiah answered and said to Shaphan the scribe, I have found the book of the law in the house of the Lord. And Hilkiah delivered the book to Shaphan.

16a. And Shaphan carried the book to the king,...

Quick referral of the scroll was made up the line until it came to King Josiah. Hilkiah gave it to Shaphan, and Shaphan took it to Josiah, where he proceeded to read it to the king (vs. 18). Considering the reaction this produced, Shaphan may have read the section from Deuteronomy 28-30 which contained threats of dire punishment to any who violated the law of God.

III. Distress: II Chron. 34:19, 21

A. Clothes: 19

19. And it came to pass, when the king had heard the words of the law, that he rent his clothes.

This incident illustrates the truth of Romans 3:20 - "By the law is the knowledge of sin." Josiah was the sensitive kind of person who was greatly distressed to learn about divine threats for neglecting or violating the law of God. He immediately tore his clothing as a sign of mourning current at that time. Other forms of expressing sorrow were sprinkling earth or ashes on one's head, wearing sackcloth (hair cloth), covering the head or lips, loud weeping, and singing or chanting of sad dirges. Professional mourners were often used at funeral processions, even in Jesus' time.

B. Concern: 21

21a. Go, enquire of the Lord for me, and for them that are left in Israel and in Judah, concerning the words of the book that is found:...

Josiah had summoned five officials to form a delegation. They were Hilkiah, Ahikam, Abdon, Shaphan, and Asaiah (vs. 20). He ordered them to go and ask the Lord what he and all the people of Israel and Judah should do in order to counteract the warnings found in the law of God. They had to find someone who had contact with Jehovah and could serve as an intermediary between Him and a sinful people.

21b. ... for great is the wrath of the Lord that is poured out upon us, because our fathers have not kept the word of the Lord, to do after all that is written in this book.

The wrath mentioned here was probably meant to refer to divine indignation, anger, and disappointment which could lead to an outpouring of judgment on the people. Josiah was so upset that he spoke of it as already happening, but it seems obvious that he wanted to prevent it from happening.

The men of the delegation decided to visit a prophetess named Huldah, wife of Shallum. She lived in the college in Jerusalem, referring to the second quarter of the city. She received them and listened to their request for help. Huldah told the men to tell the king that God would bring evil (judgment) on Jerusalem and its inhabitants for their idolatries. She also told them to tell the king that he would be spared this judgment and would die in peace, because he had humbled himself before the Lord, rent his clothes, and wept. Josiah received this report and assembled all the elders (leaders) of Judah and Jerusalem for an important convocation (II Chron. 34:22-29). As at other points in human history, a period of spiritual revival was going to precede the imposition of divine judgment, and Josiah was determined to be the leader of this revival.

IV. Declaration: II Chron. 34: 30 -32

A. Convocation: 30

30a. And the king went up into the house of the Lord, and all the men of Judah, and the inhabitants of Jerusalem, and the priests, and the Levites, and all the people, great and small:

It appears that this was a representative crowd which Josiah took with him up to the temple, for there would be children, infirm, handicapped, and aged individuals who would not be able to attend. A cross section of Judah and Jerusalem was there, including tribal elders, officials, priests, Levites, and common people both rich and poor. We might say that, in a sense, the whole nation came.

30b. ...and he read in their ears all the words of the book of the covenant that was found in the house of the Lord.

Josiah read the words of the divine covenant. This ancient document had been commanded by God to be used to guide a thousand generations (l Chron.

16:15). It is specifically referred to here as "the covenant that was found in the house of the Lord." The covenant mentioned in the next two verses was a new affirmation by Josiah and his people to follow the old covenant.

B. Covenant: 31-32

31a. And the king stood in his place, and made a covenant before the Lord,...
The special place for the king to stand was at a certain pillar at the entrance to the temple (II Kings 23:3; II Chron, 23:13). It was here that Josiah gave his majestic presence to a covenant which he made standing before the Lord, no doubt setting the example for his people to follow. This was a solemn promise to follow the law given by God to Israel through Moses long ago at Mount Sinai.

31b. ...to walk after the Lord, and to keep his commandments, and his testimonies, and his statutes, with all his heart, and with all his soul, to perform the words of the covenant which are written in this book.
There could be no doubt as to what Josiah expected Israel to do as long as he reigned. Its people were to walk the righteous path laid out by the Lord. They were to obey his commandments with all their heart and soul. They were to implement the words of the old covenant sincerely and consistently. It was the highest standard known to men at that time.

32a. And he caused all that were present in Jerusalem and Benjamin to stand to it.
The tribe of Simeon had been absorbed into the tribe of Judah. The tribe of Benjamin threw in its lot with the tribe of Judah after the death of Solomon. Jerusalem, being Judah's capital, seemed to represent the tribe of Judah. What Josiah did was to get all of the people of Judah and Benjamin to stand in confirmation of keeping the old covenant given by God through Moses at Mount Sinai.

32b. And the inhabitants of Jerusalem did according to the covenant of God, the God of their fathers.
Here, again, the phrase "inhabitants of Jerusalem" apparently refers to the whole nation, which took its example from the capital city. It was one thing to stand in confirmation of a covenant, but it was something else again to live up to it. The people of Judah tried to follow it in the spiritual revival which took place. Since no people are completely perfect, there were no doubt some infractions but the intent of the people was good.

Josiah went even further by taking away all of the abominations (idolatries) out of all the countries that pertained to the Jews. We are told that "All his days they departed not from following the Lord, the God of their fathers (II Chron. 34:33).

Josiah reinstated the celebration of the Jewish Passover in Jerusalem (II Chron. 35:1-19). When Necho, King of Egypt, went to war against Assyria to the north, Josiah went out against him and was fatally wounded, Taken back to Jerusalem in a chariot, he died there and was buried in his ancestral sepulcher. His nation mourned his passing, for he had been a good king and a leader in spiritual reforms. Jeremiah was among those who mourned his passing (II Chron, 35:20-27). It has been suggested that the reforms made by Josiah provided favorable conditions for the work done by Jeremiah during the earlier part of his prophetic ministry.

Evangelistic Emphasis

The ancient Greeks once lost the ability to write and speak their own language. For over two centuries their language was lost to them. As a result their culture perished and their civilization disappeared. In our story King Josiah and his workers find the Word of the Lord in the temple. This means that the people of God had lost the Word of God. Can you imagine God's own people trying to live without God's Word? Centuries of experience suggest clearly that when God's Word is lost, the dissipation of God's people is certain. According to the writer of II Chronicles, the people of God, separated from God's Word, followed idols.

If a nation loses its language, it can survive. When the people of God, however, lose the Word of God, they lose not only their whole way of life but also their reason for being. God's people cannot survive without the direction, guidance and power of God's word.

Recall the pointed words of Isaish: "Wherefore do ye spend money for that which is not bread? . . . Incline your ear, and come unto me: hear, and your soul shall live. (Isaiah 55:2,3). Remember the hard promise of God, "Behold the days come, saith the Lord God, that I will send a famine in the land, not a famine of bread, nor a thirst for water, but of hearing the words of the Lord" (Amos 8:11). The Word of God nourishes the hearts and minds of people with life-saving power. The Word offers grace and love and forgiveness as well as judgment. To rediscover the Word of God is to find life.

♦♦♦♦♦♦

Memory Selection

Josiah took away all the abominations from all the territory that belong to the people of Israel, and made all who were in Israel serve the Lord their God.
II Chronicles 34:33

An abomination is whatever is ethically loathsome and repugnant to God. In the Old Testament the word designated violation of established custom, unclean foods, imperfect sacrifices, magic, sexual irregularities, immorality, and idolatrous practices. In the memory verse the reference is to the idol worship of God's people. To get a feel for how much God hates idolatry, say the word "abomination". The word sort of rolls off the tongue with a sickening, destestable sound. Make no mistake. God hates the worship of idols, and abomination is just the word to describe God's attitude toward idolatry.

The action of Josiah applies to our age just as well because the church itself can be idolatrous with pompous religiosity. M. Holmes Hartshorne once remarked that "religion is regularly the most subtle and the most potent expression of human sin." We need to make sure that we worship God with purity of heart and not for the praise and honor of others.

Our individual idols are also an abomination to the Lord: technology, materialism, scientific knowledge, pleasure, and sports. We too must take away all the abominations that keep God from being the center of our lives. The idols of our time must be destroyed.

October 25, 1992

Weekday Problems

Jim is a member of his local church, First Church. He accepted Christ as his Saviour at an early age. Now he is a successful businessman as the owner-operator of a large supermarket. The business takes up most of his time.

For years Jim did not open his store on Sunday, but times changed. Before long he was open after church every Sunday. Then he started opening all day on Sunday. He told his pastor, "I think all those blue laws about not doing business on Sunday are just legalistic mumbo jumbo. I don't have to be in church every Sunday in order to worship God. Besides, I have to make a living. Every other store in town is open on Sunday." With all his rationalizations neatly worked out, Jim went about his business. Last month he started selling beer because "the profits are so high," and this month he is getting a license to sell lottery tickets. Jim has not been to church in three years. He does, however, send the church a check for $1,000 every Christmas. In slow, unconscious ways Jim has slipped into bad habits.

*What example from Josiah might help Jim understand what has happened to him?
*What could you say to Jim about the importance of priorities?
*Do you have trouble keeping your spiritual priorities in order?
*What could we say to answer Jim's rationalizations?

♦♦♦♦♦♦

Superintendent's Sermonette

The world seems to be filled with all kinds of improvement programs. Bookstores have whole sections with self-improvement books. Video cassettes are available to teach how to do things. There are probably more people involved in education as students, teachers, administrators, and publishers than in any other human activity. We are living in the midst of an explosion in knowledge and the means for distributing what is learned. There is a problem, however, for what people are learning can be evil as well as righteous, and too many are choosing what is evil. The burden of upholding what is righteous becomes greater as time goes by.

Young King Josiah struggled with evil influences in ancient Judah, but he was guided in his development by principles inherited from his ancestor, King David. Then something wonderful but frightening happened, for the law of God was discovered in the temple as it was being repaired. That law contained threats of divine judgment on sinners, and Josiah moved swiftly to prevent them from being implemented in Judah. Our best hope for defeating evil and increasing righteousness lies with the Word of God, and we should uphold it with the same intensity as Josiah did.

77

JOSIAH: KING OF REFORMS

This Lesson In Your Life

Psychologists describe neurotics as persons who prefer the security of known misery to the misery of unfamiliar insecurity. Simply put, change is never an easy experience for people. Rather than risk the dangers of change, most people prefer to maintain their own private brand of security, no matter how helpless and hopeless their situation. Another way of looking at our fear of change comes from Robert Frost's poem, "The Mountain." He has a character say, "I've always meant to go and look myself, but you know how it is: It doesn't seem so much to climb a mountain you've worked around the foot of all your life." Isn't that part of the reluctance to change. We are used to low altitudes, low goals, low ideals. Maybe we are afraid of heights, and thus afraid to make any changes at all.

The story of Josiah is about change, a total reformation of the character and spiritual make-up of an entire nation. And there is no indication that the change was automatic or easy. After all, Josiah was going against the tide of popular opinion. His faithfulness to God stands out like a single, majestic island in a wild, unruly sea. Yet Josiah, with singleminded commitment brought a whole people back to a right relationship with God.

In order for genuine change to occur, the change that leads to spiritual revival and renewal, certain elements are required. First, excellent leadership is necessary. Josiah certainly fits the description of a great leader because he did what was right in the sight of the Lord. He returned to the worship of God. To return is a basic message of the Old Testament. All the prophets bear witness to the necessity of turning from sin and returning to the Lord. There can be no significant change until God's people follow a leader who returns to the Lord.

A second necessary element of change is the complete concentration of God's leader upon the task at hand. Josiah, we are told, did not turn aside to the right or to the left. Many good intentions for change and for holy living are side tracked by other priorities. John Killinger tells the story of a man who trained his dog to go to the meat market and bring home a package of meat. The dog would go straight to the butcher, take the package in his mouth and go straight home. He paid no attention to all the little dogs barking and nipping at his heels. He "brought the bacon" home despite all manner of distractions. That's part of what our biblical author means when he says Josiah did not turn aside.

There is an old definition of the word "affirmation" that applies here: "to maintain." Josiah affirmed his faith in God, set his course toward revival, and maintained a straight path. He allowed no one to sidetrack him. There is certainly a lesson here for us because we are often inattentive. In fact, inattention may be our greatest sin. God speaks but we are not listening. God leads in the direction of revival but we are preoccupied. Listen, if there is going to be effective revival in the church we must affirm our goal and pay attention to the road leading to revival.

The third and most important element of change is attention to the Word of God. No revival is possible until people begin to hear the word of the Lord. "To hear" means to hear and to obey. Communication theorists call it "active listening." Many people think that hearing is a passive activity requiring no effort. And so we often listen to God in passive, inattentive ways. We hear but do not obey the word of God.

Seed Thoughts

1. Whose example of moral conduct and right living did Josiah follow in serving the Lord?
David. He walked in the ways of his ancestor David.

2. What does it mean to say that Josiah took away all the abominations from the land of Israel?
In our lesson an abomination refers to all the idols the Israelites were worshipping as well as the religious *paraphenelia* associated with false gods.

3. What are the two most important achievements of Josiah's reign as king?
The repair of the temple and the revival of the worship of God.

4. What is the primary cause of the religious revival and return to the worship of God under Josiah.
The finding and reading of the Word of God - the Law of Moses. All great revivals are preceded by a mighty proclamation of God's Word.

5. How does Josiah respond to the reading of God's Word and what is the significance of the king's action?
He tore his clothes as a sign of sorrow and repentance.

(PLEASE TURN PAGE)

---

1. Whose example of moral conduct and right living did Josiah follow in serving the Lord?

2. What does it mean to say that Josiah took away all the abominations from the land of Israel?

3. What are the two most important achievements of Josiah's reign as king?

4. What is the primary cause of the religious revival and return to the worship of God under Josiah.

5. How does Josiah respond to the reading of God's Word and what is the significance of the king's action?

6. To whom does Josiah turn for an interpretation of the Word of God?

7. What was the message of the prophet to the people of Judah and to King Josiah?

8. What are the implications to be drawn from the temporary results of Josiah's religious revival?

9. What promises did Josiah make in his personal covenant with God?

10. How long did the revival of Josiah last and what happened to the people after Josiah's death?

David. He walked in the ways of his ancestor David.

In our lesson an abomination refers to all the idols the Israelites were worshipping as well as the religious *paraphenelia* associated with false gods.

The repair of the temple and the revival of the worship of God.

The finding and reading of the Word of God - the Law of Moses. All great revivals are preceded by a mighty proclamation of God's Word.

He tore his clothes as a sign of sorrow and repentance.

Huldah, the prophet and wife of Shallum.

The prophet announced disaster upon the disobedient people, but mercy for the penitent king.

As great as Josiah was, his reformation was externally enforced. True revival must come from the hearts of the people. Legalism can never effect a true revival of the Spirit.

Josiah promised to follow the Lord, keep His commandments, and perform the Word of God.

All the days of Josiah the people followed God. When Josiah died, however, the people reverted to their idolatrous ways.

(SEED THOUGHTS--Cont'd)

6. To whom does Josiah turn for an interpretation of the Word of God?
Huldah, the prophet and wife of Shallum.

7. What was the message of the prophet to the people of Judah and to King Josiah?
The prophet announced disaster upon the disobedient people, but mercy for the penitent king.

8. What are the implications to be drawn from the temporary results of Josiah's religious revival?
As great as Josiah was, his reformation was externally enforced. True revival must come from the hearts of the people. Legalism can never effect a true revival of the Spirit.

9. What promises did Josiah make in his personal covenant with God?
Josiah promised to follow the Lord, keep His commandments, and perform the Word of God.

10. How long did the revival of Josiah last and what happened to the people after Josiah's death?
All the days of Josiah the people followed God. When Josiah died, however, the people reverted to their idolatrous ways.

November 1, 1992

Elijah: Prophet of Courage

I Kings 18

17 And it came to pass, when Ahab saw E-li´-jah, that Ahab said unto him, *Art* thou he that troubleth Israel?

18 And he answered, I have not troubled Israel; but thou, and thy father's house, in that ye have forsaken the commandments of the LORD, and thou hast followed Ba´-al-im.

20 So Ahab sent unto all the children of Israel, and gathered the prophets together unto mount Carmel.

21 And E-li´-jah came unto all the people and said, How long halt ye between two opinions? if the LORD *be* God, follow him: but if Ba´-al, *then* follow him. And the people answered him not a word.

22 Then said E-li´-jah unto the people, I, even I only, remain a prophet of the LORD; but Ba´-al's prophets are four hundred and fifty men.

23 Let them therefore give us two bullocks; and let them choose one bullock for themselves, and cut it in pieces, and lay *it* on wood, and put no fire *under*: and I will dress the other bullock, and lay *it* on wood, and put no fire *under*:

24 And call ye on the name of your gods, and I will call on the name of the LORD: and the God that answereth by fire, let him be God. And all the people answered and said, It is well spoken.

36 And it came to pass at *the time of* the offering of the *evening* sacrifice, that E-li´-jah the prophet came near, and said, LORD God of Abraham, Isaac, and of Israel, let it be known this day that thou *art* God in Israel, and *that* I *am* thy servant, and *that* I have done all these things at thy word.

37 Hear me, O LORD, hear me, that this people may know that thou *art* the LORD God, and *that* thou hast turned their heart back again.

38 Then the fire of the LORD fell, and consumed the burnt sacrifice, and the wood, and the stones, and the dust, and licked up the water that *was* in the trench.

39 And when all the people saw *it*, they fell on their faces: and they said, The LORD, he *is* the God; the LORD, *he* is the God.

◆◆◆◆◆◆

◀ **Memory Selection**
I Kings 18: 21

◀ **Devotional Reading**
I Kings 18:30-39

◀ **Background Scripture**
I Kings 17:1-7, 18

◀ **Printed Scripture**
I Kings 18:17-18, 20-24, 36-39

ELIJAH: PROPHET OF COURAGE

Teacher's Target

Our last five lessons this quarter deal with five Old Testament prophets (Elijah, Amos, Hosea, Micah, and Jeremiah), Elijah was a rugged individualist who served as a foretype for John the Baptist (Matt. 3:1-4; 17:10-13). He confronted the notorious King Ahab and Queen Jezebel of Israel for their sins. This lesson emphasizes a high point, for Elijah successfully challenged the prophets of Baal supported by the king and queen.

Help your students to realize that true courage in spiritual matters must rest upon implicit faith in the Lord. Satan and his hosts, both demonic and human, are strong, but they can always be defeated by God and His hosts, both angelic and human. Urge your students to place themselves firmly on the side of God and of righteousness in the midst of a sinful world-system. The battle will continue until the Prince of peace comes to reign.

Lesson Introduction

Ahab was seventh in line of the monarchs who ruled over the northern kingdom of Israel following the division from the southern kingdom of Judah. Ahab was more evil than the six kings who had preceded him. He made things worse by marrying Jezebel, daughter of Ethbaal, King of Sidon, and supporting Baal worship at a temple and altar he built for the pagan god in Samaria (I Kings 16:30-33) God was angry with him and sent Elijah to challenge him.

Elijah declared that a terrible drought would prevail in Samaria, brought on by a lack of rain and dew. God sent the prophet to dwell by the brook named Cherith, where ravens delivered food to sustain him. When the brook dried up, he found a new home with a widow at Zarephath and her son, whom he raised from the dead. After three years, Elijah was sent by God to meet Ahab. God promised to end the drought by sending rain (I Kings 17:1-18:1). Elijah did as he was told.

Teaching Outline

I. Criticism: I Kings 18:17-18
   A. Sarcasm: 17
   B. Statement: 18
II. Challenges: I Kings 18:20-24
   A. Proposal I: 20-21
   B. Proposal II: 22-24
III. Consumption: I Kings 18: 36-39
   A. Request: 36-37
   B. Response: 38
   C. Reverence: 39

Daily Bible Readings

Mon. Elijah Hides by Brook the of Cherith - *I Kings 17:1-7*
Tue. Elijah Is Fed by a Poor Widow *I Kings 17:8-16*
Wed. Elijah Resurrects the Widow's Son - *I Kings 17:17-24*
Thu. The Lord Sends Elijah to Ahab *I Kings 18:7-16*
Fri. Elijah Triumphs over Ahab at Mt. Carmel - *I Kings 18:25-29*
Sat. Elijah Builds an Altar for the Lord - *I Kings 18:30-35*
Sun. The Lord Sends Rain *I Kings 18:41-46*

November 1, 1992

VERSE BY VERSE

I. Criticism: I Kings 18: 17-18

A. Sarcasm: 17

17. And it came to pass, when Ahab saw Elijah, that Ahab said unto him, Art thou he that troubleth Israel?

The first thing that Ahab did when meeting Elijah was to accuse him of bringing the drought upon the nation. He should have realized that no mere human being could withhold rain and dew from coming upon the earth. Whatever part Elijah had had in the matter was due to his being an instrument in the hands of Jehovah. In pointing the finger of blame at Elijah, Ahab was trying to excuse his own responsibility for the trouble facing Israel. This use of sarcasm by sinners can also be found today.

B. Statement: 18

18. And he answered, I have not troubled Israel; but thou, and thy father's house, in that ye have forsaken the commandments of the Lord, and thou hast followed Baalim.

Elijah refused to be intimidated by King Ahab. He boldly stated that it was not he himself who had troubled Israel with drought and resultant famine. It was Ahab and his sinful ancestors who had brought trouble to Israel by forsaking the commandments of the true God and following Baalim, instead. Baalim is the plural of Baal, showing that Baal worship was polytheistic. Elijah was making a direct connection here between divine wrath and earthly deprivation. The drought was not merely caused by a whim of nature. It had come upon Israel as a form of divine punishment. Evidence that this was so could be found in the announcements that the drought would begin and end according to God's timetable.

Verse 19 says that Elijah challenged Ahab to gather all Israel to Mount Carmel on the coast of the Great (Mediterranean) Sea, including four hundred and fifty prophets of Baal and four hundred prophets of the groves who were fed from the queen's kitchen. Subsequent verses make no further mention of the prophets of the groves.

II. Challenges: I Kings 16:20-24

A. Proposal I: 20-21

20. So Ahab sent unto all the children of Israel, and gathered the prophets together unto mount Carmel.

We do not know if Elijah revealed to Ahab what he planned to do at Mount Carmel, but it seems reasonable to assume that he did. The king responded by complying with the prophet's request. Messengers were sent out to summon elders, prophets of Baal, and others to meet at Mount Carmel. There was some danger in assembling there, for it was considered to be the home of Canaanite gods and it was disputed territory between Israel and Phoenicia to the north. The meeting place was evidently suited to a large audience gathered on the slopes surrounding a prominent rock in the eastern end of the range running from the sea inland.

21. And Elijah came unto all the people, and said, How long halt ye between two opinions? if the Lord be God, follow him: but if Baal, then

83

follow him. **And the people answered him not a word.**

The first proposal Elijah made to the multitude was that they make a clear choice between worshiping and serving either Jehovah or Baal. There was no vocal response to this challenge. They had been used to dividing their allegiance between Jehovah and Baal and they obviously wanted to continue to do this. Elijah was trying to make them realize that Jehovah would not share His glory with any other deity produced by the imagination of man. He stood alone and unique. We can only speculate as to why the people would not answer Elijah. Perhaps they were afraid to offend Jehovah and His prophet or Baal and his prophets. Perhaps they were looking for some sign that one or the other side was more powerful. If that was their motive, they were soon to discover the truth.

B. Proposal II: 22-24

22. Then said Elijah unto the people, I, even I only, remain a prophet of the Lord; but Baal's prophets are four hundred and fifty men.

Elijah was wrong about his assessment of the situation in Israel. God later told him that there were seven thousand in Israel who had not bowed to Baal nor kissed his image (I Kings 19:18). However, Elijah felt very much alone on that day on Mount Carmel, thinking that he was God's sole servant. On the other hand, he called the people's attention to the four hundred and fifty prophets of Baal gathered at the site. If power was to be found in numbers, he was at a disadvantage.

23. Let them therefore give us two bullocks; and let them choose one bullock for themselves, and cut it in pieces, and lay it on wood, and put no fire under: and I will dress the other bullock, and lay it on wood, and put no fire under:

Elijah knew that the people needed a challenge which could be openly and easily demonstrable. It was to be a challenge which could move out of the realm of the abstract and into the realm of the concrete which could be seen. He suggested that the prophets of Baal produce two bullocks, one for him and one for themselves. They were to butcher their bull first and put its pieces on the wood of their crude altar but not set it afire. He was to do this with his bull, too, but not until later, as we shall see.

24. And call ye on the name of your Gods, and I will call on the name of the Lord: and the God that answereth by fire, let him be God. And all the people answered and said, It is well spoken.

Now came the test, and it was to be tied to unseen deity, either in the form of pagan gods or the one true God. The prophets of Baal were to call down fire from him on their sacrifice, and Elijah would do the same with Jehovah when his turn came. Baal was supposed to preside over fire, and thus it would seem only natural that he would send it down on the sacrifice. If that happened, by his own argument, Elijah would have to admit the authority of Baal and not bother offering his sacrifice.

The people felt that Elijah had presented a fair challenge, and they must have concluded that they would suffer no embarrassment from the contest. They probably thought that this was a good way to silence Elijah once and for all. We wonder how the four hundred and fifty prophets of Baal felt. Their feelings may have ranged all the way from happiness at proving their god's existence to despair from worrying that something would go wrong.

The supplication of the prophets of Baal is not in our printed text; but you would do well to summarize it from verses 25-29. They prepared their sacrifice and called on the name of Baal all morning to no avail. When there was no response, they leaped in frustration on their altar. Some versions suggest that they danced, hopped, or limped around it. Elijah watched this spectacle until noon and then began to mock the pagan prophets. He said that they should cry louder to Baal, for he might be busy talking, pursuing, traveling, or sleeping and need to be awakened. They cried out and cut themselves in frenzy until their blood flowed. They ranted and raved during the afternoon until time for the regular sacrifice came. Note that the word "evening" in verse 29 in the Authorized Version is in italics, meaning that it was not in the original manuscripts but was supplied. The regular time for the "evening", sacrifice was probably about the middle of the afternoon. Nothing the pagan prophets did produced any response from Baal.

Verses 30-35 are not in our printed text, but they tell how Elijah became busy. The people gathered around him as he repaired the Lord's altar by using twelve stones, one for each tribe in Israel. He dug a trench around it and put wood on it. He butchered his bull and placed its pieces on it. He had the people fill four barrels of water at a nearby spring and pour it over the sacrifice three times until everything was soaked and the trench was filled. Now his supplication began.

III. Consumption: I Kings 10:36-39

A. Request: 36-37

36. And it came to pass at the time of the offering of the evening sacrifice, that Elijah the prophet came near, and said, Lord God of Abraham, Isaac, and of Israel, let it be known this day that thou art God in Israel, and that I am thy servant, and that I have done all these things at thy word.

Realizing that their pagan prophets had failed miserably in their experiment to call down fire from Baal, the people were ready to pay close attention to Jehovah's prophet and even assist him in his part of the contest. They listened as he called on the Lord to make it clear that He was the God of Abraham, Isaac, and Israel (Jacob) and thus the God of the nation of Israel which had descended from them. He wanted God to convince the people that he was His servant and was doing what he did in obedience to His instructions.

37. Hear me, O Lord, hear me, that this people may know that thou art the Lord God, and that thou hast turned their heart back again.

Baal may have been discredited in the minds of the people, but Elijah wanted Jehovah to be authenticated in their minds. He also wanted them to realize that the Lord had initiated this contest in order to prove His existence and turn their hearts back toward Him. He was a covenant-keeping God, and He would forgive their sins and restore them to His favor if they repented. What was required now was for fire to fall from heaven as a demonstrable sign that Jehovah was real.

B. Response: 38

38. Then the fire of the Lord fell and consumed the burnt-sacrifice, and the wood, and the stones, and the dust, and licked up the water that was in the trench.

Contrast the prolonged supplication of the pagan prophets with the brief one of Elijah. God had obviously been waiting to send down fire when it was requested. He did this in a most dramatic manner, for His fire consumed the altar and everything on it and around it, even evaporating the water in the trench. This had to be supernatural because of its specific timing and localization. It was an affirmation of Elijah's faith in the Lord.

C. Reverence: 39

39. And when all the people saw it, they fell on their faces: and they said, The Lord, he is the God: the Lord, he is the God.

Go back to verse 21. Elijah had challenged the people to decide if God was real and then follow Him or if Baal was real and then follow him. By means of the contest on Mount Carmel, he had persuaded them that Jehovah was not only more powerful than Baal but that He was the *only* true God.

Now the worst fears of the prophets of Baal came true. Elijah ordered the people to arrest them and prevent any from escaping. He took them down to the brook Kishon and slew them there, thus putting evil out of Israel to that extent. He told King Ahab that an abundance of rain was coming to end three years of drought. Elijah sent his servant seven times to look for clouds over the sea. The prophet was so elated when they came that he ran back to Jezreel ahead of Ahab's chariot (vss. 40-46).

Evangelistic Emphasis

A contest! Whether Elijah is taking on the prophets of Baal or two favorite football teams are battling, we are familiar with contests! The mentality of competition permeates our society. Perhaps there is no older motif in literature than the contest between good and evil. We have to be careful, however, not to reduce Elijah's battle against Baal to the level of a mere game. A game between two teams is a spectator sport. The consequences of victory or defeat are peripheral and short term. The purpose of an athletic contest is really entertainment. There is much more at stake in the contest between Elijah and the prophets of Baal.

The story of Elijah's confrontation with Baal is a miniature, specific portrait of a cosmic-scale war between good and evil. The characters in the portrait change from place to place and from generation to generation. The nature of contest remains essentially the same.

When Ahab assembled the people at Mount Carmel, all eyes were on Elijah and the prophets of Baal. The real action, however, was unfolding in the hearts of the people. The ultimate winners or losers would be the people. The deciding factor would be their choice of faithfulness or unfaithfulness. Elijah already knew the power of God was superior to the assembled entourage of Baal's men. Their efforts were doomed to failure. What mattered, though, was the decision of the people. Would they choose good over evil? God over Baal?

◆◆◆◆◆◆

Memory Selection

Elijah came near to all the people, and said, "How long will you go limping with two different opinions? If the Lord is God, follow him; but if Baal, then follow him."
I Kings 18:21.

Make no mistake about Elijah's demand. Here is the build-up to the climax of life's essential drama: the choice between good and evil. The tension in the drama is provided by the ambivalence of the Israelites. For quite some time they have equivocated between God and Baal. In effect, the people are trying to stay in the middle. Somehow they want to slide by with a nebulous description of themselves as not really that good, but not all that bad either. Elijah will have none of their moral and ethical timidity. With unrelenting insistence Elijah demands a choice.

Life often comes down to choice. In fact all of our hundreds of little choices ultimately add up to one big decision. Perhaps the Israelites never intended to get caught in the middle between God and Baal. Yet with each seemingly small immoral, less-than-righteous choice, they became more and more entrapped in webs of deceit, hypocrisy, and sin. Each refusal to take a clear stand for God put the Isrealites more squarely on the side of Baal. Maybe God's people were unaware of the dire consequences of their indecision.

Not to choose is an ever worse fate. It is like being forever stuck in the middle between two causes, two loves, or two roads. Some people seem to stand still before two roads as if they were sculpted stone. Actually not to choose good is to choose evil. Elijah, knowing that, pressed hard for an answer. What is your choice?

November 1, 1992

Weekdays Problems

Jennifer, a young adult church member, had a questioning look on her face. "What's bothering you?" her husband asked.

"I listened to the preacher talk about the dramatic confrontation between Elijah and the prophets of Baal," Jennifer said. "The story was so exciting, but I feel so far removed from such biblical accounts. I've never faced down the prophets of Baal, or caused a bunch of wet logs to catch fire."

"I see what you mean," her husband remarked. "You're wondering how we are fighting the same battle between good and evil."

"Exactly," she said. Jennifer often relied on her husband to help her clarify her own doubts and thoughts. He was a much more mature Christian.

"I believe that we have to look beyond the dramatic details of the story," explained Jennifer's husband. "For us the importance of the story is its universal application to the choice between right and wrong, good and evil."

"Do you mean," asked Jennifer, "that Elijah's confrontation did not happen? Is it just a dramatic story?"

"Oh no!" her husband answered. "The event did actually take place. We have to make decisions about good and evil all the time. Our choices are just as important, but not always as dramatic."

*In what ways do you think Jennifer might have to make choices between good and evil?

*How do Christians today oppose the false gods of our society? Give some examples.

*What concepts from our Christian experience might help Jennifer clarify her thinking?

♦♦♦♦♦♦

Superintendent's Sermonette

We who live in a democracy put great emphasis on majority votes to decide various issues on the national, state, and municipal levels. We follow the same pattern in churches, clubs, or other organizations. However, there are times when truth and error or right and wrong cannot be governed by numerical majority votes. There may come times when only a single individual knows the truth and is right, while the vast majority is in error and wrong. In our text today we learn of a situation such as this. Elijah stood alone against four hundred and fifty prophets of Baal in a contest on Mount Carmel, and Elijah won with God's help.

Never underestimate your ability to influence wavering people, if you are walking with God and living according to His Holy Word. Resist the considerable pressure which people can put on you to turn aside from the path of righteousness. Even if you feel that your efforts are misunderstood and scorned, your example will have positive effects on others. You may even expect to see some of them come over to the side of righteousness. It takes courage to walk with God, and that courage must be based on implicit faith in Him. Let us ask God to increase our faith!

ELIJAH: PROPHET OF COURAGE

This Lesson In Your Life

One-time Chairman of the Board of Tenneco Dick Freeman once said, "A man's a fool to spend his whole life building a great corporation and then discover - at age seventy, when he's about to die - what life is all about." With some variation, many people play out the same theme in life. At or near the end, when life has already been lived, people realize they have made bad choices, taken wrong roads, and bowed before the altars of too many strange gods. Yet almost everyone, when asked, would indicate a desire to discover "what life is all about."

The story of Elijah and the prophets of Baal portrays a consistent biblical theme: the Word of God confronts people with a definite course for life. It offers everyone a choice between good and evil. From Joshua's appeal to the people to choose whom they would serve to Elijah's insistence that the people choose between Yahweh and Baal, from the prophets of the Old Testament to the preaching of Jesus, the Bible message offers and contrasts two ways; one way is good and true and righteous while the other way is evil and false and wicked. With unrelenting purpose, the biblical writers insist that people decide what life is all about.

Suppose for a moment that we chose to serve Baal. What are the consequences of such a choice? What kind of life would such a choice imply? A life of alienation from God would be the major consequence of a decision to bow before the altars of an idol. Baal, you see, is a stereotypical term for all kinds of idols.

One of the Baals of our time is our fascination with science and technology. Sometimes known as the scientific-rational paradigm, this idol rears its ugly head whenever man trades a biblical concept of God for the illusion of technology. The more advanced our technology, the more precise our science, the greater the tendency to believe we have created a world that no longer needs God. The result is alienation. When man feels no dependency on God, no sense of connection to the Creator, the sense of separation from meaningful life grows. The fact is we need to find God and he cannot be found in an over-reliance on science and technology. No matter that the prominent scientist, Lewis Thomas, proclaims that science is the only game in town. There is still God in this universe.

In addition the choice of Baal delimits the quality of life and produces anxiety and fear. Apart from God and a sense of eternal life, the man or woman following Baal is left only with a temporary existence. Life is no more than the accumulation of material things, the enjoyment of fleeting kicks, and the chasing after rainbows of superficiality. The emptiness, the powerless, the hopelessness of such a life is well depicted by St. Paul: "having no hope, and without God in the world." (Ephesians 2:12c). At the last Baal is no power at all. Death, not life, awaits the disciples of Baal.

On the other hand, to choose loyalty to God is to discover the power of faithfulness. Elijah's battle with the Baalites is much more than an isolated contest. Elijah is the power of God, all the power of God wrapped in courage and faithfulness. The contest with Baal was all about setting the people of Israel free for faith. Now they could let go and trust God. The decision to let go and trust God is not an easy one. We can choose, in definite ways, to shape our lives according to God's will. We can choose life over death, hope over despair, fulfillment over emptiness. The persons who do so will find a lasting satisfaction.

Seed Thoughts

1. What was the purpose of the drought that Elijah prophesied concerning Israel?
The worshipers of Baal thought their god controlled the rain. Elijah intended to prove that his God, the Lord God of Israel, controlled the rain.

2. What is the major implication of Elijah being fed by the ravens?
The element of the miraculous feeding of Elijah by the ravens demonstrates the power of God. When circumstances are beyond our control, they are still within God's providence.

3. What is the significance of the name of the prophet Elijah?
The name of Elijah means "The Lord is God." By his very name, Elijah proclaims his faith.

4. In what ways did Obadiah demonstrate his faith in God during the persecution carried out by Ahab?
Obadiah feared the Lord. When Ahab and Jezebel were killing the prophets, Obadiah hid one hundred prophets in caves, and he provided them with food and water.

5. Why was Ahab trying so hard to find the prophet Elijah?
Ahab had been searching in every nation and kingdom for Elijah. He had been seeking to apprehend Elijah in order to work out some deal with him to end the drought.

(PLEASE TURN PAGE)

---

1. What was the purpose of the drought that Elijah prophesied concerning Israel?

2. What is the major implication of Elijah being fed by the ravens?

3. What is the significance of the name of the prophet Elijah?

4. In what ways did Obadiah demonstrate his faith in God during the persecution carried out by Ahab?

5. Why was Ahab trying so hard to find the prophet Elijah?

6. Why was Obadiah reluctant to tell the king that Elijah had come out of hiding?

7. In what sense could the term, "troubler of Israel," be a badge of honor for a preacher?

8. When Baal was unable to produce fire from heaven, in what ways did Elijah mock the pagan god?

9. What was the final outcome of the prophets of Baal trying to produce fire, and what is its significance?

10. What is the theological message intended by the slaughter of the prophets of Baal?

(SEED THOUGHTS--Cont'd)

The worshipers of Baal thought their god controlled the rain. Elijah intended to prove that his God, the Lord God of Israel, controlled the rain.

The element of the miraculous feeding of Elijah by the ravens demonstrates the power of God. When circumstances are beyond our control, they are still within God's providence.

The name of Elijah means "The Lord is God." By his very name, Elijah proclaims his faith.

Obadiah feared the Lord. When Ahab and Jezebel were killing the prophets, Obadiah hid one hundred prophets in caves, and he provided them with food and water.

Ahab had been searching in every nation and kingdom for Elijah. He had been seeking to apprehend Elijah in order to work out some deal with him to end the drought.

Obadiah was afraid the king would kill him. Obadiah did not yet know that Elijah intended to take a stand against Ahab, Jezebel, and paganism.

When the preacher proclaims the prophetic truth of God and tells people the hard truths, he may not be popular.

Elijah used sharp satire to wonder if Baal was meditating, wandering, on a journey, or asleep.

There was no voice, no answer, and no response from Baal. The significance is that the worship of false gods always leads to despair.

The outcome was a matter of life and death.

6. Why was Obadiah reluctant to tell the king that Elijah had come out of hiding?
Obadiah was afraid the king would kill him. Obadiah did not yet know that Elijah intended to take a stand against Ahab, Jezebel, and paganism.

7. In what sense could the term, "troubler of Israel," be a badge of honor for a preacher?
When the preacher proclaims the prophetic truth of God and tells people the hard truths, he may not be popular.

8. When Baal was unable to produce fire from heaven, in what ways did Elijah mock the pagan god?
Elijah used sharp satire to wonder if Baal was meditating, wandering, on a journey, or asleep.

9. What was the final outcome of the prophets of Baal trying to produce fire, and what is its significance?
There was no voice, no answer, and no response from Baal. The significance is that the worship of false gods always leads to despair.

10. What is the theological message intended by the slaughter of the prophets of Baal?
The outcome was a matter of life and death.

November 8, 1992

Amos: Prophet of Justice

Amos 2

6 Thus saith the LORD; For three transgressions of Israel and for four, I will not turn away the punishment thereof, because they sold the righteous for silver, and the poor for a pair of shoes;
7 That pant after the dust of the earth on the head of the poor, and turn aside the way of the meek: and a man and his father will go in unto the same maid, to profane my holy name:
8 And they lay themselves down upon clothes laid to pledge by every altar, and they drink the wine of the condemned in, the house of their god.
9 Yet destroyed I the Am'-or-ite before then, whose height was like the height of the cedars and he was strong as the oaks; yet I destroyed his fruit from above, and his roots from beneath.
10 Also I brought you up from the land of Egypt, and led you forty years through the wilderness, to possess the land of the Am'-orite.
11 And I raised up of your sons for prophets, and of your young men for Nazarites. Is it not even thus, O ye children of Israel? saith the LORD.
12 But ye gave the Nazarites wine to drink; and commanded the prophets, saying, Prophesy not.

Amos 3

2 You only have I known of all the families of the earth: therefore I will punish you for all your iniquities.

◆◆◆◆◆◆

◀ **Memory Selection**
Amos 5:24

◀ **Devotional Reading**
Amos 2:6-16

◀ **Background Scripture**
Amos 1:6-3:2

◀ **Printed Scripture**
Amos 2:6-12; 3:2

AMOS: PROPHET OF JUSTICE

Teacher's Target

Justice is supposed to be "blind," meaning that it is objective and incorruptible. However, we know that injustice occurs because individuals in power weight things to favor themselves. Justice should be the maintenance or administration of that which is just or right. It should result in both reward for doing what is right and punishment for doing what is wrong. The greatest sources for right and wrong are personal conscience and divine revelation. It is comforting to realize that divine justice ultimately prevails, even though human justice may be perverted.

Help your students to see in Amos a man of God who boldly proclaimed the effect of divine justice on people. He set an example for believers to follow in succeeding generations. We are responsible in our generation for holding up the divine standard of justice through both precept and practice. We should never apologize but show others what God expects from men and then demand it of them.

Lesson Introduction

Amos was a herdsman and a seasonal worker on sycamore-fig trees in the little town of Tekoa south of Jerusalem in the southern kingdom of Judah. God called him to a prophetic ministry when Uzziah ruled in Judah and Jeroboam II ruled in Israel to the north. It was during Jeroboam's forty-year reign that Israel greatly enlarged its borders and prospered materially, but it was also a time of moral and spiritual corruption tied to Canaanite idolatry. Amos spoke particularly to Israel, but his vision also encompassed the whole "house of Jacob."

He began his ministry by condemning the sins of foreign people surrounding Judah and Israel—Damascus in Syria, Gaza in Philistia, Tyre in Phoenicia, and the people of Edom, Ammon, and Moab (Amos 1:3—2:3). Then he drew the noose tighter around the necks of God's Own people when he denounced Judah and Israel (Amos 2:4-16). This lesson deals primarily with his case against Israel.

Teaching Outline

I. Sins: Amos 2:6-8
   A. Indictment: 6a
   B. Iniquities: 6b-8
II. Salvation: Amos 2:9-12
   A. Amorites: 9
   B. Access: 10
   C. Apostacy: 11-12
III. Sentence: Amos 3:2
   A. Privilege: 2a
   B. Punishment: 2b

Daily Bible Readings

Mon. An Earthquake Will Be Sent to Israel - *Amos 1:1-5*
Tue. Judah and Moab Will Burn *Amos 2:1-5*
Wed. The Lord Will Punish Israel *Amos 3:1-8*
Thu. Israel Is Unfaithful *Amos 4:1-10*
Fri. Seek the Lord and Live *Amos 5:1-9*
Sat. Seek Good, Not Evil *Amos 5:10-15*
Sun. Israel's Offerings Are Rejected *Amos 5:18-24*

November 8, 1992

VERSE BY VERSE

I. Sins: Amos 2:6-8

A. Indictment: 6a

6a. Thus saith the Lord: For three transgressions of Israel, and for four, I will not turn away the punishment thereof; ...

The phrase "Thus saith the Lord" was used to introduce condemnations on the people of Damascus, Gaza, Tyre, Edom, Ammon, Moab, Judah, and Israel (Amos 1:3, 6, 9, 11, 13; 2:1, 4, 6). It showed that Amos spoke on behalf of the divine Judge. The phrase "For three transgressions, and for four" showed that God was patient with sinful people both in and surrounding Judah and Israel. In each case, His cup of wrath had filled up to the brim and then spilled over in judgment onto those who had rebelled against Him. Our particular concern in this lesson is His indictment of the northern kingdom of Israel,

B. Iniquities: 6b-8

6b. ... because they sold the righteous for silver, and the poor for a pair of shoes;

7a. That pant after the dust of the earth on the head of the poor, and turn aside the way of the meek: ...

God condemned the leaders in Israel of being guilty of oppression. This was directed toward the poor and the meek. The people of God were forbidden to sell their countrymen into slavery to foreigners. Servitude within the nation was supposed to be guided by Levitical law and have certain limits in treatment and length of time. It appears that the affluent in Israel were going beyond these regulations. Individuals were sold into slavery for the price of silver or even for a pair of sandals. Those who could not pay their debts because of various types of reverses were placed in bondage. Oppressors were not content until they saw the poor and meek laid low in the dust. They turned aside the inherent rights of these people and exploited them.

Literal slavery may be outlawed in most of the world today, but economic bondage is still very much with us. In many situations, a few wealthy, powerful people control the destinies of the vast majority by keeping them poor and helpless. Many factors are involved, including education, job opportunities, financial procedures, creativity, science, technology, and individual or group rights. Moral and spiritual values are often ignored or denied.

7b. ... and a man and his father will go in unto the same maid, to profane my holy name:

It was common for prostitutes to be connected with ancient pagan temples or shrines, and the Israelites had been influenced by the heathen. The name of Jehovah was profaned by the Israelite father and son going in to have sexual intercourse with the same woman as part of idolatrous practices.

8a. And they lay themselves down upon clothes laid to pledge by every altar, ...

The Mosaic law made it very clear that a poor person's robe left with a creditor as security for borrowed money should be returned to the debtor before sundown. It was his only covering for the coolness of the night when he slept (Exod. 22: 25- 27). This stipulation was apparently being overlooked, The rich

93

creditors kept the robes given as pledges and reclined upon them as they banqueted beside pagan altars. The debtors meanwhile shivered for lack of covering.

8b. ... and they drink the wine of the condemned in the house of their god.

Interpretation here is debatable, but it probably referred to the creditors drinking the wine bought by money unjustly taken from the debtors in fines. They held their banquets in the house of their pagan god. Having abandoned their true God, it was common for those in power to abandon their fellowmen who had been made in God's image. This was something which God would not overlook, and it was bound to result in judgment in due time. The only way to avoid this judgment was to repent, confess, seek forgiveness, and offer to make restitution to those who had been offended.

II. Salvation: Amos 2:9-12

A. Amorites: 9

9a. Yet destroyed I the Amorite before them, whose height was like the height of the cedars, and he was strong as the oaks;...

God reminded the Israelites that they had once faced a formidable foe in the Amorite nation. The Amorites are thought to have descended from Canaan, the son of Ham. They may have lived in the larger part of Mosopotamia, and Syria before being driven by the Hittites to the land of Canaan. They were finally subdued by Israel under the leadership of Joshua. The Lord recalled for Israel the fact that the Amorites had appeared as tall as the cedars of Lebanon and as strong as the mighty oaks.

These symbolic comparisons apparently referred to the military might of the Amorites at the time the Israelites encountered them in Canaan.

9b. ...yet I destroyed his fruit from above, and his roots from beneath.

Carrying through with the same symbolism, God said that He utterly destroyed the Amorites by cutting off their fruit-bearing branches from above and their life-sustaining roots from below. They could not withstand His divine power as it worked on them directly or through His people.

B. Access: 10

10. Also I brought you up from the land of Egypt, and led you forty years through the wilderness, to possess the land of the Amorite.

Reaching further back into Israel's history, the Lord reminded His people that He was the One Who had delivered them from bondage in Egypt, using Moses as His instrument. He was the One Who had led them for forty years in the Sinai wilderness when the first generation refused to go in to subdue and possess the land of Canaan. God had supplied Israel with manna and water, and He had prevented their clothing from wearing out during those four decades. He had brought the second generation across the swollen Jordan on dry land and allowed it to conquer the pagan tribes of many names who were generally called Amorites. This took extensive military campaigns to accomplish, and afterward the territory had to be divided among the twelve tribes of Israel.

C. Apostasy: 11-12

11a. And I raised up of your sons for prophets, and of your young men for Nazarites.

Included in God's blessings to Israel was the raising up by Him of young men to become prophets and Nazarites. At a time in life when there was strong temptation for them to be selfish and sinful they dedicated themselves to be pure and spiritual. The Hebrew root *nazar* means "to separate" or "to set apart." These young men were required to take a vow to abstain from wine and all ceremonial and moral defilement. They were not to shave. They were not to touch any dead body. Details regarding the law governing the Nazarites may be found in Numbers 6:1-21. Samson, Samuel, and John the Baptist were Nazarites. These are the only examples we have of perpetual Nazarites. Most were temporary, ranging from thirty days on upward. Prophets and Nazarites were respected as instructors and examples of godly living.

11b. Is it not even thus, O ye children of Israel? saith the Lord.

God asked the Israelites if they would dare to deny the truth of what He said about the prophets and Nazarites, seeing that He, the highest Authority, had affirmed it. He wanted them to admit the positive aspect of this subject before He dealt with the negative aspect of it.

12. But ye gave the Nazarites wine to drink; and commanded the prophets, saying, Prophesy not.

God condemned the Israelites for persuading the Nazarites to break their vow and drink wine. He condemned them for forbidding the prophets to speak for Him. In Isaiah's time, the Lord said, "This is a rebellious people,...that will not hear the law of the Lord: which say to the seers, See not; and to the prophets, Prophesy not unto us right things, speak unto us smooth things, prophesy deceits" (Isa. 30:9-10).

The priest of Bethel did this with Amos. "Amaziah said unto Amos, O thou seer, go, flee thee away into the land of Judah, and there eat bread, and prophesy there: but prophesy not again any more at Bethel" (Amos 7:12-13). Amos replied by stating that he had been no prophet in Judah, for his occupation was that of a herdsman and a seasonal harvester of sycamore-fig fruit. It was God Himself who had chosen him to leave that work and go up to Israel to prophesy. He condemned Amaziah for telling him not to prophesy against Israel, and he pronounced severe consequences on the priest for what he had said (Amos 7:14-17).

God was so provoked by what the Israelites had done to the prophets He had sent to them that He predicted horrible consequences on them in Amos 2:13-16. He said that He would bring pressure to bear on them similar to that of a cart filled with sheaves at harvest time. That pressure would be felt by the Israelites in time of battle, for they would lose their swiftness, strength, might, and skill in defending themselves from their enemies. The normally courageous would flee away naked in the time of trouble.

III. Sentence: Amos 3:2

A. Privilege: 2a

2a. You only have I known of all the families of the earth:

God was to bring judgment on the northern kingdom of Israel through Assyrian conquest in 722 B.C. He would bring it on the southern kingdom of Judah through Babylonian conquest in 586 B.C. Amos 3:1 mentions the Lord speaking against the whole family which He had brought up from Egypt, evidently meaning both Israel and Judah. The same seems to hold true for His comments recorded in Amos 3:2.

God certainly knew *all* of the families of the earth. Therefore, we need to determine what He meant by this designation when speaking to Israel and Judah. He obviously referred to the fact that He knew them in a *special* way by means of the covenant given to them at Mount Sinai. The particular wording is found in Exodus 20: 5-6— "If ye will obey my voice indeed, and keep my covenant, then ye shall be a peculiar treasure unto me above all people: for all the earth is mine: and ye shall be unto me a kingdom of priests, and an holy nation."

B. Punishment: 2b

2b. ...therefore I will punish you for all your iniquities.

By speaking to His chosen but wayward people in this way, the Lord was showing that He would use punishment as a means for persuading them to repent of their sins and return to fellowship with Him. This concept has been more fully developed in Hebrews 12:3-11 and applies to us, as well.

AMOS: PROPHET OF JUSTICE

Evangelistic Emphasis

In our consumer-oriented world there is a temptation to equate affluence with goodness and salvation. Even church folks buy into the illusion of wealth and affluence. As a matter of fact, we are pretty rich. Most of us have a high standard of living. Think of all the catalogs that start arriving in your post office box about the first of September. Every slick, full-color catalog is an invitation to buy and spend and charge all we can. Luxury has become a new god on our block. We are a prosperous people.

The prophetic voice of Amos cuts through the illusion of affluence. Instead of suggesting that our good fortune is a blessing, Amos insists that our prosperity is a result of our mistreatment of the poor. Even Christians are often unaware of the extent of materialism's influence on their lives. Amos calls us to judgment when he labels our lack of concern for the poor as transgression against the law.

If we are going to proclaim and live a full and complete gospel, we must make room in our hearts for the poor. We must accept our social responsibility. We must give. We must see the poor and the hungry as Jesus saw them: as our brothers and sisters.

♦♦♦♦♦♦

Memory Selection:

Let justice roll down like waters, and righteousness like an everflowing stream. *Amos 5:24*

With piercing clarity, the prophetic voice cuts through the fog of hypocrisy often associated with religious movements. The message of Amos reminds us that we don't stand on ceremony. Instead the twin pillars of godly living are justice and righteousness.

What about our world? If any qualities are lacking, justice and righteousness are certainly high on the missing virtues list. While we sing songs of glorious praise in church, we often mistreat others at work. While we pray the Lord's Prayer in worship, we often verbally abuse persons we do not like. The contrast is inescapable. We, in our Sunday best, singing and praying, act out our worship before God, but in the world we are sometimes unjust in our dealings and unrighteous in our behavior.

Justice has to do with seeing that people get their right. In the Old Testament the primary function of justice is to vindicate the oppressed. In the practical arena of ethical behavior, justice refers to treating people with fairness. Justice rolls down like waters when integrity, honesty, and compassion are the qualities manifested in our relationships.

Righteousness, on the other hand is the fulfillment of the demands of a relationship. To meet the covenant demands of one's relationships constitutes right living. In short, the righteous are those who uphold and build community. Their concern is for the well being of others.

There can be no doubt that a world like ours needs an abundance of justice and righteousness. Let it begin in our fair treatment of others and our fulfillment of the covenant demands of community.

November 8, 1992

Weekday Problems

The church board meeting was not going well. What began as a simple request to provide food and clothing for some poor families in the community, had turned into a disagreement over the role of the church in areas of social conern. Not everybody agreed on exactly what the church should do.

"I do not believe," insisted Mr. Andrews, a leading member of the board, "that the church should waste its money on these people. Let them work and earn money like the rest of us. I'd be ashamed to go around town begging for food."

"I agree," said Mrs. Henderson. "Besides, can't these people get help from the United Way agencies or the government? We pay enough taxes for that sort of thing."

The sentiment of the board seemed to be headed for a rejection of the request to help the needy people of the town. In all fairness, some board members were worried about being able to take care of the church's needs during hard times.

About that time, Jane Jones spoke up: "Do you realize that most of the money we give to the church is spent on us and our needs? It seems like we are tithing to ourselves. I believe we have a greater responsibility to the less fortunate."

*"What concept about treatment of the poor did Amos present that might help the board resolve the problem?

*"In what Christian ways could the members of the board be encouraged to accept their social responsibilities?

♦♦♦♦♦♦

Superintendent's Sermonette

American patriotism, which had fallen to low ebb following the wars in Korea and Vietnam, rose to new heights following victory over Iraq in the war in the Persian Gulf. At the same time, however, the United States realized that there were still many problems at home. Success in one area could not overshadow defeat in other areas for long.

The ancient kingdom of Israel was prosperous under the leadership of Jeroboam II, and the people in power felt good about their nation. However, a groundswell of resentment was rising among the ranks of the common people who were mistreated. They were suffering from economic oppression, and they could not find relief in their corrupt courts. Judges were being bribed to render verdicts favoring the business leaders. Justice was perverted.

We seem to face this kind of problem in every generation. This means that we have to be constantly on guard against injustice and speak out against it despite the consequences. Amos was that kind of man, and God is looking for modern counterparts. Are we willing to study situations and determine what is wrong? Are we willing to pray about them and seek righteous solutions? May our patriotism persuade us to do these things.

This Lesson In Your Life

A college English professor assigned his freshman class a 500-word paper on the topic: "Why are you attending college?" He asked them to be honest and straightforward, but the results were nevertheless unexpected. Paper after paper seemed to have been written by a machine: college was a means to an end of success, status, prosperity, and security. Only two papers stood out, dramatically different from the others. These papers talked about college enabling the writers to do something with their lives that would be good for the world, that would better the planet, and that would serve others better. The professor was at first encouraged, because it only takes one or two to make a difference. Then he became disturbed. Both students who authored these papers were not from the United States. The students who sought service over status, success, and security were from Angola and Lebanon.

The second chapter of Amos pictures the people of God as much like the majority of the students in the freshman English class: concerned only for self, status, success, and security. Amos attacks such attitudes as transgressions against God. The prophetic denunciation is chilling and provacative.

The young college students are not isolated examples. Have you noticed how much anxiety there is in our world about status, success and security? Would we need so much Madison Avenue hype if there was not widespread anxiety about looking great?

No wonder we are anxious. In a world of make-believe, we put too much emphasis on externals: how we look, what we wear or drive, status symbols, brand names! The coins of worthiness in our society are beauty, brains and brawn. All our posturing is an admission that our lives are built on a fragile foundation of external securities. By accumulating more toys and gadgets we try to set up the illusion of people who are perfectly together. Even in church we are tempted to turn worship into showtime, where the preacher does a Johnny Carson routine, tells a few funny stories, adds a few sweet Jesus vignettes, makes a moral point or two and says AMEN. Even in church we are afraid of the internal, the matters of the heart. The fact is, we are afraid and we hide our anxieties behind our toys and pretenses.

What is the answer? If the writer of Ecclesiastes is right in claiming that "all men's efforts are for his mouth, yet his appetite is never satisfied," then it will do no good to demand that people give up their toys. What we need is a whole new perspective for life, a kingdom of God. We need a kingdom where worries about fads and fashions and food are exchanged for concerns about the well-being of the entire community of persons. We need a kingdom where God's gift of life is accepted as is without the pretense of status or success or wealth added. As the gospel proclaims, "It is your Father's good pleasure to give you the kingdom." What Jesus is asking for is a whole new way of living in relation to God and to ourselves and to others.

Meanwhile, we Christians are called to responsibility for the welfare of our various communities. In a selfish world, we are called to show the priorities of kingdom life. We must not play status games or power games to protect our ego or impress our neighbors. We are to stop worrying over our toys and whining over our problems and give ourselves with abandon to creative ways of serving the poor and the oppressed. We are to live so that, in a troubled world, we never lose sight of those who need our help the most.

Seed Thoughts

1. What transgressions were committed by the Israelites according to Amos 2:6-8?

The Israelites were guilty of excessive materialism, oppression of the poor, sexual immorality, and idolatry.

2. What evidence does Amos present to prove that God has the power to carry out His judgment against Israel?

Amos reminds the people that God destroyed the Amorites, brought Israel out of Egypt, and raised some of their children to be prophets. The power of God is thus revealed in His wrath and in His election.

3. In Amos 2:12, the Israelites commanded the prophets, "Prophesy not." What contemporary significance could this have for our preachers?

Congregations may want popular preachers who do not preach judgment or bring up uncomfortable issues.

4. In what sense do you believe a preacher should carry out a prophetic role in the church?

The preacher should always proclaim the Word of God. The preacher should stand over against the culture and condemn its excesses and idolatry.

5. Why is the message of Amos so harsh and the judgment of God so fearful upon Israel?

In Amos 3:1-2, the Lord reminds Israel that her special relationship with him has created special responsibilities. Because Israel has been favored above all nations, more was expected of her.

(PLEASE TURN PAGE)

---

1. What transgressions were committed by the Israelites according to Amos 2:6-8?

2. What evidence does Amos present to prove that God has the power to carry out His judgment against Israel?

3. In Amos 2:12, the Israelites commanded the prophets, "Prophesy not." What contemporary significance could this have for our preachers?

4. In what sense do you believe a preacher should carry out a prophetic role in the church?

5. Why is the message of Amos so harsh and the judgment of God so fearful upon Israel?

6. What are God's two basic requirements for those who serve Him?

7. Who were the "Nazirites"?

8. Why does Amos insist that the punishment of God will come upon "the whole family" of Israel?

9. Does the message of Amos have contemporary relevance for Christians?

10. What is the implication of Amos 2:14-16?

(SEED THOUGHTS--Cont'd)

The Israelites were guilty of excessive materialism, oppression of the poor, sexual immorality, and idolatry.

Amos reminds the people that God destroyed the Amorites, brought Israel out of Egypt, and raised some of their children to be prophets. The power of God is thus revealed in His wrath and in His election.

Congregations may want popular preachers who do not preach judgment or bring up uncomfortable issues.

The preacher should always proclaim the Word of God. The preacher should stand over against the culture and condemn its excesses and idolatry.

In Amos 3:1-2, the Lord reminds Israel that her special relationship with him has created special responsibilities. Because Israel has been favored above all nations, more was expected of her.

God expects justice and righteousness. We are to act justly in our relationship with all people, and do right in all our dealings.

"Nazirites" were those who were separated or consecrated. They were never to cut their hair or drink wine. Yet the Israelites led even these to violate their covenant with God.

The Hebrew people had a theology of corporate sin and responsibility. Everyone was responsible. Therefore everyone would be punished.

Of course. Any message that condemns oppression and mistreatment of others is relevant in a world like ours.

No matter how independent we may think our military strength and technological clout make us, there is no salvation except in the Lord our God.

6. What are God's two basic requirements for those who serve Him?
God expects justice and righteousness. We are to act justly in our relationship with all people, and do right in all our dealings.

7. Who were the "Nazirites"?
"Nazirites" were those who were separated or consecrated. They were never to cut their hair or drink wine. Yet the Israelites led even these to violate their covenant with God.

8. Why does Amos insist that the punishment of God will come upon "the whole family" of Israel?
The Hebrew people had a theology of corporate sin and responsibility. Everyone was responsible. Therefore everyone would be punished.

9. Does the message of Amos have contemporary relevance for Christians?
Of course. Any message that condemns oppression and mistreatment of others is relevant in a world like ours.

10. What is the implication of Amos 2:14-16?
No matter how independent we may think our military strength and technological clout make us, there is no salvation except in the Lord our God.

November 15, 1992

Hosea: Prophet of God's Love

Hosea 1
1 The word of the Lord that came unto Hose´-a, the son of Be-e´-ri, in the days of Uz-zi´-ah, Jo´tham, Ahaz and Hez-e-ki´-ah, kings of Judah, and in the days of Jer-o-bo´-am the son of Jo´-ash, king of Isreal.
2 The beginning of the word of the Lord by Ho-se´-a. And the Lord said to Ho-se´-a, Go, take unto thee a wife of whoredoms and children of whoredoms: for the land hath committed great whoredom, departing from the Lord.
3 So he went and took Go´-mer the daughter of Dib´-la-im; which conceived, and bare him a son.

Hosea 3
1 Then said the Lord unto me, Go yet, love a woman beloved of her friend, yet an adulteress, according to the love of the Lord toward the children of Isreal, who took to other gods, and love flagons of wine.
2 So I bought her to me for fifteen pieces of silver, and for an ho´-mer of barley, and an half ho´-mer of barley"

Hosea 6
4 O E´-phra-im, what shall I do unto thee? O Judah, what shall I do unto thee? for your goodness is as a morning cloud, and as the early dew it goeth away.
5 Therefore have I hewed them by the prophets; I have slain them by the words of my mouth: and thy judgements are as the light that goes forth.
6 For I desired mercy, and not sacrifice; and the knowledge of God more than burnt offerings.

Hosea 11
When Isreal was a child, then I loved him, and called my son out of Egypt.
2 As they called them, so they went from them: they sacrificed unto Ba´-al-im, and burned incense to graven images.
3 I taught E´-phra-im also to go, taking them by their arms; but they knew not that I healed them.
4 I drew them with cords of a man, with bands of love:

◆◆◆◆◆◆

◀ **Memory Selection**
Hosea 6:6

◀ **Devotional Reading**
Hosea 3:1-5

◀ **Background Scripture**
Hosea 1:1-3; 3:1-2; 6:4-6; 11:1-4

◀ **Printed Scripture**
Hosea 1:1-3, 3:1-2; 6:4-6; 11:1-4a

HOSEA: PROPHET OF GOD'S LOVE

Teacher's Target

Members of a family face many challenges, and one of them is the temptation to be unfaithful to one another. A child may be unfaithful to parents or to siblings. A parent may be unfaithful to children or spouse. The results in each case can be disastrous, unless ways can be found to bind up emotional wounds and restore loyalties. God stands ready to discipline and then heal each one who turns to Him for help.

Help your students to see in the book of Hosea that what is true of a family can also be true of a nation and the Lord. Its key verse is 6:1—"Come, and let us return unto the Lord: for he hath torn, and he will heal us; he hath smitten, and he will bind us up." Gomer, Hosea's adulterous wife, was a symbol of God's sinful people. Hosea became a symbol of God and His willingness to take back sinful people who repented. Love was the antidote for adultery, whether it was literal or spiritual, and love originated with the Lord.

Lesson Introduction

Hosea prophesied in Israel as a contemporary of Amos and in Judah as a contemporary of Isaiah and Micah. His ministry spanned the years before and after the Assyrian captivity of the northern kingdom described in 2 Kings 15:29.

The book centers on a woman named Gomer and her three children. God told Hosea to marry her in spite of promiscuity. The name given to her first child was Jezreel, meaning "God sows or scatters." Her second child was named Lo-ruhamah, meaning "unloved." Her third child was named Lo-ammi, meaning "not my people." The latter two were changed to Ruhamah, meaning "God loves you," and Ammi, meaning "You are my people" (Hos. 1:4, 6, 9; 2:1).

Even as the wayward Gomer was restored to her home and family, so it is that errant Israel will one day be restored to God's eternal family. In the meantime, we may expect infidelity to continue, although individual conversions will take place.

Teaching Outline

I. Proposition: Hos. 1:1-3
   A. Message: 1
   B. Marriage: 2-3
II. Purchase: Hos. 3:1-2
   A. Order: 1
   B. Obedience: 2
III. Problem: Hos. 6:4-6
   A. Retribution: 4-5
   B. Reason: 6
IV. Provision: Hos. 11:1-4a
   A. Call: 1
   B. Contrasts: 2-4a

Daily Bible Readings

Mon. Israel Is Called a Harlot *Hos. 2:1-7*
Tue. The Lord Will Punish Israel *Hos. 2:8-13*
Wed. The Lord Will Make a New Covenant with Israel - *Hos. 2:14-23*
Thu. The Lord Has a Controversy with Israel - *Hos. 4:1-10*
Fri. Israel Is Alienated from God *Hos. 5:1-7*
Sat. Israel Will Not Return to God *Hos. 7:1-10*
Sun. God Will Forgive Israel *Hos. 11:7-12*

November 15, 1992

VERSE BY VERSE

I. Proposition: Hos. 1:1-3

A. Message: 1

1. The word of the Lord that came unto Hosea, the son of Beeri, in the days of Uzziah, Jotham, Ahaz, and Hezekiah, kings of Judah, and in the days of Jeroboam the son of Joash, king of Israel.

God gave His message to Hosea, the son of Beeri, who may have been a merchant or baker. As a member of the middle class, Hosea was probably well-educated and obviously had spiritual discernment. He was given his message during the times when Uzziah, Jotham, Ahaz, and Hezekiah ruled as kings over the southern kingdom of Judah and Jeroboam II ruled over the northern kingdom of Israel.

B. Marriage: 2-3

2. The beginning of the word of the Lord by Hosea. And the Lord said to Hosea, Go, take unto thee a wife of whoredoms and children of whoredoms: for the land hath committed great whoredom, departing from the Lord.

The first part of the verse refers to the time when God first spoke to Hosea, or it may refer to God's first message to him. An astounding proposition was presented to Hosea. Two views might be considered regarding this. One is that Hosea was told to go out and marry a prostitute with illegitimate children. Another is that he was told to go out and marry a woman destined to become promiscuous and have children with that tendency. Perhaps the latter is more plausible, for it would parallel the spiritual decline of Israel from close fellowship with the Lord to a nation of spiritual adulterers. Whatever the case, Hosea must have been shocked at God's order, because it would go against his spiritual inclinations. God had to make Hosea realize that his action would become a symbol for the massive abandonment of the Lord by His chosen people and thus serve a spiritual purpose.

3. So he went and took Gomer the daughter of Diblaim; which conceived, and bare him a son.

We are not told if God or Hosea made the choice of Gomer, daughter of Diblaim (Dib-lay´-im). It may be that God chose her, knowing what she would become. Her first child was a son, and God said to name him Jezreel (Hos. 1:4-5). It meant "God sows or scatters," and it was the name of the capital where King Ahab and his successors reigned. It was in the tribal territory of Issachar. It was also the name of a valley stretching from the Great (Mediterranean) Sea on the west to the Jordan River on the east. Hosea 1:4-5 probably referred to the downfall of Israel scheduled to come during the Assyrian invasion of 722 B.C.

II. Purchase: Hos. 3:1-2

A. Order: 1

1. Then said the Lord unto me, Go yet, love a woman beloved of her friend, yet an adulteress, according to the love of the Lord toward the children of Israel, who look to other gods, and love flagons of wine.

This pictures the degrading effects

103

of literal adultery. Hosea was told to go out and love the woman who had taken another lover. She had left home on her own or been put out of it because of her immorality. She had become a symbol of the people of Israel who had abandoned the Lord and given themselves over to paganism. They had embraced the Canaanite gods of Baalim.

B. Obedience: 2

2. So I bought her to me for fifteen pieces of silver, and for an homer of barley, and an half homer of barley:
A slave in ancient Israel was worth about thirty shekels of silver. Hosea paid fifteen pieces of silver plus a homer and a half of barley to buy back Gomer from her new master. This amounted to about twenty dollars and several bushels of grain. He took her home and reinstated her there, but he warned her not to become promiscuous again (Hos. 3:3). The spiritual application was that God was willing to forgive and redeem repentant Israel, warning her to follow the path of righteousness. We are reminded of the infinitely higher price God paid for our redemption from sin. Peter told first-century believers, "Ye know that ye were not redeemed with corruptible things, as silver and gold,.. but with the precious blood of Christ" (I Pet. 1:18-19).

III. Problem: Hos. 6:4-6

A. Retribution: 4-5

4. O Ephraim, what shall I do unto thee? O Judah, what shall I do unto thee? for your goodness is as a morning cloud, and as the early dew it goeth away.
We may be sure that God was not in the least confused about what to do with sinful Ephraim (Israel) and Judah. These were rhetorical questions to make His people realize that He was displeased with the vacillation shown toward Him by them. They were like morning clouds or dew on the ground which disappeared when the hot sun began shining. When they were under pagan pressure, they tended to move away from the Lord and into the sphere of Satan. Time and time again they had to be judged and punished in efforts to drive them back to the Lord.

5. Therefore have I hewed them by the prophets; I have slain them by the words of my mouth: and thy judgments are as the light that goeth forth.
This verse looked ahead to future judgments and upheavals. God spoke through His prophets to warn the people of what would come to pass. The prophets spoke about coming holocausts in which sinful people would be hewn down by the swords of their enemies. God's judgments were as predictable as the sun which rises every morning and sends forth its rays to warm the earth. Divine retribution was sure to come to those who failed to repent.

B. Reason: 6

6. For I desired mercy, and not sacrifice; and the knowledge of God more than burnt-offerings.
In a plaintive way God expressed sorrow at the shallowness of His people. They thought that they could sin and then please Him by offering up animal sacrifices to atone for them. What God wanted from them was inner righteousness and the mercy generated by it. The outward show of piety could never take the place of inward piety. They had acted as if they were not covenant people and thus had dealt treacherously with God (vs. 7).

IV. Provision: Hos. 11:1-4a

A. Call: 1

1. When Israel was a child, then I loved him, and called my son out of Egypt.
It had been in pagan Egypt that Israel had been born as a nations descending from the sons of Jacob. God here referred to Israel as a child at that timed and that figure continues through this text. The Lord loved Israel and was grieved when the Egyptians decided to enslave the people and mistreat them. Therefore, He called them to come up out of Egypt and go back to the land of Canaan which He had promised to Abraham. This was done through the instrumentality of Moses and his brother, Aaron. It took ten devastating plagues

to persuade the pharaoh to let the Israelites go. It took a miracle by God to drown the pursuing Egyptians in the Red Sea. It took forty years of care by God in the wilderness before the second-generation Israelites entered, subdued, and settled pagan Canaan. Despite all of the divine care God showed them, people drifted away from Him. Note the following contrasts between a loving God and an unappreciative people.

B. Contrasts: 2-4a

2a. As they called them, so they went from them:...
Parents know what it is to call their children and have them run away from them. God sent His prophets to the earth to call to the Israelites, but they chose to run away from them. As we saw in the last lesson, they even told a prophet such as Amos to stop prophesying. Cutting themselves off from the truth, they made themselves vulnerable to influence from pagan sources.

2b. ...they sacrificed unto Baalim, and burned incense to graven images.
Having turned away from Jehovah, the Israelites turned toward the Canaanite gods of Baalim. According to Joshua 24:14-15, they had idols from Mesopotamia and Egypt, as well as from Canaan. They evidently remained devoted to them until the traumatic experience of the Babylonian captivity finally ended it.

3a. I taught Ephraim also to go, taking them by their arms;...
Parents are familiar with a young child's attempts to graduate from crawling and walking by hanging onto things to walking on his own. He is likely to fall many times, and parents often take hold of his arms to steady him as he learns how to balance himself and put one foot ahead of the other to get somewhere. This was the way God pictured Himself helping Israel during the time of its toddling in the wilderness and settling of Canaan. He gave the law at Mount Sinai. He established the priesthood. He gave victory in battle. He organized the twelve tribes. He taught young Israel how to make its way in the world.

3b. ...but they knew not that I healed them.
Even as a child learning how to walk is bound to fall and hurt himself sometimes, so it was that young Israel had its share of injuries, but God was there to heal. Too often His care was not appreciated or acknowledged as it should have been.

4a. I drew them with cords of a man, with bands of love:...
This goes along with the comment about God taking Ephraim (Israel) by the arms when learning how to walk (vs. 3). As the toddler developed his ability to walk on his own, a parent would put cords into his hands and take hold of the other ends. By pulling them taut, he could pull gently on them and thus lead the child in various directions. This was a loving action performed by the parent. God had His ways of giving direction to young Israel as it sought to survive and develop as a nation.

HOSEA: PROPHET OF GOD'S LOVE

Evangelistic Emphasis

God's love for an unfaithful people dominates the landscape of Hosea's world. There is no stronger evangelistic message in the Old Testament. Make no mistake. Hosea is more than a prophet. He is love, all the love in the world. All the love of God is riding on Hosea's treatment of Gomer. Remember how Gomer left Hosea and engaged in various acts of infidelity? Well, most men would have let her go and filed for a divorce, but not Hosea. Hosea went out after Gomer. In love he brought her home again. An American author has claimed that people cannot go home again. Not so, says Hosea. With love all things are possible.

The whole world of selfish, legalistic persons would insist on writing off Gomer. Hosea obeyed God and went after Gomer. There is no starry-eyed sentimentality in the stone-washed face of Hosea. There is no illusion of a soft, easy return to a love relationship with his wife. With stark realism Hosea tracks down Gomer, sells all he possesses, and reclaims her as his wife.

There is no trace of cheap grace in our story. Gomer's return required discipline. She would have to prove once again her love for Hosea. In that sense, God, while forgiving, is also demanding.

◆◆◆◆◆◆

Memory Selection

I desire steadfast love and not sacrifice, the knowledge of God, rather than burnt offerings. - *Hosea 6:6*

Worship is not optional equipment for the people of God. When God tells Hosea that He wants steadfast love and knowledge instead of sacrifices and burnt offerings, He is not throwing out all worship. On the contrary, God is expressing the true meaning of worship.

To love God with steadfast loyalty and commitment is one side of the coin called worship. Far from demeaning worship, the text elevates worship to eternal significance. Worship rises from the grateful hearts of forgiven, redeemed people. True worship is an action verb, not a noun. It is the offering of who we are and what we have to God. No wonder Luther offered up a one line definition of worship: "The tenth leper turning back." Worship is our acting out before God the people we should be in grateful, steadfast love.

The other side of the coin of worship is knowledge. In order to know God, we must be still and silent and meditate. In worship we reflect upon the gracious acts of God in Christ Jesus. We connect our struggles with the saving grace of God.

Worship is thus based on steadfast love and knowledge. Love without knowledge can turn into mere emotionalism. Knowledge without love can turn into a sort of superior legalism that degenerates into meaningless ritualism. It is the Christian's responsibility to model love and knowledge through true worship.

November 15, 1992

Weekday Problems

Kim has been married for ten years. She has two children. She and her husband seem to have the perfect marriage. But one night during an argument he tells her that he has been having an affair for over a year.

Her first reaction is anger. She says she wants a divorce. Something in her, however, refuses to give up on the marriage. After seeking the counsel of her pastor, Kim decides to fight to save the marriage. She and her husband meet and work out a reconciliation. He promises to be faithful and loving.

The following weekend, however, the husband takes the other woman to a hotel. He returns home on Sunday afternoon. Kim confronts him with the situation. His response is that he has no intention of leaving or giving up his girlfriend. Kim, her self-esteem battered and her confidence gone, is so confused she doesn't know what to do.

*Based on the teaching of the Scripture, what advice would you give Kim?

*If her husband continues seeing the other woman, does Kim have the right to a divorce?

*Why do you think Kim would stay with an unfaithful husband? Are there biblical precedents for such action?

*As Christian what actions can you take to support Kim and help her recover her self-confidence?

♦♦♦♦♦♦

Superintendent's Sermonette

Sometimes we get so smug about our spiritual condition that we like to think that we can hold ourselves above the sins which surround us. We need to beware that spiritual pride might bring us down. Not only are we vulnerable to temptation and sin, but there are those close to us who can also fall. When something evil happens to us or them, we are face to face with Satan's power, and we need to exercise our right to call on God for help. He alone can pardon us and pour out divine love on us. It is through this continual operation of dependence on Him that we grow in spiritual strength.

Hosea lived in a time when Israel and Judah were rushing toward oblivion. Their kingdoms were due to fall under foreign domination, and their people were going to be taken into captivity to the east. It must have been difficult for Hosea to follow God's instruction and take Gomer as his wife, because she was to cause him shame by her immorality. Hosea did as he was ordered, for it was made clear to him that this would serve as a symbol of God's people being spiritually adulterous. Coupled with warnings of judgment, however, were promises of restoration for those who repented. We need to give a sinful world this same message today.

107

HOSEA: PROPHET OF GOD'S LOVE

This Lesson In Your Life

Love! The love of a man for a woman defies our attempts at explanation. Take, for example, the love of Hosea for Gomer. In all of the Old Testament there is no clearer picture of the meaning of love than Hosea's commitment to Gomer. How powerful and redemptive Hosea's love is. As a matter of fact, the love of Hosea is a mirror in which we can look to determine the quality of our love relationships.

In our society "love" has become a word devalued. The word is used for everything from feelings about a new sports car to one-night sexual escapades. In our society, love is a value that no longer carries along its necessary partner, commitment. Yet people look for love, desire love, and want love. Love is necessary for survival. Without love, relationships perish and communities die. Without love, marriages end in divorce. The cheap imitations that pass for love do not fill the emptiness which is characteristic of our world.

If Hosea's love is a mirror, then hold up your own love relationship and take a long, evaluative look. Do you love your spouse as much as Hosea loved Gomer? In your love relationships are you trying to get something for yourself or attempting to give something of yourself?

Those who are attempting to get something for themselves have missed the true meaning of love. Their selfish, greedy, vindictive attitude has been called "need-love" by C. S. Lewis. Need-love is conditional love: "I will love you if . . ." or "I will love you as long as you do what I want." The need-lover always has an ulterior motive. He gives only to get something in return. Much of what passes for love in our love-starved society is based on need-love.

If Hosea had offered Gomer only need-love, then their relationship would have been finished. After all, Gomer had committed the sin of adultery. According to the law, Hosea was entitled to a divorce. Hosea could have cut off Gomer without any legal repercussions or any continuing responsibility for her welfare. That is exactly the pattern of need-love. Need love is not capable of sacrifice and forgiveness. The good of the other person is never considered. Need-love takes care only of self.

Hosea, however, expressed his love for Gomer in more meaningful ways. Lewis labels such love as "gift-love." The purpose of gift-love is to build up not to tear down the other. Gift-love is forgiving and generous. Gift-love believes in second chances. Gomer was in a vulnerable position because of her infidelity. According to the law, she could have been stoned to death at worst and turned out of the home at best. Hosea's heart went out to her, however, and he brought her back into the marriage relationship. No law could have ever so moved Hosea. The heart of gift-love accomplished what no legalism could ever do. In the act of reconciliation, the one wronged gave Gomer another opportunity. Thus Hosea, motivated by gift-love, moved beyond the law to an act of reconciliation.

Those who are trying to give something of themselves, those who are attempting to endure pain and loss for the sake of the beloved, those who are willing to sacrifice for the well-being of another, such people are the gift-lovers of the world.

Seed Thoughts

1. Who were the kings of Israel and Judah during the ministry of Hosea?
The kings were Uzziah, Jotham, Ahaz, and Hezekiah in Judah and Jeroboam in Israel.

2. What implication can we draw about God's love from the love of Hosea for Gomer?
God loves His people even when they are rebellious and unfaithful. With steadfast love God calls His people back into a right relationship.

3. Why did God command Hosea to take a wife of harlotry?
Hosea's marriage to Gomer was a powerful analogy of God's love for Israel and Judah.

4. What were God's expectations of His people?
God expected His people to love and know Him in a faithful, constant relationship.

5. What did Hosea require of Gomer after paying a ransom for her?
After paying fifteen pieces of silver for Gomer, Hosea disciplined her and required her to be faithful.

(PLEASE TURN PAGE)

---

1. Who were the kings of Israel and Judah during the ministry of Hosea?

2. What implication can we draw about God's love from the love of Hosea for Gomer?

3. Why did God command Hosea to take a wife of harlotry?

4. What were God's expectations of His people?

5. What did Hosea require of Gomer after paying a ransom for her?

6. What does God mean by describing Judah's goodness as a "morning cloud, and as the early dew . . ."?

7. To what does God compare His love for Israel in Hosea 11:1?

8. What New Testament parable parallels Hosea's image of God as a loving parent?

9. What New Testament concept of Christ's death is prefigured in Hosea's payment for Gomer?

10. What great salvation story does God ask Israel to remember?

(SEED THOUGHTS--Cont'd)

The kings were Uzziah, Jotham, Ahaz, and Hezekiah in Judah and Jeroboam in Israel.

God loves His people even when they are rebellious and unfaithful. With steadfast love God calls His people back into a right relationship.

Hosea's marriage to Gomer was a powerful analogy of God's love for Israel and Judah.

God expected His people to love and know Him in a faithful, constant relationship.

After paying fifteen pieces of silver for Gomer, Hosea disciplined her and required her to be faithful.

The goodness of Judah has only a temporary, superficial quality. Whatever goodness Israel possesses soon evaporates when put to the test.

God's love is like that of a loving parent for a child.

In Luke 15, the parable of the prodigal son parallels the imagery of Hosea.

The idea of a ransom being paid is prominent in Hosea's action, and Christ giving His life as a ransom is prominent in the New Testament doctrine of the atonement.

The major salvation event Israel is called to remember time and again is how God delivered Israel from slavery in Egypt. In Hosea's words, God "called my son out of Egypt."

6. What does God mean by describing Judah's goodness as a "morning cloud, and as the early dew . . ."?
The goodness of Judah has only a temporary, superficial quality. Whatever goodness Israel possesses soon evaporates when put to the test.

7. To what does God compare His love for Israel in Hosea 11:1?
God's love is like that of a loving parent for a child.

8. What New Testament parable parallels Hosea's image of God as a loving parent?
In Luke 15, the parable of the prodigal son parallels the imagery of Hosea.

9. What New Testament concept of Christ's death is prefigured in Hosea's payment for Gomer?
The idea of a ransom being paid is prominent in Hosea's action, and Christ giving His life as a ransom is prominent in the New Testament doctrine of the atonement.

10. What great salvation story does God ask Israel to remember?
The major salvation event Israel is called to remember time and again is how God delivered Israel from slavery in Egypt. In Hosea's words, God "called my son out of Egypt."

November 22, 1992

Micah: Prophet of Righteousness

Micah 6

1 HEAR ye now what the LORD saith; Arise contend thou before the mountains, and let the hills hear thy voice.

2 Hear ye, O mountains, the LORD's controversy and ye strong foundations of the earth: for the LORD hath a controversy with his people, and he will plead with Israel.

3 O my people, what have I done unto thee? and wherein have I wearied thee? testify against me.

4 For I brought thee up out of the land of Egypt, and redeemed thee out of the house of servants; and I sent before thee Moses, Aaron, and Miriam.

5 O my people, remember now what Ba´-lah king of Moab consulted and what Ba´-laam the son of Be´-or answered fiim from Shit´-tim unto Gil´-gal; that ye may know the righteousnes of the LORD.

6 Wherewith shall I come before the LORD *and* bow myself before the high God? shall I come before him with burnt offerings, with calves of a year old?

7 Will the LORD be pleased with thousands of rams, Or with ten thousands of rivers of oil? shall I give my firstborn *for* my transgressions the fruit of my body for the sin of my soul

8 He hath shewed thee, O man, what is good and what doth the LORD require of thee, but to do justly, and to love mercy, and to walk humbly with thy God?

◆◆◆◆◆◆

◀ **Memory Selection**
Micah 6:8

◀ **Devotional Reading**
Micah 6:9-16

◀ **Background Scripture**
Micah 6

◀ **Printed Scripture**
Micah 6:1-8

111

MICAH: PROPHET OF RIGHTEOUSNESS

Teacher's Target

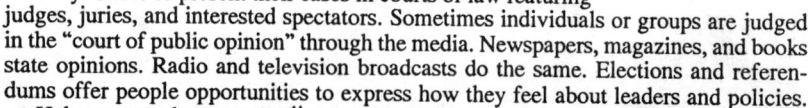

Civilized men claim to live by the rule of law. They establish elaborate judicial systems. Prosecutors and defense attorneys strive to present their cases in courts of law featuring judges, juries, and interested spectators. Sometimes individuals or groups are judged in the "court of public opinion" through the media. Newspapers, magazines, and books state opinions. Radio and television broadcasts do the same. Elections and referendums offer people opportunities to express how they feel about leaders and policies. Help your students to see, However, that above and beyond all human attempts to provide standards through law, there is God and His law. If His dealings with sinful men could be displayed in full, it would be clear that He is right and they are wrong. It would also be obvious that His concern goes beyond material and outward things and fastens itself on spiritual and inward things such as justice, mercy, and humility.

Lesson Introduction

There are several Micahs mentioned in the Bible, but Micah the Morasthite was a prophet of God from 750-710 B.C. during the reigns of Jotham, Ahaz, and Hezekiah over Judah, his homeland. His ministry, however, was directed primarily toward Samaria to the north, where Pekahiah, Pekah, and Hosea occupied the throne during his lifetime. The three parts of the book of Micah are introduced by the imperative of "Hear, all ye people" (1:2), "Hear, ...O heads of Jacob" (3:1), and "Hear ye" (6:1). This lesson's text begins that third part.

God had a controversy with Israel because of her sins. He called on nature itself to witness it. He invited the people to tell Him if He had done anything wrong in His dealings with them. He reminded them of past blessings and deliverances. He urged them to separate the outer trappings of worship from the inner realities of spiritual verities. He emphasized the importance of developing just actions, loving kindnesses, and a humble walk with Him.

Teaching Outline

I. Indictment: Mic. 6:1-2
   A. Audience: 1-2a
   B. Accusation: 2b
II. Inquiry: Mic. 6:3-5
   A. Demand: 3
   B. Deliverance I: 4
   C. Deliverance II: 5
III. Invitation: Mic. 6:6-8
   A. Examples: 6
   B. Exaggerations: 7
   C. Expectations: 8

Daily Bible Readings

Mon. God Will Not Forsake Israel
Mic. 2:6-13
Tue. God's People Will Be Exalted
Mic. 4:1-5
Wed. Israel Will Prevail Over Enemies
Mic. 4:6-13
Thu. God Will Deliver Israel
Mic. 5:5-9
Fri. God Promises to Punish Israel
Mic. 6:9-16
Sat. Israel Waits for God's Compassion - *Mic. 7:1-7*
Sun. God Will Be Faithful to Israel
Mic. 7:15-20

November 22, 1992

VERSE BY VERSE

I. Indictment: Mic. 6:1-2

A. Audience: 1-2a

**1. Hear ye now what the Lord saith; Arise, contend thou before the mountains, and let the hills hear thy voice.
2a. Hear ye, O Mountains, the Lord's controversy, and ye strong foundations of the earth:...**

The courtroom for this event is apparently the whole natural earth which had been around as long as God had dealt with mankind. The Lord wants to state His case against Israel and Judah, populated by His chosen but wayward people. The mountains, the hills, and the foundations of the earth are to make up the audience. It is easy to picture the mountains and hills. Trying to identify the foundations is more difficult. Since the earth is a sphere, the foundations cannot be the type we see underlying normal buildings. Perhaps this symbolic terminology is simply meant to refer to the totality of the earth, both infrastructure and superstructure, however these are defined. They are shown as becoming personified here.

B. Accusation: 2b

2b. for the Lord hath a controversy with his people, and he will plead with Israel.

One paraphrase puts it this way—"The Lord has an accusation against His people, and He will indict Israel" (Berkeley). Once the scene is set, the Lord will make known His controversy and prosecute Israel for her sins. An official indictment is a list of charges against the defendants which has to be proved or dismissed.

II. Inquiry: Mic. 6:3-5

A. Demand: 3

3. O my people, what have I done unto thee? and wherein have I wearied thee? testify against me.

These had to be rhetorical questions not requiring answers, for God had been fair and gracious in His dealings with His people. However, He wanted them to think about the relationship. Had He ever done anything to harm them? Had He ever done anything to wear out their patience? If they felt mistreated in any way, they were to speak out and make their feelings known to Him. The natural reaction to this invitation would have to be silence as far as sincere individuals were concerned. In That that case, God was free to move ahead with summary of outstanding dealings with Israel.

B. Deliverance I: 4

4a. For I brought thee up out of the land of Egypt, and redeemed thee out of the house of servants;...

The Lord reminded His people of past blessings. The greatest appeared to be that of deliverance from the land of Egypt. Slaves could be set free if someone was willing to pay for them and turn them loose. God was the only One powerful enough to redeem the Israelites from their cruel taskmasters. He did this by sending devastating plagues on Egypt until the one supreme authority, the pharaoh, let the Israelites go. Israel became a multitude of people in bondage, but she became a nation when liberated and moved out of the house of servants (slaves).

4b. ...and I sent before thee Moses, Aaron, and Miriam.

God used three members of one family to provide leadership for Israel when moving from bondage to freedom and from dependence on Egypt to independence. The story of how Moses escaped death by being hidden in a small ark among the reeds in the river until adopted by the Egyptian princess is well-known. He learned the arts and sciences of Egypt during his royal upbringing. He learned to meditate and be humble while serving as a shepherd in Midian. He learned to administer a large and contentious people while leading them through the wilderness for forty years. He gave them God's law and sought to hold them to it.

Aaron, Moses' brother, became his spokesman when Moses complained to God that he was inarticulate. Aaron also became the first of a long line of consecrated priests responsible for leading the people in worship and maintaining the portable tabernacle which later was replaced by the permanent temple.

Miriam, the sister who guarded Moses while he was a baby in the little ark, and who suggested to the Egyptian princess that Moses' own mother be used as his nurse, became a prophetess. She led the nation in celebration after God delivered the Israelites from the pursuing Egyptians by drowning them in the Red Sea.

C. Deliverance II: 5

5a. O my people, remember now what Balak king of Moab consulted, and what Balaam the son of Beor answered him from Shittim unto Gilgal;...

The Lord reminded His people of the incident involving Balak, evidently king over Moab and Midian when the Israelites were traveling from Egypt to Canaan. Feeling threatened by the Israelites, Balak sent repeatedly to a diviner named Balaam in the city of Pethor on the Euphrates River in Mesopotamia to come down and help. Balak wanted Balaam to put a curse upon Israel for payment. God intervened and would not let Balaam do it. Ironically, Balaam ended up giving a blessing to Israel. Balak was furious, refused to pay Balaam, and sent him away (Num. 22-24). God called on Israel to remember all that had happened on the trip from Shittim (Acacia) to Gilgal (Mic. 6:5).

5b. ... that ye may know the righteousness of the Lord.

This phrase may have climaxed all that preceded it in verses 4 and 5, making use of two examples of deliverance in Israel's history. The righteousness of the Lord had been demonstrated in His deliverance of Israel from bondage in Egypt and from the threats of King Balak.

III. Invitation: Mic. 6:6-8

A. Examples: 6

6. Wherewith shall I come before the Lord, and bow myself before the high God? shall I come before him with burnt-offerings, with calves of a year old?

It was probably Micah the prophet speaking here, and there appears to have been a progression in his remarks as recorded in verses 6-8. He began with the exemplary (vs. 6b), moved on to the exaggerated (vs. 7), and ended with the excellent (vs. 8). Keep this progression in mind as we study the verses in detail.

It was taken for granted that the high God deserved to have His people come to bow before Him in worship. The question posed was concerned with what should be brought with them to serve as offerings to please Him. What would cause Him to receive them and show favor to them?

The first thing mentioned was exemplary. In answer to the question as to whether a person should come before God with burnt-offerings, with calves one year old, one should get a positive response. Yes, year-old calves were welcome under the Levitical law, if offered sincerely and according to the proper priestly procedures.

B. Exaggerations: 7

7a. Will the Lord be pleased with thousands of rams, or with ten thousands of rivers of oil?

The answer to this question is not as simple as the answer to the first question was. King Solomon offered up thousands of animal sacrifices to God when he dedicated the temple (1 Kings 8:63), and there was nothing wrong with that. The reason for using exaggeration in Micah 6:7 was to point out the fact that excessive offerings of rams and of olive oil to the Lord would not gain favor with Him simply because of the numbers involved. God would not be favorably affected in that way, if these offerings were not made from sincere hearts. He was after quality, not quantity.

7b. ...shall I give my firstborn for my transgression, the fruit of my body for the sin of my soul?

Here was a type of sacrifice which was common among the pagans surrounding Israel. Parents were often called on to offer up their infants to heathen deities in order to propitiate them and to prove their devotion to them. This practice was abhorrent to the Lord and forbidden to Israelites. The only case in which it was permitted was in the death of Christ as atonement for the sins of men.

Your students may mention the case of Abraham and Isaac. Although God told Abraham to offer up Isaac, this was avoided and a ram caught in a nearby thicket was offered up, instead (Gen. 22:1-18).

C. Expectations: 8

8a. He hath shewed thee, O man, what is good; and what doth the Lord require of thee,...

We move now from tangible sacrifices to intangible virtues or qualities. We can take the rhetorical question here and transpose it into a declarative form. Micah was convinced that the Lord had clearly showed men what He considered to be good and acceptable when it came to sacrifices. More than that, the Lord had made it clear that he required certain things from men. They were responsible for meeting His expectations.

8b. ...but to do justly,...

Amos 5:24 gives this added force – "Let judgment [justice] run down as waters, and righteousness as a mighty stream." Justice on earth is supposed to reflect justice in heaven. God is the One Who defines it, not man. Human "justice" is sometimes perverted by discrimination, bribery, and other evils. Divine justice is always pure.

8c. ...and to love mercy,...

Mercy in the Bible may be defined as the withholding of deserved punishment because of God's grace, but there is a second meaning which seems to apply here. Mercy is shown in acts of kindness toward others. Although we often think of this in material terms, it could involve help in the physical, mental, emotional, social, and spiritual aspects of life, as well. It becomes a blessing, even as Jesus said, "It is more blessed to give than to receive" (Acts 20:35).

8d. ...and to walk humbly with thy God?

Contrition is required of those who want to walk humbly with the Lord. He said, "I dwell in the high and holy place, with him also that is of a contrite and humble spirit, to revive the spirit of the humble, and to revive the heart of the contrite ones" (Isa. 57:15). A person who walks in humility before the Lord will obey Him and go out to influence the lives of others.

The message of Micah 6:8 appears to be almost New Testament in its tone, for it looks beyond the literal aspects of the Mosaic law and points ahead to the spiritual aspects of Christ and His message.

Evangelistic Emphasis

Nothing in life is as essential as the quality of our relationships. Strong, intimate relationships give us hints of heaven. Weak, destructive relationships, however, become a form of hell on earth. By far the most significant relationship is the one we establish with God. Micah 6 is a famous text because it raises and answers a fundamental question of faith: How does a sinner enter into a relationship with God?

The emptiness of much modern life speaks of our need for a relationship with God. The hypocrisy and the dead ritualism of many churches leave many people unmoved and unsaved. They search for God in the ruins of ritualistic religion and find nothing.

The questions of Micah are at the heart of life's meaning. How do we meet God? We often act as if the only requirement is to put on our Sunday clothes and our Sunday masks and show up for some casual worship. We seem to think meeting with God is like meeting an old friend for a meaningless lunch.

Meeting God, however, has eternal dimensions. We meet God here and now in our daily lives, in the everydayness of every day, but we shall also meet God one day in judgment. Micah's question is not a casual one. It is loaded with eternal consequences

♦♦♦♦♦♦

Memory Selection

What does the Lord require of you, but to do justice, and to love kindness, and to walk humbly with your God.
Micah 6:8

Justice. Kindness. Humility. In our kind of world that doesn't sound like much of a resume, does it? In a world where winning is everything and looking out for number one is a cult religion, justice comes in near the bottom. Why? Because doing justice means being fair with people. It means telling the truth and keeping our word. Would so many human beings be abused and mistreated if justice were a top priority? In our sort of world justice appears as a lost virtue.

How can we expect much of a performance from kindness? It sounds like a fragile virtue, doesn't it? In a world where the hard-boiled get their way, kindness doesn't have much of a chance. Why? Because kindness means treating people with dignity and respect. It means going out of our way to offer help and hospitality. Americans seem to have lost their manners. There is so much pushing and shoving and shouting, so much rudeness and impatience. A world without manners puts a virtue like kindness in the intensive care unit.

Humility is no better off because arrogance seems to rule our world. People think so highly of themselves and spend so much time putting down others. It is hard to have a relationship with God when we think we are capable of taking care of ourselves. In a world where so many are conceited, humility doesn't stand much of a chance.

God commands us to do all three: justice, kindness, and humility. God will help us.

November 22, 1992

Weekday Problems

Jack had always believed that knowing the difference between right and wrong was a simple matter. As a Christian there was no point in asking a lot of complex questions. Right was right and wrong was wrong.

Now as he stood by the bed of his wife, in the Intensive Care Unit, all he saw was a beautiful woman covered with wires and bandages and machines. She is hooked to a life-support system. The doctors have said that she will never recover. Already she has been in a coma for 26 days. The reason she was in this condition was a serious automobile wreck. Her brain was so damaged that even if she woke up she would not recognize or know Jack.

The doctor has asked Jack's permission to remove Jane from the life-support system. He is baffled by the strong flood of emotions. Even more he is confused by the ambiguity concerning the rightness and wrongness of his decision.

*What concept from Micah 6 might help Jack work through his decision? What might be said about doing the most loving thing?

*How could you help Jack apply Christian principles to this complex situation?

*Should Jack continue praying and ask God for a miracle? What if his wife can be kept on the life-support system for an indefinite time?

*Should Jack consider other issues such as his own financial condition or the quality of life Jane will never have?

◆◆◆◆◆◆

Superintendent's Sermonette

A popular ballad sung years ago stated that the best things in life are free. There is some truth in that, for God providentially gives all men some things to enjoy. Jesus said, "He [God] maketh his sun to rise on the evil and on the good, and sendeth rain on the just and on the unjust" (Matt. 5:45). However, there are many things we enjoy which come at a price. We would be naive if we claimed not to appreciate or want them.

The Bible does not teach us to make light of material things, but it promotes the superior worth of spiritual things. Our lesson today deals with this subject. Micah 6:1-8 presents a courtroom encompassing the earth. God is the Judge, and He summons the mountains, hills, and foundations of the earth to witness His case against ancient Israel. In spite of His bestowal of earthly blessings, the Israelites had perverted their worship activities with hypocrisy and ostentation.

God wants us to be governed by the right heart attitudes, including justice, kindness, and humility. These virtues are as relevant now as they have always been, for they are timeless in their importance and impact. Let us determine that we are going to cultivate them in our lives.

MICAH: PROPHET OF RIGHTEOUSNESS

This Lesson In Your Life

Only the poetic can capture the pathos of a hurting God, wounded by the sins of His own people. The questions in Micah are intensely personal, but there is a cosmic setting. Court has been called into session. The most unusual trial in history is opening. At center stage is God, playing the dual roles of defendant and prosecuting attorney. Israel is the accuser of God. The mountains and foundations of the earth have been called to serve on the jury. In the powerful forsenic metaphors of Micah, the issues before the court transcend time to involve us in the complaint.

Somehow, in the mixed imagery of the courtroom God begins as the aggrieved party and later becomes the prosecuting attorney. The trial begins with God's pronouncement of His controversy with Israel. As prosecuting attorney, God asks two questions: "What have I done unto thee?" and "Wherein have I wearied thee?"

The questions are defensive ones implying the innocence of God. The Israelites have been complaining and murmuring about the circumstances in which they live. Now they have blamed God for their bad circumstances. The scene looks and sounds amazingly modern, doesn't it? To blame God for all the bad things that happen in life is a persistent theme in theology. Thus the Israelites are not the first or the last to take the road of despair and heap all blame for tough circumstances on God.

God, however, refuses to play the blame game. He reverses the charge and accuses Israel of misdirected complaining. He then challenges Israel to testify against Him. God waits for one single piece of evidence that can be scraped up against Him. Israel answers with silence. Not one word, not one incident, not a single event can be conjured up for use in court. There is no factual basis to blame God. The truth is even religious people still want to blame God for their problems.

When Israel has no answer, no evidence, God breaks into the silence with testimony. Over against the murmuring, God appeals to His mighty saving acts on behalf of Israel. While Israel has no evidence of God mistreating them, God has plenty of evidence of His saving work for Israel. God now piles up the historical evidence to help Israel remember and be grateful. To remember and to accept life with gratitude are twin cures for the blame game. God's purpose is to jog Israel's sacred memory.

To remember is a crucial act of faith. The major speech of the trial is God's reminder of His saving acts. The whole trial centers on the acts of God. Israel, despite her complaints, is forever indebted to God. In the Exodus, Israel received her first taste of redemption. The cry was, "For I brought thee up out of the land of Egypt . . ."

The Lord Himself has taken the floor. Israel and the mountains and foundations of the earth are called to witness the redemption of Israel. As Christians we can not afford to forget the redemptive act of Christ. There is always a cross in our memory. We celebrate the Lord's Supper in remembrance of Him who died for us and was raised from the dead.

Sometimes God's people suffer from amnesia. We forget that the Lord has redeemed us; the Lord has guided us; the Lord has given us eternal life. The evidence of our amnesia is everywhere in our ritualistic worship, in our casual attitude toward the spiritual, and in our come and go as we please posture.

Seed Thoughts

1. What is the meaning of the tension between sacrifices offered in worship and right conduct?

The prophet does not suggest that worship is unimportant, or that sacrifice is unnecessary. It is rather that the rituals of worship are empty when separated from right conduct.

2. What is the nature of God's controversy with Israel?

The Lord has a controversy with His people because they have forgotten the saving acts of history and what it means to do justice, love kindness, and walk humbly with God.

3. Describe the major imagery Micah uses in chapter 6 to put forth God's controversy with Israel?

The imagery is drawn from the sphere of legal practice in Israel. It is an example of what biblical scholars call a court-saying. Such imagery is common in prophecy from Hosea to Malachi.

4. Name three other prophets who sound the same major notes as Micah 6:8.

Since Micah presents the essence of the Jewish faith, it is no accident that the same notes are sounded by Amos (5:24), Hosea (2:19-20) and Isaiah (7:9, 30:15).

5. What specific historical acts does God use to remind Israel of His saving power?

God reminds Israel of their redemption from Egypt; their being led through the wilderness; and the story of Balak and Balaam.

(PLEASE TURN PAGE)

---

1. What is the meaning of the tension between sacrifices offered in worship and right conduct?

2. What is the nature of God's controversy with Israel?

3. Describe the major imagery Micah uses in chapter 6 to put forth God's controversy with Israel?

4. Name three other prophets who sound the same major notes as Micah 6:8.

5. What specific historical acts does God use to remind Israel of His saving power?

6. Why do you suppose Micah does not recount the details of the Balak and Balaam story?

7. God says that he *redeemed* Israel. What is the meaning of *redemption*?

8. What does the prophet consider offering God?

9. What is the main sin which Israel has committed?

10. What does God require of His people?

The prophet does not suggest that worship is unimportant, or that sacrifice is unnecessary. It is rather that the rituals of worship are empty when separated from right conduct.

The Lord has a controversy with His people because they have forgotten the saving acts of history and what it means to do justice, love kindness, and walk humbly with God.

The imagery is drawn from the sphere of legal practice in Israel. It is an example of what biblical scholars call a court-saying. Such imagery is common in prophecy from Hosea to Malachi.

Since Micah presents the essence of the Jewish faith, it is no accident that the same notes are sounded by Amos (5:24), Hosea (2:19-20) and Isaiah (7:9, 30:15).

God reminds Israel of their redemption from Egypt; their being led through the wilderness; and the story of Balak and Balaam.

Micah is able to assume that his audience already knows the sacred story contained in the Word of God. Micah did not face the problem of people being ignorant of God's Word.

To redeem means to free someone who is bound by legal obligation by the payment of a price. The verb is a metaphor of salvation for the helpless Israelites.

The prophet considers trying to please God with sacrifices and ritual worship.

Israel is guilty of forgetting the Lord.

God requires faithfulness, righteousness, kindness, steadfast love, and humility.

(SEED THOUGHTS--Cont'd)

6. Why do you suppose Micah does not recount the details of the Balak and Balaam story?
Micah is able to assume that his audience already knows the sacred story contained in the Word of God. Micah did not face the problem of people being ignorant of God's Word.

7. God says that he *redeemed* Israel. What is the meaning of *redemption*?
To redeem means to free someone who is bound by legal obligation by the payment of a price. The verb is a metaphor of salvation for the helpless Israelites.

8. What does the prophet consider offering God?
The prophet considers trying to please God with sacrifices and ritual worship.

9. What is the main sin which Israel has committed?
Israel is guilty of forgetting the Lord.

10. What does God require of His people?
God requires faithfulness, righteousness, kindness, steadfast love, and humility.

November 29, 1992

JEREMIAH IN DUNGEON PRISON

Jeremiah: Persistent Prophet

Jeremiah 1
9 Then the Lord put forth his hand, and touched my mouth. And the Lord said unto me, Behold, I have put my words in thy mouth.
10 See, I have this day set thee over the nations and over the kingdoms, to root out, and to pull down, and to destroy, and to throw down. to build, and to plant.

Jeremiah 20
7 O Lord, thou hast deceived me, and I was deceived: thou art stronger than I, and hast prevailed: I am in derision daily, every one mocketh me.
8 For since I spake, I cried out, I cried violence and spoil; because the word of the Lord was made a reproach unto me, and a derision daily.

9 Then I said, I will not make mention of him, nor speak any more in his name. But his word was in mine heart as a burning fire shut up in my bones, and I was weary with forbearing, and I could not stay.
10 For I heard the defaming of many, fear on every side. Report, say they, and we will report it. All my familiars watched for my halting saying, Peradventure he will be enticed, and we shall take our revenge on him.
11 But the Lord is with me as a mighty terrible one: therefore my prosecutors shall stumble, and they shall not prevail: they shall be greatly ashamed; for they shall not prosper: their everlasting confusion shall never be forgotten.

◆◆◆◆◆◆

◀ **Memory Selection**
Jeremiah 20:9

◀ **Devotional Reading**
Jeremiah 8:18-22

◀ **Background Scripture**
Jeremiah 1:1-10; 8:22-9:3; 20:7-13

◀ **Printed Scripture**
Jeremiah 1:9-10; 20:7-11

JEREMIAH: PERSISTENT PROPHET

Teacher's Target

World War II, Winston Churchill, Prime Minister of England, seemed to be the human equivalent of the tenacious British bulldog. He refused to be intimidated by Hitler's massive war machine, and he lived to see it destroyed. During the Persian Gulf War, Norman Schwartskopf, Commander of the allied forces, seemed to assume a similar role when facing Saddam Hussein's war machine. Jeremiah the prophet may not have appeared to be as tough when he faced sinful Judah, but he had the inner toughness of being persistent in proclaiming God's message to those who needed it.

Help your students to look beyond Jeremiah's reputation as "the weeping prophet" and see him as the resolute prophet. He serves as an example of the kind of persistence which ought to characterize all true believers. He experienced discouragement, but it was overcome by the Word of God in his heart which burned like a fire and caused him to renew his faith and continue his ministry. God can repeat that in His children today. We need it, for our challenges are great and our enemy is strong.

Lesson Introduction

Jeremiah spanned the years before and after the destruction of Judah by Babylon. Zephaniah and Habakkuk were contemporaries of his earlier ministry, and Daniel was a contemporary of his later ministry. Following the death of good King Josiah, Judah went rapidly downhill, headed for the Babylonian captivity. Jeremiah foresaw this seventy year period and the return of a remnant of Jews to their homeland afterward.

Jeremiah was not carried into exile to the east. He was permitted to remain with a few of his countrymen to care for the land. However, when they rebelled against Babylon and fled for safety to Egypt, he went with them to continue ministering to them, and it was there that he died. He is credited with the book bearing his name and with the book of Lamentations describing the terrible siege of Jerusalem in 587-586 B.C. He is truly one of the "major prophets."

Teaching Outline

I. Direction: Jer. 1:9-10
  A. Enablement: 9
  B. Effects: 10
II. Decision: Jer. 20:7-9a
  A. Reproach: 7-8
  B. Resolution: 9a
III. Determination: Jer. 20:9b-11
  A. Fire: 9b
  B. Fear: 10
  C. Faith: 11

Daily Bible Readings

Mon. Jeremiah Is Called to Be a Prophet - *Jer. 1:1-9*
Tue. The Lord Will Fight Jeremiah's Battles - *Jer. 1:13-19*
Wed. Israel's Heart Is Hardened toward God - *Jer. 4:14-22*
Thu. God's Wrath Will Fall upon Israel - *Jer. 6:10-15*
Fri. God Calls Israel to Repentance - *Jer. 7:1-7*
Sat. Israel's Covenant with God Is Broken - *Jer. 11:1-11*
Sun. God Will Free Israel from Captivity - *Jer. 30:1-18*

November 29, 1992

VERSE BY VERSE

I. Direction: Jer. 1:9-10

A. Enablement: 9

9. Then the Lord put forth his hand and touched my mouth. And the Lord said unto me, Behold, I have put my words in thy mouth.

The background for this is found in verses 4-8. God spoke to Jeremiah and told him that He had ordained him to be a prophet to the nations while he was still in his mother's womb. Jeremiah objected, saying that he could not speak because he was but a "child," meaning that he felt inexperienced and inadequate for the task. The Lord rebuked Jeremiah for saying this and predicted that he would go to all those to whom he was sent and tell them whatever he was commanded to tell them. He was not to be afraid of them, for God would be with him.

God's enablement of Jeremiah for his prophetic ministry was through a simple act. The Lord put forth his hand and touched Jeremiah's mouth. It was a gesture of authority, and it carried with it the divine impartation of words to be spoken. Similar actions might be mentioned here. An angel used a coal from off the altar to touch the mouth of Isaiah (Isa. 6:6-7). Ezekiel was given a scroll to eat (Ezek. 3:1-2). An angel touched Daniel's lips (Dan. 10:16). God's words are extensions of Himself, and they have great power in them. Divine truth remains the same, whether or not men will hear it, believe it, or accept it. Those who embrace it may build upon it. Those who reject it will be broken upon it.

B. Effects: 10

10. See, I have this day set thee over the nations and over the kingdoms, to root out, and to pull down, and to destroy, and to throw down, to build, and to plant.

Note the similarity of Jeremiah 31:28—"It shall come to pass, that like as I have watched over them (the houses of Israel and of Judah), to pluck up, and to break down, and to throw down, and to destroy, and to afflict; so will I watch over them, to build, and to plant, saith the Lord." The wording of these two verses makes it clear that God was the One with the power to tear down or build up Israel and Judah. Jeremiah was mentioned as if he had the power simply because he was God's spokesman to his generation. God spoke through Jeremiah and then acted according to those words. The prophet held the awesome power of prophecy given to him by the Lord. He spoke both of judgment and of restoration. By using God's inspired Word, we can do the same in our generation.

II. Decision: Jer. 20:7-9a

A. Reproach; 7-8

7a. O Lord, thou hast deceived me, and I was deceived: ...

Jeremiah had come to the Lord's house in Jerusalem and said, "Thus saith the Lord of hosts, the God of Israel; Behold, I will bring upon this city and upon all her towns all the evil that I have pronounced against it, because they have hardened their necks, that they might not hear my words" (Jer. 19:15). When Pashur, son of Immer the priest and chief governor of the temple, heard what Jeremiah had prophesied, he smote him and put him in the stocks nearby. He released him the next morning, and Jeremiah delivered a stinging oration in which he predicted the Babylonian captivity and Pashur's death in exile (Jer. 20:1-6).

Jeremiah then prayed to the Lord, expressing his complaint. He was so upset by his recent mistreatment that he blamed the Lord for deceiving him when He first gave him words of judgment and endued him with power to use them effectively for making positive changes. What Jeremiah seemed to miss was the fact that the messenger gets into trouble while giving the message at various points. He has words of divine power, but he is subjected to human persecution and weakness himself.

7b. ...thou art stronger than I, and hast prevailed:...

Jeremiah's lament now accused God of using His superior power to make him merely a helpless instrument in His hands. Paul later developed this theme in working for Christ "I take pleasure in infirmities, in reproaches, in necessities, in persecutions, in distresses for Christ's sake: for when I am weak, then am I strong (II Cor. 12:10). This is a lesson we all should learn.

7c. ...I am in derision daily, every one mocketh me.

Jeremiah not only resented feeling weak, but he also resented being ridiculed by others. We can well imagine that he suffered much from the mocking of those who gathered about him while he was helpless in the stocks near the temple. This was emotional wounding, and it could be as hard on a person as physical abuse in its own way.

8a. For since I spake, I cried out, I cried violence and spoil;...

Jeremiah seemed to be saying that he always had to give people bad messages. "You have never once let me speak a word of kindness to them; always it is disaster and horror and destruction" (Living Bible). This kind of message was bound to get a bad hearing most of the time, even though it was necessary to give it.

8b. ...because the word of the Lord was made a reproach unto me, and a derision, daily.

Jeremiah went on to say, "Lord, I am ridiculed and scorned all the time because I proclaim your message" (Today's English Version). It is easy to see that Jeremiah took the reproach personally.

B. Resolution: 9a

9a. Then I said, I will not make mention of him, nor speak any more in his name.

Jeremiah told how he came to the conclusion that he would stop being a prophet. He would refuse to mention the Lord or give His messages again. Other versions make this conditional and tie it into the latter part of the verse in this manner - "If I say that I will not make mention of him, nor speak any more in his name, then his word is in my heart as a burning fire..." We are amazed to think that Jeremiah even considered cutting off his prophetic ministry, but we have to realize that discouragement and ridicule can be powerful weapons in Satan's arsenal when used against a believer.

III. Determination: Jer. 20:9b-11

A. Fire: 9b

9b. But his word was in mine heart as a burning fire shut up in my bones, and I was weary with forbearing, and I could not stay.

Regardless of the difficulty of his work, Jeremiah felt compelled to proceed with it. The words of God were in his heart and seemed to smolder within his bones. He became tired of forbearing (holding it in). He had to let it out again. Paul expressed this kind of compulsion when he was spreading the gospel. At Corinth he "was pressed in the spirit, and testified to the Jews that Jesus was Christ" (Acts 18:5). He later wrote to the Corinthians, "Necessity is laid upon me; yea, woe is unto me, if I preach not the gospel" (I Cor. 9:16). As a true child of God and a commissioned worker, he had to speak the truth. We should examine our own hearts to see if they beat in time with the Lord and His program of redemption for mankind. Is the fire of our devotion strong enough to propel us out to the lost?

B. Fear: 10

10a. For I heard the defaming of many, fear on every side.

Jeremiah described the campaign against him. He heard the defaming made. This produced fear within him, despite the fact that God had promised to be with him in his ministry. We see the human emotion here which keeps many of God's servants from working for Him as they should.

10b. Report, say they, and we will report it.

Jeremiah not only had to bear the ridicule of the common people but also the possibility that they would carry out a threat to report him to the Jewish authorities and charge him with treason for predicting Babylonian conquest of Judah. Satan loves to use the fear of what *might* happen to keep believers from doing God's work.

10c. All my familiars watched for my halting, saying, Peradventure he will be enticed, and we shall prevail against him, and we shall take our revenge on him.

Jeremiah complained that all of his familiars (acquaintances) watched for him to slip and make a mistake. They said that they would wait for him to be enticed into saying something for which he could be accused. The implication was that they might get him sentenced to death, probably for treason.

All of us are apt to suffer somewhat from paranoia, at least in its milder forms of a persecution complex. Since ridicule may come to us for our belief in God, we will be tempted to blame Him for our predicament. We need to guard against this by maintaining a close, personal walk with the Lord and by finding the strengthening fellowship which comes through associating with other believers. "Perfect love casteth out fear" (I John 4:18). That love is best found demonstrated in the assembly of God's people.

C. Faith: 11

11a. But the Lord is with me as a mighty terrible one: ...

This referred to the Lord as a powerful warrior in the battle believers have with sinners. Faith motivates us to put our trust in the One Who is equal to every confrontation with earthly foes. We know that He and Christ are with us through the indwelling presence of the Holy Spirit.

11b. ... therefore my persecutors shall stumble, and they shall not prevail: they shall be greatly ashamed; for they shall not prosper: their everlasting confusion shall never be forgotten.

Jeremiah came to the conclusion that God would turn his situation around and bring judgment on his enemies. It was not *he* who would stumble, but *they*. It was not *they* who would prevail, but the *Lord*. All that they could look for was great shame. They could not prosper in their evil intentions. Their confusion (shame, disgrace, stigma) would never be forgotten.

We know that these predictions by Jeremiah came true. When Judah fell to the Babylonians, and they destroyed the city of Jerusalem in 586 B.C., the Jews who opposed the prophet were victims of the long siege (disease, malnutrition), slain in battle, or carried off into ignominious exile. The record of the fall of the kingdom of Judah was preserved in the records of history, including the Bible itself.

Evangelistic Emphasis

Jeremiah listened to his heart. There he discovered the strength he needed in the power of God's Spirit. The key to better living lies with God's Spirit in us. The same is true for us. We need the Spirit of God within us to help us with the difficult times.

Just look at the difficulty Jeremiah faced. No one listened to his message. Someone has said that prophets are either killed or ignored, and being ignored hurts worse. Even Jeremiah's friends were laughing at him. It is never easy to stand alone. Imagine Jeremiah caving in to peer pressure. That is exactly what would have happened without God's Spirit within Jeremiah.

Perhaps someone would complain that this approach is overly simplistic. Well, think about the available alternatives. I suppose Jeremiah could have joined an ignored prophet support group, if there had been such an organization. We certainly have options when we feel alone and unloved. There are counseling sessions, but isn't it simplistic to believe that an hour a week on the psychologist's couch will solve our spiritual problems? We could join a therapy group or read books about positive imaging. I'm not suggesting that these are bad things to do. They are not, however, magical solutions.

Suppose, on the other hand, that rather than a dependency upon psychology and secularism we opened all the windows of our soul to God's Spirit. Wouldn't our perspective be different when we brought all our burdens and aches and pains to the Lord? Wouldn't we be better equipped to handle the adversity of the world?

♦♦♦♦♦♦

Memory Selection:

If I say, "I will not mention him, or speak any more in his name," there is in my heart as it were a burning fire shut up in my bones, and I am weary with holding it in, and I cannot. - *Jeremiah 20:9*

Contrast the powerful testimony of Jeremiah with our guilty silence. He has a fire in the belly and feels compelled to speak the word of the Lord. We, however, scared by a society that no longer seems to listen, are reluctant to speak for the Lord. Perhaps we are discouraged. When was the last time you spoke to someone about his relationship with God?

Jeremiah is energized by the Spirit of God. His experience of God so dominates his life that he cannot help but preach. Even when he tries to be silent, the words about God just keep flowing. Even though Jeremiah experiences fear he cannot be quiet.

Jeremiah is a preacher with an unpopular message. The people either ignore him or laugh at him. He feels he is the laughingstock of the whole country. The fact is God calls everyone of us to preach with the same passion of Jeremiah. Will we be afraid? Yes. Will we be unpopular? Probably. Will we have a hard time? Yes. God will be with us and provide us with strength. Therefore, we preach Christ.

Weekday Problems

"I'm never going back to church," shouted Jim as he came in the door on Sunday afternoon.

"What in the world is wrong with you?" asked his wife as they entered the living room. She had never heard her husband so angry over church matters. As a matter of fact, he had always been a good member of the church. He was supportive of the pastor and the mintstry of the congregation. Something really had him disturbed. Jill, his wife, waited for Jim's response.

"I just don't think it is my responsibility to talk to people all over town about their relationship with Jesus Christ," Jim finally said. "I don't really know that much about the Bible," he remarked, "and, besides, isn't that witnessing supposed to be the preacher's job? What are we paying him to do?"

"Jim, are you afraid of what other people will think? asked Jill.

"Well, I suppose that's it. I get nervous when people start talking about religion. Shouldn't we save all that for church?"

*What can we tell Jim to help him develop a better theology of lay persons as witnesses for Christ?

*What are some other factors that cause people like Jim to be afraid of sharing their faith?

◆◆◆◆◆◆

Superintendent's Sermonette

We are intrigued by accounts of God preparing certain individuals within the womb to become His spokesmen. This was true of the prophet Jeremiah (Jer. 1:5). It was true of John the Baptist (Luke 1:13-17), Since God is sovereign, it is not presumptuous to conclude that He had a plan for every believer. He knew before we were born how we would respond to His plan of redemption, and He called us to Himself (Rom. 8:29-30). He even determined the works which we would do for Him (Eph. 2:10). We can feel a kinship to Jeremiah and John the Baptist, for God prepared us to serve Him, too.

Once we know that God has chosen us for His service, we have a responsibility to speak for Him. Jeremiah was reluctant to become God's spokesman, but the Lord made it evident that he could do the task to which he was appointed, and he could do it by saying what God told him to say. The power inherent in God's truth was thrilling, but it was counterbalanced by persecution from unbelievers who refused to hear and obey it. The same is true in our day. We have the most wonderful message in the world, but many will reject it and stay in their sins. We must not let this discourage us, even if it leads to scorn. God will be by our side.

JEREMIAH: PERSISTENT PROPHET

This Lesson In Your Life

When circumstances are beyond our control, how do we react? Jeremiah faced circumstances beyond his control. He received a powerful call from God to preach. Jeremiah felt confident, but then his message fell on deaf ears. He was ridiculed, mocked, and rejected. He did not understand.

Like Jeremiah, we too face circumstances that overwhelm us and confuse us. We come up against harsh realities. We are bombarded with complex questions and too few answers. From economic hard times to family problems, we all face circumstances beyond our control.

Most people are intimidated by situations they cannot control. We are often independent sorts, people who like to be in control. Life, however, is not parcelled out in small dosages that we can easily control. Like Jeremiah we can lose control of the situation through the acts of others. The question then becomes not "Why?" but "How?"

To ask "Why" there are circumstances beyond our control is a question not answerable in any human philosophical system. The best we can offer is that somehow the perfect will of God is involved. In the midst of difficult circumstances, all answers to the "why" question seem inadequate. So we will be better served by asking the "how."

Other people are overwhelmed by the circumstances of life and retreat into a fog of fear and anxiety. Such fear usually paralyzes people. They manage to rationalize themselves into accepting their circumstances as their just reward. They become like people whose only security is in the known hell which they inhabit.

Their security becomes their circumstances. Why? Because they can hide from responsibility. Jeremiah was tempted to give up and ignore his responsibility to preach. So are we all tempted. Remember the man by the pool whom Jesus asked if he wanted to be made whole? I always thought that everybody wanted to be well until Jesus' question opened my eyes. The man had been sick for thirty-eight years. He had no responsibility. He had accepted his fate and was now scared to live. Some people are scared to die, but many more are scared to live.

Opposite the negative coping skills there are some positive ones that deserve our attention: trust, patience, gratitude. The ability to trust God's larger purpose and plan can see us through tough circumstances. Bad times do not last forever. Our own sacred history tells us as much. There's Joseph delivered from slavery and imprisonment. There's Moses set free from Midian's wilderness to lead God's people out of Egypt. There's Job, his health, fortune, and family restored. There's Jesus raised from the dead on Easter Sunday. When we are down for the count, God is still standing. When we sink into the depths, underneath are the everlasting arms. When circumstances are beyond our control, they are within God's. Trust God and let go. They who wait upon the Lord shall renew their strength, cried Isaiah. As Paul confidently proclaims, "We know that all things work together for good to them that love God, to them who are the called according to his purpose." Romans 8:28.

With the basic assurances of God's presence and power, we, like Jeremiah, will not be able to restrain ourselves from proclaiming the word of God. After all, our task is faithful proclamation. The harvest is God's responsibility.

Seed Thoughts

1. When Jeremiah speaks of the "word of the Lord," what is he empahsizing?
Jeremiah is emphasizing that his message is God's word and not his own.

2. What are the implications of Jeremiah's being called before he was born?
God has a purpose for His world, His people, and His messengers. While we may not often see with the eyes of faith, God sees behind us and in front of us to accomplish His will.

3. What factors made Jeremiah reluctant to accept his call to serve as a prophet of God?
Jeremiah suggested that he was too young and that he was afraid. God answered these objections by promising to be with Jeremiah, and by touching his mouth and giving Jeremiah the words to say.

4. What does Jeremiah mean by the expression "balm in Gilead"?
The "balm in Gilead" was resin from the Styrax tree. Its primary use was for medicinal purposes. Jeremiah borrows the medical image to suggest that God's people are sin-sick and only God can be their "balm in Gilead."

5. In Jeremiah 9:1-3, what is God's attitude toward his people?
Actually there are two attitudes expressed by the Lord. First there is sympathy and compassion. Then there is disgust and contempt for the lying, deceiving, adulterous nation.

(PLEASE TURN PAGE)

---

1. When Jeremiah speaks of the "word of the Lord." what is he empahsizing?

2. What are the implications of Jeremiah's being called before he was born?

3. What factors made Jeremiah reluctant to accept his call to serve as a prophet of God?

4. What does Jeremiah mean by the expression "balm in Gilead"?

5. In Jeremiah 9:1-3, what is God's attitude toward his people?

6. What is the main cause of Judah's sin in the eyes of God?

7. Why does Jeremiah complain to the Lord in Jeremiah 20:7-8?

8. Jeremiah's accusation sounds blasphemous. How can we justify his anger?

9. How does Jeremiah manage to overcome his negative attitude?

10. What is Jeremiah's final response to the circumstances he faced?

(SEED THOUGHTS--Cont'd)

Jeremiah is emphasizing that his message is God's word and not his own.

God has a purpose for His world, His people, and His messengers. While we may not often see with the eyes of faith, God sees behind us and in front of us to accomplish His will.

Jeremiah suggested that he was too young and that he was afraid. God answered these objections by promising to be with Jeremiah, and by touching his mouth and giving Jeremiah the words to say.

The "balm in Gilead" was resin from the Styrax tree. Its primary use was for medicinal purposes. Jeremiah borrows the medical image to suggest that God's people are sin-sick and only God can be their "balm in Gilead."

Actually there are two attitudes expressed by the Lord. First there is sympathy and compassion. Then there is disgust and contempt for the lying, deceiving, adulterous nation.

The symptoms are lying, adultery, and falsehood. The primary sin: not knowing the Lord.

The prophet is discouraged. His message has not been well received and he believes people are laughing at him.

Jeremiah is being honest with the Lord. His crying out is a cry of pain, and is thus a prayer to the Lord.

The prophet reminds himself that the Lord is with him. Jeremiah depends upon the invincible protection of God.

In Jeremiah 20:13, Jeremiah breaks out in praise to the Lord. He borrows from the Psalms to celebrate the delivering power of the Lord.

6. **What is the main cause of Judah's sin in the eyes of God?**
The symptoms are lying, adultery, and falsehood. The primary sin: not knowing the Lord.

7. **Why does Jeremiah complain to the Lord in Jeremiah 20:7-8?**
The prophet is discouraged. His message has not been well received and he believes people are laughing at him.

8. **Jeremiah's accusation sounds blasphemous. How can we justify his anger?**
Jeremiah is being honest with the Lord. His crying out is a cry of pain, and is thus a prayer to the Lord.

9. **How does Jeremiah manage to overcome his negative attitude?**
The prophet reminds himself that the Lord is with him. Jeremiah depends upon the invincible protection of God.

10. **What is Jeremiah's final response to the circumstances he faced?**
In Jeremiah 20:13, Jeremiah breaks out in praise to the Lord. He borrows from the Psalms to celebrate the delivering power of the Lord.

December 6, 1992

God's Purpose Through Love

Hebrews 1

1 GOD, who at sundry times and in divers manners spake in time past unto the fathers by the prophets,
2 Hath in these last days spoken unto us by *his* Son whom he hath appointed heir of all things, by whom also he made the worlds;
3 Who being the brightness of his glory, and the express image of his person, and upholding all things by the word of his power, when he had by himself purged our sins, sat down on the right hand of the Majesty on high;
4 Being made so much better than the angels, as he hath by inheritance obtained a more excellent name than they.

Ephesians 1

3 Blessed be the God and Father of our Lord Jesus Christ, who hath blessed us with all spiritual blessings in heavenly places in Christ:
4 According as he hath chosen us in him before the foundation of world, that we should be holy and without blame before him in love:
5 Having predestinated us unto the adoption of children by Jesus Christ to himself, according to the good pleasure of his will,
6 To the praise of the glory of his grace, wherein he hath made us accepted in the beloved.
7 In whom we have redemption through his blood, the forgiveness of sins, according to the riches of his grace;
8 Wherein he hath abounded toward us in all wisdom and prudence;
9 Having made known unto us the mystery of his will, according to his good pleasure which he hath purposed in himself:
10 That in the dispensation of the fulness of times he might gather together in one all things in Christ, both which are in heaven, and which are on earth; even in him:
11 In whom also we have obtained an inheritance, being predestinated according to the purpose of him who worketh all things after the counsel of his own will:
12 That we should be to the praise of his glory, who first trusted in Christ.
13 In whom ye also trusted, after that ye heard the word of truth, the gospel of your salvation: in whom also after that ye believed, ye were sealed with that holy Spirit of promise,
14 Which is the earnest of our inheritance until the redemption of the purchased possession, unto the praise of his glory.

◆◆◆◆◆◆

◀ **Memory Selection**
Hebrews 1:1,2

◀ **Devotional Reading**
Ephesians 3:14-21

◀ **Background Scripture**
Hebrews 1:1-4
Ephesians 1:3-14
◀ **Printed Scripture**
Hebrews 1:1-4
Ephesians 1:3-14

Teacher's Target

Each year at this season we like to recall the incarnation of God in Christ, and the first three lessons of this quarter are designed to do that. There could have been no incarnation (enfleshment) if God had not loved man and planned for his redemption from sin. Divine love was the driving force which produced "the Lamb slain from the foundation of the world" (Rev. 13:8). What was decided in heaven in eternity past became reality on the earth several millenia later. The Babe of Bethlehem became the Savior at Calvary.

Help your students to see the Lord's master plan of redemption and the essential role played in it by His beloved Son, Jesus Christ. Hebrews 1:1-4 and Ephesians 1:3-14 provide rich doctrinal teaching on this subject. Only Christ, the God-Man, could span the gulf between God and man. Only in Him can believers be set in heavenly places and know the reality of being sealed by the Holy Spirit as belonging to God for eternity.

Lesson Introduction

Study non-Christian religions and cults, and you will note that one persistent theme is self-salvation. In other words, they tell you what *you* must do in order to be free from evil, however they may define it. In Christianity the emphasis is on divine mercy and grace. It is *God* Who withholds deserved punishment from sinners. It is *God* Who gives believers unmerited favor. Both of our lesson texts stress God as the One Who was and is active in our salvation.

Hebrews 1:1-4 tells us that God spoke in the past through His prophets. In these "last days," meaning the age of grace, He has spoken to us through His beloved Son, and the record of this is glorious. Ephesians 1:3-14 tells us what our position is in Christ. It goes back to eternity past and reveals how God chose us to be holy and blameless before Him in love. This was all made possible because God sent His Son to redeem us and His Spirit to seal us unto our purchased possession in eternity future. God gives, and we receive by faith. This makes Christianity unique.

Teaching Outline

I. Son: Heb. 1:1-4
   A. God spoke: 1
   B. God speaks: 2-4
II. Source: Eph. 1:3-6
   A. God blessed: 3
   B. God chose: 4-6
III. Summons: Eph. 1:7-12
   A. God saved: 7-8
   B. God revealed: 9-12
IV. Sealing: Eph. 1:13-14
   A. God sealed: 13
   B. God promised: 14

Daily Bible Readings

Mon. A Song for a Festival
Ps. 81:1-10
Tue. The Work of Christ
Col. 1:15-19
Wed. Prayer of Thanksgiving
Rom. 1:8-15
Thu. Called to Be God's Son
I Chron. 17:1-14
Fri. God's Chosen Son
Ps. 2:1-7
Sat. God Is Faithful and Gives Blessings - *Heb. 6:1-12*
Sun. Spiritual Blessings through Christ
Eph. 1:3-14

December 6, 1992

VERSE BY VERSE

I. Son: Heb. 1:1-4

A. God spoke: 1

1. **God, who at sundry times and in divers manners spake in time past unto the fathers by the prophets,**

We do not know for sure who wrote the epistle to the Hebrews. Suggested names have been Paul, Luke, Silas, Apollos, and Timothy. Whoever the author was, he wanted to show how Christianity built upon Judaism which preceded it and was superior to it. He said that God had spoken at sundry (various) times and in diver (different) manners in the past to the fathers (ancestors) by means of His prophets. We know that God used visions, dreams, angels direct speech, thunder, lightning, and other methods to get His message across to men. The records of many of these experiences became parts of the books of divine revelation contained in the Old Testament.

B. God speaks: 2-4

2a. **Hath in these last days spoken unto us by his Son, ...**

Looking beyond the Old Testament times, the author of Hebrews said that God had spoken in "these last days" to first-century believers by means of His Son. Although Jesus Christ had ascended to heaven before the epistle to the Hebrews was written, God was still speaking to people by means of His Son. This has remained true throughout the age of grace, which is now almost two thousand years long and will last until Christ comes back. The most extensive and clear revelation of God to men was made when Christ ministered on the earth. He was the living Word to make God real to men.

2b. **....whom he hath appointed heir of all things, by whom also he made the worlds;**

The remainder of our brief passage from Hebrews is devoted to describing the uniqueness and superiority of Christ. He is described as the God-appointed Heir to all things.This is appropriate, for He was the One used by God to make the universe in the first place. This is supported by John 1:3 and by Colossians 1:16-17. It is interesting to note that the children of God will be joint-heirs with Christ (Rom. 8:17)

3a. **Who being the brightness of his glory, and the express image of his person, and upholding all things by the word of his power,...**

This describes Christ as equal to His heavenly Father in brightness and glory (cf. John 1:14), He was called the express image (perfect likeness) of His Father. He was shown to be the One Who upholds (holds together) all things by the word of His power (cf. Col. 1:17),

3b. **...when he had by himself purged our sins, sat down on the right hand of the Majesty on high;**

Here Christ is presented as the Savior Who shed His precious blood to purge the sins of men who put their trust in Him. He is seen as the ascended Savior seated at the right hand of God in heaven. Stephen saw Him there (Acts 7:55-56).

4. **Being made so much better than the angels, as he hath by inheritance obtained a more excellent name than they.**

Christ was and is superior to men

and to angels. They were all created, but He was with His Father in eternity past. He is superior because of Who He is and what He has done. Men may be called the sons of God when adopted into His family following their redemption (Rom. 8:14-15; 1 John 3:2). Even angels are called sons of God (Job 1:6; 38:7). However, only Christ has the name or title of being *the* Son of God (cf. Phil. 2:9-11).

II. Source: Eph. 1:3-6

A. God blessed: 3

3. Blessed be the God and Father of our Lord Jesus Christ, who hath blessed us with all spiritual blessings in heavenly places in Christ:

Verses 3-14 actually comprise one long, involved sentence, with each verse building grammatically on the one preceding it. Scholars who supplied periods at the end of verses 6 and 12 failed to impede the smooth flow from beginning to end. The passage begins with a word of praise for God, the Father of the Lord Jesus Christ. That potential is theirs because they are positioned with Christ in heavenly places. Believers should spend their lives seeking to make their spiritual *practice* conform as much as possible to their spiritual *position*. Even the most mature Christian has room for improvement.

B. God chose: 4-6

4. According as he hath chosen us in him before the foundation of the world, that we should be holy and without blame before him in love:

Romans 8:29-30 sheds light on this truth. It was because God foreknew who would be saved by faith in His Son that He predestinated, called, and justified them, and He will glorify them when the right time comes. This took place before the earth was created. The passage of time has simply confirmed what God decided in eternity past. We need not think that God arbitrarily chose some to be saved and others damned. Whoever believes on Christ will not perish but will find eternal life (John 3:16). This made Christ the *potential* Savior of all men. However, He became the *actual* Savior only of those who put their trust in Him (I Tim. 4:10).

In the latter half of Ephesians 1:4 we see the character of Christians. They are to be holy in the sense that they partake of God's holy character. They are counted righteous (without blame) because they have been made "the righteousness of God in him (Christ)" (II Cor. 5:21). It is God's love in Christ to us which makes this possible.

5. Having predestinated us unto the adoption of children by Jesus Christ to himself, according to the good pleasure of his will.

God has always wanted men to be saved (2 Pet. 3:9). However, He could not *force* them to love Him and His Son or accept Him as Savior, for then it would lose its significance. It was because He knew those who would welcome being adopted into the family of faith that He predestinated (elected, chose, appointed, determined) them to be saved. He did this because it suited His plan and purpose.

6. To the praise of the glory of his grace, wherein he hath made us accepted in the beloved.

Paul praised the Lord for the glory connected with His grace. It was this unmerited favor by God which made it possible for believers to be accepted by Him because they were *in* Christ.

III. Summons: Eph. 1:7-12

A. God saved: 7-8

7. In whom we have redemption through his blood, the forgiveness of sins, according to the riches of his grace;

Verses 7 and 8 lead up to verses 9-12, which describe the summons which will come in the end times when God gathers together all believers in Christ. Verse 7 tells us that it was in Christ, "the beloved" (vs. 6), that believers have been redeemed (bought back, ransomed) from Satan's grasp. It was through the shedding of and believers' acceptance by faith of that atonement that redemption was possible (1 Pet. 1:18-19).

8. Wherein he hath abounded toward us in all wisdom and prudence;

It was in this redemption that God abounded toward us (lavished upon us, showered upon us, poured out on us) His wisdom (insight) and prudence (understanding). We may not comprehend it, but we have to accept God's superior wisdom demonstrated in His master plan of salvation.

B. God revealed: 9-12

9. Having made known unto us the mystery of his will, according to his good pleasure which he hath purposed in himself:
In the Bible, a mystery is a truth once hidden but then made known. It was through the life and death of Christ that His Father's will was made known to men. This sovereign plan of God could be ignored or ridiculed, but it could not change.

10. That in the dispensation of the fulness of times he might gather together in one all things in Christ, both which are in heaven, and which are on earth; even in him:
In the final dispensation (administration of God's dealing with men), the Lord will bring things together in Christ (Phil. 2:9-11). "When the time is ripe he will gather us all together from wherever we are—in heaven or on earth—to be with him in Christ, forever" (Living Bible).

11. In whom also we have obtained an inheritance, being predestinated according to the purpose of him who worketh all things after the counsel of his own will:
It is because believers are *in* Christ (identified with Him by faith) that they will share in His inheritance. "If [we are God's adopted] children, then [we are] heirs; heirs of God, and join theirs with Christ; if so be that we suffer with him, that we may be also glorified together" (Rom. 8:17). Even as He predestinated us to salvation, so it is that He predestinated us to our inheritance as joint heirs with Christ. God planned what He wanted to do, and He will do it.

12. That we should be to the praise of his glory, who first trusted in Christ.
Note how verses 11 and 12 repeat the wording found in verses 5 and 6. Paul had praised God for the glory of His grace and says that believers should return that praise. First-century Christians began this process, and subsequent generations were to continue glorifying Him.

IV. Sealing: Eph. 1:13-14

A. God sealed: 13

13a. In whom, ye also trusted, after that ye heard the word of truth, the gospel of your salvation: ...
It was in Him (Christ, vs. 12) that believers placed their trust after the word of truth (gospel or good news of salvation) had been preached to them and they had accepted it. By this act of faith they immediately were cleansed of sin, justified before God, and regenerated. A whole new panorama of life here and in eternity opened up before them as a result of their decision. Both Jewish and Gentile believers in Ephesus had been brought into the same household of faith in this manner (Eph. 2:11-22).

13b. ...in whom also after that ye believed, ye were sealed with that holy Spirit of promise,
In addition to cleansing, justification, and regeneration, believers had been sealed by God by means of His Holy Spirit. This means that they had been marked as belonging to God. It was His stamp of ownership after having bought them out of Satan's grasp through the blood of Christ. The promised Holy Spirit came to indwell believers on the Day of Pentecost (Acts 2:1-4).

B. God promised: 14

14. Which is the earnest of our inheritance until the redemption of the purchased possession, unto the praise of his glory.
It was the sealing of believers by the Holy Spirit which became the earnest (pledge, promise, downpayment) of believers' inheritance. Salvation of their souls was the first step in ultimate salvation of their bodies. When Christ comes, He will change the perishable bodies of believers into imperishable and glorified bodies "For this corruptible [body] must put on incorruption, and this mortal [body] must put on immortality" (I Cor. 15: 53). We can be as sure of this promise as we are of our soul's salvation today.

GOD'S PURPOSE THROUGH LOVE

Evangelistic Emphasis

In an earlier time, God revealed Himself to the world by freeing the descendants of Abraham, Isaac and Jacob from slavery and shaping them into a community.

Their mandate was a special one, unique to the nations of the ancient world. They were to live by righteousness and justice, and to be faithful to the covenant initiated with them by their God. Through their example, they would be seen as a "light" by which other nations might find their way.

The writers who chronicled the history of Israel told of times of great devotion and faithfulness, and also about long periods when the people gave up and yielded to the pressures to become just another violents superstitious tribe like their neighbors. These same chroniclers also wrote that no matter whether the people kept their side of the covenant, God was always steadfast in His love for them.

In the New Testament books of Hebrews and Ephesians, the coming of Christ is viewed in light of this great history. God's sending of the Messiah was the great climactic act of His love, and signalled that from now on, all the nations of the earth would be included in His covenant promise.

The Gospel message would now go out to touch every life of every human being. It was as though Christians were entrusted with the happy task of finding people who were heirs to a great fortune, given them by an ancestor they never knew. And since these people neither knew about the ancestor nor the inheritance, they were living as though they were poor. The exciting role of the Christian would be that of one undeserving heir telling other unsuspecting heirs of our mutal inheritance. Only the inheritance would be worth far more than any material treasure!

◆◆◆◆◆◆

Memory Selection

God, who at sundry times and in divers manners spake in time past unto the fathers by the prophets, hath in these last days spoken to us by his Son. *Hebrews 1:1-2*

In ancient times, God spoke only to certain chosen individuals, through certain persons called prophets, with specific messages that were limited in time and scope.

Through this process of revelation, a heritage of what could be know about God developed over time. The oracles of the prophets were recorded and preserved; they were studied, meditated upon, even set to music. "Thus saith the Lord" became a hallmark of a prophet's utterance, and was revered by the faithful.

Yet something was missing, which the writer of Hebrews declares is the most important dimension of who God is: God now reveals Himself through His Son!

Instead of God's revelation being only to certain people, now it would be to all people. Instead of God choosing prophets to deliver the message, now he send His own nearest and dearest. Instead of the message being for a limited time or place, now God's revelation is for all time—the most complete, most personal, most loving, most universal disclosure God has ever made.

December 6, 1992

Weekday Problems

Sam owned a convenience store that was open all night in an area that was dangerous after dark. Even though only a little cash was kept in the register, Sam lived in fear that someone would try to rob the store. So he kept two loaded guns under the counter, ready for whatever would happen.

One night he heard a noise in the back room. Taking his gun, he crept quietly to the door, and saw a figure crouched over, putting something into a large trash bag. Cocking the gun, he shouted to the figure to drop the bag. Screaming "Don't shoot!" the figure started to turn around. Responding to the sudden movement, Sam pulled the trigger. He ran to see who this intruder was, and turned over the body to look into the face of... his own daughter!

*How might this tragedy have been avoided?
*Is there any way faith in God can help us deal with our fears?
*Seen as a kind of modern "parable," what can this episode tell us about the way God has chosen to reveal Himself to us?

♦♦♦♦♦♦

Superintendent's Sermonette

The church exists in order to draw people to Jesus Christ and persuade them to accept Him as their personal Savior from sin. The texts we study today are perfectly suited to that purpose. If you are not a born again Christian, pay close attention to the doctrinal teaching of these texts. If you are a believer, be praying for those who ought to make decisions for Christ today. Never lose sight of this primary goal for the body of Christ. Be prepared to discuss the plan of salvation with unbelievers either inside or outside of the church on Sunday or any other day of the week.

Hebrews 1:1-4 paints a brief but brilliant word-picture of Christ as the beloved Son of God sent to the earth to represent Him to men through His ministry in life and then by His atoning death on the cross at Calvary. He ascended to His former glory in heaven at God's right hand, and we may inherit all things by identifying ourselves with Him by faith. Ephesians 1:3-14 lifts believers to their rightful place beside Christ and explains how this was made possible because He implemented God's master plan of redemption. The work of the Holy Spirit in sealing believers put all three Members of the Holy Trinity into union in our glorious salvation.

GOD'S PURPOSE THROUGH LOVE

This Lesson in Your Life

We are privileged to enjoy being part of the greatest family in the world, the family of God. Sometimes it's hard to grasp the magnificence of this gift; it's easier to focus on the immediate events of our own personal lives, our work, our family, the local church and community activities.

We need to step back occasionally and reflect on the great scheme of history, to try to feel the deep longings of millions of people over thousands of years who have suffered under oppression, persecution, tyranny, hunger, disease, and early death; far more often than not, this has been the common lot of most of the world's inhabitants. Unless we stop and think about the privileges we enjoy, too often we end up taking our daily blessing for granted.

Both Hebrews and Ephesians, especially the passages in today's readings, help us prepare for the season of Christmas by seeing the great scope of God's revelation, and how the coming of the Messiah brought it all to a climax.

The Devotional Reading (Ephesians 3:14-21) helps us offer a hymn of praise to God for the privilege of being part of the "whole family in heaven and earth" (verse 15). Through Christ we are enabled "to know the love of Christ which passes knowledge" (verse 19). Logically that's impossible— to know what is beyond knowledge. It's simply Paul's way of helping us say what words cannot express about the treasure of faith which we too often take for granted.

Hebrews in its own way makes a similar point: that we are privileged to be part of God's family because He has become one with us through the sending of His Son. In other times God sent messengers in the form of lawgivers, judges, kings, priests, or prophets. But in our time, God reveals Himself more fully, more intimately, through a person.

Hebrews goes on to explain how the Son of God actually fulfills all the other roles of God's earlier messengers— how Christ is priest, prophet, and king, so that now we can see more fully than ever why God chose to relate to human beings through these other kinds of messengers.

It's the difference between God's telling us in words, and His showing us in person, the true reality of who He is— loving Father— and who we are— His children.

The teachings in Hebrews and Ephesians go on to make a further point— that it was God's purpose all along to reveal Himself fully to us in this way. It's as though God was unfolding the plan only as far as people could see it— the way a parent tries to answer a child's question in words that are appropriate for the child's level of understanding. Thus when we consider that God has fully revealed Himself in Christ, we are also saying that God is entrusting this knowledge to us because we're worth it! God loves us, He trusts us, and He invites us to join Him in carrying out the joyful task of telling the world.

May we in the coming weeks prepare ourselves to celebrate this greatest gift of all. We are recipients of the priceless gift of being part of the great world family of God, the church. It is called infinite and eternal, not bound by time and space, yet life in the kingdom is also practical. Each day we are strengthened by a "power that worketh in us" given to us by the One who "is able to do exceeding abundantly above all that we ask or think,"

Can you think of a greater gift than this?

Seed Thoughts

1. Who is to be part of the family of God, if the will of God is truly honored?
Every family in heaven and on earth, Ephesians 3:15.

2. What great "riches" does God want to grant us?
His spiritual power for our inner selves, Ephesians 3:16.

3. Where can you find Christ alive and at work today?
In your heart, by faith, Ephesians 3:17.

4. What great knowledge does God want to reveal to us?
The love of Christ, "which surpasses knowledge," Ephesians 3:19.

5. What great strength is available to the person of faith?
God's ability to do far more than we can ever ask or think, Ephesians 3:20.

(PLEASE TURN PAGE)

---

1. Who is to be part of the family of God, if the will of God is truly honored?

2. What great "riches" does God want to grant us?

3. Where can you find Christ alive and at work today?

4. What great knowledge does God want to reveal to us?

5. What great strength is available to the person of faith?

6. What is the chief difference in the way God communicated to people before the coming of Christ?

7. How is it appropriate to think of ourselves as inheritors of a great fortune, spiritually speaking?

8. In what way is Christ described as superior even to angels?

9. Are the teachings of doctrine and the celebration of worship always two separate experiences?

10. Does the Bible teach that God accommodates Himself to our human limitations, like a parent who uses simple language and concepts when talking with a child?

Every family in heaven and on earth, Ephesians 3:15.

His spiritual power for our inner selves, Ephesians 3:16.

In your heart, by faith, Ephesians 3:17.

The love of Christ, "which surpasses knowledge," Ephesians 3:19.

God's ability to do far more than we can ever ask or think, Ephesians 3:20.

Earlier, God spoke at different times and places through appointed messengers; through Christ people are now in touch with God. Hebrews 1:1-2.

Christ is "the heir of all things," Hebrews 1:2

As the heir of all that God has made, Christ's inheritance is called "more excellent" than that of either earthly or heavenly messengers, Hebrews 1:40.

Not always; all of the passages in today's readings from Ephesians are part of a long hymn of praise, yet they unfold profound teaching.

Yes. Our reading today, in Ephesians 1:10, describes God acting "in the fullness of time"—in other words, when we were ready.

(SEED THOUGHTS--Cont'd)

6. What is the chief difference in the way God communicated to people before the coming of Christ?
Earlier, God spoke at different times and places through appointed messengers; through Christ people are now in touch with God. Hebrews 1:1-2.

7. How is it appropriate to think of ourselves as inheritors of a great fortune, spiritually speaking?
Christ is "the heir of all things," Hebrews 1:2

8. In what way is Christ described as superior even to angels?
As the heir of all that God has made, Christ's inheritance is called "more excellent" than that of either earthly or heavenly messengers, Hebrews 1:40.

9. Are the teachings of doctrine and the celebration of worship always two separate experiences?
Not always; all of the passages in today's readings from Ephesians are part of a long hymn of praise, yet they unfold profound teaching.

10. Does the Bible teach that God accommodates Himself to our human limitations, like a parent who uses simple language and concepts when talking with a child?
Yes. Our reading today, in Ephesians 1:10, describes God acting "in the fullness of time"—in other words, when we were ready.

December 13, 1992

God's Promise to Zechariah

Luke 1

5 There was in the days of Herod, the king of Ju-dae-a, a certain priest named Zach-a-ri´-as, of the course of A-bi´-a: and his wife *was* of the daughters of Aaron, and her name *was* Elisabeth.
6 And they were both righteous before God, walking in all the commandments and ordinances of the Lord blameless.
7 And they had no child, because that Elisabeth was barren, and they both were now well stricken in years.
8 And it came to pass, that while he executed the priest's office before God in the order of his course,
9 According to the custom of the priest's office, his lot was to burn incense when he went into the temple of the Lord.
10 And the whole multitude of the people were praying without at the time of incense.
11 And there appeared unto him an angel of the Lord standing on the right side of the altar of incense.
12 And when Zach-a-ri´-as saw *him* he was troubled, and fear fell upon him.
13 But the angel said unto him, Fear not, Zach-a-ri´-as: for thy prayer is heard; and thy wife Elisabeth shall bear thee a son, and thou shalt call his name John.
14 And thou shalt have joy and gladness; and many shall rejoice at his birth.
15 For he shall be great in the sight of the Lord, and shall drink neither wine nor strong drink; and he shall be filled with the Holy" Ghost, even from his mother's womb.
16 And many of the children of Israel shall he turn to the Lord their God.
17 And he shall go before him in the spirit and power of E-li´-as, TO TURN THE HEARTS OF THE FATHERS TO THE CHILDREN, and the disobedient to the wisdom of the just; to make ready a people prepared for the Lord.

◆◆◆◆◆◆

◀ **Memory Selection**
Luke 1:13

◀ **Devotional Reading**
Luke 1:67-79

◀ **Background Scripture**
Luke 1 : 1-25

◀ **Printed Scripture**
Luke 1:5-17

GOD'S PROMISE TO ZECHARIAH

Teacher's Target

Paul called Luke "the beloved physician" (Col. 4:14). He traveled with Paul on various journeys, as shown in the book of Acts. Luke made great contributions to the New Testament, authoring the gospel bearing his name and the book of Acts. Both were written to a man named Theophilus (Luke 1:1-4; Acts 1:1-2). Luke began his gospel with an announcement of the birth of John the Baptist, the relative and forerunner of Jesus Christ. Our text deals with the parents of John, Zacharias and Elisabeth, and with an angel of the Lord,

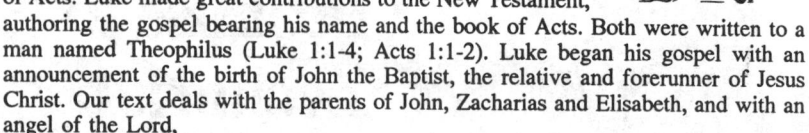

Help your students to appreciate the importance of God's promise to Zacharias both in literal terms and in Messianic significance. It was a divine miracle for the aged, barren couple to have a child, and it was a divine plan which was implemented when John was sent as herald for the coming Messiah. We also study the unusual phenomenon of John being filled with the Holy Spirit while still in the womb. We learn of a prophecy concerning his future ministry similar to that of Elijah.

Note: The name Zacharias, as it appears in the Authorized Version, is used throughout this lesson, rather than Zachariah or Zechariah, which is used in some other versions.

Lesson Introduction

Four hundred years of prophetic silence had elapsed between the completion of the Old Testament and the formation of the New Testament. Except for a brief period under the Maccabees in the second century before Christ, the Jews had remained under Gentile domination. They were now under the Roman yoke, although Herod the Great had some measure of autonomy as the king. However, there was soon to be a message proclaiming the coming of a new king. Jews who felt this would fulfill Messianic prophecies looked for the arrival of a political leader from among themselves.

Isaiah 40:3-5 had predicted the coming of a messenger who would prepare the way for the coming of the Lord. This messenger was to be John the Baptist. He was the last of the prophets pointing ahead to the Messiah, and yet he was to be the first of the prophets pointing to Him during His ministry. As with Elijah of old, John walked in a spirit of power given to him by the Lord.

Teaching Outline

I. Absence: Luke 1:5-7
   A. Coupled: 5
   B. Compliant: 6
   C. Childless: 7
II. Angel: Luke 1:8-12
   A. Appointment: 8-10
   B. Appearance: 11
   C. Alarm: 12
III. Announcement: Luke 1:13-17
   A. Marvel: 13-14
   B. Ministry: 15-17

Daily Bible Readings

Mon. Obedience to God
Ps. 128
Tue. God's Grace
Ps. 65:1-8
Wed. Giving Praise
Ps. 66:1-9
Thu. Giving Thanks
Ps. 67
Fri. Zacharias and the Angel
Luke 1:5-17
Sat. Zacharias Is Speechless
Luke 1:18-25
Sun. A Song for a Festival
Ps. 81:1-10

December 13, 1992

VERSE BY VERSE

I. Absence: Luke 1:5-7

A. Coupled: 5

5a. There was in the days of Herod, the king of Judaea, a certain priest named Zacharias, of the course of Abia:...

The event described happened during the reign of Herod the Great. He was of Edomite descent but supported the Jewish religion. An able but vicious and corrupt man, he pleased the Jews by greatly improving their temple in Jerusalem. Zacharias was a priest who belonged to the course (division) of Abia (or Abijah), one of twenty-four such divisions of priests which formed family lines descending from Aaron the brother of Moses and Miriam and the first high priest in Israel.

5b. ...and his wife was of the daughters of Aaron, and her name was Elisabeth.

Zacharias was married to Elisabeth, who also descended from Aaron. The angel Gabriel later called her the cousin of Mary (Luke 1:36), although scholars speculate whether or not they were first cousins. This couple lived in a community in the hill country of Judah (Luke 1:39).

B. Compliant: 6

6. And they were both righteous before God, walking in all the commandments and ordinances of the Lord blameless.

Luke declared that Zacharias and Elisabeth were upright individuals who walked according to all of the moral and ceremonial regulations required by the Lord and His law. We accept this as a general description of this couple, although we realize that they could not be human and sinless at the same time.

C. Childless: 7

7. And they had no child, because that Elisabeth was barren, and they both were now well stricken in years.

Barrenness was considered to be a great problem in that culture at that time. In younger years, it could be attributed to Elisabeth. Now that they both were old, it could be attributed to Zacharias, as well, as he mentioned later (Luke 1:18). It is perhaps significant that nothing is mentioned about them being bitter over this absence of a child, and we assume that they counted it as God's will. It was an assumption which was soon to change.

II. Angel: Luke 1:8-12

A. Appointment: 8-10

8. And it came to pass, that while he executed the priest's office before God in the order of his course,

9. According to the custom of the priest's office, his lot was to burn incense when he went into the temple of the Lord.

So many priests had descended from Aaron that all could not serve in the temple at the same time. They had to take turns, and it was time for Zacharias to serve with other members of his course (division). Lots were drawn to see who would serve at the altars, and Zacharias had been appointed to burn incense at the altar maintained for that purpose. It was an appropriate setting for the thing which was about to happen to him.

10. And the whole multitude of the people were praying without at the time of incense.

Men and women were standing and praying outside of the altar area, but they could look over toward it. They knew pretty well how long the ceremony of offering incense took, but it was to be prolonged this time. Verse 21 tells us, "And the people waited for Zacharias, and marvelled that he tarried so long in the temple."

B. Appearance: 11

11. And there appeared unto him an angel of the Lord standing on the right side of the altar of incense.

Verse 19 makes it clear that this was the angel named Gabriel. He described himself as one who stood in the presence of God and who had been sent by God to speak to Zacharias and show him glad tidings. He next went to Nazareth to announce the coming birth of Jesus to the virgin Mary (vss. 26-38).

C. Alarm: 12

12. And when Zacharias saw him, he was troubled, and fear fell upon him.

It is not difficult to understand that Zacharias was alarmed when he saw Gabriel standing near the altar. He became afraid, perhaps wondering if he had done something wrong in his offering of incense which would merit a divine rebuke or punishment. We note that Mary was later troubled and fearful when Gabriel appeared and spoke to her (vss. 28-30).

III. Announcement: Luke 1:13-17

A. Marvel: 13-14

13a. But the angel said unto him, Fear not, Zacharias: for thy prayer is heard;...

Gabriel spoke quickly to calm the fear felt by Zacharias. This was to be no rebuke or punishment for service performed. On the contrary, it was to be an announcement that the old priest's prayer had been heard by God in heaven.

Zacharias may have wondered what prayer this was, especially since he was so old that he had probably given up praying for a child for some time.

13b. ...and thy wife Elisabeth shall bear thee a son, and thou shalt call his name John.

Now came a marvelous announcement by Gabriel. He said that Elisabeth would conceive and bear a son in her old age, and that son was to be named John. Zacharias would not believe it (vs. 20). We might wonder if we would have believed it if we had been in his situation. One outstanding precedent, of course, had been the conception and birth of Isaac to Abraham and Sarah in their old age, but Zacharias may not have thought of that.

14. And thou shalt have joy and gladness; and many shall rejoice at his birth.

Gabriel must have seen the shock on the face of Zacharias at this unusual news, but he plunged ahead with a description of how John's birth was going to affect those who witnessed it. He said that Zacharias would experience joy and gladness, and he said that many others would rejoice when John was born. We know that Elisabeth's neighbors and relatives rejoiced with her at John's birth (vs. 58). Many others would subsequently rejoice over this event as John's ministry increased.

B. Ministry: 15-17

15a. For he shall be great in the sight of the Lord,...

It was obvious that John was called to a ministry even before he was born. Gabriel said that he was going to be great in God's estimation, and there could be no higher evaluation than that. It was Jesus Himself Who later said, "Among those that are born of women there is not a greater prophet than John the Baptist" (Luke 7:28). This commendation may have come partly because of his faithfulness in service and partly because of his position as the forerunner and herald of Christ.

15b. ...and shall drink neither wine nor strong drink;...

This suggested that John was to live a life similar to that of a Nazarite, consecrating himself wholly to his service for God. He was to allow nothing to distract him from his mission.

15c. ...and he shall be filled with the Holy Ghost, even from his mother's womb.

This is one of those scripture references which make us pause before we try to categorize people regarding when and how they are filled with the Spirit of God. Here was a case where a fetus in the womb would be suffused with the Holy Spirit. We know that this prediction came true when Mary went to visit Elisabeth. "When Elisabeth heard the salutation [greeting] of Mary, the babe leaped in her womb; and Elisabeth was filled with the Holy Ghost" (vs. 41).

16. And many of the children of Israel shall he turn to the Lord their God.

Gabriel predicted that Jews would be turned to the Lord by the ministry of John the Baptist. Details regarding this may be found in Matthew 3:1-12, Mark 1:1-8, Luke 3:1-18, and John 1:6-8 and 15-36. Mark 1:4-5 summarizes it this way—" John did baptize in the wilderness [north of the Dead Sea], and preach the baptism of repentance for the remission of sins. And there went out unto him all the land of Judaea, and they of Jerusalem, and were all baptized of him in the river of Jordan, confessing their sins."

17a. And he shall go before him in the spirit and power of Elias, to turn the hearts of the fathers to the children, and the disobedient to the wisdom of the just; ...

This sounds very similar to Malachi 4:5-6—"Behold, I will send you Elijah the prophet before the coming of the great and dreadful day of the Lord: and he shall turn the heart of the fathers to the children, and the heart of the children to their fathers, lest I come and smite the earth with a curse." Gabriel told Zacharias that John would be like Elijah, who had a rugged spirit and power for serving God. John would go before the Messiah to prepare the way for Him. "He will soften adult hearts to become like little children's, and will change disobedient minds to the wisdom of faith" (Living Bible).

17b. ...to make ready a people prepared for the Lord.

We assume that this referred to preparing people for the coming of the Messiah, for this was the expressed goal which John proclaimed during his ministry in the wilderness. When he saw Jesus coming one day, he said, "Behold the Lamb of God, which taketh away the sin of the world" (John 1:29). Speaking of Jesus, he later said, "He must increase, but I must decrease" (John 3:30).

Jesus made it clear that the "Elijah" who was to come, as foretold in Malachi 4:5, was actually John the Baptist. When he and Peter, James, and John had come down from the mount of transfiguration, His disciples asked him, "Why then say the scribes that Elias [Elijah] must first come? And Jesus answered and said unto them, Elias truly shall first come, and restore all things. But I say unto you, That Elias is come already, and they knew him not, but have done unto him whatsoever they listed [liked, referring to his beheading by order of Herod Antipas]. Likewise shall also the Son of man suffer of them. Then the disciples understood that he spake unto them of John the Baptist" (Matt. 17:10-13).

In order to complete our thoughts regarding Zacharias, we need to look further into the first chapter of Luke's gospel. When Zacharias questioned Gabriel's announcement of John's birth because both he and Elisabeth were beyond childbearing age, the angel said that the priest would be stricken dumb. When Zacharias came out of the temple, he could not speak to the people who had been wondering what took him a long time in there. After he finished his priestly appointment, he went back home. Elisabeth did conceive and was six months pregnant when Gabriel went to Nazareth to tell Mary about the coming birth of Jesus (vss. 18-26).

After John was born, neighbors and relatives gathered to rejoice with Zacharias and Elisabeth. They wanted to name him after his father, but Elisabeth insisted that he be named John. After the speechless Zacharias confirmed this in writing, God released his impediment and he spoke a Spirit-filled prophecy regarding John and the Messiah to come (vss. 57-79).

Evangelistic Emphasis

When God gets ready to do a new thing in our lives, he always gives us plenty of preparation.

Our spiritual growth requires us always to be preparing ourselves for new challenges.

John the Baptist is known as a "forerunner" who prepares the way for the coming of the Messiah.

This idea of forerunner forms a thread throughout Scripture. Israel's judges were forerunners of her kings. Samuel in particular prepared the people for the transition to the monarchy. The prophets prepared their people for both tragedy such as their captivity and for triumph, as in their return.

One problem often seemed to surface: the people equated change with discomfort. To do what was necessary to prepare for the future met with stiff resistance.

The most dramatic example: after 400 years of slavery, the descendants of Abraham, Isaac and Jacob had forgotten who they were. The slave mentality had taken over. They were suspicious of Moses and fearful of what would happen once they were free. On their way to the Promised Land they even looked back on their life in Egypt with nostalgia—how good those slave foods used to taste! It took 40 years in the wilderness to get rid of the slave mentality—as one preacher put it, they couldn't lead, they wouldn't follow, so God had to get them out of the way.

Even in individual lives, God's preparation always precedes mission. Jesus spent three years preparing the Twelve. Paul took out three years after his conversion before starting his mission to the Gentiles.

Today, God is preparing each of us for new tasks and new opportunities. Knowing what we know from God's past preparations of his people, we can look forward with eager anticipation for what He has in mind next for each of us!

Memory Selection

Fear not, Zacharias: for thy prayer is heard; and thy wife Elisabeth shall bear thee a son, and thou shalt call his name John.
- *Luke 1:13*

When a family had no children, the entire community felt uneasy, for if an inheritance was up for grabs there was no telling who might try to claim it—distant relatives, strangers claiming to be relatives, even roving bands of outlaws. When a childless couple drew nearer and nearer the end of their childbearing years, the tension built to the breaking point. No wonder so many stories in the Bible center around the crisis of a family with no heirs.

With this background in mind, we can sympathize with Zacharias and Elisabeth in their fervent prayers over many years to have a son.

But at the heart of their story is a great surprise: they received an answer to their prayers that gave them what they asked for, and more! Not only would they have a child, but this infant would grow up to play a crucial role in God's dealings with his people. Their child would be remembered and celebrated by all of God's people everywhere for all time.

Yes, their prayers were answered, beyond their wildest dreams!

December 13, 1992

Weekday Problems

A young couple, Paul and Barbara, had been trying to have a child for several years, with no success. They went to numerous doctors, endured all kinds of examinations, but nothing seemed to work. They prayed together every night that God would give them a child. They spoke often with their minister, who was very understanding and encouraging to them.

One family member, Cynthia, a sister of the young woman, began to withdraw from them. Someone had told Cynthia that being unable to have a child was a punishment that God sent upon people. Cynthia became afraid that she might be struck with the same calamity if she continued to associate with Barbara and Paul.

* What would you say to Barbara and Paul?
* How would you help Cynthia out of her fears?
* Does the Bible teach that medical conditions are divine punishments?

♦♦♦♦♦♦

Superintendent's Sermonette

We have all heard the saying, "Some news seems too good to be true!" That seemed to be the case with an old priest named Zacharias and his old wife named Elisabeth. They used to pray for a child when they were younger, but God had not given them one, Now they were beyond the normal childbearing years; and they had probably stopped praying about it. Then one day the angel Gabriel appeared to Zacharias in the temple and told him that the prayer would finally be answered. It seemed so incredible that Zacharias refused to believe it. That did not stop Gabriel from telling how John the Baptist was going to be born and have a great ministry.

How do we react to the great promises of God, especially when they seem too good to be true and applicable to us? God is not pleased when we refuse to believe what He tells us. He wants us to exercise our faith and put His promises to the test. Zacharias was stricken dumb (speechless) for his lack of faith, although God gave the power of speech back to him after John was born. We would do well to believe God in all things so that we may avoid His discipline and so that we may enjoy the fulfillment of His promises.

This Lesson in Your Life

It's common for people to long for new beginnings. Sometimes we think about moving to a new place where the weather is better. We imagine changing to another job that would be more rewarding. Couples even talk about having another child because they feel it might improve their marriage.

Obviously, not every decision to make a change turns out for the better. That's why so few of us pursue our dreams and help make them come true. More often we just let the fleeting thoughts pass and go back to business as usual.

Yet wherever people are alive, they are going to yearn for change. All through the history of the church we read of certain eras of great renewal, revival, and reform. But we also read of long periods of stagnation, controversy, and faithlessness.

Some historians are so well trained in these ups and downs that they can predict with surprising accuracy what the church will face next: a period of growth or of decline. In the same way, some experts in human behavior can pinpoint times in individuals' lives when big changes may be on the horizon.

Sometimes we might feel: wouldn't it be great if each of us could tell what the immediate future holds in our lives? Not just in a vague, general, Chinese fortune cookie kind of way, but with enough accuracy to know for sure. Wouldn't it be wonderful to know the future course of our children's lives?

It's tempting to envy Zacharias, to be told how his child would turn out even before he was born—especially to know that the child would "give light to those who sit in darkness, and to guide our feet into the way of peace."

On the other hand, suppose we could know exactly the day on which we would die. Most of us probably would just as soon not know. Or if we knew that our infant would years later as a teenager come down with a life-threatening disease, we might live in dread of that day and be unable to enjoy the intervening years.

Some people do, of course, know such things about the future. Some are battling diseases in which the statistical odds give them a rather fixed life expectancy. Even here we read of people "beating the odds" and living for years after their time supposedly was up.

As we look back on the lives of Zacharias and Elisabeth, we get the impression that they were people of such deep faith that they would handle whatever befell them. We see that the many years of childlessness had not made them bitter or resentful. Their response to conceiving a child was instantaneous praise and thanksgiving. You can't do that if you've spent years in gloom and doom. Their faith in God helped them through the difficult times, and their faith in God enabled them to celebrate the joyous times.

Did they know something we don't know? Were they perhaps comforted by a God who also knew what it would be like to have a Son?

As we reflect on the prayerful, faithful, joyous life of Zacharias, may we be strengthened to receive whatever God has in store for us, with the trusting faith of Zacharias and Elisabeth.

The old saying is still true: we may not know what the future holds, but we know Who holds the future.

As we prepare for the Christmas season, may we not be overcome by the stresses and turmoils that accompany buying presents and getting ready for company, so by the time the holiday arrives we're too exhausted to enjoy it.

Instead, may we continue to live in anticipation of God's glorious future, so we'll be able to receive the many pleasant surprises He has in store for us!

Seed Thoughts

1. In Zacharias' praise to God for the gift of a son, for what three blessings did he give thanks?
For divine visitation, redemption, and salvation, Luke 1:68-69

2. What long-ago promise did Zacharias see fulfilled in the birth of his son?
The covenant promise of God to Abraham, 1:72-73.

3. What new way of life would be made possible resulting from this new fulfillment of the covenant?
Deliverance from enemies, opportunity to serve God without fear, and to live in holiness and righteousness, 1:74-75

4. What ancient role would John play?
Prophet of god, 1:76

5. What specific duty of a prophet would John perform?
To prepare the way of the Lord, 1:76

---

1. In Zacharias' praise to God for the gift of a son, for what three blessings did he give thanks?

2. What long-ago promise did Zacharias see fulfilled in the birth of his son?

3. What new way of life would be made possible resulting from this new fulfillment of the covenant?

4. What ancient role would John play?

5. What specific duty of a prophet would John perform?

6. What message would John declare?

7. What two blessings would come to the people through John?

8. Who was Zacharias and what was his background?

9. Who was Elisabeth and what was her background?

10. Spiritually speaking, how does Scripture describe the quality of their lives?

(PLEASE TURN PAGE)

(SEED THOUGHTS--Cont'd)

For divine visitation, redemption, and salvation, Luke 1:68-69

The covenant promise of God to Abraham, 1:72-73.

Deliverance from enemies, opportunity to serve God without fear, and to live in holiness and righteousness, 1:74-75

Prophet of god, 1:76

To prepare the way of the Lord, 1:76

Knowledge of salvation by the remission of sins, 1:77

Light to those who are in darkness and near death, and a guide into the way of peace, 1:79

A priest from the family of Abijah, 1:5

She traced her ancestry back to Aaron, brother of Moses, 1:6

"Righteous," "walking in the commandments of God," "blameless," 1:6

6. What message would John declare?
Knowledge of salvation by the remission of sins, 1:77

7. What two blessings would come to the people through John?
Light to those who are in darkness and near death, and a guide into the way of peace, 1:79

8. Who was Zacharias and what was his background?
A priest from the family of Abijah, 1:5

9. Who was Elisabeth and what was her background?
She traced her ancestry back to Aaron, brother of Moses, 1:6

10. Spiritually speaking, how does Scripture describe the quality of their lives?
"Righteous," "walking in the commandments of God," "blameless," 1:6

December 20, 1992

God's Promise To The Gentiles

Luke 2

AND it came to pass in those days, that there went out a decree from Caesar Augustus, that all the world should be taxed.
2 (And this taxing was first made when Cyre'-ni-us was governor of Syria.)
3 And all went to be taxed, every one into his own City.
4 And Joseph also went up from Galilee, out of the city of Nazareth, into Ju-dae'-a, unto the city of David, which is called Beth'-le-hem; because he was of the house and lineage of David:
5 To be taxed with Mary his espoused wife, being great with child.
6 And so it was, that, while they were there, the days were accomplished that she should be delivered.
7 And she brought forth her firstborn son, and wrapped him in swaddling clothes, and laid him in a manger; because there was no room for them in the inn.

22 And when the days of her purification according to the law of Moses were accomplished, they brought him to Jerusalem, to present *him* to the Lord;
23 (As it is written in the law of Lord, EVERY MALE THAT OPENETH THE WOMB SHALL BE CALLED HOLY TO THE LORD;)
24 And to offer a sacrifice according to that which is said in the law of the Lord, A PAIR OF TURTLEDOVES, OR TWO YOUNG PIGEONS.
25 And, behold, there was a man in Jerusalem, whose name *was* Simeon; and the same man *was* just and devout waiting for the consolation of Israel: and the Holy Ghost was upon him.
26 And it was revealed unto him by the Holy Ghost, that he should not see death, before he had seen the Lord's Christ.
27 And he came by the Spirit into the temple: and when the parents brought in the child Jesus, to do for him after the custom of the law
28 Then took he him up in his arms, and blessed God, and said
29 Lord, now lettest thou thy servant depart in peace, according to thy word:
30 For mine eyes have seen thy salvation,
31 Which thou hast prepared before the face of all people
32 A light to lighten the Gentiles, and the glory of thy people Isreal.

◆◆◆◆◆◆

◀ **Memory Selection**
Luke 2: 10-11

◀ **Devotional Reading**
Luke 2:8-20

◀ **Background Scripture**
Luke 2:1-40

◀ **Printed Scripture**
Luke 2:1-7, 22-32

GOD'S PROMISE TO THE GENTILES

Teacher's Target

Micah predicted the place where the Messiah was going to be born. "But thou, Bethlehem Ephratah, though thou be little among the thousands of Judah, yet out of thee shall he come forth unto me that is to be ruler in Israel; whose goings forth have been from of old, from everlasting" (Mic. 5:2), The time of His coming was determined by God. "When the fullness of the time was come, God sent forth his Son, made of a woman, made under the law, to redeem them that were under the law, that we might receive the adoption of sons" (Gal. 4:4-5).

We should be thrilled anew with the incarnation of God in Christ almost two thousand years ago. The facts concerning His humble birth, the faithfulness of Joseph and Mary in offering Him to God in the temple, and the far-seeing prophecy concerning Him by the aged Simeon are covered in the lesson texts. Here was a light to shine not only upon God's chosen people, the Jews, but on the Gentiles, as well.

Lesson Introduction

Certain human obstacles had to be overcome in order for Jesus to be born in Bethlehem. Joseph and Mary had to move down from Nazareth in Galilee to the city of David, for they both descended from the ancient king. Although Mary was burdened by her advanced pregnancy, she made the trip in good health. The inn at Bethlehem had no room for the impending birth, and they had to make do with an animal stall. No mention is made of midwives assisting, and it is likely that Joseph helped to deliver the baby Jesus. It all went according to God's plan, for His sovereignty prevailed.

Jesus' birth was announced to shepherds who came to find Him and praise God. He was circumcised on the eighth day according to the Mosaic law. He was offered to God in the temple following Mary's days of purification. He was recognized and adored by Simeon and Anna in the temple. The incarnation unfolded in carefully orchestrated stages, and God in heaven was the Composer and the Conductor.

Teaching Outline

I. Incarnation: Luke 2:1-7
   A. Decree: 1-3
   B. Departure: 4-5
   C. Deliverance: 6-7
II. Presentation: Luke 2:22-24
   A. Service: 22-23
   B. Sacrifice: 24
III. Adoration: Luke 2:25-32
   A. Preparation: 25-27a
   B. Prayer: 27b-32

Daily Bible Readings

Mon. Words of Hope
Is. 49:1-6
Tue. One Is Chosen
Ps. 45:1-7
Wed. Successor to David's Throne
Is. 9:2-7
Thu. The Birth of Jesus
Luke 2:1-7
Fri. The Shepherds and the Angels
Luke 2:8-21
Sat. Jesus at the Temple
Luke 2:22-36
Sun. Anna and Baby Jesus
Luke 2:36-40

VERSE BY VERSE

I. Incarnation: Luke 2:1-7

A. Decree: 1-3

1. And it came to pass in those days, that there went out a decree from Caesar Augustus, that all the world should be taxed.

Caesar Augustus reigned over the Roman Empire from 27 B.C. to A.D. 14. He decided that a census should be taken so that a universal tax program might be initiated, and he decreed that this would be done. Reference here to "all the world" obviously meant all of the world under his control, and that was around the Mediterranean Sea and certain outlying parts of Europe, North Africa, and the Middle East. Palestine was one tiny part of his massive territorial holdings.

2. (And this taxing was first made when Cyrenius was governor of Syria.)

Palestine actually came under the jurisdiction of Syria, and Cyrenius (Quirinius) was governor of Syria from 4 B.C. to A.D. 1 and again from A.D. 6 onward. Adjustments to our calendar place the birth of Jesus at about 4 B.C. We are not sure when the tax itself was imposed following the census.

3. And all went to be taxed, every one into his own city.

The census on which the taxation was to be based required every Jew to be registered in his or her place of ancestral origin, regardless of current place of residence. God used this means by which Joseph and Mary could be moved down to Bethlehem for the birth of Jesus.

B. Departure: 4-5

4. And Joseph also went up from Galilee out of the city of Nazareth, into Judaea, unto the city of David, which is called Bethlehem; (because he was of the house and lineage of David:)
5. To be taxed with Mary his espoused wife, being great with child.

Joseph was spoken of as going up from Nazareth in Galilee to Bethlehem in Judaea because the Jews thought of going to the Jerusalem area as going up. Bethlehem was located a few miles south of Jerusalem, and it was the ancestral home of King David and thus of his descendants, including Joseph. It was here that Joseph came to be registered. Espousal (engagement) was as important as marriage in Jewish customs of that time. Joseph and Mary were husband and wife, although they did not have sexual intercourse and Mary remained a virgin until Jesus was born (Matt. 1:24-25). Her pregnancy was coming to full term as the couple arrived in Bethlehem.

C. Deliverance: 6-7

6. And so it was, that, while they were there, the days were accomplished that she should be delivered.

We are not told how many days Joseph and Mary had been in Bethlehem when the time for her delivery came. The exertion of making the trip may have been a contributing factor, but there is nothing to indicate that Mary's waiting period was accelerated by it.

7a. And she brought forth her firstborn son, and wrapped him in swaddling clothes, and laid him in a manger;

It is significant that Jesus was mentioned as being Mary's *firstborn* son. She did not remain a perpetual virgin, as some claim. We know that she later had other sons and daughters, who were half-brothers and half-sisters to Jesus. The sisters were unnamed, but the brothers were James, Joses, Simon, and Judas (Jude) (Matt. 13:55; Mark 6:3). Mary wrapped Jesus in a square piece of cloth with its ends folded over His feet and sides and held in place by swaddling bands of cloth going around it. This was apparently common procedure. People and animals often were housed under the same roof at that time, although they would be in separate compartments. Tradition holds that the place where Jesus was born was in a cave behind the local inn at Bethlehem. It would be natural for Jesus to be laid in a manger of soft straw there.

7b.... because there was no room for them in the inn.

Some commentators have made much of the fact that Joseph and Mary were excluded from the inn, as if this was a humiliating and heartless act. Considering the usual crowded conditions in an ancient inn, it would appear that they were far better off in a stable for the intimate matter of giving birth. The fact does remain, however, that Jesus was born in most humble circumstances, the Lord of glory coming to earth in a manner to which even the lowliest of men could relate themselves with affection.

Luke 2:8-20 tells how the shepherds that night were told by angels of Jesus' birth and how they sought and found Him. Luke 2:21 tells how Jesus was circumcised and named on the eighth day after His birth according to Jewish custom. Now we come to the record of His dedication in the temple.

II. Presentation: Luke 2:22-24

A. Service: 22-23

22. And when the days of her purification according to the law of Moses were accomplished, they brought him to Jerusalem, to present him to the Lord;

A woman bearing a child was considered ceremonially unclean and had to go through a period of ceremonial cleansing required by the Mosaic law. This lasted for forty days. After that time Joseph and Mary brought Jesus to the temple in Jerusalem in order to present (dedicate) Him to God.

23. (As it is written in the law of the Lord, Every male that openeth the womb shall be called holy to the Lord;)

The service of dedication was based on Exodus 13:2 and 12. God demanded that the firstborn of both men and beasts should be sanctified (set apart) for Him. Verse 12 specified that this applied to all male children and animals. Jesus later said of Himself, "Think not that I am come to destroy the law [of Moses], or the prophets: I am come not to destroy, but to fulfil" (Matt. 5:17). This began with His dedication to God while still an infant. Although He was already holy and perfect, He identified with mankind and was presented to the Lord so that He might be called holy. The same could be said of Him at His baptism by John the Baptist in the Jordan River (Matt. 3:13-15).

B. Sacrifice: 24

24. And to offer a sacrifice according to that which is said in the law of the Lord, A pair of turtledoves, or two young pigeons.

God required that both a burnt-offering and a sin-offering be made for either a son or a daughter. If possible, these involved a lamb, but, if the parents could not afford a lamb, they could bring two turtledoves or two young pigeons, and one would be used for each offering (Lev. 12:6-8). Since nothing is mentioned here of a lamb, we assume that Joseph and Mary brought birds, instead. This would indicate that they had little money.

III. Adoration: Luke 2:25-32

A. Preparation: 25-27a

25. And behold, there was a man in Jerusalem, whose name was Simeon; and the same man was just and devout, waiting for the consolation of Israel: and the Holy Ghost was upon him.

This was one of six Simeons mentioned in the Bible. Verses 26 and 29-30 tell us that he was an old man ready to die, but he was waiting for the Messiah to come. Simeon was a just man and a devout man. It was because of these qualities that the Holy Spirit rested upon him.

26. And it was revealed unto him by the Holy Ghost, that he should not see death, before he had seen the Lord's Christ.

All devout Jews longed for the arrival of the promised Messiah. The writings of the Old Testament prophets showed that they did not realize there would be two comings separated by many centuries of the age of grace. Therefore, they described the Messiah as both Servant and King. Jews tended to emphasize His role as reigning King, and they expected Him to come and deliver them from foreign domination. Simeon was thrilled when the Holy Spirit revealed to him that he would not die before he saw the Lord's Christ (Anointed One) come. Verse 32 would suggest that Simeon had the right perspective on the Messiah, anticipating the fact that He would come as a spiritual Light to both Jews and Gentiles.

27a. And he came by the Spirit into the temple: ...
Simeon moved under the daily guidance of the Holy Spirit, Who led him into the temple at precisely the right time to meet Joseph, Mary, and Jesus. We should pray for the same kind of guidance in our lives from day to day. If we had it, we could be prepared for whatever blessings God has for us.

B. Prayer: 27b-32

27b. ...and when the parents brought in the child Jesus, to do for him after the custom of the law,
28a. Then took he him up in his arms, and blessed God
Joseph and Mary were mentioned here as the parents of Jesus. Only Mary was His physical parent, but Joseph was considered to be His legal parent. Verses 22-24, already covered, told why they had brought Him to the temple. Simeon immediately recognized Who Jesus was, and he reached out to take Him in his arms. Joseph and Mary yielded to this, perhaps out of respect for old age and perhaps because they realized that Simeon had something special to say about their child. The first thing Simeon did was to praise God for the experience of seeing and holding the Messiah.
28b. ...and said,
29. Lord, now lettest thou thy servant depart in peace, according to thy word:
30. For mine eyes have seen thy salvation.
Simeon uttered words of resignation. He was now ready to die, and he may have even welcomed it, since he had seen God's salvation as personified in the Messiah, the infant named Jesus. Survival is a strong force in a human being, but sometimes old people have so many weaknesses and infirities that they yearn to be released into the next world. This could have been true of Simeon.

In referring to Jesus as the source of salvation, Simeon seems to have seen Him as becoming more than a political leader to rescue Israel from foreign domination. His subsequent remarks indicated that he viewed the Messiah as a spiritual light-giver.

31. Which thou has prepared before the face of all people;
32. A light to lighten the Gentiles, and the glory of thy people Israel,
Simeon may have been acquainted with the prophecies of Isaiah 42:6, 49:6, and 55:5, which refer to light shining out to Gentiles and nations running to Israel to learn about the Lord. Simeon gave God credit for preparing that light to shine to all people. It would enlighten the darkened Gentiles, and it would shine upon Israel, God's chosen people.

Verses 33-35 are not in our printed text, but they tell us about the end of this brief encounter. Luke carefully distinguished between Joseph and Mary by not calling Joseph Jesus' father but calling Mary His mother (vss. 33-34). Both of them marveled over what Simeon said about Jesus, for perhaps this raised their own concept of how wide His influence was going to be. Simeon told Mary that her Son would cause many to rise or fall in Israel. Although He would be a sign from God, many would speak out against Him. A sword would pierce Mary's heart as the thoughts of many hearts were revealed. Thus it was that the shadow of Calvary fell across the Messiah while still an infant. No more is said about Simeon, and it may be that the Lord granted his request and took Him unto Himself not long after this incident.

155

Evangelistic Emphasis

When the shepherds first witnessed an angel in their midst, their immediate reaction was fear. (So it was with Zacharias when he confronted a heavenly messenger.)

In each instance, the first task of the angle was to deal with the fear. Before the messenger could deliver the message, the hearer's state of mind had to be considered. "Do not be afraid," are the first words we hear.

Being sensitive to other people's states of mind is essential to good communication.

We can understand that many situations in which we as Christians feel comfortable are decidely strange to those whom we might want to invite into fellowship with Christ.

Sometimes the Gospel may even appear as a threat to a person who is not familiar with it. All kinds of factors may be responsible: a family member who puts on too much pressure; a friend whose life falls far short of his or her profession of faith; a sense of low self-esteem that prevents trying a new way of life for fear of failure.

Even the angel who came to announce the best news of all had to deal with the hearer's state of mind before sharing the Good News.

◆◆◆◆◆◆

Memory Selection

Fear not: for, behold, I bring you good tidings of great joy, which shall be to all people. For unto you is born this day in the city of David a Saviour, which is Christ the Lord. - *Luke 2:10-11*

The greatest news ever announced is reported in this passage. No wonder we want to commit it to memory; it's one of the most familiar of all portions of Scripture.

In thousands of churches all around the world, children will be presenting the Christmas story from the Gospel of Luke in pageants and programs to be enjoyed by millions. And that's how it should be.

Do you remember participating in these programs as a child? It seemed the most important role was the part of the angel who says the words of our Memory Selection. The director nearly always chose the tallest kid in the class to be the angel. There's something about these words that demands some special attention. And that, too, is how it should be.

Certainly these little pageants brought smiles to our faces, no matter how "amateur" they were (remember that "amateur" is Latin for "one who loves")

What's not so true to the spirit of the season is some of the other things we do, like spending too much money, worrying too much about giving or receiving the right gifts, working too hard getting ready for company—you can add to the list.

This season may the children in our midst bring us back to the true meaning of Christmas by their guileless enjoyment of what is, after all, a celebration of the birth of a child, a celebration of God in our midst.

December 20, 1992

Weekday Problems

Carol and Bill enjoyed going to the mailbox each day in December, for they could expect a stack of colorful envelopes, each one filled with beautiful cards with inspirational messages, signed by friends and relatives from all over everywhere—their hometowns, the office, the neighbors, friends in faraway places. In many of the cards they'd find mass-produced copies of end-of-the-year review letters.

This year, however, they read these letters knowing they wouldn't be sending one of their own. It was just too difficult. This was a year in which Bill's mother had died of a lingering, painful cancer. Carol's grandfather had to be placed in a nursing home that specialized in victims of Alzheimer's disease. Layoffs in the place where Bill worked left him vulnerable to the next downturn in the economy. And their own marrige was being severely tested by the strains.

Who wanted to write about such things on bright green sheets of paper decorated with lively red holly stickers?

* Do people sometimes make Christmas "off limits" to thinking about hard times and lonely people? Why does this happen?
* Can you think of some ways to include people who are going through difficulties—the homeless in your community, family members who are suffering—in your own Christmas celebrations?

◆◆◆◆◆◆

Superintendent's Sermonette

People like to be selective in their acceptance of truth and in their support of fantasy. They like the concept of Jesus as a babe in the manger and a symbol of world peace, but they reject Him as their atoning Savior and coming King. Secular people have embraced the concept of gift-giving at the Christmas season, but they reject God's gift to them. Christmas becomes a time for glitter, excessive spending, and even drunken celebration. The spiritual significance of the incarnation is buried beneath layers of superfluous fantasy. God must look down and be grieved at what He sees.

Each year true Christians have an obligation to make the incarnation of God in Christ as real as possible to themselves and to any others who will pay attention to them. We should all carefully evaluate how we celebrate Christmas and then put our emphasis on the spiritual aspects of it. This may mean that we have a more modest celebration, matching the humble circumstances which accompanied Jesus' arrival in Bethlehem. It may mean that we spend more time and effort on giving to the needy rather than the greedy. It may mean that we turn the thoughts of others from the babe in the manger to the atoning sacrifice on the cross.

This Lesson in Your Life

The coming of the Savior is the greatest news of all time. The response of all who recognize it is described over and over in Scripture with a single short word: joy.

The more you understand what joy is, the better you appreciate why receiving Christ as Savior produces this reaction in so many of us.

We have many words for happiness, and joy is only one of them.

We also have many ways of making ourselves happy, but again, not everything that makes us happy creates joy.

If you're a fan of a particular sports team, when the team wins a championship, you'll see your fellow fans screaming, jumping up and down, even running onto the playing area and mobbing the players. Winning makes people happy in a special way. Winning, after all, is a way of saying, our team beat all the other teams. And because I'm a backer of the winner, that makes me a winner too. (Obviously people don't say that in so many words, but it's certainly part of what makes our nation so sports-crazed.)

Another time you see people happy is after a successfully concluded war. The warriors come home, and they are welcomed with ceremonies at the seaports and airports, with local downtown parades and nationwide shows on TV. Here a sense of victory is mixed with a feeling of relief that our loved ones are out of danger.

A third time people are happy is at a wedding. Here two people are inviting all their friends to witness their making of vows of love to each other. It's a moving time for everyone involved.

But the joy that comes from receiving the Gospel is different.

The sports fans are jubilant because their team beat all the other teams. But the Gospel belongs to everyone, and you don't have to defeat anybody to participate in its blessings. Becoming a believer is a celebration of victory over sin and death and alienation from God and separation from other human beings. We are forgiven and reconciled. Other people are part of the great family of God, not teams to defeat.

In the same way, the Gospel is different from the celebrations when the troops come home from battle. Those celebrations are mixed with grief for those who died, a profound regret for the loss of life in other nations, and just plain relief that it's over. Whenever the full impact of the Gospel hits us, we feel a surge of joy because we see that Christ's way is the way of peace, and the more it is followed, the less likely it is for war to break out.

The Gospel is even different from a wedding though it's more like a wedding than like a team championship or the end of a war. (The New Testament is filled with comparisons of the Kingdom of God with a wedding feast.) The difference is that a wedding is such an intimate celebration that only the immediate family and friends share the feeling.

Christmas is the perfect time to rediscover the joy of being a Christian. It's better than winning a team championship, because everyone in the world can share in the victory of the Gospel. It's better than a homecoming celebration for the troops because when the peace of God breaks out, it creates no casualties. It's even better than a wedding, because the love of God can enter the hearts of every person and bring us all into the heavenly family.

So whether you're a spontaneous, exuberant person, or whether you're more reserved and restrained, find a way this season to sing with all your heart, "Joy to the World, the Lord is Come!"

Seed Thoughts

1. Why did Joseph and Mary leave their residence in Nazareth?
To obey Caesar Augustus' command to return to their native town to be enrolled in a tax census, Luke 1:1-3

2. Why did they go to Bethlehem?
Joseph, being of the lineage of King David—Luke 3:23, 31—returned to the "City of David," Luke 2:4

3. When Mary delivered her child, where was the couple staying?
Because of so many unexpected visitors and apparently only one "inn," they spent the night in a stable or animal stall, where a manger was used as a cradle, 2:7

4. Besides Mary and Joseph, who were the first people to whom the birth of Jesus was announced?
Shepherds staying out in the pastures at night with their flocks, 2:8-10

5. What was the first reaction of the shepherds to the appearance of an angel?
Great fear, 2:9

(PLEASE TURN PAGE)

---

1. Why did Joseph and Mary leave their residence in Nazareth?

2. Why did they go to Bethlehem?

3. When Mary delivered her child, where was the couple staying?

4. Besides Mary and Joseph, who were the first people to whom the birth of Jesus was announced?

5. What was the first reaction of the shepherds to the appearance of an angel?

6. How did the angel deal with the shepherds' fear?

7. What action did the shepherds take after the angelic host appeared?

8. What did the shepherds see when they got to Bethlehem?

9. What did the shepherds do after they saw the infant?

10. What is recorded about Mary's reaction to her experience?

(SEED THOUGHTS--Cont'd)

To obey Caesar Augustus' command to return to their native town to be enrolled in a tax census, Luke 1:1-3

Joseph, being of the lineage of King David—Luke 3:23, 31—returned to the "City of David," Luke 2:4

Because of so many unexpected visitors and apparently only one "inn," they spent the night in a stable or animal stall, where a manger was used as a cradle, 2:7

Shepherds staying out in the pastures at night with their flocks, 2:8-10

Great fear, 2:9

By calming them with the words, "Do not be afraid," and by announcing the good news of the birth of a Savior, 2:10-11

They agreed among themselves to go and see the infant for themselves, 2:15

They found the stable where Mary and Joseph had placed the infant Jesus in a manger, 2:16

They told large groups of people about "the saying" of the angel concerning the meaning of the birth in the stable, 2:17-18

She remembered the things that happened and "pondered" their meaning, 2:19

6. How did the angel deal with the shepherds' fear?

By calming them with the words, "Do not be afraid," and by announcing the good news of the birth of a Savior, 2:10-11

7. What action did the shepherds take after the angelic host appeared?

They agreed among themselves to go and see the infant for themselves, 2:15

8. What did the shepherds see when they got to Bethlehem?

They found the stable where Mary and Joseph had placed the infant Jesus in a manger, 2:16

9. What did the shepherds do after they saw the infant?

They told large groups of people about "the saying" of the angel concerning the meaning of the birth in the stable, 2:17-18

10. What is recorded about Mary's reaction to her experience?

She remembered the things that happened and "pondered" their meaning, 2:19

December 27, 1992

Jesus Filled with the Spirit

Matthew 3

16 And Jesus, when he was baptized, went up straightway out of the water: and, lo, the heavens were opened unto him, and he saw the Spirit of God descending like a dove, and lighting upon him:
17 And lo a voice from heaven, saying, This is my beloved Son, in whom I am well pleased.

Matthew 4

THEN was Jesus led up of the spirit into the wilderness to be tempted of the devil.
2 And when he had fasted forty days and forty nights, he was afterward an hungred.
3 And when the tempter came to him, he said, If thou be the Son of God, command that these stones be made bread.
4 But he answered and said, It is written, MAN SHALL NOT LIVE BY BREAD ALONE, BUT BY EVERY WORD THAT PROCEEDETH OUT OF THE MOUTH OF GOD.
5 Then the devil taketh him up into the holy city, and setteth him on a pinnacle of the temple
6 And saith unto him, If thou be the Son of God, cast thyself down: for it is written, HE SHALL GIVE HIS ANGELS CHARGE CONCERNING THEE: and IN *THEIR* HANDS THEY SHALL BEAR THEE UP, LEST AT ANY TIME THOU DASH THY FOOT AGAINST A STONE.
7 Jesus said unto him, It is written again, THOU SHALT NOT TEMPT THE LORD THY GOD.
8 Again, the devil taketh him up into an exceeding high mountain, and sheweth him all the kingdoms of the world, and the glory of them;
9 And saith unto him, All these things will I give thee, if thou wilt fall down and worship me.
10 Then saith Jesus unto him, Get thee hence, Satan: for it is written, THOU SHALT WORSHIP THE LORD THY GOD, AND HIM ONLY SHALT THOU SERVE.
11 Then the devil leaveth him, and, behold, angels came and ministered unto him.

◆◆◆◆◆◆

◀ **Memory Selection**
Matthew 3:16-17

◀ **Devotional Reading**
John 1:19-34

◀ **Background Scripture**
Matthew 3:1-4:11

◀ **Printed Scripture**
Matthew 3:16-4:11

JESUS FILLED WITH THE SPIRIT

Teacher's Target

Joseph and Mary took Jesus to Egypt to escape Herod's massacre of infant children (Matt. 2:13-18). They returned to Nazareth after Herod's death, and it was here that Jesus "grew, and waxed strong in spirit, filled with wisdom: and the grace of God was upon him" (Luke 2:40). The only account we have from His childhood is of a trip to the Passover in Jerusalem when He was left behind and Joseph and Mary went back to get Him from an amazing discussion He was having with temple scholars (Luke 2:41-52). He began His ministry at the age of thirty after being baptized and tempted.

Help your students to better understand why Jesus sought John's baptism and what the happy results from that experience were. Help them to understand why Jesus was tempted by Satan and how He handled the three temptations involved. This study should cause them to appreciate things Jesus did in order to identify Himself with sinful people and raise them up to righteous living.

Lesson Introduction

With men it is true that everything is theoretical until it is proved in practice. A concept may look good on paper, but it has to be put to the test before it can be accepted. This is the basis for advancement in all fields of human knowledge. Theory and practice are one and the same in the Members of the Holy Trinity. They say something, and it is as good as done, even if it takes time. What is obvious to God, Christ, and the Holy Spirit sometimes must be shown to men before they accept it.

The first theme in this lesson is the approval of Jesus shown by God the Father and God the Spirit at His baptism by John in the Jordan River. A visible sign and a vocal sign were used to convince men that Jesus met divine approval. The second theme in this lesson is the successful resistance of three temptations brought against Jesus by Satan in the wilderness. The visible appearance of angels to minister to Jesus after this experience was used to convince men that Jesus had withstood temptation well.

Teaching Outline

I. Trinity: Matt. 3:16-17
   A. God the Son: 16a
   B. God the Spirit: 16b
   C. God the Father: 17
II. Temptation: Matt. 4:1-11
   A. Trip: 1-2
   B. Test I: 3-4
   C. Test II: 5-7
   D. Test III: 8-10
   E. Treatment: 11

Daily Bible Readings

Mon. The Birth of Jesus Christ
Matt. 1:18-24
Tue. Visitors from the East
Matt. 2:1-12
Wed. The Escape to Egypt
Matt. 2:13-18
Thu. The Return from Egypt
Matt. 2:19-23
Fri. The Preaching of John the Baptist
Matt. 3:1-12
Sat. The Baptism of Jesus
Matt. 3:13-17
Sun. The Temptation of Jesus
Matt. 4:1-11

December 27, 1992

VERSE BY VERSE

I. Trinity: Matt. 3:16-17

A. God the Son: 16a

16a. And Jesus, when he was baptized, went up straightway out of the water: ...

John the Baptist had been reluctant when Jesus came down from Galilee to the Jordan River and requested to be baptized. John had responded by saying that he needed to be baptized by *Jesus*, rather than the other way around. Jesus had simply replied that John should do it, because it would help Him to fulfill all righteousness (Matt. 3: 13- 15). In other words, Jesus wanted to identify Himself with repentant humanity so that men might be open to His message of salvation. It was on this basis that John baptized Jesus. We must remember, however, that there was no sin in Jesus and no lack of righteousness in Him. He was the holy, divine, perfect second Member of the Holy Trinity. He was the same when He went into the water of baptism as He was when He came up out of it.

B. God the Spirit: 16b

16b. ...and, lo, the heavens were opened unto him, and he saw the Spirit of God descending like a dove, and lighting upon him:

Isaiah 11:2 had predicted, "The spirit of the Lord shall rest upon him," referring to the coming Messiah. John the Baptist later recalled this incident and said, "I saw the Spirit descending from heaven like a dove, and it abode upon him. And I knew him not: but he that sent me to baptize with water, the same said unto me, Upon whom thou shalt see the Spirit descending, and remaining on him, the same is he which baptizeth with the Holy Ghost" (John 1:32-33).

Heretics in the early church, who were called Adoptionists, claimed that divinity was conferred on a human Jesus at His baptism, but this was not true. Jesus had always been divine and had inhabited eternity past with His Father (John 1:1-2). His anointing by the Holy Spirit at His baptism represented empowerment for ministry, not conferral of divinity. Jesus had been praying as He came up out of the water (Luke 3:21). We assume that He had been asking His heavenly Father for a visible sign of the Spirit's blessing upon Him. It could have been no surprise to Him when the heavens opened and the dove descended to rest upon Him, but men who watched must have been surprised.

C. God the Father: 17

17. And lo a voice from heaven, saying, This is my beloved Son, in whom I am well pleased.

The dove resting on Jesus had been a visible sign of the Holy Spirit. Now the voice of God approving of Jesus came as a vocal sign of the Father. He identified Jesus as His beloved Son, and He added that He was well pleased with Him. John the Baptist was convinced, for he later said, "I saw and bare record that this is the Son of God" (John 1:34).

The clear references to the three Persons in the Godhead found in this passage help us to believe and teach the existence of the Holy Trinity. Any teaching which seeks to humanize Jesus to the point of denying His divinity is wrong. Any teaching which seeks to depersonalize the Holy Spirit and make Him some vague influence is wrong. We must accept the biblical teaching of the divinity of all three Members of the Godhead and not be swayed from it by heretical doctrines.

II. Temptation: Matt. 4:1-11

A. Trip: 1-2

1. Then was Jesus led up of the spirit into the wilderness to be tempted of the devil.

The description given in Mark 1:12 said, "The spirit driveth him into the wilderness." Luke 4:1 said that He "was led by the Spirit into the wilderness." Due to His human side, Jesus may have had to be persuaded to meet this challenge, but He was obedient to the Spirit. Jesus had been baptized in the Jordan Valley, but now He headed up into the desolate hills of the Judaean wilderness to meet His arch-enemy, Satan.

2. And when he had fasted forty days and forty nights, he was afterward an hungred.

God had performed a miracle in allowing Moses to go without food and drink for this length of time on Mount Sinai (Exod 28). He had done the same for Elijah at the same place (I Kings 19:8). He evidently did it for Jesus in the Judaean wilderness Despite the miracle of survival, the fast took its toll upon Jesus, and He was famished. We know that hunger and thirst can break down a person's resolve when faced by a trials but Jesus proved equal to the task.

B. Test I: 3-4

3. And when the tempter came to him, he said, If thou be the Son of God, command that these stones be made bread.

John the Baptist had already said that God was able to raise up stones to become children (Matt. 3:9). All that Satan was suggesting to Jesus was that He could make bread out of stones lying nearby, if He was truly the Son of God. This was definitely a physical temptation, and it must have had considerable force, for Jesus was very hungry, and He knew that He had the power to perform the miracle. Think of all the physical temptations we have.

4. But he answered and said, It is written, Man shall not live by bread alone, but by every word that proceedeth out of the mouth of God.

Jesus met this test by referring to Deuteronomy 8:3—"Man doth not live by bread only, but by every word that proceedeth out of the mouth of the Lord doth man live." Jesus refused to perform a divine miracle by turning stones into bread simply to prove to Satan that He was the Son of God. He chose to wait until later for sustenance.

C. Test II: 5-7

5. Then the devil taketh him up into the holy city, and setteth him on a pinnacle of the temple.

We are not told how Satan transported Jesus literally into Jerusalem, the holy city, and set Him up on a pinnacle of the temple, probably on the roof of Solomon's porch overlooking the Kidron Valley to the east, which was strewn with boulders.

6a. And saith unto him, If thou be the Son of God, cast thyself down:...

This had a physical aspect to it, but it was also a *mental* temptation. Satan sought to make it sound logical for Jesus to do as he suggested, because he quoted scripture for it. He invited Jesus to throw Himself off the pinnacle to substantiate scripture.

6b. ...for it is written, He shall give his angels charge concerning thee: and in their hands they shall bear thee up, lest at any time thou dash thy foot against a stone.

Satan quoted from Psalm 91:11-12— He shall give his angels charge over thee, to keep thee in all thy ways. They shall bear thee up in their hands, lest thou dash thy foot against a stone." That promise was no doubt given to encourage a believer to trust God for protection. It was not given to excuse a person for doing something foolish such as flinging himself off a roof.

7. Jesus said unto him, It is written again, Thou shalt not tempt the Lord thy God.

This was taken from Deuteronomy

6:16, recording what Moses told the Israelites about not testing God as they had done back at Massah (Exod. 17:5-7). Jesus refused to put on a show of angelic protection for Himself simply to prove to Satan that He was the Son of God. He also rebuked Satan for testing the Lord in this way. Think of all the mental temptations he uses with us.

D. Test III: 8-10

8. Again, the devil taketh him up into an exceeding high mountain, and sheweth him all the kingdoms of the world, and the glory of them;

Once more Satan was allowed to transport Jesus by some supernatural way to the top of a very high mountain. While there he managed to parade the kingdoms of the world before Jesus with all of their pomp and glory. Jesus had come to atone for the sins of men and eventually rule the world in peace and righteousness. Did Satan have some other way to give Him this without going to Calvary? We conclude that this was a spiritual temptation.

9. And saith unto him, All these things will I give thee, if thou wilt fall down and worship me.

This was the worst of the three temptations, for Satan had the audacity to suggest that Jesus bow down and worship him! It was utterly ridiculous. It was because Lucifer, Satan's original name, tried to raise himself above God in heaven that he was cast down to the earth (Isa. 14:12-17). He may be called "the god of this world" (II Cor. 4:4) and "the prince of the power of the air" (Eph. 2:2), but he will not control the kingdoms of this earth in the end. John told us, "The kingdoms of this world are [going to] become the kingdoms of our Lord, and of his Christ; and he shall reign for ever and ever" (Rev. 11:15), In the meantime, think of all the spiritual temptations Satan uses with us in his attempt to displace God and Christ.

10. Then saith Jesus unto him, Get thee hence, Satan: for it is written, Thou shalt worship the Lord thy God, and him only shalt thou serve.

Jesus may have been referring to Deuteronomy 6:13 here—"Thou shalt fear the Lord thy God, and serve him and shalt swear [only] by his name" (cf. Deut. 10:20). Along with the quotation, Jesus dismissed Satan, and he had to depart. This was apparently all Satan planned to do, anyway, "And when the devil had ended all the temptation, he departed from him for a season" (Luke 4:13). The last part implied that he would be back to test Him in the future.

E. Treatment: 11

11. Then the devil leaveth him, and, behold, angels came and ministered unto him.

It must have been a tremendous contrast to have Satan, the fallen angel, leave and to have good angels come to minister to Him. We assume that their help included food and drink to end the long fast. They no doubt encouraged Him in other ways, as well. Hebrews 1:14 describes angels as "ministering spirits, sent forth to minister for them who shall be heirs of salvation," and believers may consider themselves included in this.

As we come to the end of this exposition, we would do well to look at Hebrews 4:15-16, because it gives practical application to our study of the temptation of Jesus. "We have not an high priest which cannot be touched with the feeling of our infirmities; but was in all points tempted like as we are, yet without sin. Let us therefore come boldly unto the throne of grace, that we may obtain mercy, and find grace to help in time of need."

We have sought to bring out the fact that Jesus was tempted by Satan in the physical, mental, and spiritual aspects. Satan comes to tempt us in these same areas. When he does, we have a Savior Who understands and sympathizes with us. Therefore, we should come boldly to Him to find pardon and new courage to face future temptations.

Evangelistic Emphasis

The Scriptures link two very important events: Jesus' baptism and His temptation.

Baptistm signalled the beginning of Jesus' public ministry at the age of approximately 30 years. Then almost immediately came a great test, instigated by Satan himself.

Immediately after being designated as the one whom God had appointed to bring in His Kingdom, Jesus was confronted with three alternative ways of presenting the Kingdom of God. What kind of Messiah would Jesus be—one who feeds the people's physical needs, one who plays to people's fascination with the spectacular, or one who uses political methods.

Jesus transcended all these choices. The rest of the story of Jesus' ministry reveals the path that He did take—one that included all the others but went far beyond them to offer something far more important for meeting our deepest needs.

We should not be surprised when in our lives a high point of personal triumph is followed by a severe test of our character or even of our faith. It's common to feel immune to ordinary pressures while we are experiencing the thrill of victory.

Memory Selection

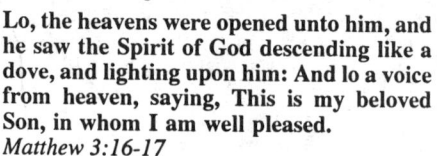

Lo, the heavens were opened unto him, and he saw the Spirit of God descending like a dove, and lighting upon him: And lo a voice from heaven, saying, This is my beloved Son, in whom I am well pleased.
Matthew 3:16-17

This most beautiful and awesome scene has inspired countless artists over the centuries to express its meaning. In many of these created scenes, a bright cloud represents the Father, a young man kneeling in a stream depicts the Son, while the Holy Spirit is symbolized by a dove. (Note, however, that our verse reads "the Spirit of God descending like a dove.")

Also coming down to us from centuries of theological reflection is an analysis of this verse as exhibiting a doctrine of the Trinity, for here Father, Son and Holy Spirit are present.

Artists may inspire us and theologians may enlighten us, but there's also something to be said for letting members of the class share how this story has made an impact on their own personal understandings.

Here is one such personal impression, to help start the process:

The story of Jesus' baptism is a vivid reminder that God is loving fellowship and intimate communion. God is not some solitary being remote and withdrawn, for the very divine nature expresses conversation and communication among Father, Son and Holy Spirit. That makes our own Christian fellowship supremely important.

As we love one another, listen to one another, bear one another's burdens, encourage one another, we are bearing witness to the very nature of the God who made us.

December 27, 1992

Weekday Problems

Now that their children are grown, on their own and doing well, Joe and Mary have a lot of time on their hands.

Joe is at the top of his career; in fact, he manages his division so well that his only challenge is when something goes wrong, which isn't very often. Mary is training for a new career, and soon she'll work outside the home for the first time since the kids were small.

The problem: Joe is bored. He's a victim of his own success on the job. He's still 15 years from retirement but can't imagine hanging on 15 more years. So he's thinking about resigning and going full time with his hobby, making Shaker style furniture. He's good at it, selling pieces at local fairs for top dollar.

However, if he goes full-time, he'll give up a sizeable pension, drop half his salary, pay his own benefits, and lose the prestige of being an executive of a nationally respected firm. He'll just be Joe, the guy in the loud flannel shirt with his power saws in the basement.

* If either Joe or Mary came to you for advice, what would you say?
* How do people decide between job satisfaction and money, prestige or power?
* Do you see any connections between the decisions Joe and Mary are making and the tests Jesus faced in the wilderness?

♦♦♦♦♦♦

Superintendent's Sermonette

Jesus Christ became our example in all things. This included baptism and resisting temptation. We profit from learning how He handled these things.

He was sinlessly perfect, and yet He went to John the Baptist to request baptism, because He wanted to identify Himself with sinful humanity and provide an example of humility for believers to follow. John's baptism unto repentance was primarily a Jewish ceremony of purification. Christian baptism is unto repentance and regeneration and is for both Jews and Gentiles who have trusted Christ for salvation. Have you followed Christ in baptism?

Jesus was tempted in all points as we are (Heb. 4:15). He was tempted physically to make stones into bread, to prove a scriptural promise by hurling Himself from a pinnacle of the temple, and to bow down and worship Satan. He defeated these physical, mental, and spiritual temptations by quoting scripture. Are you overcoming your temptations by using God's Holy Word?

JESUS FILLED WITH THE SPIRIT

This Lesson in Your Life

The word "temptation" in Scripture connotes a <u>time of testing</u>. You could call it a "pop quiz" about your life.

A temptation offers a challenge to your character, your priorities, your values. It's not really something to be feared. Notice that in the opening lines describing the temptation of Jesus, he was "led by the Spirit" to the place of testing in the desert.

The best way to respond to temptation is the way you probably used to react to pop quizzes in school. They were designed to test what you know without last-minute memory work with books.

Win or lose, pass or fail, make the best of it. Use the situation positively to look for ways you respond to temptation creatively. Give yourself credit for doing something right. Compare your response to how you might have reacted several years ago; maybe it will show that you're making progress! If you fall and yield, take note of your weakness and look for ways to build up the qualities within so you can overcome next time.

In the temptation of Jesus, He saw the innocent-sounding words of the devil as being tests of His character and mission—what means He would use to reveal His messiahship.

The temptation to turn stones into bread he saw as suggestion to use "bread alone," or meeting people's physical needs, as the way to bring people to God.

The second temptation, to leap from the temple and bring legions of angels fluttering to His rescue certainly would have been a spectacle, but Jesus resisted appealing to people's weakness for thrill-seeking to draw them to the Kingdom.

Finally, he resisted the temptation to gain the kingdoms of the world by worshipping the devil by reminding the devil that the world wasn't his to give in the first place.

Notice that the real evil in this story doesn't lie in the specific acts the devil encouraged Jesus to perform. The evil is found in the nature of the devil's motives. The devil is called the Temper (in other passages, the Accuser, or the Usurper). His motive is to exploit weakness to make things worse—

to use people's hunger to make them subservient to those with the means of supplying food;

to use the holy legions of heaven to manipulate people's penchant for cheap thrills;

to claim power to give away what doesn't really belong to him.

Jesus' responses show Him to have exactly the opposite kind of character: to heal us, not to exploit; to encourage us, not to belittle; to save us, not to destroy.

There's a kind of wonderful irony in the way Jesus continues His mission after the temptation:

He certainly does feed the hungry, but with both physical and spiritual nourishment.

He actually does receive ministry from angels (How quickly? Just read Matthew 4:11).

He ultimately receives the kingdoms of the world—not by worshipping the devil, not be armed conquest, but by becoming a suffering servant, setting the example of humble service for us all.

What a marvelous victory! Everything the devil offered, Jesus turned down. But that's not the end of the story. The Gospel is the incredible news that everything Jesus turned down because of the devil's motives, God in His wisdom and in His time gave it all to Jesus—and He wants us to share in it as well!

Seed Thoughts

1. How was Jesus prompted to go to the desert following his baptism?
He was led by the Spirit, Matthew 4:1.

2. While in the desert, how did Jesus spend his time?
He entered a period of fasting that lasted forty days and forty nights, 4:2.

3. How did Jesus' time of fasting become an opportunity for temptation?
The Tempter used Jesus' hunger to challenge him to perform a miracle of turning stones into bread, 4:3.

4. How do we know that Jesus viewed this suggestion as symbolizing much more than simply a way of feeding himself?
His reply to the tempter indicated that Jesus saw the suggestion as involving an entire way of life and attitude toward material possessions, for his reply was: "Man shall not live by bread alone," 4:4.

5. From what source did Jesus take his reply?
His words are found in Deuteronomy 8:3.

---

1. How was Jesus prompted to go to the desert following his baptism?

2. While in the desert, how did Jesus spend his time?

3. How did Jesus' time of fasting become an opportunity for temptation?

4. How do we know that Jesus viewed this suggestion as symbolizing much more than simply a way of feeding himself?

5. From what source did Jesus take his reply?

6. Where was the site of Jesus' second temptation?

7. From what source did the devil take the words of his next temptations?

8. How does Jesus indicate that this temptation involved far more than jumping off the temple pinnacle?

9. What assumption does the devil make about this connection with the kingdoms of the world?

10. How does Jesus show that the third temptation involved a basic decision about his mission and ministry?

(PLEASE TURN PAGE)

(SEED THOUGHTS--Cont'd)

He was led by the Spirit, Matthew 4:1.

He entered a period of fasting that lasted forty days and forty nights, 4:2.

The Tempter used Jesus' hunger to challenge him to perform a miracle of turning stones into bread, 4:3.

His reply to the tempter indicated that Jesus saw the suggestion as involving an entire way of life and attitude toward material possessions, for his reply was: "Man shall not live by bread alone," 4:4.

His words are found in Deuteronomy 8:3.

They went into the city of Jersualem, to the highest point of the temple, 4:5.

Read Psalm 91:11-12.

He compares it to testing or challenging God's power to respond, 4:7.

He implies that these kingdoms are his to give away, 4:8-9.

His answer cast the issue in terms of who rules the world, God or the devil, 4:10.

6. Where was the site of Jesus' second temptation?
They went into the city of Jersualem, to the highest point of the temple, 4:5.

7. From what source did the devil take the words of his next temptations?
Read Psalm 91:11-12.

8. How does Jesus indicate that this temptation involved far more than jumping off the temple pinnacle?
He compares it to testing or challenging God's power to respond, 4:7.

9. What assumption does the devil make about this connection with the kingdoms of the world?
He implies that these kingdoms are his to give away, 4:8-9.

10. How does Jesus show that the third temptation involved a basic decision about his mission and ministry?
His answer cast the issue in terms of who rules the world, God or the devil, 4:10.

The Coming of the Holy Spirit

Acts 2

AND when the day of Pentecost was fully come, they were all with one accord in one place.

2 And suddenly there came a sound from heaven as of a rushing mighty wind, and it filled all the house where they were sitting.

3 And there appeared unto them cloven tongues like as of fire, and it sat upon each of them.

4 And they were all filled with the Holy Ghost, and began to speak with other tongues, as the Spirit gave them utterance.

5 And there were dwelling at Jerusalem Jews, devout men, out of every nation under heaven.,

6 Now when this was noised abroad, the multitude came together, and were confounded, because that every man heard them speak in his own language.

7 And they were all amazed and marvelled, saying one to another, Behold, are not all these which speak Gal-i-lae'-ans?

12 And they were all amazed, and were in doubt, saying one to another, What meaneth this?

13 Others mocking said, These men are full of new wine.

14 But Peter, standing up with the eleven, lifted up his voice, and said unto them, Ye men of Ju-dae'-a, and all ye that dwell at Jerusalem, be this known unto you, and hearken to my words.

15 For these are not drunken, as ye suppose, seeing it is but the third hour of the day.

16 But this is that which was spoken by the prophet Jo'-el;

17 AND IT SHALL COME TO PASS IN THE LAST DAYS, SAITH GOD, I WILL POUR OUT OF MY SPIRIT UPON ALL FLESH:

◆◆◆◆◆◆

◀ **Memory Selection**
Acts 2:4

◀ **Devotional Reading**
Acts 2:14-21

◀ **Background Scripture**
Acts 2

◀ **Printed Scripture**
Acts 2:1-7, 12-17a

THE COMING OF THE HOLY SPIRIT

Teacher's Target

In our last lesson, we studied the baptism of Jesus and His temptation by Satan as being preparatory to His earthly ministry. We now skip over His ministry, betrayal, trial, crucifixion, death, resurrection, and ascension to heaven. As He got ready to go up, He had told His disciples, "Ye shall receive power, after that the Holy Ghost is come upon you: and ye shall be witnesses unto me both in Jerusalem, and in all Judaea, and in Samaria, and unto the uttermost part of the earth" (Acts 1:8). This lesson deals with the coming of the Holy Spirit to indwell believers on the Day of Pentecost.

Help your students to understand that it was the coming of the Holy Spirit which launched the church into its world mission. It has only been through the enablement of the Holy Spirit that the church has been able to grow and develop during the past twenty centuries. It is through His guidance that the church will continue throughout the age of grace until Christ comes back again.

Lesson Introduction

Pentecost, meaning "fiftieth day," was used by Jews to refer to a religious celebration held on the fiftieth day following Passover. They called it the Feast of Harvest (Exod. 23:16), the Feast of Weeks (Exod. 34:22), or the Day of First-Fruits (Num. 28:26). The festival was used to mark the dedication of first-fruits of the grain crop. It was on the Day of Pentecost that the Holy Spirit descended on the early believers, filling them with power to witness.

This Jewish Holy Day became the occasion for the coming of the Holy Spirit and the birth of the Christian church.

Teaching Outline

I. Empowerment: Acts 2:1-4
   A. Situation: 1
   B. Signs: 2-3
   C. Speech: 4
II. Excitement: Acts 2:5-7
   A. Assembled: 5
   B. Amazed: 6-7
III. Explanation: Acts 2:12-17a
   A. Perplexity: 12-13
   B. Peter: 14-15
   C. Prediction: 16-17a

Daily Bible Readings

Mon. The Pentecost Festival
Lev. 23:15-22
Tue. The Coming of the Holy Spirit
Acts 2:1-13
Wed. Peter's Message
Acts 2:14-21
Thu. Peter's Plea
Acts 2:22-28
Fri. Peter's Response
Acts 2:29-37
Sat. Peter's Appeal
Acts 2:38-42
Sun. Life among the Apostles
Acts 2:43-47

January 3, 1993

VERSE BY VERSE

I. Empowerment: Acts 2:1-4

A. Situation: 1

1. **And when the day of Pentecost was fully come, they were all with one accord in one place.**

As Jesus ascended to heaven, two angels appearing as men stood by His followers and promised that He would someday return in the same manner. The believers returned to Jerusalem from the mount of Olives, went into an upper room, and prayed. During the ten days which followed, they chose a man named Matthias to take the place of Judas Iscariot, the betrayer who had committed suicide (Acts 1:10-26). We assume that it was the same one hundred and twenty individuals mentioned in Acts 1:15 who were the ones assembled together in one place on the Day of Pentecost. Pentecost had always meant celebration of the harvest to the Jews. Now it was to be given new meaning by the descent of the Holy Spirit on the followers of Christ. They were unified (in one accord) spiritually. It was an ideal situation for what was about to happen.

B. Signs: 2-3

2. **And suddenly there came a sound from heaven as of a rushing mighty wind, and it filled all the house where they were sitting.**

Since the Holy Spirit was invisible, He used certain signs to make His presence known to the believers. The first sign was a noise from heaven which *sounded* like a mighty wind. Note that it was not a literal wind and no damage resulted from it. This permeated every room in the house where they were sitting. Nothing was said about it causing fear among the believers. They were no doubt startled by it but must have welcomed it.

3. **And there appeared unto them cloven tongues like as of fire, and it sat upon each of them.**

The second sign of the Holy Spirit's presence was what *looked* like a flame from which smaller flames spread out and came down to rest on each believer. Note that it was not a literal fire and no damage resulted from it. Nothing was said about it causing fear among the believers. They were no doubt startled by it but must have welcomed it.

Before moving on, let it be mentioned that these signs seemed to be unique to what happened on the Day of Pentecost when the Spirit descended on the believers. Other references to them being filled with the Spirit found in the book of Acts do not include reference to these signs.

C. Speech: 4

4. **And they were all filled with the Holy Ghost, and began to speak with other tongues, as the Spirit gave them utterance.**

Another evidence that the Holy Spirit was present on the Day of Pentecost was that He filled the believers and empowered them to speak in a variety of foreign languages. Subsequent verses reveal that this was done in order that they might witness about Christ to Jews visiting Jerusalem to celebrate the Jewish festival. It appears that what happened on that day was unique. If we want to speak about the practice of

over

173

"speaking in tongues" as a recurring evidence of being filled with the Spirit, we would have to define what that "tongue" or "tongues" happens to be. Paul wrote in I Corinthians about speaking in a heavenly or otherworldly language, but that must have been something different from the variety of worldly languages spoken by believers on the Day of Pentecost. That heavenly language also required that an interpreter be present, if what was said was supposed to benefit the hearers (I Cor. 14:27-28).

II. Excitement: Acts 2:5-7

A. Assembled: 5

5. And there were dwelling at Jerusalem Jews, devout men, out of every nation under heaven.

Jerusalem was home to many Jews who had once been dispersed to many nations but who had come back there to live. There were also Jews from many nations who had been drawn there by the religious festival of the first-fruits. They were at least outwardly devoted to God and zealous regarding the requirements of Judaism.

B. Amazed: 6-7

6. Now when this was noised abroad, the multitude came together, and were confounded, because that every man heard them speak in his own language.

It appears that the sound of the coming of the Holy Spirit went beyond the house where believers had sat. People from all over the city came running to see what was happening. By that time, the believers were out witnessing about Christ to anyone who would listen. The people were amazed to discover that the believers were speaking to them in a variety of languages which the Jews had spoken in the many lands where they had lived.

7. And they were all amazed and marvelled, saying one to another, Behold, are not all these which speak Galilaeans?

People in the gathering multitude wondered how it was possible for Galileans to talk to them in the languages of the countries where they had been born or lived before coming to Jerusalem.

Acts 2:8-11 tells us that there were people from a widespread area. Starting in the east, the counties moving westward included Parthia, Media, Elam, Mesopotamia, and Judaea. Western countries included Cappadocia, Pontus, Asia (a Turkish province, not the continent of Asia), Phrygia, and Pamphylia. Countries to the south included Egypt and parts of Libya around Cyrene. Rome, Crete, and Arabia are added at the end, and reference is made to both Jews and strangers (proselytes to Judaism). They heard believers talk about the wonderful works of God in the languages of these various lands.

III. Explanation: Acts 2:12-17a

A. Perplexity: 12-13

12. And they were all amazed, and were in doubt, saying one to another, What meaneth this?

Note the terms used to describe how the multitude felt—"confounded" (vs. 6); "amazed" and "marvelled" (vs. 7); "amazed" and "in doubt" (vs. 12). They simply could not understand this unusual phenomenon. They began to ask one another what it could possibly signify.

13. Others mocking said, These men are full of new wine.

The believers apparently had been acting somewhat ecstatically as they spoke, and some people in the crowd assumed that they had become intoxicated with new, sweet wine. They mocked them by saying this. It seems to be human nature to make negative assumptions when something cannot be understood, and this is what some of the people did. This was something which had to be corrected immediately, or the believers would have lost their testimony to those who listened to them.

B. Peter: 14-15

14a. But Peter, standing up with the eleven, lifted up his voice, and said unto them, ...

Before seeing what Peter said, we pause to consider Peter the man. He was the one who denied knowing Jesus as his Master three times around the enemies' campfire after Jesus had been arrested and taken to judgment (John 18:15-27). He had been reconciled to Jesus following His resurrection after Jesus had asked him three times if he loved Him (John 21:15-19). After the disciples had been filled by the Holy Spirit, Peter had gained new confidence and boldness. He, along with the other eleven disciples (including Matthias), stood together before the multitude on the Day of Pentecost and thus provided one another with mutual support. Peter's natural aggressiveness evidently prompted him to be the group's spokesman on this occasion.

14b. ...Ye men of Judaea, and all ye that dwell at Jerusalem, be this known unto you, and hearken to my words:
This was the beginning of a sermon by Peter which would sweep about three thousand souls into the kingdom of God on the Day of Pentecost (Acts 2:14-41), He addressed the assembled men of Judaea and others living (permanently or temporarily) in Jerusalem. He had something important to say, and he called for their attention. It appears that he was successful in getting it, for they responded in a positive way to it later on (vs. 37).

15. For these are not drunken, as ye suppose, seeing it is but the third hour of the day.
The first thing Peter wanted to do was correct the misunderstanding some people had that the believers were drunk from wine. He pointed out the fact that it was only the third hour of the day (nine o'clock in the morning according to Jewish reckoning). That was hardly the time of day for anyone to have drunk too much wine.

16. But this is that which was spoken by the prophet Joel;
Peter now switched adroitly from his remark regarding it being unlikely for anyone to be drunk at nine in the morning to a sophisticated reason for the believers' ecstatic behavior and speaking to the multitude in a variety of known languages. He attributed the phenomenon to fulfillment of a prophecy by Joel, one of the Old Testament prophets.

17a. And it shall come to pass in the last days, saith God, I will pour out of my Spirit upon all flesh:
This was a general statement, with details to follow it in verses 17 through 21.

Reference to "the last days" in Acts 2:17 has to do with the whole age of grace from Christ's first coming to His second coming. It was toward the beginning of this period that the Holy Spirit was poured out on the believers so that they all might prophesy (speak forth) the message of salvation. Note that this included participation by both men and women and by young and old. At the very start of the church, individuals were to be used by the Lord regardless of gender or age.

You might want to summarize what happened as Peter continued his sermon. He proved Jesus to be the Messiah by speaking of His works (miracles, wonders, signs), by quoting Old Testament scripture about Him, and by describing His resurrection from the dead. At this point, the people asked what they should do, and Peter urged them to repent of their sins and be baptized. Many heeded his invitation that glorious day (Acts 2:22-41).

Evangelistic Emphasis

What was the secret of the great explosive beginning that we associate with Pentecost, the birthday of the church?

Luke, the author of Acts, emphasizes the role of the Holy Spirit's timing. The people didn't get out ahead of God or lag behind. The apostles were told (see Acts 1:4) to "wait for the promise of the Father." When that promise was fulfilled only 10 days later, the apostles were ready.

Today we yearn to experience a new burst of growth led by the Holy Spirit. We can know that it will happen in God's good time - because God has kept the Pentecost dream alive all through the centuries.

Seeming periods of decline suddenly erupt into revival.

Did you know, for example, that at the time of the American Revolution, only about five percent of the people attended church regularly? A few decades later, at the height of what is called the First Great Awakening, that number had increased to a 25 percent of the population. By the year 1900 church attendance had increased to include one-third of all Americans, and by World War II, 50 percent. Today polls show that two-thirds of Americans consider themselves regular attenders of worship services.

♦♦♦♦♦♦

Acts. 2:4

Memory Selection

We may never get a clear picture of exactly what it was like on that tumultuous Pentecost morning.

Did the people speak in ecstatic languages or foreign languages? (Was it a miracle of speech or of hearing?) Was there a wind or a sound like wind? Did people see flames or something that looked like flames?

We can't be completely sure how distinct were the messages people heard - clear enough for the languages to be recognized, (Acts 2:6), yet some thought the speakers were drunk (Acts 2:13).

One thing is sure: the event belongs with the greatest of Great Beginnings in the Bible. We're reminded of the giving of the Law at Sinai, also described with images of fire and wind. The birth of Jesus is also marked by stunning sights and sounds and voices from heaven.

Jesus' baptism, the Transfiguration, and the events of high noon on the day of the Crucifixion, had such signs.

When the Bible describes such "spectacular" events, they are not an end in themselves. They point to something else that is about to happen.

Indeed, we celebrate the Day of Pentecost as the time when God's Spirit was unleashed in a new and climactic way. Pentecost means the birth of the church. It means salvation is now available to the whole world. It means the Holy Spirit will provide every one of us with the personal guidance and comfort we need to live our daily lives victoriously.

Considering the full impact of Pentecost, the spectacle that signalled it almost begins to look modest in comparison!

January 3, 1993

Weekday Problems

Jo and her husband Tom went away for a weekend retreat sponsored by another church. When they returned, they could hardly stop talking about the beautiful experiences they had, and how their lives were changed. Jo and Tom are among your best friends, so naturally they invite you to come with them next time.

You're not sure. For one thing, you're not too big on "life-changing experiences," and you prefer to take one day at a time as far as your spiritual growth goes.

* What kinds of signs would you look for in Jo and Tom to tell whether their experience might be positive for you?
* What would you look for to tell whether the changes were passing or permanent?
* If you decided to say no, how might you do so without hurting their feelings?
* If you had some genuine concerns about the effects of the weekend on Jo and Tom, how could you express them in a way that would allow the three of you to keep an open mind and a continuing conversation?

♦♦♦♦♦♦

Superintendent's Sermonette

The traumatic experiences of betrayal, arrest, judgment, torture, crucifixion, and burial demoralized the disciples and other believers. They went into hiding for fear of the Jews. It was discovery of Christ's resurrection, plus His appearances to many, which pulled the disciples and believers out of despair and renewed their hope of the coming kingdom of God. However, Jesus had to tell them that the coming of the kingdom was in His heavenly Father's hands at some future time. Meanwhile, they were to wait for the coming of the Holy Spirit and the power they needed to take the gospel to the whole world (Acts 1:6-8).

The descent of the Spirit came on the Day of Pentecost, fifty days following Christ's resurrection. A mighty sound and tongues like fire were the audiovisual signs of His coming. He filled the believers and sent them out to witness in various known languages to people in Jerusalem. The people who heard them were greatly amazed and wondered what it all meant. Peter riveted their attention by giving a sermon which persuaded three thousand to accept Christ as Savior. We need the empowerment of the Holy Spirit to continue that witness today. He stands ready to fill us with Himself.

THE COMING OF THE HOLY SPIRIT

This Lesson In Your Life

In last week's study, we witnessed the Spirit descending on Jesus; today, on His disciples. In between has come the great three-year ministry of Jesus that included all his teachings and healings, and the events of His death, resurrection, and ascension.

In fact, the last conversation on earth between Jesus and His disciples appears a few verses before today's text, in the first chapter of Acts.

Even after all that the disciples had seen and heard, they asked a rather surprising question at the end of their time with Him: "Lord, wilt thou at this time restore again the kingdom to Isreal?"

The question implied that the purpose of Jesus' coming was to "restore" something that had existed before. In fact, the mission of Jesus involved infinitely more. Ten days later, on the Day of Pentecost, the disciples would begin to receive an answer to their question.

It would be an answer far beyond their greatest hopes and dreams.

Before we criticize the disciples too quickly, let's try to put ourselves in their shoes.

On the morning of the Day of Pentecost, we are there with the twelve apostles (Matthias had been selected to replace Judas), along with Mary the mother of Jesus, his brothers, and other disciples who brought the total around one hundred twenty who "were all with one accord in the place" (Acts 2:1)

It's hard to describe what happened next. A sound came from heaven like a rushing, mighty wind. "Tongues" that looked like fire "sat upon" each if us. Then suddenly we heard voices.

The sounds were loud enough to attract a crowd. Jerusalem was filled with visitors for the annual Pentecost harvest festival, so the crowd that gathered came from all points of the Roman Empire, and spoke a variety of languages.

Instead of the usual confusing babel of tongues, each of us who were visitors heard our own languages coming from those who were speaking. What we heard sounded to many of us like inspiring exhortations concerning the mighty works of God.

(Of course, some of the more cautious and skeptical among us wondered if we were imagining things, and the speakers were just local Galileeans with a little too much to drink.)

It fell Peter's lot to try to calm things down and make sense of it all. Peter is pictured in the Gospels as the most impulsive of the Twelve, always the first to do something courageous (answer Jesus' call, confess Him as Messiah) and also the first to try something foolhardy (jump out of a boat and try to walk on water, defend Jesus against a mob with a sword).

Now Peter is the first to speak what is called "the First Gospel sermon."

The point of contact with his devout Jewish listeners was the Scriptures they revered. Peter selected some prophecies and psalms that for centuries had given hope to those who heard them read. For Peter, however, these Scriptures were more than ancient documents; they were powerful ways of understanding what was happening in our midst.

We came to see that God's working that day was as important as anything that had happened in the distant past.

We came to realize that what the Spirit was beginning on this Day of Pentecost would change the world for all time to come.

We were reminded that every generation is given a new challenge. Being faithful doesn't mean camping on the banks where our ancestors died, but taking up their cause and advancing in the way God has in mind for us.

We came to see the Spirit is truly alive and well in every generation!

Seed Thoughts

1. What is the origin of the Feast Day of Pentecost?
It was a harvest festival to celebrate the end of a hard-working season of reaping that usually began at Passover and lasted 50 days. (The word *Pentecost* in Greek means "fiftieth day.")

2. Who was gathered together in the house where the Spirit appeared?
The group included the twelve apostles (Matthias replacing Judas), a number of women including Mary, mother of Jesus, the brothers of Jesus, and others totalling about 120 people.

3. Describe the sights and sounds from Acts 2:2-6 as you envision them as they might have affected you if you had been there.
(A sound like wind; cloven tongues like fire; speaking in other languages, etc.)

4. Why are the people who are attracted by the outpouring of the Spirit from so many different places?
The Feast of Pentecost traditionally brought devout Jews from all over the Empire to Jerusalem for the major celebration.

5. Did the people hear unknown, ecstatic languages or ordinary spoken languages?
Here Luke seems to emphasize that many different known languages were heard. Other parts of the new Testament, however, describe ecstatic languages.

---

1. What is the origin of the Feast Day of Pentecost?

2. Who was gathered together in the house where the Spirit appeared?

3. Describe the sights and sounds from Acts 2:2-6 as you envision them as they might have affected you if you had been there.

4. Why are the people who are attracted by the outpouring of the Spirit from so many different places?

5. Did the people hear unknown, ecstatic languages or ordinary spoken languages?

6. What was the effect of these events on the crowd that gathered?

7. How did those who "mocked" try to explain away what people were hearing?

8. What evidence did Peter produce to challenge the charge of intoxication?

(PLEASE TURN PAGE)

(SEED THOUGHTS--Cont'd)

It was a harvest festival to celebrate the end of a hard-working season of reaping that usually began at Passover and lasted 50 days. (The word *Pentecost* in Greek means "fiftieth day.")

The group included the twelve apostles (Matthias replacing Judas), a number of women including Mary, mother of Jesus, the brothers of Jesus, and others totalling about 120 people.

(A sound like wind; cloven tongues like fire; speaking in other languages, etc.)

The Feast of Pentecost traditionally brought devout Jews from all over the Empire to Jerusalem for the major celebration.

Here Luke seems to emphasize that many different known languages were heard. Other parts of the new Testament, however, describe ecstatic languages.

They were "confounded," verse 6, "were amazed and marvelled," verse 7, "were in doubt," verse 12, and "others mocked," verse 13.

They said the speakers were full of "new wine" - made from the first drippings from the vat, and often more intoxicating than ordinary vintages.

That it was only the "third hour of the day," 9 o'clock in the morning, the time of morning prayer, before which devout Jews would not eat or drink.

6. What was the effect of these events on the crowd that gathered?
They were "confounded," verse 6, "were amazed and marvelled," verse 7, "were in doubt," verse 12, and "others mocked," verse 13.

7. How did those who "mocked" try to explain away what people were hearing?
They said the speakers were full of "new wine" - made from the first drippings from the vat, and often more intoxicating than ordinary vintages.

8. What evidence did Peter produce to challenge the charge of intoxication?
That it was only the "third hour of the day," 9 o'clock in the morning, the time of morning prayer, before which devout Jews would not eat or drink.

January 10, 1993

"FOLLOW ME IN HOLY LIVING."

A Call to Holy Living

I Peter 1

13 Wherefore gird up the loins of your mind, be sober, and hope to the end for the grace that is to be brought unto you at the revelation of Jesus Christ;
14 As obedient children, not fashioning yourselves according to the former lusts in your ignorance:
15 But as he which hath called you is holy, so be ye holy in all manner of conversation;
16 Because it is written, Be ye holy; for I am holy.
17 And if ye call on the Father, who without respect of persons judgeth according to every man's work, pass the time of your sojourning *here* in fear:
18 Forasmuch as ye know that ye were not redeemed with corruptible things, *as* silver and gold from your vain conversation received by tradition from your fathers;
19 But with the precious blood of Christ, as of a lamb without blemish and without spot:
20 Who verily was foreordained before the foundation of the world, but was manifest in these last times for you,
21 Who by him do believe in God, that raised him up from the dead, and gave him glory; that your faith and hope might be in God.
22 Seeing ye have purified your souls in obeying the truth through the Spirit unto unfeigned love of the brethren, see that ye love one another with a pure heart fervently:
23 Being born again, not of corruptible seed, but of incorruptible by the word of God, which liveth and abideth for ever.
24 FOR ALL FLESH *IS* AS GRASS, AND ALL THE GLORY OF MAN AS THE FLOWER OF GRASS. THE GRASS WITHERETH, AND THE FLOWER THEREOF FALLETH AWAY:
25 BUT THE WORD OF THE LORD ENDURETH FOR EVER. And this is the word which by the gospel is preached unto you.

◆◆◆◆◆◆

◀ **Memory Selection**
I Peter 1:13-25

◀ **Devotional Reading**
I Peter 2:1-10

◀ **Background Selection**
I Peter 1:3-25

◀ **Printed Scripture**
I Peter 1:13-25

A CALL TO HOLY LIVING

Teachers Target

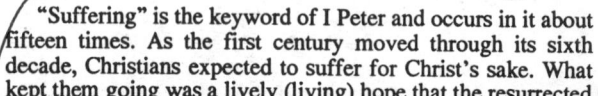

"Suffering" is the keyword of I Peter and occurs in it about fifteen times. As the first century moved through its sixth decade, Christians expected to suffer for Christ's sake. What kept them going was a lively (living) hope that the resurrected Christ would someday return and deliver His people from persecution. It has been that same hope which has sustained believers through periods of suffering for almost two millenia. God-given love has also served to bind them together when persecuted.

Help your students [WE NEED] to dedicate ourselves [WE] to living holy lives so that they [WE] may increasingly become more like God and Christ. They [WE] should feel obligated to do this, because it was through the precious blood of Christ that they [WE] were redeemed. They [WE] should feel encouraged to do this because of our [US] sure hope that He is coming again to take them [US] unto Himself. The Word of the Lord endures forever, and those who place their destiny in it will not be disappointed.

Lesson Introduction

Christians suffered much persecution in ancient Rome during the reigns of such emperors as Nero, Domitian, and Trajan (A.D. 54-117). Peter mentioned that he wrote his first epistle from Babylon, where he, Silvanus (Silas), Marcus (Mark), and other believers were living (I Pet. 5:12-13). If that "Babylon" was actually Rome, it could lend support to the tradition which states that Peter was martyred there during Nero's reign.

Believers had developed a long record of suffering from the time of Job onward. He had said that God knew his path and would bring him through trial refined as pure gold (Job 23:10). Psalm 42:8 promised a song in the night. Paul and Silas had sung praises to God while imprisoned and in stocks at the Philippian jail (Acts 16:25). Peter wrote about faith tried in the fire and being purified by it (I Pet. 1:7). His personal experiences with persecution gave force to his writings about it.

Teaching Outline

I. Challenge I: I Pet. 1:13-16
   A. Call to hope: 13
   B. Call to holiness: 14-16
II. Challenge II: I Pet. 1:17-21
   A. Call to reverence: 17
   B. Call to remembrance: 18-21
III. Challenge III: I Pet. 1:22-25
   A. Call to love: 22
   B. Call to the Word: 23-25

Daily Bible Readings

Mon. Glory to God
Ps. 8
Tue. Full Assurance of Faith
Heb. 10:19-25
Wed. Living a Life of Love
I Cor. 13:1-7
Thu. The Greatest Gift
I Cor. 13:8-15
Fri. Living in Christ
I Cor. 15:20-28
Sat. A Living Hope
I Pet. 1:3-12
Sun. A Call to Holy Living
I Pet. 1:13-25

January 10, 1993

VERSE BY VERSE

I. Challenge 1: I Pet. 1:13-16

A. Call to hope: 13

13. Wherefore gird up the loins of your mind, be sober, and hope to the end for the grace that is to be brought unto you at the revelation of Jesus Christ;

Peter had described believers as those "who are kept by the power of God through faith unto salvation ready to be revealed in the last time" (I Pet. 1:5). Having developed this thought in considerable detail in intervening verses 6-12, he now stated that believers should gird up the loins of their mind (brace themselves for righteous action). He said that they should be sober (disciplined, morally alert). He said that they should have hope (optimism), looking toward the end times when God's grace would be brought to them at the revelation (second coming) of Jesus Christ. Since they were identified by faith with Christ, they could expect to share His glory when He came. The fact that they died long before He comes does not detract from this promise. Every generation of believers should have this same hope.

B. Call to holiness: 14-16

14. As obedient children, not fashioning yourselves according to the former lusts in your ignorance:

Obedience to God was a natural requirement for believers who had hope in Christ's return. They were told to refrain from being fashioned as they had been in the past when lusts dominated them, He referred to that as a time of ignorance when divine principles were not known and not operating in their lives.

15. But as he which hath called you is holy, so be ye holy in all manner of conversation:

As far back as the time of Moses, there was a strong emphasis on holy living. God was the One Who demanded it of His people. He called them to lives of holiness in all manner of conversation (aspects of conduct).

16. Because it is written, Be ye holy; for I am holy.

"I am the Lord your God: ye shall therefore sanctify yourselves, and ye shall be holy; for I am holy" (Lev. 11:44). "Ye shall be holy: for I the Lord your God am holy" (Lev. 19:2), In other words, God's people were expected to take on His character. They could never be sinlessly perfect in this life, but that was not to prevent them from being as holy as possible within their human limitations. The measurement for holiness was found in the law of God. Obeying it helped them come increasingly closer to the ideal of being like God Himself in what they thought, felt, and did.

II. Challenge II: I Pet. 1:17-21

A. Call to reverence: 17

17. And if ye call on the Father, who without respect of persons judgeth according to every man's work, pass the time of your sojourning here in fear:

Believers who prayed to their heavenly Father were expected to pass their time on this earth in fear (reverence) for Him. They could do this, knowing that He judged all men and their actions impartially. They never had to worry about Him mistreating them. This call to reverence emphasized the fact that the kind of life a person lived was important when it came time for him to seek God's help in prayer. Psalm 66:18 says, "If I regard iniquity in my heart, the Lord will not hear me."

B. Call to remembrance: 18-21

18. Forasmuch as ye know that ye were not redeemed with corruptible things, as silver and gold, from your vain conversation received by tradition from your fathers;

Peter called on believers to remember how they had been redeemed from Satan's grasp. It had not been done by payment of such corruptible things as silver and gold. It had not been done by dependence on such things as the vain conversation (fruitless way of life) practiced by their fathers probably referring to the multitude of man-made traditions which grew up in Judaism. In the case of converted Gentiles, it may have referred to various pagan beliefs and practices which were worthless.

19. But with the precious blood of Christ, as of a lamb without blemish and without spot:

All of the animal sacrifices offered up in Old Testament times were but types of the one worthy sacrifice offered up by Christ when He died on the cross at Calvary. The lambs which had to be without blemish or spot were but types of the Lamb of God Who took away the sins of the world. No one but the God-Man could have atoned for our sins. His shed blood alone could make us clean and righteous in God's sight.

20. Who verily was foreordained before the foundation of the world, but was manifest in these last times for you.

This referred to the fact that Jesus was foreordained (appointed beforehand) to be the Savior of men. This was done before the world was created. Revelation 13:8 called Him "the Lamb slain from the foundation of the world." Once this decision was made in eternity past, it was only a matter of time before He came to the earth and died to atone for men's sins. The last times mentioned here refer to the age of grace which runs from His first coming to His second coming.

21. Who by him do believe in God, that raised him up from the dead, and gave him glory; that your faith and hope might be in God.

It was through placing their trust in Christ that believers showed their faith in the God Who raised Him up from the dead and gave Him glory. Their faith and hope had to be fixed on God.

III. Challenge: I Pet. 1:22-25

A. Call to love: 22

22. Seeing ye have purified your souls in obeying the truth through the Spirit unto unfeigned love of the brethren, see that ye love one another with a pure heart fervently:

Peter called on Christians to truly love one another. Their old selfish desires had been dealt a blow when they were converted to Christ. At least the potential for sincere love had been placed within them at that time. The Holy Spirit had used the experience in a cleansing, purifying way. Peter now wanted believers to fervently love one another with purified hearts which could look beyond selfish desires and seek the good of others. Perfect behavior could not be expected, but believers had an ideal for which to strive! Christian love for others, both inside and outside the church, could grow and develop throughout life.

B. Call to the Word: 23-25

23. Being born again, not of corruptible seed, but of incorruptible, by the word of God, which liveth and abideth for ever.

Being born again (regenerated spiritually, made new creatures in Christ) could not be done by means of mortal seed. Something immortal was required, and that was the everlasting Word of God. "Faith cometh by hearing, and hearing by the word of God" (Rom. 10:17). Peter urgently called believers to support the revealed Word of God. The Old Testament was completed, but the New Testament was still in the process of formation. Oral teachings accepted by the early Christians had to bridge the gap until the New Testament was completed and certified by the early church leaders.

The important thing was that the Word of God was an extension of Himself. It was, therefore, as eternal and unchanging as He was. The psalmist said, "For ever, O Lord, thy word is settled in heaven" (Ps. 119:89). Jesus said, "The scripture cannot be broken" (John 10:35), Regardless of what sinful men try to do with the Word of God it cannot be altered or destroyed. This makes it a worthy object of our trust.

24. For all flesh is as grass, and all the glory of man as the flower of grass. The grass withereth, and the flower thereof falleth away:

25a. But the word of the Lord endureth for ever.

Peter borrowed this from Isaiah 40:6-8—"All flesh is grass, and all the goodliness thereof is as the flower of the field; the grass withereth, the flower fadeth: because the spirit of the Lord bloweth upon it: surely the people is grass. The grass withereth, the flower fadeth: but the word of our God shall stand for ever." Contrasted with the permanence of God is the temporary state of mankind. Contrasted with the endurance of God's Word is the transitory condition of men's words. We cannot avoid the fact that God and His Word are one and the same, whereas men and their teachings can be marred by ignorance, insincerity, and deceit.

25b. And this is the word which by the gospel is preached unto you.

In case anyone wondered just what the Word of God was; Peter made it clear that it was the gospel of salvation which he and others had been proclaiming. It had to be presented in order for faith to be activated and for salvation to take place.

There was another function of studying the Word of God, but we have to go beyond the printed text for this lesson to see it. This is provided in I Peter 2:1-3. The apostle said that believers ought to lay aside malice, guile, hypocrisies, envies and evil speakings. These things had characterized them when they were living in sin, and they were surrounded by people who were still characterized by them. Peter called on them to leave them behind and, as newborn babes, desire to take in the sincere milk of the Word of God. It was through this kind of spiritual nourishment that they could expect to grow and develop. Having tasted the truth enough to become born again, they were now to keep tasting it so that they might grow into mature Christians.

We could only hope that the first-century believers took Peter's advice and followed through on it. Some of them probably did this to the best of their ability. Others may have tried it for awhile but then fallen away. Human nature being what it is, this has happened down through subsequent generations of believers.

The lesson for us, of course, is to take Peter's advice seriously and seek to implement it in our own lives. His comments were preserved in this letter so that they might become part of the completed Word of God and be available for our study and acceptance. There is the need for us to brace ourselves for righteous action, be disciplined, and optimistically look forward to the second coming of Christ.

A CALL TO HOLY LIVING

Evangelistic Emphasis

There's a good reason why Christians can be optimists, and why even the worst of times have no power to defeat our optimism.

We possess "a living hope," Peter's letter reminds us, and our hope is alive because it's grounded in "the resurrection of Jesus Christ from the dead" (I Peter 1:3).

You could say that we've read the story of our lives, that we've skipped to the end of the story, and we know already that our lives will end in victory. We know that in the end, we win!

Our sense of victory makes all the difference in the way we wake up and face each day. No matter what happens, we know we will not be defeated.

Of course there will be setbacks. Of course the forces of evil will score their points on us. Of course we'll get our share of scars and hurts. But Christ's victory over death gives us confidence to face any challenge.

In sports, all the memorable upsets occur when an underdog truly believes it can defeat the heavily favored team. There's nothing more unnerving to the favored team than to watch the underdog coming back again and again, no matter how many times the favored team moves out ahead.

That's how underdogs win: they're convinced they've got just as much right to be out there as the other team.

That's what the "living hope" gives the Christian: we don't know any better than to think we've got as much right to win as the Adversary!

◆◆◆◆◆◆

1 PETER 1:15
Memory Selection

"Be holy as Christ is holy" — talk about an impossible dream! But holy living is more practical than you might think.

Scripture gives us two essential qualities of holiness. One quality is that of purification, the other is that of wholeness.

Holiness as purification is seen in images of God as a refining fire used in tempering iron (see Job 28:1-6, Isaiah 1:25-26). The result is a hardened tool, much more resistant to breakage.

In this sense spiritual growth purifies us as we face and overcome challenges and temptations.

The other aspect of holiness, that of wholeness, is at the heart of the biblical teaching about salvation. That's why you often see the phrase "being made whole" as a synonym for Jesus' miracles of healing and also for his divine forgiveness of sins.

Becoming a whole person requires that we know our strengths and weakness. Some people are intellectually strong and emotionally weak. Others may be spiritual giants but they neglect the fitness and health of their physical bodies.

Holiness—being made stronger by the tests of life, being made whole by the grace of God—is a most practical and essential discipline!

January 10, 1993

Weekday Problems

Christine has been a Christian for more than 25 years. She reads her Bible dutifully, listens to religious broadcasts as she drives to and from work, and attends every service of her own church—often accepting invitations of friends to visit their services.

Yet after 25 years, Christine still is consumed with a feeling of unworthiness. She wants to believe what all the ministers say about the new start that the Gospel gives. In many ways her life has changed dramatically. Yet she finds herself being critical of others, quick to judge harshly the spiritual lives of others.

The worse she feels about herself, the more critical her judgments of others become, as if to say, if I can't be as good as you, I'll remind you you're not perfect yourself.

After she hurts someone's feelings, Christine is filled with remorse about her "I'm not OK and you're not either" attitude.

* What is there in the biblical teaching of holiness that might help Christine?
* Is there anything in Peter's teachings about the "living hope" that can help?

◆◆◆◆◆◆

Superintendent's Sermonette

If we have lived thus far without persecution for Christ's sake, we may consider ourselves fortunate. Not all of our Christian partners in other societies have been protected from abuse. We should not assume that we face no persecution in the future. We would do well to fortify ourselves emotionally and spiritually to face suffering for our testimony.

The epistles written by Peter, John, and Jude all deal with the subject of Christians coping with persecution. Our text from 1 Peter deals with it and thus serves as a sample for what we can learn from all six epistles. It teaches us to build up our courage, remember our redemption through Christ, and learn to love one another fervently.

We live in an age when we ought to take a stand for God, His Holy Word, and righteous positions. We ought to stand against evils of our time, such as pornography, immorality, dishonesty, drunkenness, drug-abuse, cultism, law-breaking, and all types of corruption. This will bring us ridicule, rejection, deprivation, and perhaps even threats on our health or our lives, but God will sustain us. We will become catalysts for right-thinking people who can make a difference.

A CALL TO HOLY LIVING

This Lesson in Your Life

Today's Scripture lesson, from its first verse to its last, emphasizes how our faith can make us truly alive. Our faith can give us greater energy for our work, help us get through our problems, give us more hope about the future—fortify us with everything we need to live for today and for eternity.

We can live fully because our Savior is fully alive! We can live each day to the fullest because our inheritance is imperishable—our spiritual resources can never be used up.

We don't have to be like the person who works night and day to amass a fortune, but lives in fear that a slight shift in the economy will take it away.

We don't have to be like the lottery winner who's suddenly faced with strangers offering sleazy schemes for investing.

We don't have to be like the heir to a great estate who feels tied down by the demand to make sure he doesn't lose the family's wealth.

Our inheritance "endures forever."

In the news you read almost every day about someone who faces a sudden plunge into ruin.

It may be an athlete making millions who on a single play on the field receives a career-ending injury,

A movie star stricken with inoperable cancer, or

A famous political figure facing a family scandal.

The public watches breathlessly: how will this person react to the tragedy? It's as though people see themselves in the drama—we, too, could lose everything, and we're not sure how we would handle it.

Happily, many of those thrown into the floodlight of public view to deal with their most private agonies turn out to be more spiritually rich than we might have thought. Sometimes we see a different side of these celebrities—the power that helped them in their rise to success also comforts them in their hour of need. The people they met on the way up help them on the way down.

Sadly, others are devastated by the turn of events and retreat into self-destructive behavior.

They may have thought only of themselves on the way up, and find there's no one to stop their fall on the way down.

Actually, the daily news is giving us the latest version of an old story, as Peter shows when he observes that our life is like grass, and our glory like a flower: "the grass withereth, and the flower thereof fadeth away."

However, that's not the end of the story!

The end is that "the word of the Lord endureth forever." It is that "forever gospel" that gives us the perspective to enjoy our blessings and to handle prosperity, but also to survive downfalls and tragedies.

Psychologists have observed that these are our two greatest fear:

* fear of success
* fear of failure

Does that seem strange to you? In a way, both are rooted in the same source of anxiety: a future that we can't control.

The first fear whispers: Don't use your potential to the fullest, or you might face a world you don't know anything about. Worse, you might lose it.

The second fear haunts us with a similar message: don't risk doing anything new, or you might fall flat on your face. Play it safe, don't make waves, take whatever comes your way.

How different is the perspective that the gospel makes possible!

Seed Thoughts

1. What does Peter say is the power that keeps our hope alive?
The resurrection of Christ shows that God's power conquers even death, and offers us eternal life (I Peter 1:3-4)

2. To what manufacturing process is our suffering compared? What is the point of the comparison?
The tests of our lives are like the fire that refines gold by removing the dross and making it pure. The point is that suffering can make us more compassionate toward others and better able to minister in Christ's name (1:6-7).

3. What practical benefits do we receive when we love Christ even though we have not literally seen Him?
Faith itself is a different way of life from a materialism which is based only on what we can see, hear, taste or touch. It is the source of our ability to love, or even receive salvation (1:8-9).

4. In what sense were the ancient prophets ministers to us as well as to the peoples of their own time?
"The Spirit of Christ within them" proclaimed a message of the Messiah's sufferings and glory—and we are the recipients of their message today (1:10-12).

(PLEASE TURN PAGE)

---

1. What does Peter say is the power that keeps our hope alive?

2. To what manufacturing process is our suffering compared? What is the point of the comparison?

3. What practical benefits do we receive when we love Christ even though we have not literally seen Him?

4. In what sense were the ancient prophets ministers to us as well as to the peoples of their own time?

5. What does the exhortation to "be holy" involve?

6. Peter uses the term "time of exile," a reminder of the Jewish captivity in Babylon, to describe the Christian life. What point does he want to make?

7. What effect does loving other people have on our own spiritual growth?

8. How is our new birth compared to a springtime planting?

(SEED THOUGHTS--Cont'd)

The resurrection of Christ shows that God's power conquers even death, and offers us eternal life (I Peter 1:3-4)

The tests of our lives are like the fire that refines gold by removing the dross and making it pure. The point is that suffering can make us more compassionate toward others and better able to minister in Christ's name (1:6-7).

Faith itself is a different way of life from a materialism which is based only on what we can see, hear, taste or touch. It is the source of our ability to love, or even receive salvation (1:8-9).

"The Spirit of Christ within them" proclaimed a message of the Messiah's sufferings and glory—and we are the recipients of their message today (1:10-12).

Aspects of holiness mentioned in this context by Peter include purification by suffering that empowers us to love (1:7-8) and growth in grace that moves us toward the fullness of salvation (1:13-14).

That we, too, are not yet at home in our ultimate place of residence; that we, too, live in a world where the gospel has not yet completed its ultimate work (1:17-20).

Love is a central part of our response to the truth of the Gospel, and "purifies our souls" (1:22).

We are like seed that is planted and grows and gives forth beautiful flowers—except that our seed and growth and beauty never dies (1:23-25).

5. What does the exhortation to "be holy" involve?
Aspects of holiness mentioned in this context by Peter include purification by suffering that empowers us to love (1:7-8) and growth in grace that moves us toward the fullness of salvation (1:13-14).

6. Peter uses the term "time of exile," a reminder of the Jewish captivity in Babylon, to describe the Christian life. What point does he want to make?
That we, too, are not yet at home in our ultimate place of residence; that we, too, live in a world where the gospel has not yet completed its ultimate work (1:17-20).

7. What effect does loving other people have on our own spiritual growth?
Love is a central part of our response to the truth of the Gospel, and "purifies our souls" (1:22).

8. How is our new birth compared to a springtime planting?
We are like seed that is planted and grows and gives forth beautiful flowers—except that our seed and growth and beauty never dies (1:23-25).

January 17, 1993

The Church is for All People

Acts 11

AND the apostles and brethren that were in Ju-dae´-a heard that the Gentiles had also received the word of God.
2 And when Peter was come up to Jerusalem, they that were of the circumcision contended with him,
3 Saying, Thou wentest in to men uncircumcised, and didst eat with them.
4 But Peter rehearsed the *matter* from the beginning, and expounded *it* by order unto them, saying,
5 I was in the city of Jop´-pa praying: and in a trance I saw a vision, A certain vessel descend, as it had been a great sheet, let down from heaven by four corners; and it came even to me:
6 Upon the which when I had fastened mine eyes, I considered, and saw fourfooted beasts of the earth, and wild beasts, and creeping things, and fowls of the air.
7 And I heard a voice saying unto me, Arise, Peter; slay and eat.
8 But I said, Not so, Lord: for nothing common or unclean hath at any time entered into my mouth.
9 But the voice answered me again from heaven, What God hath cleansed, *that* call not thou common.
10 And this was done three times: and all were drawn up again into heaven.
11 And, behold, immediately there were three men already come unto the house where I was, sent from Caes-a-re´-a unto me.
12 And the Spirit bade me go with them, nothing doubting. Moreover these six brethren accompanied me, and we entered into the man's house:
13 And he shewed us how he had seen an angel in his house, which stood and said unto him, Send men to Jop´-pa, and call for Simon, whose surname is Peter;
14 Who shall tell thee words, whereby thou and all thy house shall be saved.
15 And as I began to speak, the Holy Ghost fell on them, as on us at the beginning.
16 Then remembered I the word of the Lord, how that he said, John indeed baptized with water; but ye shall be baptized with the Holy Ghost.
17 Forasmuch then as God gave them the like gift as he *did* unto us, who believed on the Lord Jesus Christ; what was I, that I could withstand God?
18 When they heard these things, they held their peace, and glorified God, saying, Then hath God also to the Gentiles granted repentance unto life.

◆◆◆◆◆◆

◀ **Memory Selection**
Acts 11:18

◀ **Devotional Reading**
Ephesians 2:11-22

◀ **Background Scripture**
Acts 11

◀ **Printed Scripture**
Acts 11:1-18

THE CHURCH IS FOR ALL PEOPLE

Teacher's Target

Prejudice is preconceived judgment, usually negative and often unreasonable. It feeds on differences, on pride, and on fear. The differences may be racial, social, religious or cultural. Pride centers on self, assuming that others are inferior. Fear has a tendency to produce criticism, ridicule, and even persecution. First-century Jews were prejudiced against Gentiles and Samaritans. Jesus showed love and concern for all men, and His followers tried to do this, too, but Judaizers in the church retained their animosity toward Gentile converts.

Help your students to understand the difficulties involved in overcoming prejudice and bringing their thoughts and feelings into alignment with how God thinks and feels toward all men. This is necessary in order to maintain an effective witness to the lost and proper fellowship with other believers. The household of God has diverse members in it (Eph. 2:19-22). They are all one in Christ (Col. 3:11) Love is the antidote for prejudice.

Lesson Introduction

Pharisees in the first century considered themselves to be guardians of the law of God and of the hundreds of traditions which had grown up around it. They followed Jesus around during His earthly ministry, trying to entrap Him into saying something for which they could criticize Him and bring Him to judgment. Judaizers who developed in the early church had many of the same characteristics as the Pharisees. They were legalistic, demanding that both Jewish and Gentile converts to Christ should keep the Mosaic law, including circumcision. They were unhappy when Jewish Christians ate with Gentiles or had fellowship with them.

Our text today goes back over an experience that Peter and his companions had when they visited Caesarea, the Roman stronghold on the Mediterranean, and brought the gospel to Gentiles there. Peter's report to the believers at Jerusalem was so convincing that they had to agree that God had granted eternal life to Gentile converts. Legalism had to give way to the reality of oneness in Christ. Law had to give way to grace.

Teaching Outline

I. Rebuke: Acts 11:1-3
  A. Report: 1
  B. Resistance: 2-3
II. Recital: Acts 11:4-17
  A. Vision I: 4-6
  B. Voice: 7-10
  C. Visitors: 11-12
  D. Vision II: 13-14
  E. Visitation: 15-17
III. Recognition: 18
  A. Consideration: 18a
  B. Conclusion: 18b

Daily Bible Readings

Mon. Saul Persecuted the Church
Acts 8:1-8
Tue. The Gospel Is Preached
Acts 8:9-13
Wed. Peter's Sermon
Acts 8:14-25
Thu. The Ethiopian Official
Acts 8:26-40
Fri. Peter's Report
Acts 11:1-9
Sat. Peter's Message
Acts 11:10-18
Sun. The Church at Antioch
Acts 11:19-30

January 17, 1993

VERSE BY VERSE

I. Rebuke: Acts 11:1-3

A. Report: 1

1. And the apostles and brethren that were in Judaea heard that the Gentiles had also received the word of God.

It would be good for you and your students to be familiar with Acts 10, because it gives a fuller account of Peter's trip to Caesarea than is provided in chapter 11. Perhaps this could be done by summarizing the content of chapter 10 first. The apostles and brethren in Jerusalem had heard a report from unnamed sources that the Gentiles had received the Word of God. This probably referred to Gentiles receiving the gospel of salvation and responding to it in faith. We are not told how extensive this report was.

B. Resistance: 2-3

2. And when Peter was come up to Jerusalem, they that were of the circumcision contended with him,

3. Saying, Thou wentest in to men uncircumsised, and didst eat with them.

After Peter arrived in Jerusalem, he was met by a hostile group of Judaizers. They demanded that Jewish Christians retain barriers between themselves and Gentiles interested in the gospel. They wanted Jewish believers to continue keeping Judaistic regulations, including kosher dietary laws. The slaughter and preparation of animals for human consumption were governed by these kosher laws. Jews were not supposed to eat with Gentiles as Peter had done in Caesarea. If they did, they would be guilty of ceremonial defilement and breaking of traditions. They denounced Peter for what he had done.

Peter's defense of what he had done was in the form of a report of what had happened in Caesarea. The church in general was so happy with the results that the Judaizers were blunted for the time being. However, prejudice dies slowly, and it finally took a church council to make the decision that Gentile believers need not be bound by Jewish ceremonial regulations (Acts 15). The important point was made that salvation is by faith in Christ alone and not by works of men, as Paul clearly declared in Ephesians 2:8-9.

II. Recital: Acts 11:4-17

A. Vision I: 4-6

4. But Peter rehearsed the matter from the beginning, and expounded it by order unto them, saying,

Peter was wise not to get into a heated doctrinal debate with the Judaizers. He decided simply to tell what had happened to him before and during his trip to Caesarea. The first thing he had to do was relate the vision he had been given in the city of Joppa, for that had a direct relationship to what he later did in Caesarea.

5. I was in the city of Joppa praying: and in a trance I saw a vision, A certain vessel descend, as it had been a great sheet, let down from heaven by four corners; and it came even to me:

Peter had been praying on the flat roof of the house of Simon the tanner in Joppa. He went into a trance and had a vision of what looked like a large sheet let down from heaven by its four corners. He may not have been able to see what was in it until it came close to him, and what he saw there contained some things which disturbed him.

6. Upon the which when I had fastened my eyes, I considered, and saw fourfooted beasts of the earth, and wild beasts, and creeping things, and fowls of the air.

Peter gazed with concentration on what the sheet contained, and he saw there some domesticated animals, wild beasts, reptiles, and birds. Some of the animals in it were considered unclean by Levitical law. Ordinary Jews would probably have been as repelled by these animals as they would be by the sight of Gentiles. Peter found it hard to deal with ingrained feelings when faced with these creatures.

B. Voice: 7-10

7. And I heard a voice saying unto me, Arise, Peter; slay and eat.

Peter must have been shocked to hear an authoritative voice command him to slay and eat the animals found in the sheet. This would go against his lifelong training. It would seem to make no sense or offer any good result. It would make him feel guilty

8. But I said, Not so, Lord: for nothing common on unclean hath at any time entered into my mouth.

Peter's bold and impetuous nature prompted him to react strongly to the authoritative command, even though he recognized it as coming from the Lord. He took pride in his claim that he had never eaten any common or unclean animals in his life.

9. But the voice answered me again from heaven, What God hath cleansed that call not thou common.

Mark 7:14-23 serves as background for this verse. It tells of Jesus teaching regarding what defiles a man. It is not what enters his stomach but what comes out from his heart. Jesus was laying the groundwork for removing prohibition of certain foods once declared unclean by the Levitical law. The voice from heaven mentioned in Acts 11:9 stated that what God had cleansed ought not to be called common or unclean by Peter.

10. And this was done three times: and all were drawn up again into heaven.

Peter saw the same vision three times. It was probably shown to him three times so that he would realize it was important and that he had not misunderstood it. The details were now firmly fixed in his mind, although he did not know what they meant. The meaning was made clear after Peter and his companions arrived in Caesarea. He said to the Gentiles assembled in the home of Cornelius, "Ye know how that it is an unlawful thing for a man that is a Jew to keep company, or come unto one of another nation; but God hath shewed me that I should not call any man common or unclean" (Acts 10:28),

C. Visitors: 11-12

11. And, behold, immediately there were three men already come unto the house where I was, sent from Caesarea unto me.

The next step in the unfolding drama was the arrival of three men sent by Cornelius to Joppa to find Peter. These Gentiles may have wondered what kind of reception they would get from Peter. As it turned out, they need not have worried, because Peter was still on the roof of Simon's house when "the Spirit said unto him, Behold, three men seek thee. Arise therefore, and get thee down, and go with them, doubting nothing: for I have sent them" (Acts 10:19-20). Peter echoed these words when he told the church in Jerusalem what had happened.

12. And the Spirit bade me go with them, nothing doubting. Moreover these six brethren accompanied me, and we entered into the man's house:

Note how Peter protected his action here. Not only did he claim to be led of the Holy Spirit in going to Caesarea, but he took along six Jewish witnesses with him. Anyone who wondered what he did could check with them and be assured that he had acted properly. It gave Peter a much more solid case than he would have had if he had gone to Caesarea by himself.

D. Vision II: 13-14

13. And he shewed us how he had seen an angel in his house, which stood and said unto him, Send men to Joppa, and call for Simon, whose surname is Peter;

14. Who shall tell thee words, whereby thou and all thy house shall be saved.

Corresponding to God contacting Peter through the thrice-repeated great-sheet vision in Joppa was God contacting Cornelius through an angel in Caesarea. When Peter and his six companions arrived in Caesarea and entered the home of Cornelius, the Roman centurion told them what the angel had said. He had instructed Cornelius to send messengers to Joppa to find Simon Peter (who was at the home of Simon the tanner). These men were to persuade Peter to accompany them back to Caesarea, because he was the one whom God had chosen to tell the Gentiles there how to be saved from their sins. We now slip back to Acts 10:23-43 to see what had happened next. The house of Cornelius had been filled with family members and friends. As Peter entered, Cornelius fell at his feet to worship him, but Peter demanded that he stand up, for he was but a man. Cornelius told what had happened up to that point, and then he invited Peter to speak whatever God had given him to say. Peter said that he was now convinced that God was no respecter of persons and that He was willing to accept people of every nation who reverenced Him. Peter had launched into a gospel sermon, but he had not gone very far before it was interrupted.

E. Visitation: 15-17

15. And as I began to speak, the Holy Ghost fell on them, as on us at the beginning.

Acts 10:44-46 gives more details about what had happened in Caesarea. The Holy Spirit fell on those who heard the word of salvation. The Jews with Peter had been astonished that the Holy Spirit had been poured out on Gentile believers. They had been amazed that these Gentiles had spoken in tongues and magnified (praised) God in this manner. Peter told the Jewish Christians in Jerusalem that the event in Caesarea was similar to that which had happened on the Day of Pentecost to them.

16. Then remembered I the word of the Lord, how that he said, John indeed baptized with water; but ye shall be baptized with the Holy Ghost.

Jesus had told His followers this just before He ascended to heaven (Acts 1:5). John the Baptist had baptized in water to signify confession of sin and readiness to receive the coming Messiah, but he had said that the Messiah would baptize with the Holy Spirit.

17. Forasmuch then as God gave them the like gift as he did unto us, who believed on the Lord Jesus Christ; what was I, that I could withstand God?

Jewish believers had been saved through faith in Christ and had been baptized with the Holy Spirit. Gentile believers had had similar experiences. Peter had concluded that this was God's will, and he felt vindicated in supporting it. The old barrier between Jews and Gentiles had been removed in this way. The Judaizers might not like it, but they were now under pressure to accept it as coming from the Lord. Law had been superseded by grace.

III. Recognition: 18

A. Consideration: 18a

18a. When they heard these things, they held their peace, and glorified God,...

The Jewish Christians in Peter's audience heard what he had to say and gave it careful consideration, Criticism was stifled for the time being. Praise was given to God for this new development.

B. Conclusion: 18b

18b. ...saying, Then hath God also to the Gentiles granted repentance unto life.

The conclusion of the Jewish believers was that God had given eternal life to repentant Gentile believers. This was a tremendous admission on their part, for they had long been steeped in the teaching that Jews were spiritually superior to Gentiles. It would take a while for some of them to change their inner feelings on this matter in spite of the fact that it had been proved that Jews and Gentiles could be one in Christ.

Judaizers continued to push their views and act in a condescending way to Gentile believers. Even Peter was guilty of catering to Judaizers in Antioch, Syria, and Paul had to stand up to him when he left Gentile believers and ate only with Judaizers from Jerusalem (Gal. 2:11-14).

THE CHURCH IS FOR ALL PEOPLE

Evangelistic Emphasis

Think of Cornelius as the spiritual ancestor of just about everyone who reads this lesson!

You may remember that the word "Gentile" was a Jewish way of referring to non-Jews, just as the Greeks referred to outsiders as barbarians.

We take it for granted that the gospel is for everyone. But let's be reminded that until the conversion of Cornelius, the long unfolding story of God's creation of a spiritual community chiefly involved those who were direct descendants of Abraham, Isaac, and Jacob.

Exceptions included those known as Hellenists, also called "God-fearers." These had voluntarily joined the Jewish community and participated (at a distance) in synagogue and temple activities. A smaller number had undergone the ritual of circumcision and were accepted by the ethnic Jews as part of their number.

But Cornelius was the first non-Jewish person to become a Christian.

What's so important about that?

Well, for one thing, it caused a great deal of soul-searching for many new Christians. Most assumed that the Messiah's coming would result in the fulfillment of all the ancient prophecies and hopes about the restoration of the Jewish nation—but they expected no impact on the wider world.

Cornelius's conversion sent them looking back through the prophecies to find out if the ancient seers had envisioned a worldwide community.

♦♦♦♦♦♦

Memory Selection

How hard it must have been for Peter to change an attitude he had held all his life.

Everything he'd been taught as a child led him to take for granted the practices of ritual purity—certain foods and acts and even people were either clean or unclean, and a clear-cut system was available for telling which was which.

Now Peter is finding out how all that was about to change.

It starts with a dream. In the dream all kinds of birds and animals appear, clean mixed together with unclean. A heavenly voice tells him to go ahead and choose anything he likes and prepare it for dinner.

Proudly Peter declares his faithfulness to the rules, and says he had never let a single bit of unclean food touch his lips.

Then comes a heavenly voice that utters the momentous, and challenging, words: "What God has cleansed, do not call common or unclean."

Even today, we Christians are still learning about the magnificence of the heavenly vision. We still get hurt by old ideas about who qualifies and who doesn't for membership in the kingdom.

January 17, 1993

Weekday Problems

Larry was one of those hard-driving people, always on the go, always running behind. You'd often see him racing around town in his little sports car, screeching to a halt in front of one building to do business, then peeling out of the parking lot on to the next appointment.

One of Larry's biggest frustrations, naturally, was parking, or the lack of it. The time he spent looking for a parking space meant money lost forever.

The worst of it was that he'd see an empty space, race toward it, only to find it was zoned for the handicapped. His resentment would boil over: why do the handicapped always have parking when I don't? His anger would rage.

"I bet most people with the special stickers and plates aren't even handicapped."

"In fact, I know a guy who handicapped daughter moved away a long time ago and he still gets special privileges."

"Next time a politician wants to abolish these parking spaces, he's got my vote!"

* If you heard Larry venting his anger, what would you say to him?
* In what ways have you ever been the object of discrimination? How do you handle it?

♦♦♦♦♦♦

Superintendent's Sermonette

The Bible tells us how sorely the Hebrews were persecuted while they were slaves in ancient Egypt. History tells us how Jews suffering during the infamous Spanish Inquisition. More recent history describes how Jews were persecuted and how six million died during the Nazi Holocaust. Observers might conclude that those who suffered the most ought to have the most compassion toward other who suffer, but this is not always the case. In our text for this lesson, we study about Judaizers (Jewish critics) who denounced Peter for having fellowship with Gentiles in the home of the Roman centurion named Cornelius in the city of Caesarea.

Peter was not intimidated by them. He calmly reported the whole account of how he had been called by God to Caesarea and had given Gentiles there the gospel of salvation. His clinching argument was that God had poured out the Holy Spirit on Gentile believers the same as He had done on Jewish believers on the day of Pentecost. The Jerusalem church concluded that God had granted eternal life to repentant Gentiles. This was an important step forward in showing that law had been superseded by grace. It also showed that racial prejudice has no place in the unified body of Christ.

THE CHURCH IS FOR ALL PEOPLE

This Lesson in Your Life

The Holy Spirit again and again has changed the hearts of some and given courage to others to make it possible for the church to reach out into the world with the Gospel's vision for human life.

We can see it happening for the first time in the conversion of Cornelius.

Before Peter could even complete his sermon, the Bible says that "the Holy Spirit fell on them, as on us at the beginning" (Acts 11:15). The effect of these unexpected events on Peter was to give him the final proof he needed—now he believed that the will of God was the power behind this breakthrough to invite Gentiles to share in the coming Kingdom.

A generation or so later, other Christians would face a different challenge of change: cruel persecution that threatened to wipe out all the gains from the years of the apostles.

Would these persecuted Christians hold true to their convictions? Could they forgive those who were destroying their loved ones?

We are indebted to those who believed in the ultimate rightness of their cause, in the faces of anguishing evidence to the contrary.

A few centuries later, the persecutions ended as the Emperor Constantine professed Christ and invited the Christians to assist in ruling the Empire. Would the Christians do any better at wielding power than their pagan tormentors?

Sadly, many so-called Christian emperors and warriors picked up where earlier Roman tyrants left off. However, in those centuries there were those who saw the light of Christ and kept it burning, bequeathing us great gifts of learning, law, and spiritual insight.

A thousand years afterward, the Scriptures came to be translated into various languages, and printed for mass distribution. Would the Word of God unite people, or fall prey to divisions over interpretations?

Our inheritance is mixed: hundreds of denominations, all claiming the authority of the same Bible, and also thousands of faithful witnesses to the unifying power of the Gospel.

Two centuries ago, missionaries began to flow out of America and Europe into places where the gospel had never been before. Would the new missions enable the world's peoples to know the love of God, or would alien customs be imposed upon them?

In some places, Christianity came to be viewed as part of a foreign invasion backed by colonial powers bent on material conquest. In many regions, the Gospel has brought more peace, more democracy, and more prosperity, along with its spiritual message of salvation.

Today we, too, face great opportunities and challenges never before encountered by earlier Christians.

Like Peter and the other champions of faith over the centuries, we look for signs: which changes in our day will help spread the circle of God's love, and which ones would restrict or reverse the divine plan?

The poet Edwin Markham captured the spirit of Peter's experience, and ours, when he wrote these words in his poem, The Outwitted:

He drew a circle that shut me out—
Heretic, rebel, a thing to flout.
But Love and I had the wit to win:
We drew a circle that took him in.

Seed Thoughts

1. Why would it start a controversy to preach the Gospel to a Gentile?
Jews traditionally kept to themselves both socially and religiously (Acts 10:28).

2. What is meant by the phrase "they that were of the circumcision"?
Luke uses this phrase to refer to new Christians who were ethnic Jews (Acts 10:45 and 11:2, see also Acts 15:1ff).

3. Why did it cause a problem when Peter ate with non-Jews?
Eating a meal with a person was considered an act of close spiritual fellowship, not merely a custom showing hospitality (Acts 10:28).

4. Discuss Peter's statement "in a trance I saw a vision." Do you believe such visions are promised to believers today?
Scripture neither clearly promises nor clearly opposes dreams and visions as means that God uses, although I Corinthians 13 emphasizes love above all other experiences of the divine.

5. What was striking to Peter about the animals in his vision?
The Law of Moses distinguished between animals that were ritually clean or unclean. In the vision Peter sees both clean and unclean together, in apparent violation of Mosaic law (Acts 11:6).

(PLEASE TURN PAGE)

---

1. Why would it start a controversy to preach the Gospel to a Gentile?

2. What is meant by the phrase "they that were of the circumcision"?

3. Why did it cause a problem when Peter ate with non-Jews?

4. Discuss Peter's statement "in a trance I saw a vision." Do you believe such visions are promised to believers today?

5. What was striking to Peter about the animals in his vision?

6. Some people say God "changed the rules" concerning the ancient rituals about clean and unclean animals. What do you say?

7. As Peter arrived at Cornelius's house, he found that God had been active there as well. what did he learn?

8. What happened before Peter could finish his sermon?

9. Summarize the main events that led Peter to believe God was leading him to open the Kingdom to the world beyond Judaism.

Jews traditionally kept to themselves both socially and religiously (Acts 10:28).

Luke uses this phrase to refer to new Christians who were ethnic Jews (Acts 10:45 and 11:2, see also Acts 15:1ff).

Eating a meal with a person was considered an act of close spiritual fellowship, not merely a custom showing hospitality (Acts 10:28).

Scripture neither clearly promises nor clearly opposes dreams and visions as means that God uses, although I Corinthians 13 emphasizes love above all other experiences of the divine.

The Law of Moses distinguished between animals that were ritually clean or unclean. In the vision Peter sees both clean and unclean together, in apparent violation of Mosaic law (Acts 11:6).

Other Scriptures view the ritual practices as culminating in the death of Christ "the lamb of God" (John 1:29) so that all people, "clean" or "unclean" are now brought into God's love (Ephesians 2:14-16).

That an angel had visited Cornelius and told him to send messengers to Joppa and ask for Peter by name to come to him (Acts 11:13).

The Holy Spirit "fell upon" Cornelius and his household as on the Day of Pentecost (Acts 11:15).

His vision and its meaning; his unusual commission to go to Cornelius; the descent of the Holy Spirit even before the Gospel was preached.

(SEED THOUGHTS--Cont'd)

6. Some people say God "changed the rules" concerning the ancient rituals about clean and unclean animals. What do you say?
Other Scriptures view the ritual practices as culminating in the death of Christ "the lamb of God" (John 1:29) so that all people, "clean" or "unclean" are now brought into God's love (Ephesians 2:14-16).

7. As Peter arrived at Cornelius's house, he found that God had been active there as well. what did he learn?
That an angel had visited Cornelius and told him to send messengers to Joppa and ask for Peter by name to come to him (Acts 11:13).

8. What happened before Peter could finish his sermon?
The Holy Spirit "fell upon" Cornelius and his household as on the Day of Pentecost (Acts11:15).

9. Summarize the main events that led Peter to believe God was leading him to open the Kingdom to the world beyond Judaism.
His vision and its meaning; his unusual commission to go to Cornelius; the descent of the Holy Spirit even before the Gospel was preached.

January 24, 1993

CHRIST'S DEATH—GOD'S WISDOM

Learning God's Wisdom

I Corinthians 1
18 For the preaching of the cross is to them that perish foolishness; but unto us which are saved it is the power of God.
19 For it is written, I WILL DESTROY THE WISDOM OF THE WISE, AND WILL BRING TO NOTHING THE UNDERSTANDING OF THE PRUDENT.
20 Where is the wise? where is the scribe? where is the disputer of this world? hath God made foolish the wisdom of this world?
21 For after that in the wisdom of God the world by wisdom knew not God, it pleased God by the foolishness of preaching to save them that believe.
22 For the Jews require a sign, and the Greeks seek after wisdom:
23 But we preach Christ crucified, unto Jews a stumbling block, and unto the Greeks foolishness;
24 But unto them which are called, both Jews and Greeks, Christ the power of God, and the wisdom of God.
25 Because the foolishness of God is wiser than men; and the weakness of God is stronger than men.
26 For ye see your calling, brethren, how that not many wise men after the flesh, not many mighty, not many noble, are called:
27 But God hath chosen the foolish things of the world to confound the wise; and God hath chosen the weak things of the world to confound the things which are mighty;
28 And base things of the world, and things which are despised, hath God chosen, *yea,* and things which are not, to bring to nought things that are:
29 That no flesh should glory in his presence.
30 But of him are ye in Christ Jesus, who of God is made unto us wisdom, and righteousness, and sanctiflcation, and redemption:
31 That, according as it is written, He that glorieth, let him glory in the Lord.

◆◆◆◆◆◆

◀ **Memory Selection**
I Corinthians 1:1-21

◀ **Devotional Reading**
I Corinthians 2:1-13

◀ **Background Scripture**
I Corinthians 1:1-2:13

◀ **Printed Scripture**
I Corinthians 1:18-31

LEARNING GOD'S WISDOM

Teacher's Target

The quest for human wisdom has long been a driving force in the world. Great minds have probed for knowledge in many fields, and the masses have attempted to absorb and utilize what has been learned. For many centuries the most significant results seemed to come in philosophy and theology, and they were considered the crowning studies up through the medieval period. Then came the modern era with its emphasis on scientific research and technology, and tremendous changes were made in the lives of most people. In the midst of these fast-moving developments, many neglected God's wisdom.

Help your students to realize that wisdom from God is infinitely more important than wisdom from men. The cross on which Christ died to atone for the sins of the world has become the symbol of God's wisdom. It appears as foolishness to unbelievers, but to those who are saved it becomes the sign of the power of God. God has called Christians to rally around the cross, regardless of what the sinful world-system may think of it.

Lesson Introduction

Paul had been invited to speak to Greek philosophers on Mars' hill in Athens. When he reached the point where he spoke of the bodily resurrection of Christ, some mocked, some postponed hearing more, and only a few believed (Acts 17:32-34). When he came to Corinth, he "determined not to know any thing among [them], save Jesus Christ, and him crucified" (I Cor. 2:2), Perhaps he had learned the lesson that a straightforward approach to the gospel was the best way to evangelize. It was equally applicable to Greek philosophy, Judaism, fertility cults, eastern mystery religions, and idolatry.

We need to adapt this same approach to evangelism today. Instead of being intimidated by the wide range of philosophies, religions, cults, and isms abroad in the world, we need to present the simple truth of Christ crucified, risen, ascended, and coming again. There is power in divine truth, and we have been commissioned to proclaim it to everyone. God will use it to convert the lost to Christ.

Teaching Outline

I. Confusion: I Cor. 1:18-21
  A. Qualifications: 18-19
  B. Questions: 20-21
II. Choices: I Cor. 1:22-25
  A. Goals sought: 22-23
  B. God's wisdom: 24-25
III. Calling: I Cor. 1:26-29
  A. Rejections: 26
  B. Receptions: 27-28
  C. Reason: 29
IV. Christ: I Cor. 1:30-31
  A. Totality: 30
  B. Teaching: 31

Daily Bible Readings

Mon. Prayer of Thanksgiving
Rom. 1:8-15
Tue. Blessings in Christ
I Cor. 1:4-9
Wed. Divisions in the Church
I Cor. 1:10-17
Thu. Power in Christ's Message
I Cor. 1:18-25
Fri. Union in Christ
I Cor. 1:26-31
Sat. The Message about Christ
I Cor. 2:1-5
Sun. God's Wisdom
I Cor. 2:6-16

January 24, 1993

VERSE BY VERSE

I. Confusion: I Cor. 1:18-21

A. Qualifications: 18-19

18. For the preaching of the cross is to them that perish foolishness; ...

Paul said that the preaching (message) of the cross appeared foolish to those who refused to believe and were headed for perdition. He later wrote, "If our gospel be hid, it is hid to them that are lost: in whom the god of this world hath blinded the minds of them which believe not, lest the light of the glorious gospel of Christ, who is the image of God, should shine unto them" (II Cor. 4:3-4), The presence of superior mental intelligence in individuals seems to make no difference in this matter. Even brilliant men have failed to understand the significance of the cross.

18b. ...but unto us which are saved it is the power of God.

Those who have believed God's revelation and have trusted Him for salvation see His power personified in His Son, Jesus Christ. The cross on which He died to atone for men's sins became a symbol of the unfathomable wisdom of God. His wisdom in planning redemption is matched by His power in redeeming those who have faith in Him.

19. For it is written, I will destroy the wisdom of the wise, and will bring to nothing the understanding of the prudent.

The latter half of Isaiah 29:14 says, "The wisdom of their wise men shall perish, and the understanding of their prudent men shall be hid. These words were spoken when ancient Jews threatened by Assyria appealed to Egypt for help. They turned to pagans rather than to Jehovah. Paul adapted this to his time and situation, claiming that God would counteract that kind of thinking. Those who would qualify for true wisdom must put themselves in God's hands and do things His way.

B. Questions: 20-21

20. Where is the wise? where is the scribe? where is the disputer of this world? hath not God made foolish the wisdom of this world?

The Amplified Bible presents an interesting paraphrase of this verse—"Where is the wise man—the philosopher? Where is the scribe—the scholar? Where is the investigator—the logician, the debater—of this present time and age? Has not God shown up the nonsense and the folly of this world's wisdom?" These rhetorical questions demand answers showing that human wisdom is futile when it is applied to the subject of redemption.

21. For after that in the wisdom of God the world by wisdom knew not God, it pleased God by the foolishness of preaching to save them that believe.

Paul said that God, in His wisdom, made sure that the world, in its limited wisdom, could not know Him as it should. It pleased Him to make Himself known best through the sending of His beloved Son. Jesus died on the cross at Calvary to provide salvation for sinful men. It was the preaching of this gospel (good news) which drew criticisms of foolishness from unbelievers but which drew gratitude from believers who profited from it.

II. Choices: I Cor. 1:22-25

A. Goals sought: 22-23

22. For the Jews require a sign,

and the Greeks seek after wisdom:
Paul said that Jews had long yearned for the revelation of a sign, probably referring to the coming of the Messiah. However, when He did come, they refused to believe in Him. It is interesting that Jews today still wait for the Messiah. Paul said that the Greeks of his day sought for wisdom, mainly through philosophy. However, when the gospel concerning Jesus was preached to them, they often rejected it as being too simplistic or not in line with their own philosophical concepts.

23. But we preach Christ crucified, unto the Jews a stumblingblock, and unto the Greeks foolishness;

Christians presented Jesus as the Messiah, but He did not square up with Jewish concepts of the Messiah. This was particularly true when He allowed Himself to be nailed to the cross. Jews had expected Him to come as a reigning King, not as a suffering Servant. They stumbled over this. The Greeks, as mentioned above, thought of the cross as foolishness.

B. God's wisdom: 24-25

24. But unto them which are called, both Jews and Greeks, Christ the power of God, and the wisdom of God.

Verses 24 and 30 show Jesus Christ to be the personification of the power and wisdom of God. This truth is accepted by those who are called to salvation, whether they are Jewish or Gentile converts. We will look more closely at this in connection with our study of verse 30.

25. Because the foolishness of God is wiser than men; and the weakness of God is stronger than men.

If the preaching of the cross appears to men to be foolish and weak, that does not change it. God has declared it to be wise and powerful, and men will have to accept that and act upon it or they will be broken upon it. Human opinion, corrupted as it is by Satan, is no match for the infinite wisdom and power of God.

III. Calling: I Cor. 1:26-29

A. Rejections: 26

26. For ye see your calling, brethren, how that not many wise men after the flesh, not many mighty, not many noble, are called:

Paul mentioned here that Christians in Corinth should consider their own call to salvation through faith in Christ. Not many of them were wise, powerful (influential), or noble (socially prominent) according to worldly opinion. By inference, they were from the common people generally speaking. It was because of unbelief that most worldly leaders were rejected by God so that they could not become members of His redeemed family.

B. Receptions: 27-28

27. But God hath chosen the foolish things of the world to confound the wise and God hath chosen the weak things of the world to confound the things which are mighty;

The Living Bible puts it this way—"God has deliberately chosen to use ideas the world considers foolish and of little worth in order to shame those people considered by the world as wise and great." The Berkeley Version sees it differently—"God has chosen the world's unschooled to shame the learned; and God has chosen the weak in the world to shame the strong." Therefore, you have to decide if the term "things" refers to ideas or persons.

28. And base things of the world, and things which are despised, hath God chosen, yea, and things which are not, to bring to nought things that are:

The Living Bible puts it this way—"He [God] has chosen a plan despised by the world, counted as nothing at all, and used it to bring down to nothing those the world considers great." The Berkeley Version renders it this way, "God also has chosen the world's lowborn and contemptibles and nobodies in order to annihilate what amounts to something." Here, again, does the term "things" refer to ideas or persons?

C. Reason: 29

29. That no flesh should glory in his presence.

This verse gives the reason why God

chose the "things" which had little or no worth in the eyes of the world in order to promote the plan of redemption. It guarded against any flesh (persons) boasting that they had come up with a plan of redemption by human reasoning. God did not want anyone bragging of such a thing in His presence.

IV. Christ: I Cor. 1:30-31

A. Totality: 30

30a. But of him are ye in Christ Jesus, ...

This is a tremendous verse and is worthy of careful and extensive analysis. It begins by stating that believers have their existence in Christ. Paul said that "God has brought you into union with Christ Jesus" (Today's English Version). This, and what is said in the remainder of the verse, infers that there is a totality of union involved. Potential is there for full and mature development as believers walk faithfully with Christ.

30b. ...who of God is made unto us wisdom, ...

We pause here, because, as was mentioned when we considered verse 24, Christ was personified as the wisdom and power of God. Another way to put it is that Christ was made wisdom unto believers by God. The term "wisdom" here seems to refer to Christ and the plan of salvation which He implemented. He is our only Source of redemption from sin.

30c. ...and righteousness, and sanctification, and redemption:

It is because of identification by faith with Jesus Christ that believers partake of salvation. Out of that salvation flow three blessings, and we should take a look at each one.

The first blessing is righteousness. We are put right with God when we are born again spiritually. We become acceptable to Him, because we are cleansed of our sins by the shed blood of Christ. He paid the penalty for sin by His death on the cross, and we are freed from Satan's grasp. God sees us in His Son, "for he hath made him to be sin for us, who knew no sin; that we might be made the righteousness of God in him" (II Cor. 5:21). We are cleansed, justified, regenerated, and sealed as belonging to Him eternally.

The second blessing is sanctification. We are set apart from sin and set apart unto righteousness. The initial act of salvation is followed by a lifelong growth in grace as we use the various means of grace, such as Bible study, prayer, stewardship, fellowship, worship, and witnessing. We should be engaged in the continual process of narrowing the gap which exists between our position with Christ in heavenly places and our practice here on the earth. We should be growing day by day into more mature followers of Christ.

The third blessing is redemption. This probably refers to the ultimate redemption of our mortal bodies when Christ comes to give us glorified bodies fit for eternity (Rom. 8:23; I Cor. 15:51-53; 1 Thess. 4:13-18). Paul wrote, "In whom [Christ] ye trusted, after that ye heard the word of truth, the *gospel of* your salvation: in whom [Christ] also after that ye believed, ye were sealed with the holy Spirit of promise, which is the earnest [pledge, down payment] of our inheritance until the redemption of the purchased possession" (Eph. 1:13-14).

B. Teaching: 31

31. That, according as it is written, He that glorieth, let him glory in the Lord.

In contrast to flesh (people) glorying (boasting, bragging) in God's presence (I Cor. 1:29), Paul invited believers to give God all glory. He seemed to draw this from Jeremiah 9:23-24—"Thus saith the Lord, Let not the wise man glory in his wisdom, neither let the mighty man glory in his might, let not the rich man glory in his riches: but let him that glorieth glory in this, that he understandeth and knoweth me, that I am the Lord which exercises lovingkindness, judgment and righteousness, in the earth: for in these things I delight, saith the Lord."

Evangelistic Emphasis

If we take a closer look at the Corinthian Christians, we can learn a lot about how people are drawn to Christ.

It wasn't that Paul possessed great speaking skills. Indeed, both he and his critics agreed that public speaking wasn't his strong suit.

Nor were the Corinthians great examples of moral or religious fervor. They would have been the last people to show up for a revival.

Furthermore, neither Paul nor the Corinthians were known as builders of great institutions. They would not have been asked to help draw big crowds to a favorite cause.

Well, then, what was it? Something drew these people into a spiritual fellowship. Something helped them begin the long process of overcoming their faults and failures—and forgive each other.

Paul the Apostle writes the Corinthians with a rare candor. He tells them there was nothing special in their abilities that led God to call them. Instead, Paul tells them, God called you precisely because you're so ordinary—you've got the same weakness as everyone else (perhaps a few more).

Through your innocence and ignorance, Paul writes, God's wisdom will challenge the arrogance of those who trust too much in their own talents.

Through your powerlessness, God's power will challenge those who got where they are through brutality and terror.

Working with you who are so hard to get along with, God will create a new community, and thus show the extent of his love.

◆◆◆◆◆◆

I Cor 1:21

Memory Selection

Some of the most important things we can know about God come from ordinary experience. Through our five senses—sight, hearing, touch, taste, and smell—we can know the goodness of God's creation. We can behold a glorious sunrise; hear the rippling of ocean waves; feel the wind against our skin; taste a sweet, juicy peach; and smell baking bread. These are all parts of God's plan to reveal Himself to us.

However there is more, much more.

God has also created in us a moral sense that we can cultivate or leave undeveloped. This inborn sense of right and wrong can help us do the things that make for peace and justice and love. If neglected it can lead us to behavior that destroys community and ultimately ourselves. Both the inner moral law and the "powers that be" are given to us by God for our benefit.

Yet there is more, much more.

God has also revealed His personal love for us, and the depth to which He is willing to go on our behalf. God has become one of us in Jesus Christ. Now we know how important we are to Him.

Christ brings a message that neither nature nor law could fully reveal. The "foolishness" of the Gospel is God's most important revelation of all.

January 24, 1993

Weekday Problems

Jimmy Learner is a first-year college student, the first in his family to go beyond high school. Since Jimmy's college is far away, his first trip home is at Christmas time.

At first everyone wants to hear Jimmy tell what it's like to be a college man. But after a couple of days their curiosity pales considerably. Jimmy has changed a lot and doesn't care who knows it. He tells his family how uncultured they are, how outdated their politics, and how low their musical tastes are. He even makes fun of the old framed hunting scene on the living room wall.

Still, the family suffers in silence till Jimmy starts in on their religion. At last, Grandpa Learner speaks. "How dare you attack the old-time religion!" he booms. "It was good for Paul and Silas," he sings, tauntingly, "and it's good enough for me." Even Jimmy's brothers and sisters joined the fray: "If this is what it means to be 'educated', we'll stay 'ignorant.' "

Finally Mother Learner intervenes. Quietly she says she doesn't think the most important thing is whether one is educated or uneducated, old-fashioned or modern. What counts is something far more important. She begins to read to the family from I Corinthians chapter one.

* From your reading of the passage, what point do you think Mother Learner might have made?

* What insights can you find in the passage to bring the Learner family closer together?

♦♦♦♦♦♦

Superintendent's Sermonette

Daniel 12:4 mentions "the time of the end" and states that "many shall run to and fro, and knowledge shall be increased." We live in a time when knowledge is exploding throughout the earth. There are probably more people involved in research and education than in any other human activity. We are aware of the proliferation of nursery, elementary, secondary, college, and graduate schools. We are aware of the proliferation of books, magazines, newspapers, broadcasts, and audio-visual materials. We are aware of the vast programs to train people in business, industry, and the military services.

We ought to parallel this world-wide interest in education by promoting Christian education in the church. This should involve Sunday programs, weekday programs, the library, the audio-visual center, and Christian training at home. We can support the educational programs sponsored by extra-church agencies for children, youth, and adults. We can encourage Christians schools at all levels. We can do the same for Christian publishers.

Let us never apologize for the message of the cross. Today's text should help us to know it better, love it more, and make it known to others.

207

LEARNING GOD'S WISDOM

This Lesson in Your Life

This certainly is the education generation. For the first time in history, more than 50% of American young people are attending college. The changes are dramatic.

More and more young people are discovering that a college degree is the expected passport to a decent career.

A high school diploma by itself has a lot less clout than in earlier generations, when it could earn one a foothold where he could learn on the job.

Back then there was always work to do where one might hide the fact the his reading, writing and arithmetic skills were weak.

Today even the fast-food checkout registers are computerized.

Sadly, our moral values haven't caught up with our educational progress. While we have more muggars and burglars than ever, the real growth in violence has come in "white-collar" crime.

Today people steal millions of dollars through stock market manipulations, bank fraud, computer system break-ins, and many other techniques, including some that are so advanced that laws have yet to catch up.

These high-tech criminals harm us without our even knowing it, without our getting mad and demanding that somebody do something.

Most of us seem caught between the old and the new worlds, struggling with real issues of job security, paying for a home, rearing children, caring for health, and hoping for a pleasant retirement.

Today's lesson from Paul the Apostle is particularly appropriate.

Paul was highly educated for his time. Yet for him the ultimate issue was not how much education you have.

Paul could always get a decent living as a professional tent maker (not bad work in a day when millions of people lived in tents). But for him job security wasn't the most important thing.

He knew human nature all too well. He knew that no matter how much money we have, we always could use "just a little more."

He realized that no matter how much influence and political power one might be able to exert, he would always be prone to use it for his own ends.

That's why Paul helped the Corinthians see things in a different perspective. God didn't call them because they were rich or poor, powerful or weak, ignorant or expert. God called the believers in the Corinthian church to start a new way of life in the world. He called them to be a community based on divine love.

The symbol of this new community was not the dollar sign or the flag or the diploma on the wall.

The new sign was a cross, and object of scorn, an instrument of execution. It became a symbol of hope to those who felt trapped, a sign of God's care for those who felt abandoned, a proof of spiritual presence for people whom the trappings of life have passed by.

To the high rollers, Paul in effect paraphrases Jesus' words where much is given, much shall be required. Money and power and success don't belong to us. If they are embraced, they will betray. If they are used for higher purposes one's life begins to experience the promised blessings of the Kingdom of God.

The way of the cross is the way of "loving people and using things"—to live the abundant life here on earth, and then to anticipate the even more glorious promises of eternity.

Seed Thoughts

1. What is there in the cross that might appear "foolish" to someone who doesn't understand its full meaning?
Crucifixion was a common method of executing criminals, and had the same effect on people as electric chairs, gas chambers, firing squads, or lethal injections have on people today.

2. Why does Paul teach that we cannot save ourselves or build a just society, using only our knowledge, even our obedience to moral law?
He points to the killing of the Son of God by "the princes of this world" (2:8) as proof of the poor judgment of even the wisest and most powerful of human beings.

3. Paul warns against excessive confidence in the abilities of "the wise, the scribe, the disputers of this age." Who were they?
The wise were sages who applied the wisdom of the past to the practical problems of their day. The scribes were the preservers and interpreters of the Law. The disputers were teachers who debated their positions in public.

4. What does Paul mean by the phrase "the foolishness of the preaching"? Is he putting down the work of pulpit proclamation?
"The preaching" refers to the content of what Paul proclaims, not the method (1:21). He means the message of the cross, which some see as foolish.

(PLEASE TURN PAGE)

---

1. What is there in the cross that might appear "foolish" to someone who doesn't understand its full meaning?

2. Why does Paul teach that we cannot save ourselves or build a just society, using only our knowledge, even our obedience to moral law?

3. Paul warns against excessive confidence in the abilities of "the wise, the scribe, the disputers of this age." Who were they?

4. What does Paul mean by the phrase "the foolishness of the preaching"? Is he putting down the work of pulpit proclamation?

5. To what human tendencies does Paul refer when he laments that "the Jews look for signs" and "the Gentiles look for wisdom" (1:22)?

6. What does Paul recommend to help us get past the need to look for spectacular signs or impressive wisdom to grow spiritually?

7. Many people in Paul's time found it hard to believe that God would allow evil people to kill His very own Son. How does Paul deal with this "stumbling block"?

8. Does Paul literally mean that God is ever foolish or weak?

9. In our time, we will always run into people who have better education, more money, or more power. How can we deal with this?

10. What does Paul say is the only power that can bring everyone together into a new community?

Crucifixion was a common method of executing criminals, and had the same effect on people as electric chairs, gas chambers, firing squads, or lethal injections have on people today.

He points to the killing of the Son of God by "the princes of this world" (2:8) as proof of the poor judgment of even the wisest and most powerful of human beings.

The wise were sages who applied the wisdom of the past to the practical problems of their day. The scribes were the preservers and interpreters of the Law. The disputers were teachers who debated their positions in public.

"The preaching" refers to the content of what Paul proclaims, not the method (1:21). He means the message of the cross, which some see as foolish.

Signs are omens, either astrological or historical, to which ancient seers pointed as signals by which people could know the future. Wisdom in Paul's usage referred to the practical application of ancient tradition.

The cross is the clue to God's nature and God's plan for us, hidden from the wise, but revealed to ordinary people through faith (2:7).

By saying that God turned our most evil intent into our greatest blessing— the ultimate revelation of an all-good, all-powerful God (1:27-31).

Paul uses the literary structure called "paradox"—the placing of apparent opposites to teach a deeper truth.

By remembering that God can use our gifts, no matter how humble (1:27-28).

Our faith in Christ's power to grant us "wisdom, righteousness, sanctification, and redemption" (1:30).

(SEED THOUGHTS--Cont'd)

5. To what human tendencies does Paul refer when he laments that "the Jews look for signs" and "the Gentiles look for wisdom" (1:22)?

Signs are omens, either astrological or historical, to which ancient seers pointed as signals by which people could know the future. Wisdom in Paul's usage referred to the practical application of ancient tradition.

6. What does Paul recommend to help us get past the need to look for spectacular signs or impressive wisdom to grow spiritually?

The cross is the clue to God's nature and God's plan for us, hidden from the wise, but revealed to ordinary people through faith (2:7).

7. Many people in Paul's time found it hard to believe that God would allow evil people to kill His very own Son. How does Paul deal with this "stumbling block"?

By saying that God turned our most evil intent into our greatest blessing— the ultimate revelation of an all-good, all-powerful God (1:27-31).

8. Does Paul literally mean that God is ever foolish or weak?

Paul uses the literary structure called "paradox"—the placing of apparent opposites to teach a deeper truth.

9. In our time, we will always run into people who have better education, more money, or more power. How can we deal with this?

By remembering that God can use our gifts, no matter how humble (1:27-28).

10. What does Paul say is the only power that can bring everyone together into a new community?

Our faith in Christ's power to grant us "wisdom, righteousness, sanctification, and redemption" (1:30).

January 31, 1993

One Body in Christ

Ephesians 4

1 THEREFORE, the prisoner of the Lord, beseech you that ye walk worthy of the vocation wherewith ye are called,
2 With all lowliness and meekness, with longsuffering, forbearing one another in love;
3 Endeavoring to keep the unity of the Spirit in the bond of peace.
4 *There* is one body, and one Spirit even as ye are called in one hope of your calling;
5 One Lord, one faith, one baptism,
6 One God and Father of all, who is above all, and through all, and in you all.
7 But unto every one of us is given grace according to the measure of the gift of Christ.
8 Wherefore he saith, WHEN HE ASCENDED UP ON HIGH, HE LED CAPTIVITY CAPTIVE, AND GAVE GIFTS UNTO MEN.
9 (Now that he ascended, what is it but that he also descended first into the lower parts of the earth?
10 He that descended is the same also that ascended up far above all heavens, that he might fill all things.)
11 And he gave some, apostles; and some, prophets; and some, evangelists; and some, pastors and teachers;
12 For the perfecting of the saints, for the work of the ministry, for the edifying of the body of Christ:
13 Till we all come in the unity of the faith, and of the knowledge of the Son of God, unto a perfect man, unto the measure of the stature of the fulness of Christ:
14 That we *henceforth* be no more children, tossed to and fro, and carried about with every wind of doctrine, by the sleight of men, *and* cunning craftiness, whereby they lie in wait to deceive;
15 But speaking the truth in love, may grow up into him in all things, which is the head, *even* Christ:
16 From whom the whole body fitly joined together and compacted by that which every joint supplieth, according to the effectual working in the measure of every part, maketh increase of the body unto the edifying of itself in love.

◆◆◆◆◆◆

◀ **Memory Selection**
Ephesians 4:4

◀ **Devotional Reading**
I Corinthians 12:12-27

◀ **Background Scripture**
Ephesians 4

◀ **Printed Scripture**
Ephesians 4:1-16

ONE BODY IN CHRIST

Teacher's Target

Chapters 1-3 of Paul's letter to the Ephesians are doctrinal, telling us about the nature of the church. Chapters 4-6 are practical, telling us how the church operates in the world. The text for this lesson comes from the beginning of the practical latter half of the epistle. It points out the importance of Christians being unified in the Spirit. It deals with spiritual gifts and with spiritually-gifted individuals given by God to the church. It describes the purpose of these spiritual gifts and spiritually-gifted individuals at work in the church.

Help your students to understand the unity to which God has called them in Christ. Help them to realize that every believer has one or more spiritual gifts to use in edifying the whole body of Christ. Help them to know and appreciate the special kinds of leaders God uses in the church. Help them to know what Christian maturity is and how to attain to it.

Lesson Introduction

Earlier in Ephesians, Paul compared the church to a holy temple built upon the foundation of the apostles and prophets and featuring Jesus Christ Himself as the chief cornerstone (Eph. 2:19-22). In this lesson text, Paul compared the church to a living organism with Christ as its Head and believers as members fitted together and edifying (building up) one another in love (Eph. 4:15-16). Too much emphasis has been put on the material aspects of church development during the history of the church, such as properties, buildings, rituals, and pageantries.

We need to see that the church is primarily a spiritual entity and should be dedicated to winning souls to Christ and building them up in Him. Jesus Himself gave the great commission involving evangelism and education (Matt. 28:19-20). It can be implemented only if the church is united, well-led, and using the spiritual gifts provided. Mature, dependable, loving believers mean more to a church than the finest facilities ever could mean to it, and that is the emphasis of this lesson.

Teaching Outline

I. Meekness: Eph. 4:1-6
   A. Obligation: 1-3
   B. Oneness: 4-6
II. Measure: Eph. 4:7-10
   A. Grace: 7
   B. Gifts: 8-10
III. Maturity: Eph. 4:11-16
   A. People: 11
   B. Perfection: 12-13
   C. Progress: 14-16

Daily Bible Readings

Mon. One in Christ
Eph. 2:11-22
Tue. A Prayer for Wisdom
Eph. 3:1-13
Wed. The Love of Christ
Eph. 3:14-21
Thu. Show Your Love
Eph. 4:1-6
Fri. Special Gifts
Eph. 4:7-16
Sat. New Life in Christ
Eph. 4:17-24
Sun. Members of Christ's Body
Eph. 4:25-32

VERSE BY VERSE

I. Meekness: Eph. 4:1-6

A. Obligation: 1-3

1. I therefore, the prisoner of the Lord, beseech you that ye walk worthy of the vocation wherewith ye are called.
Paul's letter to the Ephesians was the first of his prison epistles. Part of his ministry while confined to house-arrest for two years in Rome was to reach out by his letters and help believers in various places. This epistle was carried to Ephesus by the hand of Tychicus, and he was assigned to strengthen them in the faith while there (Eph. 6:21-22). Although Paul was Rome's prisoner, he thought of himself as the Lord's prisoner (or a prisoner for the Lord's sake). He urged believers to behave in such a way that they would be a credit to the One Who had called then to a vocation of service to Him. This was a spiritual obligation.

2. With all lowliness and meekness, with longsuffering, forbearing one another in love;
Paul wanted believers to cultivate certain virtues. They should be humble (lowly, meek). They should be patient (longsuffering). They should be tolerant (forbearing) toward one another in love. Let it be mentioned here that forbearance is needed by believers when they deal with unrepented sins. Forgiveness is needed by them when they deal with repented sins (Luke 17:3-4; Gal. 6:1).

3. Endeavoring to keep the unity of the Spirit in the bond of peace.
Paul was a good student of human nature, and he knew that it was sinful and weak. He saw in the assembly of believers opportunities for them to help one another through difficult experiences. However, they would not be able to do this if they were arguing with one another. He said that they would have to make a conscious effort to maintain unity among themselves. They would need help from outside of themselves. That is where the Holy Spirit came in. If they were obedient to His guidance, believers could be bound together in peace. This was important, not only for their own sakes, but also for their testimony to the unsaved world. People would not be attracted to the church if believers were continually bickering with each other. They would be attracted to them if they sincerely loved one another both in words and in deeds.

B. Oneness: 4-6

4. There is one body, and one Spirit, even as ye are called in one hope of your calling;
Paul developed the theme of unity by reminding believers that they were members of one body under the guidance of the Holy Spirit. They had been called to a glorious hope, and that was the second coming of Jesus Christ to take them up to heaven. While they waited for that event, they were to devote themselves to harmonious relationships.

5. One Lord, one faith, one baptism.
Since the Holy Spirit is mentioned in verse 4, and God the Father is mentioned in verse 6, it is probable that the "one Lord" mentioned in verse 5 refers to the Lord Jesus Christ. It was believing faith in Him which bound believers

to Him, and, by inference, to one another.

6. One God and Father of all, who is above all, and through all, and in you all.

God the Father is sovereign over all creatures and things in the universe. He is superior to all. He is everywhere present. He is in believers by means of the indwelling Holy Spirit. The union of the Holy Trinity and believers is indivisible.

II. Measure: Eph. 4:7-10

A. Grace: 7

7. But unto every one of us is given grace according to the measure of the gift of Christ.

We have heard of saving grace, but the grace mentioned here seems to refer to enabling grace within believers. This is grace given to them by the Holy Spirit so that they might serve Christ effectively. "To each one of us grace has been given as Christ has apportioned it" (New International Version). "Christ has given each of us special abilities— whatever he wants us to have out of his rich storehouse of gifts" (Living Bible).

B. Gifts: 8-10

8. Wherefore he saith, When he ascended up on high, he led captivity captive, and gave gifts unto men.

This comes from Psalm 68:18— "Thou hast ascended on high, thou hast led captivity captive: thou hast received gifts for men." It may describe the ascension of Christ to heaven and His sending down of spiritual gifts to believers by means of the Holy Spirit. For lists of such gifts, see Romans 12: 6-8 and I Corinthians 12:4-11 and 28. Reference to Christ leading "captivity captive" is uncertain. It may mean that Christ caught what had captured us and cancelled its influence. It may refer to Christ taking the righteous dead out of Abraham's bosom and transporting them to heaven at the time of His resurrection.

9. (Now that he ascended, what is it but that he also descended first into the lower parts of the earth?

10. He that descended is the same also that ascended up far above all heavens, that he might fill all things.)

This parenthetical material is given to explain what was recorded in verse 8, but it, too, is uncertain. Some think that it refers to Christ coming down to the earth as a man for some thirty-three years and then ascending back up to heaven. Others suggest that it refers to Christ going down into the depths of the earth after His death at Calvary and leading the righteous souls out and upward to His Father. Whatever the case, He gave saving grace to believers and enabling grace to equip them for effective service. He ascended up above the heavens in order that He might fill the whole universe with His presence and power.

III. Maturity: Eph. 4:11-16

A. People: 11

11. And he gave some, apostles; and some, prophets; and some, evangelists; and some, pastors and teachers;

Paul said that God gave four or five types of spiritually-gifted individuals to the church. Apostles were literally "sent ones," but the term came to be applied to the twelve disciples of Jesus (minus Judas Iscariot, plus Matthias) and to such men as Barnabas and Paul. Prophets were those who had a special message from God. Apostles, prophets, and teachers are also mentioned in I Corinthians 12:28. Evangelists were those specially gifted in winning souls to Christ. Pastors were shepherds over God's flock, nourishing them with God's Word. Some think that pastors and teachers were separate, while others put them together in pastor/teacher roles.

Hebrews 13:7 seems to refer to such leaders, "Remember them which have the rule over you who have spoken unto you the word of God: whose faith follow, considering the end of their conversation [conduct]." These were examples for believers to emulate.

B. Perfection: 12-13

12. For the perfecting of the saints, for the work of the ministry, for the edifying of the body of Christ:

This is a general, three-pronged statement showing why God gave the church spiritually-gifted people. First, it was to help the saints (believers) become perfect (mature). This does not refer to sinless perfection, but rather to a state of Christian maturity in which the positive increasingly outweighs the negative. Second, it was to equip believers to carry on the ministry of the church. This involved inspiration and education. Third, it was to edify (build up) the body of Christ by means of instruction, love, and cooperation. Elaboration on these points is given in subsequent verses in this passage.

13. Till we all come in the unity of the faith, and of the knowledge of the Son of God, unto a perfect man, unto the measure of the stature of the fulness of Christ.

Every local church had a wide range of believers in it. Paul said that God's gifted leaders would help these believers to draw together through their pursuit of a common faith (body of truth). This would lead to experiential knowledge of Jesus Christ. He stood as the ideal One to imitate.. They could not attain fully to His exalted stature, but they could move in that direction. They could also look forward to a glorious fulfillment in the future—"Beloved, now are we the sons of God, and it doth not yet appear what we shall be; but we know that, when he [Christ] shall appear, we shall be like him; for we shall see him as he is" (1 John 3:2).

C. Progress: 14-16

14. That we henceforth be no more children, tossed to and fro, and carried about with every wind of doctrine, by the sleight of men, and cunning craftiness, whereby they lie in wait to deceive;

In contrast to the growing spiritual maturity described in verse 13, Paul spoke of the immaturity of some believers. He may have been thinking of some of the shallow Christians in Ephesus. He described such individuals as those who were blown this way and that by every wind of doctrine coming their way. He called them vulnerable to men stalking them in cunning, crafty, deceitful ways.

15. But speaking the truth, in love, may grow up into him in all things, which is the head, even Christ.

Here Paul came back to the same tone he used in verses 12-13. He urged believers to speak the truth in love. There is a similarity here to what is found in Colossians 2:8-10 and 18-19, and you may want to turn to those verses with your students. Through mutual sharing of divine truth, believers could grow (develop) up into the form provided for them in the character of Christ, the Head of the church. Becoming spiritually mature involved becoming more and more like Christ. Love for Him, plus obedience to His commandments, promoted spiritual progress.

16. From whom the whole body fitly joined together and compacted by that which every joint supplieth, according to the effectual working in the measure of every part, maketh increase of the body unto the edifying of itself in love.

The "whom" here refers to Christ. He is the Source from Whom the body draws its wisdom and strength. If He is followed, harmony among the members of His body will prevail. Spiritual health, growth, and unity will be present. Strong members will take over for weak members until they can develop and carry their own weight. Spiritual gifts will be identified and utilized in each member for the good of the whole. As a result, the church will hold together the way it should, and it will have an effective testimony to the unsaved world. This is the goal to which each congregation called.

Evangelistic Emphasis

Some see the world as made up of either saints or sinners, one or the other. Paul the Apostle would disagree. Paul would say that all of us, himself included, are sinners.

Do you know the most common reason people stay away from church? Surveys by evangelism researchers show that a person's own self-image is the biggest factor. If people have very low self-esteem, their reaction is likely to be:

No, it's not for me; I'm not qualified. I've had too much of a checkered past. People wouldn't accept me. I couldn't live up to the expectations of "church people." It would be nice, but I could never be accepted.

Isn't that tragic? You probably know folks who feel that way about themselves. Jesus understood their hesitancy and treated it with great compassion. His invitation was wide open: "Whosoever will may come!" He was especially sensitive to the outcast and the downtrodden, the homeless and the public sinner. You rarely see him accusing such people, for they have already accused themselves. (He saves most of his harshest words for "religious" people who make others feel rejected.)

Today's lesson can help us invite others into the great circle of fellowship to which all of us are invited, and to which all of us have something to receive and something to give.

◆◆◆◆◆◆

Memory Selection

Many Christian conferences and meetings have composed slogans based on Ephesians 4:5: "One Lord, One Faith, One Baptism." However, in order of priority, our memory verse for today, Ephesians 4:4, contains a vision that's just as crucial:

One Body, One Spirit, One Hope.

Majestic words. Yet the experience is one that's both urgent and practical.

Think of it this way.

Suppose you look under your porch one day and far in a dark back corner you spy a tiny puppy, whimpering and shivering. You call to her, make familiar "come here" noises and motions, but the puppy seems more frightened than ever.

You come to realize this little puppy has received a lot of abuse from its contacts with human beings in its short life.

How will you distinguish yourself from those other harmful humans?

In a way, this is the problem of a loving God trying to reach out to hurting people.

The solution he offers is found in this threefold Oneness:

The One Body — a loving, supportive fellowship where we encourage each other and draw strength from Him.

The One Spirit — who leads us into the Body and nurtures and empowers us.

The One Hope — the new perspective on life that kindled in us based on trust and faith.

One Body. One Spirit. One Hope. It's how God has, spiritually speaking, coaxed us out from under the porch.

January 31, 1993

Weekday Problems

You never have to ask Candide what she thinks. Candor is her trademark. She's honest, direct, and forthright; in fact, she's blunt to the point of insensitivity that wounds people's feelings.

Her brother Shyler is just the opposite. He is a reserved, painfully sensitive fellow, who wouldn't hurt anyone for the world.

If you get to know Candide really well, however, you'll find she's not as open with all her feelings as she appears. The truth is, she knows that people steer clear of her. She knows her directness gets her into trouble. For all her outward bravado, Candide is lonely and discouraged.

Shyler is also struggling. In his attempt to get along with everyone, resentments have accumulated over the years with no way to deal with them. He hates the fact that he's "too nice."

*Applying the principle of "speaking the truth in love" (Ephesians 4:15), how might both Candide and Shyler develop more balanced ways of dealing with people?

◆◆◆◆◆◆

Superintendent's Sermonette

We like to live in a way which allows us to avoid being arrested and going to jail or prison. We want to avoid the humiliation, confinement, and loss of earning power involved. Other Christians, however, have had to suffer these things, and the Apostle Paul was one of them. Falsely arrested and condemned, he exercised his right as a Roman citizen to appeal his case to Caesar. After a long and arduous journey, he finally reached Rome and was held under house-arrest for two years. During that time, he wrote several letters to various churches, and they became known as "prison epistles." His letter to the Ephesians was the first of these.

In spite of his own negative circumstances Paul used his time in Rome to encourage believers to live for Christ and for one another. He knew that the strength of individual churches depended on the ministry of the Holy Spirit working through spiritually gifted leaders and laymen. He made it very clear that this was the only way a group could avoid being sidetracked by false teachers and could go ahead in spiritual development. We need to remind ourselves today that Christ is the Head of the church, and we, as individual members, must draw our wisdom and strength from Him.

This Lesson in Your Life

Today lets talk about "calling."

Let's leave aside discussions about hearing voices in the night, and other aspects of the "hows" of God's calls. There's something much richer in store for us. Let's look instead at the kinds of calls that Scriptures says we may expect God to make on our lives.

1. The call to salvation. This is the first call God makes to our lives — to make a personal decision. God invites us to accept the greatest gift ever offered, that of salvation in Jesus Christ. God also invites us to accept the great invitation to attend the non-stop spiritual banquet, the moveable feast, known as God's worldwide community, the church.

2. The call to commitment. This is the call to become not only part of the great throng of the saved, but also to be a disciple, to put oneself under the discipline of Christ. If the call to salvation feels like a religious experience, the call to commitment is a wider call. It involves one's whole life — values, family life, work life, attitudes, politics — everything. In this call God promises to make every moment of life into a blessing.

3. The call to ministry. God also calls each of us to "equip ourselves for the work of ministry" (Ephesians 4:12). For some this means choosing ministry as a full-time vocation, with all the preparation and training this entails. For others the call to ministry involves re-directing our secular training or experience toward the needs of the spiritual community — teaching, travelling, serving on behalf of various age groups, needs, or lifestyles where we have something special to offer.

4. The call to office. This is the call of God that is echoed in the calls of others. Your fellow Christians recognize your special gifts and ask you to serve the church in some capacity. You might be called to serve in the work of a local congregation. It might be that you've been called to serve as a teacher, department head, committee head, or other church officer. The call might also extend to the wider church, to serve as a missionary, as a director of a regional or national level of church work.

5. The call to task. At certain times in your life you will be asked to take on a particular task that matches your training and interests with the needs of a certain time and place. For example, a minister might be called to serve a particular congregation; a church member to teach a certain age group in the church; an executive to accept a secular position in a distant city which results in using his spiritual gifts in a new way.

6. The call to world vision. This is the call to pioneer a ministry in totally new ways. This could be something as dramatic as Mother Teresa's work among the poorest of the poor in India or Martin Luther King's work that broke down legal barriers to brotherhood. Or it could be something as unheralded as being the first person in your congregation to innovate a particular practice in the classroom or the worship service, or to start a new outreach to an urgent need in the community. With such a call comes the gift to persevere in spite of opposition, apathy, or lack of encouragement. To a person called to serve God from the perspective of the pioneer, the fact that there is a job to be done and he has the heart to carry it out is all that's necessary.

How many of these levels of call to ministry have come to you? As you recognize the many aspects of God's call, why not share some of your experiences with your Bible study group today?

Seed Thoughts

1. Paul describes himself as "a prisoner of Jesus Christ for you" (Ephesians 3:1; see also 4:1). What does he mean?
   He was likely serving time in prison. Even imprisonment failed to stop Paul: He used the time to write great epistles to the churches.

2. "The unity of the Spirit in the bond of peace" — does Paul view it as an ideal to strive for, or as a gift already received which we are to maintain?
   Paul instructs us to "endeavor to keep" unity that is given us already by the Spirit (4:3).

3. What are the seven aspects of the unity we are to preserve?
   One body, one spirit, one hope, one Lord, one faith, one baptism, one God (4:4-6).

4. What gifts has Christ given the church to help us maintain unity?
   Apostles, prophets, evangelists, pastors, teachers (4:7-11).

---

1. Paul describes himself as "a prisoner of Jesus Christ for you" (Ephesians 3:1; see also 4:1). What does he mean?

2. "The unity of the Spirit in the bond of peace" — does Paul view it as an ideal to strive for, or as a gift already received which we are to maintain?

3. What are the seven aspects of the unity we are to preserve?

4. What gifts has Christ given the church to help us maintain unity?

5. What is the ultimate purpose of the gifts Christ has given us?

6. What does the mature Christian look like?

7. The Greek word for "cunning" in 4:14 means "to play with loaded dice." In what ways do some people play with loaded dice, spiritually speaking?

8. What does a church look like when it is led into spiritual maturity?

(PLEASE TURN PAGE)

(SEED THOUGHTS--Cont'd)

He was likely serving time in prison. Even imprisonment failed to stop Paul: He used the time to write great epistles to the churches.

Paul instructs us to "endeavor to keep" unity that is given us already by the Spirit (4:3).

One body, one spirit, one hope, one Lord, one faith, one baptism, one God (4:4-6)

Apostles, prophets, evangelists, pastors, teachers (4:7-11).

The perfecting of the saints, the work of ministry, the edifying of the body of Christ (4:12).

Stable and deep-rooted in the faith, able to detect counterfeit teachings and fraudulent leaders, able to speak the truth in love (4:13-15).

The term refers to taking unfair advantage of others. It is the opposite of being "lowly, meek, patient, forbearing" (4:2).

Each person receives the personal encouragement and teachings needed and all bring their unique gifts to work together for a higher cause. (4:16).

5. What is the ultimate purpose of the gifts Christ has given us?
The perfecting of the saints, the work of ministry, the edifying of the body of Christ (4:12).

6. What does the mature Christian look like?
Stable and deep-rooted in the faith, able to detect counterfeit teachings and fraudulent leaders, able to speak the truth in love (4:13-15).

7. The Greek word for "cunning" in 4:14 means "to play with loaded dice." In what ways do some people play with loaded dice, spiritually speaking?
The term refers to taking unfair advantage of others. It is the opposite of being "lowly, meek, patient, forbearing" (4:2).

8. What does a church look like when it is led into spiritual maturity?
Each person receives the personal encouragement and teachings needed and all bring their unique gifts to work together for a higher cause. (4:16).

February 7, 1993

Commissioned To Witness

IS WITNESSING IN THE PLANS?

Luke 24

36. And as they thus spake, Jesus himself stood in the midst of them, and saith unto them, Peace be unto you.
37. But they were terrified and affrighted, and supposed that they had seen a spirit.
38. And he said unto them, Why are ye troubled? and why do thoughts arise in your hearts?
39. Behold my hands and my feet, that it is I myself: handle me, and see; for a spirit hath not flesh and bones, as ye see me have.
40. And when he had thus spoken, he shewed them his hands and his feet.
41. And while they yet believed not for joy, and wondered, he said unto them, Have ye here any meat?
42. And they gave him a piece of a broiled fish, and of an honeycomb.
43. And he took it, and did eat before them.
44 And he said unto them, These *are* the words which I spake unto you, while I was yet with you, that all things must be fulfilled, which were written in the law of Moses, and *in* the prophets, and in the psalms, concerning me.
45. Then opened he their understanding, that they might understand the scriptures,
46 And said unto them, Thus it is written, and thus it behoved Christ to suffer, and to rise from the dead the third day:
47. And that repentance and remission of sins should be preached in his name among all nations, beginning at Jerusalem.
48. And ye are witnesses of these things.
49. And, behold, I send the promise of my Father upon you: but tarry ye in the city of Jerusalem, until ye be endued with power from on high.
50. And he led them out as far as to Beth´-a-ny, and he lifted up his hands, and blessed them.
51. And it came to pass, while he blessed them, he was parted from them, and carried up into heaven.
52. And they worshipped him, and returned to Jerusalem with great Joy:
53. And were continually in the temple, praising and blessing God. A´-men.

◆◆◆◆◆◆

◀ **Memory Selection**
Luke 24:47

◀ **Devotional Reading**
Acts 1:1-8

◀ **Background Scripture**
Luke 24:13-53

◀ **Printed Scripture**
Luke 24:36-53

COMMISSIONED TO WITNESS

Teacher's Target

The followers of Jesus were on an emotional roller coaster. They had thought that the triumphal entry into Jerusalem signified the establishment of the kingdom of God on earth with Jesus as its King. He had warned them of coming suffering and death, but they chose to put it out of their minds, Then came the dark days of betrayal, arrest, judgment, suffering, and crucifixion. He had been laid in a tomb. On the third day He rose again just as He had promised. When they saw Him again, they thought He was a ghost, and He had to prove that He was real. Then came His great commission to carry the gospel to the ends of the earth.

Help your students to be convinced that Jesus is truly alive in heaven, and we are commissioned to carry on the work which He began. They cannot do this in their own strength. They have to be endued with power from on high through the ministry of the indwelling Holy Spirit. They can witness by means of personal contact, letters, literature, broadcasting, and other ways and by supporting believers who go in our place.

Lesson Introduction

Men do not like to be called cowards or wimps. Sometimes they go to ridiculous extremes to bolster a *macho* image. How should we evaluate the disciples of Jesus? When He was betrayed and arrested in the garden of Gethsemane, "they all forsook him and fled" (Mark 14:50). "Peter followed him afar off" when He was taken to judgment (Mark 14:54). In the evening of the day Jesus rose from the dead, His disciples were in hiding for fear of the Jews (John 20:19). They needed an infusion of courage and boldness before they could carry on His work.

When Jesus appeared to them, they were terrified, thinking that He was a ghost. He calmed their fear and proved that He was real. He told them that their future work was to evangelize the world. This was later reinforced when He spoke to them just prior to His ascension to heaven (Matt. 28:16-20). Their problem of cowardice was solved on the Day of Pentecost, just as He had predicted (Luke 24:49; Acts 1:8; 2:4; 4:8; 4:31). We can solve our problem, too, as we are empowered by the Holy Spirit.

Teaching Outline

I. Appearance: Luke 24:36-45
   A. Extension: 36-37
   B. Examination: 38-43
   C. Explanation: 44-45
II. Announcement: Luke 24:46-48
   A. Purpose: 46-47
   B. Participants: 48
III. Ascension: Luke 24:49-53
   A. Demand: 49
   B. Departure: 50-51
   C. Delight: 52-53

Daily Bible Readings

Mon. Jesus Is a Witness
Luke 23:26-34
Tue. Jesus Is Crucified
Luke 23:35-43
Wed. Jesus' Death
Luke 23:44-56
Thu. The Resurrection
Luke 24:1-12
Fri. The Walk to Emmaus
Luke 24:13-27
Sat. Breaking Bread
Luke 24:28-35
Sun. Jesus Appeared to the Disciples
Luke 24:36-49

February 7, 1993

VERSE BY VERSE

I. Appearance: Luke 24: 36-45

A. Extension: 36-37

36. And as they thus spake, Jesus himself stood in the midst of them, and saith unto them, Peace be unto you.

This passage should be studied in conjunction with John 20:19-23. Cleopas and his unnamed companion had met Jesus on the road to Emmaus, and they had returned to Jerusalem to find the disciples and others with them so that they could report on what had happened (Luke 24:33-35). At the time, the disciples were evidently called "the eleven," much as they had once been called "the twelve," but there were actually only ten of them present. Thomas was missing (John 20:24). As this report was given, Jesus suddenly appeared in the room in spite of the doors being shut (and probably bolted) (John 20:19). He stood in their midst and greeted them with the usual "Peace be unto you."

37. But they were terrified and affrighted, and supposed that they had seen a spirit.

This was a normal reaction because of the circumstances. When He had come earlier to them walking on the sea, "they were troubled, saying, It is a spirit; and they cried out for fear" (Matt. 14: 26). Even as they had not expected Him to walk on the sea at night, they had not expected Him to come to them now by extending Himself through a solid door or wall. They were also amazed to note that He looked normal, rather than being battered and bruised from His torture and crucifixion, Their conclusion was that this must be His spirit (ghost).

B. Examination: 38-43

38. And he said unto them, Why are ye troubled? and why do thoughts arise in your hearts?

Jesus asked two questions which served as rebukes to the disciples. He wanted to know why they were disturbed and why they had doubts in their minds at seeing Him. This probably was based on the fact that He had repeatedly told them about His coming death and resurrection before they came.

39. Behold my hands and my feet, that it is I myself: handle me, and see; for a spirit hath not flesh and bones, as ye see me have.

John 20:20 adds that He also showed them His side. It was by looking at the nail prints in His hands and feet and at the mark made by the spear in His side that He identified Himself to them. He mentioned that a spirit would not be composed of flesh and bone as He obviously was at that moment.

40. And when he had thus spoken, he shewed them his hands and his feet.

Perhaps Jesus had first merely had them look at His hands and feet. His invitation to handle (or touch) him (vs. 39) may now have been literally accepted by them, for it says that He showed them His hands and his feet and perhaps urged them to feel them to see that they were indeed flesh and bone.

41. And while they yet believed not for joy, and wondered, he said unto them, Have ye here any meat?

42. And they gave him a piece of a broiled fish, and of an honeycomb.

43. And he took it, and did eat before them.

Luke, the physician, made this known to us, perhaps because of his scientific outlook. While the disciples were still doubting the reality of Jesus being among them, the Master asked for meat (food). Given a piece of broiled fish and part of a honeycomb, Jesus ate before them, something a ghost would not have done. They had to be convinced. Their physical examination of Him was over, and it was now time for Him to give them spiritual teaching.

44. And he said unto them, These are the words which I spake unto you, while I was yet with you, that all things must be fulfilled, which were written in the law of Moses, and in the prophets, and in the psalms, concerning me.

Jesus declared that things written about the Messiah in the Old Testament had been fulfilled in Him. Divisions in the Old Testament included the law of Moses (the Pentateuch), writings of the prophets (major and minor prophets, plus some historical books), and the psalms (plus other poetic books). He was no doubt referring particularly to events which had just recently transpired connected with His death and resurrection.

45. Then opened he their understanding, that they might understand the scriptures.

Cleopas and his companion had already had this kind of marvelous experience. They said, "Did not our heart burn within us, while he talked with us by the way, and while he opened to us the scriptures?" (Luke 24:32). Now the disciples were allowed to have this experience, as well. Imagine what it must have been like to have the Master Himself go back through the Jewish Scriptures and pull out references to Himself and show what had been fulfilled up to that time. He may also have told what was yet to happen to Him such as His ascension, second coming, and establishment of a worldwide kingdom.

II. Announcement: Luke 24:46-48

A. Purpose: 46-47

46. And said unto them, Thus it is written, and thus it behoved Christ to suffer, and to rise from the dead the third day:

Jesus' stated purpose in giving the disciples a scripture lesson that evening was to make it clear that his death and resurrection were required in order to fulfill Old Testament prophecies concerning the Messiah. Therefore, what had happened was actually right and for the best, regardless of how unfair and disastrous things may have seemed at the time they happened. These facts were to form the basic message to be preached by the disciples from that time forward. An analysis of New Testament sermons shows that this was done.

47. And that repentance and remission of sins should be preached in his name among all nations, beginning at Jerusalem.

This verse fits nicely with Matthew 28:19-20 and with Acts 1:8. Jesus announced that His followers were destined to spread the gospel of repentance and remission of sins to the whole world, starting at Jerusalem. It was a message of liberation and hope for all who sincerely wanted to please God.

B. Participants: 48

48. And ye are witnesses of these things.

The events seen and heard by the followers of Jesus had been traumatic, but they were all the more impressive because of their stark reality. They could not be forgotten, and they would remain in their minds during their lifetime. They had been participants in many of the things which had happened to Jesus, and they had been observers of the rest. This was not limited to the disciples who formed His inner circle, for there were others involved. There were "men which have companied with us all the time that the Lord Jesus went in and out among us, beginning with the baptism of John, unto that same day that he was taken up from us" (Acts 1:21-22), Thus spoke Peter on the day that a vote was taken to replace Judas Iscariot as one of the twelve. We know that two of these men were named Barsabas Justus and Matthias, and that it was Matthias who was chosen to replace Judas Iscariot (Acts 1:23-26).

III. Ascension: Luke 24:49-53

A. Demand: 49

49. And, behold, I send the promise of my Father upon you: but tarry ye in the city of Jerusalem, until ye be endued with power from on high.

Jesus had already foretold the coming of the Holy Spirit upon believers (John 14:16-17; 15:26; 16:13). The Spirit had been described as a Comforter, Witness concerning Christ, and Teacher. To that was now added His role as an Empowerer. The followers of Jesus would be able to accomplish nothing in the realm of spiritual matters unless they were guided and empowered by the Holy Spirit.

Luke 24:49 and Acts 1:8 agree in the sense that Jesus' followers were to remain in Jerusalem until the Holy Spirit came upon them, and then they were to spread the gospel by beginning at Jerusalem and going out to the provinces of Judaea and Samaria before going out further to the nations of the earth. What they began was to be completed by subsequent generations of believers, and we may count ourselves as being included in that number.

B. Departure: 50-51

50. And he led them out as far as to Bethany, and he lifted up his hands, and blessed them.

Jesus led His followers out to Bethany, a town on the slope of the Mount of Olives. Here He put up His hands over them in a gesture of benediction. It must have been a thrill to hear Him personally teach about Himself from the Jewish Scriptures (Luke 24:32, 45). It must have also been a thrill to hear Him pronounce a personal benediction. This had to be a blessing with substance, and it was obviously one of spiritual importance, for it came from the divine Son of God.

51. And it came to pass, while he blessed them, he was parted from them, and carried up into heaven.

This is a beautiful picture of Christ, blessing His followers while He Himself was transported upward to heaven by a cloud until He vanished from their sight (Acts 1:9). Two angels (appearing as men) stood by and told the believers that Jesus would come back in like manner as He went up (Acts 1:10-11). He will come back to the earth at this same place (Zech. 14:4).

C. Delight: 52-53

52. And they worshipped him, and returned to Jerusalem with great joy:

It appears that the believers remained at the Mount of Olives for awhile in order to worship Jesus, even though He was no longer with them. They must have felt a great loss, for they had hoped to see Him set up His earthly kingdom at this time instead of leaving them (Acts 1:6). The forty days in which he had appeared to many between His resurrection and ascension had passed too quickly. However, still basking in the glow of His benediction upon them, they turned to walk back to Jerusalem with great joy. They may also have rejoiced in His promise to send them another Comforter soon.

53. And were continually in the temple, praising and blessing God. Amen.

We are not sure of the timing mentioned here. It is probable that the believers went to the temple for daily times of prayer and praise to God. Acts 1:12-26 tells us that they also spent time in an upper room praying and deciding who should replace Judas Iscariot as a member of the twelve. There were around a hundred and twenty believers gathered there.

Scriptural proof that Jesus reached heaven maybe found in several places. Stephen saw Him there as he was being martyred (Acts 7:55-56). We are told that He intercedes for believers at the right hand of God (Heb. 7:25; 1 John 2:1). He helps believers to keep from falling (Jude 24). John saw Him in his heavenly vision (Rev. 1:9-17). Living believers and resurrected believers will see Him when He comes again to take them to heaven (1 Thess. 4:13-18). All nations will see Him when He comes to rule the world (Matt. 25:31-32; Rev. 19:11-16).

Evangelistic Emphasis

You see it on the comic pages of your newspaper— the white-robed character standing haplessly on a busy street corner, holding a sign that says, "Repent!"

Is this what is meant in the Bible by repentance?

Properly understood, repentance is far more than a futile cry against a heedless world. Biblical repentance is the first step in spiritual revival. It is the awakening of moral responsibility in a dormant conscience.

Jonah preached in Nineveh and the people proclaimed a public fast. The king call for the citizens to count the ways they acted violently and corruptly. (See Jonah, chapter 3.)

John the Baptist preached a message of repentance and then got specific. To the people: share your food and your clothing with those who have none. Tax collectors: create a new system that's fair to the taxpayers. Soldiers: live within your budget, and don't exploit the people you're supposed to protect (See Luke 3:10-14.)

Great reformers of all times have linked the personal experience of repentance to major change in society. Their message is, Get your heart right; look at the evils around you; see how your actions or inactions are contributing to the problem; then resolve to make a turnaround.

Everything God does starts with one person who decides to change: that's *biblical repentance!*

◆◆◆◆◆◆

Memory Selection

The Gospel begins and ends with a message of repentance and forgiveness. What a powerful combination! Repentance... the sensitizing of the conscience to the point that we must act. Forgiveness the experience of the all-embracing love of God that lets us start over, no matter how many times we fall.

Repentance and forgiveness are the two essential elements of abounding grace. Repentance without forgiveness can produce harsh harangues and paralyzing guilt. Forgiveness without repentance can produce apathy in the face of deadly sin. They are like the sodium and the chloride that make up common table salt. As separate elements sodium and chlorine gas can kill. In combination, and used properly, they are essential to life.

Resolve to open your heart to the cries of need all around you, even though that openness may produce some profound changes in your life Determine also to let God's forgiveness cleanse you and energize you to live each day full of joy and love for everyone you meet.

Experience for yourself the ever-renewing and regenerating power of the simple gospel of repentance and forgiveness of sin.

February 7, 1993

Weekday Problems

Hank knows he eats too much. He knows it everytime he puts on a pair of pants that are more than six months old. He knows it every time he meets a friend he hasn't seen for awhile, and watches the surprised survey of his widening physique.

Hank has tried to diet again and again. Whenever he loses weight, it seems to come back more quickly than the last time. His self esteem takes a dive after each attempt to diet. The worst part of it is the advice he gets from friends— all kinds of suggestions for this or that surefire new approach. His friends make it sound so easy. If only someone could understand how he feels, and take him from where he is to where he'd like to be, now there would be a true friend!

*What are some examples of some ways insensitive friends make matters worse for persons struggling with problems?

*What are some ways truly caring friends can help?

*How might a clearer understanding of repentance and forgiveness help make constructive life changes such as health or diet?

♦♦♦♦♦♦

Superintendent's Sermonette

We could save ourselves a lot of worry and grief if we studied the Scriptures carefully and matched them up with what is happening in the world. The disciples of Jesus had an insufficient or imperfect comprehension of the Jewish Scriptures and the way in which Jesus was fulfilling predictions regarding the Messiah. When He moved into His suffering Servant role, rather than His reigning King role, they were confused and depressed. They went into hiding for fear of the Jews, and it was not until they became convinced that Jesus had been raised from the dead that they were able to rejoice again. He restored their joy and He gave them the solemn responsibility of evangelizing the world.

We have the completed revelation of God's Word in both the Old and New Testaments. There are predictions there which have not yet been fulfilled. The way for us to keep our equilibrium in this fast-paced and ungodly world is to know what the Bible teaches and match it up with what is happening. We need to do this in order to retain our joy. We need to do it in order to keep alive our responsibility for evangelizing the world. The Holy Spirit, sent to believers in the first century, is indwelling us and will help us to go forward with confidence.

COMMISSIONED TO WITNESS

This Lesson in Your Life

What would it be like to have the Resurrected Lord appear to you suddenly in the midst of your daily activities?

Luke tells us two stories about such appearances and the results aren't what we might expect. But they do give us food for thought about how resurrection power works in our lives today.

The story of Jesus' appearance to the two disciples on the road to Emmaus is one of the most endearing in the Bible. Here are these two devoted followers of Jesus who have been to Jerusalem during the very events of the crucifixion of the One in whom they had placed their hopes. Now He comes alongside them as they make their way to their home in Emmaus.

He asks them why they are so sad. They answer, in effect, are you the only person around here who doesn't know what happened? They begin to tell Him the whole story— what Jesus taught, how people felt about Him, His arrest, trial, and crucifixion— even the claims, which they seem to doubt, about His still being alive.

He answers by referring to various Scriptures that prophesy about a suffering Christ.

It makes us want to say to them. "Look! Don't you recognize who it is who walks with you?"

They walk on, uncomprehending. . . until the stranger stays for supper. Then, when He takes bread, and blesses it and breaks it and gives it to them. . . *then* they know! As Luke puts it, "their eyes were opened."

Resurrection power, Luke wants us to know, is a different kind of power. It's more than sanctified common sense for these two hapless disciples weren't the sharpest observers, or they might have noticed some scars on the stranger's hands and feet. What is it?

Luke tells another story.

The two disciples leave Emmaus and rush back to Jerusalem to tell the twelve apostles what had happened. Just as they were getting into it, the Risen Lord appears in their midst.

This time He does call attention to His scars. But Luke tells us the people's reaction: "they believed not, for joy." Again, however, Jesus asks to share a meal with them This time He eats a piece of fish. He also interprets more prophecies for them.

At last, they recognized Him. Or to use Luke's words, "He opened their understanding."

Resurrection power is the conviction that love is stronger than death. It's what opens our eyes to know who Jesus really is. Our eyes may be opened in many ways—by a word of Scripture, by an especially meaningful worship experience, by our own encounter with suffering, or by a life infused with divine love and forgiveness. Each of these played a role in opening the eyes of the individuals in today's lesson. In the same marvelous ways, God still works to bring us to faith!

Seed Thoughts

1. What did the two disciples from Emmaus know about Jesus and how did they feel about Him?
They had close ties to the Apostles. They knew something about Jesus' life and teachings and His trial and crucifixion, as well as the eyewitness accounts of the empty tomb.

2. What was Jesus' response to their disappointment?
Luke says Jesus opened the Scriptures and taught from the prophecies, particularly those about the Messiah's suffering and glory (Luke 24:25-27).

3. Why didn't Jesus simply announce who He was and show them His scars?
Luke implies that it was part of God's plan to keep certain things hidden from the two disciples, at least for the time being (24:16).

4. What did "open their eyes" to recognize Jesus?
As they were eating, He took bread, blessed it, broke it, and gave it to them— a reminder of the Last Supper and many other meals with Jesus.

5. What were some other initial reactions of people who saw the Risen Lord?
Many were afraid. and some thought they had seen a ghost. Even those who were invited to see and touch His scars still did not fully understand (24:6-41).

(PLEASE TURN PAGE)

---

1. What did the two disciples from Emmaus know about Jesus and how did they feel about Him?

2. What was Jesus' response to their disappointment?

3. Why didn't Jesus simply announce who He was and show them His scars?

4. What did "open their eyes" to recognize Jesus?

5. What were some other initial reactions of people who saw the Risen Lord?

6. How did people respond to Jesus' teaching from Scripture regarding His crucifixion and resurrection?

7. What do these two accounts teach us about faith in Christ?

8. What was there about eating fish that might have identified Jesus to them?

9. What did Jesus ask the disciples to do?

10. How was the mood of the disciples changed after the ascension?

They had close ties to the Apostles. They knew something about Jesus' life and teachings and His trial and crucifixion, as well as the eyewitness accounts of the empty tomb.

Luke says Jesus opened the Scriptures and taught from the prophecies, particularly those about the Messiah's suffering and glory (Luke 24:25-27).

Luke implies that it was part of God's plan to keep certain things hidden from the two disciples, at least for the time being (24:16).

As they were eating, He took bread, blessed it, broke it, and gave it to them—a reminder of the Last Supper and many other meals with Jesus.

Many were afraid, and some thought they had seen a ghost. Even those who were invited to see and touch His scars still did not fully understand (24:6-41).

They believed only when Jesus "opened their understanding" (24:45).

Christ had to "open the eyes" of people before they could appreciate Scripture or the breaking of bread, or even seeing and touching Him.

The taking of food demonstrated that He was a physical reality and not an apparition.

Stay in the city until they were empowered from heaven for their mission.

Their anxiety and fear were replaced by great joy.

(SEED THOUGHTS--Cont'd)

6. How did people respond to Jesus' teaching from Scripture regarding His crucifixion and resurrection?
They believed only when Jesus "opened their understanding" (24:45).

7. What do these two accounts teach us about faith in Christ?
Christ had to "open the eyes" of people before they could appreciate Scripture or the breaking of bread, or even seeing and touching Him.

8. What was there about eating fish that might have identified Jesus to them?
The taking of food demonstrated that He was a physical reality and not an apparition.

9. What did Jesus ask the disciples to do?
Stay in the city until they were empowered from heaven for their mission.

10. How was the mood of the disciples changed after the ascension?
Their anxiety and fear were replaced by great joy.

February 14, 1993

"PASTOR, THANKS, I'VE FOUND JESUS"

Proclaim the Gospel

Romans 10

5. For Moses describeth the righteousness which is of the law, That the man which doeth those things shall live by them.
6. But the righteousness which is of faith speaketh on this wise, Say not in thine heart, Who shall ascend into heaven? (that is, to bring Christ down *from above:*)
7. Or, Who shall descend into the deep? (that is, to bring up Christ again from the dead.)
8. But what saith it? The word is nigh thee, in thy mouth, and in thy heart: that is, the word of faith, which we preach;
9. That if thou shalt confess with thy mouth the Lord Jesus, and shalt believe in thine heart that God hath raised him from the dead, thou shalt be saved.
10. For with the heart man believeth unto righteousness; and with the mouth confession is made unto salvation.
11. For the scripture saith, Whosoever believeth on him shall not be ashamed.
12. For there is no difference between the Jew and the Greek: for the same Lord over all is rich unto all that call upon him.
13. For whosoever shall call upon the name of the Lord shall be saved.
14. How then shall they call on him in whom they have not believed? and how shall they believe in him of whom they have not heard? and how shall they hear without a preacher?
15. And how shall they preach, except they be sent? as it is written, How BEAUTIFUL ARE THE FEET OF THEM THAT PREACH THE GOSPEL OF PEACE, AND BRING GLAD TIDINGS OF GOOD THINGS!
16. But they have not all obeyed the gospel. For E-sa′ias saith, Lord, who hath believed our report?
17. So then faith *cometh* by hearing, and hearing by the word of God.

◆◆◆◆◆◆

◀ **Memory Selection**
Romans 10:17

◀ **Devotional Reading**
I Corinthians 9:19-27

◀ **Background Scripture**
Romans 10

◀ **Printed Scripture**
Romans 10:5-17

Teacher's Target

Human reasoning makes it difficult for some people to understand the gospel. They think of cause and effect. They think of action and reaction. They find it almost impossible to conceive of salvation as anything separate from their own efforts. They feel it is necessary for them to do things in order to merit redemption. World religions stress activities designed to bring their devotees merit. Against this background, the gospel of Christ stands forth in sharp contrast, because it proclaims divine grace as the means of salvation.

Help your students to realize that righteousness originates in heaven and is available to human beings only by faith in Jesus Christ. The Mosaic law held up a standard of righteousness which only Christ Himself could fulfill. It demanded a penalty for sin which only He could pay. It is through identification with Him that we may know true righteousness in this life and the life to come. This is a message of hope for all men, and on us rests the responsibility for helping them hear it.

Lesson Introduction

Paul expressed deep concern for his fellow Jews in Romans 9-11. Note opening comments in each of these chapters. "I could wish that myself were accursed from Christ for my brethren, my kinsmen according to the flesh" (Rom. 9:3). "My heart's desire and prayer to God for Israel is that they might be saved" (Rom. 10:1). "God hath not cast away his people which he foreknew" (Rom. 11:2). Until the time came for Israel to turn to Christ as a nation, Paul wanted to win individual Jews to Him one by one. Although he had a special ministry to Gentiles, he did not forget the spiritual needs of the Jews.

Our text for this lesson is taken from the middle of this three-chapter passage. It is addressed to both Jews and Gentiles. It begins with reference to the law of Moses and what Jews could expect under the law as far as righteousness was concerned. It then moves on to the righteousness which comes by faith in Christ and shows that this is a matter of the heart and leads to confession by the mouth. It concludes that "faith cometh by hearing, and hearing by the word of God" (Rom. 10:17).

Teaching Outline

I. Righteousness: Rom. 10:5-9
  A. Righteousness of law: 5
  B. Righteousness of faith: 6-9
II. Richness: Rom. 10:10-13
  A. What man does: 10-11
  B. What God does: 12-13
III. Reception: Rom. 10:14-17
  A. Witnesses: 14-15a
  B. Writings: 15b-16
  C. Ways: 17

Daily Bible Readings

Mon. The Law Proclaims
Gal. 3:21-29
Tue. God's People
Rom. 9:1-5
Wed. God's Promise
Rom. 9:6-18
Thu. God's Mercy
Rom. 9:19-26
Fri. Gospel for Israel
Rom. 9:27-33
Sat. Salvation for All
Rom. 10:1-13
Sun. Message of Salvation
Rom. 10:14-21

VERSE BY VERSE

I. Righteousness: Rom. 10:5-9

A. Righteousness of law: 5

5. For Moses describeth the righteousness which is of the law, That the man which doeth those things shall live by them.

God spoke to Israel through Moses, saying, "Ye shall therefore keep my statutes, and my judgments: which if a man do, he shall live in them: I am the Lord" (Lev. 18:5), What was the best a person could do to be considered righteous while living under the law? He could try to keep (obey) all of God's statutes, judgments, and commandments. Being human, of course, he could not accomplish this. What he did do, however, was to show his faith in God by attempting to keep His law.

Souls of those who were righteous by this definition were kept in "Abraham's bosom" until they were justified at the time Christ died to atone for sin (Luke 16:22; Rom. 3:24-26). Many believe Jesus led them out and up to heaven between the time of His crucifixion and resurrection (Eph. 4:8) and that they are included in the great cloud of heavenly witnesses mentioned in Hebrews 12:1.

B. Righteousness of faith: 6-9

6. But the righteousness which is of faith speaketh on this wise, Say not in thine heart, Who shall ascend into heaven? (that is, to bring Christ down from above:)

7. Or, Who shall descend into the deep? (that is, to bring up Christ again from the dead.)

Since no one was capable of obtaining righteousness by keeping the law of God perfectly, how was righteousness to be found? Paul did not want anyone to go searching for it by ascending into the heavens or descending into the depths of the earth. He may have been thinking of Deuteronomy 30:11-13 or Proverbs 30:4. He applied it to Christ here in a parenthetical way by suggesting that He need not be brought down from above or raised up from the dead. His ascension to heaven following His resurrection from the dead was a known fact. The truth He taught about righteousness coming by faith was well known. Let it be studied and understood.

8. But what saith it? The word is nigh thee, even in thy mouth, and in thy heart; that is, the word of faith, which we preach;

What does the righteousness which is by faith say? It says that the word of truth regarding salvation by faith in Christ is close to every believer. It is in his mouth and in his heart. This was evidently taken from Deuteronomy 30:14—"The word is very nigh unto thee, in thy mouth, and in thy heart that thou mayest do it." Even as God's will was to be found in His law, so it was also to be found in His Son. Note the fact that Paul had written, "For Christ is the end of the law for righteousness to every one that believeth (Rom. 10:4).

9. That if thou shalt confess with thy mouth the Lord Jesus, and shalt believe in thine heart that God hath raised him from the dead, thou shalt be saved.

Truth obviously moves in two directions. It first moves inward to the heart and stirs belief. Faith centers on the Lord Jesus and accepts Him as the divine Son of God and the Savior from sin. His death and His resurrection are seen as focal points in salvation. He had to die to atone for sin, and He had to rise again in order to validate that atonement. Salvation is an inward experience. Truth also moves outward when the mouth of the believer confesses that salvation comes by no other means than placing one's faith in Christ and His atoning work. Self-righteousness is worthless. Imputation of Christ's righteousness into a believer is worthwhile.

II. Richness: Rom. 10:10-13

A. What man does: 10-11

10. For with the heart man believeth unto righteousness; and with the mouth confession is made unto salvation.

Note that verse 9 mentioned confessing with the mouth first and believing in the heart second. In verse 10 the reverse order is used. Man believes unto righteousness in his heart, and then he confesses it to others with his mouth. The inward work must be done before the outward work can be done, but both are important.

11. For the scripture saith, Whosoever believeth on him shall not be ashamed.

Are there those who are afraid that they will believe on Christ and be ashamed by His rejecting them? Paul said that there was scripture to allay that fear. He may have been thinking of various references. Psalm 34:22 says, "The Lord redeemeth the soul of his servants: and none of them that trust in him shall be desolate." Isaiah 28:16 says, "He that believeth shall not make haste [run away in panic]." Isaiah 49:23 says, "They shall not be ashamed that wait for me."

B. What God does: 12-13

12. For there is no difference between the Jew and the Greek: for the same Lord over all is rich unto all that call upon him.

Judged from the human viewpoint, there were many cultural and religious differences between Jews and Greeks (Gentiles). However, there was no difference between them from the divine viewpoint when it came to the crucial matter of salvation. Richness of grace flowed from the same Lord Jesus Christ to all who called on Him to save them.

13. For whosoever shall call upon the name of the Lord shall be saved.

This is a summary verse, stating concisely the effect which the gospel of Christ can have on people. Whoever calls on the name of the Lord Jesus will be saved. "Everyone who calls out to the Lord for help will be saved" (Today's English Version). Joel 2:32 says, "Whosoever shall call on the name of the Lord shall be delivered." Peter quoted this in his sermon on the Day of Pentecost (Acts 2:21). It was a statement with universal meaning and application.

III. Reception: 10:14-17

A. Witnesses: 14-15a

14a. How then shall they call on him in whom they have not believed?

This is the first of four questions asked in this passage, each one leading logically to the next one. If whoever calls on the name of the Lord Jesus Christ will be saved, then it follows that those who do not call on Him will not be saved. The propagation of the gospel is absolutely necessary in order to win the lost and give them hope of eternal life.

Paul chose to work his way backwards through the process. Transposing his first question into a declarative statement, we could say, "People must believe on Christ before they can call on Him." The facts concerning Who Christ is and what He did at Calvary to atone for sin must be presented before people can commit themselves to Him in faith and ask for pardon of their sins.

14b. ...and how shall they believe in him of whom they have not heard?

This question can be transposed into the statement, "People must hear about Christ before they can believe on Him." This requires exposure to someone who knows the truth about Christ and who is willing to share it with others. This involves the whole matter of witnessing through home missions and foreign missions.

14. ...and how shall they hear without a preacher?

This question can be transposed into the statement, "A preacher must tell people what they need to hear." Whether it is a clergyman, layman, literature, broadcast, or some other form of communication involved, truth about Christ has to be given to the lost. Divine information must penetrate the darkness of the human souls of men and bring them needed light.

15a. And how shall they preach, except they be sent?

This question can be transposed into the statement, "Preachers cannot preach unless they are sent to do this work." Witnessing can be done on the local level, as well as through limited travel, by Christians of all types. However, an organized effort to fulfill Christ's great commission to evangelize and educate the world demands that those who remain at home support those who staff home and foreign missions programs. That support should involve training, assignment, financial aid, prayer, and continual encouragement.

Christians in the early church were slow to move out of Jerusalem to the provinces of Judaea and Samaria and then to the ends of their known world in the first century. However, there seemed to be no doubt in their minds that witnesses had to carry the gospel to the lost if they were to have any hope of eternal life. Ever since that time there have been critics of missions who claim that people are better off if left in their own religions. We have often heard the statement, "It does not matter what you believe, as long as you are sincere," or the statement, "All religions reach for the same God," We need to resist this kind of error. The Bible makes it very clear Christ is the only answer for all sinful people.

B. Writings: 15b-16

15b. ...as it is written, How beautiful are the feet of them that preach the gospel of peace, and bring glad tidings of good things!

Quoting from Isaiah 52:7, Paul remembered how God had saved Jerusalem and messengers had brought the good news. He applied this same thought to the arrival of the gospel, the good news regarding salvation from sin available to all who believed on Christ.

16. But they have not all obeyed the gospel. For Esaias saith, Lord, who hath believed our report?

Paul realized, of course, that hearing of the gospel did not automatically convince all people to be saved from their sins through faith in Christ. He quoted from Isaiah 53:1 to show that the Jews historically had rejected truth regarding the Messiah, Jehovah's suffering Servant (described in Isaiah 52:13—53:12). That passage told of the rejection which would be experienced by the Messiah when He came to atone for sin. In another place, Paul told us that even good news is not received and absorbed by individuals who are blinded by Satan (II Cor. 4:3-4).

C. Ways: 17

17. So then faith cometh by hearing, and hearing by the word of God.

This is obviously a summary statement, similar to verse 13. "Faith comes from hearing the message, and the message is heard through the word of Christ" (New International Version). "Faith comes from listening to this Good News—the Good News about Christ" (Living Bible). Regardless of the reception or rejection of it, the gospel truth does its work. Not all accept it, but some do. Over the past nineteen-and-a-half centuries of church history, we have noted the various results of evangelism all over the world. The important thing has not been success or failure, but consistency of witnessing.

Evangelistic Emphasis

You've probably seen this little slogan: "The only Gospel some people ever see is the Gospel According to YOU."

It's a way of saying your life and your example bear witness to people who may never hear a sermon or attend a Bible study.

The reason is that the Word of God is alive in your heart— it's a part of your thoughts, it affects what you say, it's behind the attitudes you express toward the things that happen to you.

People may see you coping with tough situations and wonder what it is that enables you to get through it all. They may hear you talk about someone in a way that shows compassion or understanding and wonder why you don't join in the cutting remarks and gossip that others direct toward that person.

In these and a thousand others ways each day you bear witness to your faith— to the values you live by, to the spiritual strength that energizes you, to the One whose allegiance you pledge.

That's what Paul is talking about when he describes the dynamics of faith in Romans 10. The Word of God starts first in your heart, then moves to your words, then molds your attitudes, and then influences your actions.

That's how faith works.

Except one thing has been left out: the very first step. Faith, Paul says comes from hearing the Word of God. We don't have to it alone: God takes the initiative.

Pray today that you will sense the presence of God in your heart more powerfully than ever before. Then watch as the Word of God affects your words attitudes and actions. Others will notice, too!

◆◆◆◆◆◆

Memory Selection

When we read that faith comes by *hearing*, we're not being taught a lesson about how the auditory nerve picks up information. The word Paul uses in Romans 10:17 carries the meaning of *heeding*. not just hearing.

Hearing is a physical process; heeding is a spiritual process. We may *hear* a loud noise involuntarily without knowing or caring where it comes from or what it means. To *heed* what we hear involves a process of trust. We act on what we hear only when we believe in the trustworthiness of the messenger.

For example if we're driving down the highway and we see a sign marked "Detour" and it's orange and black, and diamond shaped, we've been taught that this is the official highway symbol for road construction ahead. We slow down and watch for a change in road conditions.

Suppose we see the word "Detour" on a neon sign flashing out in front of a truck stop. We immediately conclude that it's a gimmick to attract customers. Maybe we "heed" it and maybe we don't.

The more we come to trust God, the more likely we are to heed each new aspect of the faith as we discover it. This is what is meant by the teaching that faith comes by heeding the Word of God.

February 14, 1993

Weekday Problems

Sally is a devout local Christian whose mother was a famous church leader, known throughout her denomination as an eloquent speaker and a gifted organizer.

Sally lives a fine personal life. and is deeply loved by her family and friends. Her burden is her name. Every time she attends a conference, people see that famous name on her name tag. It almost always prompts the response, "your mother was such a great person."

Sally accepts the comment graciously, but somewhere deep down inside. she is nursing a hurt she doesn't want to admit to herself: "Why can't I be judged on my own merits like everyone else?"

*What encouragement could you give to Sally, or to anyone who feels his or her life doesn't measure up to expectations?

*What is there in the Christian teaching about grace that could help the Sallys of the world accept their own unique talents as God-given?

*Is there any value in the concept of heeding the Word as involving trust that could help us when we feel that we are underachieving?

◆◆◆◆◆◆

Superintendent's Sermonette

Terms such as compromise, give and take, conciliation, and arbitration have become so acceptable to us that we may be tempted at times to let down our biblical standard. The concept of the "golden mean" suggests that extremes on either side of a subject are always poor choices. In morality, for example, a person is considered normal if he is neither too good nor too bad by prevailing attitudes and practices of society. He is said to do well if he walks down the middle of the road on all issues. This overlooks the fact that walking in the middle of the road can be a dangerous thing to do.

It is certainly dangerous when it comes to divine truths. These are not issues for debate or for compromise. If they are right, then they are right, and we do well to uphold them, even if it means we are considered extremists by the world. Paul made no apology for the gospel of Christ. He made no room for righteousness coming by any means except through identification by faith with Christ, the only truly righteous One. He made no room for any false religions or isms. People of all locations, cultures, and classes had to come humbly to the foot of the cross to be saved. We need to give as strong a support to that gospel as he did in his time.

237

PROCLAIM THE GOSPEL

This Lesson in Your Life

Almost everyone discovers sooner or later that life brings a bitter unexpected disappointment.

Sometimes a breadwinner will sacrifice for years in an intolerable job only to be let go in a company cutback without so much as a thank you from the boss.

Sometimes a child will work as hard as possible for honor grades in school, only to find that a parent fails to appreciate the effort and says of every report card. "You could do better."

Bitter disappointment is directly tied to our expectations. We expect that on the job our loyalty will be met by loyalty. We expect that in the family our parents will be our biggest encouragers. Life isn't always fair and sometimes people betray our expectations.

Saul of Tarsus came to feel that way about certain religious teachings he adopted early in life. He was taught and deeply believed that if a person was sincerely obedient to God in every way possible, God would bring prosperity and peace of mind.

Then along came a band of believers in a new way of life, who said that the Messiah had come and had lived a life innocent of sin, yet had been executed as a common criminal by crucifixion. This could not be the work of God, Saul immediately concluded. If this were truly the Messiah, God would bestow special blessing on Him, give him special prosperity, even special powers to rule the world.

Eventually, we know, Saul of Tarsus came to view the Messiah very differently. He came to contrast what he called "the righteousness which is based on law" with "the righteousness which is based on faith." The first is a way of life in which we do certain things and then expect God to reward us for our good deeds. Anytime we suffer failure or loss, it must mean that we haven't lived up to our end of the deal. This is the attitude that enabled the friends of Job to keep insisting that he must have done very evil things that brought about his suffering.

The way of life that brought about Saul's conversion to become Paul the Apostle presented a very different picture. The heart of God bursts with sorrow whenever any of his creatures suffer, according to this new view. Innocent suffering, unjust affliction far from being a sign of God separating Himself from us is actually the revelation of God's true nature. It means that we are never closer to the heart of God than when we approach the cross where His Son died for us.

Living by this philosophy of "the righteousness that comes from faith" gives us new strength to overcome our disappointments, and to heal our feelings of being let down by others.

We learn that in the eyes of God, seeming failure can become the beginning of new success. We learn that although others may hurt us God gives us new strength to start over and "turn our scars into stars."

Seed Thoughts

1. How would you explain the difference between "righteousness which is of the law" and "righteousness which is of faith" (Romans 10:5-6)?
The first refers to a way of life based on our own efforts and merits, while the second is based on our trust in God and our reliance on Him.

2. What is Paul's point about people who ask."Who shall ascend into heaven to bring Christ down" (10:6)?
To some people Christ seems very far away— so far away that we almost have to go all the way to heaven to approach Him.

3. Where does faith begin?
Faith begins with God's loving redemptive acts on our behalf. The more we come to know about God's love, the more we come to love Him in return.

4. How does true faith affect the way we view other people?
We come to see that the same God who loves us also loves every person, regardless of his station in life (10:12).

5. What is the role of the preacher of the Word in bringing faith to the peoples of the earth?
The person who bears witness to the Word of God is an essential link in the process. It could be any person whose life exemplifies the power of God (10:14).

(PLEASE TURN PAGE)

---

1. How would you explain the difference between "righteousness which is of the law" and "righteousness which is of faith" (Romans 10:5-6)?

2. What is Paul's point about people who ask."Who shall ascend into heaven to bring Christ down" (10:6)?

3. Where does faith begin?

4. How does true faith affect the way we view other people?

5. What is the role of the preacher of the Word in bringing faith to the peoples of the earth?

6. What is the role of the person who contributes financial and moral support to the work of ministry?

7. What should we keep in mind when our efforts seem to fail?

8. What is the difference between hearing and heeding?

9. How can a person believe in one in whom he has never heard?

10. What is the meaning of the phrase "believe in your heart?"

(SEED THOUGHTS--Cont'd)

The first refers to a way of life based on our own efforts and merits, while the second is based on our trust in God and our reliance on Him.

To some people Christ seems very far away— so far away that we almost have to go all the way to heaven to approach Him.

Faith begins with God's loving redemptive acts on our behalf. The more we come to know about God's love, the more we come to love Him in return.

We come to see that the same God who loves us also loves every person, regardless of his station in life (10:12).

The person who bears witness to the Word of God is an essential link in the process. It could be any person whose life exemplifies the power of God (10:14).

Such a person is an equally essential link: "how shall they preach, except they be sent? (10:15)."

Even the great prophets of Israel met with resistance. Sometimes people listened, but did not believe: heard but did not heed (10:16).

Hearing is a simple mental process, involving sensory impressions on the auditory nerve. Heeding is trusting, accepting, and obeying.

It would be impossible. That is why it is so important that we speak of Jesus to others though they may not appear interested.

Belief must come from within and be more than a verbal expression of faith.

6. What is the role of the person who contributes financial and moral support to the work of ministry?
Such a person is an equally essential link: "how shall they preach, except they be sent? (10:15)."

7. What should we keep in mind when our efforts seem to fail?
Even the great prophets of Israel met with resistance. Sometimes people listened, but did not believe: heard but did not heed (10:16).

8. What is the difference between hearing and heeding?
Hearing is a simple mental process, involving sensory impressions on the auditory nerve. Heeding is trusting, accepting, and obeying.

9. How can a person believe in one in whom he has never heard?
It would be impossible. That is why it is so important that we speak of Jesus to others though they may not appear interested.

10. What is the meaning of the phrase "believe in your heart?"
Belief must come from within and be more than a verbal expression of faith.

February 21, 1993

Serve and Honor

Romans
15. We then that are strong ought to bear the infirmities of the weak, and not to please ourselves.
2. Let every one of us please his neighbour for his good to edification.
3. For even Christ pleased not himself, but as it is written, The reproaches of them that reproached thee fell on me.
4. For whatsoever things were written aforetime were written for our learning, that we through patience and comfort of the scriptures might have hope.
5. Now the God of patience and consolation grant you to be likeminded one toward another according to Christ Jesus:
6. That ye may with one mind and one mouth glorify God, even the Father of our Lord Jesus Christ.
7. Wherefore receive ye one another as Christ also received us to the glory of God.
8. Now I say that Jesus Christ was a minister of the circumcision for the truth of God, to confirm the promises made unto the fathers:
9. And that the Gentiles might glorify God for *his* mercy; as it is written, FOR THIS CAUSE I WILL CONFESS TO THEE AMONG THE GENTILES, AND SING UNTO THY NAME.
10. And again he saith, REJOICE, YE GENTILES, WITH HIS PEOPLE.
11. And again, PRAISE THE LORD, ALL YE GENTILES; AND LAUD HIM, ALL YE PEOPLE.
12. And again, E-sa´ias saith, THERE SHALL BE A ROOT OF JESSE, AND HE THAT SHALL RISE TO REIGN OVER THE GENTILES; IN HIM SHALL THE GENTILES TRUST.
13. Now the God of hope fill you with all joy and peace in believing, that ye may abound in hope, through the power of the Holy Ghost.

♦♦♦♦♦♦

◀ **Memory Selection**
Romans 15:1-2

◀ **Devotional Reading**
Colossians 3:9-17

◀ **Background Scripture**
Romans 15:1-13

◀ **Printed Scripture**
Romans 15:1-13

Teacher's Target

Chapters 12-15 of Paul's epistle to the Romans emphasize Christian life and service. The section begins with a challenge to present yourself to God as a living sacrifice, resist being conformed to the sinful world-system, and be transformed by the renewing of your mind. The law of love regarding doubtful things is covered in 14:1-15:3, and the relationship between Jewish and Gentile believers is covered in 15:4-13. The thrust of this lesson's text (Rom. 15:1-13) is on interpersonal relationships among Christians.

Help your students to realize that they have a responsibility within the Christian fellowship to serve and honor others. Jesus Himself set the example for this when He ministered to the multitudes, washed His disciples' feet, and died to save sinners. Servants are not greater than their Master, and believers are expected to serve both Him and one another. Herein lies our hope for a strong inner unity and a strong outer testimony.

Lesson Introduction

A person is usually quick to defend his right to be different from others, but he may be just as quick to challenge differences in others. For most of human history, conformity was highly prized, just as it still is in primitive and backward societies. In more recent history, however, individualism has gained ascendancy in more highly developed and democratic societies. The question arises as to what stand Christians should take in this matter.

When appearing before" the Sanhedrin (Jewish Council) in Jerusalem, Peter and other apostles said, "We ought to obey God rather than men" (Acts 5:21), referring to spiritual things. Peter later wrote that Christians should be submissive to government leaders (1 Pet. 2:13-17), referring to earthly things. Therefore, Christians need to follow a mixture of individuality and conformity, guided by the indwelling Holy Spirit. This is true in contacts with the world and also in contacts within the church. Forbearance (tolerance) and forgiveness help to make this possible.

Teaching Outline

I. Goodness: Rom. 15:1-3
   A. Expectation: 1
   B. Edification: 2
   C. Example: 3
II. Grant: Rom. 15:4-7
   A. Patterns: 4
   B. Prayer: 5-6
   C. Proposal: 7
III. Gentiles: Rom. 15:8-13
   A. Restatement: 15:8-9a
   B. References: 9b-12
   C. Request: 13

Daily Bible Readings

Mon. Paul's Prayer
Phil. 2:1-11
Tue. How to Treat Others
Rom. 13:8-14
Wed. Do Not Judge Others
Rom. 14:1-12
Thu. Do Not Let Others Fail
Rom. 14:13-23
Fri. Serve Others, Not Self
Rom. 15:1-6
Sat. The Gospel for the Gentiles
Rom. 15:7-13
Sun. Paul's Reason for Writing
Rom. 15:14-21

February 21, 1993

VERSE BY VERSE

I. Goodness: Rom. 15:1-3

A. Expectation:

1. We then that are strong ought to bear the infirmities of the weak, and not to please ourselves.

Taken in context, this appears to refer to mature Christians dealing with new converts. It was expected that believers would be weaned from the milk of the Word (elementary teachings) and go on to strong meat (advanced teachings). Even as adults are normally stronger than infants and small children, veteran believers were supposed to be spiritually stronger than babes in Christ. Along with growing spiritual strength came the temptation to become proud and domineering when dealing with immature believers. Paul suggested that those who were spiritually strong ought to help bear the infirmities of those who were spiritually weak. Mature believers should not try to please themselves, but please God by helping weak believers.

In another place, Paul wrote, "If meat make my brother to offend, I will eat no flesh while the world standeth, lest I make my brother to offend" (I Cor. 8:13). Paul was mature enough to eat such meat without having it offend his own conscience, but he was willing to give it up for life if there was a chance that eating it would offend the conscience of a weaker brother. That person's conscience was more precious to him than his own personal feelings. This was but one example of how his approach would work.

B. Edification: 2

2. Let every one of us please his neighbour for his good to edification.

This advice assumed that a mature believer was aware of what an immature believer needed for spiritual growth. This required discernment and sensitivity on his part. He had to get to know the other person on something deeper than a surface level, so that he would know how he thinks, feels, and acts. It took time and effort to learn these things. As time went by, he would decide what was needed in order to edify (build up) that person's spiritual character and then do what was necessary to make it happen. Dealing with the immature believer's confusion and doubts would require patience.

C. Example: 3

3. For even Christ pleased not himself; but, as it is written, The reproaches of them that reproached thee fell on me.

Paul evidently took Psalm 69:9-10 as background for this statement regarding Christ, for David wrote, "The zeal of thine house hath eaten me up; and the reproaches of them that reproached thee are fallen upon me. When I wept, and chastened my soul with fasting, that was to my reproach." The fact that Christ took severe mistreatment from sinful men in order to die and redeem sinners provided the primary example of what Paul meant by mature believers pleasing not themselves but devoting themselves to the edification of others.

II. Grant: Rom. 15:4-7

A. Patterns: 4

4. For whatsoever things were written aforetime were written for our learning, that we through patience and comfort of the scriptures might have hope.

Having just referred to an Old Testament reference, Paul added this general thought. Whatever was written before this time in the Jewish Scriptures was put there to instruct believers. It was useful in motivating them to be patient and to feel encouraged, so that they might keep hope alive that sin would ultimately be dealt with and laid aside in the life to come. From that source came instruction which formed workable patterns to follow when helping others.

B. Prayer: 5-6

5. Now the God of patience and consolation grant you to be likeminded one toward another according to Christ Jesus:

This verse and the next verse record a sort of benediction by Paul on his readers. He wanted God to grant them patience, consolation, and likemindedness toward one another, using Christ as their example. It is implied" here that the virtues mentioned were in God's character and could be in their own characters, as well. Their part was to open themselves up to this kind of development and allow the Holy Spirit to bestow these graces on them to be used in interpersonal relationships.

6. That ye may with one mind and one mouth glorify God, even the Father of our Lord Jesus Christ.

The end result of having patience, consolation, and likemindedness would be a unified way of thinking and speaking both inside and outside the body of believers. This would bring glory (praise, honor) to God, the Father of the Lord Jesus Christ. Paul knew that Christian harmony would attract people to the church. By inference, disharmony would drive people away from the church.

C. Proposal: 7

7. Wherefore receive ye one another, as Christ also received us to the glory of God.

There seems to be a parallel mode of thought here to that presented in verse 3. Christ was held up as the primary example of One Who pleased not Himself but bore the reproaches required to die for the redemption of sinners. Mature believers should not seek to please themselves but to edify others. In verse 7 He is held up as the primary example of One Who received sinners to bring glory to God. Mature believers are supposed to receive one another in love, and this will also bring glory to God.

III. Gentiles: Rom. 15:8-13

A. Restatement: 8-9a

8. Now I say that Jesus Christ was a minister of the circumcision for the truth of God, to confirm the promises made unto the fathers:

9a. And that the Gentiles might glorify God for his mercy;...

Paul was a Jew by race and by religion when he was converted to Christ on the road to Damascus. A man named Ananias was sent to him three days later to tell him that he was God's chosen vessel to bear His name before Gentiles, kings, and the children of Israel (Acts 9:1-19). He ministered to Jews wherever he went, but his greatest response came from Gentiles. Paul said that Jesus Christ came to minister to the Jews (the circumcision) concerning the truth of God. He confirmed the Messianic prophecies in the Jewish Scriptures by fulfilling them in Himself. His ministry, however, went beyond the Jews and out to the Gentiles, too. It was largely through the work of His followers that the gospel of God's mercy was spread to the Gentiles. Those who heard and accepted it brought glory to God. The old barriers between Jews and Gentiles came tumbling down when they met together in love in the household of faith (Eph. 2:11-22; Col. 3:11). It was a marvelous development!

B. References: 9b-12

9b. ...as it is written, For this cause I will confess to thee among the Gentiles, and sing unto thy name.

This was taken from a psalm of David—"Therefore will I give thanks unto thee, O Lord, among the heathen

[Gentiles], and sing praises unto thy name" (Ps. 18:49).

10. And again he saith, Rejoice, ye Gentiles, with his people.

It might be better to substitute "it" for "he" here, referring to the Old Testament. This was taken from Deuteronomy 32:43—"Rejoice, O ye nations [Gentiles], with his people [God's people, the Jews]." In other words, Paul knew that the time had come for Gentiles and Jews to rejoice together as they became one in Christ.

11. And again, Praise the Lord, all ye Gentiles; and laud him, all ye people.

Psalm 117 is only two verses long, making it the shortest of the psalms. Paul quoted the first verse. The psalm used the term "nations" instead of "Gentiles." Some translations make the term "people" plural, probably referring to all nations outside of Israel. God's merciful kindness and enduring truth is featured in the second verse. The implication is clear that Paul believed this short psalm supported conversion of Gentiles to Christ and thus predicted what happened in the first century of the Christian era.

12. And again, Esaias saith, There shall be a root of Jesse, and he that shall rise to reign over the Gentiles; in him shall the Gentiles trust.

This refers to Isaiah 11:10—"In that day there shall be a root of Jesse, which shall stand for an open ensign of the people; to it shall the Gentiles seek." The root (descendant) of Jesse, David's father, mentioned here was Jesus. He would stand up as the Source of salvation for the nations, and even Gentiles would come to Him. During the age of grace, individual Gentiles would come to claim Him as their Savior. In the end times, all nations would have to bow before Him, whether they accepted Him as Savior and Lord or not (Matt. 25:31-32; Phil. 2:1-11; Rev. 19:11-16).

These four references to Gentiles coming to the light of the gospel are by no means exhaustive, for there are many more in the Old Testament. Paul simply chose these as examples to prove that God always intended for Jews and Gentiles to be made one in Christ. He hoped and prayed that the differences which had long separated them and fostered hatred between them would be replaced by harmony and love.

C. Request: 13

13. Now the God of hope fill you with all joy and peace in believing, that ye may abound in hope through the power of the Holy Ghost.

Paul had given a benediction earlier, as recorded in verses 5-6. Now he gave another one to his readers. He prayed that the God of hope, meaning that God was the Source of believers hope, would fill them with joy and peace through their believing, so that they might abound in hope. This would be possible through the power of the Holy Spirit at work within them.

Reading between the lines of this passage, it may be that Paul had heard of friction arising between Jewish and Gentile believers. Perhaps some Judaizers had been spreading their legalistic propaganda. Inclusion of four references regarding Gentiles from the Jewish Scriptures suggests that Paul wanted them to realize that they had just as much right to be in the church as Jews did.

This was elementary truth by now. Paul wanted Jewish and Gentile Christians to go beyond it and develop the deep, loving, mutually edifying attitudes and practices which would unite them as one in Christ. More important than their racial backgrounds were the differences in spiritual development which had to be resolved. Let the mature believers be solicitous of the immature believers. Let the patterns of harmony and love presented in the Scriptures be worked out in the church.

SERVE AND HONOR

Evangelistic Emphasis

Why should we put the needs of others before our own? Paul offers three reasons. Two of them we might expect. The third may surprise us.

1. First, the concerns of the weak come first because it's ethically more sound. If the strong think only of themselves. the weak die out, until only one is left as king of the mountain— but then the human race is gone. Most societies know that ignoring this brings collapse.

2. Paul adds a second reason: we think of others because Christ put others first. Christ's ministry was not done for Himself, but for us. We serve others as Christ served us.

3. The third reason to put others first: it lets us participate in God's great redemptive plan. Paul writes that the Messiah's mission was to expand God's Kingdom to include the Gentiles. Christ stretched the borders of the kingdom far beyond the limits of race or creed or class or any other human boundary.

Our own need for salvation is linked to the salvation of others. Our need for God is linked to the needs of others. If we think only of our own salvation, we may miss it! This is Paul's last and most important reason for putting others first.

♦♦♦♦♦♦

Memory Selection

Do you know the immeasurable satisfaction that comes from truly "edifying" other people?

It's what keeps school teachers going year after year, enduring low pay, endless paperwork, and unruly classrooms, for the thrill of seeing a spark come alive in a young mind.

It's what keeps ministers hanging in there, putting out fires, grabbing a few moments for study, convening hundreds of meetings, all for the joy of sharing grace with someone everybody else had written off.

When God invites us to think about others first, He's not asking us to do something against our own best interests. It's God's way of letting us in on the great secret of the universe: that community is more fulfilling than isolation. Even heaven itself enjoys the fellowship of Father, Son, and Holy Spirit (not to mention the company of the great angelic host). God wants His people to discover that "the fellowship of kindred minds is like to that above."

Next time you find yourself retreating into your own little world— thank God instead for the heavenly and earthly examples of the joys of caring for others!

Weekday Problems

Curt never misses a church service. He never misses a planning meeting. Nobody works harder in the church than Curt.

So why do people dread getting placed on a committee with Curt?

Curt is a complainer, not a leader. When he sees a problem that needs addressing, his approach is to tell everyone in earshot that somebody needs to do something about it. Actually, Curt's way seems to work. People often work on his issues instead of other more pressing needs just to get him to quiet down.

* In terms of Paul's teaching in Romans 15, is Curt a "strong" Christian or a "weak" one?

* If he is considered a weak Christian, does that mean the stronger church members should rush to solve whatever he complains about?

* What is Curt's real problem, and how can the church deal with it in a way that frees the members to move on to more important tasks?

◆◆◆◆◆◆

Superintendent's Sermonette

If there are several Bible-believing churches in a given area, do individual churches attract certain types of people? We know that doctrinal differences will draw people to particular assemblies. What we may not know, or want to admit, is that sociological differences and racial differences can do the same thing. Certain churches seem to attract those who are lower, middle, or upper class, featuring some overlap but not much. Certain churches attract people, while others attract those who are very proper and dignified. You may be able to think of other differences.

What happens if a Bible-believing church stands alone in its location? Christians who attend it will obviously have to make personal adjustments to tolerate and even love one another. Some would say that this is good discipline, and it could be. Others would hope for more choices so that they can find a church where they feel more comfortable.

Our text today features the Apostle Paul urging believers to get along with one another in as harmonious a way as possible despite their differences. We should try to do this, too. The unity we find in Christian conferences, conventions, and camps can be developed in our local church, as well.

SERVE AND HONOR

This Lesson in Your Life

At least 50 wars are going on at any given time in the world today. We don't even hear about most of them, but they affect us all the same, whether by influxes of refugees, higher prices for products we depend on from the war zones, or, on a more spiritual plane, from the sorrow and suffering added to the world by the endless killing and destruction.

The citizens of any country experiencing war long for a way to live in peace. They don't always understand the causes of war, but they dream of a day when harmony will be restored.

Given a chance, people everywhere would do anything to leave behind the violence and live in a loving, joyful, industrious community. Exactly this is the glorious privilege given to us as citizens of the Kingdom of God: to establish outposts of harmony throughout the whole earth!

We can start with our own homes. Then we can bear witness to Christ's peace where we work. Then we can come together with our brothers and sisters in the church as we celebrate God's love in praise and adoration.

We can also help to heal the places in the world where the hurting is greatest, by going there ourselves, and by supporting those who go, through our prayers and with our treasure.

The Kingdom of God exists wherever people have caught the great vision. It doesn't have to be a spectacular breakthrough that makes the history books: it's just as important when one person resolves to be more loving, more just, more faithful. This is what Paul wants his readers to remember— each of us can play a role in the great story of salvation.

Paul understands the Gospel as a magnificently unfolding story. For him it started with Abraham— just one person who believed a promise. Following him came a tribe of people, and then a nation, and then a worldwide church— each a chapter that reveals a portion of God's redeeming purpose.

The people of God in Paul's day had a hard time seeing how they could allow Gentiles into a community that for centuries was composed only of Jews.

The people of God in our day may have a hard time seeing how we can invite—whomever is considered an outcast in our community—to share the blessings of salvation.

In every generation we are challenged to do our part to extend the borders of the Kingdom. A hundred years ago, slaves were cast out, and had to create their own churches. Fifty years ago, foreigners were made unwelcome, and were forced to hold their own services. Today in your community, probably there are many who long to accept God's great invitation. Society puts up obstacles to their acceptance, so the church, as always, will have to create new ways to assure their inclusion.

You probably know who the outcasts are in your world. What can you do to invite them in? By doing something, however small a step it may seem, you help God write today's unfolding chapter in the great redemptive drama we call the Kingdom of God.

Seed Thoughts

1. What are some ways to distinguish between the spiritually strong and the spiritually weak, according to Paul?
The strong are those who can think about others, while the weak think only of themselves (Romans 15:1-2).

2. How can self-centered persons be encouraged to become more sensitive to the needs of others?
By being steadfast in modeling the example of Christ— not losing patience and attacking weaker individuals for their weakness.

3. What source of strength does Paul recommend?
He turns to the Scriptures, which he says "were written for our learning."

4. Paul speaks of "the God of patience and comfort" (15:5). In what ways has God been patient with you?
Recall for your class, experiences in which God has allowed you more time or given you second chances.

5. What is the purpose of God's patience toward us?
God's purpose is to bring us into closer unity with each other and with Christ (15:5-6).

(PLEASE TURN PAGE)

---

1. What are some ways to distinguish between the spiritually strong and the spiritually weak, according to Paul?

2. How can self-centered persons be encouraged to become more sensitive to the needs of others?

3. What source of strength does Paul recommend?

4. Paul speaks of "the God of patience and comfort" (15:5). In what ways has God been patient with you?

5. What is the purpose of God's patience toward us?

6. For what purpose was Christ born a Jew (a "minister of the circumcision")?

7. How does Paul see the mission of Christians as a continuation of the work of God began with the Jewish people?

8. How does Paul relate God's special relationship with Jews to the conversion of Gentiles?

9. What gifts does Paul mention that are available to us?

10. What experiences have you had with these gifts?

(SEED THOUGHTS--Cont'd)

The strong are those who can think about others, while the weak think only of themselves (Romans 15:1-2).

By being steadfast in modeling the example of Christ— not losing patience and attacking weaker individuals for their weakness.

He turns to the Scriptures, which he says "were written for our learning."

Recall for your class, experiences in which God has allowed you more time or given you second chances.

God's purpose is to bring us into closer unity with each other and with Christ (15:5-6).

To fulfill the promise that through the descendants of Abraham. God's blessings would spread throughout the whole world.

In Romans (15:9-12), He cites numerous Scriptures that foretell the expansion of God's blessings to the Gentile world.

He sees the spread of the gospel to Gentiles as the fulfillment of promises made to the Jews.

Joy, peace, believing, abounding, hope, and the power of the Holy Spirit.

Recount an incident or two where your Christian faith has helped you through a difficult period of life.

6. For what purpose was Christ born a Jew (a "minister of the circumcision")?
To fulfill the promise that through the descendants of Abraham. God's blessings would spread throughout the whole world.

7. How does Paul see the mission of Christians as a continuation of the work of God begun with the Jewish people?
In Romans (15:9-12), He cites numerous Scriptures that foretell the expansion of God's blessings to the Gentile world.

8. How does Paul relate God's special relationship with Jews to the conversion of Gentiles?
He sees the spread of the gospel to Gentiles as the fulfillment of promises made to the Jews.

9. What gifts does Paul mention that are available to us?
Joy, peace, believing, abounding, hope, and the power of the Holy Spirit.

10. What experiences have you had with these gifts?
Recount an incident or two where your Christian faith has helped you through a difficult period of life.

February 28, 1993

Teach the Truth

TEACH THE TRUE GOSPEL!

II Timothy 2
14 Of these things put them in remembrance, charging them before the Lord that they strive not about words to no profit, but to the subverting of the hearers.
15 Study to shew thyself approved unto God, a workman that needeth not to be ashamed, rightly dividing the word of truth.
16 But shun profane *and* vain babblings: for they will increase unto more ungodliness.
17 And their word will eat as doth a canker: of whom is Hy-me-nae´-us and Phi-le'-tus;
18 Who concerning the truth have erred, saying that the resurrection is past already; and overthrow the faith of some.
19 Nevertheless the foundation of God standeth sure, having this seal, The Lord knoweth them that are his. And, Let every one that nameth the name of Christ depart from iniquity.
20 But in a great house there are not only vessels of gold and of silver, but also of wood and of earth; and some to honour, and some to dishonour.
21 If a man therefore purge himself from these, he shall be a vessel unto honour, sanctified, and meet for the master's use, and prepared unto every good work.
22 Flee also youthful lusts: but follow righteousness, faith, charity, peace, with them that call on the Lord out of a pure heart.
23 But foolish and unlearned questions avoid, knowing that they do gender strifes.
24 And the servant of the Lord must not strive; but be gentle unto all men, apt to teach, patient,
25 In meekness instructing those that oppose themselves; if God peradventure will give them repentance to the acknowledging of the truth;
26 And that they may recover themselves out of the snare of the devil, who are taken captive by him at his will.

◆◆◆◆◆◆

◀ **Memory Selection**
II Timothy 2:15

◀ **Devotional Reading**
Titus 2

◀ **Background Scripture**
II Timothy 2:14-3:9

◀ **Printed Scripture**
II Timothy 2:14-26

TEACH THE TRUTH

Teacher's Target

When Jesus appeared before Pilate, He said, "For this cause came I into the world, that I should bear witness unto the truth. Every one that is of the truth heareth my voice. Pilate saith unto him, What is truth?" (John 18:37-38). Jesus was speaking of truth theologically. Pilate was referring to it philosophically. This contrast has been going on ever since that time. We as Christians, are called upon to present the simple truth of the gospel from a theological or doctrinal viewpoint.

Help your students to see that our time and effort is best used in presenting and defending divine truth as it has been revealed in the Word of God. There are always people who want to argue about spiritual matters from a philosophical viewpoint, and getting involved with them can be time-consuming and worthless. To rightly divide the word of truth should be our goal. This will save us from heresy, and it will bring others to the truth which God wants them to have.

Lesson Introduction

Paul put great emphasis on evangelism in his effort to fulfill Christ's great commission to "teach all nations, baptizing them in the name of the Father, and of the Son, and of the Holy Ghost" (Matt. 28:19). He also put great emphasis on education in his effort to fulfill Christ's great commission to be "teaching them [converts] to observe all things whatsoever I have commanded you" (Matt. 28:20). His advice to young Timothy was that he should promote the great commission by motivating others to fulfill it too (II Tim. 2:2).

Our lesson text carries this forward. Paul urged Timothy to remind and challenge his workers to avoid superfluous teachings of men. He urged Timothy to be a good student of the Word of truth and to avoid heretical ideas such as the one put forth by Hymenaeus and Philetus that the resurrection was already past. He urged Timothy to purge himself from evil and be a vessel unto honor. He urged him to flee youthful passions and to develop Christian virtues. By serving God, he could please Him and rescue people held captive by Satan.

Teaching Outline

I. Intention: II Tim. 2:14-15
   A. Worthless act: 14
   B. Worthy act: 15
II. Illustrations: II Tim. 2:16-21
   A. Vanities: 16-19
   B. Vessels: 20-21
III. Instructions: II Tim. 2:22-26
   A. Recommendation: 22-24
   B. Restoration: 25-26

Daily Bible Readings

Mon. Be Encouraged
II Tim. 1:3-14
Tue. A Worker of Christ
II Tim. 2:1-13
Wed. An Approved Worker
II Tim. 2:14-19
Thu. Work Toward Love
II Tim. 2:20-26
Fri. How Some People Act
II Tim. 3:1-9
Sat. Sound Doctrine
Titus 2:1-8
Sun. God's Grace
Titus 2:9-15

February 28, 1993

VERSE BY VERSE

I. Intention: II Tim. 2:14-15

A. Worthless act: 14

14. Of these things put them in remembrance, charging them before the Lord that they strive not about words to no profit, but to the subverting of the hearers.

Paul wanted Timothy to remind and challenge the individuals under his care. He was to do this in a sober manner "before the Lord." Paul had previously charged Timothy "before God, and the Lord Jesus Christ, and the elect angels" (1 Tim. 3:21), and that expands our concept of the challenge made here. Timothy was to urge Christian workers to avoid arguing about words. This could lead to a situation in which no profit would be found and which might actually subvert those who heard it. The idea seems to be that debate over subtle nuances of semantics can produce frivolous argument and thus obscure important truths.

B. Worthy act: 15

15. Study to shew thyself approved unto God, a workman that needeth not to be ashamed, rightly dividing the word of truth.

In contrast to the useless arguing mentioned in verse 14, Paul urged Timothy to perform a worthy act.

He wanted him to study so thoroughly that he would become a worker for God who would never need to be ashamed of himself. The term "approved" has in it the concept of being tested through trial, meaning that Timothy would have to know from experience what he was teaching. Paul wanted Timothy to rightly divide the word of truth, meaning that he would handle it properly. Therefore, Paul encouraged Timothy to study, apply, and dispense divine truth in order to please God and help others. In doing these things, Timothy would serve as a good example for his co-workers to emulate. Beginning with this intention, he could work toward its implementation

II. Illustrations: II Tim. 2:16-21

A. Vanities: 16-19

16. But shun profane and vain babblings: for they will increase unto more ungodliness.

Paul told Timothy to avoid (stand above or apart from) "vain babblings." This could refer to "godless chatter" (New International Version), "idle talk" (Amplified Bible), "foolish discussions" (Living Bible), or "unholy, empty discussions" (Berkeley Version). All that could result from this would be an increase in "ungodliness," referring to a diversion from truth and a growth in impiety.

17. And their word will eat as doth a canker: of whom is Hymenaeus and Philetus;

18. Who concerning the truth have erred, saying that the resurrection is past already; and overthrow the faith of some.

Paul said that the teachings of imprudent men would erode spiritual truth as a canker (ulcer, gangrene) eats away flesh. He named Hymenaeus and Philetus as examples of those teaching error. They, for example, said that the resurrection of believers was already past, and they had overthrown the faith of some by doing this. This probably referred to the Gnostic teaching that resurrection was to be considered allegorical rather than literal and that it described spiritual resurrection of souls from the death of sin.

Philetus is not mentioned elsewhere

253

in the Bible. Hymenaeus is mentioned in 1 Timothy 1:19-20, along with Alexander, as having made shipwreck of the faith and having been delivered over to Satan so that they might learn not to blaspheme.

19a. Nevertheless the foundation of God standeth sure, having this seal, The Lord knoweth them that are his.

God's foundation stands firm, despite the doctrinal errors of heretics. This foundation is inscribed with the statement that the Lord knows those who truly belong to Him. There seems to be agreement that the foundation refers to the church. It is "built upon the foundation of the apostles and prophets, Jesus Christ himself being the chief corner stone; in whom all the building fitly framed together groweth unto an holy temple in the Lord: in whom ye also are builded together for an habitation of God through the Spirit" (Eph. 2:20-22). Paul also described it to Timothy as "the house of God, which is the church of the living God, the pillar and ground of the truth" (1 Tim. 3:15).

19b. And, let every one that nameth the name of Christ depart from iniquity.

When Korah in ancient Israel led a delegation to Moses and Aaron, he said, "Ye take too much upon you, seeing all the congregation are holy,...wherefore then lift ye up yourselves above the congregation of the Lord?" Moses replied, "Tomorrow the Lord will shew who are his, and who is holy" (Num. 16:3-5). Paul may have been thinking of that when he told Timothy that the Lord knows who are His. Then he added that every person who takes upon himself the name of Christ should depart from iniquity. In other words, it is by their lives that they prove their identification with Christ. They have given up the vanities of the world in order to devote themselves to Him.

B. Vessels: 20-21

20. But in a great house there are not only vessels of gold and of silver, but also of wood and of earth; and some to honour, and some to dishonour.

Paul set the stage here for what he wanted to say as recorded in verse 21. He referred to a great house as having vessels made of gold and silver, but also some made of wood and clay. The gold and silver vessels were obviously for honorable use and the wooden and earthen vessels for ordinary use. If one could become a vessel, he would naturally want to be among those used for honorable purposes. Paul was now ready to make his spiritual analogy.

21. If a man therefore purge himself from these, he shall be a vessel unto honour, sanctified, and meet for the master's use, and prepared unto every good work.

Paul said that a man who wants to purge himself from these things (errors, iniquities) can become a vessel unto honor. He will be sanctified (set apart from evil and set apart to righteousness). He will be meet (suitable, useful, profitable) to his Master, ready for every good work to which he is assigned by Him. Every form of service for Him is ennobled by the fact that it is done for His honor and glory. This could include such things as cleaning the church, digging ditches for a new mission station, or tending those sick and dying from a cholera plague.

III. Instructions: II Tim. 2:22-26

A. Recommendation: 22-24

22a. Flee also youthful lusts:...

This may seem to be a strange thing for Paul to say to a fine, young man such as Timothy. Perhaps it was a general warning to avoid encroaching sins common to that time and culture which surrounded the young pastor, for no one was immune to them. On the other hand, it might be suggested that Paul was warning Timothy to avoid the passion generated by such spiritual sins as impatience and pride.

22b. ...but follow righteousness, faith, charity peace, with them that call on the Lord out of a pure heart.

Paul wanted Timothy to pursue Christian virtues such as righteousness, faith, charity (love), and peace. These were the things sought by believers who called on the Lord out of pure hearts. "If I regard iniquity in my heart, the Lord will not hear me: but verily God hath heard me; he hath attended to the voice of my prayer" (Ps. 66:18-19)." In contrast to chasing after sins prompted by lusts, believers stretch forth to lay hold of virtues prompted by devotion to their Savior and Lord.

23. But foolish and unlearned questions avoid, knowing that they do gender strifes.

This obviously goes back to what was covered in verses 14 and 16. Hot arguments over the various shadings of meaning in words accomplished nothing good. It was better to keep away from foolish and unlearned questions, realizing that they stir up quarrels. From what was said before, we know that such quarrels as these can lead to heresies (vss. 17-18).

24. And the servant of the Lord must not strive; but be gentle unto all men, apt to teach, patient,

We know from experience that there are some individuals who like to argue and fight. There can be legitimate times when we all have to argue or fight, but our basic desire is to have peace. This certainly should be true of Christians in their approach to one another and to unbelievers. A servant of God will find that his witness is enhanced by being gentle, apt (able) to teach, and patient (willing to suffer wrong treatment). These are not automatic virtues. They have to be cultivated. The Holy Spirit stands ready to help. As in every other aspect of personal development, experience facilitates having and using these virtues.

B. Restoration: 25-26

25. In meekness instructing those that oppose themselves; if God peradventure will give them repentance to the acknowledging of the truth;

A Christian must remind himself that unbelievers are often their own worst enemies in the sense that they reject what is good for them. Coming at them with a condescending and arrogant manner usually offends them and makes them unwilling to listen or agree with what is said to them. Therefore, a believer must come to them in meekness (humility). He must hope and pray that God by His Spirit will touch their hearts, persuading them to repent of their sins and acknowledge divine truth regarding salvation through Jesus Christ. It is only divine persuasion which is valid.

26. And that they may recover themselves out of the snare of the devil, who are taken captive by him at his will.

The "repentance" mentioned in verse 25 finds its counterpart here in the term "recover." Sinners must first recover themselves (come to their senses) before they can take the important step of repenting of their sins. They may not realize that they have been caught in a trap all of their lives. Thinking that they are free and unfettered, they may resist the concept that Satan holds them fast in his grip.

Thus it is that we come to the end of a passage in which Paul challenged young Timothy to make his life count for Christ. If you have time, move over to II Timothy 4:1-8 to read Paul's final challenge to Timothy and his remarks regarding his own coming death. There were souls to be won, heretics to be resisted, and a crown of righteousness to be won.

TEACH THE TRUTH

Evangelistic Emphasis

Today's lesson focuses on some wise advice to a young Christian leader. It offers a rich variety of ways to reduce conflict in churches and families.

Timothy knew (as do Christians today) how easy it is to get into arguments over words and issues, and how hard it is to regain the high ground. Whenever people do find ways to keep Christ central, and handle controversies delicately that achievement in itself is a witness to the community. People who need healing for brokenness in their own lives will be attracted to a church that knows how to heal its own conflicts.

Scripture offers no justifiable reason to divide a church over issues or words. Even an issue as central as the doctrine of the resurrection was not enough to disqualify someone automatically from the body of Christ, according to II Timothy 2:17-19. Even here, there is a proper way and an improper way to proceed.

Some churches— and families— are spiritually immature and brittle, and break under a little pressure. Others are more mature and can survive and thrive even after severe testing. What makes the difference? It's not the weight of the problems, but the depth of dependence on Christ, that affects the outcome!

◆◆◆◆◆◆

II Timothy 2:15

Memory Selection

Even though the Letters to Timothy and Titus reveal the counsel of an older minister to a younger one, many of the instructions apply to anyone who wants to be a servant leader for Christ.

That's particularly true of the exhortation in II Timothy 2:15. Here Paul shows how to avoid having our energies drained off by side issues, and to "keep our eyes on the prize" to do everything we can to develop competence in handling the Word of God.

The words "study" and "workman" refer not just to head knowledge, but to craftsmanship or artisanship—the kind of knowledge you see in an accomplished carpenter or musician or athlete. There, theory and application are combined so smoothly that the work doesn't call attention to itself. An observer hardly notices the masterful way the work is being done.

It brings to mind the old proverb. "Great art conceals art." To be "approved unto God," a teacher or preacher doesn't have to use big words or dense thoughts. In fact. many of today's true masters of Scripture "make it look easy."

In many churches, those who sit through sermons and Bible classes week after week take for granted the work involved in preparation and delivery. That's as it should be, for the ultimate goal of preaching and teaching is not a memorable performance, but a group of people more and more nourished by the Word of God, more and more committed to a life of loving service.

256

February 28, 1993

Weekday Problems

It's a small church, and their fine young minister has been on the job for just a year. Enthusiasm is growing, and much-needed new life is in store for the congregation.

Naturally, new life means change. In this situation, it means changing some things that a few of the longtime members really cherish. Friction and conflict are on the horizon, unless proper action is taken.

A majority of the members want to encourage the new minister and the new approaches, but they also respect and love the older members.

* What principles are mentioned in II Timothy 2 that might head off conflict?
* Suppose someone sees the new approach as a violation of essential doctrine, while someone else views the changes as necessary for the church's growth and survival. What can be done to "lower the temperature" and keep the situation from polarizing?

♦♦♦♦♦♦

Superintendent's Sermonette

The Apostle Paul had suffered many things during the time that he served Christ. An extensive list is provided in II Corinthians 11:23-28. He was thankful for God's sustaining grace and expressed this by saying, "Though our outward man perish, yet the inward man is renewed day by day" (II Cor. 4:16). However, Paul realized that his life was coming to an end, and he was concerned about the work of the gospel being continued. He turned to young Timothy and wrote him two letters to encourage and challenge him and others under his care. Paul saw Timothy and others like him as replacements for himself when God called him home to heaven.

Christian leaders today need to follow Paul's procedure. Christians today need to see themselves as developing replacements for those leaders. Lifetimes rush by, and there is continual need for individuals to step into the gaps created by the passing of valued workers. The whole church should recognize how the system works. Let those who have promise be singled out and given the training and experience they need to carry on God's program. Each of us needs to determine where he or she fits into this and then do what is required. Let's take Paul's challenge to Timothy seriously for ourselves.

TEACH THE TRUTH

This Lesson in Your Life

Paul urges Timothy to become proficient at "rightly dividing" the Word. The original Greek words for "to rightly divide" mean "to cut straight."

It's a term that might describe a farmer plowing a straight furrow or a tailor who makes a straight cut on a piece of fabric. The idea is to keep heading in the right direction, not being distracted or taken off course.

Jesus Himself makes a very similar point. He says for us not to be like the farmer who keeps looking over his shoulder while he's plowing. In other words, let's not waste time checking the work we've already done. Let's concentrate on what's out in front of us (see Luke 9:62).

Today you'll see the same point made in a familiar TV comedy setup: a parent is driving the car with the kids acting up in back. When the driver turns around to straighten out the kids, something always happens— a near accident, running off the road— and the parent is shown to be no better than the kids.

This is the message to the young evangelist Timothy: master the Scriptures in such a way that you'll keep on course. Don't let disputes about side issues, or even, quarrels about central issues, draw you into a fight. Instead, work diligently to become the kind of leader who can point people to Christ as the center of life in all circumstances. How easy it is to go off course. How often we are distracted by the "tyranny of the urgent" and have to struggle to give proper attention to the truly important. We can be going along having a great day when one ugly remark from somebody sends us reeling. The rest of the day is ruined.

The exhortation to "rightly divide" the Word encourages us to know that we can find ways to handle getting knocked off course. Nothing has the power to keep us from working toward our goals unless we choose to let it. Clearly it's not easy, especially at first.

In fact, studying the Scriptures itself at first seems to be a challenge in how to separate central issues from peripheral ones.

There's so much to learn in the Bible! Beginners often find themselves beguiled by a particular interpretation or a theory that promises to reduce everything in the Bible to a few simple points.

Once we get past the oversimplifiers we may notice that some religious traditions emphasize certain parts of the Bible over others. In some places, Bible prophecies seem to get the most attention. Others return over and over to the Book of Acts. Learning to "rightly divide" the Word is much more than figuring out a scheme for arranging Scripture teachings according to some particular method of interpretation. It means, rather, that we learn to center on the true goal of Scripture, Jesus Christ.

Once our understanding of the Word of God centers on Christ, everything else in our lives begins to fall into place. We can set proper goals and reach them. We can keep distractions out. We won't let worry or criticism or temptation or anything else distract us.

That's the promise of what's in store for us when we are able to "rightly divide" the Word!

Seed Thoughts

1. How often do you find that conflicts are caused by misunderstandings?
It's more common than we suppose, which is perhaps the reason Paul warns Timothy away from "strife about words" (II Timothy 2:14).

2. Is it possible to know a Scriptural answer to every question that comes up?
No, for the mature student of Scripture is the one who knows the difference between a significant issue and a distracting side issue.

3. Who were Hymenaeus and Philetus, and what problems were they causing for Timothy?
They believed that "the resurrection is past already," perhaps meaning believers would never die.

4. What advice does Paul give for dealing with a person who causes conflict?
We can withstand a lot more than we might think and it's not our task to straighten out every problem (2:19).

5. What is the most important resource for creating unity in a church or family?
Appreciation of and forbearance for one another, whether we are at our worst or at our best.

(PLEASE TURN PAGE)

---

1. How often do you find that conflicts are caused by misunderstandings?

2. Is it possible to know a Scriptural answer to every question that comes up?

3. Who were Hymenaeus and Philetus, and what problems were they causing for Timothy?

4. What advice does Paul give for dealing with a person who causes conflict?

5. What is the most important resource for creating unity in a church or family?

6. What big struggle does Paul say younger Christians will face?

7. What help is promised to grow out of impulsiveness?

8. What will be the big struggle of more mature Christians, according to Paul?

9. What help is promised to deal with impatience?

10. Is there a hope for those who have been caught up in senseless quarrels and conflict?

(SEED THOUGHTS--Cont'd)

It's more common than we suppose, which is perhaps the reason Paul warns Timothy away from "strife about words" (II Timothy 2:14).

No, for the mature student of Scripture is the one who knows the difference between a significant issue and a distracting side issue.

They believed that "the resurrection is past already," perhaps meaning believers would never die.

We can withstand a lot more than we might think and it's not our task to straighten out every problem (2:19).

Appreciation of and forbearance for one another, whether we are at our worst or at our best.

Impulsiveness— anything from unpremeditated sexual activity to thoughtless changes in career or studies— is included in the term "youthful lust" (2:22).

A life that develops righteousness, faith, love, and peace— and associating with those with similar values (2:22).

Impatience with those who are less mature, especially when they stir up senseless conflicts (2:23).

Knowing that it's not the leader's responsibility to force change on anyone. God can bring change in His own good time (2:24-26).

If they are treated with kindness and forbearance, it is possible that they may escape the snare of the devil.

6. What big struggle does Paul say younger Christians will face?
Impulsiveness— anything from unpremeditated sexual activity to thoughtless changes in career or studies— is included in the term "youthful lust" (2:22).

7. What help is promised to grow out of impulsiveness?
A life that develops righteousness, faith, love, and peace— and associating with those with similar values (2:22).

8. What will be the big struggle of more mature Christians, according to Paul?
Impatience with those who are less mature, especially when they stir up senseless conflicts (2:23).

9. What help is promised to deal with impatience?
Knowing that it's not the leader's responsibility to force change on anyone. God can bring change in His own good time (2:24-26).

10. Is there a hope for those who have been caught up in senseless quarrels and conflict?
If they are treated with kindness and forbearance, it is possible that they may escape the snare of the devil.

March 7, 1993

In Him Was Life

John 1

1 IN the beginning was the Word and the Word was with God, and the Word was God.
2 The same was in the beginning with God.
3 All things were made by him; and without him was not any thing made that was made.
4 In him was life; and the life was the light of men.
5 And the light shineth in darkness; and the darkness comprehended it not.
6 There was a man sent from God, whose name was John.
7 The same came for a witness, to bear witness of the Light, that all *men* through him might believe.
8 He was not that Light, but *was sent* to bear witness of that Light.
9 *That* was the true Light, which lighteth every man that cometh into the world.
10 He was in the world, and the world was made by him, and the world knew him not.
11 He came unto his own, and his own received him not.
12 But as many as received him, to them gave he power to become the sons of God, *even* to them that believe on his name:
13 Which were born, not of blood, nor of the will of the flesh, nor of the will of man, but of God.
14 And the Word was made flesh, and dwelt among us, (and we beheld his glory, the glory as of the only begotten of the Father,) full of grace and truth.
15 John bare witness of him, and cried, saying, This was he of whom I spake, he that cometh after me is preferred before me: for he was before me.
16 And of his fullness have all we received, and grace for grace.
17 For the law was given by Moses, *but* grace and truth came by Jesus Christ.
18 No man hath seen God at any time; the only begotten Son, which is in the bosom of the Father, he hath declared *him*.

◆◆◆◆◆◆

◀ **Memory Selection**
John 1:14

◀ **Devotional Reading**
John 1:19-23, 29-34

◀ **Background Scripture**
John 1:1-18

◀ **Printed Sculpture**
John 1:1-18

IN HIM WAS LIFE

Teacher's Target

God had communicated with men from Adam and Eve onward. He used direct speech, angelic messengers, dreams, visions, priests, Urim and Thummim, seers, and prophets. The best way, however, was in sending His beloved Son to the earth to minister, die, be raised, and ascend back to heaven. The Apostle John began his gospel by immediately mentioning these things. He placed Christ in eternity past with the heavenly Father and called Him the Word (Communicator). He ascribed creative power to Him. He introduced John the Baptist as a witness of the Light to come. He declared Jesus to be that Light and the Savior of all who believe on Him.

Help your students to define life in both physical and spiritual terms and to realize that Jesus Christ is the Source of both. "These are written, that ye might believe that Jesus is the Christ, the Son of God; and that believing ye might have life through his name (John 20:31). Identification by faith with Christ should be the end result of God's communication with us.

Lesson Introduction

Modern scientists talk about things happening millions or billions of years ago as if they have evidence to support their theories. We actually know nothing of the distant past except what God has revealed to us in His Holy Word, and that is minimal. The Bible begins with a graphic description of the creation of the universe and particularly of the earth. The period before that is called "the beginning" and refers to eternity past without mentioning time as we know it. God, Christ, and the Holy Spirit have always existed.

When it pleased God to create the universe using His Son as the Creator (John 1:3; Col. 1:16; Heb. 1:2), it was also decided that Christ would assume a human form, becoming the unique God-Man. This was necessary in order that He might become the only worthy and valid sacrifice to atone for the sins of mankind. To those who received Him, and who do today, He gave the power to become the sons of God. This assures them of salvation in eternity future.

Teaching Outline

I. Two Beings: John 1:1-5
   A. Christ: 1-2
   B. Creation: 3
   C. Coverage: 4-5
II. Two Messengers: John 1:6-14
   A. John: 6-8
   B. Jesus: 9-14
III. Two Witnesses: John 1:15-18
   A. John the Baptist: 15
   B. John the Apostle: 16-18

Daily Bible Readings

Mon. The Word Was God
John 1:1-5
Tue. A Witness to Jesus
John 1:6-13
Wed. God With Us
John 1:14-18
Thu. John Identified Himself
John 1:19-28
Fri. John Identifies Jesus
John 1:29-34
Sat. We Have Found the Messiah
John 1:35-42
Sun. The Call to Follow
John 1:43-51

March 7, 1993

VERSE BY VERSE

I. Two Beings: John 1:1-5

A. Christ: 1,2

1. In the beginning was the Word, and the Word was with God, and the Word was God.
2. The same was in the beginning with God.

As already mentioned in the Lesson Introduction, "the beginning" referred to eternity past as a period of infinite and indeterminate time as we know it. God the Father, God the Son, and God the Holy Spirit always existed. God and the Son are the two divine Beings mentioned here, but the Holy Spirit was there, too, and had a part in creation (Gen. 1:2).

Greek philosophers used the term *Logos* (Word) to refer to deities communicating with men. The Apostle John personalized it, applied it to Christ, and described Him as Communicator with men. This is certainly its meaning in John 1:14. Christ was able to reveal God the Father to men because He was with Him in eternity past and up to the time He came to earth at Bethlehem in the body of a baby. This is certainly supported in John 1:18, which we study later in this lesson. The eternality of Christ is an important biblical doctrine. There was never a time when He was *not* divine. The Word was God!

B. Creation: 3

3. All things were made by him; and without him was not anything made that was made.

The fact that Christ was the One Whom God used in creating the universe finds ample support in the New Testament. John 1:3 states it. Ephesians 3:9 refers to "God, who created all things by Jesus Christ." Colossians 1:16, speaking of Christ, says that "by him were all things created, that are in heaven, and that are in earth, visible and invisible, whether they be thrones, or dominions, or principalities, or powers: all things were created by him, and for him." Hebrews 1:2 refers to Christ when stating it was He "by whom also he (God) made the worlds."

Scientists tell us that all matter can ultimately be reduced to energy. It was divine energy which spoke the universe into being and then populated and furnished it with all living things. This is in keeping with the following verse's reference to life, both temporal and eternal.

C. Coverage: 4-5

4 In him was life; and the life was the light of men.

This simply means that Christ was the Source of all life in the universe, including angelic, human, animal, and plant forms. Life was not accidently sparked by some electrical or chemical reaction and then set on a path of upward evolution. It was deliberately infused by divine power into all creatures and things designed to live. It was Christ, the Source of temporal and spiritual life, Who became the Light of men. Light is a biblical term used to denote truth, and Jesus Himself claimed to be "the way, the truth, and the life" leading men to the Father (John 14:6).

5. And the light shineth in darkness; and the darkness comprehended it not.

Some feel that this verse describes truth shining out to the world and men failing to understand or accept it. We know that many have not. Others feel

263

this verse describes truth shining out to the world and the darkness (ignorance) of men failing to cover it. We know that truth has persisted in spite of human attempts to suppress it. Providing coverage of the world with divine truth has been the responsibility of believers throughout human history.

II. Two Messengers: John 1:6-14

A. John: 6-8

6. There was a man sent from God, whose name was John.

The Apostle John never referred to himself by his personal name in his gospel. In this verse he was obviously referring to John the Baptist as the man sent by God. Chapter 1 of the gospel of Luke explains in detail the fact that God did indeed send John the Baptist to herald the coming of Jesus. This was in fulfillment of Old Testament prophecies such as Isaiah 40:3-5 and Malachi 3:1.

7. The same came for a witness, to bear witness of the Light, that all men through him might believe.

8. He was not that Light, but was sent to bear witness of that Light.

Verse 8 repeats what was said in verse 7, and we can analyze them together. John the Baptist did not pretend to be the Light sent by God. That specific term was used to denote the Messiah Who originated in heaven but took on the form of a man when conceived by the Holy Ghost in Mary and was born in Bethlehem. Light is a synonymn for truth in the Bible, and Jesus claimed to be "the light of the world" (John 8:12) and "the truth" (John 14:6). John the Baptist clearly stated, "I am not the Christ (John 1:20). He was the forerunner of Christ, trying to get all men to believe on Him. He practised water baptism as a form of Jewish purification on those who repented of sin who waited for the Messiah to come. After Jesus began His ministry, John the Baptist said, "He must increase, but I must decrease" (John 3:30).

John the Baptist was a transitional figure between the Old Testament and the New Testament, between law and grace, and between Judaism and Christianity. He might be called the last of the Old Testament type of prophets and the first of the New Testament type of prophets.

B. Jesus: 9-14

9. That was the true Light, which lighteth every man that cometh into the world.

John the Baptist was a worthy witness of Christ, but Christ was His Own best witness. Does verse 9 state that He was the true Light Who lights (or enlightens) every man coming into the world, or does it state that He was the true Light, the One Who lights (or enlightens) every man, and that He was coming into the world? The latter would appear to be the more likely statement. Christ did enlighten men in various ways long before He came into the world to minister. He did this through nature, conscience, and revelations.

10. He was in the world, and the world was made by him, and the world knew him not.

Christ came into the literal world which He had created, and that natural world recognized and respected Him. He multiplied a boy's lunch to feed a multitude. He calmed a Galilean storm. He healed many sick people. He raised the dead. However, the sinful world-system was largely unreceptive.

11. He came unto his own, and his own received him not.

Jesus came to His Own people, the Jews. Some believed on Him as being their long-awaited Messiah and the divine Son of God. Most chose to reject His claim to divinity. His humble birth in peasant circumstances did not fit into their idealized picture of the Messiah. His enemies plotted until they persuaded the Roman governor, Pilate, to send Him to the cross.

12. But as many as received him, to them gave he power to become the sons of God, even to them that believe on his name:

13. Which were born, not of blood, nor of the will of the flesh, nor of the will of men, but of God.

The comparative few who accepted Jesus and His message of salvation were given the power (right, authority) to become redeemed sons of God. This was made possible when they believed on His name and all that the name meant (Messiah, Savior, Lord). Natural birth required the mingling of bloods from parents through the joining of sperm and ovum. Human (fleshly) passions were involved. Spiritual new birth, however, was quite different. This involved the impartation of spiritual life by God from above and outside of men's usual experiences. We will look more closely at this in our next lesson when we study Jesus' conversation with Nicodemus on how to be born again of the Spirit of God.

14. And the Word was made flesh, and dwelt among us, (and we beheld his glory, the glory as of the only begotten of the Father,) full of grace and truth.

The Word (Communicator) mentioned in John 1:1 was Jesus Christ in spirit form existing in eternity past. He became flesh (human) and dwelt among men by coming to the earth as the Babe of Bethlehem and growing to manhood in Egypt and Nazareth. He ministered throughout Palestine and even over the border in Phoenicia. Although He was truly human, He was also truly divine, the unique God-Man. His divine majesty revealed itself through His sinless life, sublime teachings, sensational miracles, sacrificial death, and subsequent resurrection and ascension to heaven. He was filled with grace and truth (vss. 14 and 17). It was through grace and truth that sinners could be converted to Christ and become adopted members of God's redeemed family (Rom. 8:14-17).

III. Two Witnesses: John 1:15-18

A. John the Baptist: 15

15. John bare witness of him, and cried, saying, This was he of whom I spoke, He that cometh after me is preferred before me: for he was before me.

Ancient people loved riddles, and this may have been cast in that form. John the Baptist bore witness (testified) regarding Jesus by saying that He came *after* he did but was preferred over him because He came *before* him. Jesus came *after* John in the sense that he was born some six months afterward. However, Jesus came *before* John in the sense that He existed in eternity past. Jesus was superior to John because He was divine as well as human. Therefore, Jesus was preferred over John due to His unique position as the Son of God.

B. John the Apostle: 16-18

16. And of his fulness have all we received, and grace for grace.

Scholars suggest that verses 16-18 were spoken by John the Apostle rather than by John the Baptist. This would seem to be supported by verse 14, because the flow of thought continues on in verse 16. It was because Jesus was filled with grace and truth that He was able to bestow "grace for grace" on men. It might also be translated as "grace upon grace" or an accumulation of gracious acts by Him upon men.

17. For the law was given by Moses, but grace and truth came by Jesus Christ.

Both John the Baptist and John the Apostle were Jews brought up in the Mosaic law and respectful of it. They recognized the fact that God had given the law to Israel through Moses, and they respected him. However, both also knew that the new era would feature grace and truth as given by God to men through Jesus Christ. The law provided a preparation for grace, but it could not save men as grace could. Moses was superseded by Christ, and law was superseded by grace.

18. No man hath seen God at any time; the only begotten Son, which is in the bosom of the Father, he hath declared him.

God could not be seen, for He is an invisible Spirit (John 4:24). Stephen saw the glory of God prior to his martyrdom (Acts 7:55). It was in the coming of Jesus, however, that God was best revealed to men. Jesus came from His Father's side in heaven, and He returned there at His ascension (Acts 1:9-10; 7:55-56).

IN HIM WAS LIFE

Evangelistic Emphasis

Life! Encased in a seedling tree, it cracks open great boulders. Emerging from a woman's womb, life brings unequalled joy to a young couple. Hanging by a fragile thread, life martials the concerted skills of an entire hospital emergency room staff intent on preserving it against all odds. How powerful and valued life is! And it is life — eternal life — that is the basis of the good news proclaimed in John's Gospel.

The *temporary* quality of much contemporary life underlines our need for *eternal* life—not simply life unending, but life like that of the eternal God. Instant gratification, throwaway goods, rootlessness and fleeting relationships prompt many to ask, Is that all there is?

The answer of John's Gospel is that life of the quality we seek is available through Christ. This is especially good news for a rootless age because the life Jesus offers reconnects us to the *source* of all life. Since "all things were made by him" (John 1:3), those whom Christ enlivens are in touch with the creative power of the universe. John also relates this power to creation by connecting it with the light of creation's first Day: "In him was life; and the life was the light of men" (vs. 4).

◆◆◆◆◆◆

Memory Selection

And the Word was made flesh, and dwelt among us, (and we beheld his glory, the glory as of the only begotten of the Father) full of grace and truth. *John 1:14*

John's Gospel comes to us in Greek dress. The Greeks were very familiar with the Word as a concept. But Jesus comes to us as a Jew, from a religious heritage more concerned with *doing* religion than with religious concepts. Jesus comes to us as the *enfleshed* Word.

How important it is to remember that Jesus was the divine Word *in the flesh*. Although existing in the form of God, He voluntarily assumed fleshly form, being "made in the likeness of men" (Phil. 2:7). Hence, when we behold His glory — when we gasp in amazement at Jesus' glorious deeds and self-giving life — our gaze is also drawn to God, Who reveals His true nature through Jesus.

There is also an important principle here for Christian living. We need to enflesh our own "glorious" words! The world has never lacked for religious words and ideas. But this passage is an implicit challenge for us to back up our godly words with godly deeds. In Jesus' day, the scribes and Pharisees earned the criticism, "They say, and do not" (Matt. 23:3). Their words about religious duties were not enfleshed. So Jesus warns, "You must not imitate their lives! For they preach but do not practice" (*Phillips*).

March 7, 1993

Weekday Problems

Greg, a high school junior, had a frown on his face. "What's wrong?" his dad asked.

"I just heard a radio preacher warn against 'living after the flesh,'" Greg said. "He was talking about sex, and...ahem." Embarrassed, his voice trailed off.

Mr. Frye obligingly finished the sentence. "And you're wondering about boy-girl stuff and marriage and making babies — am I right?"

"Right," his son grinned. He could always count on his dad to knife directly, if painfully, through to the point.

"I was just studying for my Sunday lesson" Mr. Frye continued. "Here in John 1 it speaks of the flesh, too. It says that Jesus was divine, but *became* flesh."

"Then how could 'flesh' be so wrong?" Greg asked.

"Maybe it's not, in itself," his father answered. "In fact, this chapter also claims that as the Word, Jesus had a hand in creating the world — and I suppose that includes our fleshly bodies."

"So what did the preacher mean?" Greg asked.

*What concept from John 1 might help answer Greg's question? What else might be said?

*Look up the word *flesh* in a Bible dictionary. What are the main ways the word is used in Scripture?

*"Gnostic" is a term often given to ancient views of human sexuality as "bad." How should such "gnostic" ideas today be countered?

◆◆◆◆◆◆

Superintendent's Sermonette

The gospels written by Matthew and Luke revealed early biographical material regarding John the Baptist and Jesus. Mark's gospel briefly profiled John the Baptist and went directly into a description of Jesus' ministry beginning at the time of His baptism by John in the Jordan River. John's gospel described Jesus as being with His Father in eternity past and told about His creative work. As in Mark's case, John moved directly to the ministries of John the Baptist and Jesus without early biographical references.

The three synoptic (seeing together) gospels of Matthew, Mark, and Luke presented Jesus' ministry as a whole. John's gospel, written toward the end of the first century, selected certain discourses and miracles of Jesus to emphasize. Chapter 1, on which Lessons 1, 9, and 10 for this quarter are based, plays a large role in this series.

As we begin the quarter, let us ask God to give us a new vision of the greatness and blessing of Jesus upon men, including ourselves. If we already belong to Him by faith, let us rejoice in our sonship and all that this relationship means to us both now and for eternity. If there are those among us who have not yet become redeemed sons of God, let us hope and pray that this series will help them to become His sons.

267

This Lesson In Your Life

BIGGER THAN LIFE

Columnist and humorist Art Buchwald once described the traits of U. S. presidents and the opportunities they offer for good-natured jokes. John F. Kennedy flattered the press, according to Buchwald, sometimes making them reluctant to poke fun at him. Nixon came on like a corporation executive whose PR line made journalists wonder who the real Nixon was. Lyndon Johnson was Buchwald's favorite target because he was "bigger than life." All presidents wield power, but LBJ brandished it in oversized portions. All presidents have ears, but LBJ's were a cartoonist's delight since they were "bigger than life."

The first 18 verses of John's Gospel, often viewed as its Prologue, portray Jesus as bigger than life, too. It describes Him as a person of flesh, *and then some*: He is also a pre-existent figure, the Word, present with the Father before creation. The ancient heresies countered by this portrayal of Christ are a continual temptation in our own day.

There is a view of Jesus that wants Him to remain *apart from life*. In this view, Christ can become so spiritual He is of no earthly good. This picture of Jesus affirms that He is an eternal Spirit, and emphasizes the preexistent aspect that John touches on in 1:1-3. His miracles are dwelt on to the point of making Him little more than a divine Magician. A second century legend describes even the boy Jesus as a miracle-worker, patting clay into the form of a dove and "blowing life" into it so that it flies away.

In addition to being unscriptural, this view of Jesus has little relevance to everyday life. It too easily separates Christ from urgent human and social concerns. It tempts us to long to be with Jesus in heaven, while ignoring responsibilities such as caring for the earth of which He was the creative Agent. While also tempting us to retreat from the street to the altar, this view is not even very helpful there. When we are burdened with cares it is of little comfort to have a Lord who knows nothing of our daily struggle in the flesh. It is no favor to the real Jesus to pay Jesus what philosopher A. N. Whitehead called "excessive metaphysical compliments."

Another extreme is perhaps more common in our day. This is the view of Jesus that is *limited to life*. Some naturalistic people want to celebrate the humanity of Jesus while denying His divinity. They seek the "Jesus of history" but have no interest in "the Christ of faith." They emphasize John's statement that the Word became flesh (1:14), while discounting claims of His preexistence and divinity.

Ironically, as modern as this view seems, it actually harks back to a "flat world" mentality. It is unable to deal profoundly with the mystery and depth of human needs. The Bible's claim that we can have a vertical relationship with God through His Son is traded for the horizontal relationships among people. Sadly, as one adherent of this view said, "the front page of the newspaper is the benediction of the day."

Neither of these views of Jesus is as big as life, according to John's Gospel. John affirms Christ's divinity so clearly that his Gospel is sometimes called "the mystic Gospel." It is John who records the astounding confession of Thomas, when confronted with the resurrected Lord: "My Lord and *my God*" (John 20:28). Yet John also insists, more than any other Gospel writer, on speaking of Christ "in the flesh." In other words, John's view is that the spiritual aspect of Jesus is as "real" as His "natural" aspects; and that His natural qualities are in fact an actual part of spiritual reality.

Seed Thoughts

1. What implication can we draw from the fact that everything—including our fleshly bodies—can be attributed to the creative work of the Word?

All creation—including our bodies—is "very good," just as Genesis 1 repeatedly affirms.

2. What does it mean to say that darkness does not "comprehend" the light? (See John 1:5 in other versions, too.)

Understood as "comprehend" the meaning may be that those who oppose Christ cannot truly understand Him.

3. Who is the "John" in verses 6 and 15? Is he the John who wrote this Gospel?

No, verses 6 and 15 refer to John the Baptist, not the author of this Gospel.

4. Who were those in verse 11 who did not receive the Word?

Jesus' own people, the Jews.

5. What power is lacking in those who do not receive the Word? (John 1:12)

The power (right, authority) to become children of God.

(PLEASE TURN PAGE)

---

1. What implication can we draw from the fact that everything—including our fleshly bodies—can be attributed to the creative work of the Word?

2. What does it mean to say that darkness does not "comprehend" the light? (See John 1:5 in other versions, too.)

3. Who is the "John" in verses 6 and 15? Is he the John who wrote this Gospel?

4. Who were those in verse 11 who did not receive the Word?

5. What power is lacking in those who do not receive the Word? (John 1:12)

6. Why are those born "of blood" or of the flesh (vs. 13) not necessarily among those who become children of God?

7. What "glory" do you "behold," as in verse 14, as you think of Jesus?

8. Discuss the difference between the contributions of Moses and of Christ to the way of salvation.

9. What unique perspective or vision can we gain from Christ according to verse 18?

10. What else besides the visible world does Colossians 1:16 say Christ was involved in creating?

(SEED THOUGHTS--Cont'd)

All creation—including our bodies—is "very good," just as Genesis 1 repeatedly affirms.

Understood as "comprehend" the meaning may be that those who oppose Christ cannot truly understand Him.

No, verses 6 and 15 refer to John the Baptist, not the author of this Gospel.

Jesus' own people, the Jews.

The power (right, authority) to become children of God.

Because they are merely born naturally— "once" instead of being born spiritually— "again," as in John 3:3-5.

Answers might include His miracles, His compassion and love, His willingness to die for our sins, the glory of His resurrection, His presence with us today.

Moses' law system tended to emphasize salvation by one's ability to be righteous. A grace system places more emphasis on salvation as a free gift.

Since the Son is the only One who has lived with the Father, He is the primary source of our vision of God.

The invisible world (the world of angels and spirits?).

6. Why are those born "of blood" or of the flesh (vs. 13) not necessarily among those who become children of God?
Because they are merely born naturally— "once" instead of being born spiritually— "again," as in John 3:3-5.

7. What "glory" do you "behold," as in verse 14, as you think of Jesus?
Answers might include His miracles, His compassion and love, His willingness to die for our sins, the glory of His resurrection, His presence with us today.

8. Discuss the difference between the contributions of Moses and of Christ to the way of salvation.
Moses' law system tended to emphasize salvation by one's ability to be righteous. A grace system places more emphasis on salvation as a free gift.

9. What unique perspective or vision can we gain from Christ according to verse 18?
Since the Son is the only One who has lived with the Father, He is the primary source of our vision of God.

10. What else besides the visible world does Colossians 1:16 say Christ was involved in creating?
The invisible world (the world of angels and spirits?).

March 14, 1993

ETERNAL LIFE INSURANCE IS FREE!

Rebirth Into Eternal Life

John 3

THERE was a man of the Pharisees, named Nic-o-de´-mus, a ruler of the Jews:

2. The same came to Jesus by night, and said unto him, Rabbi, we know that thou art a teacher come from God: for no man can do these miracles that thou doest, except God be with him.

3. Jesus answered and said unto him, Verily, verily, I say unto thee, Except a man be born again, he cannot see the kingdom of God.

4. Nic-o-de´-mus saith unto him, How can a man be born when he is old? can he enter the second time into his mother's womb, and be born?

5. Jesus answered, Verily, verily, I say unto thee, Except a man be born of water and of the Spirit, he cannot enter into the kingdom of God.

6. That which is born of the flesh is flesh; and that which is born of the Spirit is spirit.

7. Marvel not that I said unto thee, Ye must be born again.

8. The wind bloweth where it listeth, and thou hearest the sound thereof, but canst not tell whence it cometh, and whither it goeth: so is every one that is born of the Spirit.

9. Nic-o-de´-mus answered and said unto him, How can these things be?

10. Jesus answered and said unto him, Art thou a master of Israel, and knowest not these things?

11. Verily, verily, I say unto thee, We speak that we do know, and testify that we have seen and ye receive not our witness.

12. If I have told you earthly things, and ye believe not, how shall ye believe, if I tell you of heavenly things?

13. And no man hath ascended up to heaven, but he that came down from heaven, *even* the Son of man which is in heaven.

14. And as Moses lifted up the serpent in the wilderness, even so must the Son of man be lifted up:

15. That whosoever believeth in him should not perish, but have eternal life.

16. For God so loved the world, that he gave his only begotten Son, that whosoever believeth in him should not perish, but have everlasting life.

17. For God sent not his Son into the world to condemn the world; but that the world through him might be saved.

◆◆◆◆◆◆

◀ **Memory Selection**
John 3:3

◀ **Devotional Reading**
John 3:22-36

◀ **Background Scripture**
John 3:1-21

◀ **Printed Scripture**
John, 3:1-17

REBIRTH INTO ETERNAL LIFE

Teachers Target

Everyone enjoys accomplishing something worthwhile and having his work recognized. Nicodemus rose into the membership of the Sanhedrin (Jewish Council). The Romans allowed this group to monitor religious regulations of the Jews. However, Nicodemus was obviously a man with a conscience and a desire to know truth. He had heard about Jesus and may even have observed Him teach and perform miracles. He wanted to know more by talking directly with Him, but he did not want to jeopardize his position in the Sanhedrin. He came to Jesus at night in an effort to keep the meeting secret.

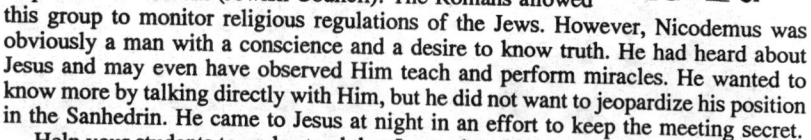

Help your students to understand that Jesus placed life's most demanding requirement before Nicodemus, and the same is true for us today. The new birth by the Spirit of God is necessary for those who want to enter the kingdom of God. Illustrations such as Jesus used (wind and serpent) may help grasp the meaning of this truth. It is impossible to be born again without the ministries of the Holy Spirit and of Jesus Christ, the One lifted up to atone for our sins.

Lesson Introduction

Nicodemus provided an example of the difficulties a person follows when trying to walk the line between two opposing sets of beliefs and practices. He was mentioned in the Bible only in the gospel of John and only three times. John 3:1-21 tells of his nighttime conversation with Jesus regarding the new birth. John 7:50-52 tells of his attempt to get the Sanhedrin to give Jesus a fair hearing, only to have other members give him a severe rebuke. John 19:38-42 tells how he assisted Joseph of Arimathaea in preparing the body of Jesus for burial following His crucifixion.

His actions have resulted in him being labeled "a secret believer" in Jesus. We can only speculate as to what happened to him after that last recorded incident. If he had joined the early Christians and become prominent in the work of the church, probably something would have been written about him. Since the New Testament contains nothing more about him, we suspect that he may have stayed on the sidelines. We are left to wonder about his subsequent spiritual condition.

Teaching Outline

I. Seeker: John 3:1-7
   A. Investigation: 1-2
   B. Insight: 3
   C. Inquiry: 4
   D. Information: 5-7
II. Spirit: John 3:8-12
   A. Comparison: 8
   B. Confusion: 9
   C. Complaint: 10-12
III. Salvation: John 3:13-17
   A. Ascension: 13
   B. Allusion: 14-15
   C. Appropriation: 16-17

Daily Bible Readings

Mon. Born of the Spirit
John 3:1-8
Tue. Christ Lifted Up
John 3:9-15
Wed. Christ, the Way
John 3:16-21
Thu. He Must Increase
John 3:22-30
Fri. He Is Above All
John 3:31-36
Sat. Eternal Life in Christ
John 17:1-11
Sun. Born of God
1 John 4:7-12

VERSE BY VERSE

I. Seeker: John 3:1-7

A. Investigation: 1-2

1. There was a man of the Pharisees, named Nicodemus, a ruler of the Jews:

The name Nicodemus means "victor over the people" in Greek, but we do not know the significance of it. Nicodemus was a member of the strict party known as Pharisees, who considered themselves to be "guardians of the law (of Moses)" and of longstanding Jewish religious traditions. Some of them were members of the Sanhedrin (Jewish Council), and it appears that Nicodemus was one of that number. The Romans ruled Palestine politically, but they left administration of religious matters to the Sanhedrin.

2. The same came to Jesus by night, and said unto him, Rabbi, we know that thou art a teacher come from God: for no man can do these miracles that thou doest, except God be with him.

This verse reveals several things regarding the character of Nicodemus. John put stress on the fact that Nicodemus came to Jesus at night (John 3:2; 7:50; 19:39). We assume that this revealed a reluctance on the part of Nicodemus to be seen talking to Jesus openly. This timidity seems to have been shown in the other two references and in the absence of further mention of him elsewhere. Nicodemus flattered Jesus by calling Him by the title of Rabbi. He must have known that Jesus was not a graduate of the rabbinical system, but he honored Him as a teacher. Nicodemus assumed that Jesus had been sent by God, as witnessed by His wisdom and miracles, but this did not mean that Nicodemus considered Jesus to be divine. He probably placed Him in the category of a prophet. Despite his timidity, we have to give Nicodemus credit for sincerely seeking truth. It is unfortunate that he did not appear to act openly on it afterward.

B. Insight: 3

3. Jesus answered and said unto him, Verily, verily, I say unto thee, Except a man be born again, he cannot see the kingdom of God.

Jesus looked into the heart of Nicodemus and told him what he really needed. Jews thought that they had a bright future because they had been born into God's chosen people. Jesus wanted Nicodemus to be aware of the fact that he would have to be born again in order to please God and live with Him for eternity. Nicodemus had trouble with this concept, as we see in his response.

C. Inquiry: 4

4. Nicodemus saith unto him, How can a man be born when he is old? can he enter the second time into his mother's womb and be born?

We can hardly be expected to think that Nicodemus asked this in a literal sense. We assume that this was his way of trying to discover the spiritual meaning of what Jesus meant by the new birth.

D. Information: 5-7

5. Jesus answered, Verily, verily, I say unto thee, Except a man be born

of water and of the Spirit, he cannot enter into the kingdom of God.

6. That which is born of the flesh is flesh; and that which is born of the Spirit is spirit.

Two types of births are mentioned here. Jesus said that the first one was of water, probably referring to "the water breaking" just prior to a physical birth. He said that the second one was of the Spirit, referring to spiritual rebirth at the time of salvation. The first type produces a fleshly body. The second type awakens the dormant soul and spirit to God-consciousness.

7. Marvel not that I said unto thee, Ye must be born again.

We can have sympathy for Nicodemus. Jesus was telling him that physical birth must be followed by spiritual rebirth, but Jesus had not yet died to atone for men's sins. It is much easier for us to grasp this concept today, because we have a fuller record and revelation in the New Testament, plus the accumulated experience of church history.

II. Spirit: John 3:8-12

A. Comparison: 8

8. The wind bloweth where it listeth, and thou hearest the sound thereof, but canst not tell whence it cometh, and whither it goeth: so is every one that is born of the Spirit.

Jesus used the wind as an illustration. The term pn*euma* can be translated as "wind," "breath," or "spirit." It can be heard but not seen. It goes wherever it wants and cannot be controlled by men. Spiritual rebirth comes from outside of men's experience and is ministered by the Holy Spirit.

B. Confusion: 9

9. Nicodemus answered and said unto him, How can these things be?

It is difficult to know what Nicodemus was actually thinking when he asked this question. He must have had better-than-average intelligence to hold the position he did, but he seemed to be confused. Perhaps he was sincere about wanting to know how these things could be. On the other hand, he may have been deliberately antagonizing Jesus. The subsequent three verses show that Jesus was upset with Nicodemus, who apparently reflected the reluctance of his colleagues to accept the teachings of Jesus regarding Himself and salvation.

C. Complaint: 10-12

10. Jesus answered and said unto him, Art thou a master of Israel, and knowest not these things?

Jesus seemed to use sarcasm here. He asked Nicodemus how he could be a master (teacher) of Israel and not understand what He was teaching. For example, Ezekiel 11:19 might have helped, and that was from the Jewish Scriptures—"I (God) will give them (repentent Jews) one heart, and I will put a new spirit within you; and I will take the stony heart (sinful heart) out of their flesh, and will give them a heart of flesh (repentant heart)."

11. Verily, verily, I say unto thee, We speak that we do know, and testify that we have seen; and ye receive not our witness.

Jesus said that He and his companions had spoken about what they knew and had testified about what they had seen; but men such as Nicodemus had refused their claims.

12. If I have told you earthly things, and ye believe not, how shall ye believe, if I tell you of heavenly things?

Jesus bluntly suggested that Nicodemus and men like him would also be unwilling to believe whatever heavenly or spiritual things Jesus and His disciples told them. Following this rebuke by Jesus, Nicodemus is not recorded as saying more, although he evidently remained to hear the remainder of what Jesus had to say (vss. 13-21).

III. Salvation: John 3:13-17

A. Ascension: 13

13. And no man hath ascended up to heaven, but he that came down from heaven, even the Son of man which is in heaven.

The best manuscripts omit the last four words of this verse. What Jesus appeared to be saying was that no man had gone from earth up to heaven in order to learn the spiritual truths He was teaching. He Himself had come down from heaven with them. He gave Himself the title of Son of man, which was Messianic. He would be going back to heaven when His ministry on earth was done, as described in John 17:4-5.

B. Allusion: 14-15

14. And as Moses lifted up the serpent in the wilderness, even so must the Son of man be lifted up:

15. That whosoever believeth in him should not perish, but have eternal life.

Jesus had used wind as an illustration of the Holy Spirit ministering the new birth to a believer. He now used a serpent as an illustration of Himself and the role He would play in redemption. Historical background for this is found in Numbers 21:5-9. The ancient Israelites had murmured against God for bringing them out into the wilderness to die. He punished them for this by sending fiery serpents to bite them, and many died. Moses prayed for the people and obeyed God in putting a brass serpent up on a pole. When the Israelites looked at it, they were healed. This served as a type of Christ. He predicted that He would also be lifted up so that sinners might not perish for their sins but be given eternal life.

C. Appropriation: 16-17.

16a. For God so loved the world, that he gave his only begotten Son,...

This verse in the Bible is probably the best known and most used throughout the world. It contains the gospel in concise form. Salvation began within the loving heart of God. He loved the world of men, not the sinful world-system. He saw that men had forfeited their divine blessings by their waywardness, and yet He loved them so much that He was willing to give His only begotten Son to atone for their sins To say that Jesus was "begotten" has nothing to do with reproduction. Jesus had a unique standing with His heavenly Father which no one else could claim. The fact that He was much loved by God made His sacrifice at Calvary all the more poignant and precious to us who believe.

16b. ...that whosoever believeth in him should not perish, but have everlasting life.

God made His commitment of His Son to the plan of redemption. It then became the responsibility of sinners to accept Christ as Savior and appropriate the grace offered to them. The sacrifice was *sufficient* for all men, but it is *efficient* only in those who reach out to take it by faith. The moment a person believes wholeheartedly in Christ as Savior, the guilt of sin drops away and the dire threat of perishing is lifted. In its place comes the promise of everlasting life with God and Christ in heaven. Let it be mentioned here that perishing is not annihilation, as some teach, but is eternal condemnation and suffering in the lake of fire (Rev. 20:15). That may be difficult to comprehend, but it is scriptural truth.

17a. For God sent not his Son into the world to condemn the world;...

This simple statement declares that God's purpose in sending His Son to the earth was not to condemn it. Those who end up condemned are those who choose to remain in sin and seal their own doom.

17b. ...but that the world through him might be saved.

God's purpose in sending His Son to the earth was to save its people. That general purpose, of course, has been modified by the reception given to His Son. Those wise enough to commit their destiny to Him receive assurance of salvation and are adopted into the redeemed family of God.

You may never have a better time than this to invite unsaved members of your class to accept Jesus Christ as their Savior. Try to allow enough time to make a personal appeal at the end of this lesson and let them know that they can contact you, the pastor, or any other church leader for help. Close the class session with prayer for them and for your saved students and the need for them to share their faith with others throughout the coming week.

Evangelistic Emphasis

The evangelical revival of the 1970s was accompanied by unprecedented talk of being "born again." Although, as John 3:3-5 shows, the phrase is based on Scripture, its use in recent times has sometimes been protested. More than one busy traveler accosted at the airport with the question, "Have you been born again, brother?" has replied, "No thanks— once is quite enough for me!"

We can understand the protest if it is an objection to pop theology presented like a quiz by an over-zealous believer. But when we stop to think about it, many of us need to stop to think about it! Life itself has a way of asking whether it might be possible to make new beginnings—as it were, to be "born again."

The businessman, so deep into shady deals that he is faced with charges of mishandling company funds—is there no way for him to come clean, reshaping his values and rebuilding his life? The teenage girl, pregnant but without a husband—is there no grace, no supportive community, no further chance for her to experience the joys of a godly Christian home? The purposeless drifter, living only for the moment— is there no possibility that he might catch a new vision of life as a means of "glorifying God and enjoying Him forever" (as in the Westminster Shorter Catechism)?

The fact is, Nicodemus' question about whether we can be born again is a universal question. It is the question of whether God's grace exists for once-born but failed and flawed people. And the answer is more than a *requirement.* It's the glad affirmation, the gospel: You can be born again!

♦♦♦♦♦♦

Memory Selection

Jesus answered and said unto him, verily, verily I say unto thee, Except a man be born again, he cannot see the kingdom of God. *John 3:3*

Jesus found it necessary to correct a mistaken idea in his day that is sometimes found in our own times—the idea that merely being born into the right group (race, church, nation) earns people special favor in the heart of God. Not so, the Lord teaches. Entering the kingdom requires being born a second time.

To Jews who thought that their racial heritage or first birth automatically placed them in the kingdom Jesus said: "Think not to say within yourselves, We have Abraham to our father: for I say unto you, that God is able of these stones to raise up children unto Abraham" (Matt. 3:9). K*ingdom* people are twice-born people: you must be born again.

To illustrate Christ's point even more strongly, the word translated "again" in our passage can also mean born "from above." As verses 5-6 emphasize, our Lord speaks here of a *spiritual,* not a fleshly, birth. John has already referred to this in 1:12-13, where he affirms that those who belong to Christ are born not merely "by the will of the flesh"—not just because a Jewish couple (or any other) decides to have children—but by a divine decision, the will of God.

March 14, 1993

Weekday Problems

Clarence's new job at the automobile manufacturing plant was so demanding that he was surprised at what was going on in his head. Maybe it was the move that had brought them to the new job, or his favorite uncle's recent death. Whatever the reason, for the first time in his life Clarence was asking himself about the value of his life, and what he really wanted to make of himself over the long haul.

Then Clarence met Jeff. A foreman on the second shift, Jeff had the clear-eyed look of someone who knew exactly where he was going. Many of the workers secretly laughed at him because he had started a Bible study at lunch break. Although this intrigued Clarence, he hesitated to attend the studies because of the ridicule. After all, he had a shot at the foreman's slot on his own shift. Why should he risk being bad-mouthed, when Jeff might prove to be another religious fanatic, anyway?

*Have you ever felt embarrassed by your religious inclinations?

*What would you do if you were Clarence? (Would it be helpful to take a lesson here from the story of Nicodemus?

*Do you think public demonstrations of faith such as offering thanks at meals in public, or marching for Christian causes, usually help or hurt Christianity in the eyes of non-Christians?

♦♦♦♦♦♦

Superintendent's Sermonette

Ecclesiastes 9:10 says, "Whatsoever thy hand findeth to do, do it with thy might." In other words, set your goal and do your best to attain it. We have little patience with those who want to succeed but who vacillate. When it comes to spiritual matters, we think of those who want to keep one foot in the world and the other foot in God's kingdom. It does not work. We have to make our choice for the Lord and then stay with it.

Our lesson text refers to Nicodemus. He was a Pharisee and a ruler of the Jews in religious matters as a member of the Sanhedrin (Jewish Council). He heard of the teachings and miracles of Jesus and wanted to talk to Him. He came at night so that the meeting could be secret and not jeopardize his position among the Jews. Jesus let him know that he needed to be born again by the Spirit of God. The implied tragedy of Nicodemus is that he wanted to hold onto what he had.

How is it with you? Have you been born again by placing your faith in Jesus Christ and His atoning sacrifice at Calvary? He calls for a complete commitment and will not settle for less. Listen carefully to the lesson today and make your decision. If you are already a believer, witness for Christ.

REBIRTH INTO ETERNAL LIFE

This Lesson in Your Life

Many people today can identify with Nicodemus' bewilderment at Jesus' teaching. When we view Christ and the Bible from the standpoint of our own everyday lives we may ask, "How can these things be?" (John 3:9). The issues we confront in the modern world can seem foreign to the world in which Jesus lived. Bible study and theological talk can seem "so spiritual it's of no earthly good." Some of us can well imagine Christ asking us, "How can I connect with you to tell you about heavenly things, when you're on such a worldly wave-length?" (see v. 12).

If you sometimes feel this way, you may want to remember two seemingly opposite approaches that can help. Picture yourself standing on one side of a deep gash in the earth, with Christ and his Word on the other side. How can you get across?

One approach is to find a narrow spot in the chasm and to build a bridge that connects your side with the other in as short a span as possible.

A method used by a missionary to Australia's aboriginal people illustrates this approach. For years, the message of the gospel had fallen on deaf ears. The aboriginals continued to worship ancestral spirits, with special attention to various "totems"—animals from kangaroos to caterpillars that were venerated as founders or guardians of the tribe. When the missionaries would pull out their Bibles, the native Australians would turn to their "totem sticks"—sacred sticks on which their tribal animals and myths were carved. Their response to the message of Christ was like that of Nicodemus: "How can these things be"?

Then the missionary had an idea about building a bridge. Selecting similar "totem sticks" of his own, the missionary told his audience that he was going to carve another sacred story on them. Then he painstakingly etched on them, in crude pictures the story and the meaning of Christ's birth, death and resurrection. Suddenly there were tears of appreciation—*Christian* tears—in the very eyes that only days earlier had been unable to "see" the truth of the gospel. The missionary had moved naturally from an "earthly" starting point to "heavenly things."

As effective as this method can be, it's not infallible. Sometimes it seems that the very earthly concepts with which we are most familiar become obstacles instead of bridges. The Danish theologian Soren Kierkegaard found this situation in the Europe of his day. Natural structures such as the family, the state and the state church were assumed to be "bridges" between God and persons.

"Not so!" Kierkegaard protested. Christians are people who are passionately involved in burning questions that are answered not by the culture but by Christ. The way from my side of the chasm across to God is not a bridge but a "leap of faith." Reaching out to God is not just a rational process but an emotional gamble, Kierkegaard cried.

Whether one or the other of these approaches helps you get more "in synch" with the teachings of Christ may depend on your own personality, as well as the situation. The challenge is to come to see, by whatever means, that the Christian message is not foreign to life. When it "jars and clashes" with everyday life, we are challenged to look for the problem in our own perspective or attitude, rather than with the message.

Seed Thoughts

1. Suppose Nicodemus had been your teacher. Would it have been a problem for you to know that he came to Jesus to ask him questions "by night"?

Most people appreciate the humility of a teacher who is willing to learn, but a lack of courage can cost a leader his or her effectiveness.

2. What did Jesus' signs mean for Nicodemus and how does this relate to the purpose of the Gospel of John?

The miracles indicated Jesus was a divinely appointed teacher, and John recorded them in order to produce or strengthen faith in Jesus.

3. According to verse 8, will human eyes always be able to tell just who is and is not born of the Spirit?

No. Although being born of the Spirit ordinarily results in the fruits of the Spirit, we cannot look into others' hearts and see the Spirit.

4. What fruits should those born of the spirit bear? (Gal. 5:22-23.)

Love, joy, peace, long suffering, gentleness, goodness, faith, meekness and temperance.

5. What similarity do you find between Jesus' question to Nicodemus in John 3:10, and the comment about teachers in Hebrews 5:12?

Both are rebukes of religious leaders who have not learned fundamentals of the faith.

(PLEASE TURN PAGE)

---

1. Suppose Nicodemus had been your teacher. Would it have been a problem for you to know that he came to Jesus to ask him questions "by night"?

2. What did Jesus' signs mean for Nicodemus and how does this relate to the purpose of the Gospel of John?

3. According to verse 8, will human eyes always be able to tell just who is and is not born of the Spirit?

4. What fruits should those born of the spirit bear? (Gal. 5:22-23.)

5. What similarity do you find between Jesus' question to Nicodemus in John 3:10, and the comment about teachers in Hebrews 5:12?

6. To what event does the reference to the Son of man's being "lifted up" apply? (See 12:32-33.)

7. Find these "superlatives" in John 3:16: the greatest emotion...the greatest gift...the widest audience...the simplest requirement...the greatest promise.

8. Compare John 3:16 with 3:36. What does the present tense in verse 36 add to our concept of "eternal life"?

9. Why did Jesus not have to condemn an unbelieving world? (See 3:17-18.)

10. What evidence do we have that an unbelieving world lies condemned?

(SEED THOUGHTS--Cont'd)

Most people appreciate the humility of a teacher who is willing to learn, but a lack of courage can cost a leader his or her effectiveness.

The miracles indicated Jesus was a divinely appointed teacher, and John recorded them in order to produce or strengthen faith in Jesus.

No. Although being born of the Spirit ordinarily results in the fruits of the Spirit, we cannot look into others' hearts and see the Spirit.

Love, joy, peace, long suffering, gentleness, goodness, faith, meekness and temperance.

Both are rebukes of religious leaders who have not learned fundamentals of the faith.

To the crucifixion.

The emotion: God's love. The gift: God's Son. The audience: "whosoever." The requirement: to believe in Christ. The promise: everlasting life.

It indicates that it is a *quality* of life—life that is kin to the divine life—available to believers now.

Because unbelief condemns itself.

Because it chooses evil over righteousness.

---

6. To what event does the reference to the Son of man's being "lifted up" apply? (See 12:32-33.)
To the crucifixion.

7. Find these "superlatives" in John 3:16: the greatest emotion...the greatest gift...the widest audience...the simplest requirement...the greatest promise.
The emotion: God's love. The gift: God's Son. The audience: "whosoever." The requirement: to believe in Christ. The promise: everlasting life.

8. Compare John 3:16 with 3:36. What does the present tense in verse 36 add to our concept of "eternal life"?
It indicates that it is a *quality* of life—life that is kin to the divine life—available to believers now.

9. Why did Jesus not have to condemn an unbelieving world? (See 3:17-18.)
Because unbelief condemns itself.

10. What evidence do we have that an unbelieving world lies condemned?
Because it chooses evil over righteousness.

Marcch 21, 1993

Light of the World

John 9

AND as *Jesus* passed by, he saw a man which was blind from *his* birth
2 And his disciples asked him, saying, Master who did sin, this man, or his parents, that was born blind?
3 Jesus answered, Neither hath this man sinned, nor his parents: but that the works God should be made manifest in him.
4 I must work the works of him that sent me, while it is day: the night cometh, when no man can work.
5 As long as I am in the world, I am the light of the world.
6 When he had thus spoken, he spat on the ground, and made clay of the spittle, and anointed the eyes of the blind man with the clay
7 And said unto him, Go, wash in the pool of Si-lo'-am, (which is by interpretation, Sent.) He went his way therefore, and washed, and came seeing.
8 The neighbours therefore, and they which before had seen him that he was blind, said, Is not this he that sat and begged?
9 Some said, This is he: others said, He is like him: but he said, I am he.
10 Therefore said they unto him, How were thine eyes opened?
11 He answered and said, A man that is called Jesus made clay, and anointed mine eyes, and said unto me, Go to the pool of Si-lo´-am, and wash: and I went and washed, and I received sight.
12 Then said they unto him, Where is he? He said, I know not.

35 Jesus heard that they had cast him out; and when he had found him, he said unto him Dost thou believe on the Son of God?
36 He answered and said, Who is he, Lord, that I might believe on him?
37 And Jesus said unto him, Thou hast both seen him, and it is he that talketh with thee.
38 And he said, Lord, I believe. And he worshipped him.
39 And Jesus said, For judgment I am come into this world, that they which see not might see; and that they which see might be made blind.
40 And some of the Pharisees which were with him heard these words, and said unto him, Are we blind also?
41 Jesus said unto them, If ye were blind, ye should have no sin: but now ye say, We see; therefore your sin remaineth.

◆◆◆◆◆◆

◀ **Memory Selection**
John 9:5

◀ **Devotional Reading**
John 8:48-59

◀ **Background Scripture**
John 9

◀ **Printed Scripture**
John 9:1-12, 35-41

LIGHT OF THE WORLD

Teacher's Target

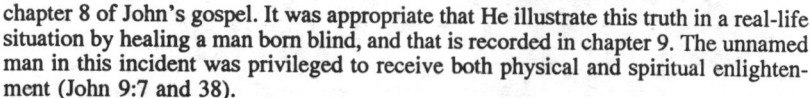

Jesus said, "I am the light of the world: he that followeth me shall not walk in darkness, but shall have the light of life" (John 8:12). He built a whole discourse around that theme in chapter 8 of John's gospel. It was appropriate that He illustrate this truth in a real-life situation by healing a man born blind, and that is recorded in chapter 9. The unnamed man in this incident was privileged to receive both physical and spiritual enlightenment (John 9:7 and 38).

Help your students to appreciate what spiritual enlightenment brings to believers both now and in eternity. Help them also to see the tragedy of continuing in spiritual darkness both now and in eternity. The healed blind man was an example of enlightenment, while the Pharisees were an example of darkness. We will see how their response to Jesus in each case made the crucial difference. Our response to Him determines our destiny, too.

Lesson Introduction

Woven into the general themes of physical and spiritual enlightenment and darkness covered in our texts are interesting secondary themes. See what they were and how Jesus handled them.

Delay of deliverance: The man had suffered blindness from birth and was now at least thirty or more years old, for his parents said that he was "of age" (John 9:21). He apparently was "reserved" all that time until his healing fitted into Jesus' teaching ministry and brought glory to God (John 9:3-4).

Faith and obedience: Jesus anointed the blind man's eyelids with clay and spittle and told him to wash in the pool of Siloam. He obeyed and was healed (John 9: 6-7). Was the anointing therapeutic or symbolic? What part did faith play?

Teaching Outline

I. Predicament: John 9:1-5
   A. Reason: 1-3
   B. Radiation: 4-5
II. Provision: John 9:6-12
   A. Reward: 6-7
   B. Reactions: 8-10
   C. Report: 11-12
III. Postludes: John 9:35-41
   A. Conversion: 35-38
   B. Condemnation: 39-41

Daily Bible Readings

Mon. Before Abraham, I Am
John 8:48-59
Tue. Delivered from Blindness
John 9:1-7
Wed The Man Called Jesus
John 9:8-12
Thu He Is a Prophet
John 9:13-23
Fri. I Was Blind, Now I See
John 9:24-34
Sat. Lord, I Believe
John 9:35-41
Sun. Jesus the Shepherd
John 10:1-9

Marcch 21, 1993

VERSE BY VERSE

I. Predicament: John 9:1-5

A. Reason: 1-3

1. And as Jesus passed by, he saw a man which was blind from his birth.

Jesus had completed a long discourse on Himself as the Light of the world. His opponents had been irritated by what He said. They planned to stone Him, but He hid Himself from them and went out of the temple and into the streets of Jerusalem (John 8:12-59). It was as He was passing along one of these streets that He saw a man who had been born blind. Jesus used this man to illustrate the fact that He could bring both physical and spiritual enlightenment. The man may have been out on the street begging, for this is what his neighbors later said that he was accustomed to doing (John 9:8). He must have been at least thirty years old, for his parents later stated that he was "of age" (John 9:21, 23). The reason that he suffered this longstanding handicap is explained in a subsequent verse.

2. And his disciples asked him, saying, Master, who did sin, this man, or his parents, that he was born blind?

Jesus' disciples were prompted by the blind man's predicament to ask Him a theological question. They wanted to know if his blindness had been caused by his sin or sin by his parents. There were two things wrong with their thinking.

First, a handicap did not necessarily result from sin. God might have another reason for allowing it, as He did in this case.

Second, sin by a person's parents did not necessarily produce a handicap in that person, although it could happen.

3. Jesus answered, Neither hath this man sinned, nor his parents: but that the works of God should be made manifest in him.

Jesus was not saying that the blind man and his parents were sinless. He simply stated that the blindness the man suffered had not resulted from sin. It had been allowed by God in order that the power of God might be manifested in him. Taken in context, we know that this was to be done when Jesus healed the man by removing his handicap. This verse should be of comfort to everyone who suffers from illness or handicap, because God can use each situation to bring glory to His name. He can give grace to endure, and He can give deliverance if He chooses to do that. Observers will be impressed by whatever help He gives. Ultimate grace and deliverance will come, even if coming by death and passing into His presence.

B. Radiation: 4-5

4. I must work the works of him that sent me, while it is day: the night cometh, when no man can work.

Jesus made it clear here that the works of God were to be done through Himself. His Father had sent Him to the earth to perform miracles which would substantiate Jesus' claim to divinity and would impress the world with His power and love. Jesus had only three years in which to do His works, and He called this "day." He looked ahead to the time when He would cease His ministries and ascend to heaven, and He called this "night." We, as followers of Jesus, have our "day" and "night" as far as working for God is concerned. God has appointed us to do certain works, and we are responsible for them (Eph. 2:10).

5. As long as I am in the world, I am the light of the world.

Truth focused in Jesus during the few years He ministered on the earth. He planned for truth to focus in His disciples after He ascended to His heavenly Father. The light of truth has been shining ever since; through the ministries of Christ's followers in succeeding generations. It is a spiritual radiation which persists.

II. Provision: John 9:6-12

A. Reward: 6-7

6. When he had thus spoken, he spat on the ground and made clay of the spittle, and he anointed the eyes of the blind man with the clay,

7a. And said unto him, Go, wash in the pool of Siloam, (which is by interpretation, Sent.)

What Jesus did here was to call for faith on the part of the blind man and perhaps to draw the attention of the onlookers who had gathered. There is nothing here to indicate that the paste made any literal difference in the blind man's condition. It was put on the man's eyelids, but his physical problem was internal. He was ordered to go and wash the mixture off in the pool of Siloam. This was located in southeastern Jerusalem, was fed by a spring, and was thought by the Jews to have been sent to them by God. Perhaps the man thought that a combination of the paste on his eyelids and the water sent from God would be beneficial to him.

7b. He went his way therefore, and washed, and came seeing.

The blind man demonstrated obedience and faith by doing as Jesus instructed him. We can only speculate on the thrill it must have been for him to gain his sight for the first time in his life. What he had known only by sound and touch he could now envision, and it must have been a grand experience as he made his way back to his own neighborhood. He was to enjoy his gain of physical sight for a brief period before he was confronted with his need for spiritual sight. One reward preceded the other.

B. Reactions: 8-10

8. The neighbours therefore, and they which before had seen him, that he was blind, said, Is not this he that sat and begged?

It appears that the size of the crowd had grown, including neighbors and others who had been aware of his lifetime of blindness. When they saw him walking normally, instead of groping his way along, some were not sure it was the same man who once sat and begged.

9. Some said, This is he: others said, He is like him: but he said, I am he.

Reactions were mixed, with some declaring it was the same man and others saying he only looked like him. It must have given the man great satisfaction to speak up and declare that he was the one in question and to see the surprise on the faces of those who doubted it.

10. Therefore said they unto him, How were thine eyes opened?

Convinced of the man's identity, his questioners wanted to know how he had received his sight. This may have simply denoted curiosity on their part, but it was a curiosity which was to have serious implications and call for more investigation.

C. Report: 11-12

11. He answered and said, A man that is called Jesus made clay, and anointed mine eyes, and said unto me, Go to the pool of Siloam, and wash: and I went and washed, and I received sight.

The man had somehow learned that the name of his benefactor was Jesus. He reported that Jesus made a paste of spittle and clay, anointed his eyelids, and sent him to wash off the mixture in the pool of Siloam. He had done as he had been told, and now he could see. Subsequent verses reveal that this man did not yet know the spiritual significance of Jesus or of the miracle.

12. Then they said unto him, Where is he? He said, I know not.

Then began a period of trial for the healed man and his parents. His neighbors and others wanted to know who this Jesus was, but the healed man did not know where He had gone. It soon became obvious that some viewed this as Satan's work performed by some type of magic. John 9:13-34 tells what happened, and this should be summarized. The healed man was brought before the Pharisees, evidently because the miracle had taken place on the Jewish Sabbath and had involved "work" on the part of Jesus and of the man himself. Jesus was denounced for desecrating the Sabbath. The Pharisees tried to question the man's parents, but they insisted that he was of age and could speak for himself. When the Pharisees tried to get the man to denounce Jesus, He refused and was thrown out of the synagogue. These religious legalists over-looked the divine miracle and concentrated on their rules and regulations.

III. Postludes: John 9:35-41

A. Conversion: 35-38

35. Jesus heard that they had cast him out; and when he had found him, he said unto him, Dost thou believe on the Son of God?

Jesus heard the news of the expulsion and sought for the healed man. He found him and asked him if he believed on the Son of God, but He did not refer to Himself as being that One.

36. He answered and said, Who is he, Lord, that I might believe on him?

Some versions change the term "Lord" to "Sir," but it is quite possible that the healed man already thought Jesus was the Son of God but wanted to be sure of it before committing himself to Him.

37. And Jesus said unto him, Thou hast both seen him, and it is he that talketh with thee.

Jesus stated that the Son of God was One Whom the man had previously seen and Who was even now talking to him. This probably confirmed what the man had already decided rather than being news to him.

38. And he said, Lord, I believe. And he worshipped him.

Confession of belief was immediately followed by worship of Jesus. We accept this as recording the fact that the man had now received not only physical sight but spiritual sight. His conversion was real from this point onward.

B. Condemnation: 39-41

39. And Jesus said, For judgment I am come into this world, that they which see not might see; and that they which see might be made blind.

Jesus used this moment to declare that He had come to the earth to judge people. Those who yearned for spiritual sight would be given it, but those who falsely claimed to have it would remain in a state of spiritual blindness.

40. And some of the Pharisees which were with him heard these words, and said unto him, Are we blind also?

These were apparently Pharisees who traveled around with Jesus, hoping to entrap Him into saying something for which they could condemn Him. It was obvious that they thought themselves to be spiritually enlightened and resented what He said.

41. Jesus said unto them, If ye were blind, ye should have no sin: but now ye say, We see; therefore your sin remaineth.

What Jesus bluntly told these Pharisees was that they could have admitted their spiritual blindness, confessed it, and found forgiveness. However, by claiming to have spiritual sight where none existed, they remained in the darkness of sin. It was a strong indictment of their spiritual hypocrisy. They lacked the discernment required to see Jesus as the Light of the world and as the Son of God.

LIGHT OF THE WORLD

Evangelistic Emphasis

Elton Trueblood, the great Quaker philosopher-theologian, once said that "there is something faintly embarrassing about all evangelism." Many Christians who take seriously the call to share the saving message of Christ know the feeling. Like the Pharisees in John 9, some people ridicule the idea that Jesus can change lives to the extent claimed by the young man born blind.

There are many reasons for this, and several are revealed in this very incident. The Pharisees seem to have challenged the healing because they had a vested interest in maintaining the religious status quo. After all, they were supposed to be the leaders, and people were following Jesus instead. They felt "in charge" of what people believed, and they were threatened because the blind man believed something they did not.

Since Jesus had healed the man on the Sabbath, the newly-healed man also threatened the establishment's rules about Sabbath-keeping. Jesus was causing more excitement than they felt the occupying Romans would tolerate. He might bring oppressive measures down on their heads. Anyone who testified in His behalf would be painted with the same brush.

No matter! Those who have experienced genuine conversion, those who know the truth about the power of God to change people, cannot be deterred by nay-sayers from sharing the message. The joy is too full to keep it from overflowing to others. The light finally seen by those who were "blind" is too brilliant to keep hidden under a bushel.

◆◆◆◆◆◆

Memory Selection

I am the light of the world. *John 9:5*

John's Gospel is full of references to light and darkness. Christ is the light of the world, while those who oppose him dwell in darkness, deliberately blind. The Word enlightens everyone who comes into the world. Following Jesus sheds light on our pathway, while rejecting him plunges us into darkness.

This symbolism appeals to our questing, searching natures. We know instinctively that light enlightens, and ordinarily we much prefer that state of affairs over dwelling in the dark. We speak of learning something new as light dispelling darkness, saying "It dawned on me," or "I finally saw the light." We speak disparagingly of "the Dark Ages," when learning ebbed. Even physically, we sit before a fireplace and are mesmerized by its dancing flames of light.

No wonder that Christians have historically been leaders in educational fields. And how poorly do we represent the Light when we oppose the quest for knowledge. Christians affirm that Jesus, the preexistent Word who was the agent of creation, is the Sun that enlightens the world as well as the Son sent to earth by the Father. In giving Christ first place in our lives we affirm our allegiance to light over darkness, truth over error, good over evil.

Marccch 21, 1993

Weekday Problems

The John Adkins family was a pillar in the community. The president of the largest bank in town, John was also active in civic clubs and city politics. His wife Joanna was prominent in social circles. They and their three children were regular church attenders. No one had anything bad to say about the Adkins.

Then Justin, the eldest son, went off to college. And did he ever "go off"! He became involved in a religious group that some called a "cult." They met for Bible study and prayer every night of the week. Rigid rules and tight structure governed every aspect of their lives. Members had to get permission from the group's leader even to date. It was ironic, thought Mr. and Mrs. Adkins, that a son who had never given them a minute's problem about drugs or other such activity had "flipped out" over religion!

*If you were the Adkins, would you be concerned about Justin? Why or why not?

*Typically, would there be any parallels between the Adkins' concern and the family of the young man Jesus healed in John 9? (See especially vss. 18-23.)

*Do you suspect any relationship between the reasons some youths get involved with religious cults and others with drug-abusing groups or gangs?

*Can the church do better at meeting the needs felt by people such as Justin?

♦♦♦♦♦♦

Superintendent's Sermonette

We live in a world where communication and publicity play important roles. Various forms of media (broadcasts, newspapers, magazines, books, tapes) compete with one another for attention. Something unusual can happen to a person, and he will be lifted from obscurity and have his story flashed around the globe in a short time. When he becomes a celebrity, however fleetingly, he is affected for good or ill by the experience. The Christian world, with its penchant for imitating the secular world, creates its own celebrities from time to time.

Today we study an unusual event in ancient Jerusalem. Jesus gave sight to a man born blind. This man has become well known to Bible students wherever they have met around the Word of God, but we have not been told his name. Did the Apostle John forget that name, or did he omit it deliberately?

The man healed of his blindness also received his spiritual sight, but we are not told if he became a strong member of the early church. Perhaps it is just as well. No churches, schools, or programs are named after him. He lived in darkness and beggary for over thirty years in order to illustrate that Jesus is the Light of the world. That is enough.

This Lesson in Your Life

People still often ask, "Who sinned?" when tragedies such as being born blind occur. It seems to be instinctive for us to suppose that either God or Satan is catching up with someone whose life seems especially tragic. Even when we suffer in our personal lives we may cry out, at least in our secret heart, "Why me, Lord?"—as though protesting our innocence or at least asking God to reveal the sin that triggered the punishment. The problem of human suffering still conjures up the echo of the question Job's counselors asked: "Whoever perished, being innocent? or where were the righteous cut off?" (Job 4:7). In other words, isn't suffering the result of sin?

Not in this case, Jesus says in John 9. He does not take the time to explain that there is a sense in which living in a fallen world means that we must suffer the consequences of the Fall. He does not warn that some sins, such as drunkenness, can bring the terrible, swift sword of consequence in judgment on the sinner. He doesn't pause to acknowledge that some suffering may be sent in order to discipline us (Heb. 12:5-11).

Instead, Jesus uses the occasion to correct the instinct that insists on being able to connect past deeds with present punishment. Some unhappiness, as in this situation, simply serves as the arena in which God's power can be shown victorious over tragedy: "that the works of God should be made manifest" (vs. 3).

Outward circumstances simply don't always reveal inner causes. This is true not only in the case of suffering but of blessings, too. God maketh his sun to rise on the evil and on the good, and sendeth rain on the just and the unjust (Matt. 5:45). There is a sense in which nature is marvelously indifferent to morals. The message is clear: we must not insist, as did Christ's disciples and Job's friends, on fathoming a cause-effect connection for everthing that happens.

Yet haven't we all been guilty of presuming to do so? We may say to a sorrowing mother, grieving over the loss of her little child, "There, there—God took your dear one so He could have another lovely flower in His heavenly garden." As well-meaning as such opinions are, they can hurt as much as it would to pick up on the disciples' question and tell the mother just what sin she or the child had committed to earn such punishment!

Our well-meaning intent breaks down at that little word so. "This tragedy has happened, so...." At this point we are presuming to intrude into a mystery only God can penetrate.

Of course philosophers do this regularly. An entire field of thought called theodicy—the attempt to justify the ways of God—has challenged the best of minds from ancient times. More recently, Rabbi Harold Kushner dealt with the problem in his best-selling book, Why *Do Bad Things Happen to Good People?* While such studies can correct mistaken notions and provide helpful insights, they do not fully explain the ways of a good God in an evil world.

Yet, scripture does offer an answer, of sorts. As in John 9, it does not explain human suffering, connecting specific tragedies with specific reasons. The answer it gives is more personal than philosophical. If we accept it, it will be more by faith than by reason. It is the answer of the Incarnation, the event with which John began his Gospel.

The Incarnation means that while God does not answer our questions for us, He asks them with us. He refuses to stay in some heavenly parlor, abstractly contemplating the problem of evil. Instead, He immerses himself in the life we live, struggling with us in our pain, weeping with us in our sorrow. When we turn to Christ we do not receive a flood of "so's," or answers; but we receive incarnate love, the divine presence.

Seed Thoughts

1. What assumption did the disciples reveal by their question in verse 2? Is this a safe assumption?
They assumed that suffering is always the result of sin. As Jesus' answer shows, this isn't a safe assumption.

2. Does Jesus' answer in verse 3 deal with all possible questions about why people suffer?
No, but it does suggest that "the works of God" are more powerful than tragic circumstances.

3. Why do you think this particular miracle is described in connection with Jesus' claim in verse 5?
The opening of blind eyes illustrates Jesus' teaching that he is the light of the world.

4. Why do you suppose the formerly blind man was not recognized by everyone, as verses 8-9 indicate?
Such a radical change as having his sight restored may have changed the blind man's entire appearance.

5. Why did the Pharisees claim that healing the blind man constituted breaking the sabbath? (See Exod. 20:8-11.)
Because it violated their definition of working, which was forbidden on the sabbath.

---

1. What assumption did the disciples reveal by their question in verse 2? Is this a safe assumption?

2. Does Jesus' answer in verse 3 deal with all possible questions about why people suffer?

3. Why do you think this particular miracle is described in connection with Jesus' claim in verse 5?

4. Why do you suppose the formerly blind man was not recognized by everyone, as verses 8-9 indicate?

5. Why did the Pharisees claim that healing the blind man constituted breaking the sabbath? (See Exod. 20:8-11.)

6. How did Jesus answer the charge of breaking the sabbath in Mark 2:27-28, and what did he mean?

7. What principle can be drawn from the blind man's parents' statement in verse 21b?

8. Would you classify the reason for faith given in verse 25 as theological, practical, or second-hand?

9. Compare verse 22 with verse 34, and define the meaning of being "cast out."

10. Who is Jesus referring to as "they which see not" and "they which see," in verse 39?

(PLEASE TURN PAGE)

(SEED THOUGHTS--Cont'd)

They assumed that suffering is always the result of sin. As Jesus' answer shows, this isn't a safe assumption.

No, but it does suggest that "the works of God" are more powerful than tragic circumstances.

The opening of blind eyes illustrates Jesus' teaching that he is the light of the world.

Such a radical change as having his sight restored may have changed the blind man's entire appearance.

Because it violated their definition of working, which was forbidden on the sabbath.

In saying that the sabbath was made for man, not man for the sabbath, Jesus meant that human needs were of higher priority than religious ritual.

Youth reach an age when they deserve to be treated with the dignity of being allowed to answer for themselves.

Practical. (A somewhat theological reason is given in verses 30-33.)

The term refers to being dismissed or excluded from the synagogue.

Those who "see not" accept the truth when they hear it. Those who "see" are the ones who, like the Pharisees, cannot admit their need for Christ.

6. How did Jesus answer the charge of breaking the sabbath in Mark 2:27-28, and what did he mean?
In saying that the sabbath was made for man, not man for the sabbath, Jesus meant that human needs were of higher priority than religious ritual.

7. What principle can be drawn from the blind man's parents' statement in verse 21b?
Youth reach an age when they deserve to be treated with the dignity of being allowed to answer for themselves.

8. Would you classify the reason for faith given in verse 25 as theological, practical, or second-hand?
Practical. (A somewhat theological reason is given in verses 30-33.)

9. Compare verse 22 with verse 34, and define the meaning of being "cast out."
The term refers to being dismissed or excluded from the synagogue.

10. Who is Jesus referring to as "they which see not" and "they which see," in verse 39?
Those who "see not" accept the truth when they hear it. Those who "see" are the ones who, like the Pharisees, cannot admit their need for Christ.

March 28, 1993

JESUS!—MY BROTHER IS DEAD!

Coming to Life

John 11
NOW a certain *man* was sick, *named* Laz´-a-rus, of Beth´-a-ny, the town of Mary and her sister Martha.
2. (It was *that* Mary which anointed the Lord with ointment, and wiped his feet with her hair whose brother Laz´-a-rus was sick.)
3. Therefore his sisters sent unto him, saying, Lord, behold, he whom thou lovest is sick.
4. When Jesus heard *that*, he said, This sickness is not unto death, but for the glory of God, that the son of God might be glorified thereby.

21. Then said Martha unto Jesus, Lord if thou hadst been here, my brother had not died.
22. But I know, that even now, whatsoever thou wilt ask of God, God will give it thee.
23. Jesus said unto her, Thy brother shall rise again.
24. Martha said unto him, I know that he shall rise again in the resurrection at the last day.
25. Jesus said unto her, I am the resurrection, and the life: he that believeth in me, though he were dead, yet shall he live:
26. And whosoever liveth and believeth in me shall never die. Believest thou this?
27. She saith unto him, Yea, Lord: I believe that thou art the Christ, the Son of God, which should come into the world.

38. Jesus therefore again groaning in himself cometh to the grave. It was a cave, and a stone lay upon it.
39. Jesus said, Take ye away the stone. Martha, the sister of him that was dead, saith unto him, Lord by this time he stinketh: for he hath been *dead* four days.
40. Jesus said unto her, Said I not unto thee, that, if thou wouldst believe, thou shouldest see the glory of God?
41. Then they took away the stone from the place where the dead was laid. And Jesus lifted up his eyes, and said, Father, I thank thee that thou hast heard me.
42. And I knew that thou hearest me always: but because of the people which stand by I said it, that they may believe that thou hast sent me.
43 And when thus he had spoken, he cried with a loud voice, Laz´-a-rus, come forth.
44 And he that was dead came forth, bound hand and foot with graveclothes: and his face was bound about with a napkin. Jesus saith unto them, Loose him, and let him go.

◆◆◆◆◆◆

◀ **Memory Selection**
John 11:25

◀ **Background Scripture**
John 11:1-44

◀ **Devotional Reading**
John 11:45-54

◀ **Printed Scripture**
John 11:1-4, 21-27, 38-44

COMING TO LIFE

Teacher's Target

Note how this quarter's lessons thus far build on one another. Lesson 1 showed Jesus to be the Source of life and light (truth). Lesson 2 showed Jesus to be the Way to eternal life. Lesson 3 showed how Jesus, as the Light of the world, gave physical and spiritual sight to a man born blind. Lesson 4 now shows Jesus to be the Giver of physical life to a friend named Lazarus. This is in line with the fact that in two weeks we celebrate the resurrection of Jesus Himself.

Help your students to gain confidence in Jesus as the Resurrection and the Life (John 11:25). By personalizing this in Him, we can see that the raising of Lazarus flowed naturally from His power and love. The dramatic manner in which this resurrection was performed was no doubt designed to impress onlookers and encourage them to place their faith in Jesus. It also gives comfort to all believers since that time, because the One Who raised Lazarus can also guarantee their resurrection unto eternal life as described in 1 Thessalonians 4:13-18.

Lesson Introduction

According to Luke 10:38-42, Jesus had been a guest in the home of Mary and Martha. Mary spent her time at Jesus' feet listening to Him teach. Martha concentrated on preparing a meal for Him and His disciples. When Martha complained that Mary did not help her, Jesus said that Mary had chosen the better thing to do. In Luke 11 we learn about the illness, death, and resurrection of Lazarus at a later time. We also learn that the chief priests and Pharisees called a council to discuss what Jesus had done and to plot His death.

In Luke 12:1-11 we learn that the day before Jesus' triumphal entry into Jerusalem He shared a meal with Lazarus, Mary, and Martha at their home in Bethany. Mary anointed Him with expensive ointment. Judas Iscariot objected, but Jesus rebuked him and praised Mary's act. Many Jews believed on Jesus because of His raising of Lazarus. This caused the chief priests to plot Lazarus' death, as well.

Teaching Outline

I. Despair: John 11:1-4
   A. Assistance: 1-3
   B. Assessment: 4
II. Definition: John 11:21-27
   A. Rebuke: 21-22
   B. Resurrection: 23-26
   C. Response: 27
III. Deliverance: John 11:38-44
   A. Preparation: 38-41a
   B. Prayer: 41b-42
   C. Performance: 43-44

Daily Bible Readings

Mon. For the Glory of God
John 11:1-11
Tue. He Will Rise Again
John 11:12-23
Wed. I Am the Resurrection
John 11:24-29
Thu. Jesus Wept
John 11:30-37
Fri. Unbind Him and Let Him Go
John 11:38-44
Sat. Jesus Must Die
John 11:45-53
Sun. Looking for Jesus
John 11:54-57

March 28, 1993

VERSE BY VERSE

I. Despair: John 11:1-4

A. Assistance: 1—3

1. Now a certain man was sick, named Lazarus, of Bethany, the town of Mary and her sister Martha.

Jesus had escaped out of the hands of Jewish opponents in Jerusalem and taken refuge in Bethabara (Bethany beyond Jordan) where He had been baptized by John the Baptist (John 10:39-40). While He was there, Lazarus became ill at his home with his sisters, Mary and Martha, at Bethany on the eastern side of Mount Olivet near Jerusalem. The only biblical references to this Lazarus are found in John 11:1-12:17.

2. (It was that Mary which anointed the Lord with ointment, and wiped his feet with her hair, whose brother Lazarus was sick.)

This parenthesis identified Mary by referring to her anointing of Jesus as recorded in John 12:3, something taking place at a later time. It also identified Lazarus as being brother to the two sisters mentioned in Luke 10:38-42, since he had not been mentioned in that other passage.

3. Therefore his sisters sent unto him, saying, Lord, behold, he whom thou lovest is sick.

John 11:5 says, "Now Jesus loved Martha, and her sister, and Lazarus." The sisters appealed to Jesus on the basis of His love for Lazarus, informing Him that their brother was ill and no doubt implying that He should come and heal him. Note that they referred to Jesus as "Lord," revealing their faith in Him. We assume that they contacted Jesus through a personal messenger. It was a touching plea for assistance.

B. Assessment: 4

4. When Jesus heard that, he said, This sickness is not unto death, but for the glory of God, that the Son of God might be glorified thereby.

Receiving the message, Jesus responded, but we do not know if what He said was spoken to the messenger to be taken back to Martha and Mary. Jesus declared that this sickness of Lazarus would not result in death. It would ultimately bring glory to God and to His Son. Jesus and His disciples stayed in Bethabara for two days after this, and Lazarus had been dead for four days when they finnally arrived in Bethany (John 11:6,17,39). This suggests that Lazarus may already have been dead when Jesus spoke, but it did not matter. What He meant to imply was that the sickness would not result in permanent death for Lazarus.

After two days, Jesus suggested that He and His disciples go to Judaea. The disciples resisted, because they did not want to face their enemies there again. He said that Lazarus was sleeping, and the disciples assumed this meant that he was recovering, but Jesus plainly said that he was dead. They finally decided to go with Jesus, even if it meant they would be killed with Him. As they approached Bethany, Martha left home to come out to meet Jesus (John 11:7-20).

II. Definition: John 11:21-27

A. Rebuke: 21-22

21. Then said Martha unto Jesus, Lord, if thou hadst been here, my brother had not died.

It appears that Mary stayed at home and did not know Jesus was coming until she was informed of it by Martha later that day (John 11:20 and 28). We cannot be sure what was in Martha's mind when she appeared to rebuke Jesus for not being present to keep Lazarus from dying. It may have actually been a statement of confidence in His power to heal, along with a desire on her part that Jesus had been around to use that power when it was needed.

22. But I know, that even now, whatsoever thou wilt ask of God, God will give it thee.

This was a remarkable statement for

Martha to make. She implied that even death could not hold her brother in its grasp, if Jesus asked His heavenly Father to bring him back to life. Her statement also suggested that she saw Jesus primarily as a channel of God's power, rather than as a source of power in Himself. Subsequent verses would indicate that Jesus wanted to instruct her on this point.

B. Resurrection: 23-26

23. Jesus saith unto her, Thy brother shall rise again.

Jesus had an immediate meaning in what He said, but Martha evidently had some future time in mind regarding resurrection, as shown by her response.

24. Martha saith unto him, I know that he shall rise again in the resurrection at the last day.

Martha agreed wholeheartedly that Lazarus would live again, but she thought only of the general resurrection scheduled for the end time. She may have been thinking of a number of Old Testament texts. Job had said, "I know that my redeemer liveth, and that he shall stand at the latter day upon the earth: and though after my skin worms destroy this body, yet in my flesh shall I see God" (Job 19:25-26). The psalmist said, "God will redeem my soul from the power of the grave: for he shall receive me" (Ps. 49:15). Daniel was told, "Many of them that sleep in the dust of the earth shall awake, some to everlasting life, and some to shame and everlasting contempt" (Dan. 12:2).

25. Jesus said unto her, I am the resurrection and the life: he that believeth in me, though he were dead, yet shall he live:

26a. And whosoever liveth and believeth in me shall never die.

Jesus wanted to focus Martha's attention on Himself as the Source of life, both physical and eternal. He wanted to draw her from thinking about the future to thinking about the present. Even if someone were dead, he could live through His power right now. When Jesus had healed the crippled man at the pool of Bethesda, He had said, "As the Father raiseth up the dead, and quickeneth them; even so the Son quickeneth whom he will" (John 5:21).

Jesus also stated that believers in Him would never permanently die. They would inherit eternal life.

26b. Believest thou this?

Martha had already said that she believed in a coming general resurrection. Jesus now asked her if she believed in Him being the Resurrection and the Life, the Source of eternal life to all who believe in Him. Contrast this with Martha's statement that Jesus could ask God for whatever He wanted and have it given to Him (John 11:22). Jesus wanted her to realize that He Himself had power to raise the dead whenever He wished.

C. Response: 27

27. She saith unto him, Yea, Lord, I believe that thou art the Christ, the Son of God, which should come into the world.

Martha's response might be interpreted various ways, but it appeared to be respectful but evasive. She assured Jesus that she considered Him to be the Christ (Anointed One sent by God) and the Son of God Whose appearance had been predicted. However, she did not say that she saw Him as the Resurrection and the Life with all that this implied for the present situation involving the death of her brother. This view is supported by her later resistance to have the sepulcher opened when Jesus requested it (John 11:39).

Martha went back into town to get Mary and have her come to meet Jesus. Mourners in the house assumed that Mary was going to the grave to weep for Lazarus, and they followed her. When Mary met Jesus, she fell at His feet and plaintively said that her brother need not have died if He had been present to heal him. Jesus was grieved at the sorrow displayed by her and the other mourners, and He wept Himself. The Jews took this as a sign that Jesus loved Lazarus, but some complained that He could have prevented His friend's death (John 11:28-37).

III. Deliverance: John 11:38-44

A. Preparation: 38-41a

38. Jesus therefore again groaning

in himself cometh to the grave. It was a cave, and a stone lay upon it.

Having wept, Jesus was sighing in His spirit as He came to the gravesite. Lazarus had been placed in a sepulcher made from a cave, and a round stone had been rolled across the entrance to it. Since Jews normally buried their dead immediately, the body of Lazarus had probably been there for most of the four days since he had died.

39. Jesus said, Take ye away the stone. Martha, the sister of him that was dead, saith unto him, Lord, by this time he stinketh: for he hath been dead four days.

Jesus was preparing the scene for the miracle about to take place. He dramatically ordered the stone door rolled away from the tomb's opening. Martha was resistant to this, for she rightly assumed that a body dead for four days would stink horribly. It would be a desecration of the dead to have the corpse displayed in a state of putrifaction. She apparently had not understood that Jesus planned to set aside the usual circumstances and make the reappearance of Lazarus something wonderful and welcomed.

40. Jesus saith unto her, Said I not unto thee, that, if thou wouldest believe, thou shouldest see the Glory of God?

Note the similarity of this to what Jesus had told His disciples previously—"This sickness is not unto death, but for the glory of God, that the Son of God might be glorified thereby" (John 11:4). His remarks to Martha previously had carried the same meaning (John 11:25-26). Now the stage was set for the miracle to begin.

41a. Then they took away the stone from the place where the dead was laid.

It probably took several men to roll the stone away from the opening. The first step in performance of the miracle may have been the prevention of noxious odor from the body of Lazarus issuing from the tomb.

B. Prayer: 41b-42

41b. And Jesus lifted up his eyes, and said, Father, I thank thee that thou hast heard me.

42. And I knew that thou hearest me always: but because of the people which stand by I said it, that they may believe that thou hast sent me.

The next step in performance of the miracle was for Jesus to offer up prayer to His heavenly Father. He simply offered praise rather than petition. He thanked His Father for hearing Him at this time and at all times. He said that His reason for doing this vocally and publicly was to impress onlookers with the fact that God had sent Him to do His will. The miracle to take place was but one facet in the teaching that Jesus was engaged in at this time. It was to be an audio-visual aid to His teaching regarding resurrection and eternal life.

C. Performance: 43-44

43. And when he thus had spoken, he cried with a loud voice, Lazarus, come forth.

44a. And he that was dead came forth, bound hand and foot with graveclothes: and his face was bound about with a napkin.

Jesus had ordered men to roll away the stone from the tomb opening. Now He ordered Lazarus by name to come forth from the tomb. He spoke in a loud voice with authority, and Lazarus could do nothing else but rise up and come out. We wonder if he floated out under divine power, because we are told that he was bound hand and foot with grave wrappings. Even his face was obscured by the grave cloth wrapped around it. He was still a prisoner of these things, although he was now alive again.

44b. Jesus saith unto them, Loose him, and let him go.

Jesus ordered onlookers to remove the confining wrappings from Lazarus so that they could ever afterward claim to be witnesses of this miracle and testify to the fact that Jesus had performed it. Many did believe on Jesus because of this event (John 11:45; 12:11). Others reported the incident to the Pharisees, and the chief priests and Pharisees convened a council to decide what to do to bring the ministry of Jesus to an end (John 11: 46-53). Meanwhile, Mary and Martha rejoiced that their brother had been restored to them.

Evangelistic Emphasis

The story of the raising of Lazarus retains its power as a witness to "the glory of God, that the Son of God might be glorified thereby" (John 11:4). Along with the other "signs" or miracles in this Gospel, it has the potential of producing and maintaining faith (see vs. 15, with 20:30-31).

This glory, this potential faith factor, shines through at more than one level. Of course the fact that Jesus raised the dead has its own unique impact. Yet it is remarkable that even so mighty a sign had little effect on Christ's enemies, the Pharisees. Although they could not deny his miracles (see v. 47), the signs produced political plots instead of faith! (See vss. 47—50).

Moderns may also be underwhelmed by miracles. They not only have a secular mind-set; in a day of technological wonders, some take it for granted that they can't explain any physical phenomena, so the miracles in the Bible may be no more startling than the wonders of nuclear fission.

But there is another faith-building element in this story that can prove convincing. That is the moving account of the way Jesus and his disciples converged with compassion and concern on Lazarus' family. Even though he planned to raise Lazarus from the dead, Christ was so moved by Mary's sadness that he wept. The scene took on its own testimony, as observers said, "Behold how he loved him!"

Millions today are lonely, cynical and disillusioned about finding anyone who really cares. While we may not be able to bring them to faith by raising the dead, we can show them that Christians *care*. We can raise the "sign" of compassion carried by Jesus and His disciples in this story. We can create the miracle of community—not only for its inherent value as one way of defining the church, but to say to the lost and the lonely: "Come see the miracle... the miracle of love."

Memory Selection

I am the resurrection, and the life: he that believeth in me, though he were dead, yet shall he live. *John 11:25.*

It's a source of wonder and abiding encouragement for Christians to be able to look about them and see evidence for faith in the natural world. We thrill at a crocus pushing up through the warming spring soil, and see in it a tiny "resurrection." We watch breathlessly as a butterfly sheds its cocoon and we recall the empty tomb.

In this passage, however, a topsy-turvy view is suggested that is perhaps even more breath-taking. Here Jesus says that *he* is the resurrection. Not a crocus. Not a butterfly. A *Person*, instead.

Imagine! The bright crocus doesn't just point to or illustrate the resurrection; it *receives* its powers of "resurrection" from him who is *the* regenerative power in the universe. Lazarus, dead and decaying, receives new life not from "nature" as a god, but from Christ. We may wonder: Without Christ as the resurrection principle, would the brown earth of winter simply have no power to adorn itself with the garments of spring?

Whatever, Christ's claim reaches deep into our hearts to inspire the faith that our own loved ones who have gone before lie not in the grip of "nature," but in the bosom of Abraham—and in the loving care of Him who is the resurrection and the life.

March 28, 1993

Everyday Problems

Jill Blakeley was one of the most active laypersons to be found at First Church. She served on several committees, hosted a home Bible study and even found time to take a peer counseling course—all this in spite of her job as a travel agent, which required that she be gone some.

As a result of this involvement, many people at First Church learned to depend on Jill as a supportive Christian friend and mentor. In fact, when Marge Jackson's husband fell critically ill, she called Jill first. As usual, Marge found Jill warm and supportive. She promised to visit Philip Jackson in the hospital the next day.

Unfortunately, however, Jill had to fly to Honolulu unexpectedly to make arrangements for a convention. When she returned, she found to her great sorrow that Philip Jackson had died.

Marge was angry and hurt. Here she was, needing her friend Jill as never before, and she wasn't there. What was worse, she was gone to *Hawaii*. What a time to be away at an international playground, Marge thought bitterly.

*Should Marge talk about her anger to Jill, or simply be more understanding?
*How might Jill respond to Marge in her grief and anger?
*What do you suppose the disciples thought when Jesus delayed going to Lazarus for two days? (See John 11:5-6.)

♦♦♦♦♦♦

Superintendent's Sermonette

We have heard a great deal in recent years about near-death or after-death experiences. Even secular sources seem intrigued with cases in which individuals are clinically dead and are then revived and given a new lease on life. Common reports tell of individuals viewing their bodies while their spirits float near the ceiling, entering a long dark tunnel, and ending up in a place of brightness, peace, and comfort. Some claim to have seen relatives and friends. Most, say they would rather have stayed there than to come back. Those who report a visit to a place of terror and torment no doubt were glad to return to this life.

Today we study the resurrection of Lazarus by Jesus after he had been dead and buried for four days. This was no temporary, fleeting brush with death. It was the real thing. No doubt the soul of Lazarus was in Abraham's bosom, the place of the righteous dead, during those four days (Luke 16:22-26). We have no biblical record of what he experienced there, but it must have affected his outlook when he returned to the land of the living. We can have confidence in facing death, for we who belong to Christ know that our destiny is determined by Him, the Resurrection and the Life.

This Lesson In Your Life

Is the Christian belief in the resurrection of any practical influence in your everyday life? Or is it just one of the doctrines that you are expected to believe?

When you picture Jesus standing before the tomb of Lazarus and calling out, "Lazarus, come forth!" can you put yourself in the scene, enfolded in the embrace of the earth until Christ calls *you* to new life, too? And does that picture carry over into any attitudes and behaviors in your life now?

Such questions are at the heart of what it means to be a Christian instead of a member of another faith, or of none, in a practical sense. Belief in a personal resurrection distinguishes Christianity from several world religions. Yet it is a doctrine that must be reflected in daily life if the distinction is to be anything but arm-chair philosophy.

God's people in Old Testament times did not have the resurrection hope that Christ brought. From a point of view limited to life "under the sun," the author of Ecclesiastes gathered that both persons and beasts "go unto one place; all are of the dust, and all turn to dust again" (3:20). "Sheol," or the grave, was widely assumed to be the only known human destiny.

This does not mean that Old Testament people went about their daily activities long-faced and bereft of hope. They had a few hints of something better. There is Job's remarkable confidence that "I know that my redeemer liveth, and that he shall stand at the latter day upon the earth, And though after my skin worms destroy this body, yet in my flesh shall I see God" (Job 19:25-26). And there is David's hope that "Thou wilt not leave my soul in hell (Sheol); neither wilt thou suffer thine Holy One to see corruption" (Ps. 16:10).

By the time of Christ, these hints of hope had grown into buds ready to bloom. When Jesus told Martha that her dead brother Lazarus "shall rise again," she indicated an already well-developed belief in the resurrection: "I know that he shall rise again in the resurrection at the last day" (John 11:24). With such miracles as the raising of Lazarus... with Jesus' affirmation that *He* in fact is "the resurrection and the life" (vs. 25)...and later with His own resurrection, the Christian hope came into full flower.

The development of resurrection faith must be more than an historical sketch. It must result in our being able, as those who bask in the light of the ultimate revelation of Christ, to reflect in our lives the fuller confidence in life after death that Jesus brought. The divine Sonship of Jesus was fully revealed by His resurrection (Rom. 1:4). Does my own belief in the resurrection reveal *my* identity also as a child of God? What might Christ reasonably expect to see in my life, as a result of resurrection faith?

He might expect to see *indomitable optimism*. If the resurrection is true, *nothing* can turn out ultimately *wrong*! This isn't just a future hope. People with resurrection faith bring the future into the present. They are constantly looking for a brighter point of view in the face of what others can see only as dismal reality. It's just hard to confront them with a problem they can't stare down!

This isn't "Polyanna thinking." Christian optimism is based on what we view as history—the actual event of Christ's resurrection. His empty tomb functions something like *the exodus* did for Old Testament Jews. When times were tough, the reality of their deliverance from Egypt was recalled, recited and celebrated. The historical fact that God had rescued Israel in their distress was brought into the present in the form of a dynamic hope that he would relieve their present distress in equally marvelous ways (see, for example, Psalm 105).

Seed Thoughts

1. Why is John 11:2 so careful to identify this Mary?
Probably because there are several other Marys associated with the story of Jesus (Mary the mother of Jesus, Mary Magdalene, etc.).

2. How can *death* ever bring glory to the Son of God, as in verse 4?
In the way Christians deal with it when it strikes our own loved ones; the way we help others who must deal with it.

3. What references does John 11 make to Jesus' quite human love for Lazarus and his sisters?
"Whom thou lovest" (vs. 3); "Jesus loved..." (vs. 5); "our friend" (vs. Il); "he groaned...and was troubled" (vs. 33); he wept at the tomb (vss. 34-35).

4. Why did Jesus' disciples protest when he decided to go to Judea at Lazarus' death?
Because his opponents in Judea had already sought to stone him (see 10:31).

5. How did Jesus' reply possibly indicate that he knew what he would be "walking" into by returning to Judea?
Perhaps His reference to walking "in the day" indicated that because He was "the light of the world" He knew exactly what awaited him.

(PLEASE TURN PAGE)

---

1. Why is John 11:2 so careful to identify this Mary?

2. How can *death* ever bring glory to the Son of God, as in verse 4?

3. What references does John 11 make to Jesus' quite human love for Lazarus and his sisters?

4. Why did Jesus' disciples protest when he decided to go to Judea at Lazarus' death?

5. How did Jesus' reply possibly indicate that he knew what he would be "walking" into by returning to Judea? (See vss. 9-10.)

6. Why was Jesus glad the disciples were not at Lazarus' side when he died?

7. What else do you know about Thomas that balances his enthusiastic outburst of faith in verse 16?

8. Why is *timing* important in tending to those in bereavement or other crises?

9. How did Jesus transform Martha's belief in the *doctrine* of the resurrection into a more personal faith?

10. Did Jesus' *compassion* or *the miracle* make the better impression on the Jews?

(SEED THOUGHTS--Cont'd)

Probably because there are several other Marys associated with the story of Jesus (Mary the mother of Jesus, Mary Magdalene, etc.).

In the way Christians deal with it when it strikes our own loved ones; the way we help others who must deal with it.

"Whom thou lovest" (vs. 3); "Jesus loved..." (vs. 5); "our friend" (vs. Il); "he groaned...and was troubled" (vs. 33); he wept at the tomb (vss. 34-35).

Because his opponents in Judea had already sought to stone him (see 10:31).

Perhaps His reference to walking "in the day" indicated that because He was "the light of the world" He knew exactly what awaited him.

Apparently because He knew their faith would be strengthened by witnessing the raising of Lazarus.

This is also "doubting Thomas" (John 20:24-25).

People who hurt can have mood swings. For example, the bereaved may want to talk at some times but not others.

By saying that He Himself is the resurrection—and of course by personally raising Lazarus from the dead.

"The Jews" marveled at how Jesus loved Lazarus, while the miracle prompted the Pharisees to plot against him.

6. Why was Jesus glad the disciples were not at Lazarus' side when he died?
Apparently because He knew their faith would be strengthened by witnessing the raising of Lazarus.

7. What else do you know about Thomas that balances his enthusiastic outburst of faith in verse 16?
This is also "doubting Thomas" (John 20:24-25).

8. Why is *timing* important in tending to those in bereavement or other crises?
People who hurt can have mood swings. For example, the bereaved may want to talk at some times but not others.

9. How did Jesus transform Martha's belief in the *doctrine* of the resurrection into a more personal faith?
By saying that He Himself is the resurrection—and of course by personally raising Lazarus from the dead.

10. Did Jesus' *compassion* or *the miracle* make the better impression on the Jews?
"The Jews" marveled at how Jesus loved Lazarus, while the miracle prompted the Pharisees to plot against him.

April 4, 1993

Do As I Have Done

John 13

1 Now before the feast of the passover, when Jesus knew that his hour was come that he should depart out of this world unto the Father, having loved his own which were in the world, he loved them unto the end.
2 And supper being ended, the devil having now put into the heart of Judas Is-car´-i-ot, Simon's son, to betray him;
3 Jesus knowing that the Father had given all things into his hands, and that he was come from God, and went to God;
4 He riseth from supper, and laid aside his garments; and took a towel, and girded himself.
5 After that he poureth water into a basin, and began to wash the disciples' feet, and to wipe them with the towel wherewith he was girded.
6 Then cometh he to Simon Peter: and Peter saith unto him, Lord, dost thou wash my feet?
7 Jesus answered and said unto him, What I do thou knowest not now; but thou shalt know hereafter.
8 Peter saith unto him, Thou shalt never wash my feet. Jesus answered him, If I wash thee not, thou hast no part with me.
9. Simon Peter saith unto him, Lord, not my feet only, but also my head.
10 Jesus saith to him. He that is washed needeth not save to wash his feet, but is clean every whit: and ye are clean, but not all.
11 For he knew who should betray him; therefore said he, Ye are not all clean.
12 So after he had washed their feet, and had taken his garments and was set down again, he said unto them, know ye what I have done to you.
13 Ye call me Master and Lord: and ye say well; for so I am.
14 If I then, your Lord and Master, have washed your feet; ye also ought to wash one another's feet.
15 For I have given you an example, that ye should do as I have done to you.
16 Verily, verily, I say unto you, the servant is not greater than his lord; neither he that is sent greater than he that sent him.

◆◆◆◆◆◆

◀ **Memory Selection**
John 13:15

◀ **Devotional Reading**
John 13:31-36

◀ **Background Selection**
John 13: 1-20

◀ **Printed Scripture**
John 13:1-16

DO AS I HAVE DONE

Teacher's Target

One day James and John told Jesus that they wanted to rule with Him in His kingdom, one on either side of Him. Jesus reminded them that they would have to suffer much before His kingdom came, and it was not up to Him to say where they would be seated. He then taught His disciples that those who would be great must first be servants. He concluded by saying, "Even the Son of man came not to be ministered unto, but to minister, and to give his life a ransom for many" (Mark 10:45). As He neared the end of His earthly ministry, Jesus emphasized this theme again in the upper room when He washed the disciples' feet.

Help your students to see that believers' service to one another serves two important objectives. It promotes unity among the brethren. It gives a good testimony to those outside the church circle. Washing feet was but a symbol of the many ways in which believers can serve one another.

Lesson Introduction

Jesus and His disciples were the only characters in the incident of foot-washing recorded in our text. Two of the disciples provide interesting studies in similarities and contrasts. Jesus knew that Satan had already persuaded Judas Iscariot to betray him, but He washed his feet along with those of the others. Jesus did remark that they were not all "clean," for He knew betrayal was coming. Jesus met resistance when he began to wash Peter's feet, but He overcame it.

Subsequent scripture shows that both Judas and Peter denied their Lord during His passion. However, one became so remorseful that he committed suicide. The other repented and was restored to his place of service. These cases taught the early Christians that disloyalty and sin led to disaster, while renewed loyalty and pardon led to fruitful ministry. Judas Iscariot went "to his own place" (Acts 1:25). Peter went on to a life of service and to eternal life.

Teaching Outline

I. Resolve: John 13:1-5
   A. Affection: 1-2
   B. Action: 3-5
II. Resistance: John 13:6-11
   A. Refusal: 6-8a
   B. Reversal: 8b-10a
   C. Reference: 10b-11
III. Reminder: John 13:12-16
   A. Perspective: 12-15
   B. Principle: 16

Daily Bible Readings

Mon. Jesus Is Anointed
John 12:1-6
Tue. The King Is Coming
John 12:12-19
Wed. Jesus Predicts His Death
John 12:23-36
Thu. Jesus Washes the Disciples' Feet
John 13:1-11
Fri. The Servant Role
John 13:12-17
Sat. Jesus Predicts His Betrayal
John 13:18-30
Sun. Bear Witness to Christ
John 15:18-27

April 4, 1993

VERSE BY VERSE

I. Resolve: John 13:1-5

A. Affection: 1-2

1a. Now before the feast of the passover, when Jesus knew that his hour was come that he should depart out of this world unto the Father,...

The first part of this verse deals with the time involved in the foot-washing incident. It was actually during celebration of the Passover Feast that Jesus realized His hour (time) had come to suffer, die, rise again, and then ascend to His heavenly Father. It was with this in mind that He decided to do something special to illustrate the need for unity fostered by mutual service.

1b. ...having loved his own which were in the world, he loved them unto the end.

Jesus accepted all converts to Himself as gifts from His Father (John 17:6) Therefore, He loved them right up to the end of His ministry among them. These were the ones who were expected to carry on His work after He ascended back up to heaven, with the obvious exception of Judas Iscariot, who would betray Him and lose both his life and ministry. Even in the case of Judas, Jesus was willing to wash his feet and show him His love.

2. And supper being ended, the devil having now put into the heart of Judas Iscariot, Simon's son, to betray him;

This verse, along with verses 10-11, reveals the knowledge Jesus had regarding Judas Iscariot and His concern about him. The regular Passover meal had now ended. The first Lord's supper had not yet been initiated, and it would not be until the betrayer had left the upper room. However, Jesus allowed Judas to remain there to take part in the foot-washing ceremony. He knew that Satan was even then working in the heart of Judas, but this did not deter Him from including him in this event.

B. Action: 3-5

3. Jesus knowing that the Father had given all things into his hands, and that he was come from God, and went to God;
4 He riseth from supper, and laid aside his garments; and took a towel, and girded himself.

Mental preparation for the foot-washing involved Jesus overlooking the negative influence of Judas and his opinion of Him. It involved looking at the positive influence of His Father Who had given all things into His hands, had sent him to the earth, and expected Him to come back up to heaven. Physical preparation for the foot-washing involved Jesus rising up from His place at the supper table, laying aside His outer robe to stand in His inner tunic, and tying a long towel around His waist. Now He was ready for action.

5. After that he poureth water into a basin, and began to wash the disciples' feet, and to wipe them with the towel wherewith he was girded.

The pitcher of water and the basin were already on hand, ready to be used. This task of foot-washing was normally done by a servant, but Jesus had wanted to be alone in the upper room with His disciples and apparently had excluded servants. The disciples must have been surprised and shocked that Jesus would volunteer to wash their feet and wipe them with the towel about His waist. Each may have been embarrassed for not offering to do this job himself. Jesus intended for them to learn an important lesson from His action, but first He had

303

to deal with determined resistance from Peter.

II. Resistance: John 13:6-11

A. Refusal: 6-8a

6. Then cometh he to Simon Peter: and Peter saith unto him, Lord, dost thou wash my feet?

It was almost as if Peter said, "Lord, do you really intend to wash my feet?" In his usual outspoken way, Peter planned to resist this. Perhaps he thought that the other disciples had not put up enough resistance to this unusual procedure and that it was up to him to put a stop to it. It evidently did not seem right to him.

7. Jesus answered and said unto him, What I do thou knowest not now; but thou shalt know hereafter.

Another way to put this is, "You do not understand now what I am doing, but you will understand it later on" (Amplified Bible). Jesus was asking Peter to accept His action for the time being, even if it seemed strange or inappropriate to him

8a. Peter saith unto him, Thou shalt never wash my feet.

This was not the first, nor would it be the last, time that Peter's impulsive mouth got him into trouble. He may have had the best of intentions in resisting Jesus at this point, but he should have avoided telling Jesus that He was never going to wash his feet. This amounted to rebellion against the Master, and it could not be tolerated. The result would be alienation of the relationship, as Jesus was quick to point out to him.

B. Reversal: 8b-10a

8b. Jesus answered him, If I wash thee not, thou hast no part with me.

This may have seemed to be a minor matter, but Jesus was stern with Peter. He told him that he must submit to the foot-washing or sever his relationship with the Master. This prompted a sudden reversal on the part of Peter.

9. Simon Peter saith unto him, Lord, not my feet only, but also my hands and my head.

Peter was so appalled at the bluntness of Jesus' warning and its punishment that he swung over to the opposite extreme. He called on Jesus to rinse not only his feet, but his hands and head, as well. This would have been more than Jesus had been doing with the other disciples, thus singling Peter out for special treatment. Although Peter's suggestion may have been meant to compensate for his original resistance to Jesus, it was rejected.

10a. Jesus saith to him, He that is washed needeth not save to wash his feet, but is clean every whit:...

We should look at the literal situation described here before looking for the spiritual application. Jesus said that a person who had bathed in preparation to go anywhere would only have to have his feet rinsed to take off the dust picked up on the way. Otherwise, he was considered to be clean. Peter's suggestion that Jesus wash his hands and head, as well as his feet, had been inappropriate and unnecessary in this situation.

C. Reference: 10b-11

10b. ...and ye are clean, but not all.

11. For he knew who should betray him; therefore said he, Ye are not all clean.

This must have sounded like a riddle to the disciples, and they may have spent time trying to figure it out as Jesus finished washing their feet. By the time the Apostle John wrote his gospel, the early Christians knew its meaning. Jesus had been referring to Judas Iscariot and there was a spiritual application. The disciples were loyal, except for Judas Iscariot. He was not "clean" in the same sense. Satan had already planted the idea of betraying Jesus in his mind, and he would shortly leave to implement his plan (John 13:2, 21-30).

III. Reminder: John 13:12-16

A. Perspective: 12-15

12. So after he had washed their feet, and had taken his garments, and was set down again, he said unto them, Know ye what I have done to you?

We are not told if Jesus washed the dust off His Own feet or if anyone else offered to do it. When He had finished with the disciples, He set the pitcher and basin aside, put on His outer robe, and sat down at the table again. It was time to examine the event and determine what it meant. He asked if they understood what He had done to them. There is no record that they responded. Perhaps no one knew the significance of His strange action. He now had their attention and was; ready to teach. He wanted to develop their perception of servanthood as it was to be worked out in a group of believers. He had to sharpen their perspective on this concept.

13. Ye call me Master and Lord: and ye say well; for so I am.

Jesus began by stating something which seemed obvious to the disciples. They referred to Him as Master and Lord, implying that they were His servants. He commended them for this, because He was indeed their Master and Lord, although one of them was soon to turn away from Him.

14. If I then, your Lord and Master, have washed your feet; ye also ought to wash one another's feet.

Jesus had previously told His disciples, "It is enough for the disciple that he be as his master, and the servant as his lord" (Matt. 10:25). Another way to put it would be, "It is sufficient for a student to be as his teacher is and for a slave to be as his owner is." In other words, the standard of measurement rested with the master and lord through precept and example. Jesus had certainly laid down a high standard for His followers to try to emulate. They were able to comprehend this in many things, but would they be able to understand it when it came to servanthood within the body of believers?

15. For I have given you an example, that ye should do as I have done to you.

Jesus knew that events in upcoming days would threaten to tear the disciples apart. They would undergo tremendous stress as their hope for the establishment of the kingdom of God on earth seemed to vanish away with His betrayal, arrest, judgment, torture, crucifixion, and burial occurring rapidly.

Jesus wanted them to be sustained by a unity produced through shared service to one another. The example of service shown through foot-washing was but a symbol of the multifaceted program of services. He wanted His followers to develop among themselves. He elevated humble service to a high plane.

B. Principle: 16

16a. Verily, verily, I say unto you, The servant is not greater than his lord:

Jesus' use of "Verily, verily, I say unto you" usually prefaced statement of an important principle. Here He wanted to emphasize the fact that a servant should not consider himself to be greater than his master. At that time a slave had few rights and was completely subservient to his owner, who often had the power of life or death over him. We should be thankful that slavery is outlawed in our society and that we have the right to resign from employment if we do not like what an employer demands of us. However, the same principle is at work today. One slogan in use states, "I may be right, or I may be wrong, but I am still the boss!" The employer holds the power over an employee as long as that person works for him.

16b. ...neither he that is sent greater than he that sent him.

This referred to an envoy sent to represent a ruler. This person could never consider himself to be greater than the one who sent him. He had to speak only what he had been told to speak in his contact with the foreign leader. We know that the same principle operates in diplomatic circles today. The diplomat may have more flexibility in negotiating than in ancient times, but he is still allowed to move only within certain guidelines prepared at home by the political leadership.

Jesus said that each disciple of His had to see himself in the role of servant or envoy. Each had to take directions from Him. He was commanding His disciples to serve one another, even as He had served them by washing their feet. It was to be service prompted by love, and it was to unite them in the face of their common enemies.

Evangelistic Emphasis

Some Christians have suggested that *the towel* is a more fitting symbol of the Christian faith than the cross. The idea is that while *the cross* is an appropriate symbol of Christ's work for us, it's in a class by itself. On the other hand, the towel more aptly symbolizes the work we are to do for each other.

In a way, of course, the cross serves that purpose, too. Jesus said, "He that taketh not his cross, and followeth after me is not worthy of me" (Matt. 10:38). The self-sacrifice implied in crossbearing surely includes putting the needs of others above our own. Still, the point is well-taken. As Jesus said, "If I then, your Lord and Master, have washed your feet; ye also ought to wash one another's feet" (John 13:14). If the cross symbolizes the essential Christian lifestyle, the towel is an essential element in our tool kit.

Hence, it's no accident that at least from the fourth century on, Christians were in the forefront of establishing hospitals, homes for the homeless and facilities to care for the aged. More than one pagan in the ancient world marveled at the way these earliest Christians wielded "the towel" instead of a sword. It became a way not only to meet human needs, but to be for others a lamp on a stand, a city set on a hill.

Does an unbelieving world, looking at our own lives, see a similar willingness to serve?

♦♦♦♦♦♦

Memory Selection

For I have given you an example, that ye should do as I have done to you.
John 13:15

You may have heard of the old epitaph that read:
As you are now, so once was I,
Before too long you too will die.
As I am now, soon you will be.
Prepare, my friend, to follow me.
But someone added, in a crude scrawl:
To follow you I'm not content
Until I learn which way you went.

Do we feel this hesitant when we learn that following Jesus leads not just to heaven but to the wash basin and the towel?

It's liberating when Christ promises, "Ye shall know the truth, and the truth shall make you free" (John 8:32). It's comforting when He invites, "Come unto me, all ye that labor and are heavy laden, and I will give you rest" (Matt. 11:28). But when we hear Him call us to follow his example in service to others we may respond, "Does he know how smelly my neighbor's feet are?" Or, "He doesn't understand my schedule—how can I squeeze foot-washing in between car-pooling and the evening meal?" Or even, in our secret heart, "I can't see how doing that will win me any status."

But Jesus doesn't just call us to lives of service to add yet another item to an over-crowded schedule, or to eat "humble pie." In his divine system of values, serving is a style of thinking and acting perfectly suited for use during the carpool and the evening meal.

April 4, 1993

Weekday Problems

Although Covenant Church was formerly in a thriving, upscale part of town, the neighborhood has changed. Now the church is surrounded by human needs. Many of its low-income families have absentee fathers. Most members now drive in to church from other parts of town. The elementary school suffers from absenteeism, and students' grades are plummeting. Teenagers roam the streets with the complaint, "There's nothing to do!"

Tom Jenkins, a social worker and a member at Covenant, knows what to do. He has all sorts of ideas about how the church could sponsor tutoring programs, job fairs, a recreation center and child care services. It's what Tom calls a "basin and towel" style of ministry.

But every time Tom tries to get something started along these lines he is met with resistance from church members who question how far the church should be involved in such ministries. Where is the message of salvation in a recreation center? they ask.

*Do you feel a tension between "social" ministries and evangelism?

*If Covenant Church built a gymnasium for the community, should it find a way to supplement "recreation" with the gospel message? If so, how could it happen?

*Would it be better for the church just to move to another part of town?

♦♦♦♦♦♦

Superintendent's Sermonette

World leaders are often disappointments to us. Too often they seek for power and possessions by oppressing their people and draining everything they can away from them. The reason that there are revolutions continually fermenting around the globe is that people will not endure mistreatment. They rise up to overthrow their oppressors, but those leaders often go into luxurious exile elsewhere instead of paying for their crimes. We are fortunate if we live in a society where we can get rid of bad leaders through the ballot box rather than through revolution.

Jesus came to display a new type of leadership. He saw Himself in the role of a Servant, ready to minister and to die in order to help other people. He said of Himself, "The Son of man came not to be ministered unto, but to minister, and to give his life a ransom for many" (Mark. 10:45), In today's text, we study how Jesus taught His disciples the importance of service by washing their feet in the upper room. He then taught them the importance of serving one another to promote unity and love. We need to be concerned about this today. Let us be leaders devoted to service, not to the acquisition of power or possessions.

DO AS I HAVE DONE

This Lesson In Your Life

A Realistic Outlook on Life

This section of John's Gospel portrays Jesus' advance knowledge of two sobering facts: *His approaching death*, and *His betrayal by Judas Iscariot*. It is no light evidence for His divinity that he should be able to peer into the future in this way.

There is also a gap between Jesus' calm acceptance of these facts, and the way we often deal with such knowledge.

The Way of Denial

Some people deal with life's hard realisms from a stance of denial. In recent years we have been told how our society has encouraged us to deny or ignore the facts of death and dying. Thanks to the leadership of persons such as Elizabeth Kubler-Ross, some strides have been taken to improve the situation. Yet, many are still reluctant to think and speak openly about death.

Many of us are equally reluctant to admit that there are Judases in the world. We want to think the best of everyone. It's painful to admit that a friend might actually spread false rumors about us—much less betray us as Judas did his Lord. A generation ago, social analysts encouraged this attitude with the message that people are all basically good; only bad environments made some people go wrong. Even now, for most of us to admit that even a friend might let us down would require a painful, personal experience of actual betrayal.

A general life-stance of denial can manifest itself in two opposite ways. If we sense that life will go wrong if we don't suppress its darker side, we may take on a doleful, joyless demeanor. On the other hand, if we sense that our denial has the dismal facts of life on the run, it may prompt us to paste on a happy face in even the saddest situations. We may become super-optimists, having found that a cheerful exterior can chase away the hosts we don't admit are real.

The Morbid View

Perhaps we have also seen the other extreme— people who are a little paranoid about both death and relationships. It's no healthier to be obsessed with death than it is to deny it. Both the hypochondriac and the person who won't venture outdoors for fear of catching a fatal virus have a morbid preoccupation with death.

People who are invariable suspicious of others have a view of people that is as distorted as that of those who live in denial. If we are thoroughly suspicious of others, we cannot have close friends, as Jesus did among the inner circle of the Twelve. Somehow it builds a barrier between ourselves and others if we're perfectly sure that everyone we know would do us in if they could collect the insurance!

The Divine Realism

In contrast with these extremes, Jesus faced both death and betrayal calmly and realistically. He knew that "It is appointed unto men once to die" (Heb. 9:27). That knowledge didn't make Him spend His remaining days wringing His hands. It only inspired Him to make His remaining days count for good.

Neither did Christ's knowledge that Judas would betray Him make Him suspicious of humanity in general. More than any of us, "he knew what was in man" (John 2:2 5)—including our capacity for betrayal and other evils. Yet we see no hints of paranoia or inability to trust others just because of this awareness.

The point is that, for Jesus, both death and flawed relationships were simply facts of life. Can we learn from Him how to face life and death and people with both faith and clear-eyed realism?

Seed Thoughts

1. Does the fact that Jesus' "hour" had now come (John 13:1) shed any light on His blunt statement to His mother in 2:4?

In his statement to Mary, Jesus simply meant that it was not time for his true purpose, that would lead to his death, to be revealed.

2. What reassuring knowledge did Jesus have that can also help us face death?

We can know, as Jesus did, that just as we came from God, He also holds our destiny.

3. In what practical ways can you as an individual follow Jesus' intent in giving us the example of washing the disciples' feet?

(Encourage specific—not generalized—suggestions of how class members can minister to those in need.)

4. Discuss similar ways *the church* can engage in such ministries.

(Are specific class or church projects appropriate?)

5. Is it sometimes as hard to accept "foot-washing" or ministry as to perform it for others?

Yes, we must sometimes swallow our pride in order to accept such humble service.

(PLEASE TURN PAGE)

---

1. Does the fact that Jesus' "hour" had now come (John 13:1) shed any light on His blunt statement to His mother in 2:4?

2. What reassuring knowledge did Jesus have that can also help us face death?

3. In what practical ways can you as an individual follow Jesus' intent in giving us the example of washing the disciples' feet?

4. Discuss similar ways *the church* can engage in such ministries.

5. Is it sometimes as hard to accept "foot-washing" or ministry as to perform it for others?

6. At what other occasion did Peter object to what Jesus was doing, and what attitude does he reveal?

7. In verse 8, Jesus moves from washing feet as a sign of humble service to washing as what other kind of symbol?

8. In what other way besides service does Jesus apply the saying about the servant's not being greater than his master?

9. Who do you think was the disciple "whom Jesus loved" (vs.23).

10. Does the fact that Satan entered Judas' heart mean that Judas was not personally responsible for betraying Jesus?

(SEED THOUGHTS--Cont'd)

In his statement to Mary, Jesus simply meant that it was not time for his true purpose, that would lead to his death, to be revealed.

We can know, as Jesus did, that just as we came from God, He also holds our destiny.

(Encourage specific—not generalized—suggestions of how class members can minister to those in need.)

(Are specific class or church projects appropriate?)

Yes, we must sometimes swallow our pride in order to accept such humble service.

Peter also objected to Jesus' intent to suffer and die in Jerusalem. Both incidents reflect Peter's failure to understand the role of a "servant Messiah."

Peter's response in verse 9 indicates that Jesus refers in verse 8 to washing as a symbol of spiritual cleansing.

Since their Master was persecuted, Christ's servants can also expect persecution.

Traditionally it has been thought that this is the way the apostle John, our author, refers to himself, modestly refraining from using his name.

No, Judas participated with his own will, as Matthew 26:14-15 makes clear.

6. At what other occasion did Peter object to what Jesus was doing, and what attitude does he reveal?
Peter also objected to Jesus' intent to suffer and die in Jerusalem. Both incidents reflect Peter's failure to understand the role of a "servant Messiah."

7. In verse 8, Jesus moves from washing feet as a sign of humble service to washing as what other kind of symbol?
Peter's response in verse 9 indicates that Jesus refers in verse 8 to washing as a symbol of spiritual cleansing.

8. In what other way besides service does Jesus apply the saying about the servant's not being greater than his master?
Since their Master was persecuted, Christ's servants can also expect persecution.

9. Who do you think was the disciple "whom Jesus loved" (vs.23).
Traditionally it has been thought that this is the way the apostle John, our author, refers to himself, modestly refraining from using his name.

10. Does the fact that Satan entered Judas' heart mean that Judas was not personally responsible for betraying Jesus?
No, Judas participated with his own will, as Matthew 26:14-15 makes clear.

April 11, 1993

I Have Seen The Lord

John 20
1. The first day of the week cometh Mary Mag-da-le′-ne early, when it was yet dark, unto the sepulchre, and seeth the stone taken away from the sepulchre.
2 Then she runneth, and cometh to Simon Peter, and to the other disciple, whom Jesus loved, and saith unto them, They have taken away the Lord out of the sepulchre, and we know not where they have laid him.
3 Peter therefore went forth and that other disciple, and came to the sepulchre.
4 So they ran both together: and the other disciple did outrun Peter, and came first to the sepulchre.
5 And he stooping down, and *looking in*, saw the linen clothes lying; yet went he not in.
6 Then cometh Simon Peter following him, and went into the sepulchre, and seeth the linen clothes lie,
7 And the napkin, that was about his head, not lying with the linen clothes, but wrapped together in a place by itself.
8 Then went in also that other disciple, which came first to the sepulchre, and he saw, and believed.

9 For as yet they knew not the scripture, that he must rise again from the dead.
10 Then the disciples went away again unto their own home.
11 But Mary stood without at the sepulchre weeping: and as she wept, she stooped down, and looked into the sepulchre,
12 And seeth two angels in white sitting, the one at the head, and the other at the feet, where the body of Jesus had lain.
13 And they say unto her, Woman, why weepest thou? She saith unto them, Because they have taken away my Lord, and I know not where they have laid him.
14 And when she had thus said, she turned herself back, and saw Jesus standing, and knew not that it was Jesus.
15 Jesus saith unto her, Woman, why weepest thou? whom seekest thou? She supposing him to be the gardener, saith unto him, Sir, if thou have borne him hence tell me where thou hast laid him, and I will take him away.
16 Jesus saith unto her, Mary. She turned herself, and saith unto him, Rab-bo′-ni; which is to say, Master.

◆◆◆◆◆◆

◀ **Memory Selection**
John 20:19-23

◀ **Devotional Reading**
John 20:19-23

◀ **Background Scripture**
John 20:1-16

◀ **Printed Scripture**
John 20:1-16

I HAVE SEEN THE LORD

Teacher's Target

The disciples of Jesus had been on an emotional rollercoaster. They had exulted when He made His so-called triumphal entry into Jerusalem. They had been depressed when He was betrayed by one of their own, taken into judgment, and condemned to die. They went into hiding for fear of the Jews. Then Sunday, the first day of the week, dawned, and the situation changed dramatically. Mary Magdalene discovered His tomb was empty. Peter and John ran to investigate this. Mary met Jesus.

Help your students to realize that Behind every dark circumstance stands the One Who is Light and Life. To know, understand, and remember His words can save us from much despair. The disciples had been told several times that Jesus would suffer, die, and rise again, but they had put it out of their minds. They paid a high price for this neglect, and we are in danger of doing the same thing if we are not careful. By remembering Christ's promises, we can face the future unafraid.

Lesson Introduction

Mary Magdalene is the central character in the text for today. She probably came from an area called Magdala on the southwestern coast of the Sea of Galilee. Jesus met her and cast seven devils (demons, evil spirits) out of her (Mark 16:9; Luke 8:2). She became an ardent follower of Jesus. She was at His grave when He was buried (Matt. 27:61). She had the honor of finding the tomb empty early Sunday morning. She ran to tell Peter and John about it, prompting them to race to the sepulcher to find out for themselves.

Mary must have caught up to them, because she was weeping there after they left. She now came into contact with supernatural beings. Two angels appearing as men, asked why she wept. She replied that some unknown individuals had stolen the body of her Lord, and she did not know where they had laid it. Turning around, she met Jesus, supposing Him to be the gardener, but she soon became aware of His true identity. The Master was alive again!

Teaching Outline

I. Mary Reporting:
   John 20: 1-10
   A. Discovery I: 1-2
   B. Discovery II: 3-5
   C. Discovery III: 6-8
   D. Departure: 9-10
II. Mary Vindicated:
   John 20: 11-16
   A. Inquiry I: 11-13
   B. Inquiry II: 14-15
   C. Impact: 16

Daily Bible Readings

Mon. Jesus Sentenced
John 19:1-16
Tue. The Via Dolorosa
John 19:17-21
Wed. The Crucifixion
John 19:22-27
Thu. Jesus' Death
John 19:28-37
Fri. The Empty Tomb
John 20:1-9
Sat. Jesus Appears to Mary
John 20:10-18
Sun. Jesus Appears to the Disciples
John 20:19-30

April 11, 1993

VERSE BY VERSE

I. Mary Reporting: John 20:1-10

A. Discovery I: 1-2

1. The first day of the week cometh Mary Magdalene early, when it was yet dark, unto the sepulchre, and seeth the stone taken away from the sepulchre.

It appears that Mary Magdalene was accompanied to the sepulcher by Mary (mother of James and Joses) and by Salome. It was very early in the predawn with the sun about to rise. They brought *sweet spices* with which to anoint the body of Jesus. They wondered who would roll away the heavy stone from the doorway (Mark 16:1-3). However, this task had already been done when an earthquake took place and an angel rolled the stone away and sat upon it. Guards at the tomb were so frightened that they shook and then fell paralyzed as dead men (Matt. 28:2-4). They evidently recovered, for some went into Jerusalem and reported what had happened. The chief priests and elders paid them money to say that the disciples of Jesus had come at night to steal His body and take it away as the soldiers slept (Matt. 28:11-15). Mary saw the *stone* rolled away and must have checked to see that the tomb was empty (John 20:2).

2. Then she runneth, and cometh to Simon Peter, and to the other disciple, whom Jesus loved, and saith unto them, They have taken away the Lord out of the sepulcher, and we know not where they have laid him.

Greatly distressed over what she had discovered, Mary Magdalene ran to find Jesus' disciples and apparently found Peter and John first. She assumed that their enemies had come to the sepulcher, removed the body of Jesus, and hidden it elsewhere. It did not seem to cross her mind that Jesus had been resurrected from the dead as He had predicted would happen on the third day. She was anxious to find a corpse, not a living person.

B. Discovery II: 3-5

3. Peter therefore went forth, and that other disciple, and came to the sepulcher.

4. So they ran both together: and the other disciple did outrun Peter, and came first to the sepulcher.

Compare the brief account found in Luke 24:12—"Then arose Peter, and ran unto the sepulcher; and stooping down, he beheld the linen clothes laid by themselves, and departed, wondering in himself at that which was come to pass." When the Apostle John wrote his gospel at the end of the first century, he expanded on what happened. He had been in a race with Peter to get to the sepulcher, and John reported here that he had won. Whatever bit of pride John might have had in his success, note his modesty in referring to himself simply as "that other disciple."

5. And he stooping down, and looking in, saw the linen clothes lying; yet went he not in.

We can only speculate on John's reason for not entering the tomb after he looked in and saw that the body of Jesus was gone and only the linen wrapping materials remained. Perhaps he was afraid to go in by himself and wanted to wait for Peter to come. Perhaps the shock of the empty tomb caused him to rest until he could calm himself before taking further action. Mary had discovered the empty tomb and run. John had discovered it and waited. Now we will see what Peter did.

C. Discovery III: 6-8

6. Then cometh Simon Peter following him, and went into the sepulcher and seeth the linen clothes lie.

Peter, impetuous and curious, plunged through the sepulcher opening and discovered only the burial wrappings which had once enclosed Jesus' body.

7. And the napkin, that was about his head, not lying with the linen clothes, but wrapped together in a place by itself.

As Peter's eyes adjusted to the gloom of the tomb, he noticed that the cloth which had encased the head of Jesus was laid aside in a place by itself. It was neatly folded, as if Jesus or a resurrection angel had taken time to do it. This hinted at the fact that the removal of the body from the sepulcher had been deliberate, rather than hurried.

8. Then went in also, that other disciple, which came first to the sepulcher, and he saw, and believed.

Perhaps shamed by Peter's courage, John now went into the tomb, too. He saw the linen wrappings by themselves and had to admit that the body of Jesus was gone. This seems to be the only meaning to this report that he "believed," referring to the fact that he now believed what Mary and Peter said about the tomb being empty.

D. Departure: 9-10

9. For as yet they knew not the scripture, that he must rise again from the dead.

Mary, John, and Peter were bewildered by the absence of the body of Jesus. The reason for their bewilderment was that they had not understood or acknowledged predictions made by Jesus that He would rise again on the third day after He died. It was obvious that Mary thought His body had been stolen and taken to some unknown place by His opponents (John 20:13), and John and Peter probably thought the same thing. This was the natural assumption to be made, since they were unaware of the fulfillment of Jesus' predictions.

10. Then the disciples went away again unto their own home.

John 19:27 and 20:10 refer to a "home" in Jerusalem which may have been owned by John, or it may have belonged to both John and Peter. Jews who traveled several times a year to religious festivals held in the city would find it convenient to own a place there. On the other hand, the term may have simply referred to temporary quarters which had been rented or to a place offered by relatives or friends for the sake of hospitality.

II. Mary Vindicated: John 20:11-16

A. Inquiry I: 11-13

11. But Mary stood without at the sepulcher weeping: and as she wept, she stooped down, and looked into the sepulcher,

12. And seeth two angels in white sitting, the one at the head, and the other at the feet, where the body of Jesus had lain.

After John and Peter had left the sepulcher, Mary Magdalene remained behind to observe it and to mourn. She may have felt that, as a woman, none of the authorities would bother her. The male disciples seemed to be more vulnerable to arrest, and they stayed in hiding for at least a week (John 19:20 and 26). It appears that John and Peter going to the tomb for a quick inspection was an exception. We do know that Thomas was away from the rest part of the time (John 20:24).

Mary stood outside the sepulcher weeping, but then she decided to stoop down and look inside to see what John and Peter had seen. Imagine her surprise when she beheld two angels dressed in white robes, one sitting at the head of the slab where the body of Jesus had rested and the other sitting at the foot of it. These were probably the same angels mentioned in Luke 24:4-7, who announced that Jesus was alive as He had predicted. Mary apparently had not yet heard this or had heard it and could not seem to believe it.

13. And they say unto her, Woman, why weepest thou? She saith unto them, because they have taken away my Lord, and I know not where they have laid him.

We do not know how much angels can do. Could these angels read Mary's mind and use their question simply to get her talking, or did they really have to get the information by asking her to respond? Whatever the case, they expressed an interest, and Mary probably surmised that they might be able to help her. She frankly told them what she *thought* had happened. Acknowledging Jesus to be her Lord, she *assumed* that His enemies had taken His body away and put it in some unknown place.

Her thinking here illustrates the fact that even followers of Christ can make wrong conclusions. When facts are not readily available, there is a tendency for them to let their imaginations take over and produce false ideas. The angels did not correct Mary. That was left to Jesus to do.

B. Inquiry II: 14-15

14. And when she had thus said, she turned herself back, and saw Jesus standing, and knew not that it was Jesus.

We suspect that Mary felt disappointed in not receiving an enlightening reply from the angels. She turned away from them, evidently heading back out of the sepulcher area and perhaps planning to rejoin the disciples in the city. As she turned, she saw a man standing nearby, but she did not recognize Him to be Jesus.

Jesus' appearance had been cruelly altered before and during His crucifixion. The Scofield paraphrase of Isaiah 52:14 describes it this way—"So marred from the form of man was His aspect that His appearance was not that of a son of man—i.e. not human." If Jesus' normal appearance was restored after His resurrection, Mary should have recognized Him. In the case of Cleopas and his unnamed companion, who met Jesus on the road to Emmaus but did not recognize Him, we are told, "Their eyes were holden that they should not know him" (Luke 24:16). Later "their eyes were opened, and they knew him" (Luke 24:3 1). Mary may have had the same kind of experience with Him.

15a. Jesus saith unto her, Woman, why weepest thou? whom seekest thou?

Jesus' inquiry came in two parts. He first asked Mary the same question that the angels had asked "Why weepest thou?" (John 20:13). He next asked a question which showed that He knew she was searching for someone, "Whom seekest thou?" Mary apparently thought of these as normal questions which would be asked by the caretaker of a cemetery. Mourners would be expected to weep, and they would want to find where their loved ones were buried.

15b. She, supposing him to be the gardener, saith unto him, Sir, if thou have borne him hence, tell me where they have laid him, and I will take him away.

Mary's response may have been affected by her grief, for through her tearful eyes she assumed that Jesus was the gardener. She was seized by the idea that this man might have taken the body of her Lord to a new location in the garden. She rashly offered to take it away, if he would only tell her where it was. Mary was desperately seeking for a corpse which no longer existed.

C. Impact: 16

16. Jesus saith unto her, Mary. She turned herself, and saith unto him, Rabboni; which is to say, Master.

Jesus spoke Mary's name, evidently in a certain tone and manner. She turned to face Him directly, and recognition rushed in upon her. She called Him by the title of Rabbi (Master, Teacher), and she must have made a move to embrace Him, because He told her not to touch Him, for He had not yet ascended to His heavenly Father. We are unsure of the significance of this statement and should be careful not to speculate on it unduly. Jesus told Mary to go and tell His disciples that He was ascending to His Father and their Father, His God and their God (John 20:17)

Mary thus prepared the way for other post-resurrection appearances by Jesus during the forty-day period between His resurrection and His literal ascension to heaven. The one who had once been controlled by seven demons became a central character in the drama regarding the resurrection of her Lord.

Evangelistic Emphasis

We can hear the pain and dismay in Mary Magdalene's voice when she finds no one occupying her Lord's tomb: "They have taken away the Lord... and we know not where they have laid him" (John 20:3). Mary had come to know and love Jesus in life. Now that He was dead, could she not at least console herself by visiting the body—as at a modern viewing or wake?

No; and the void she felt is a poignant reminder of our need for the message of Easter. Not only were Mary and the other disciples robbed of the companionship and presence of the living Christ, but there discovery that even His body was gone plunged them into deeper grief and despair. We who read the story from this side of the resurrection may miss the pathos. We know that in a little while the glory of the resurrected Lord will burst upon the scene. From the *other* side of Easter, however, the absence of Christ in both life and death made Easter Sunday begin like a very bleak and blue Monday.

It is important to remember the disciples' response in order for us to identify with the void Christ's absence creates in a human life. David Woodyard, an unbeliever, wrote of it movingly:

The center of me is always and eternally a terrible pain—a curious wild pain—a searching for something beyond what the world contains, Something transfigured and infinite, the beatific vision—God. *(To Be Human Now)*

Memory Selection

Mary Magdalene came and told the disciples that she had seen the Lord, and that he had spoken these things unto her.
John 20:18

What an honor God granted Mary Magdalene to be the first witness to the risen Lord! (According to the other Gospel writers, it was an honor shared with other women.) Mary was privileged to bring the message that brightened the skies that had been darkened by Golgotha on Good Friday.

Of all the things the Messiah had been expected to do for the faithful, dying was not one of them. Even the Twelve were disillusioned and saddened. Some may have wondered whether, if Jesus was in some sense God, God himself had died! Who would be blessed with the privilege of first announcing the good news, "He lives!"?

The fact that Mary Magdalene and the other women were involved is remarkable from several standpoints. As Jewish women, they were not even regularly expected to receive religious instruction. Furthermore, Mary was a woman who had been "demonized" by seven evil spirits (Luke 8:2). Some even suppose that she was the prostitute who washed Jesus' feet with her tears, and dried them with her hair (Luke 7:37-50).

Isn't that just like God—to put such glorious news in such a very earthen vessel? And it's a continuing grace that those of us today—sinful and inadequate that we are—still are entrusted with the glad task of bearing witness to the empty tomb.

April 11, 1993

Weekday Problems

Ethel's friend Patricia wasn't very interested in church, attending only special days such as Christmas and Easter. Ethel often took Pat's two children to Sunday School, but Pat did not attend. Even in their private conversations, Pat would always change the subject when matters of faith came up.

Then Pat's elderly mother died. Pat was still grieving when she and Elaine met for lunch the week after the funeral. Wanting to reach out, Elaine took the opportunity to urge her friend to take up a more active life in the church. "I know you want to see your mother again someday," she said.

Unfortunately, Pat didn't respond well to this remark. She felt Elaine had caught her at a vulnerable moment, and had used a sensitive issue unfairly. It was a little like a "death bed" approach, with a twist. She and Elaine were never as close after that—and now Pat shows even less interest in church.

*Can you identify with Pat in being hurt by Elaine's comment?

*Have you ever been put off by Christian people trying to interest you in spiritual matters?

*What better approach could Elaine have used in order to offer Pat some spiritual encouragement?

♦♦♦♦♦♦

Superintendent's Sermonette

It has been said, "It is better to have loved and lost than never to have loved at all." Some might argue against this, claiming that it is better not to love than to risk losing it. Consider the situation of Jesus' followers. For centuries Jews had waited for the Messiah to come, lead them out of foreign domination, and give them a golden age. Jesus came to teach, perform miracles, and bring spiritual liberation. Those who believed on Him were optimistic. They heard the loud "Hosannah's" when He made His triumphal entry into Jerusalem, but within a week His glorious advent seemed to collapse His passion began, and He ended up in a borrowed tomb.

Jesus' followers seemed to have loved and then lost their Source of hope. However, God in heaven was still alive. He raised up His Son from the dead. On Sunday morning reports began to circulate that the tomb was open and empty. They thought someone had stolen His body, and they were more depressed. Then His promise to rise on the third day was fulfilled. They could hardly believe it, but they *had* to believe it. He will live forever, and those who belong to Him will live with Him. Let us not be afraid to love Him, for we need never lose Him. Celebrate Easter with confidence and joy!

This Lesson In Your Life

MORE REAL THAN FLESH AND BLOOD

Perhaps Mary's vision was distorted by her tears. Perhaps Jesus' face was drawn and disfigured from lying in the tomb without food—especially after the ordeal of His trial and crucifixion. Or it may be that Christ's resurrected body was already transformed in a way Mary was not expecting. At any rate, we are not surprised when Mary does not recognize the risen Lord (John 20:14). In fact, Mary's experience may prompt us to ask our own questions about life after death.

The Christian hope of a personal after life is reassuring, but mysterious. We understand why people in the church at Corinth asked such questions as: "How are the dead raised up? and with what body do they come?" (1 Cor. 15:35). And many of us seek answers beyond that of the Sunday School lad, who based his confident reply on many a visual aid: "They just use Scotch tape and pull you up!"

We do know that the Christian view of life after death is not precisely the same as the ancient Greek view of immortality. For many Greeks, the body was an embarrassing encumbrance shed at death in favor of a wispy, vaporous spirit that lived on unembodied. In direct conflict with that view, Paul taught that the faithful will be given some sort of new body at the resurrection: "It is sown a natural body; it is raised a spiritual body" (1 Cor. 15:44). More glorious than our present body, it will not have "flesh and blood" (vs. 50) — such time-bound substances, subject to decay, will have no place in eternity. Even the bodies of those who are alive at Christ's Second Coming will be "changed" —touched with a glory that transforms corruptible flesh into incorruptible (vss. 51-53).

Yet, after His own resurrection, Jesus was careful to appear in a body of flesh, at least temporarily, to convince His followers that the resurrection is *real*. Here in John 20 He appears to "doubting Thomas," who is encouraged to touch his Lord's wounds—a gesture that would have been repugnant to non-Christian Greeks. Luke's account goes to even more pains to affirm the fleshly nature of Christ's resurrection body. Jesus says, "Handle me, and see; for a spirit hath not flesh and bones, as ye see me have" (Luke 24:39). Then the Lord even goes to the trouble of *eating* before His disciples, apparently to prove that His bodily processes still worked!

Yet the mystery persists. For all the tangible nature of Christ's resurrected body, He is able to appear through closed doors in order to be with His disciples (John 20:19). And there is the curious state of His body *before* he invites Thomas to touch Him, when He warns Mary, "Touch me not" (vs. 17). Was some wondrous transformation effected between the two incidents?

Speculative minds can go on endlessly with such questions. A wiser course is to allow the firm promise of life after death to be so heartening that it overwhelms our need for specific details. It is enough to look forward to reunion with loved ones who have gone before. It is enough to know that all our ailments, large and small, from cancer to flat feet, bunions to blindness, will no longer plague us. It is enough to envision a world where lion and lamb will lie down together in peace. It is enough to be confident that our questions will be overwhelmed by the living presence of Him who is not only the supreme Answer, but who will also wipe away every tear from our eyes.

Seed Thoughts

1. What explanation of the empty tomb did Jesus' enemies concoct? (See Matt. 28:11-15.)
They fabricated the story that Christ's disciples stole the body while the guards slept.

2. Who is meant by the "other disciple" in John 20:2-4?
Probably John, the author of this Gospel, whose reticence in referring to himself by name has traditionally been taken as literary modesty.

3. Why do you think verses 5-7 go to such remarkable detail in describing the position of the grave clothes?
Perhaps to emphasize the factuality and accuracy of the disciples' report about the empty tomb.

4. Note the frank confession about the disciples in verse 9. Why do you think the disciples did not understand the scriptures about Christ's resurrection?
Perhaps their expectations of a Messiah simply did not include His death, much less His resurrection.

5. What emotions did the disciples experience at the death and resurrection of Christ?
The disciples experienced fear, amazement and disbelief, then gladness and faith; and it's common to find the same reactions among modern people.

(PLEASE TURN PAGE)

---

1. What explanation of the empty tomb did Jesus' enemies concoct? (See Matt. 28:11-15.)

2. Who is meant by the "other disciple" in John 20:2-4?

3. Why do you think verses 5-7 go to such remarkable detail in describing the position of the grave clothes?

4. Note the frank confession about the disciples in verse 9. Why do you think the disciples did not understand the scriptures about Christ's resurrection?

5. What emotions did the disciples experience at the death and resurrection of Christ?

6. Have you ever had the glad task of sharing good news that produced similar reactions to Mary's announcement?

7. What possible excuse did "doubting Thomas" have for being skeptical of Christ's resurrection? (see John 20:24-25.)

8. Do you find yourself with similar questions or doubts?

9. Will we recognize our loved ones in the general resurrection?

10. Do you think spring, and any other elements in nature, point to the reality of the Christian hope?

(SEED THOUGHTS--Cont'd)

They fabricated the story that Christ's disciples stole the body while the guards slept.

Probably John, the author of this Gospel, whose reticence in referring to himself by name has traditionally been taken as literary modesty.

Perhaps to emphasize the factuality and accuracy of the disciples' report about the empty tomb.

Perhaps their expectations of a Messiah simply did not include His death, much less His resurrection.

The disciples experienced fear, amazement and disbelief, then gladness and faith; and it's common to find the same reactions among modern people.

(Encourage the group to share freely, drawing out the joy and privilege of such responsibility.)

He was not present when Jesus appeared to the other disciples.

(Encourage open sharing, accepting all statements without judgmentalism, while being alert to opportunities to affirm the biblical witness.)

Almost certainly. Jesus was fully recognizable. Paul affirms the reality of a "spiritual body" (see "This Lesson in Your Life").

Nature may *illustrate* the resurrection, but our hope lies more in the apostolic witness (especially the Gospels) than in nature.

---

6. Have you ever had the glad task of sharing good news that produced similar reactions to Mary's announcement?
(Encourage the group to share freely, drawing out the joy and privilege of such responsibility.)

7. What possible excuse did "doubting Thomas" have for being skeptical of Christ's resurrection? (see John 20:24-25.)
He was not present when Jesus appeared to the other disciples.

8. Do you find yourself with similar questions or doubts?
(Encourage open sharing, accepting all statements without judgmentalism, while being alert to opportunities to affirm the biblical witness.)

9. Will we recognize our loved ones in the general resurrection?
Almost certainly. Jesus was fully recognizable. Paul affirms the reality of a "spiritual body" (see "This Lesson in Your Life").

10. Do you think spring, and any other elements in nature, point to the reality of the Christian hope?
Nature may *illustrate* the resurrection, but our hope lies more in the apostolic witness (especially the Gospels) than in nature.

April 18, 1993

Peter's Love Not Enough

To Love Is To Serve

John 21

12 Jesus saith unto them, Come and dine. And none of the disciples durst ask him, Who art thou? knowing that it was the Lord.
13 Jesus then cometh, and taketh bread, and giveth them, and fish likewise.
14 This is now the third time that Jesus shewed himself to his disciples, after that he was risen from the dead.
15 So when they had dined, Jesus saith to Simon Peter, Simon, son of Jo'-nas, lovest thou me more than these? He saith unto him, Yea, Lord; thou knowest that I love thee. He saith unto him, Feed my lambs.
16 He saith to him again the second time, Simon, son of Jo'-nas, lovest thou me? He saith unto him, Yea, Lord thou knowest that I love thee. He saith unto him, Feed my lambs.
17 He saith unto him the third time, Simon, son of Jo'-nas, lovest thou me? Peter was grieved because he said unto him the third time, Lovest thou me? And he said unto him, Lord, thou knowest all things; thou knowest that I love thee. Jesus saith unto him, Feed my sheep.
18 Verily, verily, I say unto thee When thou wast young, thou girdedst thyself, and walkedst whither thou wouldest: but when thou shalt be old, thou shalt stretch forth thy hands, and another shall gird thee, and carry thee whither thou wouldest not.
19 This spake he, signifying by what death he should glorify God. And when he had spoken this, he saith unto him, Follow me.
20 Then Peter, turning about, seeth the disciple whom Jesus loved following; which also leaned on his breast at supper, and said, Lord, which is he that betrayeth thee?
21 Peter seeing him saith to Jesus, Lord, and what shall this man do?
22 Jesus saith unto him, If I will that he tarry till I come, what is that to thee? follow thou me.

◆◆◆◆◆◆

◀ **Memory Selection**
John 21:17

◀ **Devotional Reading**
John 21:1-14

◀ **Background Scripture**
John 21

◀ **Printed Scripture**
John 21:12-22

TO LOVE IS TO SERVE

Teacher's Target

We do not know where Jesus was nor what He was doing all of the time during the forty-day post-resurrection period before His ascension. He did make several contacts with individuals and groups during this time. When Peter said that he was going fishing on the Sea of Galilee, some others went with him. They fished all night and caught nothing. Jesus appeared on the shore, although these disciples did not know it was He at first. Jesus told them to cast their net on the right side of the ship to get a good catch, and the results were unusual. John recognized Jesus, and Peter cast himself into the water to go toward Him.

Help your students to understand what Jesus was teaching His disciples when they dined on the fish that morning and how it pertained particularly to Peter and John. Peter, who had denied Jesus three times at the enemy campfire, now was questioned three times by Jesus. He was also given a glimpse of the circumstances of his eventual death. He was told not to concern himself with John's destiny.

Lesson Introduction

An angel told women at the tomb on Sunday morning, "Go quickly, and tell his disciples that he is risen from the dead; and, behold, he goeth before you into Galilee; there shall ye see him" (Matt. 28:7). Jesus made two important appearances to followers in Galilee.

John 21:4-23 describes Jesus' appearance to a few disciples on the shore of the Sea of Galilee, and our lesson text is taken from this passage. He dealt primarily with Peter and John, but the others learned from what He said to them.

Matthew 28:16-20 describes Jesus' appearance to all eleven remaining disciples on a mountain somewhere in Galilee. It was there that He gave them His great comission to evangelize and educate the world.

Both incidents emphasize the fact that love for *Christ* should be the motive for serving Him.

Teaching Outline

I. Dining: John 21:12-14
   A. Refreshment: 12-13
   B. Record: 14
II. Declaring: John 21:15-17
   A. Question I: 15
   B. Question II: 16
   C. Question III: 17
III. Dying: John 21:18-22
   A. Destiny: 18-19a
   B. Discussion: 19b-22

Daily Bible Readings

Mon. Jesus Appears Again
John 21:1-8
Tue. Jesus Dines with the Disciples
John 21:9-14
Wed. Jesus Challenges Peter
John 21:15-19
Thu. Who Will Remain
John 21:20-25
Fri. Wait for the Spirit
Acts 1:1-5
Sat. Jesus Is Lifted Up
Acts 1:6-11
Sun. Judas Is Replaced
Acts 1:12-16, 21-26

April 18, 1993

VERSE BY VERSE

I. Dining: John 21:12-14

A. Refreshment: 12-13

12a. Jesus saith unto them, Come and dine.

The wording here suggests breakfast. The New International Version reads, "Jesus said to them, 'Come and have breakfast.'" This would be in line with the fact that these disciples had fished all night and caught nothing, and it was morning when Jesus stood on the shore (John 21:3-4).

12b. And none of the disciples durst ask him, Who art thou? knowing that it was the Lord.

None of the disciples there (Peter, Thomas, Nathanael, James, John, and two unnamed men—John 21:2) dared ask Jesus Who He was, for they were convinced that He was the Lord. They realized that He would be offended if they asked His identity, even though He may have appeared somewhat different from the way He had looked previously.

13. Jesus then cometh, and taketh bread, and giveth them, and fish likewise.

Jesus had already prepared a small fire on the sand and had laid fish to cook on it. He also had bread (John 21:9). He came to the disciples and invited them to partake of the food. He still took on the role of a servant with them, even as He had done in washing their feet in the upper room.

B. Record: 14

14. This is now the third time that Jesus shewed himself to his disciples, after that he was risen from the dead.

Just for the record, the first time had been on the evening of the resurrection Sunday. He had appeared in the room where the disciples were hiding. He had identified Himself by showing them wounds in His hands and side. He bestowed peace upon them and breathed on them to receive the Holy Spirit in some special manner (John 20:19-23). The second time He had appeared to them had been "after eight days" and evidently in the same place. He had convinced doubting Thomas that He was indeed alive again (John 20:24-29).

We are not told how much time had elapsed between Jesus' second and third appearances to His disciples, but it must have been enough days for them to travel from Jerusalem up to the Sea of Galilee.

The disciples had toiled all night and caught no fish. They harvested one hundred and fifty-three fish after obeying Jesus' command to let down their net on the right side of the ship (John 21:6 and 11). It is suggested that Jesus may have been seeking to remind them that they were supposed to be fishing for men (Matt. 4:18-20).

Jesus now turned His attention to Simon Peter, but the metaphor changed from that of catching fish to feeding sheep. The principle remained the same.

II. Declaring: John 21:15-17

A. Question I: 15

15a. So when they had dined, Jesus saith to Simon Peter, Simon, son of Jonas, lovest thou me more than these?

On the night on which Jesus was betrayed by Judas Iscariot, Jesus had told His disciples that they would all be offended because of Him. Peter had said, "Though all men shall be offended because of thee, yet will I never be offended. Jesus said unto him, Verily I say unto thee, That this night, before the cock crow, thou shalt deny me thrice. Peter said unto him, Though I should die with thee, yet will I not deny thee. Likewise also said all the disciples" (Matt. 26:33-35). The remainder of Matthew 26 tells how Peter denied Jesus and that "all the disciples forsook him and fled" (Matt. 26:56).

With that background in mind, we now see Jesus concentrating on Peter, the one who had boasted of loving Jesus more than all others and even being willing to die with Him. He had failed miserably to back up his boasting with supportive action. Jesus wanted to know if Peter still thought that he loved Him more than the other disciples.

15b. He saith unto him, Yea, Lord; thou knowest that I love thee.

Peter responded by telling Jesus that He knew that he loved Him. He used the Greek word *phileo*, which referred to fondness of a lesser, human type of emotion. Perhaps Peter was afraid to use the stronger term of *agape* because he had failed Jesus during His time of trial.

15c. He saith unto him, Feed my lambs.

On the basis of Peter's admission, Jesus turned his attention toward service. He told Peter to feed His lambs, perhaps referring to children or to new converts in this instance.

B. Question II: 16

16a. He saith to him again the second time, Simon, son of Jonas, lovest thou me?

Note that this time Jesus did not ask Peter if he loved Him "more than these" (John 21:15). He simply asked him if he loved Him, making no comparison with how others might love Him.

16b. He saith unto him, Yea, Lord; thou knowest that I love thee.

Peter's answer to the second question was identical with that given to the first question.

16c. He saith unto him, Feed my sheep.

Note that the term changed here from "lambs" to "sheep." Perhaps Jesus was referring here to young people or to partially-trained converts.

C. Question III: 17

17a. He saith unto him the third time, Simon, son of Jonas, lovest thou me?

This time Jesus switched to the word *phileo* when asking Peter if he loved Him, but we do not know why.

17b. Peter was grieved because he said unto him the third time, Lovest thou me? And he said unto him, Lord, thou knowest all things; thou knowest that I love thee.

Peter was getting frustrated with Jesus repetition of the same question, especially when he believed that Jesus already knew his heart and mind. He expressed his exasperation. However, having denied Jesus three times, he deserved to be made to state his love for Him three times.

17c. Jesus saith unto him, Feed my sheep.

This may have referred to adults or to welltrained converts. Peter and the other faithful disciples would be expected to carry on Christ's work after He ascended back up to heaven. Love for Him would have to be their compelling motivation for service in His name. They would be required to work with children, young people, and adults. They would have to deal with brand-new converts, partially-trained converts, and well-trained converts as the church developed and grew.

III. Dying: John 21:18-22

A. Destiny: 18-19a

18a Verily, verily, I say unto thee, When thou wast young, thou girdest thyself, and walkedst whither thou wouldest: ...

Jesus was apparently referring here to the fact that when Peter was young he could tie his belt or sash around his waist to hold his robe in place, and he could walk wherever he wanted to go. References to Peter as a fisherman suggest that he was a strong and able man. Even on this day, he was capable of swimming about three hundred feet from the boat to shore and help pull in a net loaded with one hundred and fifty-three fish when the boat came in (John 21:6-11).

18b. ...but when thou shalt be old, thou shalt stretch forth thy hands, and another shall gird thee, and carry thee whither thou wouldest not.

Jesus predicted that when Peter grew older he would lose control of his own movements. Someone else would belt him into his robe, perhaps because his own hands were bound. Stretching forth his hands when unbound may refer to him being crucified on a cross. Tradition says that he was crucified upside down at his own request so that his crucifixion would be different from that of Jesus.

19a. This spake he, signifying by what death he should glorify God.

It was Jesus who foretold Peter's death. Peter may have taken comfort in the fact that his death was going to bring glory to God. He knew that he was going to be a martyr. This was the man who impetuously declared his intention of dying with Jesus, if that was required, but who shamefully deserted Him and denied Him three times during His time of betrayal, arrest, and judgment. Now Peter knew that Jesus had forgiven him. He knew that he would serve the Master for the rest of his life. He knew that he would die for God's glory.

B. Discussion: 19b-22

19b. And when he had spoken this, he saith unto him, Follow me.

When Jesus had faced suffering and death, Peter had insisted on facing it with Him, but Jesus had said, "Whither I go, thou canst not follow me now; but thou shalt follow me afterwards" (John 13:36). Jesus was now at the point where the reinstated Peter was told to follow Him in service, implying that Peter was to do this even after Jesus ascended to heaven.

20. Then Peter, turning about, seeth the disciple whom Jesus loved following; which also leaned on his breast at supper, and said, Lord, which is he that betrayeth thee?

As Peter turned, he noticed that John was following him and Jesus. John never referred to himself by name in his gospel. Here he described himself as the disciple whom Jesus loved dearly. He also identified himself as the one who leaned on Jesus' chest during the last supper in the upper room. It was at that time that Peter had asked John to find out from Jesus the identity of His betrayer (John 13:23-25). We are not told why John was following Jesus and Peter by the Sea of Galilee during the post-resurrection appearance, but perhaps he was curious about what they were discussing.

21. Peter seeing him saith to Jesus, Lord, and what shall this man do?

Having heard his own death predicted, Peter now wanted Jesus to tell him what was going to happen to John. He was no doubt curious, and he may also have been motived by concern for his friend.

22. Jesus saith unto him, If I will that he tarry till I come, what is that to thee? follow thou me.

We do not know if Jesus appreciated the curiosity of Peter or his concern for John, but He did rebuke him for asking the question. In effect, He told Peter that John's destiny was none of his business. The thing Peter was supposed to concentrate upon was his responsibility to follow Jesus in devoted service for the rest of his life.

Jesus had chosen to ask a hypothetical question stating the possibility that He might want John to tarry (stay alive) until He came back again. This was misinterpreted by some of the brethren to suggest that John would never die. John set the record straight as he finished writing his gospel toward the end of the first century of the Christian era by stating, "Jesus said not unto him [Peter], He [John] shall not die; but, If I will that he tarry till I come, what is that to thee ?" (John 21:23).

John lived many more years. He was exiled to the Isle of Patmos by the Roman emperor, and it is thought that it was here he wrote his gospel, three epistles, and the book of Revelation. Tradition claims that he was the only apostle to die a natural death rather than a martyr's death.

Evangelistic Emphasis

Christians are nourished on Easter faith. Our souls are fed by Scripture's inspirational pictures of Christ's triumph over death. Christians are warmed by Easter's hope. The cold winter of doubt gives way to the confidence that because He lives, we will live with him.

Now what? It's not uncommon for us to experience a let down after the build-up and excitement of such holidays (Holy Days) as Christmas and Easter. The 21st chapter of John has an antidote: *share the nourishment and the warmth with others.*

One of Jesus' first post-resurrection acts was to share a meal with His disciples (John 20:13). The account of His appearance to the two disciples on the road to Emmaus includes an evening meal, when "he was made known of them in breaking of bread" (Luke 24:35). Only a few days earlier, they had shared the Passover feast together. In fact, it is remarkable how often the Gospels portray Christ and his disciples eating together. More than any other Gospel, John focuses on Jesus' activities on and near Jewish feast days. The point seems to be that apart from the temporary sadness of Good Friday, sharing with Christ—especially in His resurrection—is a time of filling and feasting.

In turn, after assessing the genuineness of Simon Peter's love, Christ urges him now to share the filling he had experienced: "Feed my lambs" (vs. 15). It's as though Jesus is saying, "Now that you have been fed on resurrection faith, look about you at others who are hungry for it. Now that you have warmed yourselves at resurrection fires, share the warmth with others who long to come in from the cold."

Memory Selection

Lovest thou me?... Feed my sheep.
John 21:17

The train of Jesus' thought moves abruptly in this passage from loving Jesus to tending his flock. The "leap" is repeated again and again as Christ tests Peter (John 21:15-17). The connection may not be immediately apparent. Isn't the call of Christ to love *him*? Where do "the sheep" come in?

Peter had been in Christ's "school" for nearly three years. He was among the Twelve who were graced with a special measure of the Spirit and given a special commission. Now Jesus points out that all this had not just been to draw Peter close to Jesus; he was now to prove that intimacy, that love, by turning and tending to others.

As has often been said, Christianity is *personal*, but not *private*. Salvation does not just consist of individuals plucked one by one from unbelief; Jesus is the Savior of "the body," the church (Eph. 1:22-23; 5:23). There is a social and relational dimension to the faith. We are saved to serve.

In this light we can see that the mandate to Peter is broader than any "official" pastoral ordination Jesus may have had in mind for him and subsequent pastors. All Christians who have similarly schooled themselves at the feet of the Good Shepherd have opportunities to share what they have learned.

April 18, 1993

Weekday Problems

"Do you love me?" Jesus asked Peter—not once, but three times. We may wonder whether Peter felt that his word wasn't good enough the first time. Did Christ's persistence make Peter feel he wasn't trusted...that Jesus hadn't forgiven him for denying that he knew Him...or that from now on he would have to continually prove himself, over and over again? Perhaps it was only Peter's deep devotion to his Lord that kept him from stomping off indignantly, saying, "You don't trust me, so who needs this relationship?"

Without Christ's divine insight into people's true feelings, and the depth of their commitment, we can sometimes alienate others by skeptical attitudes.

*Do you know of a business relationship where an atmosphere of mistrust was created by continual questioning, suspicion or even "snooping"?

*Does this atmosphere ever damage a marriage relationship?

*Does our society in general seem to require that some people "prove" themselves more than others? If so, what might be done about it?

*Is skepticism about people's true motives, feelings and commitment sometimes warranted?

*What reaction can suspicion sometimes generate?

♦♦♦♦♦♦

Superintendent's Sermonette

Two developments among twentieth-century evangelical Christians have caused considerable trouble. "Easy believism" has featured a superficial appeal to sinners to believe on Christ and be saved in order to reap positive benefits. "Repent and rebound" teaching has promoted a flippant and shallow treatment of sin. Both have ignored the scars created by sin or the need for making restitution whenever that is appropriate. God does forgive, pardon, and restore those who confess their sins, but there are residual effects which remain and need to be treated with humble concern.

Peter was a robust, energetic, impetuous fisherman who left his nets at the Sea of Galilee to become an outspoken disciple of Jesus. Although he offered to die with Jesus, he found himself denying Him three times when He was taken into judgment.

In our text, we see Peter back fishing with other disciples at the Sea of Galilee. Jesus appeared, and He asked Peter three times if he loved Him. When Peter assured Him that he did, Jesus told him to feed His lambs and sheep. Only deep love would make Peter a devoted servant for the rest of his life. Let us also put our failures behind us, and let us be motivated by loving service for Christ.

This Lesson In Your Life

Jesus must have been deeply hurt when Peter denied Him — *three times*— even though He had predicted as much (John 13:38). And Peter—we can imagine how disappointed he was in himself. After affirming with such bravado that he would even lay down his life for his Lord (13:37), he buckled under pressure—three times, underlining his lies and disloyalty with curses. It was a failure so blatant and painful that it wrung from this strong fisherman tears of regret (see Mk. 14:66-72).

Peter was faced not only with total failure in his career as a witness for Christ. Now he had to face the Lord he had denied, as well. And His probing, piercing questions! Three denials balanced by three questions, all alike— *Do you love me?*

Peter might well have expected to receive three stinging rebukes—verbal lashes commensurate with his failure of nerve. But, wonder of wonders, the Master makes a remarkable substitution for any rebuke Peter had earned. Christ gives Peter a renewed commission instead: "*Feed mv sheep*"! And the lofty responsibility is repeated three times, too, as though to balance precisely Peter's three denials.

Peter had been given an object lesson on the very issue he had asked Jesus about much earlier. "How oft shall my brother sin against me, and I forgive him? till seven times?" Peter had asked. Now, he was experiencing the meaning of Christ's figurative answer: "Seventy times seven," or an unlimited number of times (Matt. 18:21).

How can those of us with less than divine insight into people make practical application of the principles in this scene? It's not just that people like Peter need to be given new starts, new opportunities to redeem their past failures. Families, businesses, schools—society in general—can benefit from the productivity and improved attitudes that forgiven people, with renewed self-concepts, bring to life and relationships.

The story of a teenage girl who was abusing drugs will be familiar ground to many modern families. After discovering her problem, her parents went with her to counseling to get at the root of the problem. She promised to quit, but was soon into the drug scene again. This time she dropped out of school and left home in order to pursue her lifestyle in "freedom." She was arrested and jailed. Her parents let her stay there overnight as a stern lesson, then bailed her out and allowed her to return home, forgiven. Within three days she returned to her life of drug abuse—and wound up in jail again.

Having violated parole, she faced a stern judge with her father, who had signed for her bail. "Will you renew your daughter's bail?" the judge asked. Having realized he was only "enabling" his daughter's drug abuse, the father knew what he had to do. Taking a deep breath, he said, "No"—knowing that, sure enough, with bail denied, the daughter would be jailed again—this time for a longer sentence.

The father went through some anguish at not having "given my daughter one more chance." He wondered whether he had been forgiving of his daughter as Christ was of Peter. But later, when his firmness helped his daughter reject her self-destructive lifestyle, he felt he had made the right choice, painful though it was. Some situations such as this seem to call for the wisdom that says we can forgive a thief without putting him in charge of the cash register. Other situations challenge us to do as Christ did—to help people who have failed to imagine themselves as faithful, and to live up to the dream. Deciding which course is better calls not only for the forgiving spirit of Christ, but for the wisdom of Solomon as well.

Seed Thoughts

1. What significance for the disciples' future work is there in Jesus' appearing to them while they were fishing? (See Mk. 1:16-17.)

It was while fishing that Christ had called some to be "fishers of men." Now that he had arisen from the grave, their "bait" (message) was completed.

2. Why do you think the disciples did not recognize Jesus, as indicated in John 21:4?

Perhaps he was emaciated after his ordeal; perhaps simply because of the distance; or perhaps "their eyes were holden."

3. What might the disciples have been reminded of when Jesus broke bread with them in John 21:13?

Perhaps of the Last Supper, and Christ's promise that he would share it with them again in the kingdom.

4. What are the chief responsibilities of a shepherd, and why is this a good symbol of caring for God's people?

As a shepherd guides the sheep to good pasture, water and shelter, so God's people need guidance.

5. Do you think most people rise to the occasion when given another chance after failing?

(Encourage open sharing. Be sensitive to group members who may share intense personal experiences such as the recovery of a failing marriage.)

---

1. What significance for the disciples' future work is there in Jesus' appearing to them while they were fishing? (See Mk. 1:16-17.)

2. Why do you think the disciples did not recognize Jesus, as indicated in John 21:4?

3. What might the disciples have been reminded of when Jesus broke bread with them in John 21:13?

4. What are the chief responsibilities of a shepherd, and why is this a good symbol of caring for God's people?

5. Do you think most people rise to the occasion when given another chance after failing?

6. How can Jesus' command, "Feed my sheep," be carried out today?

7. How does Jesus' prediction of Peter's death in 21:18-19 seem to have come true? (See I Pet. 5:1.)

8. In what way can a death "glorify God," as indicated in verse 19?

9. What note does John add that indicates his Gospel does not tell us every detail about Jesus' life?

(PLEASE TURN PAGE)

(SEED THOUGHTS--Cont'd)

It was while fishing that Christ had called some to be "fishers of men." Now that he had arisen from the grave, their "bait" (message) was completed.

Perhaps he was emaciated after his ordeal; perhaps simply because of the distance; or perhaps "their eyes were holden."

Perhaps of the Last Supper, and Christ's promise that he would share it with them again in the kingdom.

As a shepherd guides the sheep to good pasture, water and shelter, so God's people need guidance.

(Encourage open sharing. Be sensitive to group members who may share intense personal experiences such as the recovery of a failing marriage.)

Through the preaching, teaching and counseling programs of the church. Through lay witness, mentoring, peer counseling and other works of ministry and outreach.

Peter refers to his sufferings in 1 Peter (possibly in Rome, often called "Babylon" by the early Christians—see vs. 13).

By giving one's life for the faith; by patient endurance of suffering without giving up the faith.

He adds that the world "could not contain" the books that could be written about Christ.

6. How can Jesus' command, "Feed my sheep," be carried out today?
Through the preaching, teaching and counseling programs of the church. Through lay witness, mentoring, peer counseling and other works of ministry and outreach.

7. How does Jesus' prediction of Peter's death in 21:18-19 seem to have come true? (See I Pet. 5:1.)
Peter refers to his sufferings in 1 Peter (possibly in Rome, often called "Babylon" by the early Christians—see vs. 13).

8. In what way can a death "glorify God," as indicated in verse 19?
By giving one's life for the faith; by patient endurance of suffering without giving up the faith.

9. What note does John add that indicates his Gospel does not tell us every detail about Jesus' life?
He adds that the world "could not contain" the books that could be written about Christ.

April 25, 1993

The Bread of Life

JOHN 6

35 And Jesus said unto them, I am the bread of life: he that cometh to me shall never hunger; and he that believeth in me shall never thirst.
36 But I said unto you, That ye also have seen me, and believe not.
37 All that the Father giveth me shall come to me; and him that cometh to me I will in no wise cast out.
38 For I came down from heaven, not to do mine own will, but the will of him that sent me.
39 And this is the Father's will which hath sent me, that of all which he hath given me I should lose nothing, but should raise it up again at the last day.
40 And this is the will of him that sent me, that every one which seeth the Son, and believeth in him, may have everlasting life: and I will raise him up at the last day.
41 The Jews then murmured at him, because he said, I am the bread which came down from heaven.
42 And they said, Is not this Jesus, the son of Joseph, whose father and mother we know? how is it then that he saith, I came down from heaven?
43 Jesus therefore answered and said unto them, Murmur not among yourselves.
44 No man can come to me, except the Father which hath sent me draw him: and I will raise him up at the last day.
45 It is written in the prophets, AND THEY SHALL BE ALL TAUGHT OF GOD. Every man therefore that hath heard, and hath learned of the Father, cometh unto me,
46 Not that any man hath seen the Father, save he which is of God, he hath seen the Father.
47 Verily, verily, I say unto you, He that believeth on me hath everlasting life.
48 I am that bread of life.
49 Your fathers did eat man'-na in the wilderness, and are dead.
50 This is the bread which cometh down from heaven, that a man may eat thereof, and not die.
51 I am the living bread which came down from heaven: if any man eat of this bread, he shall live for ever: and the bread that I will give is my flesh, which I will give for the life of the world.

◆◆◆◆◆◆

◀ **Memory Selection**
John 6:51

◀ **Devotional Reading**
John 6:22-29

◀ **Background Scripture**
John 6

◀ **Printed Scripture**
John 6:35-51

THE BREAD OF LIFE

Teacher's Target

People look to government leaders to help them protect and preserve what they have and to shield them from enemies, domestic or foreign, who would try to take it away from them. Unfortunately, those government leaders in some countries become enemies of the people and take what they have.

Jews had lived under foreign domination for a long time. Some of their own leaders had oppressed them, too. When Jesus came on the scene with His teaching and miracles, multitudes began to follow Him. Some wanted to make Him their Bread-King, especially after He fed five thousand with a boy's lunch of five barley loaves and two small fish.

~~Help your students to see how~~ Jesus used this situation to present Himself as the Bread of life. He did not want to be a literal Bread-King. He wanted to provide spiritual nourishment for people. Some were willing to accept Him in this role, while others chose to reject Him. We may expect the same kinds of reactions to Him today.

Lesson Introduction

John designed his gospel so that it featured certain discourses and miracles of Jesus, which he hoped would cause people to believe in Him as the Son of God and find eternal life in Him (John 20: 30-31). Chapter six illustrates this. Verses 1-14 describe Jesus feeding five thousand on a hill overlooking the Sea of Galilee. Verses 15-21 present another miracle, for that night He came walking to a boat carrying His disciples across the sea. He not only walked on water, but the boat immediately arrived at its destination once He came aboard.

The next day the people hurried around by land to Capernaum. Verses 22-71 tell about this and record His discourse on the Bread of life, along with reactions to it. When He called for people to eat His flesh and drink His blood, many misunderstood His meaning and walked no more with Him. Our text is taken from the middle of this long section. People wanted a sign, such as manna, but Jesus tried to help them see that He was the Bread of life and could satisfy spiritual hunger.

Teaching Outline

I. Jesus' Analogy: John 6:35-40
   A. Father's gift: 35-37
   B. Father's will: 38-40
II. Jesus' Complaint: John 6:41-46
   A. Rejection: 41-42
   B. Revelation: 43-44
   C. Reference: 45-46
III. Jesus' Invitation: John 6:47-51
   A. Salvation: 47-48
   B. Symbol: 49
   C. Sacrifice: 50-51

Daily Bible Readings

Mon. Feeding the Five Thousand
John 6:1-14
Tue. Jesus Calms the Storm
John 6:15-21
Wed. Doing the Works of God
John 6:22-29
Thu. The Bread from Heaven
John 6:30-40
Fri. Jesus, the Source of Life
John 6:41-50
Sat. Spirit and Life
John 6:51-65
Sun. The Holy One of God
John 6:66-71

April 25, 1993

VERSE BY VERSE

I. Jesus' Analogy: John 6:35-40

A. Father's gift: 35—37

35. And Jesus said unto them, I am the bread of life: he that cometh to me shall never hunger; and he that believeth on me shall never thirst.

Jesus had already presented Himself as the Water of life (John 4:10-14; cf. John 7:37-39). He had spoken about bread from heaven— "The bread of God is he which cometh down from heaven, and giveth life unto the world. Then said they unto him, Lord, evermore give us this bread" (John 6:33-34).

Jesus now presented Himself as being both the Bread of life and the Water of life. Those who came to Him for spiritual nourishment and refreshment would never hunger or thirst. He had to do what He could to help the people understand that He was talking in spiritual, not literal, terms. This is important, because people both then and now misunderstood His teaching regarding "partaking" of His flesh and blood. The latter part of John 6 makes it very clear that partaking of the Lord's supper (communion) is symbolic, not literal, in its meaning and application.

36. But I said unto you, That ye also have seen me, and believe not.

The problem with some of the people, as Jesus saw it, was that they had been told before about Him, but they had not believed on Him even though they had seen Him. Their unbelief had prevented them from accepting Him as God's sign from heaven (John 6:30).

37. All that the Father giveth me shall come to me; and him that cometh to me I will in no wise cast out.

Jesus considered believers to be gifts from God. Note how this is supported by His own words in John 17:6—"I have manifested thy name unto the men which thou gavest me out of the world: thine they were, and thou gavest them [to] me; and they have kept thy word." Jesus was so confident that these people would be drawn to Him that He stated His intention never to cast them away from Himself.

B. Father's will: 38-40

38. For I came down from heaven, not to do mine own will, but the will of him that sent me.

Jesus made it clear here that there was no difference between His Own will and the will of His heavenly Father. He was in full accord with God's master plan of redemption, even though it meant much humiliation and suffering for Himself as He moved ever closer to the cross of atonement.

39. And this is the Father's will which hath sent me, that of all which he hath given me I should lose nothing, but should raise it up again at the last day.

Jesus was making the point that He was acting according to God's will, something not accepted by cynics in His audience. He was claiming to be the Christ (Anointed One sent by God). He was stating that God had given Him people as believers. He was predicting that He would lose none of those who sincerely followed Him and put their trust in Him. He was foretelling that He would raise them up from the dead in the end time.

40. And this is the will of him that sent me, that every one which seeth the Son, and believeth on him, may have everlasting life: and I will raise him up at the last day.

This verse says essentially the same things as verse 39 says, but Jesus made it more individualistic. He said it was God's will that every person who meets the Son and believes on Him as Savior and Lord will have eternal life, even though this requires him to be raised from the dead in the last day. This was a message of comfort and hope to believers, but it was a message to be debated by unbelievers, as we now see.

II. Jesus' Complaint: John 6:41-46

A. Rejection: 41-42

41. The Jews then murmured at him, because he said, I am the bread which came down from heaven.

Jewish religious leaders in the audience disagreed with Jesus' assessment of Himself. They murmured against Him for saying that He was the Bread sent down from heaven to sustain believers. They probably considered this statement to be blasphemous. How did He dare to be the Christ, the Messiah?

42. And they said, Is not this Jesus, the son of Joseph, whose father and mother we know? how is it then that he saith, I came down from heaven?

The Jewish leaders rejected Jesus' claim to be the divine Son of God because they felt that they knew His earthly origin, and that blinded them to His heavenly origin. They knew Joseph and assumed that he was Jesus' father. We know that Joseph was only the legal, not the natural, father of Jesus (Matt. 1:18-25). We know that Mary was Jesus' natural mother, although she became pregnant with Him by supernatural means when the Holy Spirit overshadowed her as a virgin (Luke 1:34-35). Despite all of the unusual phenomena which had surrounded the birth of Jesus, the Jews evidently thought of Him as a normal human being all of the time He was growing up in Nazareth. Even those who came to hear Him teach and perform miracles often thought that He was only a prophet blessed by God.

B. Revelation: 43-44

43. Jesus therefore answered and said unto them, Murmur not among yourselves.

This suggests that the Jewish leaders had been huddling together and murmuring among themselves rather than doing it openly where others could hear it. We are not told if He knew what they were saying because He had superior hearing or because He used divine discernment, but it could have been either. He confronted them to let them know that He knew what they were saying.

44. No man can come to me, except the Father which hath sent me draw him: and I will raise him up at the last day.

Jesus had already said this before (John 6:37), and He would repeat it again later (John 6:65) Repetition underscored its importance. Jesus was determined to make the point that God forced no one to believe in His Son. Each was drawn by God by faith to a place of commitment. The latter part about being raised up at the last day was repeated from verses 39 and 40.

C. Reference: 45-46

45. It is written in the prophets, And they shall be all taught of God. Every man therefore that hath heard, and hath learned of the Father, cometh unto me.

This apparently referred to the first part of Isaiah 54:13— "And all thy children shall be taught of the Lord." Jesus applied this to His current situation by claiming that every person who had heard and learned of the Father (or had been taught by the Father) gravitated toward His Son. Jesus later said to His disciples, "Therefore said I unto you, that no man can come unto me, except it were given unto him of my Father" (John 6:65).

46. Not that any man hath seen the Father, save he which is of God, he hath seen the Father.

This seems contradictory until we realize that Jesus was speaking about Himself. God is a Spirit Who cannot be seen (John 4:24), but Jesus was with His Father from eternity past, and He came to reveal Him to men (John 1:18). He was unique.

III. Jesus' Invitation: John 6:47-51

A. Salvation: 47-48

47. Verily, verily, I say unto you, He that believeth in me hath everlasting life.

Compare this with what was said in verse 40— "Every one which seeth the Son, and believeth on him, may have everlasting life." Jesus merely repeated this central truth as he completed this segment of His discourse. Salvation was available to those who believed in Him as Savior. He was evidently looking ahead to His atoning death at Calvary and the redemption it would provide.

48. I am that bread of life.

Jesus returned to His previous analogy of Himself being the Bread of life, the Source of spiritual nourishment leading to eternal life. It was another way for Him to declare Himself to be the Savior of all who believed on Him. It also set the tone for the remainder of His discourse.

B. Symbol: 49

49. Your fathers did eat manna in the wilderness, and are dead.

When the Jews had told Jesus that their ancestors had eaten manna in the desert, they had accepted it as a sign or symbol from heaven (John 6:31). Jesus now came back to that subject to lay it to rest. He simply said that the Jews' ancestors had eaten manna in the wilderness but were all dead.

C. Sacrifice: 50-51

50. This is the bread which cometh down fron heaven, that a man may eat thereof, and not die.

Those who ate literal manna were now dead. Those who ate (partook) of the Bread of life sent down from heaven in the form of Jesus could avoid eternal death and find eternal life.

51a. I am the living bread which came down from heaven: if any man eat of this bread, he shall live for ever: ...

This repeats what was said according to verse 50, except that Jesus declared Himself to be "the living bread." Included in this was all that He taught and did through His life and death to make redemption and eternal life possible for believers.

Hopefully, there will be time in your class period to deal with certain ramifications regarding the Lord's supper (communion) which grow out of our text and should be covered.

There are three main positions regarding the elements used in the ordinance of communion. One is called transubstantiation. This claims that the bread and wine consecrated by a priest becomes within the partaker the actual body and blood of Christ. A second view is called consubstantiation. This claims that the "real presence" of Christ is in the elements much as heat is in an iron. A third view, the one generally held by evangelical Christians, is called the memorial or symbolic position. This claims that the elements are representations of the body and blood of Christ.

Keep in mind all that Jesus said about Himself being the Bread of life found in our text. Then look at the rest of John, chapter 6, beginning with verse 52. Misunderstanding what Jesus said about Himself, the Jews wondered if He was offering them His literal flesh to eat. Jesus then stated that men should eat His flesh and drink His blood to find eternal life, but He obviously was talking in symbolic terms and not literal terms.

John 6:57 makes this point. Jesus said that He lived by His connection with His heavenly Father, and believers should live by their connection with Himself. God is a Spirit, and Jesus was referring to living by spiritual connection with Him. The same is true of the connection between Christ and believers.

John 6:63 makes this point. "It is the spirit that quickeneth; the flesh profiteth nothing: the words that I speak unto you, they are spirit, and they are life." See also John 5:24 on this point.

John 6:67-68 makes this point. "Then said Jesus unto the twelve, Will ye also go away? Then Simon Peter answered him, Lord, to whom shall we go? Thou hast the words of eternal life."

The broken body and shed blood of Christ were essential for the atonement, but they were offered once to put away sin by the sacrifice of Christ (Heb. 9:26). It is the *truth* about Christ and salvation which bring us eternal life.

Evangelistic Emphasis

World hunger is a massive and perplexing problem in our day. Who has not winced as pictures of starving children are portrayed on our television screens? "Natural disasters" such as drought and floods are only part of the problem. We also face "human disasters" such as bureaucratic blockades that prevent food from reaching the hungry for political purposes.

Without detracting from this very real physical problem, we should also note evidence of spiritual famine in our world. It is "not a famine of bread, nor a thirst for water, but of hearing the words of the Lord" (Amos 8:11). Sometimes this famine, too, seems to spread by "natural disasters" such as being born in areas with predetermined mind-sets against the good news. At other times, political and racial barriers must be hurdled.

John 6 describes the remedy to all this: Jesus, the bread of life. Now that Jesus has returned to the Father's side, how can we supply people with the bread of His presence?

Jesus gives a clue in John 6:63: "The words that I speak unto you, they are spirit, and they are life." By sharing the words of the Gospel with the spiritually hungry, we enable them to feast on Him as the bread of life (see vs. 51).

◆◆◆◆◆◆

Memory Selection

I am the living bread which came down from heaven: if any man eat of this bread, he shall live for ever: and the bread that I give is my flesh, which I will give for the life of the world. *John 6:51*

Reminding ourselves of John's purpose in writing this Gospel can help us understand language that might otherwise seem crude, or even pagan (see also the commentary section).

John was concerned to challenge two main opponents of the Gospel: Jews who denied that Jesus is the Messiah, and people (later called "gnostics") who were embarrassed by the flesh. John gives his adversaries no quarter. Jesus was the Word become flesh (1:14). He had a real body even after the resurrection (20:25). And here the imagery is even extended to saying that being nourished on Christ as the bread of life is like eating His flesh.

Such language cut two ways. To gnostic types it insisted on the significance of the actual body of Christ. He was not a spook; he did not merely "seem" to have a body, as one ancient Christian heresy had it. The real Son was really wounded and really died.

Cutting the other way, John's language challenged Jews who could not see God's larger providence in the manna on which their ancestors were nourished in the flight from Egypt. *Christ*, not manna, is the true bread of life, and believing Jews were therefore actually nourished on Him when they ate the manna.

April 25, 1993

Weekday Problems

Willis is an auto mechanic who has always barely scraped by, financially. Yet he had been taught to include the Lord's work in his budget, so he always put some money in the collection plate at church on Sunday, regardless of whether the bills were paid.

On a recent Sunday when he was sick, Willis tuned in a TV evangelist who preached a "prosperity" gospel. Willis was convinced by the argument that God will bless financially those who put Him first in their budgets. He decided to send the evangelist $100 "seed money," with the virtual promise that he would receive ten-fold or more in return.

The next week Willis was laid off work for lack of business—and his nine-year-old boy had to have an appendectomy. Now he is not only broke, but angry at God for not coming through. His friend Grif chided Willis, saying, "You were in it just for the loaves and fishes. No wonder it didn't work!"

*Do you think Grif used John 6:26 appropriately?
*What do you think of the message that God will prosper those who put Him first? (Have you ever experienced either negative or positive evidence of this?)
*How does Matthew 5:45 bear on the "prosperity gospel"?

◆◆◆◆◆◆

Superintendent's Sermonette

Bread has been called the staff of life because of its importance to men's diets from earliest times onward to the present. However, "Man doth not live by bread only, but by every word that proceedeth out of the mouth of the Lord doth man live" (Deut. 8:3). When Jesus was tempted by Satan to make bread out of stones, He quoted this (Matt. 4:4; Luke 4:4). It was not surprising, therefore, when Jesus referred to Himself as the Bread of life. Those who had eaten manna in ancient Israel eventually died. Those who partook of Jesus and His teaching found the way to eternal life.

Parents today are concerned that their children have sufficient food to eat, even though sometimes they yield to pressure to get "junk food" which lacks adequate nourishment. We all feel sorry if we see pictures of starving children in other parts of the world. We feel uncomfortable when we see examples of homeless and undernourished adults in our own country.

More important than literal lack of food is the scarcity of spiritual nourishment today. People are seriously ignorant of biblical truths we take for granted. May God challenge us to take knowledge of the Bread of life to others everywhere.

THE BREAD OF LIFE

This Lesson In Your Life

KEEPING BODY AND SOUL TOGETHER

Some Bible scholars believe that the teaching about Jesus as the bread of life in John 6 is related to the Christian practice of the Lord's Supper. When John's Gospel was written, the church was concerned to underline the importance of Christ's commandment, "This do in remembrance of me." Christians needed encouragement to partake regularly of the bread and wine in the Communion, in memory of the body and blood of Christ. In this view, we can take references to "eating" Christ's flesh and "drinking" his blood (vs. 53) not only as reflecting the teaching of Jesus but also the early church's insistence on the importance of the Communion.

Whether or not this approach to John is correct, this important chapter speaks to our need to balance the physical and the spiritual aspects of life. The teaching here not only relates to our view of such rites as the Lord's Supper, but to our daily lives as well.

With the poet, we sometimes feel that "the world is too much with us." We wish we could be more "spiritual." But we have feet of clay, and we must confess that we live in a very material world. Few of us can flee to the desert in total rejection of material concerns. What clues to being truly spiritual, in our own time and place, can we find in this chapter?

Verse 27 warns us not to labor for literal food, but to value food that leads to "everlasting life." Here is a call for us to think seriously about the kind of nourishment we value. If our only priority is to belabor our tables with rich foods, we will not only slight spiritual *nourishment*; we'll end up overweight.

Yet this call to value spiritual food over the physical occurs in the same chapter as the miracle of the loaves and fishes (vss. 5-14). Jesus was no ascetic. Quite the opposite—he seems to be on the list of those who made the banquet circuit (John 2:1-11)! The call here is to live *whole* lives. The joys of physical food can remind us to stay connected to the Source of spiritual nourishment— not *"laboring for"* meat alone, but recalling that, after all, Christ's richest spiritual blessings are pictured in the New Testament as a great feast! (See Matt. 22:1-10.)

Again, Jesus reveals something about a spiritual versus a material *purpose in life* in this chapter. His purpose, He says in verse 38, is to do the will of God, rather than His own will. (In John 4:34 He actually says that doing the Father's will is his "meat" or food!).

Again, this doesn't mean that we should give no attention at all to goals that provide physical goods for ourselves and our families. It is intended to *relate* such material ends to spiritual. Does providing for our families mean merely giving them so much they don't appreciate even the material joys of life? What could be less appropriate than for those of us who have heard God's call to do *His* will to exhibit to our families interest only on selfish ends? If we are citizens of heaven, what business do we have spending all our time and money on short-lived matters that won't last past our own brief life? How much more appropriate to use earthly treasures to lay up heavenly gain, by making the good of others a part of our aim in life. Again, the challenge is not to reject one or the other, spiritual or material goals, but to see their essential relatedness.

Seed Thoughts

1. In light of this entire chapter, was the miracle of the loaves and fishes only to exhibit Jesus' miraculous powers, or did it have an inner meaning?

No doubt Jesus meant for us to learn about "true" or spiritual food from this miracle (see vss. 26-27)

2. When Jesus retreated from the crowds, why was He concerned that the people not make Him a king?

Because the excitement created by that kind of move would have been bad timing.

3. What did Simon Peter do at another time when Jesus was involved with the disciples in a storm at sea?

He walked part way to Jesus on the water, and sank when he was distracted by the storm.

4. Why are such stories recorded? (See John 20:30-31.)

As John says, they are recorded to produce (or maintain) faith. They also provide a hint that Christ can still the inner storms of life.

5. How can Jesus' recommended "work" in verses 28-29 be harmonized with Paul's insistence that we are saved by grace, not works?

Believing is a work of God, not a work of human righteousness or law-keeping, which Paul opposed.

(PLEASE TURN PAGE)

---

1. In light of this entire chapter, was the miracle of the loaves and fishes only to exhibit Jesus' miraculous powers, or did it have an inner meaning?

2. When Jesus retreated from the crowds, why was He concerned that the people not make Him a king?

3. What did Simon Peter do at another time when Jesus was involved with the disciples in a storm at sea?

4. Why are such stories recorded? (See John 20:30-31.)

5. How can Jesus' recommended "work" in verses 28-29 be harmonized with Paul's insistence that we are saved by grace, not works?

6. Do you think the people really knew what they were asking for in verse 34?

7. Can you share an illustration of Christ's having satisfied spiritual hunger in a way mere bread could not?

8. What promise in verse 39 can bring comfort to believers who wonder about their power to resist temptation?

9. Why do you think "familiarity breeds contempt," as happened to Jesus according to verses 41-42?

10. What did Jesus say might be harder to believe than His sayings about "eating" his body and "drinking" His blood? (See vss. 56-62.)

No doubt Jesus meant for us to learn about "true" or spiritual food from this miracle (see vss. 26-27)

Because the excitement created by that kind of move would have been bad timing.

He walked part way to Jesus on the water, and sank when he was distracted by the storm.

As John says, they are recorded to produce (or maintain) faith. They also provide a hint that Christ can still the inner storms of life.

Believing is a work of God, not a work of human righteousness or law-keeping, which Paul opposed.

It's doubtful, since they are apparently the very people Jesus said in verse 26 were seeking mere bread.

(Encourage open sharing, from personal experience or Scripture.)

They have the promise of God's aid, since it is His will that Christ appear at the last day with all the faithful "intact."

Perhaps because we view the ordinariness of our lives as too mundane a setting for extraordinary people. (We forget that all important people have to come from somewhere!)

Seeing Him actually ascend to heaven from earth.

(SEED THOUGHTS--Cont'd)

6. Do you think the people really knew what they were asking for in verse 34?
It's doubtful, since they are apparently the very people Jesus said in verse 26 were seeking mere bread.

7. Can you share an illustration of Christ's having satisfied spiritual hunger in a way mere bread could not?
(Encourage open sharing, from personal experience or Scripture.)

8. What promise in verse 39 can bring comfort to believers who wonder about their power to resist temptation?
They have the promise of God's aid, since it is His will that Christ appear at the last day with all the faithful "intact."

9. Why do you think "familiarity breeds contempt," as happened to Jesus according to verses 41-42?
Perhaps because we view the ordinariness of our lives as too mundane a setting for extraordinary people. (We forget that all important people have to come from somewhere!)

10. What did Jesus say might be harder to believe than His sayings about "eating" his body and "drinking" His blood? (See vss. 56-62.)
Seeing Him actually ascend to heaven from earth.

May 2, 1993

BEHOLD—THE LAMB OF GOD!

The Witness of John the Baptist

JOHN 1

19. And this is the record of John, when the Jews sent priests and Levites from Jerusalem to ask him, Who art thou?
20. And he confessed, and denied not; but confessed, I am not the Christ.
21. And they asked him, What then? Art thou E-li′-as? And he saith, I am not. Art thou that prophet? And he answered, No.
22. Then said they unto him, Who art thou? that we may give an answer to them that sent us. What sayest thou of thyself?
23. He said, I am THE VOICE OF ONE CRYING IN THE WILDERNESS, MAKE STRAIGHT THE WAY OF THE LORD, as said the prophet E-sa′-ias.
24. And they which were sent were of the Pharisees.
25. And they asked him, and said unto him, Why baptizest thou then, if thou be not that Christ, nor E-li′-as, neither that prophet?
26. John answered them, saying, I baptize with water: but there standeth one among you, whom ye know not;
27. He it is, who coming after me is preferred before me, whose shoe's latchet I am not worthy to unloose.
28. These things were done in Beth-ab′-a-ra beyond Jordan, where John was baptizing.
29. The next day John seeth Jesus coming unto him, and saith, Behold the Lamb of God, which taketh away the sin of the world.
30. This is he of whom I said, After me cometh a man which is preferred before me: for he was before me.
31. And I knew him not: but that he should be made manifest to Israel, therefore am I come baptizing with water.
32. And John bare record, saying, I saw the Spirit descending from heaven like a dove, and it abode upon him.
33. And I knew him not: but he that sent me to baptize with water, the same said unto me, Upon whom thou shalt see the Spirit descending and remaining on him, the same is he which baptiseth with the Holy Ghost.
34. And I saw, and bare record that this is the Son of God.

◆◆◆◆◆◆

◀ **Memory Selection**
John 1:34

◀ **Devotional Reading**
John 1:35-42

◀ **Background Scripture**
John 1:19-34

◀ **Printed Scripture**
John 1:19-34

THE WITNESS OF JOHN THE BAPTIST

Teacher's Target

In most fields of human endeavor, an ambitious individual tries to work his way up the ladder to the highest position he can get. If he becomes an assistant or deputy to a leader, he becomes anxious to reach the top himself. If he does not make it, he may leave to join another organization, or he may form his own organization. There is also the rare person who realizes that he could never be as great as the leader he serves. This individual finds fulfillment" in taking second place and promoting his leader in every way possible.

John the Baptist was the kind of person who knew his God-appointed role as a herald of Christ and was content with it. John served as an example of what every follower of Christ ought to be. Each believer should seek to magnify Christ before men and keep in the background as much as possible. It was John himself who said of Jesus, "He must increase, but I must decrease" (John 3:30).

Lesson Introduction

The coming of the Messiah was foretold throughout the Old Testament. He was portrayed in various types and in prophecies. Then a four-century period of prophetic silence fell upon Israel until it was time for Him to appear. John the Baptist might be viewed as the last of the Old Testament type of prophet and the first of the New Testament type of prophet. He helped to tie the old and the new together, and it demanded creativity on his part. He was a rugged individual, made in the mold of Elijah, and he shunned cities so that he might minister in the Judaean wilderness north of the Dead Sea.

People came to John the Baptist from all over Palestine. They were impressed by his strong message calling for repentance. They submitted to the Jewish ceremony of purification he practiced in water baptism. They made themselves ready to receive the Messiah when He came. John pointed them to the Lamb of God Who takes away the sin of the world (John 1:29). He prepared them to be baptized spiritually into the body of Christ (John 1:33; I Cor. 12:13).

Teaching Outline

I. Inquiry I: John 1:19-23
   A. Who he was not: 19-21
   B. Who he was: 22-23
II. Inquiry II: John 1:24-28
   A. Badgering: 24-25
   B. Baptizing: 26-27
   C. Bethabara: 28
III. Inquiry III: John 1:29-34
   A. Declaration: 29-31
   B. Descent: 32-34

Daily Bible Readings

Mon. The Birth of John
Luke 1:57-66
Tue. Zechariah's Prophecy
Luke 1:67-80
Wed. John Opposes Herod
Mark 6:14-20
Thu. Herod's Revenge
Mark 6:21-29
Fri. A Way in the Wilderness
Isa. 40:3-8
Sat. John Preached the Christ
Luke 3:15-20
Sun. More than a Prophet
Matt. 11:7-15

May 2, 1993

VERSE BY VERSE

I. Inquiry I: John 1:19-23

A. Who he was not: 19-21

19. And this is the record of John, when the Jews sent priests and Levites from Jerusalem to ask him, Who art thou?

It was the record, testimony, or confession of John the Baptist which is in view in verses 20-27. Jewish religious leaders (probably members of the Sanhedrin authorized by the Romans to enforce religious laws) sent priests and Levites from among the sect of Pharisees to question John (vs. 24). They journeyed from Jerusalem out across the Judaean wilderness to the eastern side of the Jordan River before it emptied into the Dead Sea. This was called Bethabara beyond Jordan (vs. 28) and was therefore in the province of Peraea. Some versions call it Bethany beyond Jordan to distinguish it from the town of Bethany on Mount Olivet. The Jewish authorities wanted John to state his identity so that they might decide whether or not he made valid claims about himself.

20. And he confessed, and denied not; but confessed, I am not the Christ.

The ministry of John the Baptist drew considerable attention among the common people. "All men mused in their hearts of John, whether he were the Christ or not" (Luke 3:15). Reports of this had apparently reached the religious leaders, and they wanted to hear from John himself whether he thought he was the Messiah or the Christ (Anointed One sent by God). John openly proclaimed that he did not consider himself to be that Person.

21a. And they asked him, What then? Art thou Elias? And he saith, I am not.

It had been predicted that God would send Elijah the prophet back to the earth before the coming of the dreadful day of the Lord (Mal. 4:5). We know that Elijah did not die but was taken up to heaven by a whirlwind (2 Kings 2:11). We know that he appeared with Moses to Jesus, Peter, James, and John on the mount of transfiguration (Matt. 17:1-8). We know that Jesus considered Malachi 4:5 to be fulfilled in John the Baptist in the sense that John was similar to Elijah (Matt. 17:9-13). However, John did not consider himself to be Elijah.

21b. Art thou that prophet? And he answered, No.

In some versions that Prophet is capitalized. It probably referred to the unnamed man mentioned in Deuteronomy 18:15-19, but Jews were divided as to whether or not this referred to the Messiah. John laid no claim to being the Prophet.

B. Who he was: 22-23

22. Then said they unto him, Who art thou? that we may give an answer to them that sent us. What sayest thou of thyself?

These questions sought the identity of John following his denial of being the Christ, Elijah, or the Prophet. The Pharisees from Jerusalem were now ready to hear John define his own identity. They told him that they dared not return to Jerusalem without an answer to this inquiry. The second question suggests that they might be satisfied with even John's general explanation of his vocation, even if he refused to accept any title.

23. He said, I an the voice of one crying in the wilderness, Make straight

the way of the Lord, as said the prophet Esaias.

John applied the prophecy of Isaiah 40:3 to himself. He described his work as being the herald of the Messiah to come. In preparation for the King, people were urged to repent of their sins and forsake them. They were invited to go through the Jewish rite of purification called water baptism. This was not to be confused with baptism by the Spirit which the Messiah would bring. John's baptism symbolized repentance. Christian baptism symbolizes repentance and regeneration, and it could not be instituted until after Christ died to provide new life for those dead in sin.

II. Inquiry II: John 1:24-28

A. Badgering: 24-25

24. And they which were sent were of the Pharisees.

Pharisees were proud, legalistic, self-appointed guardians of the Mosaic law and Jewish religious traditions. They were known later to join forces with even the Sadducees and Herodians in order to oppose Jesus during His ministry. Their questioning of John was not friendly but badgering in tone.

25. And they asked him, and said unto him, Why baptizest thou then, if thou be not that Christ, nor Elias, neither that prophet?

The Pharisees from Jerusalem may have taken time to go into a huddle and discuss John's remarks. They now approached him with a threatening question, wanting to know why he baptized people if he did not consider himself to be the Christ, Elijah, or the unnamed Prophet. In other words, they questioned his authority to perform a Jewish ceremony without having cleared it first with the religious leaders in Jerusalem. They must have concluded that John had no real connection with the Messiah and His kingdom, and, therefore, he had no right to represent Him.

B. Baptizing: 26-27

26. John answered them, saying, I baptize with water: but there standeth one among you, whom ye know not;

John's enigmatic response must have been frustrating to the Pharisees. He said that he baptized with water those who repented of their sins and prepared themselves to receive the Messiah when He came. John's comment that one was standing among them but remained unknown to them had to refer to the Messiah Who was near at hand. John implied that the Messiah would do something greater than baptize with water. We have to skip ahead to verse 33 to see what it was going to be—baptism with or by the Holy Ghost. Further comment will be given when we study that verse later in this lesson.

27. He it is, who coming after me is preferred before me, whose shoe's latchet I am not worthy to unloose.

We know that Jesus was born six months after John the Baptist was born (Luke 1:35-36). Therefore, He came into the world after John did. However, Jesus was preferred *before* John in the sense that He had infinitely higher rank as the divine Son of God. John said that he was not worthy of loosening His sandal thongs, the job of a slave. John considered his role to be one who simply pointed people toward the peerless Messiah and then faded into the background. He had the kind of humility which all followers of Christ should strive to have.

C. Bethabara: 28

28. These things were done in Bethabara beyond Jordan, where John was baptizing.

We are not sure of the exact location of Bethabara (or Bethany beyond Jordan). It was on the eastern side of the Jordan River somewhere north of the Dead Sea. It has been suggested that it might have been Bethbarah, a major ford over the Jordan, but this is uncertain, as well. Jesus went there to be baptized at the beginning of His ministry (Matt. 3:13-17), and He went there with His disciples later on to get away from persecution in Jerusalem (John 10:40-42).

III. Inquiry III: John 1:29-34

A. Declaration: 29-31

29. The next day John seeth Jesus

coming unto him, and saith, Behold the Lamb of God, which taketh away the sin of the world.

Some think that verse 26 implied that Jesus was in John's audience the previous day, while others think it merely referred to Him being somewhere in the surrounding area, perhaps on His way there. Whatever the case, Jesus made an open entrance into the gathering on this day and was recognized by John the Baptist, who declared Him to be the Lamb of God taking away the sins of the world.

Jews were accustomed to sacrificial lambs used in ceremonies of atonement at the temple in Jerusalem. Some in John's audience may have even had enough spiritual discernment to realize that the Messiah would serve in the role of a sacrifice. Most Jews, however, preferred to think of the Messiah not as a suffering Servant but as a reigning King. It was likely, then, that they did not comprehend why John referred to Jesus as the Lamb taking away the sins of the world. This concept would require time.

30. This is he of whom I said, After me cometh a man which is preferred before me: for he was before me.

This was first introduced in verse 27. Jesus was born six months after John, but he was preferred *before* him as being higher in rank, for He had existed *before* John in eternity past as the divine Son of God. Divinity outranked humanity. The eternal outranked the temporal.

31. And I knew him not: but that he should be made manifest to Israel, therefore am I come baptizing with water.

This may have been a continuation of John's answer to the question the Pharisees had asked as to why he baptized people (vs. 25). John remembered the time when he did not yet know the Messiah. He believed that He would be revealed to Israel, and, therefore, he had baptized people with water as a sign or symbol of their repentance and their readiness to receive the Messiah.

B. Descent: 32-34

32. And John bare recored, saying, I saw the Spirit descending from heaven like a dove, and it abode upon him.

John further reminisced about the time when Jesus had come to him to be baptized. The Holy Spirit had descended on Him in the form of a dove, and God the Father had declared that Jesus was His beloved Son in Whom He was well pleased (Matt. 3:13-17). All Members of the Trinity had been there.

33. And I knew him not: but he that sent me to baptize with water, the same said unto me, Upon whom thou shalt see the Spirit descending, and remaining on him, the same is he which baptizeth with the Holy Ghost.

John went even further back in his reminiscing to recall the time when he did not know the identity of the Messiah, but he had been told by God (Who had sent him to baptize with water) that the One on Whom the Spirit descended and remained would be the One Who would some day baptize with the Spirit. In order to explain what this meant, we must go forward into the New Testament to see what happened at a later time. Jesus told His disciples that He would ask His Father to send the Spirit down to dwell within believers and empower them for service (John 14:16; Acts 1:8). The Holy Spirit fulfilled this promise on the Day of Pentecost (Acts 2:1-6). The Spirit came at various other times, as well (Acts 4:8, 31; 10:44-45). Every time a believer is brought into the redeemed family of God, the Holy Spirit is involved (Rom. 8:9, 14-16; 1 Cor. 12:13).

34. And I saw, and bare record that this is the Son of God.

It is thought that John the Baptist and Jesus were closely related through their mothers, Elizabeth and Mary, although they lived a good distance from each other, John in the hill country of Judaea and Jesus in Nazareth. They may have met often at religious festivals in Jerusalem. However, it appears that Jesus lived in such a normal manner that even John did not realize He was the Messiah until the time he baptized Him. From that point on, however, he was fully convinced that Jesus was the divine Son of God and the Messiah long awaited by the Jewish people.

Evangelistic Emphasis

The work of John the Baptist can be compared with springtime on a farm. It's a time for preparing the soil, planting the seed and cultivating the young growth. John the Baptist came to "Make straight the way of the Lord"—to plow good furrows in which the seed of the gospel could be planted. His stern prophetic call to "Repent!" weeded out those who would not listen to Jesus. The baptism he administered was like watering the soil in preparation for the saving seed, the word of Christ. No matter that Christ's work of harvesting would be more at center stage in the gospel story. John's work of preparing people for the message was still essential.

The work of preparing the soil of people's hearts for the gospel message is just as essential today. It may not be as sensational as the work of the mass evangelist who sees hundreds coming down the aisles at an evangelistic campaign. We cannot always count the results as we might count bushels of wheat at harvesttime. But no wheat was ever harvested without first having been planted and cultivated in prepared soil.

Harvests of converts are often preceded by years of cultivation by Christians whose work is less visible but no less essential.

◆◆◆◆◆

Memory Selection

And I saw, and bare record that this is the Son of God.
John 1:34

The word translated "bare record" ("have borne witness," *New American Standard Bible*) is from a word that also gives us our term, "martyr." How did a word that simply meant to "testify" in a court of law come to imply death for a cause?

Under the iron rule of Rome, many early Christians were arrested for their Faith. After all, refusing to say, "Caesar is Lord" was both a theological heresy and treason. So when the Christians "testified" to their faith in Christ in a Roman court, they often received the sentence of death. Fortunately for John the Baptist, "bearing witness" to Christ's divine Sonship was not yet a capital offense.

Not so for Polycarp, a second-century bishop in what is now Turkey. The Roman soldiers who were sent to arrest him felt that Polycarp was a harmless old man who did not deserve to die. They urged him to renounce his faith and save his life. Refusing, Polycarp was hauled to the arena to face the lions. Again he had the chance to deny his faith. Instead, Polycarp "martyred," or testified of Jesus: "I have served Him 86 years, and He has done me no wrong; how can I blaspheme the king who saved me?" Of course this testimony cost him his life.

Surely we cannot be ashamed today to bear our own witness to a faith that has been so heroically confessed by our forebears!

May 2, 1993

Weekday Problems

"The Jews" in John 1:19 sent their representatives to investigate the work of John the Baptist, instead of going themselves. "The Jews," in John's Gospel, usually refers to those who opposed Jesus' claim to be the Messiah. Verse 24 states that they were Pharisees, who were among Christ's most vocal opponents. No doubt many of them in this account already had their own presuppositions about the report their representatives would bring back.

This sets up an interesting possibility. What if, after interviewing John the Baptist, some of these representatives became believers? What if they discovered that they could not return to the Pharisees with the kind of report they expected?

*Have you ever found yourself in a similar situation, where you could not honestly "testify" in a way your superiors expect? What did (or should) you do?

*As a student, have you ever been expected to give an answer on an exam that you disagreed with? What did you do?

*Have you ever been faced with implementing policies with which you disagree? What can be done in such circumstances? (Compare and discuss the testimony of soldiers, placed on trial for alleged war crimes, who have protested that they were only carrying out orders.)

◆◆◆◆◆◆

Superintendent's Sermonette

People are very proud of their names. Some want to be called by their names, rather than by nick-names, abbreviations, or general terms. They want their names to be spelled and pronounced correctly. They work hard to establish reputations so that they will have "good" names.

There are those who think that they have names to be proud of because of their geneology and the prestige connected with famous relatives, especially if large inheritances are involved. There are others who are proud of their names because they have worked their way up from nothing and have been highly successful in their chosen professions or vacations.

One of the most distressing experiences a person can have is to develop amnesia and forget who he is. This is very frustrating to older people who have Alzheimer's disease and forget many things, including the identity of their loved ones and friends.

John the Baptist knew who he was. He knew that he was the son of Zacharias the priest and of Elisabeth. He knew that he was the forerunner of the coming Messiah and was delighted to discover this was his relative, Jesus. John was happy to submerge his identity in that of Jesus, and we would do well to do the same as we witness to others about Him.

This Lesson In Your Life

"I'M NOT NUMBER 1"

John the Baptist made it painfully clear that he played second fiddle to Christ. "I am not the Christ," he protested (John 1:20). He was not even worthy to unlace the sandals of Him who "is preferred before me" (vs. 15). "He (Christ) must increase, but I must decrease (3:30).

All this can sound strange in the ears of a society that places a high premium on being "No. 1." Can you imagine the language of John the Baptist as a cheer at a basketball game? Somehow shouting "WE'RE NUMBER 2!" or "WE'RE NUMBER 3!" just doesn't fit. On a national and international scale, our vast resources, "Yankee ingenuity" and enterprising immigrants have helped America grow from a tiny band of rebel colonies to Number 1 in many categories.

More importantly, we have developed a mentality that virtually requires that we occupy the top spot. One could almost hear a national sigh of despair when it was reported a few years ago that Sweden was Number 1 in its standard of living. Surveys show that most Americans feel that being Number 1 in armaments and arsenals is essential to national safety and defense.

We teach our children that they can be in Number 1 their personal lives and careers if they work hard enough. We want them to dream big, to feel that "the sky's the limit," that "anyone can become President." When they enter their chosen fields of work, we hope they'll become the best.

It's ironic, in the light of all this, that most of us can't be Number 1. Like John the Baptist, we must point to someone else who occupies the top spot. In any given group there must be more followers than leaders, more junior executives than senior executives, more vice presidents than CEOs. Some social psychologists say that many of the problems in the national psyche stem from the frustration of being urged to become 1, while having to settle for less.

Even if you're chairman of the board or president of the company, similar positions in larger companies can make you feel less than Number 1. A person may aspire to "move up" from teaching high school to being a college professor, only to find after making the leap that there's an overbearing college president above him. You move up to a larger house in a better neighborhood, but after a few years you long for that still nicer place. The better car calls for one still more expensive. Number 1 is still somewhere up ahead.

How do you handle not being Number 1? How do you accept a lower rung on the ladder? Some guidelines are available from the world of the corporate climb. For one thing, if you're Number 2 or lower, you must learn to be supportive of Number 1. This can be galling if you want his job. Christians are warned against envy and jealousy, but dealing with the green-eyed monster can be tough if we *must* be Number 1. Tough or not, leaders in business and industry say that the most successful people are those who make their superiors look good...those who can say, "I'm not Number 1— *he* is.

There will always be only one Christ, but many who, like John the Baptist, only point to Him. But remember that th*ere was also only one John the Baptist*. Your uniqueness and value depends not on Number 1 in some external value framework, but in yours and God's measurement.

Seed Thoughts

1. What personal traits were required for John the Baptist to admit that he only pointed to the One people should ulimately seek?
   Humility. The willingness to be Number 2." Self-acceptance, rather than longing to be someone else.

2. Although John the Baptist was not literally Elijah (or "Elias," KJV), was there a connection? (See vs. 21; Mal. 4:5-6; Matt. 17:10-13.)
   Yes. John the Baptist came in the spirit of Elijah, in fulfillment of the Old Testament prophecy.

3. Have you ever been mistaken for someone else? How does it make a person feel?
   It can be something of a letdown, since we really like to be recognized for ourselves.

4. How was John the Baptist's mission similar to the work to be done on a farm, in the spring?
   It was "preparing the way," like the work of preparing the soil, planting the seed and cultivating young growth.

5. Do you sometimes feel that Christians are also lonely voices "crying in the wilderness"?
   (Encourage open discussion of the Christian message as it confronts unbelief in the modern world.)

(PLEASE TURN PAGE)

---

1. What personal traits were required for John the Baptist to admit that he only pointed to the One people should ulimately seek?

2. Although John the Baptist was not literally Elijah (or "Elias," KJV), was there a connection? (See vs. 21; Mal. 4:5-6; Matt. 17:10-13.)

3. Have you ever been mistaken for someone else? How does it make a person feel?

4. How was John the Baptist's mission similar to the work to be done on a farm, in the spring?

5. Do you sometimes feel that Christians are also lonely voices "crying in the wilderness"?

6. What was John referring to when he said Jesus would baptize with the Holy Spirit and with fire?

7. What is the significance of calling Jesus "the Lamb of God," as in verse 29?

8. What was the significance of the dove at Jesus' baptism?

9. What is the relationship of the Holy Spirit and baptism (see Acts 2:38).

10. What price would later often be paid for daring to "bear witness" or testify to faith in Christ?

(SEED THOUGHTS--Cont'd)

Humility. The willingness to be "Number 2." Self-acceptance, rather than longing to be someone else.

Yes. John the Baptist came in the spirit of Elijah, in fulfillment of the Old Testament prophecy.

It can be something of a letdown, since we really like to be recognized for ourselves.

It was "preparing the way," like the work of preparing the soil, planting the seed and cultivating young growth.

(Encourage open discussion of the Christian message as it confronts unbelief in the modern world.)

Probably to (a) The outpouring of the Holy Spirit at Pentecost, in Acts 2; and (b) the fires of persecution.

The term relates Christ to the Jewish sacrificial system in which the blood of lambs signified atonement for sin.

It signified the Holy Spirit, and indicated to John that Jesus was truly as God's Son.

The Holy Spirit was given as a gift at Christian baptism.

Under Roman persecution it might cost Christians their life—hence the word for "witness" came to mean "martyr."

---

6. What was John referring to when he said Jesus would baptize with the Holy Spirit and with fire?
Probably to (a) The outpouring of the Holy Spirit at Pentecost, in Acts 2; and (b) the fires of persecution.

7. What is the significance of calling Jesus "the Lamb of God," as in verse 29?
The term relates Christ to the Jewish sacrificial system in which the blood of lambs signified atonement for sin.

8. What was the significance of the dove at Jesus' baptism?
It signified the Holy Spirit, and indicated to John that Jesus was truly as God's Son.

9. What is the relationship of the Holy Spirit and baptism (see Acts 2:38).
The Holy Spirit was given as a gift at Christian baptism.

10. What price would later often be paid for daring to "bear witness" or testify to faith in Christ?
Under Roman persecution it might cost Christians their life—hence the word for "witness" came to mean "martyr."

May 9, 1993

...ANDREW

We Have Found Him

JOHN 1
35. Again the next day after John stood, and two of his disciples;
36. And looking upon Jesus as he walked, he saith, Behold the Lamb of God!
37. And the two disciples heard him speak, and they followed Jesus.
38. Then Jesus turned, and saw them following, and saith unto them, What seek ye? They said unto him, Rabbi, (which is to say, being interpreted, Master,) where dwellest thou?
39. He saith unto them, Come and see. They came and saw where he dwelt, and abode with him that day: for it was about the tenth hour. 40. One of the two which heard John *speak*, and followed him, was Andrew, Simon Peter's brother.
41. He first findeth his own brother Simon, and saith unto him, We have found the Mes-si'-as, which is, being interpreted, the Christ.
42. And he brought him to Jesus. And when Jesus beheld him, he said, Thou art Simon the son of Jona: thou shalt be called Ce'-phas, which is by interpretation, A stone.

43. The day following Jesus would go forth into Galilee, and findeth Philip, and saith unto him, Follow me.
44. Now Philip was of Beth-sa'-i-da, the city of Andrew and Peter.
45. Philip findeth Na-than'-a-el, and saith unto him, We have found him, of whom Moses in the law, and the prophets, did write, Jesus of Nazareth the son of Joseph.
46. And Na-than'-a-el said unto him, Can there any good thing come out of Nazareth? Philip saith unto him Come and see.
47. Jesus saw Na-than'-a-el coming to him, and saith of him, Behold an Israelite indeed, in whom is no guile!
48. Na-than'-a-el saith unto him, Whence knowest thou me? Jesus answered and said unto him, Before that Philip called thee, when thou wast under the fig tree, I saw thee.
49. Na-than'-a-el answered and saith unto him, Rabbi, thou art the Son of God; thou art the King of Israel.
50. Jesus answered and said unto him, Because I said unto thee, I saw thee under the fig tree, believest thou? thou shalt see greater things than these.

◆◆◆◆◆◆

◀ **Memory Selection**
John 1:41

◀ **Devotional Reading**
Matthew 10:1-10

◀ **Background Scripture**
John 1:35-50

◀ **Printed Scripture**
John 1:35-50

WE HAVE FOUND HIM

Teacher's Target

We have all heard of "a chain reaction" and of "the domino theory," referring to something at one end of a line influencing results on down to the end of that line. It may seem sometimes as if the church of Christ developed in a haphazard fashion, but we may be sure that He built it according to a master plan. In today's text we see how individuals were contacted and challenged to become followers of Jesus. Some were drawn to Him easily, while others required more persuasion.

Help your students to realize that witnessing for Christ is part of the divine plan for expanding the church. Every believer should be involved. It is included among the works for which Christians have been foreordained. "We are his workmanship created in Christ Jesus unto good works, which God hath before ordained that we should walk in them" (Eph. 2:10). We should not expect *others* to do what God has planned for *us* to do.

Lesson Introduction

Most Jews living in the first century no doubt yearned for the coming of the Messiah. However, they must have expected Him to be born to a prominent couple, receive the best education available, and surround Himself with learned scholars and influential associates who could help Him end Israel's foreign occupation and lead her on to a new, golden age. They assumed that Jesus, though He was virgin-born of Mary, to be the son of Joseph the carpenter. He had been taken by His peasant parents to Egypt and then home to Nazareth up in Galilee, far from the center of power in Jerusalem.

When He made His bid for attention at the age of thirty, He did not go to the religious leaders in the capital but was baptized by a hermit-like preached named John the Baptist out in the wilderness. He gathered about himself an assorted group of fishermen, a tax collector, and other common men. He worked outside of "the establishment," "and the common people heard him gladly" (Mark 12:37). Thus it was that He began to build His church against which the gates of hell could not prevail (Matt. 16:18).

Teaching Outline

I. Contact I: John 1:35-39
   A. John plus two: 35-37
   B. Jesus plus two: 38-39
II. Contact II: John 1:40-42
   A. Andrew plus Peter: 40-41
   B. Jesus plus Peter: 42
III. Contact III: John 1:43-44
   A. Jesus plus Philip: 43
   B. City of three: 44
IV. Contact IV: John 1:45-50
   A. Philip plus Nathanael: 45-46
   B. Jesus plus Nathanael: 47-50

Daily Bible Readings

Mon. Disciples Given Authority
Matt. 10:1-7
Tue. Disciples Given Instructions
Matt. 10:8-15
Wed. The Call to Endure
Matt. 10:16-23
Thu. Be Like Your Teachers
Matt. 10:24-28
Fri. A God of Detail
Matt. 10:29-33
Sat. A Sword that Separates
Matt. 10:34-42
Sun. Good News to All
Matt. 11:1-6

May 9, 1993

VERSE BY VERSE

I. Contact I: John 1:35-39

A. John plus two: 35-37

35. Again the next day after John stood, and two of his disciples;

The witness given by John the Baptist on the day that he declared Jesus to be the Lamb of God taking away the sins of the world began a "chain reaction." It was on the following day that John was standing in his accustomed place of ministry, and he was accompanied by two of his own followers.

36. And looking upon Jesus as he walked, he saith, Behold the Lamb of God!

In these transition verses, we see the desire of John the Baptist to turn his followers away from himself so that they might focus on Jesus, Whom he again declared to be the Lamb of God. The title implied that Jesus was the Source of salvation by means of atonement.

37. And the two disciples heard him speak, and they followed Jesus.

One of these men was Andrew, Peter's brother (vs. 40). The other is thought by some to have been John, author of this gospel, who never mentioned himself by name while writing it. These men accepted the endorsement of Jesus by John the Baptist and approved of it. They took it for granted that he was advising them to follow Jesus.

B. Jesus plus two: 38-39

38a. Then Jesus turned, and saw then following, and saith unto them, What seek ye?

Jesus could read the hearts of these two men, and He opened a conversation with them by gently asking what they were seeking. They were no doubt happy for this contact and wanted to expand on it.

38b. They said unto him, Rabbi (which is to say, being interpreted, Master,) where dwellest thou?

The two men referred to Jesus as Rabbi, meaning Master or Teacher, and asked Him where He was staying. Since this was a wilderness area, it may have been a campsite or some local home rented or offered for the sake of hospitality. In asking this question, the two men seemed to imply that they wanted to spend some time with Jesus to learn more of Him and His teachings.

39. He saith unto them, Come and see. They came and saw where he dwelt, and abode with him that day: for it was about the tenth hour.

Jesus responded positively to the two men's request by inviting them to go to His place of lodging. It was about the tenth hour (four o'clock in the afternoon), and they spent the rest of that day with Him. It made such an impression on John, assuming him to be the unnamed man here, that he remembered the time several decades later while writing about it.

II. Contact II: John 1:40-42

A. Andrew plus Peter: 40-41

40. One of the two which heard John speak, and followed him, was Andrew, Simon Peter's brother.

Andrew was also favorably impressed by his time with Jesus, and he was anxious for his brother, Simon, to meet the Master, too.

41. He first findeth his own brother Simon, and saith unto him, We have found the Messias, which is, being interpreted, the Christ.

It appears that the first thing Andrew did after leaving Jesus was to find his brother, Simon, and report to him that he and the other man (John?) had discovered the Messias (Messiah). The Greek counterpart for Messiah was Christ, meaning Anointed One sent from God. This was momentous news!

B. Jesus plus Peter: 42

42. And he brought him to Jesus. And when Jesus beheld him, he said, Thou art Simon the son of Jona: thou shalt be called Cephas, which is by interpretation, A stone.

When Andrew brought his brother to Jesus, the Master looked into the future and created a new name for Simon. Using the Aramaic, Jesus said he would be known as Cephas. We know him better as Peter, which means "a stone." Although such a name suggests stability, we know that Peter went through periods of vacillation. However, following the descent of the Holy Spirit on the believers on the Day of Pentecost, Peter became more stable, and he did make significant contributions to the growth and development of the church.

III. Contact III: John 1:43-44

A. Jesus plus Philip: 43

43. The day following Jesus would go forth into Galilee, and findeth Philip, and saith unto him, Follow me.

Having spent a period of time in Judaea and with John the Baptist at the Jordan River, Jesus wanted to go northward to His home province of Galilee. He sought for a man named Philip, perhaps upon the recommendation of Andrew and Peter (vs. 44), and invited him to follow Him. Whatever the reason was, Jesus took the initiative with Philip, and he accompanied Him on the way north. It gave them time to talk, and Philip became one of His disciples.

B. City of three: 44

44. Now Philip was of Bethsaida, the city of Andrew and Peter.

Bethsaida may have been the fishing district associated with the city of Capernaum on the northern shore of the Sea of Galilee. If it was a separate city elsewhere, it appears that Andrew and Peter moved to Capernaum, because Mark 1:29 speaks of a house they had there. It may be that this was actually Peter's mother-in-law's house (Mark 1:30). Whatever the explanations, Bethsaida was called the city of Philip, Andrew, and Peter.

IV. Contact IV: John 1:45-50

A. Philip plus Nathanael: 45-46

45. Philip findeth Nathanael, and saith unto him, We have found him, of whom Moses in the law, and the prophets, did write, Jesus of Nazareth, the son of Joseph.

We are not told where Philip found Nathanael (or Bartholomew as he is sometimes called). We do know that Nathanael came from Cana, not far from Nazareth, west of the Sea of Galilee and in the hill country, according to John 21:2. Philip told Nathanael that he and others had found the Messiah. He said that the writings of Moses and of the prophets in the Jewish Scriptures (Old Testament) had predicted His coming. Jesus Himself later said that Moses had written about Him, probably referring to Deuteronomy 18:15-18, which described the Prophet to come. We know that there are almost forty references to the Messiah in the writings of the prophets describing His birth, life, death, resurrection, and post-resurrection events. Philip was convinced that Jesus of Nazareth, known as the son of Joseph the carpenter, was this promised Messiah.

46a. And Nathanael said unto him, Can there any good thing come out of Nazareth?

Although the Old Testament had predicted that the Messiah would be born in Bethlehem (Mic. 5:2), it had not mentioned that He would grow up in Nazareth. Nathanael, coming from Cana nearby, had a low opinion of Nazareth and its people. He wondered if anything good could come from it. We know that the people of Nazareth once tried to throw Jesus off a cliff to end His life, although He managed to escape (Luke

4:29-30). If this was typical of their tendency to be violent, we can better understand why Nathanael felt negative about anyone coming from there.

46b. Philip saith unto him, Come and see.

Philip's reply was wonderful in its simplicity. Rather than argue with Nathanael about whether or not the Messiah could come from a place such as Nazareth, he invited him to come and see for himself. We too often forget that the best kind of witnessing is to put aside our fragile arguments and introduce individuals to Christ. He has the ability, through His Holy Spirit, to draw people to Himself once they are put in contact with Him.

B. Jesus plus Nathanael: 47-50

47. Jesus saw Nathanael coming to him, and saith of him, Behold an Israelite indeed, in whom is no guile!

Here was an interesting reaction by Jesus to a common Jew in need of a Savior the same as all the others. He saw something special in Nathanael. He said that he was an Israelite without guile, meaning that he was sincere and not a hypocrite. He seemed to be free from deceit, duplicity, falsity, and dishonesty. This was an amazing testimony by the Son of God for a child of Abraham. We assume that Nathanael had become this way by carefully following the teachings of the Jewish Scriptures in his everyday living. It showed what the Old Testament could do in preparing a person to meet and become a follower of the Messiah. We are reminded of Galatians 3:24—"The law was our schoolmaster to bring us unto Christ, that we might be justified by faith."

48a. Nathanael saith unto him, Whence knowest thou me?

Nathanael was amazed to realize that Jesus, Whom he had not yet met, could know about his guileless character. He realized there was something special about the Master, and he inquired about it.

48b. Jesus answered and said unto him, Before that Philip called thee, when thou wast under the fig tree, I saw thee.

Jesus told Nathanael that He had "seen" him under a fig tree before Philip had come to invite him to meet Him. Sitting under a fig tree had the connotation of meditation, and Jesus may have known what Nathanael was thinking about or praying about when he was there. Nathanael was once again amazed that Jesus could "see" him at a distance not normally possible with regular sight. He must have concluded that Jesus was supernatural in this way, and his heart was stirred to believe that Philip was right about Him being the Messiah.

49. Nathanael answered and saith unto him, Rabbi, thou art the Son of God; thou art the King of Israel.

Nathanael quickly discerned that Jesus was the Messiah, and he was thrilled about it. He expressed his delight by declaring Jesus to be the Son of God and the King of Israel, with perhaps the first referring to His person and the second to His office. Nathanael was declaring Jesus to be divine and sovereign.

50a. Jesus answered and said unto him, Because I said unto thee, I saw thee under the fig tree, believest thou?

Jesus appeared to be surprised that Nathanael would accept Him as the Messiah as quickly as he did and on only the evidence of "seeing" him under the fig tree. However, we know that Jesus already knew Nathanael's heart and mind and that he had become a believer.

50b ...thou shalt see greater things than these.

This, plus verse 51, was probably an allusion to Jacob's vision of a ladder reaching from earth to heaven with the angels of God ascending and descending it (Gen. 28:13), Some think that reference to Daniel seeing in night visions one like the Son of man coming with the clouds of heaven may have been in mind (Dan. 7:13).

As we conclude this lesson on selection of disciples by Jesus, let us consider Paul's comments in 1 Corinthians 1:26-27—"Ye see your calling, brethren, how that not many wise men after the flesh, not many mighty, not many noble, are called: but God hath chosen the foolish things of the world to confound the wise; and God hath chosen the weak things of the world to confound the things which are mighty."

Evangelistic Emphasis

Have you played the game "Gossip"? A leader starts a whispered sentence around the circle. You whisper it to the person next to you only once—you're not allowed to repeat it, even if the next person doesn't understand it. One by one the whispered sentence gets passed along, with all its distortions, until it reaches the last person—and by then, like many tales, it bears no resemblance to the original sentence.

Spreading the good news of Christ often follows a more positive version of this game. When precautions are taken to keep the original sentence intelligible, the process of repetition through the chain is invaluable. It happened with the earliest disciples of John the Baptist and Jesus. "Peter!" John's disciple Andrew exclaimed to his brother. "We have found the Lord!" "Nathanael!" said Philip, "We have found the One the prophets foretold!"

Through the years, efforts to squelch the message have failed. The news is too good not to share, and people of good faith endeavor to keep its original clarity and content. The only way Satan has found to stop it is to interrupt the chain reaction, persuading one link in the chain to remain silent; or to affect our hearing or speech in a way that distorts the message beyond recognition. Our task is to keep the process of the game alive, while not changing the essentials of the good news.

♦♦♦♦♦♦

Memory Selection

We have found the Messias.
John 1:41

"Messias" (Messiah), meaning "anointed," is a word used in the Old Testament more broadly than just in reference to Him who would one day come as the Savior of the world. Yet it always refers to something valued and precious and honored.

The tabernacle—that portable Jewish "temple" in the wilderness—was anointed, along with the holy vessels and altars within. Priests were anointed with oil to signify their holy office. Kings and prophets were anointed as a sign of being set apart for God's special use. The term could also indicate the joy of God's special favor, as in Psalm 45:7—"God, thy God, hath anointed thee with the oil of gladness."

You may have heard the word used in this way even today. When a ministry seems to be going especially well, people may describe it as being "anointed." And in many communities of faith, the ordination of ministers and other special servants is accompanied by an anointing with oil, just as it was used in Bible times.

For isn't it still our nature to seek to follow and be a part of those activities that are specially blessed of God? We have many calls in the modern world for our time, attention and allegiance—just as John the Baptist's disciples already had plenty to do when they found Jesus. Because Christ was *the* Anointed One, following Him was the best choice. Can we also give Him the anointed place in our own priorities?

May 9, 1993

Weekday Problems

Fortunately for Andrew and Simon Peter, following the Messiah became a family affair. Both brothers became a part of Christ's inner circle of the Twelve, and were kinsmen both by blood and by faith.

Lillian and her sister Betsy weren't so fortunate. While serving in the Peace Corps, Lillian became involved in a cult that conducted seances and other rituals designed to contact the dead. When she returned, she approached her sister much like Andrew did Peter. "Come with me to one of our meetings," she urged.

Betsy, an active Christian, was reluctant. The very mention of contacting the dead frightened her, and she thought she remembered that the Bible forbids such practices. During one argument she called Lillian a witch, and the atmosphere between the two sisters has been very tense.

For her part, Lillian is trying to put her newfound interests into some kind of framework that is compatible with Christianity. Betsy sees this, and is considering going to a meeting with Lillian after all. Maybe it would restore some of their closeness, and even help Lillian to reconsider her involvement.

*Would you accept Lillian's invitation if you were Betsy?
*Should Betsy protest that the Bible takes a dim view of contacting the dead (as in Deut. 18:10-11), and try to get her sister to leave the cult?
*Should she decline to visit on the basis that she is afraid?

◆◆◆◆◆◆

Superintendent's Sermonette

If something is good, it ought to grow. We know that a Sunday school is good, but it often does not seem to grow, and we can become discouraged. However, someone figured it out mathematically that ten per cent growth per year would double the size of a Sunday school in just eight years! Even allowing for attrition by death, loss of interest, or people moving away, a Sunday school should be able to double in size in ten years.

How does growth take place? It comes from good teaching and counseling. It comes from having adequate facilities, equipment, and curriculum. It comes from capable administration. It comes from an active calling program. It comes from prayer.

In many cases, the burden for the work to be done falls on a small percentage of a church's members. The majority all too often sit on the sidelines. The fact is, however, that steady growth is hard to find unless more people get involved. It is on an individual basis that believers must make contacts which will produce converts. Our lesson today shows how it happened in Jesus' time. Disciples came to Him in one's and two's. Let us be willing to make the effort to persuade others to accept Him as Savior and see His church grow.

This Lesson In Your Life

"Come and see"... "We have found him"... "Follow me." Such expressions in our text are explicitly used to invite people to faith in Christ. In turn, they also invite us to investigate other sources of faith—how and why and by whom do other people become and maintain themselves as believers? The highlights of recent research in this area may help us be more intentional in the Christian task of nurturing faith.

Of course one of the most important ways to develop believers is in *the family* and the *family of faith*. This process was at work in John 1, which depicts family members and fellow-Jews telling others within their circle about Jesus. To no one's surprise, recent studies show how children typically absorb at least some of the elements of their parents' faith. One study even showed that a high percentage even of rebellious children who reject parental values for a time, eventually return to an affirmation of core family values.

Christian institutions are credited with being an important factor in faith-formation. The Sunday School, Christian day schools and Christian colleges are at the forefront. Even some businesses (such as Christian publishing firms) have mission statements that include passing along the faith to others.

In recent years some have questioned whether the Christian college or university can adequately support the kind of free enquiry that makes education vital and progressive, while maintaining a protectionist position over Christian values. But the numbers of church related institutions of higher education that continue to turn out Christian men and women equipped for various professions indicate that these schools are still considered by their constituents to be viable ways of "traditioning" people in the faith.

Heroes and *mentors* have been identified as influential in handing along Christian faith and values. Recent scandals showing that Christians with high visibility also have feet of clay only highlight their influence on others. Tracing the roots of your own faith may lead to someone—a relative or family friend, a minister or layperson, a Boy Scout leader or teacher—whose life you admired, and who came along at a moment when you were especially open to his way of modeling the faith.

Crises are often crucially involved in a person's faith development. We are often reminded that the word "crisis" means "opportunity" in some Eastern languages. Similarly, in faith development, a crisis denotes an event that may push us *toward* or *away from* deeper faith, depending on choices and circumstances. War, for example, has the capacity to point us toward God, or away from Him. Generally, the population as a whole becomes more outwardly religious during wartime; but individuals caught up in its brutality have returned with their faith damaged, or destroyed by the inevitable and agonizing question of why God allows such evils.

Historically, *the culture* itself has been an important bearer of the faith. Although our nation was founded partly in response to a demand for religious liberty, Christian values were imbedded in its foundation. We can debate whether one or another of our forefathers was explicitly "Christian" or just "deist"; but the fact remains that our society's civic fabric early assumed shared Christian principles.

We can see that the wellsprings of faith are diverse. Furthermore, a sovereign God can surprise us by using unpredictable events and sources to point us toward Himself. But whether or not we can catalogue them precisely, we want to be a part of a "Yes!" answer to Christ's searching question in Luke 18:8: "When the Son of man cometh, shall he find faith on the earth?"

Seed Thoughts

1. What is the significance of the expression "Lamb of God," which John again applies to Christ in 1:36?
It related Christ and His work to the Jewish sacrifical system in which the blood of lambs signified atonement for sins.

2. From what group were two of Jesus' earliest disciples recruited?
From among the disciples of John the Baptist.

3. How do you think John felt about this, in view of such statements as those in 1:20 and 3:28-30?
The indication is that John would not have resented it, since he did not envy Jesus His role, and since he knew his ministry was to "decrease."

4. Have you had a personal experience in which someone introduced you to Jesus as did Andrew and Nathanel, or in which you yourself were able to tell someone of Him?
(Encourage group sharing.)

5. What significance is there in the title "Messiah" that Andrew uses in verse 41?
It referred to "the Anointed One," the long-awaited Deliverer of Israel promised in their Scriptures.

---

1. What is the significance of the expression "Lamb of God," which John again applies to Christ in 1:36?

2. From what group were two of Jesus' earliest disciples recruited?

3. How do you think John felt about this, in view of such statements as those in 1:20 and 3:28-30?

4. Have you had a personal experience in which someone introduced you to Jesus as did Andrew and Nathanel, or in which you yourself were able to tell someone of Him?

5. What significance is there in the title "Messiah" that Andrew uses in verse 41?

6. What two translation helps does the Gospel writer offer in verses 38 and 41?

7. What word play does Jesus make on the meaning of Peter's name ("rock") in Matthew 16:18?

8. If Nathanael knew the scripture Micah 5:2, would it help explain his statement in John 1:46?

9. What astounded Nathanael and prompted him to confess that Jesus is the son of God? (see vss. 47-48).

10. What Old Testament incident may be behind Christ's saying in verse 51? (See Gen. 28:10-15.)

(PLEASE TURN PAGE)

(SEED THOUGHTS--Cont'd)

It related Christ and His work to the Jewish sacrifical system in which the blood of lambs signified atonement for sins.

From among the disciples of John the Baptist.

The indication is that John would not have resented it, since he did not envy Jesus His role, and since he knew his ministry was to "decrease."

(Encourage group sharing.)

It referred to "the Anointed One," the long-awaited Deliverer of Israel promised in their Scriptures.

He explains that Rabbi means "master" (or teacher), and that Messiah means "Christ" (which is from the Greek word for Messiah, or the Anointed One).

Jesus relates it to the rock-like foundation of the Church (probably the foundational truth of His Sonship).

Very likely, since he would have expected the Messiah to come from Bethlehem, not Nazareth.

The fact that Jesus somehow saw him and knew him even before He met him.

The incident is "Jacob's ladder," when God renewed His promise to Abraham.

6. What two translation helps does the Gospel writer offer in verses 38 and 41?
He explains that Rabbi means "master" (or teacher), and that Messiah means "Christ" (which is from the Greek word for Messiah, or the Anointed One).

7. What word play does Jesus make on the meaning of Peter's name ("rock") in Matthew 16:18?
Jesus relates it to the rock-like foundation of the Church (probably the foundational truth of His Sonship).

8. If Nathanael knew the scripture Micah 5:2, would it help explain his statement in John 1:46?
Very likely, since he would have expected the Messiah to come from Bethlehem, not Nazareth.

9. What astounded Nathanael and prompted him to confess that Jesus is the son of God? (see vss. 47-48).
The fact that Jesus somehow saw him and knew him even before He met him.

10. What Old Testament incident may be behind Christ's saying in verse 51? (See Gen. 28:10-15.)
The incident is "Jacob's ladder," when God renewed His promise to Abraham.

May 16, 1993

Can This Be The Christ?

John 4

7 There cometh a woman of Sa-ma´-ri to draw water: Jesus saith unto her, Give me to drink.
8 (For his disciples were gone away unto the city to buy meat.)
9 Then saith the woman of Sa-ma´-ri-a unto him, How is it that thou, being a Jew, askest drink of me, which am a woman of Sa-ma´-ri-a? for the Jews have no dealings with the Sa-ma'-ri-tans.
10 Jesus answered and said unto her, If thou knewest the gift of God, and who it is that saith to thee, Give me to drink; thou wouldest have asked of him, and he would have given thee living water.
11 The woman saith unto him, Sir, thou hast nothing to draw with, and the well is deep: from whence then hast thou that living water?
12 Art thou greater than our father Jacob, which gave us the well, and drank thereof himself, and his children, and his cattle?
13 Jesus answered and said unto her, Whosoever drinketh of this water shall thirst again:
14 But whosoever drinketh of the water that I shall give him shall never thirst; but the water that I shall give him shall be in him a well of water springing up into everlasting life.
15 The woman saith unto him, Sir, give me this water, that I thirst not, neither come hither to draw.

20 Our fathers worshipped in this mountain; and ye say, that in Jerusalem is the place where men ought to worship.
21 Jesus saith unto her, Woman, believe me, the hour cometh, when ye shall neither in this mountain, nor yet at Jerusalem, worship the Father.
22 Ye worship ye know not what: we know what we worship: for salvation is of the Jews.
23 But the hour cometh, and now is, when the true worshippers shall worship the Father in spirit and in truth: for the Father seeketh such to worship him.
24 God is a Spirit: and they that worship him must worship him in spirit and in truth.
25 The woman saith unto him, I know that Mes-si´-as cometh, which is called Christ: when he is come, he will tell us all things.
26 Jesus saith unto her, I that speak unto thee am he.

◆◆◆◆◆◆

◀ **Memory Selection**
John 4:42

◀ **Devotional Reading**
John 4:43-54

◀ **Background Scripture**
John 4:1-42

◀ **Printed Scripture**
John 4:7-15, 20-26

CAN THIS BE THE CHRIST?

Teacher's Target

Jesus minstered first to Jews, then to Samaritans, and even to Gentiles in Phoenicia. Our focus today is on His ministry to one Samaritan woman, but that contact led to His ministry to the whole town of Sychar in Samaria. Just prior to His ascension to heaven, Jesus told His disciples that they would receive power from the Holy Spirit and become His witnesses in Jerusalem, Judaea, Samaria, and the uttermost part of the earth (Acts 1:8).

Help your students to analyze Jesus' dealing with the unnamed Samaritan woman at the well outside of Sychar to learn His personal evangelism techniques. As these are grasped, look for ways to transpose those techniques in witnessing for Christ today. Face honestly the problems which can be raised by racial prejudice in witnessing situations, and determine how Jesus was able to be free from them. We need to follow His example in this in a shrinking world where we are bound to come into contact with many racial groups.

Lesson Introduction

Jesus began His conversation with the Samaritan woman by asking for a drink of literal water. He then talked to her about the availability of living water. She obviously did not catch His meaning. In spite of this, she did ask Him for living water. The conversation then veered off to talk about the woman's five previous husbands and a current lover, the proper place to worship God, and Jesus' statement that location of worship was secondary to worshiping God in spirit and in truth. As the woman's spiritual perception grew, Jesus declared Himself to be the Messiah, and she accept Him as such.

It seemed as if the concept of living water had been lost in the convolutions of the conversation. However, John 7:37-39 later made it clear that living water referred to the Holy Spirit and blessings He bestows on those who accept Jesus as Savior. The thought was further developed by Paul in Romans 8:14-17. It was put perhaps most succinctly put by Paul in 1 Corinthians 12:3—"No man can say that Jesus is the Lord, but by the Holy Ghost."

Teaching Outline

I. Literal Water: John 4:7-9
   A. Request: 7-8
   B. Racism: 9
II. Living Water: John 4:10-15
   A. Suggestion: 10
   B. Source: 11-12
   C. Superiority: 13-15
III. Loving Revelation: John 4: 20-26
   A. Place: 20-22
   B. Person I: 23-24
   C. Person II: 25-26

Daily Bible Readings

Mon. The Water of Life
John 4:1-14
Tue. True Worship
John 4:15-24
Wed. Can This Be the Christ?
John 4:25-30
Thu. White for Harvest
John 4:31-38
Fri. A Personal Experience
John 4:39-42
Sat. Looking for Signs
John 4:43-48
Sun. The Second Sign
John 4:49-54

May 16, 1993

VERSE BY VERSE

I. Literal Water: John 4:7-9

A. Request: 7-8

7a. There cometh a woman of Samaria to draw water: ...

John 4:3-6 tells us that Jesus and His disciples were on their way from Judaea to Galilee. Since Jews did not like Samaritans, they would often go around Samaria by crossing over the Jordan River and traveling up through Peraea, instead. However, John said that Jesus had to go through Samaria, and we assume it was because He had a spiritual reason. A well dug in Jacob's time was outside the city of Sychar, and the group arrived there about the sixth hour of the day (noontime). The woman who came out from Sychar to draw water at that hour had a bad reputation (vss. 16-18). She probably came in the heat of the day in order to avoid contact with the other women who would shun her.

7b. ...Jesus saith unto her, Give me to drink.

Jesus was wearily resting on the edge of the well when the woman arrived (vs. 6). He was thirsty and decided to ask the woman for some water. This reference to literal water was a prelude to His later reference to living water. We do not even know if she ever gave Jesus a drink, for it is not mentioned in subsequent verses.

8. (For his disciples were gone away unto the city to buy meat.)

Jesus' disciples had left Him at the well and proceeded into the city to buy provisions. Jews and Samaritans may not have had good relationships in social or religious matters, but they carried on business with one another. Jesus may have sent the disciples into the city so that He could have time alone to deal with the woman who came out to the well. She was to be the key to open up the whole populace to the gospel.

B. Racism: 9

9. Then saith the woman of Samaria unto him, How is it that thou, being a Jew, askest drink of me, which am a woman of Samaria? for the Jews have no dealings with the Samsritans.

The woman was surprised that Jesus would ask her for a drink of water. Even in as simple a matter as this, she realized that Jews and Samaritans had racial barriers separating them. She must have known Jesus was a Jew by His clothing and accent. She may have thought it odd for Jesus to ask her for a drink, realizing that a Jew would normally refuse to drink from a Samaritan vessel.

When Assyrians conquered the northern kingdom of Israel in 722 B.C., they allowed some Jews to remain in the land and deported the rest. Gentiles were brought in from the east to be resettled in Israel. Marriages between these Jews and Gentiles produced the mixed breed known as Samaritans, and their descendants were generally despised by Jews.

Jesus was not prejudiced toward Samaritans. He proved this at Sychar, as we shall see. At another time He told the parable of the good Samaritan and then urged a Jewish scribe to follow this example of compassion (Luke 10:25-37). At still another time He commended one healed leper out of ten who came back to thank Him, and that man was a Samaritan (Luke 17:11-19). Jesus loved all races, but the same has not always been true of those who have borne His name. This deserves serious discussion.

II. Living Water: John 4:10-15

A. Suggestion: 10

10. Jesus answered and said unto

her, **If thou knewest the gift of God, and who it is that saith to thee, Give me to drink; thou wouldest have asked of him, and he would have given thee living water.**

Jesus began the process of turning attention from literal water to living water. Subsequent remarks made by the woman suggest that she did not comprehend the shift from literal water to spiritual refreshment, and that may explain why Jesus moved on to other topics as the conversation continued. Jesus did imply here that He was someone special who could give her living water if she requested it.

B. Source: 11-12

11. The woman saith unto him, Sir, thou has nothing to draw with, and the well is deep: from whence then hast thou that living water?

The woman seemed to pick up on the thought that Jesus was someone special, for she addressed Him as "Sir." This trend continued, with her calling Him "Sir" again (vs. 15), "a prophet" (vs. 19), and "the Christ" (vs. 29). Still thinking of living water as being literal water, she commented that Jesus had no vessel or rope with which to draw any out of the deep well there. How, then, could He offer to give any to her?

12. Art thou greater than our father Jacob, which gave us the well, and drank thereof himself, and his children, and his cattle?

It would appear that the woman spoke sarcastically when she asked if Jesus thought Himself to be greater than her ancestor, Jacob, who had caused the well to be dug which supplied water for himself, his family, and his herds. It had served other generations for many centuries, as well. Both Jews and Samaritans claimed Jacob as a prestigious ancestor. Did Jesus dare to claim that He was a source equal to Jacob when it came to water?

C. Superiority: 13-15

13. Jesus answered and said unto her, Whosoever drinketh of this water shall thirst again:

Once again Jesus attempted to help the woman realize that the water from Jacob's well was only literal. It would satisfy a person's thirst for a brief time and then need to be replenished. He was stating the obvious, for the woman had to come often to the well to get more water.

14. But whosoever drinketh of the water that I shall give him shall never thirst; but the water that I shall give him shall be in him a well of water, springing up into everlasting life.

Jesus declared that the water He had to offer was superior to water from the well. He said that the water He gave would prevent a person from ever thirsting again. Taken from a literal viewpoint, this was an amazing statement, and the woman seemed to take it this way. She had to decide whether or not Jesus Himself was superior to Jacob, and she must have concluded that He was, unless she was being sarcastic again. Let us look at her response.

15. The woman saith unto him, Sir, give me this water, that I thirst not, neither come hither to draw.

We would have to have heard the tone of voice she used in making this remark. She may have been sincere and really anxious for Jesus to give her water which would permanently slake her thirst and relieve her of coming out to draw water from Jacob's well. On the other hand, she may have smirked and spoken in such a way that she ridiculed the idea that anyone could give her water which did not have to be constantly replaced to take care of thirst. Whatever the case, it seems clear that she was *still* thinking of literal water and that Jesus had not convinced her that He could supply spiritual refreshment. He now seemed to change topics.

Jesus told the woman to call her husband and have him come to Him. Jesus was testing her, for He knew that she had had five husbands and was now living with a man to whom she was not married. When she admitted this and heard what He said, she discerned that He must be a prophet (vss. 16-19).

III. Loving Revelation: John 4:20-26

A. Place: 20-22

20. Our fathers worshipped in this mountain; and ye say, that in Jerusa-

lem is the place where men ought to worship.

Shifting away from further discussion of her private life, the woman began to talk about worship. She said that her ancestors taught that worship should be done at Mount Gerizim nearby, while Jews said that it should take place at Jerusalem. She wanted to know what Jesus thought about this. If He was a real prophet, perhaps He could explain this discrepancy and enlighten her.

21. Jesus saith unto her, Woman, believe me, the hour cometh, when ye shall neither in this mountain, nor yet at Jerusalem, worship the Father.

Jesus suggested that the woman trust Him when He said that the time was coming when location for worship would not matter. We see here a hint of coming events. Judaism and the Samaritan religion were going to be superseded by Christianity. Jerusalem would be destroyed by the Romans in A.D. 70, leaving the temple in ruins. Under the new order worship would not require geographical placement in order to be correct.

22. Ye worship ye know not what: we know what we worship: for salvation is of the Jews.

Jesus wanted to make it clear that, for the time being, Jews held the edge over Samaritans on spiritual understanding. Samaritans groped in the darkness, while Jews had enlightenment regarding salvation. It was obvious that Jesus would not have agreed with the modern idea that *all* religions are equally valid. God had committed His ordinances to the Jews, and truth was to be found in them. Any deviations would have to be set aside.

B. Person I: 23-24

23. But the hour cometh, and now is, when the true worshippers shall worship the Father in spirit and in truth: for the Father seeketh such to worship him.

Jesus declared that the time was now at hand in which true worshipers would worship God the Father in spirit (spiritually) and in truth (sincerely). These were the kind of people God was seeking, and, it might be implied, the only kind He received. Worship was not a matter of location as much as it was a condition of the heart. Elaborate buildings, sophisticated clergy, rich vestments, and ritualistic ceremonies could be no substitutes for honest yearning for God and His will.

24. God is a Spirit: and they that worship him must worship him in spirit and in truth.

This was an elaboration on what had been said as recorded in verse 23. The reason that God must be worshiped in spirit (spiritually) and in truth (sincerely) was that He was a Spirit Himself. Literal things were of the earth, but spiritual things were of heaven. God demanded spiritual communion from His people. That is why the Holy Spirit had to come and lead people in maintaining contact with God and Christ. The spiritual aspect of our lives should be considered more *real* than any other aspect, including material things.

C. Person II: 25-26

25. The woman saith unto him, I know that Messias cometh, which is called Christ: when he is come, he will tell us all things.

The woman wanted Jesus to know that she believed in a coming Messiah, the One called Christ. She said that He would reveal things to come. It may be that she now thought of Jesus not only as *a* prophet (vs. 19) but as *the* Prophet foretold in Deuteronomy 18:15-19.

26. Jesus saith unto her, I that speak unto thee am he.

Jesus had led the woman along gradually by first turning her attention from literal water to living water and then to the meaning of true worship and the realization that He Himself was the Messiah, the Christ. Spiritual discernment flooded over her. As Jesus' disciples returned from Sychar, the woman left her waterpot and hurried into the city to invite people to come out and meet Him (vss. 27-28). Jesus taught them for two days before moving on, and many believed on Him (vss. 40-43). Thus was laid a foundation of belief in Samaria which was later enlarged by the ministry of Philip (Acts 8:5-8).

Evangelistic Emphasis

An interesting sidelight to Jesus' encounter with the Samaritan woman at Jacob's well is the insight it offers into communicating the gospel across racial and national lines. It emerges from the way Jesus interacted with a person from a race that most Jews considered "unclean"—"For the Jews have no dealings with the Samaritans" (John 4:9).

Thankfully, overtly expressed attitudes of cultural superiority are becoming a thing of the past as missionaries from the West enter new lands. Yet some unevangelized peoples still expect it—as did the Samaritan woman. How can this suspicion be overcome? Jesus' request for a drink of water illustrates one way: *He Placed himself in a position of need.* Instead of intimating that only He was in a position to give something of value, He communicated respect for the Samaritan woman by indicating that she, too, had something to offer him.

Contrast this with what a missionary to Thailand a generation ago wrote home: "When I see these Buddhist temples it makes me want to get in a Sherman tank and smash them all." Granted that the missionary was there to present the claims of Christ against those of other religions. Still, could he not have created more openings for ministering the water of life if he had some appreciation at least for such enriching elements as the culture's architectural marvels?

◆◆◆◆◆◆

Memory Selection

We know that this is indeed the Christ, the Savior of the world.
John 4:42

None of us can be too grateful to those who first enabled us to learn about Christ—just as the villagers of Sychar must have appreciated the woman who told them of her encounter with Jesus at the well.

Yet our Memory Selection moves to a deeper level, from the hearing of ears and mind to the experiencing of the soul from hearsay...evidence to personal knowledge...from "they say" to *"we know."*

Are we today handicapped because we cannot know Jesus "in the flesh"? Christian history says otherwise. Since empire-wide persecution of Christians did not begin until long after Christ's death, most of the martyrs "knew" Him with the heart, not their eyes and ears. People rarely give their lives for a cause they merely know *about*. Their death testifies to the reality of Christ's continuing life, through the Spirit.

In fact, the Spirit Himself was given, like earnest money, as a "guarantee" that Christ is real. This spirit guided the writers of New Covenant Scriptures "into all truth" (John 16:13). Thus, when we come to know Christ through scripture, and allow the Spirit to imbed this knowledge in our hearts, we *know* Him. And the same Spirit assures us that our future hope of life with Him is real (2 Cor. 5:4-5).

May 16, 1993

Weekday Problems

Fran was sure that Yusuf, the new member Bob introduced to the church's singles group, was Middle Eastern. He looked just like the Iraqi soldiers she had seen on TV during the brief war there early in 1991—when her brother Stan had been killed. Her stomach tightened as Bob and Yusuf sat down at her table for coffee. Although she managed to say "Hi," her tightly drawn lips could hardly let a smile slip by.

"Yusuf here is from Iraq," Bob said. Fran stiffened inadvertently. Why couldn't he have been from Egypt or Saudi Arabia? For a crazy instant she imagined herself screaming an insult at the man and stalking off.

For his part, Yusuf was animated and talkative. He showed no indication of being apologetic about his country, or even self-conscious about being the only dark-skinned person in the group. Fran soon excused herself, saying she had to say hello to someone at another table. Maybe this wasn't the right singles group for her after all, she thought.

*What can Fran do to deal honestly with her feelings, while having a Christian attitude toward Yusuf?

*Do unhappy experiences with individuals of another race often affect people's attitude toward the race in general?

*How would you define the term "racism"? What biblical principles does racism violate?

♦♦♦♦♦♦

Superintendent's Sermonette

We may not think of Jesus' conversation with the woman at the well outside of Sychar as a study in personal evangelism, but that is what it was. Jesus used techniques with her which we can imitate in our contacts with others today. He began the conversation by referring to something close at hand and of interest to her. He asked her for a drink of water from Jacob's well. He told her that she lacked something of value which He could give to her, although she did not at first seem to understand what He meant by living water. We know that it was spiritual refreshment. Jesus let her know that He was aware of her bad reputation and her need of a Savior.

Jesus turned aside the woman's emphasis on *where* worship of God should take place and helped her to understand that it was *how* God is worshiped that really counted. He stressed the need to worship God in spirit (spiritually) and in truth (sincerely) regardless of location or material circumstances. He revealed Himself to her as being the Messiah, the Christ, and she believed on Him. She did what we as converts also ought to do—she invited others to come and meet Him so that they might believe on Him. May God help us to follow these examples and be the kind of personal evangelists He wants us to be.

This Lesson In Your Life

TO CATCH THE SUN

The account of Jesus and the woman at Jacob's well almost turned out to be the story of two ships passing in the night. At first, the conversation depicts two people who are on totally different tracks. The woman is simply not in a position to understand what Jesus was talking about. It reminds us of the way we ourselves may find "Jesus talk" strange, and unrelated to our "real" life-work of drawing water from our various wells.

It's a matter of *attitude*—in the sense scientists speak of the attitude of a satellite, referring to the way it is turned or positioned. A satellite's attitude determines whether or not it catches the sun's rays in a way that reflects them so trackers can spot it. In a similary way, our ability to grasp the teachings of Christ depends as much on our mental position as on His words.

We may also see ourselves in the way the woman at the well seems gradually to turn herself toward the Son, in order to catch the light from His words. At first, she is surprised that Jesus even speaks to her. Not only is she a "mere woman," but a member of a race of half-castes whom Jews despised. Is this Jewish man from another planet? Were it not for some openness on her part, she may have dropped her water pot and fled.

Then there is the matter of the water. Obviously, she has access to the well and He doesn't, but He talks as if *she* should be asking *Him* for it (John 4:10-11). What sort of water is He referring to, anyway, with all that talk about "living water" and never thirsting, once you drink it?

Is the man an angel or a prophet, seeing into her personal life that way, knowing that she has had five husbands, and isn't married to the man she is with now? She must change the subject. Religion—let's try that, to move the man to a more comfortable orbit. Let's talk about the proper place of worship—is it here in Samaria, or are you one of those strict Jews who insist that the Temple in Jerusalem is the only place to worship?

No, there's more to the man that that, she can tell. She may not fully understand, but she is intrigued about His talk about the spirit of worship being more important than the physical place. Maybe she can talk with Him after all. If spirituality is His angle, she'll try bringing up the Messianic hope. And sure enough, their previously separate conversational paths seem, finally, to begin to converge with Jesus' direct thrust: "*I that speak to thee am he*." There! She understands that so clearly that she hurries off to the village to spread the good news, leaving her water pot behind (an indication that she plans to return to hear more!).

Isn't all this something like our own attitude toward theological language? Often it seems that talk about Christ, the church and the Bible can be at once intriguing and a little strange. There's something there that we need, but we aren't always sure how it fits in our world—except for the times when our personal lives are "judged" by such high standards of morality—then it fits all too well! Sometimes we want to change the subject, switching to sports or politics.

Does it take a special gift from God to get on Christ's wave length? Theologians will always debate the question, but there are some clear biblical principles required for us to be able to understand Christ. We must have a love for the truth, else God promises to actually assist us in believing falsehood (2 Thess. 2:10-12). We must be careful not to have a hardened heart: "If ye will hear his voice, harden not your hearts" (Heb. 3:15). This is simply the precondition of being willing to understand if we *were* to hear His voice.

Seed Thoughts

1. Why did Jesus leave Judea at this time and go to Galilee? (John 1:1-3).
Because the Pharisees had learned that Jesus was winning more converts than John the Baptist.

2. Explain verse 3 with the help of a Bible map.
Since Samaria lay between Judea to the south and Galilee to the north, Jesus had to go through it or around it.

3. How can Christians today can turn conversations toward spiritual matters, as Jesus did?
(Encourage open discussion on how to do this naturally.)

4. Contrast literal water with "living water," and explain this latter term (see vss. 10-14).
Jesus' teachings quench our spiritual thirst, and thus have an eternal quality literal water lacks.

5. What prompted the woman's belief that Jesus was "a prophet"? (vss. 16-19.)
Jesus' divine knowledge of her personal life.

---

1. Why did Jesus leave Judea at this time and go to Galilee? (John 1:1-3).

2. Explain verse 3 with the help of a Bible map.

3. How can Christians today can turn conversations toward spiritual matters, as Jesus did?

4. Contrast literal water with "living water," and explain this latter term (see vss. 10-14).

5. What prompted the woman's belief that Jesus was "a prophet"? (vss. 16-19.)

6. What situation does Jesus seem to predict when he says that true worship will be neither in Samaria or Jerusalem (vss. 21-24).

7. Give an example of worship that is not "in spirit and in truth," as stipulated in verses 23-24.

8. What was more important than physical food, to Jesus (vss. 31-34)?

9. Who had previously "sown seed" that Christ's disciples were now able to harvest (as in vss. 35-38)?

10. What exemplary spirit was exhibited by those who heard the woman's testimony about Jesus? (Vss. 40-42.)

(PLEASE TURN PAGE)

Because the Pharisees had learned that Jesus was winning more converts than John the Baptist.

Since Samaria lay between Judea to the south and Galilee to the north, Jesus had to go through it or aroumd it.

(Encourage open discussion on how to do this naturally.)

Jesus' teachings quench our spiritual thirst, and thus have an eternal quality literal water lacks.

Jesus' divine knowledge of her personal life.

A time when acceptable worship will not be tied to a "holy place," but will be a matter of the heart—probably the Christian era.

Worship that is insincere or thoughtless worship in which outward ritual is not accompanied by awareness of its significance.

Doing God's will.

John the Baptist and his disciples (see John 3:28- 30, for example).

They asked Jesus to stay in order to hear Him for themselves, instead of settling for hearsay evidence.

(SEED THOUGHTS--Cont'd)

6. What situation does Jesus seem to predict when he says that true worship will be neither in Samaria or Jerusalem (vss. 21-24).
A time when acceptable worship will not be tied to a "holy place," but will be a matter of the heart—probably the Christian era.

7. Give an example of worship that is not "in spirit and in truth," as stipulated in verses 23-24.
Worship that is insincere or thoughtless worship in which outward ritual is not accompanied by awareness of its significance.

8. What was more important than physical food, to Jesus (vss. 31-34)?
Doing God's will.

9. Who had previously "sown seed" that Christ's disciples were now able to harvest (as in vss. 35-38)?
John the Baptist and his disciples (see John 3:28- 30, for example).

10. What exemplary spirit was exhibited by those who heard the woman's testimony about Jesus? (Vss. 40-42.)
They asked Jesus to stay in order to hear Him for themselves, instead of settling for hearsay evidence.

May 23, 1993

"THE LAW SAYS—JESUS MUST DIE!"

Confronting The Galilean

John 7
37. In the last day, that great day of the feast, Jesus stood and cried, saying, If any man thirst, let him come unto me, and drink.
38. He that believeth on me, as the scripture hath said, out of his belly shall flow rivers of living water.
39. (But this spake he of the Spirit, which they that believe on him should receive: for the Holy Ghost was not yet *given*; because that Jesus was not yet glorified.)
40. Many of the people therefore, when they heard this saying, said, Of a truth this is the Prophet.
41. Others said, This is the Christ. But some said, Shall Christ come out of Galilee?
42. Hath not the scripture said, That Christ cometh of the seed of David, and out of the town of Beth´-le-hem, where David was?
43. So there was a division among the people because of him.
44. And some of them would have taken him; but no man laid hands on him.
45. Then came the officers to the chief priests and Pharisees; and they said unto them, Why have ye not brought him?
46. The officers answered, Never man spake like this man.
47. Then answered them the Pharisees, Are ye also deceived?
48. Have any of the rulers or of the Pharisees believed on him?
49. But this people who knoweth not the law are cursed.
50. Nico-de´-mus saith unto them, (he that came to Jesus by night, being one of them,)
51. Doth our law judge *any* man, before it hear him and know what he doeth?
52. They answered and said unto him, Art thou also of Galilee? Search, and look: for out of Galilee ariseth no prophet.

◆◆◆◆◆◆

◀ **Memory Selection**
John 7:41

◀ **Devotional Reading**
John 7:1-13

◀ **Background Scripture**
John 1:37-52

◀ **Printed Scripture**
John 7:37-52

CONFRONTING THE GALILEAN

Teacher's Target

Along with the growing popularity of Jesus among the common people of His day was the growing resistance to Him by the Jewish religious leaders. The common people heard Him gladly, but the entrenched religious leaders felt threatened by Him. Jesus used even times of opposition to His ministry to teach people about Who He was and what He came to do. As sides were being chosen for or against Him, some were caught in the middle, such as Nicodemus and Joseph of Arimathaea, whom some have labeled as "secret believers."

Help your students to see that no one could harm Jesus until the proper time for His suffering and death was at hand. God and His angels protected Him during the time of His earthly ministry. We should take our cue from this, realizing that we, too, are under God's divine care as long as He has service for us to do. We must expect opposition from those who ignore or oppose the truth and trust in God's sovereign grace to sustain us.

Lesson Introduction

Jesus was in Galilee, because He could no longer walk openly in Jewry (Judaea) where Jewish religious leaders were plotting His death (John 7:1). The chapter goes on to tell how His unbelieving brothers urged Him to accompany them to the annual Feast of Tabernacles in Jerusalem. He chose to remain behind at that time and go secretly afterward. While there, Jesus appeared in the temple, where He evidently was protected by the general support of the people who wanted to hear Him teach. He climaxed His teaching by declaring Himself to be capable of satisfying any man's thirst.

Jesus was referring to the Holy Spirit Who would be given to those who believed in Himself. People were confused, many thinking Him to be the Prophet predicted in Deuteronomy 18:15-19, while others thought of Him as the Christ (Messiah). Still others could not believe that the Messiah could come out of Galilee, not realizing Jesus had been born in Bethlehem of Judaea. Officers sent to arrest Him failed. Nicodemus sought to defend Him and was scorned. Tensions finally eased.

Teaching Outline

I. Declaration: John 7:37-39
   A. Statement: 37-38
   B. Spirit: 39
II. Division: John 7:40-44
   A. Prophet: 40
   B. Perplexity: 41-42
   C. Protection: 43-44
III. Discussions: John 7:45-52
   A. Report: 45-46
   B. Ridicule: 47-49
   C. Reminder: 50-51
   D. Ridicule: 52

Daily Bible Readings

Mon. Jesus in Galilee
John 7:1-9
Tue. Jesus Teaches
John 7:10-15
Wed. The Authority of Jesus
John 7:16-24
Thu. The People Marvel
John 7:25-31
Fri. Come and Drink
John 7:32-39
Sat. This Is the Christ
John 7:40-44
Sun. Nicodemus Defends Jesus
John 7:45-52

May 23, 1993

VERSE BY VERSE

I. Declaration: John 7:37-39

A. Statement: 37-38

37. In the last day, that great day of the feast, Jesus stood and cried, saying, If any man thirst, let him come unto me, and drink.

The last day of the Feast of Tabernacles was also the last day of the Jewish festival year, and, therefore, it was the greatest (most important, final) day. Whereas it was customary for priests to bring water in golden vessels each day from the pool of Siloam or the stream of Shiloh and pour it out on the temple altar, it has been suggested that this was not done on the eighth day of the feast. If so, this may have prompted Jesus to declare Himself to be One Who could satisfy spiritual thirst to all who came to Him for it.

Using water as a symbol for spiritual refreshment was well-rooted in the Old Testament. For example, Isaiah 12:2-3 read, "The Lord JEHOVAH is my strength and my song; he also is become my salvation. Therefore with joy shall ye draw water out of the wells of salvation." Jesus had already said, "He that believeth on me shall never thirst" (John 6:35), thus showing Himself to be a Source of salvation.

38. He that believeth on me, as the scripture hath said, out of his belly shall flow rivers of living water.

We are not sure if Jesus had a specific reference in mind here. He may have been thinking of Himself as the Rock which God told Moses to strike in order to bring literal water out for the ancient Israelites to drink in the wilderness (Exod. 17:6) and the fact that this served as a type of Himself and spiritual refreshment. Paul later wrote, "[Our fathers or ancestors] did all drink the same spiritual drink: for they drank of that spiritual Rock that followed them: and that Rock was Christ" (1 Cor. 10:4). Other possibilities are Isaiah 44:3; 58:11; Ezekiel 47:1-9; and Zechariah 14:8. Jesus said that believers not only became personally satisfied, but they also became channels of blessing so that spiritual refreshment came to others.

B. Spirit: 39

39. (But this spake he of the Spirit, which they that believe on him should receive: for the Holy Ghost was not yet given; because that Jesus was not yet glorified.)

The Apostle John provided this explanation of Jesus' remarkable statement. He said that it referred to the Holy Spirit as the One to be given to believers. At the time that was a future event, for Jesus had not yet died, been resurrected, glorified, and ascended to heaven. We know that the Spirit descended on believers on the Day of Pentecost following Jesus' ascension (Acts 2:1-4). The point being made was that the Holy Spirit was the One through Whom believers in Christ received spiritual blessings and with Whose help they themselves became channels of spiritual blessing to others.

II. Division: John 7: 40-44

A. Prophet: 40

40. Many of the people therefore, when they heard this saying, said, Of a truth, this is the Prophet.

With this verse we begin to see division among the people at the feast regarding Jesus. Reference to "the Prophet" here evidently came from

373

Deuteronomy 18:15—"The Lord thy God will raise up unto thee a Prophet from the midst of thee, of thy brethren, like unto me; unto him ye shall hearken." However, we do not know how these people defined the title "Prophet" with regard to Jesus. Many may have considered Him to be only a great prophet.

B. Perplexity: 41-42

41. Others said, This is the Christ. But some said, Shall Christ come out of Galilee?

There were those who saw Jesus as being more than a great prophet. They considered Him to be the Messiah, the Christ (Anointed One sent by God). Even in their case, however, we do not know if they all accepted Him as being the divine Son of God.

Those who refused to believe that Jesus was the Messiah or Christ were perplexed by the fact that He came from Galilee, for this did not line up with their belief that the Messiah must come from Judaea.

42. Hath not the scripture said, That Christ cometh of the seed of David, and out of the town of Bethlehem, where David was?

We know the facts. Micah 5:2 had predicted that the Messiah would be born in Bethlehem of Judaea. Luke 2:4-7 records that Jesus was born in Bethlehem. After a brief time in Egypt, Joseph, Mary, and Jesus had returned to Nazareth to live, and it was there that Jesus grew to maturity over the next twenty-some years. When Jesus went out to minister at the age of thirty, He appeared to be thoroughly Galilean in appearance, mannerisms, and speech. His birth in Bethlehem, ancestral home of King David, had been forgotten by some who had been aware of it. Others had never heard about it.

C. Protection: 43-44

43. So there was a division among the people because of him.

44. And some of them would have taken him; but no man laid hands on him.

Contending forces had already been in place when Jesus began to speak in the temple. What He said caused the lines to be more clearly drawn. We know that the religious leaders had been arrayed against Him. The battle now seemed to be among the common people, some of whom believed on Him and others who did not. Those who opposed Him tried to have Him taken (arrested), probably by temple officers. However; no man dared lay hands upon Him. Some might assume that this was due to protection from the many people who supported Him. Others would say that He was protected by God's divine power. Verse 30 seems to support the latter view—"They sought to take him: but no man laid hands on him, because his hour was not yet come." In other words, He could not be harmed until His ministry was completed. Those of us involved in His service might take comfort in the fact that God does the same for us.

III. Discussions: John 7:45-52

A. Report: 45-46

45. Then came the officers to the chief priests and Pharisees; and they said unto them, Why have ye not brought him?

It appears that the religious leaders, sensing opposition to Jesus among the common people, had sought to exploit the situation for their own purpose. They had sent officers, presumably temple officers, to arrest Jesus. When these men returned emptyhanded, they wanted to know what had happened. Why had they not brought Jesus with them?

46. The officers answered, Never man spake like this man.

It was apparent that the officers had been favorably impressed by Jesus. Their only answer to the religious leaders' question was that no one ever spoke the way Jesus did. It appears that this was the second time the officers had failed in their mission (vss. 30, 44). Something strange was going on here, and the leaders were ready to discuss it and defend their intention of arresting Jesus.

B. Ridicule: 47-49

47. Then answered them the Pharisees, Are ye also deceived?

48. Have any of the rulers or of the Pharisees believed on him?

Ridicule can be a powerful weapon, especially when used by superiors. The Pharisees suggested that the officers had been stupid and therefore deceived in their conclusion about Jesus. They asked the rhetorical and sarcastic question as to whether any of the rulers (religious authorities, chief priests) or Pharisees had believed on Him. Their assumption that the leaders presented a solid front against Jesus was not entirely true, as we shall see in our study of verses 50-52.

49. But this people who knoweth not the law are cursed.

This was probably a reference to Deuteronomy 28:15—"If thou wilt not hearken unto the voice of the Lord thy God, to observe to do all his commandments and his statutes which I command thee this day; that all these curses shall come upon thee, and overtake thee." This ancient warning by Moses was appropriated by the Pharisees and applied to this situation, implying that people who were ignorant of the law of God were cursed. No response by the officers was recorded. Perhaps they were frightened by the warning. However, one of the leaders was not intimidated into remaining silent but spoke out to defend Jesus.

C. Reminder: 50-51

50. Nicodemus saith unto them, (he that came to Jesus by night, being one of them,)

51. Doth not our law judge any man, before it hear him, and know what he doeth?

We have three main references to Nicodemus. He had previously come to Jesus one night, probably to shield himself from being discovered by his associates on the Sanhedrin (Jewish Council), and had talked with Him about His teachings. Jesus had emphasized the fact that Nicodemus had to be born again by the Spirit of God in order to enter the kingdom of God (John 3:1-21). Nicodemus now spoke up for Jesus' right to be heard before being condemned. He may have been thinking of what Moses had said to the Israelites in the wilderness—"Ye shall not respect persons in judgment, but ye shall hear the small as well as the great." Finally, Nicodemus had later assisted Joseph of Arimathaea in burying the body of Jesus in Joseph's rock-hewn tomb (John 19:38-42).

D. Ridicule: 52

52a. They answered and said unto him, Art thou also of Galilee?

The religious leaders turned on Nicodemus. They ignored his call for justice according to the law of God. They scorned him by asking him if he also came from Galilee, as they assumed that Jesus did. Their pride in being from Judaea was evident, and this would also show itself in their next statement.

52b. Search, and look: for out of Galilee ariseth no prophet.

Ridicule of Nicodemus continued as the religious leaders suggested that he search the Jewish Scriptures to determine that no prophet arose from the province of Galilee. One manuscript renders the word "prophet" here as "Prophet," referring to the Messiah or the Christ (Deut. 18:15-19). The attempt to make Nicodemus appear ignorant showed the ignorance of the religious leaders, because Jesus had come from Bethlehem in Judaea as the Scriptures had predicted that He would.

We find no response recorded for Nicodemus, and we assume that he considered it wise to be silent. We may feel somewhat sorry for Nicodemus and Joseph of Arimathaea for their status as secret believers who wanted to maintain their privileged positions. However, we feel a sense of shame for them in the fact that they did not openly become part of Jesus' followers. We are not told how they spent the remainder of their lives.

Categories of individuals regarding their relationship to Jesus are much as they were in His lifetime. Some remain ignorant of Him. Some are hostile to Him or ignore Him. Some give Him only limited support. Some are fervently devoted to Him. Our text today helps us to once again face ourselves and determine our relationship to Him.

Evangelistic Emphasis

The seventh chapter of John raises the matter of Jesus' timing in revealing His true identity. Apparently, it's a delicate issue. When his brethren try to persuade Him to go to the feast in Jerusalem for a great public display of His powers, He replies, "My time is not yet come" (vss. 2-6). Yet, later He decides to attend after all, with less fanfare. It's a question of timing and approach.

A curious thread often called "the Messianic secret" runs throughout the Gospels. At times, Jesus' identity is carefully guarded. It is not to be broadcast by demons. Sometimes, even those who experience Christ's healing firsthand are told sternly to "see that no man know it" (Matt. 9:30). The announcement that this miracle-worker is actually the Messiah is to be made by His followers, but only in circumstances that Jesus Himself carefully controls.

Timing is also important in sharing the message of Christ today. Missionaries may work for years in a country without much visible fruit—until circumstances become so favorable that thousands are converted in only a matter of months. Closer to home, people whom we try to introduce to Christ may resist every overture until a moment of crisis or other event—perhaps even the unseen work of the Spirit—triggers an openness to the gospel.

All this, plus the fact that we cannot share Christ with everyone, everywhere, all at once, is a call for the sensitivity to discern appropriate moments for sharing the message. It is also a call for patience and steadfastness, and for trust in God's own timing.

Are there those in your circle of acquaintances whose "hour" may be come—whose personal stories have brought them to a point of readiness to hear the greatest story ever told?

Memory Selection

This is the Christ.
John 7:41

The dust of 20 centuries tends to obscure the significance of reaching the conclusion that "this is the Christ," and daring to admit it publicly.

Early Christians under Roman rule were pressured to say something like this about Caesar. Many were willing to give up their lives rather than to say "Caesar is Lord," or to sprinkle a bit of incense on an altar to the goddess Roma, the spirit of the Empire. Would we be willing to commit both treason and "heresy" by insisting that Jesus, not Caesar, is Lord?

Why make so much over such a simple statement? Because it shows where our loyalty is. It is a public statement of which king we serve, and in whose realm we are, first and foremost, citizens. The statement even aligns us with the mind of the eternal God. In the Greek, "confession" means to "say alike" It is God who first "confessed" that Jesus is the Christ, His only begotten Son. When we say the same thing, our lone voice is caught up into an eternal echo, joining the voice of God and of uncounted thousands booming down the corridors of time: <u>This is the Christ</u>!

May 23, 1993

Weekday Problems

It must have been unsettling to the Pharisees when the officers they sent to entrap Jesus returned with admiration for Him instead of accusations. How could they trust agents who could only report the truth!?

Richard, an assistant district attorney and a Christian, thought of this incident recently when he was asked to prosecute a young man for robbery. Richard's superior, the district attorney, was certain that the culprit was Jerome Johnson, who was out on bail after serving time for a similar robbery. The community was clamoring for a conviction, and the D.A. assigned Richard to see that the robbery was pinned on Jerome.

The trouble was that Richard knows Jerome's family. He believes Jerome learned his lesson from the first incident, and he buys Jerome's alibi this time. But no one can back it up, and Richard has little more than a hunch as a defense. The D.A. has hinted that Richard will be replaced if he does not prosecute Jerome vigorously.

*As an assistant P.A., is Richard's first responsibility to the truth, or to his superiors?

*Statistically, Jerome is likely to become a repeat offender. Should this weigh as much in Richard's thinking as his hunch?

*What would you do if you were Richard?

♦♦♦♦♦♦

Superintendent's Sermonette

By creating people with freedom of choice, God made sure that there would be differences of opinion. However, resolution of those differences is sometimes a serious and complicated matter. This is true in government, industry, business, education, and many other aspects of modern life. A number of frightening trends demand our attention as children of God. One of these is that the majority is always right. We recognize the value of this in democratic procedures, but sometimes the minority is right. Another trend is that people want to determine truth by thesis, antithesis, and synthesis. This can also lead to errors, for the middle of the road can be a dangerous place.

In this lesson's text we hear Jesus declaring Himself to be the Source of spiritual life, made available to believers by the ministry of the Holy Spirit. We follow the debate regarding the identity of Jesus between believers and unbelievers. Even as people in His time were forced to choose sides, so it is that we must choose sides today. We cannot hide behind majority opinion or synthesis. What is true and right should be our goal, regardless of whether others agree with us or not. If we have to choose between reason and revelation, let it be the latter.

CONFRONTING THE GALILEAN

This Lesson In Your Life

Doubting Our Doubts

During a recent presidential election, a young man was trying to fulfill what he believed to be his Christian civic responsibility by "voting his conscience." The trouble was that the candidate he admired most in general was "pro-choice" on the abortion issue, while the young man was "pro-life." But the pro-life candidate had been implicated in several violations of a state senate's ethics code. How should he cast his vote? Finally, after a valiant struggle to weigh the pros and cons of each candidate, the young man marched boldly into the voter's booth—and found himself paralyzed. He walked out without voting at all.

John 7 gives a realistic picture of people in just such a pro/con dilemma about Jesus, unable to make up their minds about Him. While we today want black-and-white faith, in moments of radical honesty we may also find ourselves with unanswered questions. Are there clues in this section of Scripture about what we, as believers, can do about our doubts?

Jesus' brothers must have seen many signs that Jesus was a special boy, growing up; yet they doubted (vs. 5). On the other hand, "the Jews," John's favorite term for Jesus' enemies, were quite ready to disbelieve; yet their doubt weakened when they observed and marveled at His learning (vs. 15).

People who perhaps were prejudiced against Jesus' claims because their leaders opposed Him seemed to doubt their doubts when they saw how openly and boldly He taught—apparently He had nothing to hide. Could it be that He was the Christ, after all, and their leaders did not know it (vss. 25-27)? If the real Messiah were to appear, would He work any more wonders (vs. 31)? Back and forth the argument went in their minds.

The Pharisees' henchmen came to Jesus fully prepared to gather material that would prove Him to be an impostor. But their unbelief was weakened and they, too, vacilated when they discovered that "Never man spake like this man" (v. 46). Nicodemus, a member of the very Council that wanted to put Jesus to death, was not so sure they should, but at this point seems reluctant to openly affirm his faith.

Critics might accuse the Bible writers of being so prejudiced that they contrived this picture of Jesus' enemies doubting their doubts, and coming around to faith after all. But, as we have seen, Scripture is disarmingly frank in portraying the other side of the coin: believers have doubts, too. Perhaps this fact can enable us to deal with our own doubts, and those of others, with equal openness and courage.

John 7 has just such a tone of openness. It pictures people weighing evidence on both sides. Jesus' works and magnetically authoritative teaching are on the faith side of the scales. But, not knowing that He was born in Bethlehem of Judea, the people must also weigh the fact that He hails from Galilee (vss. 41-42). On the one hand, "He is a good man"; but on the other, "He deceiveth the people" (vs. 12). It's revealing just to scan the chapter to see how many questions it contains about Christ.

All this suggests that God is quite willing for us to ask questions about Jesus. He seems only to require that we be ready to believe, on good evidence; and that we have the courage to say so when we do believe, and act on our faith. In Scripture, people are not commended for blind faith.

God is big enough to handle honest doubt, and to deal with our questions. It remains for us to be big enough to affirm, and to live by, the faith we have.

Seed Thoughts

1. Why do you think Jesus chose to go to Jerusalem on a feast day?
Perhaps because it was an opportunity to get His teachings before many people.

2. How does verse 5 relate to John 4:44?
Both illustrate the difficulty some "home-town" people have in recognizing the significance of a hometown celebrity.

3. Why does Jesus say that the world "hates" Him? (See vs 7.)
Because He judges the evil works that the world wants to cling to.

4. How does Jesus explain His being able to teach despite His lack of formal religious training? (vss. 15-16.)
By maintaining that His teaching came directly from the Father.

5. What requirement is given in verse 17 for knowing whether Christ's claims are of God?
That we be willing to do His will when we learn it.

---

1. Why do you think Jesus chose to go to Jerusalem on a feast day?

2. How does verse 5 relate to John 4:44?

3. Why does Jesus say that the world "hates" Him? (See vs 7.)

4. How does Jesus explain His being able to teach despite His lack of formal religious training? (vss. 15-16.)

5. What requirement is given in verse 17 for knowing whether Christ's claims are of God?

6. What "work" on the Sabbath is Jesus referrring to in verse 21? (See 5:8-9).

7. Verses 6 and 30 refer to Christ's hour or time not yet having come. What does this mean?

8. To what was Jesus referring when He said that He was going to a place where His enemies could not find Him? (See vs. 33.)

9. What member of the godhead does the "living water" of verses 38-39 represent?

10. Why did the agents of the Pharisees not return with Christ as their superiors had ordered? (vss. 45-49.)

(PLEASE TURN PAGE)

(SEED THOUGHTS--Cont'd.)

Perhaps because it was an opportunity to get His teachings before many people.

Both illustrate the difficulty some "home-town" people have in recognizing the significance of a hometown celebrity.

Because He judges the evil works that the world wants to cling to.

By maintaining that His teaching came directly from the Father.

That we be willing to do His will when we learn it.

Healing the cripple at the pool of Bethesda.

Apparently He was not yet ready for the inevitable reaction His claims to Messiahship would cause. He had His own sense of the right timing.

He was anticipating His return to the Father, who sent Him.

The Holy Spirit.

Because they were awed by His teaching. (Also, there may have been some divine protection—see vs. 44.)

6. What "work" on the Sabbath is Jesus referrring to in verse 21? (See 5:8-9).
Healing the cripple at the pool of Bethesda.

7. Verses 6 and 30 refer to Christ's hour or time not yet having come. What does this mean?
Apparently He was not yet ready for the inevitable reaction His claims to Messiahship would cause. He had His own sense of the right timing.

8. To what was Jesus referring when He said that He was going to a place where His enemies could not find Him? (See vs. 33.)
He was anticipating His return to the Father, who sent Him.

9. What member of the godhead does the "living water" of verses 38-39 represent?
The Holy Spirit.

10. Why did the agents of the Pharisees not return with Christ as their superiors had ordered? (vss. 45-49.)
Because they were awed by His teaching. (Also, there may have been some divine protection—see vs. 44.)

May 30, 1993

The Promise of the Spirit

John 14

15. If ye love me, keep my commandments.

16. And I will pray the Father, and he shall give you another Comforter, that he may abide with you for ever;

17. *Even* the spirit of truth; whom the world cannot receive, because it seeth him not, neither knoweth him: but ye know him; for he dwelleth with you, and shall be in you.

18. I will not leave you comfortless: I will come to you.

19. Yet a little while, and the world seeth me no more; but ye see me: because I live, ye shall live also.

20. At that day ye shall know that I *am* in my Father, and ye in me, and I in you.

21. He that hath my commandments, and keepeth them, he it is that loveth me: and he that loveth me shall be loved of my Father, and I will love him, and will manifest myself to him.

22 Judas saith unto him, not Is-car'-iot, Lord, how is it that thou wilt manifest thyself unto us, and not unto the world?

23 Jesus answered and said unto him, If a man love me, he will keep my words: and my Father will love him, and we will come unto him, and make our abode with him.

24 He that loveth me not keepeth not my sayings: and the word which ye hear is not mine but the Father's which sent me.

25. These things have I spoken unto you, being *yet* present with you.

26. But the Comforter, *which is* the Holy Ghost, whom the Father will send in my name, he shall teach you all things, and bring all things to your remembrance, whatsoever I have said unto you.

27 Peace I leave with you, my peace I give unto you: not as the world giveth, give I unto you. Let not your heart be troubled, neither let it be afraid.

◆◆◆◆◆◆

◀ **Memory Selection**
John 14:26

◀ **Devotional Reading**
John 16:5-15

◀ **Background Scripture**
John 14

◀ **Printed Scripture**
John 14:15-27

THE PROMISE OF THE SPIRIT

Teacher's Target

Jesus had come from His Father's side in heaven in order to reveal Him to men (John 1:18). Jesus now promised to send the Holy Spirit to make Himself (Jesus) known to men. "When the Comforter is come, whom I will send unto you from the Father, even the Spirit of truth, which proceedeth from the Father, he [the Holy Spirit] shall testify of me" (John 15:26). WE HAVE A responsibility for keeping Christ's commandments. God the Father, God the Son, and God the Holy Spirit will bless those who sincerely believe in Christ and seek to do His will. Our text presents some of those blessings which believers can expect to receive. They include comfort, love, spiritual wisdom, and peace. God and Christ give these things to believers through the indwelling presence and ministry of the Holy Spirit. Spiritual development is absolutely dependent on the work done by the Spirit in our hearts and minds.

Lesson Introduction

It is difficult for us, as finite beings, to comprehend the Godhead called the Holy Trinity and composed of God the Father, God the Son, and God the Holy Spirit. They are separate identities, and yet they are unified as one. They have distinct functions, and yet They operate in perfect harmony. They have individual personalities, and yet they have the same attributes. Each had a part to play in the origin and implementation of the master plan of redemption offered to men.

It may also be difficult for us to comprehend the fact that the Holy Trinity planned for redeemed men to be united with the Godhead. Our text makes it clear that redeemed individuals may be *in* Christ, and, therefore, *in* God. It makes it clear that the Holy Spirit was sent to dwell *in* believers. What concept could be grander than this, that sinful people might be cleansed and joined to Those Who are divine and holy? All other goals and experiences fade when compared with this.

Teaching Outline

I. Comforter: John 14:15-20
   A. Proof: 15
   B. Presence: 16-17
   C. Promise: 18-20
II. Commandments: John 14:21-24
   A. Consequences: 21
   B. Contrast: 22-24
III. Comfort: John 14: 25 -27
   A. Instructor I:25
   B. Instructor II: 26
   C. Imputation: 27

Daily Bible Readings

Mon. A Place Prepared
John 14:1-7
Tue. The Authority of God
John 14:8-14
Wed. A. Counselor Is Promised
John 14:15-20
Thu. Keeping His Commandments
John 14:21-25
Fri. Jesus Leaves Peace
John 14:26-31
Sat. The Spirit's Witness
Rom. 8:12-17
Sun. The Spirit's Intercession
Rom. 8:18-27

VERSE BY VERSE

I. Comforter: John 14:15-20

A. Proof: 15

15. If ye love me, keep my commandments.

Jesus had just said, "If ye shall ask any thing in my name, I will do it" (John 14:14). He had a partnership with believers in mind, and it was His responsibility to provide them with what they would need. He followed this by saying that they should prove their love for Him by keeping His commandments. Love was supposed to produce obedience. This was very important to Jesus. Note how the concept was repeated in verses 21 and 23, as well as Him commenting that the Holy Spirit would come to bring to their remembrance all the things He had taught them (vs. 26).

B. Presence: 16-17

16. And I will pray the Father, and he shall give you another Comforter, that he may abide with you for ever.

17a. Even the Spirit of truth;...

Jesus knew that His followers were imperfect, and He knew that they would sometimes fail and be remorseful. At those times they would need comfort and encouragement. He promised to ask His Father to send them another Comforter. Jesus had come and served as a Comforter, but He was planning to leave them soon. The Holy Spirit would come and abide with them forever. He was called here "the Spirit of truth," meaning that He "leads into all truth" (Living Bible) or "reveals the truth about God" (Today's English Version). This agrees with John 15:26 which refers to "the Comforter" and "the Spirit of truth" Who will testify of Jesus.

17b. Whom the world cannot receive, because it seeth him not, neither knoweth him: ...

Jesus said that people in the sinful world-system could not receive the Holy Spirit, because they did not see Him or know Him. The Holy Spirit would not force Himself upon them.

17c. ...but ye know him; for he dwelleth with you, and shall be in you.

Only sincere believers had the spiritual discernment to see and know the Holy Spirit. Up to the time of the Spirit's descent on the Day of Pentecost, believers experienced the Holy Spirit being *with* them. Afterward they were to experience His presence being in them. "They were all filled with the Holy Ghost" (Acts 2:4).

C. Promise: 18-20

18. I will not leave you comfortless: I will come to you.

Some might think that Jesus referred to His second coming here. The early Christians thought that, if He left them, He would return soon. We know that this was not the case, for He has been gone for over nineteen centuries already. It is more likely that Jesus meant He would come to comfort believers *through* the Holy Spirit. This would explain His statement as recorded in Matthew 18: 20— "Where two or three are gathered together in my name, there am I in the midst of them." He would be geographically located in heaven, but He would come to them by means of the Spirit.

19a. Yet a little while, and the world seeth me no more; ...

Jesus said that it would be only a short time and He would be gone from the earth. The world, which saw Him only literally, would miss Him.

19b. ... but ye see me: ...

Believers would continue to "see" Jesus by the eyes of faith, even after He literally ascended to heaven. The Holy Spirit would make Jesus real to them.

19c. ... because I live, ye shall live also.

Those who walked by faith, and not by sight, were to have a sure hope for the future. The eternality of Jesus was only temporarily interrupted when He died for a few days and was then resurrected. The statement that it was because He lived that believers would have eternal life held true in spite of fleeting circumstances. In due time Jesus' followers would understand Paul's explanation of resurrected life in Christ as described in l Corinthians 15:20-23. This would all come to a head at the rapture to take place when He comes again as described in 1 Thessalonians 4:13-18.

20. At that day ye shall know that I am in my Father, and ye in me, and I in you.

Jesus may have been referring to either a day or a time here. Much was to happen before it came, for He would die, be raised, and ascend to heaven. Although the comment that believers would eventually understand the unity existing between Jesus and His Father and Jesus and His followers might be taken by some to describe the post-resurrection but pre-ascension period, others would look into the future and say that this understanding will come following the Second Coming."

A. Consequences: 21

21a. He that hath my commandments and keepeth them, he it is that loveth me:

Note how this echoes verse 15, although the order is reversed. Once again, proof of love for Christ is shown through obedience to His commands.

21b. ...and he that loveth me shall be loved of my Father, and I will love him, and will manifest myself to him.

This part of the verse carries believers along to a new dimension. Those who sincerely love Christ will be loved by God the Father, for God appreciates those who love His Son. They will also be loved by Christ, and He will manifest (reveal) Himself to them. We assume this to have two meanings. He would reveal Himself to them while He was absent in heaven through the ministry of the Holy Spirit. He would also reveal Himself to them when He came again in the end times.

B. Contrast: 22-24

22. Judas saith unto him, not Iscariot, Lord, how is it that thou wilt manifest thyself unto us, and not unto the world?

Since Judas Iscariot had already left the upper room (John 13:30), this was Judas Lebbaeus whose surname was Thaddaeus (Matt. 10:3; Mark 3:18). He was also called Judas the brother of James (Luke 6:16). He asked Jesus how He could reveal Himself to the disciples but not to the unbelieving world. He apparently was thinking of a literal, physical manifestation of Jesus, rather than a spiritual one by means of the Holy Spirit. Here was a contrast in perceptions of revelation.

23. Jesus answered and said unto him, If a man love me, he will keep my words: and my Father will love him, and we will come unto him, and make our abode with him.

This was essentially a restatement of what was recorded in verse 21. Jesus was trying to help Judas Lebbaeus and the other remaining disciples understand that different geographical locations (in heaven and earth) could not hinder fellowship between God, Christ, and believers. As believers loved Jesus and kept His words (commandments), God the Father would love them, and God and Jesus would come to dwell in them spiritually by the agency of the indwelling Holy Spirit.

24a. He that loveth me not keepeth not my sayings: ...

In contrast to the person described in verse 23, who loved Jesus and kept His words (commandments), here was a person who did not love Him or keep His sayings (commandments). We infer that this individual would *not* experience communion with God the Father and God the Son through the Holy Spirit.

24b. ...and the word which ye hear is not mine, but the Father's which sent me.

This may sound like a paradox at first. Jesus said that His message was not His Own, but that it came from His heavenly Father. However, we know that He and His Father were completely in harmony on the message and its intended effect. What Jesus probably meant to do here was to assure His disciples that His teaching had divine backing. It was not contrast, but harmony, which characterized the message.

III. Comfort: John 14:25-27

A. Instructor I: 25

25. These things have I spoken unto you, being yet present with you.

Jesus presented Himself as the disciples' current Teacher. Indeed, they often referred to Him by title as Master or Rabbi. Jesus implied here that His time as their Instructor was now limited, for He would be leaving them soon. Their capacity to learn was also limited, for Jesus later said, "I have yet many things to say unto you, but ye cannot bear them now" (John 16:12).

B. Instructor II: 26

26a. But the Comforter, which is the Holy Ghost, whom the Father will send in my name, ...

This part of the verse described the Holy Spirit and told how He would reach the earth. The Comforter, also called the Spirit of truth (vss. 16-17), would be sent by God the Father in Jesus' name. It is interesting to note that Jesus later said that *He* would send the Comforter to believers from His Father (John 15:26).

26b. ...he shall teach you all things, and bring all things to your remembrance, whatsoever I have said unto you.

This description of the coming Instructor is continued in John 15:27— "When he, the Spirit of truth, is come, he will guide you into all truth: for he shall not speak of himself; but whatsoever he shall hear, that shall he speak: and he will shew you things to come."

Note two kinds of instruction mentioned here. The Holy Spirit would teach believers all they needed to know, including what Jesus had taught them but which they might forget. The Holy Spirit would also teach believers about things to come, meaning prophecies of future events. It has been suggested that this verse served as a foundation for the completion of the New Testament in the first century of the Christian era.

Our text makes it clear that the ministries of the Holy Spirit include comforting and teaching. These include convicting, cleansing, regenerating, sealing (with God's stamp of ownership), prompting (to righteousness), restraining (from evil), and sanctifying those yielded to His control. This gives a more well-rounded picture of what the Holy Spirit does in believers.

C. Imputation: 27

27a. Peace I leave with you, my peace I give unto you: not as the world giveth, give I unto you.

The Messiah, described as "The Prince of Peace" (Isa. 9:6), bestowed peace upon His disciples. He knew that they would become emotionally drained when He was taken into judgment and crucified. He wanted them to develop an inner peace which the world could not destroy through harsh circumstances. This was a gift, an imputation, an infusion of calm to prepare them to face the coming storm.

27b. Let not your heart be troubled, neither let it be afraid.

Jesus wanted His disciples to meet fear with faith. Unfortunately, they failed miserably. Judas Iscariot betrayed Him and led temple officers to arrest Him in the garden of Gethsemane. All of Jesus' disciples forsook Him and fled. Peter denied Him three times. Darkness closed in, and the disciples went into hiding to avoid arrest. A new bestowal of peace by Jesus was required after His resurrection (John 20:21). A new boldness had to come to them through the Holy Spirit (Acts 2. 4; 4:8; 4:31).

Evangelistic Emphasis

The "signs and wonders" accomplished by Jesus intrigue us. Surely healing the sick, opening the eyes of the blind, multiplying loaves and fishes and even raising the dead far exceed any miracles we could imagine.

Perhaps not. Jesus makes a remarkable promise to the believer in John 14:12—*"Greater works than these shall he do"!*

What could possibly be a greater work than the healings and other physical wonders worked by Jesus? Perhaps the *spiritual* wonders His followers can facilitate. Perhaps ministering Christ's peace (vs. 27) to the anxiety-ridden is a wonder in its own right. Perhaps the miracle of the seed of the Word enabling a person to be born again (3:3-5) is as much of a marvel as raising him from the dead. Perhaps bringing the light of the gospel to those who have previously lived in darkness is as marvelous as opening the eyes of the blind.

◆◆◆◆◆◆

Memory Selection

But the Comforter, which is the Holy Ghost, whom the Father will send in my name, he shall teach you all things, and bring all things to your remembrance, whatsoever I have said unto you. *John 14:26*

The work of the Holy spirit in the human heart remains one of the mysteries of the Christian faith. In a scientific age, some would reduce mind and spirit to electrical impulses or chemical reactions. But however science may describe *how* the mind functions, Scripture affirms that the human spirit can be penetrated, guided and comforted by the *Holy* Spirit.

The apostles and other writers of Scripture experienced this reality. They accepted the promise that the Spirit would guide them into all truth (John 16:13). The world will forever be indebted to the Spirit's power to reach deep within the memories of those who heard Christ teach, and to inspire ("in-Spirit"!) them to hand His words on to others—to us.

The crowd on the first Pentecost after Christ's resurrection experienced the Spirit. Hovering over their heads as tongues of fire, the Spirit enabled strangers from many lands to understand each other's languages (see Acts 2:1-6). The apostle Paul experienced the guidance of the Spirit in making his missionary plans (see Acts 13:4; 16:6-7).

Uncounted Christians since those days have called on the Spirit's aid in healing relational problems, the Spirit's comfort in times of pain and sorrow, the Spirit's intercession when their prayers seem thwarted and the Spirit's presence in guiding them into the truth.

The Holy Spirit is the "breath" of God. As well deny that we ourselves have breath as to deny the reality of God's Spirit.

May 30, 1993

Weekday Problems

Nothing had been the same since Loretta's husband died. For 25 years their lives had been so intertwined that Loretta felt she was only half a person without Jim. Their friends were all couples; and now that she was alone she found herself not invited to the bridge parties and other social occasions she had enjoyed.

They had been active in First Church's hospital visitation program, but as a couple. On her own, Loretta found that she lacked the aggressiveness to enter hospital rooms to which she had not been invited. She hadn't realized how much she had leaned on Jim.

Loretta recently read Christ's promise in John 14 that He would not leave His followers "comfortless" and alone. She found that the passage actually made her a little angry, and not comforted at all. She was alone, and she was not comforted. Why couldn't she experience the Spirit's comfort and presence?

*Have you ever wondered about the reality of the Holy Spirit in your life? What can be done in such cases?

*Can *people* minister the presence of the Holy Spirit to people like Loretta, or is it a purely spiritual presence that must well up from within?

*What would you say to Loretta if she expressed some guilt over being angry at God?

*What are some practical ways your church or class can minister to the lonely?

♦♦♦♦♦♦

Superintendent's Sermonette

We normally think of orphans as children whose parents have died or who were abandoned by them. We hear about orphaned children running the streets of some countries in packs, trying to survive as best they can. We pride ourselves on the fact that in more developed nations they are given institutional or foster-home care.

However, we might define orphans as people of all ages who lack proper care. Among these we might include shut-ins, the impoverished, mentally-ill street people, the homeless, and those who are so ugly, odd, and irritating that society avoids them. Many face a bleak future without hope.

Jesus looked at His adult disciples and said, "I will not leave you comfortless: I will come to you" (John 14:18). He knew the empty feeling the disciples would experience when He was taken from them into judgment and death. He promised that it would not be the end for Him. He said that He would come to them again. He did this after His resurrection. He will do it at His second coming yet in the future. In the meantime, He comes to all believers through the ministry of the Holy Spirit. Are you experiencing His presence daily as you obey His commandments? Are you trying to help others of all ages who feel "orphaned"?

THE PROMISE OF THE SPIRIT

This Lesson in Your Life

We can well imagine why Jesus goes to such lengths to reassure His followers that they need not despair after He returned to the Father. For three years they had walked by His side, learned from His lips, felt the warmth of His love along with the strength of His discipline. What *in the world* would they do when He left them?

Of course we are faced with the same question. How can the promise that we will one day have a room in heaven be of any earthly good during the times when we feel lonely, discouraged and afraid—bereft of Christ's presence? Are we to surrender to the despairing and cynical portrait of believers in Samuel Beckett's play, "Waiting for Godot"? Godot stands for God; and, in the play, He never comes. On what basis can Christians affirm a different outcome to life's drama?

We can respond with "biblical" hope to Christ's promises. Promise after promise overflows from the heart of Jesus in John 14: "I go to prepare a place for you"... "I will come again"..."the Father shall give you another Comforter"... "Because I live, ye shall live also." Both the presence of Christ now, through His Spirit, and the hope of being with Him in the future are based on God's promises.

But we don't always respond to such promises *biblically*. Our concept of a promise is too often shaped by a world in which they are regularly and glibly broken. Our concept of "hope" in the fulfillment of a promise is often shallow—like the man on his way home from work who sees smoke toward his part of town and says, "I hope that's not my house burning." (If it's burning, hoping doesn't help!)

God doesn't break promises, and our expectations that they will be fulfilled are based on something more than wishful thinking. In the Bible, hope in God's promise is based on *history*. The exodus from Egypt, God's care of Israel in the wilderness, past judgment on the wicked and past blessings for the faithful—all these historical events form a solid basis for hope, in Scripture. The God who acted in past known events will act again in the unknown future.

A distinctive use of the Hebrew word for *remember* seems to have helped God's people in the Old Testament take heart during times when He seemed absent. When the worshipping community recalled or remembered the redeeming acts of God, the individual worshipper was caught up in the acts once again. They were *reliving* history, not just *reciting* it. As Old Testament scholar Brevard Childs put it, "The biblical events have the dynamic characteristic of refusing to be relegated to the past."

In much the same way, the early Christians found God's mighty acts through Jesus Christ "catching up" with them in the present and infusing them with hope for the future. Picture a little band of persecuted Christians huddling around the Lord's Table in a Roman catacomb. When they take the bread and wine in response to Christ's invitation, "This do in remembrance of me," the crucifixion-resurrection is "represented" to them. Biblical remembering infuses them with courage to live faithfully in the absence of Christ.

In John 14:15, Jesus offers another important way to keep the faith in His absence: *"Keep my commandments."* Quite often we have it the other way around: if Jesus will just make Himself more real in His absence, then we will believe and obey. If He will "show us a sign," then we will respond faithfully. But Christ insists that there is another way to faith: the way of obedience.

Seed Thoughts

1. Why was Jesus so concerned at this time that His followers not be troubled?
Facing death and returning to the Father would throw His followers on their own, and would test their faith.

2. In what way does Jesus say that His followers came to know God?
By having known the son. ("He that hath seen me hath seen the Father," vs. 9.)

3. Who among Christ's followers besides "doubting Thomas" appears shaken by the news about Jesus' impending departure?
Philip, who apparently still needs to be convinced that to know Jesus is to know the Father.

4. How does Jesus describe His relationship with the Father?
Jesus says that He and the Father are "in" each other; and that it is actually the Father who is speaking and working through Him.

5. What sure sign of loving Jesus is given in this chapter?
Keeping His commandments.

---

1. Why was Jesus so concerned at this time that His followers not be troubled?

2. In what way does Jesus say that His followers came to know God?

3. Who among Christ's followers besides "doubting Thomas" appears shaken by the news about Jesus' impending departure?

4. How does Jesus describe His relationship with the Father?

5. What sure sign of loving Jesus is given in this chapter?

6. Who does Jesus promise would come to be with the disciples after He returned to the Father?

7. In verse 26, what functions does Jesus say the Holy Spirit would have?

8. Have you ever felt that you experienced such guidance by the Spirit?

9. It has been said that a good leader doesn't ask his followers to do anything he wouldn't do. How does Jesus illustrate this principle?

10. Who is meant by "the prince of this world," in verse 30?

(PLEASE TURN PAGE)

(SEED THOUGHTS--Cont'd.)

Facing death and returning to the Father would throw His followers on their own, and would test their faith.

By having known the son. ("He that hath seen me hath seen the Father," vs. 9.)

Philip, who apparently still needs to be convinced that to know Jesus is to know the Father.

Jesus says that He and the Father are "in" each other; and that it is actually the Father who is speaking and working through Him.

Keeping His commandments.

The Holy Spirit, the "Comforter" or "Advocate," who would abide with them forever.

He would teach Christ's followers, and enable them to remember Christ's message.

(Encourage open sharing.)

He is proving His love for God by obedience, in going to the Cross, just as He has called His own followers to obedience.

Satan, or the devil (see also John 12:31).

6. Who does Jesus promise would come to be with the disciples after He returned to the Father?
The Holy Spirit, the "Comforter" or "Advocate," who would abide with them forever.

7. In verse 26, what functions does Jesus say the Holy Spirit would have?
He would teach Christ's followers, and enable them to remember Christ's message.

8. Have you ever felt that you experienced such guidance by the Spirit?
(Encourage open sharing.)

9. It has been said that a good leader doesn't ask his followers to do anything he wouldn't do. How does Jesus illustrate this principle?
He is proving His love for God by obedience, in going to the Cross, just as He has called His own followers to obedience.

10. Who is meant by "the prince of this world," in verse 30?
Satan, or the devil (see also John 12:31).

June 6, 1993

PAUL COMMENDS PHILLIPIANS

A Worthy Life

Philippians 1

3. I thank my God upon every remembrance of you,

4. Always in every prayer of mine for you all making request with joy,

5. For your fellowship in the gospel from the first day until now;

6. Being confident of this very thing, that he which hath begun a good work in you will perform it until the day of Jesus Christ:

7. Even as it is meet for me to think this of you all, because I have you in my heart; inasmuch as both in my bonds, and in the defence and confirmation of the gospel, ye all are partakers of my grace.

8. For God is my record, how greatly I long after you all in the bowels of Jesus Christ.

9. And this I pray, that your love may abound yet more and more in knowledge and in all judgment;

10. That ye may approve things that are excellent; that ye may be sincere and without offence till the day of Christ;

11. Being filled with the fruits of righteousness which are by Jesus Christ, unto the glory and praise of God.

12. But I would ye should understand, brethren, that the things which happened unto me have fallen out rather unto the furtherance of the gospel:

13. So that my bonds in Christ are manifest in all the palace, and in all other places;

14. And many of the bretheren in the Lord, waxing confident by my bonds, are much more bold to speak the word without fear.

27. Only let your conversation be as it becometh the gospel of Christ: that whether I come and see you, or else be absent, I may hear of your affairs, that ye stand fast in one spirit, with one mind striving together for the faith of the gospel;

28. And in nothing terrified by your adversaries: which is to them an evident token of perdition, but to you of salvation, and that of God.

29. For unto you it is given in the behalf of Christ, not only to believe on him, but also to suffer for his sake;

30. Having the same conflict which ye saw in me, and now hear to be in me.

◆◆◆◆◆◆

◀ **Memory Selection**
Philippians 1:27

◀ **Devotional Reading**
II Corinthians 5:1-15

◀ **Background Scripture**
Philippians 1

◀ **Printed Scripture**
Philippians 1:3-14, 27-30

A WORTHY LIFE

Teacher's Target

Paul was fully aware that first-century Christians lived in a hostile world. He had once been part of that world, chasing down believers, committing them to prison, and rejoicing when some were put to death (Acts 26:9-11), His encounter with Jesus Christ on the road to Damascus, his three days of blind isolation in that city, and his contact by a believer named Ananias turned him around and set him on the path to a powerful ministry (Acts 9:1-20), His first stop as a missionary in Europe had been Philippi, where he had suffered arrest, beating, and imprisonment for Christ's sake (Acts 16:6-40).

Help your students to keep Paul's historic background in Philippi in mind as they begin to study his epistle to believers there. He revealed how he felt about them, prayed for them, and wanted them to regard his imprisonment in Rome. Despite his own harsh circumstances, he sought to encourage them to live faithfully for Christ. He intended to teach them that suffering for Christ's sake was normal and worthwhile in spreading the gospel.

Lesson Introduction

While Paul was under house-arrest for two years in Rome, he had an active preaching and teaching ministry to those who visited him (Acts 28:30-31). As mentioned often in his prison epistles, he kept up a steady program of prayer for believers everywhere. His epistles were a form of ministry themselves, and he still ministers to us through them. He sent out individuals to visit various churches in order to teach, raise money for poor saints, and report back to him on the conditions they found.

Another form of ministry which Paul had may not have been as obvious, but he did mention it in Colossians 1:24—"Part of my work is to suffer for you; and I am glad, for I am helping to finish up the remainder of Christ's suffering for his body, the church", (Living Bible). In other words, Paul felt that he and Christ were partners in suffering for the sake of the gospel and its establishment. He welcomed the opportunity to suffer, and he left a list of what he endured in II Corinthians 11:23-28.

Teaching Outline

I. Evaluation: Phil. 1:3-7
   A. Prayer: 3-5
   B. Prospect: 6
   C. Partakers: 7
II. Expectation: Phil. 1:8-11
   A. Passion: 8
   B. Prayer: 9-11
III. Explanation: Phil. 1:12-14
   A. Benefit: 12-13
   B. Boldness: 14
IV. Expectation: Phil. 1:27-30
   A. Conduct: 27
   B. Confidence: 28
   C. Conflict: 29-30

Daily Bible Readings

Mon. Partakers Together of God's Grace - *Phil. 1:1-11*
Tue. Rejoice! Christ is Being Proclaimed - *Phil. 1:12-18*
Wed. A Lifestyle Worthy of the Gospel - *Phil. 1:19-30*
Thu. We Share Both Suffering and Comfort - *II Cor. 1:3-11*
Fri. God Establishes and Commissions Us - *II Cor. 1:12-22*
Sat. Christ Always Leads Us in Triumph - *II Cor. 2:12-17*
Sun. Preach Christ as Lord, and Serve - *II Cor. 4:1-6*

June 6, 1993

VERSE BY VERSE

I. Evaluation: Phil. 1:3-7

A. Prayer: 3-5

3. I thank my God upon every remembrance of you.

Paul and Timotheus (Timothy), servants of Jesus Christ, sent greetings to all the saints (believers) in Jesus Christ who were at Philippi. They wished them to have grace and peace from God the Father and from the Lord Jesus Christ (vss. 1-2). Paul said that he thanked God for the Philippian believers every time he thought of them.

4. Always in every prayer of mine for you all making request with joy,

5. For your fellowship in the gospel from the first day until now;

Here is another way of putting verse 4—" In all my prayers for all of you, I always pray with joy" (New International Version). The reason Paul rejoiced when thinking of the Philippian believers was that they were fellows (partners) with him in upholding and spreading the gospel of salvation. This partnership had begun when he first met them in Philippi, and it had continued up to the time he wrote this letter to them.

B. Prospect: 6

6. Being confident of this very thing, that he which hath begun a good work in you will perform it until the day of Jesus Christ.

Note that Paul's confidence was based on his trust in the Lord, not on frail and changeable human beings. He believed that the good work of grace which God had begun in the hearts of Philippian believers was going to continue until it succeeded. Spiritual nourishment would produce good fruits of the Spirit in them. This process would proceed right up to the day of Jesus Christ, apparently referring to the time of Christ's second coming.

C. Partakers: 7

7a. Even as it is meet for me to think this of you all, because I have you in my heart; . . .

Paul felt that it was proper and natural for him to think as he did regarding the Philippian believers, since he held them in special concern in his heart. His optimism for the future was based on their past and present performance.

7b. . . .inasmuch as both in my bonds, and in the defence and confirmation of the gospel, ye all are partakers of my grace.

Paul's Philippian partners supported him whether he was in bonds (imprisoned) or free to move out to defend and confirm the gospel. They shared in the grace which God bestowed on him, because they supported him with money, material things, prayer, and encouragement.

II. Expectation: Phil. 1:8-11

A. Passion: 8

8. For God is my record, how greatly I long after you all in the bowels of Jesus Christ.

Paul called on God to witness the fact that he yearned greatly for the Philippian believers. Paul attributed this passion (strong emotion) to love placed in his heart by Jesus Christ. The term "bowels" now refers to the intestinal tract, but the Greek term used by Paul referred to the chest area including the heart, lungs, and liver. The ancients believed that this area was the source for love. We know that our emotions are located in the brain, but the heart *can* beat faster when it is stirred.

B Prayer: 9-11

9. And this I pray, that your love may abound yet more and more in knowledge and in all judgement;

Paul said that he prayed for the Philippian believers, asking God to help their love to grow increasingly in knowledge (of doctrinal and practical matters) and in all judgment (spiritual perception and discernment). He wanted their love to grow toward himself and toward one another. He was aware of some divisions among them (Phil. 2:2; 4:2), God-given love (*agape*) would have to cover disagreements.

10. That ye may approve things that are excellent; that ye may be sincere and without offence till the day of Christ.

Paul's prayer included his desire that the Philippian believers would approve things which were not merely good and acceptable but which were excellent. He wanted them to be sincere and without offence until the day of Christ's return. He knew that no one was perfect, but he wanted to hold up a high ideal toward which believers might strive.

11. Being filled with the fruits of righteousness, which are by Jesus Christ, unto the glory and praise of God.

The oldest manuscripts made "fruits" singular. Paul did this in Galatians 5:22-23—"The fruit of the Spirit is love, joy, peace, longsuffering, gentleness, goodness, faith, meekness, temperance." Righteousness and holiness include these nine Christian virtues or graces (Rom. 6:22; Eph. 5:8-9; Heb. 12:11; Jas. 3:18). They all come to believers because of their spiritual identification with Jesus Christ by means of the Holy Spirit, and they bring glory and praise to God the Father. This was Paul's expectation for believers.

III. Explanation: Phil. 1: 12-14

A. Benefit: 12-13

12. But I would ye should understand, brethren, that the things which happened unto me have fallen out rather unto the furtherance of the gospel;

The Philippian believers had been concerned about Paul's imprisonment in Rome, although it actually had been a milder case of house-arrest. He wanted to explain to them that his situation had a positive side to it. Behind his comments here was the realization that God could use any kind of circumstances to bring about good results in the lives of His Own children. Paul said that his being in Rome had promoted the gospel.

13. So that my bonds in Christ are manifest in all the palace, and in all other places;

The literal bonds restraining Paul were thought of as "bonds in Christ," meaning that they were permitted by the Lord so that the gospel of Christ might be propagated. Therefore, he was a prisoner of the Lord Jesus Christ more than he was a prisoner of the Romans. Members of the Praetorian Guard had evidently been favorably impressed with Paul's courage in holding to his testimony for Christ. They told others in the emperor's palace about him, as well as people in other places.

B. Boldness: 14

14. And many of the brethren in the Lord, waxing confident by my bonds, are much more bold to speak the word without fear.

It was not only the Roman guards who had been impressed by Paul's testimony as a prisoner, but the other Christians in Rome had been impressed too. His example gave them confidence to boldly testify about Christ on their own. Impetus was given to the spread of the gospel in a pagan environment. Paul could later conclude his letter to the Philippians by saying, "All the saints salute you, chiefly they that are of Caesar's household" (Phil. 4:22). The gospel had permeated Roman society from top to bottom. Too often we shy away from witnessing to the rich and powerful, and that is unfortunate, for they need the gospel as much as the middle and lower classes do.

Philippians 1:15-26 is not in our printed text for this lesson, but you would do well to summarize it for your students. Paul mentioned people who spoke about Christ in an envious, spiteful, contentious manner and those who spoke about Him in love. However, he rejoiced that, whether people were for him or against him, the gospel was proclaimed. Paul wanted the Philippian believers to keep praying for him, in order that Christ might be magnified through his body. He did not care if this was done through his life or his death. He was anxious to move on to be with Christ in heaven, but he was willing to remain on earth if it would help them and other believers. We now come to another stated expectation Paul had for them.

IV. Expectation: Phil. 1:27-30

A. Conduct: 27

27a. Only let your conversation be as it becometh the gospel of Christ: ...

The term "conversation" can be translated as "conduct" or as "citizenship." The Berkeley Version renders this as "Be sure to conduct yourselves as citizens of Christ." Their guide was to be the gospel of Christ.

27b. ...that whether I come to see you, or else be absent, I my hear of your affairs, that ye stand fast in one spirit, with one mind striving together for the faith of the gospel:

Paul reminded believers from time to time of his apostolic authority over them, but he more often seemed to try persuasion rather than force. He expressed his desire that, whether he could be with them or had to be absent from them, they would move forward in their spiritual development. He said that he wanted to hear reports that they were doing well. A good report would state that they stood united in one spirit, single-mindedly striving for the faith set forth in the gospel. They would thus be worthy of the description of being "citizens of Christ."

B. Confidence: 28

28a. And in nothing terrified by your adversaries: ...

Paul knew that enemies of the gospel could be very intimidating, but he advised believers to develop confidence in Christ and not allow fear to dominate them. He did not want them paralyzed by fear.

28b. ...which is to them an evident token of perdition, but to you of salvation, and that of God.

Paul wanted believers to face their foes in such a way that two things were apparent. First, believers would see that unbelievers were headed for perdition. Second, they would see that they as believers were headed toward salvation.

C. Conflict: 29-30

29. For unto you it is given in the behalf of Christ, not only to believe on him, but also to suffer for his sake;

Paul said that believers must realistically face the fact that believing on Christ and receiving His spiritual blessings would lead to suffering for His sake. He did not teach an "easy believism" sometimes found in our modern world. He had known much conflict for the sake of the gospel, and he wanted other believers to be ready to face it, too. Those who knew the *comfort* Christ brought would have to be ready to experience the *conflict* which their testimony for Him would produce.

30. Having the same conflict which ye saw in me, and now hear to be in me.

Paul said that the Philippian believers were going through the same kind of struggle which they had seen him experience in the past and which they had now heard that he was enduring in the present. By implication, Paul was saying that the same sustaining grace God gave him was available to the believers in Philippi, as well.

Two references in II Corinthians help show how Paul handled suffering for Christ. In one place he spoke collectively for himself and other team members by saying, "We faint not; but; ... though our outward man perish, yet the inward man is renewed day by day" (II Cor. 4:16). In another place, having asked the Lord three times to remove "a thorn in the flesh," God replied, "My grace is sufficient for thee: for my strength is made perfect in weakness. Most gladly therefore will I rather glory in my infirmities, that the power of Christ may rest upon me" (II Cor. 12:9).

A WORTHY LIFE

Evangelistic Emphasis

The church is not what it ought to be if it is not reaching out to those who do not know Jesus Christ. From Abraham on God had planned to reach out and invite all His estranged children back home. Over the centuries God pursued His plan to call His family back to Himself. He called the Hebrews and made covenant with them, not to be an exclusive club, but to be an outreach to all peoples. The church is not to be an exclusive private club of people who think, look and act just alike. It is called to be God's outreach to all kinds of people. Our reconciliation with God is not a gift we can selfishly hold to ourselves without losing something of its richness and meaning. The church experience has sometimes been a barrier to the person inquiring about the faith. To come to know Jesus Christ, to see His beauty and His love often brings the person to the brink of commitment. Then experience with a church which is discordant, dead, and defeated can cool the inquirer's interest. Conversely, nothing is more winsome than a community of believers sharing faith, hope and love. Jesus called the twelve, not just to Himself, but to fellowship with one another. They would need each other to remember his teachings, to share encouragement during the hard times, to remind one another of their hope and to fulfill the mission to take the gospel to all nations. "By this will all know that you are my disciples," Jesus said at the Last Supper, "that you love one another." Loving Christians make their lives reflect honor on the gospel and unbelievers receive the blessing. For ourselves and for those who do not know Christ it is a matter of first importance to live lives worthy of the gospel.

◆◆◆◆◆◆

Memory Selection

"Only let your conversation be as becometh the gospel of Christ. . ."
Philippians 1:27

"Remember who you are," we say to our young people as they drive away to college. It's no time for giving them rules and regulations. By now they should have a clear sense of who they are and what they believe; they know the difference between right and wrong. The real guarantor of their behavior is not a load of fear, guilt, anxiety. The solid ground of responsible living is a sure sense of identity. That's what Paul was saying to the Christians at Philippi: "Remember who you are, live lives worthy of the gospel." To us Paul might say: "Remember who you are. You are God's children created in His image, the objects of His redeeming love over the centuries, the treasure He purchased at the cross. You are His helpers in the world, 'workers together with God' to bring order out of chaos in this world, light into darkness, life where there was no life. You have the honor of helping Him 'subdue the earth.' Every time you try a law case and seek justice, tend a patient to cure disease, share knowledge with a student you are helping Him 'subdue the earth.' When your work is over here you have a glorious future forever with Him. Now act like that's who you are. Secure in the knowledge of your identity, live lives 'worthy of the gospel.'"

June 6, 1993

Weekday Problems

Charles did not advance up the professional ladder as fast as some. It wasn't because he didn't have what it took. He had received the finest training, graduated near the top of his class, was expected to go far in his field of work. As expected, he was competent, even exceptional as a novice. He worked hard, was loyal to the company, cared about others and was a team player. But as the years slipped by he seemed to be stuck near his entry level position. His problem seemed to be a moral one. Not unethical behavior or that he lived in the gray area, shaving the rules whenever necessary. He would not do that. Charles had trouble because he was perceived as too good. Despite his great loyalty to the company, he let it be known that work was not the only important matter in his life, not number one on his list of priorities. He was not willing to work every weekend, miss Christian fellowship and worship and sacrifice his time for physical and spiritual rebuilding. In a section meeting he remarked that he would choose fewer sales rather than engage in questionable techniques. He wanted, not only to be legal, but to be moral. Some were calling him "holy Joe" behind his back.

*Shouldn't someone tell him he has to "go along" to get along?

♦♦♦♦♦♦

Superintendent's Sermonette

Christians have to be careful that the hedonistic approach to life which is popular in the sinful world-system does not change their thinking and influence their righteous lifestyle. Many people today either avoid work or complain about the work they have to do. The big goal for some unbelievers is to "party" as much as possible. This often involves alcoholism, drug-abuse, sexual immorality, and loud, inconsiderate, and dangerous behavior. Others devote their whole lives to the acquisition of money, material things, power, and popularity.

Paul saw life from the Christian perspective. After he left a life of privilege behind him, he spent the rest of his life spreading the gospel and establishing churches. Even house-arrest in Rome did not stop him from ministering to others. He taught the believers in Philippi how to turn a harsh circumstance into a beneficial one. He helped them to understand that suffering for Christ's sake need not terrify them or hinder their testimony.

Do you have a worldly or a Christian perspective on life? Your answer will determine whether or not you are really going to count for Christ. Let us ask God to make us willing to suffer for Christ's sake, depending on divine, sustaining grace.

A WORTHY LIFE

Lesson in Your Life

Christianity is a group activity. Many protest that the church is the problem.

Nevertheless, the community of believers was a part of the Master's plan from the beginning. He not only called Peter, James, and John to Himself, He called them to follow Him *together*. "By this will all know that you are my disciples, that you love one another," Jesus said at the Last Supper.

Christian fellowship is a double-edged sword. On the one hand there are many times in our lives when we would not know what to do if it were not for the love and support of our church family. On the other hand, there are times when the maintenance cost of a vital Christian fellowship is so high we wonder if it is worth it. If we were totally candid we would admit that it is easier sometimes to love our enemy on the other side of the world or the less fortunate on the other side of the tracks than to put up with our brothers and sisters in the Lord. Our relationships become stagnant, the battle lines are drawn, nothing can change. "That's just the way she is!" "What do you expect from him, he'll never change." "I can barely speak to that man without resorting to violence." Maybe Jesus' hardest command was not to love our enemies, but that "you love one another."

Nothing about all of this is new. Life was not all peaches and cream for the earliest Christians. Paul himself found it hard from time to time working with others. He and Barnabas came to a parting of the ways. The younger man, John Mark, felt the sting of Paul's disapproval. Outside the close circle of Christian co-workers Paul was constantly in conflict with legalistic brethren. He had experienced tension with some of the leaders at Jerusalem from the first. So we can learn much about Christian fellowship from Philippians.

Paul was writing this letter from prison, waiting to be tried on capital charges. His enemies and detractors had worked overtime to discredit him and undermine his work. The little church Paul had founded at Philippi is the nearest to ideal we find in the New Testament. They had been faithful to the gospel and hearty in their support of Paul's mission from the first. But they had problems. The teachers mentioned in chapter 3 were trying to hijack the church and take it back into salvation by works of the Law. Two of the sisters in the Ladies' Bible Class, Euodia and Syntyche, were at odds. We do not know the nature of their disagreement whether it was a personality conflict, a doctrinal dispute, or a procedural tussle. Whatever the problem, the whole church was soon involved. Of course, their families and friends in the church lined up behind them and so a division was possible.

We notice that Paul was not shocked, surprised, or alarmed that there were problems in the church. Unbecoming attitudes among believers were not fatal to Paul's faith and mission. He did not expect such a total transformation of human beings at conversion that selfishness and pride were banished from the heart. Notice also that Paul did not give the Philippians permission to leave the fellowship. He did not say: "Well, if church isn't 'doing it for you' anymore why not just bail out?" That's because Paul grew up believing in the reality of sin, the hopelessness of mankind without God, God's mighty acts of salvation and the covenant community. God made covenant with His people and they made covenant with God. At that same time God's people also made covenant with one another to be His people. It was a serious commitment.

Seed Thoughts

1. What confidence did Paul have about the Philippians?
That God would finish what He had started in them.

2. How had Paul's sufferings turned out to be blessings in disguise?
His imprisonment had sent the gospel even into Caesar's household.

3. How can one possibly live life "in a manner worthy of the gospel of Christ"?
By loving the fellowship and not fearing the opposition.

4. When is suffering a privilege?
When it is endured for the kingdom and in the service of Christ.

5. Why did Paul write to the Philippians, a nearly perfect church?
Because every church needs encouragement, direction, and instruction.

(PLEASE TURN PAGE)

---

1. What confidence did Paul have about the Philippians?

2. How had Paul's sufferings turned out to be blessings in disguise?

3. How can one possibly live life "in a manner worthy of the gospel of Christ"?

4. When is suffering a privilege?

5. Why did Paul write to the Philippians, a nearly perfect church?

6. Why should I be a member of an imperfect church?

7. Why should a church accept a sinner like me?

8. What should be your first and most basic identity?

9. Why is the teacher's presence not required for Christians to continue living "worthy of the gospel"?

10. What special privilege had Jesus granted Paul and the Philippians?

(SEED THOUGHTS--Cont'd)

That God would finish what He had started in them.

His imprisonment had sent the gospel even into Caesar's household.

By loving the fellowship and not fearing the opposition.

When it is endured for the kingdom and in the service of Christ.

Because every church needs encouragement, direction, and instruction.

Because there is no other kind.

Because Jesus died for all human beings. All are sinners like you.

You are God's child, made in His image, redeemed at the cross.

Because their primary relationship is to Jesus.

To suffer with Him for His cause.

6. Why should I be a member of an imperfect church?
Because there is no other kind.

7. Why should a church accept a sinner like me?
Because Jesus died for all human beings. All are sinners like you.

8. What should be your first and most basic identity?
You are God's child, made in His image, redeemed at the cross.

9. Why is the teacher's presence not required for Christians to continue living "worthy of the gospel"?
Because their primary relationship is to Jesus.

10. What special privilege had Jesus granted Paul and the Philippians?
To suffer with Him for His cause.

June 13, 1993

THE BELIEVER'S ROLE MODEL

Christ, Our Model

Philippians 2

2 If *there be* therefore any consolation in Christ, if any comfort of love, if any fellowship of the Spirit, if any bowels and mercies,

2. Fulfil ye my joy, that ye be likeminded, having the same love, *being* of one accord, of one mind.

3. *Let* nothing *be done* through strife or vainglory; but in lowliness of mind let each esteem other better than themselves.

4. Look not every man on his own things, but every man also on the things of others.

5. Let this mind be in you, which was also in Christ Jesus:

6. Who, being in the form of God, thought it not robbery to be equal with God:

7. But made himself of no reputation, and took upon him the form of a servant, and was made in the likeness of men:

8. And being found in fashion as a man, he humbled himself, and became obedient unto death, even the death of the cross.

9. Wherefore God also hath highly exalted him, and given him a name which is above every name:

10. That at the name of Jesus every knee should bow, of *things* in heaven, and *things* in earth, and *things* under the earth;

11. And *that* every tongue should confess that Jesus Christ is Lord, to the glory of God the Father.

12. Wherefore, my beloved, as ye have always obeyed, not as in my presence only, but now much more in my absence, work out your own salvation with fear and trembling.

13. For it is God which worketh in you both to will and to do of *his* good pleasure.

14. Do all things without murmurings and disputings:

15. That ye may be blameless and harmless, the sons of God without rebuke, in the midst of a crooked and perverse nation, among whom ye shine as lights in the world;

16. Holding forth the word of life that I may rejoice in the day of Christ, that I have not run in vain, neither laboured in vain.

♦♦♦♦♦♦

◀ **Memory Selection**
Philippians 2:5

◀ **Devotional Reading**
John 14:1-14

◀ **Background Scripture**
Philippians 2:1-18

◀ **Printed Scripture**
Philippians 2:1-16

CHRIST, OUR MODEL

Teacher's Target

We are all familiar with the agony and the ecstasy which characterize family relationships. The same parents who are driven to distraction by rebellious children also love them enough to die for them, if that became necessary. Sibling rivalries which may threaten to destroy a household can be matched with acts of concern when a brother or sister needs help. A husband and wife may indulge in some strong-minded disagreements, but beware of interposing yourself between them for both may turn against you as they defend one another. Members of the redeemed family of God may also reveal mixed types of relationships.

Help your students to appreciate what Paul exhorted believers to do in order to improve their relationships with one another and with the world in general. Paul urged them to be unified, loving, and humble. He urged them to serve one another. He held up Jesus Christ as the greatest Servant, willing to humble Himself to become a Man and die on the cross. God exalted Him, and all will humble themselves before Him. If we follow Christ's example, God will also exalt us and make us lights in the world.

Lesson Introduction

Individuals who voluntarily place themselves under the tutelage of a respected person seem willing to accept instruction and even reprimands from him. In other types of situations, people usually resent others telling them what they ought to do. Paul no doubt came in contact with both kinds of situations. The believers in Philippi obviously were anxious for Paul to help them in their spiritual growth, and he was ready and able to make strong suggestions for them to follow. He called on them to fill him with joy by patterning themselves after Christ.

Forsaking self-centered concerns, they were to esteem others as better than themselves. Laying aside their own concerns, they were to put attention on the concerns of others. They were urged to have the mind of Christ, willing to be humbled before exalted. They were to work out their glorious salvation experience by being optimistic, blameless, harmless sons of God, shining as lights in the world and holding forth the Word of life to all.

Teaching Outlines

I. Exhorting: Phil. 2:1-4
   A. Request: 1-2
   B. Respect: 3-4
II. Emptying: Phil. 2:5-8
   A. Attitude: 5-6
   B. Action: 7-8
III. Exalting: Phil. 2:9-11
   A. Promotion: 9
   B. Prediction: 10-11
IV. Encouraging: Phil. 2:12-16
   A. Workers: 12-13
   B. Witnesses: 14-16

Daily Bible Readings

Mon. Follow Christ's Example
I Pet 2:18-25
Tue. Hold Fast the Word of Life
Phil. 2:12-18
Wed. Honor Faithful Servants of Christ - *Phil. 2:19-30*
Thu. Christ Our Reconciler
II Cor. 5:16-21
Fri. Christ Our Standard
II Cor. 13:5-14
Sat. Walk in Christ's Spirit
Gal. 5:13-25
Sun. Love as Christ Loved
John 15:12-17

June 13, 1993

VERSE BY VERSE

I. Exhorting: Phil. 2:1-4

A. Request: 1-2

**1. If there be therefore any consolation in Christ, if any comfort of love, if any fellowship of the Spirit, if any bowels and mercies,
2. Fulfil ye my joy, that ye be likeminded, having the same love, being of one accord, of one mind.**

The first verse looked to the past. In effect, Paul said that the Philippian believers had been a consolation to him as fellow members of the body of Christ. They had comforted him with their love. They had provided fellowship to Him in the Spirit. They had shown compassion and kindness to him. He appreciated all of these things; and he wanted them to continue, for this would fill up his joy.

Paul had previously urged them to "stand fast in one spirit, with one mind striving together for the faith of the gospel" (Phil. 1:27). He now returned to this theme by urging them to be likeminded, mutually loving, and "being one in spirit and purpose" (New International Version). If this kind of internal unity could be developed, they would be better able to withstand external pressure from adversaries such as those mentioned in Philippians 1:28. As each believer was drawn closer to Christ by the in-dwelling Holy Spirit, each would also be drawn closer to one another.

B. Respect: 3-4

3. Let nothing be done through strife or vainglory; but in lowliness of mind let each esteem other better than themselves.

Paul wanted believers to avoid strife and vainglory. The right thing to do was to keep a subdued opinion of one's own self and give proper respect to others. Paul did not expect believers to be wimps or hypocrites in their evaluation of themselves, but He hoped that they would be infused by divine love so they would truly love others. In another place; he wrote; "Be kindly affectioned one to another with brotherly love; in honour preferring one another" (Rom. 12:10). There should be times when our own rights and preferences are kept to ourselves while those of others are honored.

4. Look not every man on his own things, but every man also on the things of others.

Paul may have had more in mind here than selfish concerns versus the concerns of others. Perhaps he sought to show that Christians should be somewhat extroverted. This is easier for some than for others; but all believers have to reach out to contact one another for fellowship and outsiders for evangelism. One good way to make friends is to show an interest in their concerns; rather than talking about one's own interests all of the time.

II. Emptying: Phil. 2:5-8

A. Attitude: 5-6

5. Let this mind be in you, which was also in Christ Jesus:

Paul told believers that they should have the same mind which Jesus Christ had. No human being could hope to have His wisdom, but a believer could have His attitude. Thus begins the great emptying, passage of Philippians 2:5-8, which describes how Jesus laid aside

403

heavenly prerogatives in order to carry out His part in redemption of sinful men on the earth.

6. Who, being in the form of God, thought it not robbery to be equal with God:

Paul said that Jesus was on an equal footing with God. He shared His Father's glory and appearance. However, Jesus did not feel that divine glory was something to be grasped and held. He was willing to set it aside for a good purpose.

Let it be said here that Jesus did *not* lay aside His essential divinity in order to come to the earth. His ministry showed that He demonstrated divine wisdom and power many times. His divine glory did show through innumerable times (John 1:14), but the full force of His divinity was held in check until He returned to His Father's right hand in heaven (John 17:5; Acts 7:55).

B. Action: 7-8

7. But made himself of no reputation, and took upon him the form of a servant, and was made in the likeness of men:

Nothing like this had happened before nor would happen again. The unique action taken by Jesus was to leave the spirit-form He had in heaven and take on a human form. It was only in this form as the God-Man that He could be a Servant capable of atoning for men's sins. He became the only valid link to close the gap between a holy God and sinful men.

8. And being found in fashion as a man, he humbled himself, and became obedient unto death, even the death of the cross.

Jesus humbled Himself in three ways. He became a Man. He agreed to die as all men die. He submitted to death by crucifixion, probably the most shameful type of execution in ancient times. Why did He do this? He allowed God to make Him perfect (mature, experienced) through sufferings (Heb. 2:10). He became the Author of eternal salvation to those that obey Him (Heb. 5:9). It was "for the joy that was set before him (that Jesus) endured the cross; despising the shame, and is set down at the right hand of the throne of God" (Heb. 12:2).

III. Exalting: Phil. 2:9-11

A. Promotion: 9

9. Wherefore God also hath highly exalted him, and given him a name which is above every name:

The exaltation of Jesus from the humility of crucifixion, death, and burial began on the third day afterward when God raised Him from the dead. His exaltation continued when God caught Him back up to heaven at His ascension forty days later. There could be no exaltation greater than being at God's right hand. What was the name given to Jesus which ranked higher than any other name? Verse 10 suggests that it was simply Jesus, but the name now carried with it even greater honor than it had held before. The compelling power of that name will be demonstrated in the end times.

B. Prediction: 10-11

10. That at the name of Jesus every knee should bow, of things in heaven, and things in earth, and things under the earth;

Paul was probably thinking of Isaiah 45:23— "(God said) Unto me every knee shall bow, every tongue shall swear." He applied this to the honor which will one day be given to Jesus. At the sound of His name, all beings in heaven, all beings on the earth, and all beings under the earth will come together to bow before Him.

11. And that every tongue should confess that Jesus Christ is Lord, to the glory of God the Father.

All created beings will not only have to bow before Christ but will have to proclaim Him as Lord. Those who do not do it voluntarily will have to do it under force. All doubts by agnostics and all denials by atheists will be wiped away in that awesome spectacle. The honoring of the Son will bring glory to the Father, for they are One. No matter how difficult life becomes for believers, they know that in the end they will be on the winning side and unbelievers will be on the losing side. The exaltation of Christ will be their exaltation, too.

IV. Encouraging: Phil. 2:12-16

A. Workers: 12-13

12a. Wherefore, my beloved, as ye have always obeyed, not as in my presence only, but now much more in my absence, . . .

Paul commended the believers in Philippi for their obedience, but he did not say to whom they had been obedient. Was he talking about them obeying God, himself, or both? It is suspected that he referred to both. God, Christ, and the Holy Spirit gave the commandments, and believers sought to carry them out. Paul was thankful for their obedience while he had been with them, and he was thankful for a report that they were continuing their obedience in his absence. They were doing better now than before.

12b. . . .work out your own salvation with fear and trembling.

We know that Paul taught that salvation was by faith, not by works (Eph. 2:8-9). Why did he make this statement about working out salvation? One paraphrase puts Paul's reference to his absence in with the last part of the verse—"Now that I am away you must be even more careful to do the good things that result from being saved, obeying God with deep reverence, shrinking back from all that might displease him" (Living Bible). It appears that Paul was encouraging believers to see that their initial salvation experience should be followed through in spiritual growth and development.

13. For it is God which worketh in you both to will and to do of his good pleasure.

Paul did not expect believers to make spiritual progress all on their own. He said that it was God Who sought to work *in* them, giving them the desire and the power to do what pleased Him. It was workers who were led and controlled by the indwelling Holy Spirit who would be effective.

B. Witnesses: 14-16

14. Do all things without murmurings and disputings:

Paul felt that the testimony of believers would be enhanced if they worked without murmurings and disputings. Unbelievers were unlikely to be attracted to believers who failed to heed this advice.

15a. That ye may be blameless and harmless, the sons of God, without rebuke, in the midst of a crooked and perverse nation, . . .

Here was the positive side of Paul's thought. He wanted believers, here called "the sons of God," to be blameless innocent, harmless, without rebuke, while living in the midst of a crooked and perverse nation.

15 b. . . .among whom ye shine as lights in the world;

16a. Holding forth the word of life; . . .

The torchbearer in the Olympics ran with the torch held high and out before him. Christians were expected to hold forth the Word that brings life in the same manner but in a functional and spiritual sense. They themselves were to be lighted by the Word of God and then shine forth to a world lost in the darkness of sin. Light in the Bible refers to truth, and particularly to divine truth revealed by God to men. Our generation is just as responsible for studying, understanding, absorbing, applying, and propagating truth as other generations have been. We live in a society where false religions, cults, and philosophies have created desperate darkness. The only antidote is the pure, unadulterated Word of God. Many will ignore or reject it, but some will accept and embrace it if we are faithful witnesses.

16b. . . that I may rejoice in the day of Christ, that I have not run in vain, neither laboured in vain.

One paraphrase puts it this way— "If you do so (shine as lights and hold forth the word of life), I shall have reason to be proud of you on the Day of Christ, because it will show that all my effort and work have not been wasted" (Today's English Version). It was in their role as lightbearers that Paul thought of believers as working out the effects of their initial salvation, mentioned in verse 12. Works did not save them, but the fact that they were saved was supposed to motivate them to shine as lights in the world.

CHRIST, OUR MODEL

Evangelistic Emphasis

What can we do to make the gospel more attractive to unbelievers? Our television-conditioned world has become more and more indifferent to potent sales promotion. It takes more and more creativity and excitement to hold the attention of the viewer. Our culture is now so sophisticated, so entertained, so jaded that it cannot be captured by glitzy sales techniques.

What hope do we have to compete with the television industry for the minds of the people? We should learn by observing the advertising industry that human appetite for entertainment is a bottomless pit. Perhaps we should also recall that Jesus refused to jump off the pinnacle of the temple to wow people into His kingdom.

God has provided the uniqueness of Christianity. We do not have to keep coming up with gimmicks to create sales appeal. For one thing, the Christian community has a special kind of love not experienced in any other group. A second distinctive feature is that Christians can be secure enough in themselves to empty themselves in the service of God and others.

A modern example shows the power of such an attitude. She was a tough businesswoman used to the hard realities of the "real world." She met three Christian ladies at the bedside of her friend who was dying of AIDS. The ladies had cared for him constantly for months, knowing from the first that they would suffer great loss when he died. Later she came to worship saying about the Christian women: "I tried to figure their angle and couldn't. I asked them where they went to church. I just wanted to know what kind of group these ladies belong to. I've never seen such unselfish love." Self-emptying love is the truest of all methods of evangelism. It never fails to get the attention of a self-centered world.

♦♦♦♦♦♦

Memory Selection

"Let this mind be in you, which was also in Christ Jesus."
Philippians 2:5

Paul does not mean when he says "have this mind in you" that Christian unity and fellowship arise out of complete agreement on some particular intellectual theory or philosophy of religion. We should engage our minds to study the faith and to develop true theology. Jesus called His own to love God with their whole minds. Paul was, himself, a theologian, the first great Christian theologian. But in this passage he means: "Have this spirit in you, the attitude of Christ..." And he does not leave us wondering where we might find that attitude. "Which was also in Christ" means that by looking to Christ each day, by dwelling on his example we can come to have His spirit. Paul specifically had in mind the self-emptying of Christ who left heaven to come here and serve, to suffer the hardships of human existence, to know loneliness and betrayal, to die on a cross at the hands of those He came to save, trusting His Father to raise Him. The Christlike spirit is not an achievement of our own. In II Corinthians 3 Paul explained that we are transformed when we gaze with unveiled face day by day upon Jesus Christ. Who He is rubs off on us the more we focus our lives on Him.

June 13, 1993

Weekday Problems

Sally grew up with the idea that she had little worth in herself. She was everybody's doormat and slave. Her mother was a quiet women who worked behind the scenes and never questioned the authority of her husband. Sally's father generally treated women as his servants. Even though he loved her, he never confirmed Sally as a person in her own right. In the schools she attended Sally met the same attitude in the male faculty and administration. After many years of painful experience, including a failed marriage, she began exploring books and seminars advancing personal self worth. In ladies' meetings at church she began asking why the women were systematically ignored when important policies and decisions were made. She was just beginning to venture out on her own as a person when a Christian friend confronted her. She said Sally was becoming arrogant and proud in violation of the spirit of Christ. "Jesus was a servant," Sally's friend said. "You are denying the faith when you begin asserting that you are no one's servant." She went on to quote from Philippians 2: "He emptied himself and became a servant . . .

*What does it mean that Jesus was a servant? Was he a doormat?
*Where can Sally find a healthy balance between self-assertion and concern for others?

♦♦♦♦♦♦

Superintendent's Sermonette

Humility without sincerity becomes hypocrisy. We have too much of that among believers today. If we fail to live up to our claims for righteousness, unbelievers may condemn us as fakes. If we lack courage, they may equate our humility with weakness and cowardice. They may think humble individuals are incapable of strong, determined actions.

Moses proved this concept wrong. "Moses was very meek; above all the men which were upon the face of the earth" (Num. 12:3). However, when the Israelites made a golden calf to worship, Moses burned it, ground it to powder, spread it on water, and made the people drink it (Exod. 32:20).

Jesus proved this concept wrong. He "found in the temple those that sold oxen and sheep and doves, and the changers of money sitting: and when he had made a scourge of small cords, he drove them all out of the temple, . . . and poured out the changers' money, and overthrew the tables" (John 2:14-15).

In today's text, Paul shows that Jesus' humility in becoming a Man and dying on the cross led to His exaltation. Are we willing to suffer and die for Christ's cause? If we are, we can expect God to exalt us, too. Let us serve Him without complaining, shining as lights in the world, holding forth the Word of life!

CHRIST, OUR MODEL

This Lesson For Your Life

Wherever two or three Christians gather together two things are certain. First, the Lord is among them. He promised to be there. "Where two or three of you are gathered in my name, I am there in your midst." Second, wherever two or three are gathered they will have problems arising from interpersonal conflict. From their various experiences, needs, personalities and agendas stresses will come. The little church at Philippi had its problems: struggles with legalists cited in chapter three, in chapter four mention was made of Euodia and Syntyche who were in conflict.

Today inside the church and out there is no shortage of easy formulas for solving interpersonal tensions. Perhaps it would be instructive to notice what Paul did not go to help the Philippians with their problems. He didn't pour sugary moralisms over the problem: "Now be nice, children should play sweetly together." That kind of advice may make the speaker feel better, but it only insults the adult listener and makes him feel rage. Nor did Paul keep people busy to distract them: "If you'll just get to work these problems will take care of themselves." Assignment of tasks does relieve the tension for a while, but is no real solution. Nor did he separate them. "Maybe you should just start another church." We have hundreds and hundreds of denominations. Some divisions in church history may have been understandable, inevitable, the lesser of two evils. But beginning a new church the first time a problem arises is not the answer. It grieves Christ to see His body torn apart because of the selfishness of His disciples.

All of these answers fail because they do not penetrate the surface. They do not reach down to the heart of the matter and treat the disease at its origin. They are small answers for what might seem to be small problems. Paul did not give small answers for small problems. For him the whole faith flowed from the death, burial, and resurrection of Jesus. (I Corinthians 15:1-4). So Paul called attention to Jesus. He was to be the model of self-worth, self-emptying, and faith in the Father.

First, Jesus is our example in secure self-worth. He was "equal with God" enjoying "all the rights and privileges appertaining to that station in life." He did not have to strive after power, position, and prestige. No one had to convince Him that He had worth and significance. He knew His rights, understood His worth, and saw clearly the value of the gift He was giving. He understood completely what coming here would mean. In John 10 He said, "I lay my life down and I take it up, no one takes it from me." In John 13, knowing His own identity and mission, He took the towel and basin and washed feet. In John 18 He challenged the servant of the High Priest: "If I have said anything untrue, what was it? Otherwise, why did you slap me?"

Second, knowing His own dignity and worth, He became our example in self-emptying. He became a human being, a servant, and even died a criminal's death on the cross. He "became obedient even unto death." That is, Jesus came to do the Father's will, struggled honestly with Him in the garden, and finally said "Not my will but thine be done." Even so, He never forgot who He was, never lost His sense of self-worth. Jesus chose to empty Himself in obedience to the Father and in love for mankind. He gave *Himself* for us on Golgotha.

Third, God highly exalted Him. Most people in our society think Christians who empty themselves in service to others are fools. "What's in it for you? How can you afford to give yourself away like that?" Jesus is our model, not only in that He knew His own worth, not only in His self-emptying, but also in His reliance on the Father.

Seed Thoughts

1. Does Christianity care anything about personal rights?
Yes, but not only one's own rights, the rights of others also.

2. Why do we need a model for living the Christian life?
Otherwise, we try to make it up as we go along.

3. Are there times when I should not give up my own rights?
Yes, when doing so means that God's image in yourself or in others is not recognized.

4. Where can I go to find the model of perfect balance between self-respect and self-emptying?
No one has ever got it just right except Jesus.

5. Who were the first "grasping" persons in the Bible?
Adam and Eve.

(PLEASE TURN PAGE)

---

1. Does Christianity care anything about personal rights?

2. Why do we need a model for living the Christian life?

3. Are there times when I should not give up my own rights?

4. Where can I go to find the model of perfect balance between self-respect and self-emptying?

5. Who were the first "grasping" persons in the Bible?

6. What did the grasping of Adam and Eve produce?

7. What did Jesus' self-emptying produce?

8. What can you do to underwrite this Christian adventure in self-emptying?

9. How do we know that it will all turn out all right?

10. How can you and I pull off imitating Jesus?

(SEED THOUGHTS--Cont'd)

Yes, but not only one's own rights, the rights of others also.

Otherwise, we try to make it up as we go along.

Yes, when doing so means that God's image in yourself or in others is not recognized.

No one has ever got it just right except Jesus.

Adam and Eve.

Disaster for them and for the whole human race.

Salvation for us, achievement of God's redemptive plan, and the glorification of the Father and the Son.

Nothing, only God can underwrite risky suffering service.

In the end "every knee will bow, every tongue confess that Jesus is Lord to the glory of the Father."

We can't, God is at work in us to will and to do His good pleasure.

6. What did the grasping of Adam and Eve produce?
Disaster for them and for the whole human race.

7. What did Jesus' self-emptying produce?
Salvation for us, achievement of God's redemptive plan, and the glorification of the Father and the Son.

8. What can you do to underwrite this Christian adventure in self-emptying?
Nothing, only God can underwrite risky suffering service.

9. How do we know that it will all turn out all right?
In the end "every knee will bow, every tongue confess that Jesus is Lord to the glory of the Father."

10. How can you and I pull off imitating Jesus?
We can't, God is at work in us to will and to do His good pleasure.

June 20, 1993

GET UP MAN! THERE'S HELP AHEAD!

Keep on Keeping on

Philippians 3

1 FINALLY, my brethren, rejoice in the Lord. To write the same things to you, to me indeed is not grievous, but for you it is safe.

2. Beware of dogs, beware of evil workers, beware of the concision.

3. For we are the circumcision, which worship God in the spirit, and rejoice in Christ Jesus, and have no confidence in the flesh.

4. Though I might also have confidence in the flesh. If any other man thinketh that he hath whereof he might trust in the flesh, I more:

5. Circumcised the eighth day, of the stock of Israel, *of* the tribe of Benjamin, an Hebrew of the Hebrews; as touching the law, a Pharisee;

6. Concerning zeal, persecuting the church; touching the righteousness which is in the law, blameless.

7. But what things were gain to me, those I counted loss for Christ.

8. Yea doubtless, and I count all things *but* loss for the excellency of the knowledge of Christ Jesus my Lord: for whom I have suffered the loss of all things, and do count them *but* dung, that I may win Christ.

9. And be found in him, not having mine own righteousness, which is of the law, but that which is through the faith of Christ, the righteousness which is of God by faith:

10. That I may know him, and the power of his resurrection, and the fellowship of his sufferings, being made conformable unto his death;

11. If by any means I might attain unto the resurrection of the dead.

12. Not as though I had already attained, either were already perfect: but I follow after, if that I may apprehend that for which also I am apprehended of Christ Jesus.

13. Brethren, I count not myself to have apprehended: but this one thing I do, forgetting those things which are behind, and reaching forth unto those things which are before,

14. I press toward the mark for the prize of the high calling of God in Christ Jesus.

15. Let us therefore, as many as be perfect, be thus minded: and if in any thing ye be otherwise minded, God shall reveal even this unto you.

16. Nevertheless, whereto we have already attained, let us walk by the same rule, let us mind the same thing.

◆◆◆◆◆◆

◀ **Memory Selection**
Philippians 3:14

◀ **Background Scripture**
Philippians 3

◀ **Devotional Reading**
Romans 15:1-13

◀ **Printed Scripture**
Philippians 3:1-16

KEEP ON KEEPING ON

Teachers Target

There was a time when Paul, originally called Saul of Tarsus, depended on fleshly, carnal things for his reputation. He was putting his confidence in being a Jew from the tribe of Benjamin, a thorough Hebrew, and a strict, legalistic Pharisee. He zealously persecuted the young church. He trusted in his self-righteous adherence to the Mosaic law and the traditions which had built up around it. He was proud, arrogant, and cruel. Help your students to understand What caused Paul to count all of these things as loss in order that he might win Christ? What does it mean to have righteousness which is of God by faith? Why did Paul want to know the power of Christ's resurrection and the fellowship of His sufferings? What was the prize for which Paul sought? What were believers to do if they could not agree on something? These and other questions are posed in our text, and we will search for answers to them, for they are still relevant to us today.

Lesson Introduction

Paul was harsh in his condemnation of Jews who insisted on being mutilators of the flesh by demanding literal circumcision as a sign of spiritual excellence. He went so far as to label them "dogs" and "evil workers" (Phil. 3:2), and he said that true circumcision is spiritual and involves acceptance of God, Christ, and the Holy Spirit. Having laid down this doctrinal foundation, he proceeded to describe his own experience of forsaking Jewish assurances of a favored position in order to find assurance of identification with Jesus Christ.

Paul was not content to rest on past laurels. He had a forward look. He wanted his identification with Christ to be so thorough that he could at least symbolically suffer, die, and be raised to newness of power. In other words, Paul wanted to grow and develop to maturity in Christ. He wanted to become increasingly more Christlike. If all Christians want this, and if they will encourage one another to strive for it, all will profit.

Teaching Outline

I. Warning: Phil. 3:1-6
 A. Safeguard: 1
 B. Spirituality: 2-3
 C. Stock of Israel: 4-6
II. Winning: Phil. 3:7-14
 A. Refuse: 7-8
 B. Righteousness: 9
 C. Resurrection: 10-11
 D. Reach: 12-14
III. Walking: Phil. 3:15-16
 A. Convictions: 15
 B. Continuance: 16

Daily Bible Readings

Mon. Be Faithful even to Death
Phil 3:1-11
Tue. Press on toward the Goal
Phil. 3:12-16
Wed. The Savior Will Come
Phil. 3:17-21
Thu. Give Yourselves in Service
Rom. 12:1-8
Fri. Follow Christ's Example
Rom. 12:9-20
Sat. Bear One Another's Burdens
Gal. 6:1-5
Sun. Do Good to All People
Gal. 6:6-10

June 20, 1993

VERSE BY VERSE

I. Warning: Phil. 3:1-6

A. Safeguard: I

1a. Finally, my brethren, rejoice in the Lord.

Paul seemed to use "finally" as a transition term when going from one subject to another. It has been suggested that Paul actually meant to close his letter by urging believers to rejoice in the Lord (Phil. 4:4ff.), but he felt compelled to insert other subjects as found in Philippians 3:1—4:3. If that was the case, he picked up the theme about rejoicing again in Philippians 4:4. In both Philippians 3:1 and 4:4 we take note that rejoicing by believers is to be based not on circumstances, which can be good or bad, but on the Lord himself, for He stands above all circumstances and can control them.

1b. To write the same things to you, to me indeed is not grievous, but for you it is safe.

Paul prefaced his warning about Judaizers by saying that writing the same things repeatedly to believers in Philippi was not grievous to him. He evidently had written to them before, but we have no record of it. Paul wanted them to realize that his warnings were designed as a safeguard for them against dangers.

B. Spirituality: 2-3

2. Beware of dogs, beware of evil workers, beware of the concision.

Jews, and even Jesus Himself, referred to Gentiles as dogs (Matt. 15:26). Paul turned this around by calling troublesome Jews dogs. He was probably referring to extreme Judaizers or to antagonistic Jews. He had low regard for their *character*. Paul called them evil workers or mischief makers. He had low regard for their *conduct*. Paul called them the concision (mutilation or cutting of the flesh), a term used only here in the Bible. It designated literal, physical, ceremonial circumcision devoid of spiritual meaning. Even Gentile converts to Christ were told to be circumcised and observe Jewish regulations. Paul had low regard for this *creed*.

3. For we are the circumcision which worship God in the spirit, and rejoice in Christ Jesus, and have no confidence in the flesh.

In contrast to the Judaizers or Jews who demanded physical circumcision for all males, Paul said that true circumcision was spiritual and that it was available to all who worship God in the Spirit, who rejoice in salvation through faith in Christ, and who put no confidence in works of the flesh. In this sense, circumcision becomes a symbol involving cutting away from sin and devoting oneself to righteousness. It is circumcision of the heart, and it is open to all, Jews and Gentiles.

C. Stock of Israel: 4-6

4. Though I might also have confidence in the flesh. If any other man thinketh that he hath whereof he might trust in the flesh, I more:

Paul remembered that there was a time in his life when he put great confidence or trust in earthly credentials. He had been raised in Tarsus of Cilicia (southeastern Asia Minor or Turkey) in an orthodox Jewish home. He had later studied at the feet of the renowned scholar named Gamaliel in Jerusalem. He felt that he had all of the advantages Judaism could offer a young man.

5. Circumcised the eighth day, of

413

the stock of Israel, of the tribe of Benjamin, an Hebrew of the Hebrews; as touching the law, a Pharisee;

Paul had prided himself on being thoroughly Jewish, believing that he had all of the unique privileges available only to pure Jews. He had been circumcised on the eighth day after his birth according to longstanding custom. He was of the pure stock of Israel, not of mixed blood. He came from the tribe of Benjamin, descended from Jacob and Rachel. Saul, Israel's first king, was of the tribe of Benjamin, and Saul (Paul) may have been named after him. Paul was a Hebrew of the Hebrews, because both his father and mother were Hebrews, and they kept the Hebrew language and customs current in their home. Paul was a Pharisee, "the straitest sect of our religion" (Acts 26:5). Pharisees considered themselves to be guardians of the Mosaic law and the traditions which grew up around it.

6. Concerning zeal, persecuting the church; touching the righteousness which is in the law, blameless.

This verse seems to present Paul's personal character traits when he was young. He was zealous in his efforts to curtail the church which had sprung up in the first century. In his own testimony to King Agrippa in Caesarea he once said, "I verily thought with myself that I ought to do many things contrary to the name of Jesus of Nazareth. Which thing I also did in Jerusalem: and many of the saints did I shut up in prison, having received authority from the chief priests; and when they were put to death, I gave my voice against them. And I punished them oft in every synagogue, and compelled them to blaspheme; and being exceedingly mad against them, I persecuted them even unto strange cities (Acts 26:9-11). Paul was very loyal to the Jewish religion. He followed the requirements of the Mosaic law scrupulously, although this was evidently a slavish adherence to the letter of the law and not to its spirit.

Paul had gone on to tell Agrippa how his life had been dramatically changed by an encounter with Jesus. "As I went to Damascus . . ., I saw in the way a light from heaven . . .When we were all fallen to the earth, I heard a voice speaking unto me, and saying in the Hebrew tongue, Saul, Saul, why persecutest thou me? ...And I said, Who art thou, Lord? And he said, I am Jesus whom thou persecutest. But rise, and stand upon thy feet: for I have appeared unto thee for this purpose, to make thee a minister and a witness both of these things which thou hast seen, and of those things in the which I will appear unto thee; delivering thee from the people and from the Gentiles, unto whom now I send thee, to open their eyes, and to turn them from darkness to light, and from the power of Satan unto God, that they may receive forgiveness of sins, an inheritance among them which are sanctified by faith that is in me. Whereupon, O king Agrippa, I was not disobedient unto the heavenly vision" (Acts 26:12-19). This is the background for what Paul was about to tell the Philippian believers regarding loss and gain.

II. Winning: Phil. 3:7-14

A. Refuse: 7-8

7. But what things were gain to me, those I counted loss for Christ.

In this brief statement, Paul put together all the former advantages of his life and counted them to be only losses when compared to what he gained in Christ.

8. Yea doubtless, and I count all things but loss for the excellency of the knowledge of Christ Jesus my Lord: for whom I have suffered the loss of all things, and do count them but dung, that I may win Christ.

This verse elaborates on the preceding one. Paul declared that he reckoned all the things in which he formerly placed his confidence were without value, after he had learned by experience the excellence of knowing Jesus Christ, his Lord. It was for His sake that Paul suffered the loss of all of those things, which he counted as dung (manure, refuse), for they could not compare with what he had won in committing himself to Christ.

B. Righteousness: 9

9. And be found in him, not having mine own righteousness, which is

414

of the law, but that which is through the faith of Christ, the righteousness which is of God by faith:

Paul considered himself to be in Christ, meaning that he was united with Him. The old self-righteousness which he had previously claimed by adhering to the law was gone. He now enjoyed the righteousness which came through faith in Christ. It was righteousness imparted by God to those who placed their trust in His Son and the atonement for sin He made at Calvary.

C. Resurrection: 10-11

10. That I may know him, and the power of his resurrection, and the fellowship of his sufferings, being made conformable unto his death;
11. If by any means I might attain unto the resurrection of the dead.

Paul knew that Jesus had suffered, died, and been resurrected before He ascended to heaven. Paul was anxious to share His Savior's experiences and do it during his own lifetime. He was not worried about the final resurrection. What Paul wanted was the same power which raised Jesus from the dead to operate in his current life. He wanted to "attain to the resurrection out from among the dead" (Amplified Bible).

D. Reach: 12-14

12. Not as though I had already attained, either were already perfect: but I follow after, if that I may apprehend that for which also I am apprehended of Christ Jesus.

Using racing terms here, Paul said that no one should assume that he felt he had reached his spiritual goal. He was pursuing it during his lifetime. He was trying to lay hold of that for which Christ had laid hold of him.

13. Brethren, I count not myself to have apprehended: but this one thing I do, forgetting those things which are behind, and reaching forth unto those things which are before,
14. I press toward the mark for the prize of the high calling of God in Christ Jesus.

Paul was not content to rest on past victories in his spiritual development. He was continually stretching forward to new victories. He referred to these collectively when he said, "I press toward the mark for the prize of the high calling of God in Christ Jesus." In other words, Paul wanted to become increasingly Christlike as he moved toward union with God and Christ in heaven.

III. Walking: Phil. 3:15-16

A. Convictions: 15

15a. Let us therefore, as many as be perfect, be thus minded: . . .

Having stated his aim of seeking maturity in Christ, Paul urged the Philippian believers to imitate him. The term "perfect" here might better be translated as "mature." No believer was sinlessly perfect, but he could become spiritually mature.

15b. . . . **and if in any thing ye be otherwise minded, God shall reveal even this unto you.**

Paul was so confident that he had the right goal in mind that he felt anyone who disagreed would eventually be convinced of it by God Himself. Paul was wise enough to know that he could not force his convictions on others. Only God could persuade them of something and cause them to live by it.

B. Continuance: 16

16. Nevertheless, whereto we have already attained, let us walk by the same rule, let us mind the same thing.

One paraphrase of this is, "However, where we have arrived, let us keep moving in the same direction" (Berkeley Version). Paul wanted believers who had attained a certain level of spiritual maturity to keep walking in the light of God's truth and look for more truth to guide them. There is always a danger that Christians will think they have arrived at a plateau where further improvement is either not possible or not needed. That conclusion would cut them off from further improvement and would probably cause them to slip backward. They should always seek to close the gap between their *position* in Christ and their practice of Christian living.

Evangelistic Emphasis

What is so attractive and fascinating about an older person who is determined to squeeze every drop out of life to the very end? A retired college professor who has had an illustrious career, has taught thousands of students, published dozens of books and hundreds of papers continues in retirement to research and write books!

A minister spends a lifetime serving in difficult places and then at the age of sixty-five takes a difficult and unglamorous assignment with a troubled church. "Never be afraid to tackle a new challenge," he says. "That's what keeps you young!" A fine doctor gives herself 100 percent to serve others far beyond the call of duty, to say nothing of the call of gold, and then dedicates her sunset years to a mission's clinic. She works harder for less money than ever in her life. Her devotion to others is reminiscent of Albert Schweitzer who left the comforts of Europe to practice in an African jungle when most men his age were looking for the rocking chair. What's wrong with these people? How can such strange actions be explained.

In John's gospel the gift Jesus brings is called "eternal life." It's not really length of life so much as a quality of existence. It doesn't begin after death, it starts here and now. Jesus said, "I came to bring life, and to bring it abundantly." Since the Christian's goal is to know Christ fully, to serve Him in His kingdom, to be like Him, life never runs out before death arrives. What a wonderful and attractive feature of the faith for sharing with others!

◆◆◆◆◆◆

Memory Selection

" I press on toward the mark for the prize of the high calling of God in Christ Jesus."
Philippians 3:14

The apostle was probably in his forties when he wrote the letter to Philippi. He didn't look a day over sixty-five. Not the years, the miles had taken their toll. As a young man Saul of Tarsus was full of promise. Endowed with great natural ability, privileged to attend school in Jerusalem, he was well on his way to a promising career. He lost his career, his standing with his peers, the endorsement of his teachers when he "got religion" or religion got him on the Damascus road. He lost the favor of the Jerusalem religious establishment when he came home talking of Jesus of Nazareth. In this letter to the Philippians we see Paul at the other end of his life, counting the losses and gains. He had lost much; everything from the world's point of view. But Paul had no regrets. His pedigree as a Jew, his diplomas and awards, his shiny hopes for position, power and prominence had all been trashed. He gave it all up for a personal relationship and knowledge of Jesus Christ. "Jesus Christ, my lord" he writes in deep loyalty to the one who called him. Not in years, but in experience, Paul was an old man. How refreshing to hear his zest for life. "I don't spend my life looking back. I have too much to do today, too much waiting for me tomorrow. I press on!"

June 20, 1993

Weekday Problems

Bob and Charles were brothers. Bob was "Mr Everything" in high school. He made it big on his athletic ability, charm and good looks. Charles was "Mr. Nothing" and, then, worse, he got with the wrong crowd and became "Mr. Trouble."

After the school days were over both boys found life hard. Bob went from job to job always unsatisfied. No one ever appreciated him for his true worth. They seemed not to care in the least what he had been in school. But he could not forget the golden days. Charles on the other hand, had trouble shaking his past. He paid dearly for not applying himself to his studies when in school. He had reformed his ways, dedicated himself completely to a constructive life, but lacked the tools to make a success of it. In his own mind he was still, and would always remain "Mr. Nothing."

"Bob kept going from job to job, from relationship to relationship saying: "Don't you know that I was outstanding in school? Why are you not giving me a chance?" Charles did the same with the unspoken inner feeling: "I know I am a loser, who can blame you for not giving me a chance?"

*If you were their favorite uncle or aunt and they came to you with their problems what would your advice be?

*Which is harder from your own experience: forgetting past failures or past successes?

◆◆◆◆◆◆

Superintendent's Sermonette

Unless we live very sheltered lives, we are bound to be frequently influenced by the world. We may not even realize the effect this has on us in bold or subtle ways, pulling us downward and out of the orbit of righteousness where God wants us to live. Another negative influence on us can be legalism which others seek to impose on us in the church. Judaizers of the first century have their modern counterparts. They go beyond the Scriptures and try to regulate us by man-made rules which rob us of our liberty in Christ.

When Paul realized that legalists such as this posed a threat to Philippian believers, he warned them against it. He showed the distinction which existed between ceremonial circumcision devoid of spiritual meaning and circumcision of the heart which featured love for God, Christ, and the Holy Spirit. He explained how his earthly credentials were laid aside in order that he might gain heavenly credentials through identification with Christ.

Let us ask God to sever us from all unworthy human controls and keep us open to all valuable divine controls on what we think, say, and do. We need to move forward to spiritual maturity and keep developing it until Jesus comes to take us home.

This Lesson for Your Life

This text applies in different ways to all the various stages of our lives. For the youth it suggests priorities for goal setting and dreaming. Toward the end of his life Paul made observations about what he had found to be most important. Young people are well served to study his story and observe how he came to his conclusions. Young professionals who experience enormous pressures to live according to the world's values can adjust their thinking by absorbing Paul's testimony. He, too, was a bright young professional with worlds to conquer. Those in mid-life can benefit. This passage could pose important questions before they knock themselves out for the bread which perishes. Those who "hit the wall" in the mid-life crisis might pause to use Paul's words for inventory. Perhaps they could ask whether they will ever find their life's blood in that same old turnip they have squeezed for twenty or thirty years. Older people who feel that life is behind them should be braced and stimulated by this older man who was determined to "press on" to the prize at life's end.

Why did Paul discard his most beautiful trophies, the brightest medals, his most impressive diplomas and citations? What would inspire so promising a young man to forfeit a lifestyle of power, prestige and comfort for the hand to mouth existence of a vagabond missionary? It takes no imagination at all to see what young Saul encountered as a student in Jerusalem. For example, Gamaliel was a teacher of great prestige, honored by all who met him on the street with a title of honor. Then there was Nicodemus who was not only a teacher in Israel, but very rich and very powerful. He sat on the Supreme Court and enjoyed all the prestige of that position. We imagine that when Nicodemus suggested that a street be paved in Jerusalem it was paved. Who would not enjoy such power? It appears that young Saul of Tarsus had the "stuff" such outstanding teachers and leaders are made of. Why would he turn his back on all of that to accept a no prestige job like Christian missionary to the Gentiles? To modern American values the change makes no sense. And, yet, we Christians are all eternally grateful that he responded to the call of Christ to bring us the good news. There was something greater, nobler, more important for young Saul than his own plans allowed. "Is there something better than my best dreams?" It's a question we should all ask ourselves.

The older we get the more we have our future behind us. At least that's true for most people today who have no vital confidence in a life after death. Senior citizen Christians more than most should ponder Paul's view of life. The past was simply prelude for the best of life stretching out before him. An older person tells the young person of past glories and receives an indulgent smile with the comment: "It must have been something to see." The storyteller hears: "I guess you had to be there." The sad part of it all is that many older people are still there, in days gone by.

Most tragic of all, living in the past robs us of present opportunities and future joys. An accident on the freeway of a major city a few years ago is a parable for older people. A number of cars were involved, several people were hurt and there was considerable property loss. Investigating officers found the cause. The driver at fault had rear ended another car and set up the a chain reaction collision. On closer inspection the officers discovered inside and outside the car seven rear view mirrors! No wonder the driver could not see what was ahead of him; his preoccupation was with what lay behind. How many of us live our lives looking back? What a shame when our God is a God of the future, Who had more wonderful things ahead of us that we dare dream or imagine!

Seed Thoughts

1. Judging by his own words, was young Saul of Tarsus a "winner" or a "loser" by today's standards?
   In every way then and now he was a winner.

2. What were Saul's most impressive achievements and credentials?
   Birth, family, academic achievement, religious zeal, head of his class.

3. Judging by today's standards was Paul at the end of his life a success in comparison with his potential plans?
   No, none of his most cherished plans came true.

4. In what endeavor did Paul say: "I'm not looking back, I'm pressing on"?
   In his effort to know Christ fully and to meet Him face to face.

5. What does religious pedigree have to do with finding Paul's kind of zest for life?
   Nothing, Paul did not rest on his family history for meaning in life.

(PLEASE TURN PAGE)

---

1. Judging by his own words, was young Saul of Tarsus a "winner" or a "loser" by today's standards?

2. What were Saul's most impressive achievements and credentials?

3. Judging by today's standards was Paul at the end of his life a success in comparison with his potential plans?

4. In what endeavor did Paul say: "I'm not looking back, I'm pressing on"?

5. What does religious pedigree have to do with finding Paul's kind of zest for life?

6. How can a person with a soiled past hope to find joy in living?

7. In terms of joy in life, what is the difference between being driven and being called?

8. Does "keeping on" mean there is no time for rest and rejuvenation?

9. Where did Paul in prison on trial for his life find the will to keep looking forward in joy?

10. What, in this text, is the sign of real Christian maturity?

(SEED THOUGHTS--Cont'd)

In every way then and now he was a winner.

Birth, family, academic achievement, religious zeal, head of his class.

No, none of his most cherished plans came true.

In his effort to know Christ fully and to meet Him face to face.

Nothing, Paul did not rest on his family history for meaning in life.

By coming to know Jesus Christ personally coming to love him and yearning to know him better.

Cattle are driven; Jesus calls disciples to follow him and that makes all the difference.

No, Jesus sometimes took the disciples aside for rest.

From his Lord who obeyed His Father and loved us "to the end."

The determination to keep on keeping on.

---

6. How can a person with a soiled past hope to find joy in living?
By coming to know Jesus Christ personally coming to love him and yearning to know him better.

7. In terms of joy in life, what is the difference between being driven and being called?
Cattle are driven; Jesus calls disciples to follow him and that makes all the difference.

8. Does "keeping on" mean there is no time for rest and rejuvenation?
No, Jesus sometimes took the disciples aside for rest.

9. Where did Paul in prison on trial for his life find the will to keep looking forward in joy?
From his Lord who obeyed His Father and loved us "to the end."

10. What, in this text, is the sign of real Christian maturity?
The determination to keep on keeping on.

June 27, 1993

"I'LL COME OVER AND WE'LL GIVE GOD THANKS FOR IT TOGETHER..."

"I JUST HAD TO TELL YOU... SO YOU CAN REJOICE WITH ME."

Rejoice in the Lord

Philippians 4

4. Rejoice in the Lord alway: and again I say, Rejoice.
5. Let your moderation be known unto all men. The Lord is at hand.
6. Be careful for nothing, but in every thing by prayer and supplication with thanksgiving let your requests be made known unto God.
7. And the peace of God, which passeth all understanding, shall keep your hearts and minds through Christ Jesus.
8. Finally, brethren, whatsoever things *are* true, whatsoever things *are* honest whatsoever things *are* just, whatsoever things *are* pure, whatsoever things *are* lovely, whatsoever things *are* of good report; if *there* be any virtue, and if *there* be any praise, think on these things.
9. Those things, which ye have both learned, and received, and heard, and seen in me, do: and the God of peace shall be with you.
10. But I rejoiced in the Lord greatly, that now at the last your care of me hath flourished again; wherein ye were also careful, but ye lacked opportunity.
11. Not that I speak in respect of want: for I have learned, in whatsoever state I am, *therewith* to be content.
12. I know both how to be abased, and I know how to abound: every where and in all things I am instructed both to be full and to be hungry, both to abound and to suffer need.
13. I can do all things through Christ which strengtheneth me.
14. Notwithstanding ye have well done, that ye did communicate with my affliction.
15. Now ye Phi-lip´-pi-ans know also, that in the beginning of the gospel, when I departed from Macedonia, no church communicated with me as concerning giving and receiving, but ye only.
16. For even in Thes-sa-lo-ní-ca ye sent once and again unto my necessity.
17. Not because I desire a gift: but I desire fruit that may abound to your account.
18. But I have all, and abound: I am full, having received of E-paph-ro-dí-tus the things *which were sent* from you, an odour of a sweet smell, a sacrifice acceptable, well pleasing to God.
19. But my God shall supply all your need according to his riches in glory by Christ Jesus.
20. Now unto God and our Father *be* glory for ever and ever. A´-men.

◆◆◆◆◆◆

◀ **Memory Selection**
Philippians 4:4

◀ **Devotional Reading**
Romans 5:1-11

◀ **Background Selection**
Philippians 4

◀ **Printed Scripture**
Philippians 4:4-20

REJOICE IN THE LORD

Teacher's Target

Paul evidently intended to close his epistle to the Philippians by encouraging his readers, "Rejoice in the Lord" (Phil. 3:1). However, he had other concerns intrude on his mind and dealt with them in the remainder of chapter 3 and the first three verses of chapter 4. He returned to his theme by writing, "Rejoice in the Lord alway: and again I say, Rejoice" (Phil. 4:4). This time he stayed with this subject to finish out his letter.

Help your students to see the relevance in Paul's suggestions for dealing with anxiety. He not only provided several helpful, general directives, but he also gave specific applications from his own experience before making the summary statement that he could "do all things through Christ which strengtheneth me" (Phil. 4:13). He touched on specific information before making the summary statement that "my God shall supply all your need according to his riches in glory by Christ Jesus" (Phil. 4:19). Thus Paul showed that strength and resources find their source in God and Christ.

Lesson Introduction

There are many programs, seminars, workshops, books, tapes, and other sources of help offered to the public today for dealing with personal problems. Advertisements hold out the advantages of purchasing care-free products. Peace movements are popular. There is a general desire in society to avoid all difficulties whenever possible. The good life is supposed to be the life which runs smoothly and without negative interruptions. Perhaps the concept of utopia is not dead. (DREAMS)

In the real world, however, we know that there are always going to be problems and difficulties to face and overcome. Christians need to have their feet planted solidly on the ground, but they can look upward for the divine help they need in order to work through their hard experiences. The secret for dealing with problems is not to avoid or ignore them but to move through them with God, Christ, and the Holy Spirit beside us. Today's text helps us to do that.

Teaching Outline

I. Rejoicing: Phil. 4:4-9
   A. Suggestion I: 4
   B. Suggestion II: 5
   C. Suggestion III: 6-7
   D. Suggestion IV: 8
   E. Suggestion V: 9
II. Readjusting: Phil. 4:10-13
   A. Circumstances: 10-12
   B. Christ: 13
III. Re-examining: Phil. 4:14-20
   A. Supply by men: 14-18
   B. Supply by God: 19-20

Daily Bible Readings

Mon. Rejoice in the Creator God
Ps. 33:1-12
Tue. Rejoice in the Reigning God
Ps. 96
Wed. Rejoice in the Sustaining God
Ps. 104:24-35
Thu. Rejoice in the Saving God
Ps. 118:19-29
Fri. Rejoice in the God of Peace
Phil. 4:1-7
Sat. Rejoice in the Strengthening God
Phil. 4:8-13
Sun. Rejoice in the God of Grace
Phil. 4:14-23

June 27, 1993

VERSE BY VERSE

I. Rejoicing: Phil. 4:4-9

A. Suggestion I: 4

4. Rejoice in the Lord always: and again I say, Rejoice.

Eastern religions have been known for their emphasis on ignoring or denying harsh circumstances in an effort to reach a state of release and peace. Christianity takes a different approach. Paul urged believers to rejoice *in the Lord*, even when faced by harsh circumstances. We have to accept the fact that the Lord may allow us to encounter opposition and the discouragement, fear, and oppression which it may generate. However, the Lord stands above all circumstances, and our trust is in Him. He offers us sustaining grace to endure, and He offers us deliverance in due time, even if deliverance takes the form of death and entrance into His Own presence. Meeting challenges with God's help is necessary for us to develop strong faith.

B. Suggestion II: 5

5. Let your moderation be known unto all men. The Lord is at hand.

Paul urged believers to be moderate with all men, even those who mistreated them. They could afford to do this, for the Lord Jesus Christ was "at hand," meaning that Paul thought He was coming back soon. Even though we know that Jesus has not yet returned, Christians are to practise forbearance toward the unrepentant and forgiveness toward the repentant (Luke 17:3; Rom. 12:17-21).

C. Suggestion III: 6-7

6. Be careful for nothing; but in every thing by prayer and supplication with thanksgiving let your requests be made known unto God.

Paul did not tell believers to be careless. He told them to let nothing fill them with care (anxiety). Added to this was the suggestion that they roll over all of their cares onto the Lord in prayer. This should include not only supplication but also thanksgiving.

7. And the peace of God, which passeth all understanding, shall keep your hearts and minds through Christ Jesus.

It was before Christ's disciples had to face His suffering and death that He bestowed peace upon them (John 14:27). Paul may have had that in mind when he told the Philippian believers that they could experience peace from God which went beyond men's normal understanding of peace. It was a kind imparted by the Lord which would stabilize believers' hearts and minds despite hard circumstances. Anxiety and faith in God cannot coexist.

D. Suggestion IV: 8

8. Finally, brethren, whatsoever things are true, whatsoever things are honest, whatsoever things are just, whatsoever things are pure, whatsoever things are lovely, whatsoever things are of good report; if there be any virtue, and if there be any praise, think on these things.

Personal character is tied to thought-life. In Proverbs 23:7 we read, "As he thinketh in his heart so is he." We ought to pay more attention to guarding our minds, especially today when we are daily bombarded with worldly ideas by the media. We would not like to eat out of garbage pails, but we often allow our minds to be filled with harmful materials. Paul urged believers to reduce anxiety by concentrating on things which were true, honest, just, pure, lovely, of good report, virtuous, and praise-worthy. We live in an age in which things which are false, bizarre, and ugly seem to be featured, and we need to avoid them and put our minds on positive things.

E. Suggestion V: 9

9. Those things, which ye have both learned, and received, and heard, and seen in me, do: and the God of peace shall be with you.

Paul urged the Philippian believers to remember what they had learned from his teaching and his example and put it into practice in their own lives. He felt certain that, if they did this, the God of peace (Who gives the peace of God, vs. 7) would be with them in everyday experiences. Here, then were Paul's five suggestions for dealing with anxiety: (1) Rejoice in the Lord, not necessarily in circumstances, (2) Be gentle with all men, for Jesus is coming to set things straight, (3) Be anxious for nothing, but pray to God and know His inner peace, (4) Think about wholesome things, and (5) Practice doing wholesome things, and experience God's peaceful presence.

II. Readjusting: Phil. 4:10-13

A. Circumstances: 10-12

10a. But I rejoiced in the Lord greatly, that now at the last your care of me hath flourished again; . . .

Connect this with verse 18, which mentions the fact that Paul had received material help from the Philippian believers through Epaphroditus. Paul was thankful for their generosity and praised God for them and what they had sent to him.

10b. . . .wherein ye were also careful, but ye lacked opportunity.

Paul wanted the believers in Philippi to understand that he knew why there had been a delay in getting the materials to him. They had cared for him, but they had lacked a means by which to get the things to him. This may have been due to illness suffered by Epaphroditus (Phil. 2:25-30).

11. Not that I speak in respect of want: for I have learned, in whatsoever state I am, therewith to be content.

12. I know both how to be abased, and I know how to abound: every where and in all things I am instructed both to be full and to be hungry, both to abound and to suffer need.

Paul told the Philippian believers that he had been taught by God to be content, regardless of circumstances. He knew how to be abased (suffer deprivation) and still be content, something other believers failed to do. He knew how to abound (enjoy abundance) and be content, something some believers may have been unable to do because they felt guilty about it. Paul could readjust his life to fit into whatever circumstances faced him, because he was centered on the Lord and not on his own personal attitudes and preferences.

Note how Paul dealt with material deprivation by using the formula laid down in verses 4-9. He rejoiced in the Lord. He was careful not to blame others for his predicament. He refused to become anxious, and he prayed to the Lord. He kept his mind on wholesome things. He practised what he preached. He knew God would not forsake him.

13. I can do all things through Christ which strengtheneth me.

This was a summary statement to say that Paul met all challenges through strength imparted to him by the Holy Spirit on behalf of Christ. The ancient Greek Stoics taught people to cope with suffering by exercising courage, but it was a joyless experience. Paul taught that suffering could be endured with joy by being sustained through divine grace and thus growing in faith. Suffering could produce a positive result.

III. Re-examining: Phil. 4:14-20

A. Supply by men: 14-18

14. Notwithstanding ye have well done, that ye did communicate with my affliction.

Paul commended the believers in Philippi for doing well in communicating with his affliction. By this he meant that they had contributed things to meet his material need. He used similar language in another place —"Let him that is taught in the word communicate unto him that teacheth in all good things" (Gal. 6:6).

15. Now ye Philippians know also, that in the beginning of the gospel, when I departed from Macedonia, no church communicated with me as concerning giving and receiving, but ye only.

The first city Paul had visited with the gospel in Europe had been Philippi. It was there that he and Silas had been arrested, beaten, and put into jail. After their release, they had headed westward in Macedonia (northern Greece) before going southward to Achaia (southern Greece). Paul said that no church but theirs had sent him anything to support him at that time. This was one of the reasons that he felt a special closeness to these people as partners in the spread of the gospel.

16. For even in Thessalonica ye sent once and again unto my necessity.

Paul and his missionary team had traveled from Philippi through Amphipolis and Apollonia before coming to Thessalonica, where hostile Jews started a riot which resulted in Paul moving on to Berea (Acts 17:1-10). The church in Philippi, still in its infancy, had taken up a collection and sent it westward to Paul, not once but twice, during the brief time he was in Thessalonica.

17. Not because I desire a gift: but I desire fruit that may abound to your account.

Paul appreciated receiving a gift from the Philippian believers, but he saw something even more important in their generosity. He said that a notation would be written in their heavenly account, implying that God would reward them in due time.

18a. But I have all, and abound: I am full, having received of Epaphroditus the things which were sent from you, . . .

As mentioned in connection with verse 10, Paul now rejoiced in the abundance he enjoyed due to the things sent by the Philippian church through Epaphroditus after he recovered from his illness and was able to make the trip to Philippi and back to Rome where Paul was a prisoner.

18b. . . .an odour of a sweet smell, a sacrifice acceptable, wellpleasing to God.

The generosity of the Philippians was counted by Paul as being similar to the odor of a sweetsmelling sacrifice offered up at the temple in Jerusalem. This was an offering of a different kind, but it pleased the Lord just as much as the other.

B. Supply by God: 19-20

19. But my God shall supply all your need according to his riches in glory by Christ Jesus.

This verse has been frequently quoted by God's people down through the centuries. It stated succinctly the fact that God would meet all the needs of believers. The Living Bible reads, "It is he (God) who will supply all your needs from his riches in glory, because of what Christ Jesus has done for us." Note that it does not promise help from God for our desires, but rather for our needs. Whatever we ask Him to give us must be according to His Own will (I John 5:14-15).

20. Now unto God and our Father be glory for ever and ever. Amen.

In his benediction, Paul ascribed to God, our Father, eternal glory. He followed this with greetings from all the saints (believers in Rome), including converts from within Caesar's household. He closed by wishing that the grace of the Lord Jesus Christ would be with the Philippian believers (Phil. 4:21-23).

The text for this lesson has been fairly simple and easy to understand. The difficulty comes in applying it to our own everyday lives. Satan will try to get us discouraged and oppressed by a negative attitude as problems surround us. We will have to be willing to take the prescription found in Philippians 4:4-9 in order to have an antidote for anxiety. If we are faced by deprivation or abundance, we shall have to be flexible as Paul was, drawing strength from Christ Who indwells us by His Holy Spirit. If we have needs, we shall have to tap the unlimited resources of God which have been made available to us because of our identification with Christ by faith.

REJOICE IN THE LORD

Evangelistic Emphasis

Sometimes we wait until all the conditions are perfect to share our faith with others. We want to feel good physically, emotionally, and spiritually. The other person must be in just the perfect mood for hearing the gospel. Sometimes we wonder about technique, approach, the mechanics of sharing our faith with others. The approach must be well calculated and precisely on target if we are to risk speaking of Jesus. Paul was sharing his faith in the most unlikely of all situations. He must not have felt at the top of his form much of the time he was held prisoner in Rome. His living conditions were far less than desirable. After his many missionary tours and campaigns he must have had an assortment of aches and pains. Who would be less a likely listener than a Roman guard? What would a soldier of Rome want to know about a Jewish carpenter Messiah who died to become king? Paul had no equipment, no audio visuals to maximize his presentation. He did not lie awake worrying about approach and technique. How is it that even members of Caesar's own household heard the good news of Jesus Christ from Paul's detention cell in a remote corner of Rome? It happened because the guards who stayed with Paul had never met a person with such zest and joy for living, with such resilience and peace. Certainly no one in the chain of command all the way up to Caesar had such a view of life. John Wesley was once asked what his secret was which produced such amazing results in evangelistic meetings. "The Lord sets me on fire and the people come to watch me burn," was the answer. That's what was happening in that unmarked house where Paul was held prisoner. He was set on fire and others came to watch him burn. Before they left God's love in Christ had ignited their souls also.

Memory Selection

"Rejoice in the Lord always; again I will say, Rejoice."
Philippians 4:4

The key to Paul's admonition is the phrase, "in the Lord." Much of the time there is nothing in this fallen world about which to rejoice. National and international problems continue to plague us. Interpersonal and family relationships blow hot and cold. Others disappoint us and leave us stranded. Even worse, we often fail ourselves. We set high goals and fall short. We make noble claims and live at a somewhat lower level. To look at others and ourselves we have trouble finding reason to rejoice.

Yet, "in the Lord" there is much about which to rejoice. God created the world beautiful and healthful. He has loved His children ever since. He even came to us in Jesus Christ to participate in our human existence, to know our sorrow and joy, to share our laughter and our tears. He loved little children, the rejects of society, the little people and older people who fell victim to the movers and shakers. He told the truth, even in the face of those who had power over him. He went to a cross for loving all the wrong people and was raised victorious over Satan and death. He lives today in His church and in His world. "In the Lord" there is always occasion to rejoice.

June 27, 1993

Weekday Problems

Florence is the mother of three grade school children. She is a working mother, struggling from one pay check to the next to keep bread on the table. She doesn't make much at the department store. Her husband left her for someone else and vanished without a trace. She has never heard a word from him and so has no hope of alimony or child support. Her father with whom she was very close died last year of cancer. She has no brothers or sisters, no close relations who might be expected to help her through the tough times.

If it were not for friends at work and some people at church who come to her assistance she wouldn't make it. While none of the church members themselves have an easy answer for Florence, they surely had problems with the one the preacher gave a few Sundays ago. "Rejoice in the Lord, always" he quoted from Paul to mean that one should rejoice over everything that happens. "Even if times are hard God is teaching us. He has no children He does not correct and discipline from time to time. When you have trouble take an inventory of your life to see where the sin is. Repent and turn to the Lord and he will save you from your trouble. Whatever is happening to you praise the Lord, anyway!"

*What would you say to Florence?
*What would you say to her preacher?

◆◆◆◆◆◆

Superintendent's Sermonette

We have heard it said, "Everyone has his boiling point!" With some the boiling point seems to be very low. Strangers will meet in a public place, become annoyed, and immediately get into a shouting or shoving match. Mothers in a supermarket can be heard screaming at their disobedient children. Fathers can be heard venting their wrath half-way down the neighborhood block, With others the boiling point appears to be very high or non-existent. Professionals and diplomats pride themselves on being able to keep control of themselves even when they are deliberately goaded.

Individual personal temperament may have a lot to do with whether or not someone becomes agitated or stays calm when faced with negative circumstances. It is more likely, however, that a persons learns how to act in crisis situations by observing how others handle similar challenges. If we respect someone, we often try to imitate them.

Paul faced many difficult situations, and he was taught by God how to handle them and himself in ways which brought glory to the Lord instead of shame. Let us study his distilled wisdom in our text and find out how we can do the same. We need to avoid being mastered by our emotions. We need to let God control them for His glory.

This Lesson for Your Life

Paul's middle name was not Pollyanna. In II Corinthians 11 he recited a partial list of the sufferings he had endured as an ambassador of Christ. "Five times I have received at the hands of the Jews the forty lashes less one. Three times I have been beaten with rods; once I was stoned. Three times I have been ship-wrecked; a night and a day I have been adrift at sea; on frequent journeys, in danger from rivers, danger from robbers, danger from my own people, danger from Gentiles, danger in the city, danger in the wilderness, danger at sea, and danger from false brethren; in toil and hardship, through many a sleepless night, in hunger and thirst, often without food, in cold and exposure. And, apart from other things, there is the daily pressure upon me of my anxiety for all the churches." In chapter one of that same letter he admitted to depression so severe upon occasion that he longed to die. So when Paul says "Rejoice in the Lord always, and again I say, rejoice" he is not speaking of lofty abstractions. One remembers that this most joy-filled letter of all, this book of Philippians, is a prison epistle. The writer is aware that his time is quickly drawing to a close.

So whatever "rejoice in the Lord always" means it certainly does not mean the kind of joy known to the novice or the armchair general. We have already observed that "in the Lord" is the key. One of the writers of the Great Depression observed that "there are so many things that can knock the stuffing out of a man." It's hard to maintain the joy we feel at those special times in our lives: births, graduations, weddings, and so on. Nor can we perform well enough consistently to find abiding joy in ourselves. But "the steadfast love of the Lord never ceases, His mercies never come to an end" is the assurance we read in Lamentations, in Lamentations of all books! In the Old Testament God is pictured, not only as Creator of all things who sustains and moves the creation in a predictable way, but also as the Lord of history who holds all lives in his hand from beginning to end. He made covenant and was faithful regardless of the faithlessness and sin of His people. One scholar has observed that the faith of the Old Testament is captured in the single word, *hesed* That is the word for God's unwavering, steadfast, abiding love and faithfulness.

When God came to us in Jesus Christ He showed that same faithfulness. Jesus called disciples to follow Him. At first they followed Him eagerly, then out of obedience, and finally they parted ways with Him. He approached His passion. But He was faithful to them to the end. He called the church at Smyrna to be faithful up to and including death and He would give them the crown of life. The writer of Hebrews continually calls his readers back to their first confession by showing Jesus the faithful pioneer and high priest of their faith who obeyed the Father at Golgotha to win their access to the heavenly court.

Notice how joy in the Lord is maintained day by day. Observe what Paul says is opposite of anxiety. Our society answers anxiety with analysis, planning, action, perseverance and problem solving. Paul was also certainly a man of action. But he said the answer for anxiety is faith in God. Prayer which begins in thanksgiving for God's faithfulness in the past, which pours out the heart's concerns, which looks to God for answers produces a peace that passes all human understanding.

Paul's joy was not rooted in the hope that life would be easy or that he would be resourceful enough to meet every crisis. "My God will supply your every need" was his witness to the Philippians. The noble words were not copied from a greeting card, quoted from a favorite hymn, or even repeated from his favorite teacher.

Seed Thoughts

1. Can we pick Christians out of a crowd by their smiles and laughter?
Sometimes. But sometimes a Christian's joy is deeper, known even through suffering and heartache.

2. Is it a sin to worry?
No, but it's rejection of God's love to carry the world on one's shoulders, pretending to do His job.

3. What is the most common problem with prayer?
Unprayed prayers.

4. Does God care about my daily needs and cares?
Jesus said He who cares for the flowers and the birds cares even more for us.

5. Was Paul egotistical in urging other Christians to imitate him?
No, he was imitating Christ and all of us need to see it done.

(PLEASE TURN PAGE)

---

1. Can we pick Christians out of a crowd by their smiles and laughter?

2. Is it a sin to worry?

3. What is the most common problem with prayer?

4. Does God care about my daily needs and cares?

5. Was Paul egotistical in urging other Christians to imitate him?

6. How does one learn to be content in all kinds of circumstances?

7. "Keep a good thought" the saying goes. Does that make for joy?

8. Are Christians self-sufficient rugged individualists?

9. Are Christians self-reliant in themselves to get the job done?

10. Does God promise to grant our every request?

(SEED THOUGHTS--Cont'd)

Sometimes. But sometimes a Christian's joy is deeper, known even through suffering and heartache.

No, but it's rejection of God's love to carry the world on one's shoulders, pretending to do His job.

Unprayed prayers.

Jesus said He who cares for the flowers and the birds cares even more for us.

No, he was imitating Christ and all of us need to see it done.

By many years of giving one's life to Jesus and calling on Him for help.

Yes, Paul mentioned a long list of beautiful things and admonished Christians to dwell on them.

No, they receive all they have from above, often through others.

No, Paul said he could do all things—through Christ.

No, but to supply our every need "according to his riches in Christ Jesus."

---

6. How does one learn to be content in all kinds of circumstances?
By many years of giving one's life to Jesus and calling on Him for help.

7. "Keep a good thought" the saying goes. Does that make for joy?
Yes, Paul mentioned a long list of beautiful things and admonished Christians to dwell on them.

8. Are Christians self-sufficient rugged individualists?
No, they receive all they have from above, often through others.

9. Are Christians self-reliant in themselves to get the job done?
No, Paul said he could do all things—through Christ.

10. Does God promise to grant our every request?
No, but to supply our every need "according to his riches in Christ Jesus."

July 4, 1993

The Pre-eminent Christ

Colossians 1

3 We Give thanks to God and the Father of our Lord Jesus Christ, praying always for you,
4. Since we heard of your faith in Christ Jesus, and of the love *which ye* have to all the saints,
5. For the hope which is laid up for you heaven,
11 Strengthened with all might, according to his glorious power, unto all patience and longsuffering with joyfulness;
12. Giving thanks unto the Father, which made us meet to be partakers of the inheritance of the saints in light:
13. Who hath delivered us from the power of darkness, and hath translated *us* into the kingdom of his dear Son:
14. In whom we have redemption through blood, even the forgiveness of sins:
15. Who is the image of the invisible God firstborn of every creature:
16. For by him were all things created, that are in heaven, and that are in earth visible and invisible, whether *they* be thrones, or dominions, or principalities, or powers: all were created by him, and for him:
17. And he is before all things, and by him all things consist.
18. And he is the head of the body, the church: who is the beginning, the firstborn from the dead; that in all *things* he might have preeminence.
19. For it pleased *the Father* that in him should all fulness dwell;
20. And, having made peace through the blood of his cross, by him to reconcile all things unto himself; by him, I say whether *they be* things in earth, or things in heaven.
21. And you, that were sometime alienated and enemies in your mind by wicked works, yet now hath he reconciled
22. In the body of his flesh through death, to present you holy and unblameable and unreproveable in his sight:
23. If ye continue in the faith grounded and settled, and be not moved away from the hope of the gospel, which ye have heard, *and* which was preached to every creature which is under heaven; whereof I Paul am made a minister;

◆◆◆◆◆◆

◀ **Memory Selection**
Colossians 1:17

◀ **Devotional Reading**
I Corinthians 3:10-23

◀ **Background Scripture**
Colossians 1

◀ **Printed Scripture**
Colossians 1:3-5a, 11-23

THE PRE-EMINENT CHRIST

Teacher's Target

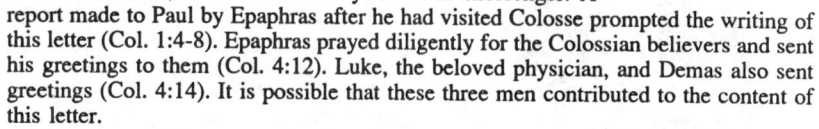

Paul's epistle to the Colossians, another prison epistle, was probably written at the same time as his epistles to the Ephesians and to Philemon, and it was sent by the same messenger. A report made to Paul by Epaphras after he had visited Colosse prompted the writing of this letter (Col. 1:4-8). Epaphras prayed diligently for the Colossian believers and sent his greetings to them (Col. 4:12). Luke, the beloved physician, and Demas also sent greetings (Col. 4:14). It is possible that these three men contributed to the content of this letter.

Help your students to see the epistle to the Colossians as a masterpiece on Christology, the study of Christ. In this, the first of three lessons based on selected texts from the letter, we see Christ extolled as King, Redeemer, God's Representative, Creator, Sustainer, Head of the church, and Reconciler of men to God. Believers should seek fulness in Christ and not be drawn away by legalism, false mysticism, or asceticism.

Lesson Introduction

People have long had various views regarding Jesus Christ. Some have seen Him as merely a man who had high ideals and a charismatic personality capable of attracting large audiences to Himself. Others may admit to Him being a special prophet with divine approval. Some might give Him the status of a demi-god, a cut above the angels, and a link between men and the Supreme Being. However, the Bible teaches that Christ is eternal, divine, and a Member of the Holy Trinity, the Godhead. Any definition less than that is inadequate and blasphemous.

Paul gave the Colossian believers strong doctrinal meat to chew and digest, and he suggested that this be shared with the church at Laodicea (Col. 4:16). His introduction expressed appreciation for the believers' faith, love, and hope (Col. 1:3-5), but he soon moved on to powerful teaching about the Lord Jesus Christ. This is helpful in guiding us to a proper and enduring view of Who Christ is, and that is vital to our Christian faith.

Teaching Outline

I Delight: Col. 1:3-5a
   A. Thanksgiving: 3
   B. Three things: 4-5a
II. Deliverance: Col. 1:11-14
   A. Resources: 11-12
   B. Rescue: 13-14
III. Description: Col. 1:15-20
   A. Creation: 15-17
   B. Church: 18-20
IV. Determination: Col. 1:21-23
   A. Reconciliation: 21-22
   B. Responsibility: 23

Daily Bible Readings

Mon. Christ, the Word of Truth
Col. 1:1-8
Tue. Christ, Our Example
Col. 1:9-14
Wed. Christ, the Fulness of God
Col. 1:15-20
Thu. Christ, Revelation of God's Glory
Col. 1:21-29
Fri. Christ, Our Reconciler
Rom. 5:6-11
Sat. Christ, the One Who Justifies
Rom. 5:12-16
Sun. Christ, the Righteous
Rom 5:17-21

July 4, 1993

VERSE BY VERSE

I. Delight: Col. 1:3-5a

A. Thanksgiving: 3

3. We give thanks to God and the Father of our Lord Jesus Christ, praying always for you,

Paul said that he and his colleagues gave thanks to the One Who is called both God and the Father of our Lord Jesus Christ. Praise for the Colossian believers was expressed in their prayers. Paul wrote in I Corinthians 13:13, "Now abideth faith, hope, charity (love)." He referred to these three virtues in other places, as well (Eph. 1:15; Col. 1:4-5; I Thess. 1:3; 5:8). He thanked God that the believers in Colosse had them.

B. Three things: 4-5a

4a. Since we heard of your faith in Christ Jesus, . . .

The beginning of Christian development had to be saving faith in Jesus Christ. The ability to trust in God and Christ continued to increase as converts walked the Christian path and developed spiritual muscles in a variety of experiences.

4b. . . .and of the love which ye have to all the saints,

"The love of God is shed abroad in our hearts by the Holy Ghost which is given unto us," wrote Paul in Romans 5:5. This was divine love imparted to believers and superior to any kind of human love. Paul commended the Colossian believers for showing it toward all the saints, even those they did not know and might never meet in person.

5a. For the hope which is laid up for you in heaven, ...

Paul referred here to the hope which believers had deposited in heaven, something which sustained them while they were on the earth. It was the coming of the gospel through Epaphras which had made faith, love, and hope possible for believers in Colosse to acquire (Col. 1:5b-8).

Thankful for what had already been accomplished, Paul and his team members continued to pray that the Colossian believers would be filled with a knowledge of God's will through spiritual wisdom and understanding. They wanted them to walk in a worthwhile way so that God would be pleased and they would be fruitful in good works, increasing in their experiential knowledge of God (Col. 1:9-10) We now pick up this theme in our printed text.

II. Deliverance: Col. 1:11-14

A. Resources: 11-12

11. Strengthened with all might, according to his glorious power unto all patience and longsuffering with joyfulness;

12. Giving thanks unto the Father, which hath made us meet to be partakers of the inheritance of the saints in light:

Paul and his friends in Rome prayed that the believers in Colosse might be spiritually strengthened. "We are praying. . .that you will be filled with his (God's) mighty, glorious strength so that you can keep going no matter what happens—always full of the joy of the Lord" (Living Bible). Some place reference to joy with verse 12 ("And with joy give thanks to the Father—Today's

433

English Version or "And joyfully giving thanks to the Father— New International Version).

Paul did not want Colossian believers to be intimidated by Greek intellectuals or Gnostic mystics. He wanted them to realize that God's wisdom and power was superior to these pagans and heretics, and divine resources were available to Christians. They could face challenges with patient endurance.

Note in verse 12 the move from petition to praise. God was thanked for making believers qualified to receive the inheritance reserved for them in the kingdom of light. Light in the Bible usually is a symbol or a synonymn for truth. Believers walk in the light of truth because of their identification with Christ, Who is "the way, the truth, and the life (John 14:6) John also used this symbolism in another place—"God is light, and in him is no darkness at all... If we walk in the light, as he is in the light, we have fellowship one with another, and the blood of Jesus Christ his Son cleanseth (or keeps on cleansing) us from all sin" (I John 1:5, 7). We are rescued from sin by accepting the truth about Christ's blood.

B. Rescue: 13-14

13. Who hath delivered us from the power of darkness, and hath translated us into the kingdom of his dear Son:
14. In whom we have redemption through his blood, even the forgiveness of sins:

These are all spiritual terms. God has delivered believers from the power of darkness. He has translated them into the kingdom of light regarding His beloved Son. It is in Christ that they have redemption, having been redeemed from Satan who held them in bondage. The price paid was "the precious blood of Christ" (I Pet. 1:19). If His atoning blood covers a person's sins, that person is justified before God. He is forgiven.

Although redemption of sinners through His shed blood appears to be Christ's greatest ministry, there are several other things for which He should receive credit. These are described next in our text and include representation, creation, preservation, headship of the church, and reconciliation.

III. Description: Col. 1:15-20

A. Creation: 15-17

15. Who is the image of the invisible God, the firstborn of every creature:

Jesus functioned as His heavenly Father's representative on the earth. He was the image of the invisible God seen by men. Three references support this. "God is a Spirit" (John 4:24) and is invisible to men, although His glory has been seen (Acts 7:55). "No man hath seen God at any time; the only begotten Son, which is in the bosom of the Father, he hath declared him" (John 1:18). "(Christ was) the brightness of his (God's) glory, the express image of his person" (Heb. 1:3).

Be careful how you explain the reference here to Christ being "the firstborn of every creature." He always existed in eternity past with God the Father and God the Spirit. He did, therefore, antedate all created beings. Although He became man by being born of Mary, He remained divine and was thus the God-Man.

16. For by him were all things created, that are in heaven, and that are in earth, visible and invisible, whether they be thrones, or dominions, or principalities, or powers: all things were created by Him, and for him:

When the time came for God to create the universe, He did it through Christ. This included all things which could be seen or not seen. Four things which appear to refer to the spirit world were made by Him—thrones, dominions, principalities, and powers. It may be that angels and their spheres of action were meant here. We know that some of them "kept not their first estate, but left their own habitation" (Jude 6).

Two references give strong support to Christ's creative role. "All things were made by him; and without him was not any thing made that was made" (John 1:3). "[God] hath in these last days spoken unto us by his Son, whom he hath appointed heir of all things, by whom also he made the worlds (Heb.

1:2). A paraphrase of the latter part of the verse says, "All [things] were made by Christ for his own use and glory" (Living Bible).

17. And he is before all things, and by him all things consist.

The first part of the verse emphasizes the eternality of Christ. He existed before all things in the universe were created. The latter part of the verse is supported by Hebrews 1:3, which states that Christ upholds all things by the word of his power He is the cohesive Force holding things together.

B. Church: 18-20

18. And he is the head of the body, the church: who is the beginning, the firstborn from the dead; that in all things he might have the preeminence.

Paul now turned to Christ's role as Head of the body composed of Himself and believers, which refers to the church universal. He was its beginning, its Founder, and He was the first to rise from the dead within its membership. He was and is its Leader, its primary Member.

19. For it pleased the Father that in him should all fulness dwell;

In contrast to the Gnostics, who taught that fulness of divine power came from God through an accumulation of angelic emanations, Paul taught that God was pleased to make fulness of divine power reside in His Son.

20. And having made peace through the blood of his cross, by him to reconcile all things unto himself; by him, I say, whether they be things in earth, or things in heaven.

Paul said that God made peace between Himself and sinful men by means of Christ's atoning blood shed at Calvary. God reconciled, or will reconcile, all things to Himself through Christ. People on the earth may be reconciled to God by placing their faith in Christ (II Cor. 5:18-19).

All must conform to the divine will.

IV. Determination: Col. 1:21-23

A. Reconciliation: 21-22

21. And you, that were sometime alienated and enemies in your mind by wicked works, yet now hath he reconciled

22. In the body of his flesh through death, to present you holy and unblameable and unreproveable in his sight:

Having referred to reconciliation by redemption and "reconciliation" by judgment, Paul now centered his thoughts on personal reconciliation of believers to God through Christ. The language here is similar to that found in Ephesians 2:11-18. The Gentile Colossians who had once been alienated from God and enemies of Him due to their sinful works were now reconciled to Him through Christ's death at Calvary. They could now be presented to a holy God as being themselves holy, unblamable, and unreprovable in His sight, for they had been justified by identifying themselves with Christ by faith.

B. Responsibility: 23

23. If ye continue in the faith, grounded and settled, and be not moved away from the hope of the gospel, which ye have heard, and which was preached to every creature which is under heaven; whereof I Paul am made a minister;

In order to remain holy, unblamable, and unreprovable, believers would have to maintain a stable and firm grip on their beliefs and not allow themselves to be deprived of their hope in the gospel. Paul said that this gospel had been heard by them and preached to every creature under heaven, probably referring to "every conceivable rank and condition of men" (Berkeley Version). He declared himself to be a minister of that gospel.

Evangelistic Emphasis

These days we hear much about how evangelism is to be done. We are told that our television culture will not tolerate dull preaching, routine worship services, and predictable teaching. These are good reminders; there is no virtue in mediocrity just because we are Christians. That is a fair and important concern.

An even more important question is, "To what are we trying to convert people?" Assuming that the first apostles had it straight, we ask to what did they convert people? The gospel was good news, saving news, the best news the world would ever hear. In response to it the church was founded and individuals were forgiven and reconciled with God. On the basis of that good news the Christian community was founded, found its identity, defined its mission, and formed its fellowship.

So what did the earliest disciples preach as the gospel? Perhaps it would be instructive first to observe what they did not preach as the gospel. They had enjoyed many exciting experiences with Jesus. They had been in the boat with Him when He stilled the tempest. But they never preached their experiences as the gospel. They stood in a centuries old tradition. While Jesus taught them to treasure their heritage and that he was its fulfillment, he never commissioned them to preach their tradition for gospel. They had each been lifted, made better, helped to understand their worth as persons in their time with Jesus. But they did not preach a gospel of self worth. In one day the church grew from a few hundred to several thousand, but they did not preach church growth.

A survey of the book of Acts shows what they preached as gospel or good news. The first apostles preached Jesus Christ, the servant of God, crucified and raised by God's design and for the redemption of mankind. From Him all other blessings would flow.

◆◆◆◆◆◆

Memory Selection

"And he is before all things, and by him all things consist:"
Colossians 1:17

The little church at Colossae was confused by a clash of doctrines and philosophies current in their area of the world. One view presented Jesus as only one of thousands of beings between man and God. The whole arrangement of spirits and intermediaries was called the "fullness" of the cosmic system. Some Christians were finding this intricate system and being "in on the know" appealing.

Paul was determined to show that Jesus was not one among many. In bold terms he reassured these Christians that Jesus was the creator of all things, that in Him all things consist, and that all things were created for Him and to Him. In Him and Him alone the "fullness" of God pleased to dwell. Many matters in Christianity are debatable. Church history is replete with debates over unimportant matters. Often trivial concerns have torn apart the body of Christ. But the center of the faith is not open to negotiation. The nature of the believing community is determined by its understanding of Jesus Christ. Those who present Jesus as just one among many great moralists deny the ancient faith witnessed to in the New Testament.

July 4, 1993

Weekday Problems

Jim is a bright young lawyer in his first year with a large, prestigious metropolitan law firm. He is one of over one hundred rookies, each trying to win a place for himself or herself. In an effort to stand out in the crowd the young laywers work seven days a week, ten or twelve hours a day. They attend all the firm social functions, a requirement for advancement. Each one is making a studied attempt to get to know the right people and make the right impressions.

The head of Jim's division liked him right away, noticed that he worked hard, did excellent work and was a team player. He had only one item on the agenda for getting Jim into shape for further advancement. One day he called him in and laid out the program. "You need to sell that old Volkswagen of yours and buy a BMW. I know a dealer who will give you the best possible deal. You need to go to the men's store downstairs and buy a half dozen dark suits with accessories to match, including a new briefcase. You have a bright future, but you must upgrade your image. No one will advance in this firm who does not project the image of competence and success.

*How should Jim respond to these instructions,
*Where will Jim stop on this principle of obedience and conformity for success?

♦♦♦♦♦♦

Superintendent's Sermonette

People look at Christ and have different views of Him, ranging from adoration to rejection. However, the important thing is not how people see Him but how God sees Him. If we look at Christ through God's eyes, everything about Him is acceptable and glorious. In his letter to the Colossians, Paul left us an incomparable record of how Christ ought to be viewed and described.

He is the King of the kingdom of light, presiding over divine truth which can save us from our sins. He is the Redeemer Who shed His blood at Calvary in order that we might have our sins forgiven and be covered with His righteousness. He is the Revealer of God the Father to us, a perfect Representative in visible form of the invisible Lord, He was the Creator of the universe and every creature and thing in it. He is the Sustainer of the universe by His power.

He is the Head of the church of which we are, as believers, functioning members. He is the Reconcilar of all created beings and things to God, conforming all to His will, whether that is by imparted righteousness or forced judgment. Let us rejoice in the fullness of Christ. Let us seek for supplemental power in no one or anything else.

This Lesson for Your Life

Chances are no one will ever approach you with the demanding words; "You will have to ditch all of that God-stuff around here. We don't allow mumbo-jumbo religious talk around here." If an employer made such demands the choice for the Christian would be clear and simple. The truth is that society almost never makes such demands in that way. Most of us have been in Sunday School classes when the subject of the early Christian martyrs came up. "What would you do, what would I do if faced with that kind of alternative?" the teacher might ask. We talk of the Roman coliseum and of the Nazi prison camps. Few if any of us are brave enough to claim that we would be faithful unto death. Most of us are thankful that we live in a free land where we are allowed to believe and worship as we see fit. Often someone will say it's a good thing that we do not have those kinds of pressures, the rolls of the church might be thinned considerably under persecution. The class ends on a general note of thanksgiving, a prayer of gratitude that we do not have such challenges to our faith in this free land.

But we may be missing something in all of that. While the threats to our faith are not as obvious as those martyrs faced, in some ways they are just as lethal. Not in the sense that we die for our faith. In the sense that we go on living, eaten up on the inside like trees which look healthy but are mere shells because of dry rot. On second glance we see that the pressures on us are much more subtle.

Subtlety is not a new weapon in the arsenal of the Evil One. When the Hebrews entered the Promised Land they knew nothing about farming or vine keeping. They had wandered the desert for two generations and before that had been slaves in Egypt. Before that they were herdsmen and shepherds. They noticed that the native farmers and vineyard keepers knew their business. Their crops were plentiful and their vines were heavy with beautiful grapes. "How do you do that?" was the natural question the newcomers asked. "Well, you plant, cultivate and irrigate just so, trim the vines this way, and, oh, by the way, don't forget to worship the Baals."

The Baals were local fertility gods worshipped in drunken sexual orgies up in the hills, on the "high places." The Hebrews were turned off at first. But as time went by they worked out a more sensible, less extreme position regarding the Baals. "Of course Yahweh is our main God. That goes without saying. So, as long as that is clear, what can it hurt to go along and worship these lesser fertility gods? No one who really knows God can take these gods as serious rivals to Him. So if that is settled, why not go along with the local customs? As far as the crops are concerned, one should cover all the bases. These locals have been gracious to us, we should not insult them by telling them their gods are nothing and that Yahweh is the only true God. Everyone sooner or later learns that you have to go along to get along."

Jesus had claimed to be the disciples' avenue to the Father, the only way. The Christians knew that, so far as they were concerned, Jesus would always be their only Lord and Savior. But accommodation to the thought forms of the time and place would be necessary for the church to live and grow in this new atmosphere.

Paul explained that the Christians were in danger of compromising the very heart of the gospel. Jesus was the only mediator between God and man. He had made peace by his cross. In Him the fullness of God had lived among men. Only in His cross had God reconciled the world to Himself. Paul preached a strong intolerance for any and all gospels which would diminish the place of Jesus Christ in the life and thought of the church.

Seed Thoughts

1. Is there still a scandal about Christianity?
Yes, the story of God becoming man to die a criminal's death sounds like nonsense to many.

2. Is salvation from sin an outdated concept?
No. People still suffer from guilt, shame, and estrangement.

3. Is Christianity exclusive and intolerant?
God loves all of His children. But He brooks no rivals.

4. Must one believe Jesus was God in order to be a Christian?
Yes, "for in him the fullness of God pleased to dwell."

5. Is it possible to go to church every week and still be an idolater?
Yes, if anyone or anything rules with Christ in our lives.

(PLEASE TURN PAGE)

---

1. Is there still a scandal about Christianity?

2. Is salvation from sin an outdated concept?

3. Is Christianity exclusive and intolerant?

4. Must one believe Jesus was God in order to be a Christian?

5. Is it possible to go to church every week and still be an idolater?

6. Was the cross God's idea or simply the end result of human evil?

7. Were just the pagan Gentiles rescued from darkness or were the religious Jews redeemed as well?

8. Can one be a disciple of Christ and slip by the pagan world unnoticed?

9. What does it mean that the "fullness of God" dwelt in Jesus?

10. Was the cross really necessary?

Yes, the story of God becoming man to die a criminal's death sounds like nonsense to many.

No. People still suffer from guilt, shame, and estrangement.

God loves all of His children. But He brooks no rivals.

Yes, "for in him the fullness of God pleased to dwell."

Yes, if anyone or anything rules with Christ in our lives.

"It pleased God to reconcile. . . through the blood of His cross."

Paul said "He rescued us from the power of darkness."(Colossians 1:13)

Not unless the pagan world has become Christian or the Christian a pagan.

Jesus said, "If you have seen Me you have seen the Father." (John 14:9)

God's children were estranged without resources to mend the relationship, God gave His Son (Himself) to bring us back home.

(SEED THOUGHTS--Cont'd)

6. Was the cross God's idea or simply the end result of human evil?
"It pleased God to reconcile. . . through the blood of His cross."

7. Were just the pagan Gentiles rescued from darkness or were the religious Jews redeemed as well?
Paul said "He rescued us from the power of darkness."(Colossians 1:13)

8. Can one be a disciple of Christ and slip by the pagan world unnoticed?
Not unless the pagan world has become Christian or the Christian a pagan.

9. What does it mean that the "fullness of God" dwelt in Jesus?
Jesus said, "If you have seen Me you have seen the Father." (John 14:9)

10. Was the cross really necessary?
God's children were estranged without resources to mend the relationship, God gave His Son (Himself) to bring us back home.

July 11, 1993

The Sufficient Christ

Colossians 2

5 For though I be absent in the flesh, yet am I with you in the spirit, joying and beholding your order, and the stedfastness of your faith in Christ.
6 As ye have therefore received Christ Jesus the Lord, so walk ye in him:
7 Rooted and built up in him, and stablished in the faith, as ye have been taught, abounding therein with thanksgiving.
8 Beware lest any man spoil you through philosophy and vain deceit, after the tradition of men, after the rudiments of the world, and not after Christ.
9 For in him dwelleth all the fulness of the Godhead bodily.
10 And ye are complete in him, which is the head of all principality and power:
11 In whom also ye are circumcised with the circumcision made without hands, in putting off the body of the sins of the flesh by the circumcision of Christ:
12 Buried with him in baptism, wherein also ye are risen with *him* through the faith of the operation of God, who hath raised him from the dead.
13 And you, being dead in your sins and the uncircumcision of your flesh, hath he quickened together with *Him*, having forgiven you all trespasses;
14 Blotting out the handwriting of ordinances that was against us, which was contrary to us, and took it out of the way, nailing it to His cross;
15 *And* having spoiled principalities and powers, he made a shew of them openly, triumphing over them it it.
16 Let no man therefore judge you in meat, or in drink, or in respect of an holyday, or of the new moon, or of the sabbath days:
17 Which are a shadow of things to come; but the body is of Christ.
18 Let no man beguile you of your reward in a voluntary humility and worshipping of angels, intruding into those things which he hath not seen, vainly puffed up by his fleshly mind.
19 And not holding the Head, from which all the body by joints and bands having nourishment ministered, and knit together, increaseth with the increase of God.

◆◆◆◆◆◆

◀ **Memory Selection**
Colossians 2:6

◀ **Devotional Reading**
Hebrews 10:11-25

◀ **Background Scripture**
Colossians 2

◀ **Printed Scripture**
Colossians 2:5-19

THE SUFFICIENT CHRIST

Teacher's Target

Paul twice said that he had been made a minister of the gospel (Col. 1:23, 25). He explained that this involved revealing the mystery of God to others (Col. 1:26, 27; 2:2). That mystery (a truth once hidden but now revealed) was simply "Christ in you, the hope of glory, Whom we preach, warning every man, and teaching every man in all wisdom; that we may present every man perfect in Christ Jesus" (Col. 1:27-28). "The mystery of God is Christ, as incarnating the fulness of the Godhead, and all the divine wisdom and knowledge for the redemption and reconciliation of man" (Scofield Reference Edition).

Help your students to understand that Nothing can be added to completeness found in Christ. Men have found various ways to attempt going beyond this, but these are futile. We are to beware of their enticing words (Col. 2:4). Spiritual development will be hampered or halted if we succumb to false philosophy, numbing traditional legalism, or bizarre mysticism involving angel-worship.

Lesson Introduction

We should be sympathetic toward the plight faced by unbelievers today. They find themselves in a labyrinth with a maze of paths to follow and they do not know which way to go. Modern improvements in transportation and communication open them up to a bewildering array of man-made teachings. They often become entrapped in false religions, cults, and isms. Even if they end up in some branch of Christianity, they may find much that is humanly contrived rather than biblical. What they need is unadulterated scriptural exposition.

If this lesson's text is handled carefully, it offers helpful warnings against confusion regarding Jesus Christ. Those who receive Him as their Savior can profit from this information as they proceed to walk in Him. The daily guidance of the indwelling Holy Spirit is needed to help us follow a clear path through many doctrinal hazards. Mature guidance from Spirit-led believers will also help us on our spiritual journey.

Teaching Outline

I. Avoid Detours: Col. 2:5-7
  A. Partnership: 5
  B. Perseverence: 6-7
II. Avoid Deception: Col. 2:8-13
  A. Spoiled: 8
  B. Sustained: 9-13
III. Avoid Legalism: Col. 2:14-17
  A. Blot: 14-15
  B. Body: 16-17
IV. Avoid Mysticism: Col. 2:18-19
  A. Heresy: 18
  B. Head: 19

Daily Bible Readings

Mon. Christ Reveals God's Treasures
Col. 2:1-7
Tue. God's Fullness Dwells in Christ
Col. 2:8-15
Wed. Christ Is Head of the Church
Col. 2:16-23
Thu. Christ Frees Us from Slavery
Gal. 5:1-t2
Fri. Christ Fulfilled the Scriptures
I Cor. 15:3-8
Sat. Christ Is God's Word to Us
Heb. 1:1-13
Sun. Christ Is Our Perfect High Priest
Heb. 7:23-28

July 11, 1993

VERSE BY VERSE

I. Avoid Detours: Col. 2:5-7

A. Partnership: 5

5. For though I be absent in the flesh, yet I am with you in the spirit, joying and beholding your order, and the stedfastness of your faith in Christ.

Paul was concerned that believers in Colosse avoid being beguiled by enticing words of false teachers such as the Gnostics (Col. 2:4, 8, 18). Although he was absent from them as a prisoner in Rome, he felt that his partnership with them was real. He was with them in spirit, and he rejoiced in hearing about their orderly behavior and the firmness of their faith in Christ. They evidently were following Paul's advice as given in I Corinthians 14: 40 —"Let all things be done decently and in order."

B. Perseverence: 6-7

6. As ye have therefore received Christ Jesus the Lord, so walk ye in him:

A parallel concept is found in Galatians 5: 25— "If we live in the Spirit, let us also walk in the Spirit." We receive Christ as Savior through the convicting and cleansing ministry of the Holy Spirit. The conversion experience is wonderful, but it is only the first step in a long process of spiritual development for believers. A Christ-centered life is one which affects what one thinks, says, and does. The goal should be maturity in Christ, and this demands perseverence on the part of believers.

7. Rooted and built up in him, and established in the faith, as ye have been taught, abounding therein with thanksgiving.

The analogy changes here from walking on a path to being planted in soil. As a seed develops, it sends roots downward to draw sustaining mineral laden water. It thrusts a shoot upward to break the soil and receive the sun's warming rays. The more it grows downward, upward, and outward, the more stable it becomes. The same is true with followers of Christ. They put their roots down into the truth about Him and send shoots of faith up into their daily lives to feel His presence there. Faith is developed as they meet challenges and trust in Him to help them. They should know the abundant life Jesus mentioned (John 10:10), and they should express thanksgiving for it.

II. Avoid Deception: Col. 2:8-13

A. Spoiled: 8

8. Beware lest any man spoil you through philosophy and vain deceit, after the tradition of men, after the rudiments of the world, and not after Christ.

Paul did not want believers to have their faith and joy spoiled by anyone's hollow philosophy and by anyone's vain deceit. The tradition of men seemed based on ideas of the material world rather than of the spiritual world.

All these were to be avoided, and spiritual development was to be centered on Christ and all of the truth about Him that was available.

Throughout our lesson text, keep in mind the possibility that Paul was counteracting the Gnostics of the first century. In their arrogance, they taught people to "touch not; taste not; handle not" (Col. 2:21), They taught "neglecting of the body" by asceticism (Col. 2:23), They could spoil the faith and joy of believers with these teachings.

B. Sustained: 9-13

9. For in him dwelleth all the fulness of the Godhead bodily.

We now enter a passage which teaches that nothing can be added to completeness in Christ. Verse 9 introduces the subject by repeating what had already been stated in Colossians 1:19 about all fulness dwelling in Christ and adding that this fulness referred to the Godhead (Father, Son, and Holy Spirit) and dwelt in His bodily form. Christ was human, but He was also divine. This served to counteract the Gnostic heresy that divinity could not reside in physical form, which was considered evil.

10. And ye are complete in him, which is the head of all principality and power:

Paul said that believers are complete in Christ. They have everything they need to grow and develop in Him throughout their lifetime. They will become like Him when they see Him face to face (1 John 3:2).

11. In whom also ye are circumcised with the circumcision made without hands, in putting off the body of the sins of the flesh by the circumcision of Christ:

Under the Mosaic law, all Jewish males had to have the foreskin of their penises circumcised (cut away) as a physical sign that they belonged to Jehovah. Gentiles in Colosse had not had this experience, and Paul said that it was not required of them. By converting to Christ, they had been spiritually circumcised by having sins of the flesh cut away from them. This type of cleansing would continue as they walked in the light of divine truth and were cleansed by the blood of Christ (1 John 1:7-9).

12. Buried with him in baptism, wherein also ye are risen with him through the faith of the operation of God, who hath raised him from the dead.

The symbol now changes from circumcision to baptism. Literal water baptism was a symbol of spiritual death and burial to self will and spiritual resurrection when believers placed their faith in God, the One Who raised Christ from the dead. References to being baptized into the body of Christ are found in I Corinthians 12:13 and Ephesians 4:4-5. Perhaps the best parallel reference to Colossians 2:12 is found in Romans 6:4—"We are buried with him (Christ) by baptism into death: that like as Christ was raised up from the dead by the glory of the Father, even so we also should walk in newness of life."

13. And you, being dead in your sins and the uncircumcision of your flesh, hath he quickened together with him, having forgiven you all trespasses;

Read Ephesians 2:1-6 in connection with this verse. Gentile believers who had been "dead in trespasses and sins" and physically uncircumcised had been quickened (made alive) in Christ, and God had forgiven their trespasses. Neither they, nor anyone else, could add anything to their position in Christ. That position was "in heavenly places in Christ Jesus" (Eph. 1:3; 2:6). They were to do all that they could to match that position in their daily practice here on the earth.

III. Avoid Legalism: Col. 2:14-17

A. Blot: 14-15

14. Blotting out the handwriting of ordinances that was against us, which was contrary to us, and took it out of the way, nailing it to his cross;

The handwriting of ordinances (written code with regulations) which once condemned believers had been removed and figuratively nailed to the cross of Christ. This must have referred to the law of God which prevailed until grace came through the sacrifice of Christ at Calvary.

15. And having spoiled principalities and powers, he made a shew of them openly, triumphing over them in it.

By His death on the cross, Jesus spoiled (conquered) Satan and the other demonic powers. He paraded them before the world and showed His victory over them. We assume that this was and is still done through the righteous living of believers.

B. Body: 16-17

16. Let no man therefore judge you in meat, or in drink, or in respect of an holyday, or of the new moon, or of the sabbath days:
Paul said that Gentile believers in Colosse ought not to let anyone judge them as far as food, drink, or special days were concerned. Peter had learned that prohibition against eating certain kinds of animals had been cancelled (Acts 10:9-16). The church council in Jerusalem had not even mentioned Gentile converts keeping Jewish holy days (Acts 15:19-20).The Jewish Sabbath (Saturday) was replaced by the Christian Lord's Day (Sunday).

17. Which are a shadow of things to come; but the body is of Christ.
Paul called the various references to Christ in the Mosaic law but a shadow of things to come. When Christ came, He became the body (reality) of those types. Christians were not required to offer up animal sacrifices, for Christ had offered Himself up. Those types became reality when they were fulfilled in Him. Jewish legalism, as practised by the Judaizers, hindered Christian spiritual development and was laid aside as the first-century church matured.

IV. Avoid Mysticism: Col. 2:18-19

A. Heresy: 18

18. Let no man beguile you of your reward in a voluntary humility and worshipping of angels, intruding into those things which he hath not seen, vainly puffed up by his fleshly mind,
Paul was probably referring here to Gnostics who dabbled in mysticism, teaching that God had to be approached through angelic intermediaries. Paul condemned their heresy and arrogance for proposing that believers voluntarily humble themselves before angels and worship them. This was wrong and completely unnecessary.

B. Head: 19

19. And not holding the Head, from which all the body by joints and bands having nourishment ministered and knit together, increaseth with the increase of God.
A parallel reference is Ephesians 4:16. Paul stated that it was from Christ that "the whole body fitly joined together and compacted by that which every joint supplieth, according to the effectual working in the measure of every part, maketh increase of the body unto the edifying of itself in love." All that believers had to do was to hold fast to Christ, the Head of the body, in order to receive all of the spiritual nourishment they needed. Growth and development was possible only as Christ, through the Holy Spirit, caused believers to mature and become more Christlike.

Colossians 2:20-23 is not in our printed text, but you might want to mention it to your students, because Paul also told Colossian believers to avoid asceticism, probably referring to that fostered by the Gnostics. The prohibitions they put in force with their followers involved touching, tasting, and handling things which were to eventually perish when used. The commandments and doctrines of human origin provide a show of wisdom in "self-imposed worship, their false humility, and their harsh treatment of the body, but they lack any value in restraining sensual indulgence" (Col. 2:23, New International Version).

THE SUFFICIENT CHRIST

Evangelistic Emphasis

In the nineteenth century British and American missionaries carried the gospel to various parts of the world. Travel was slow and cumbersome by today's standards. Huge trunks were loaded on trains, then ships before they finally came to rest on the mission field. That was not all the baggage these missionaries carried with them. Most of them carried the British or American ways of life in the trunk marked, "Gospel." We have been learning since then by painful experience that the Lord never asked us to make British Christians or American Christians of all nations. It's been a struggle to realize that the faith takes different shapes according to local customs and cultures. Missionaries must be flexible

In order to adapt the message without losing it they must understand clearly the difference between the core gospel and its many expressions. One might draw a parallel with nuclear power. The nuclear reactor with all its many parts is the necessary housing and instrumentation for what happens inside. But the secret of the power plant resides at the very center of the operation, at the nuclear core. While the reactor must contain certain basic elements, those elements may look different from place to place. In the same way, missionaries in foreign lands and witnessing Christians here at home must understand clearly what the core gospel is and what they are communicating to unbelievers. Paul said the matter of "first importance" was the death, burial, and resurrection of Jesus Christ. (I Corinthians 15:1-4) That is the irreducible core gospel which must be proclaimed at all times and places where Christians would share their faith.

Memory Selection

"As ye have therefore received Christ Jesus as Lord, so walk ye in Him."
Colossians 2:6

Plants cannot survive and grow if they are transplanted too often. Christians cannot survive and grow if they accept and feed upon every new theory that comes along. They cannot bear fruit if they keep changing their basic beliefs every time an interesting idea appears. "Grow where you were planted" was Paul's admonition to the Christians at Colossae. These disciples had originally heard of Jesus Christ the carpenter from Nazareth Who lived a life of service, Who told the truth, Who revealed the Father and was crucified and raised from the dead. The story was not as fancy as some of the theories that had come along since. Some were embarrassed about the story and wanted to dress it up in more respectable philosophical categories.

Paul lived and died by the scandalous story of Jesus Christ. He knew the disciples would only flourish if they held faithfully to the story of Jesus. Our world today is awash in strange, curious, and sometimes appealing philosophies and religions. Many Christians grow ashamed of the story that called them to faith. In this context Paul's words are good medicine for our souls. We should grow where we were planted. The day will come for each of us, if it has not already come, when we see that the story of Jesus is the most profound and valuable of all stories ever told.

July 11, 1993

Weekday Problems

Bill grew up in a Christian home. He could not remember a time when he didn't attend church regularly. Throughout high school and college he maintained a strong involvement in Christian activities. In the third year of his professional life he was disturbed about his convictions. Since his junior year in college he planned to marry Elizabeth. But now she had met someone else on her new job and had broken their engagement. He began asking questions about prayer and God's loving care over his life.

An office mate saw Bill in distress, expressed his concern and suggested that Bill attend church with him. At Ron's church no cross appeared in the sanctuary. Nor did one appear in the sermons or worship service. The speaker affirmed that answers for life did not come fronm God "up there" or "out there" but from the god inside each individual. Bill understood that "up there" and "out there" were merely spatial terms to express the transcendence of God. But he was disturbed about the idea that there was no God outside of himself. He was being asked to believe that religion was only about self-fulfillment and self-realization. He had always believed that God came to us in Jesus Christ who did not come for self-realization but to rescue us by the blood of his cross.

*What are the implications for Bill's life should he embrace this new religion'?
*How can Bill rediscover the source and solid ground of his Christian faith?

♦♦♦♦♦♦

Superintendent's Sermonette

We live in a world where knowledge increases at an alarming rate. Some scientists and professionals feel under pressure to choose early retirement because they cannot keep up with all new developments in their fields and feel obsolete. Life has become so complicated that specialists have become commonplace and continue to proliferate. The older generation seems swept aside by the computer trained younger generation. Demands in modern society range from recycling our trash to diplomats racing off on efforts to bring peace to trouble spots all over the world. Even individuals who opt for the "simple life" find it difficult or impossible to achieve it.

We have the same type of situation in spiritual matters. Intellectuals and exploiters want to make our personal beliefs a complicated regimen involving mind-bending concepts and long lists of regulations. They enslave people's minds and drive them to frustration and despair. In the midst of all of this confusion, we read what Paul wrote regarding holding fast to Christ, the Head of the body. It sounds simple, and it is simple. Let us accept it and walk each day with Him as we grow and develop into mature Christians.

447

THE SUFFICIENT CHRIST

This Lesson In Your Life

Shepherds in the field trembled before a heavenly chorus, wise men came from some distant place, Mary and Joseph wondered what had happened to them. One might get the idea that the first Christmas found the world waiting with bated breath for the coming of Jesus, the Messiah. But the rest of the story makes it clear: that was not the case. There was no room for Joseph and Mary in the inn. Nor was there any place in Herod's crusty old heart for another baby who might become king.

Christianity has always had to compete with other more popular religions and philosophies. Judaism was divided into sects when Jesus came. The Roman world knew many gods. There has never been a vacuum where faith and philosophy are concerned. Our society is no different. We have hundreds of forms of Christianity, a variety of world religions and many pragmatic philosophies of life which claim religious devotion. During a given week a Christian who is out and about will encounter a variety of beliefs."God helps them that help themselves." "I want it all." "Focus your life." "Just do it!" "God loves you." "Jesus is Lord," and so on. Not since the first century when Paul wrote to the Colossians have Christians been enticed in so many directions.

If you are persuaded that God has revealed Himself most fully in Jesus Christ how will you continue to grow in Him? Paul's advice to the Colossians gives us the beginning place. First, we should grow where we have been planted. One should go back to his or her roots to find the beginnings. Was it a Bible story book on our mother's knee where we first met God? Perhaps it was a flannel-graph story in Sunday School where the loving teacher first introduced us to Jesus. Maybe a good friend first told us the story of God and mankind. Whatever the case, very few of us began with theology and philosophy. Philosophy (the love of wisdom) and theology (reasoning about God) are legitimate pursuits. Even without knowing it, we engage in these enterprises to discover the meaning of life, the meaning of our faith. But the beginning was the story itself.

The Bible is many stories which make up one grand story. It begins with God and ends with God. He is before all things and after all things. He made the creation, including mankind, and pronounced it good. When human beings were not content to have the dignity of walking with God, when they grasped to be as God everything was distorted. When mankind "fell" this loving God did not desert us or extinguish the race. He pursued in His faithful love over the centuries to bring all His children back home. Finally, he came to us in Jesus of Nazareth. He is thoroughly human and completely understands what we struggle through each day. On the other hand, He is also "God with us" and is able to save us to the uttermost. While no human being could live as God intended us to live, Jesus did. He chose to serve rather than to be served and gave His life a ransom for all mankind. He was raised victorious over Satan and death. He lives in His church today and promises to return to receive His faithful to live with Him forever.

This story is for all human beings of all races, classes, sexes, and positions in life. All are saved by trusting God in His goodness. In one way or another most of us have based our lives on this story. It was where we were planted in the beginning. The rest of our lives we will think and theologize about the story. That is as it should be. The story was meant to furnish us a lifetime of spiritual nutrition. But we must never move away from the story to embrace another scheme or story. That is what Paul meant when he wrote to the Colossians about the all-sufficient Christ.

Seed Thoughts

1. Can Christians state their confession "while standing on one foot" as the scribes used to say?
Yes, the earliest confession was "Jesus is Lord."

2. What was the great mystery Paul prayed that all would come to know?
Christ Himself in Whom are hidden all the treasures and wisdom and knowledge of God.

3. What made Paul rejoice about the Colossians?
Their works and the firmness of their faith.

4. What, according to Colossians 2:6 is the basic Christian tradition?
"Christ Jesus the Lord."

5. What is the first rule for continued growth as a Christian?
To grow where one was rooted, in Christ.

(PLEASE TURN PAGE)

---

1. Can Christians state their confession "while standing on one foot" as the scribes used to say?

2. What was the great mystery Paul prayed that all would come to know?

3. What made Paul rejoice about the Colossians?

4. What, according to Colossians 2:6 is the basic Christian tradition?

5. What is the first rule for continued growth as a Christian?

6. Do we need an updated gospel?

7. What is assumed when we are told to "grow where we were planted"?

8. What is the difference between "human tradition" and the gospel tradition?

9. What is the meaning of Christian baptism?

10. How are Christians made one in Christ?

Yes, the earliest confession was "Jesus is Lord."

Christ Himself in Whom are hidden all the treasures and wisdom and knowledge of God.

Their works and the firmness of their faith.

"Christ Jesus the Lord."

To grow where one was rooted, in Christ.

Every age must find its own language for expressing it, but the essential gospel is eternally and universally the same good news.

That we were planted in Christ.

Human tradition is man's own thought by itself, the gospel tradition is a revelation from God.

The believer is buried with Christ and raised with Him in the power of God to new life.

They were all dead with him and are "made alive together in Christ."

(SEED THOUGHTS--Cont'd)

6. Do we need an updated gospel?
Every age must find its own language for expressing it, but the essential gospel is eternally and universally the same good news.

7. What is assumed when we are told to "grow where we were planted"?
That we were planted in Christ.

8. What is the difference between "human tradition" and the gospel tradition?
Human tradition is man's own thought by itself, the gospel tradition is a revelation from God.

9. What is the meaning of Christian baptism?
The believer is buried with Christ and raised with Him in the power of God to new life.

10. How are Christians made one in Christ?
They were all dead with him and are "made alive together in Christ."

July 18, 1993

Life in Christ

Colossians 3

1. If ye then be risen with Christ, seek those things which are above, where Christ sitteth on the right hand of God.
2. Set your affection on things above, not on things on the earth.
3. For ye are dead, and your life is hid with Christ in God.
4. When Christ, *who is* our life, shall appear, then shall ye also appear with him in glory.
5. Mortify therefore your members which are upon the earth; fornication, uncleanness, inordinate affection, evil concupiscence, and covetousness, which is idoatry:
6. For which things sake the wrath of God cometh on the children of disobedience:
7. In the which ye also walked some time, when ye lived in them.
8. But now ye also put off all these; anger, wrath, malice, blasphemy, filthy communication out of your mouth.
9. Lie not one to another, seeing that ye have put off the old man with his deeds;
10. And have put on the new *man*, which is renewed in knowledge after the image of him that created him:
11. Where there is neither Greek not Jew, circumcision nor uncircumcision, Barbarian, Scyth´-i-an, bond *nor* free: but Christ *is* all, and in all.
12. Put on therefore, as the elect of God, holy and beloved, bowels of mercies, kindness, humbleness of mind, meekness, longsuffering;
13. Forbearing one another, and forgiving one another, if any man have a quarrel against any: even as Christ forgave you, so also *do* ye.
14. And above all these things *put on* charity, which is the bond of perfectness.
15. And let the peace of God rule in your hearts, to the which also ye are called in one body; and be ye thankful.
16. Let the word of Christ dwell in you richly in all wisdom; teaching and admonishing one another in psalms and hymns and spiritual songs, singing with grace in your hearts to the Lord.
17. And whatsoever ye do in word or deed *do* all in the name of the Lord Jesus, giving thanks to God and the Father by him.

◆◆◆◆◆◆

◀ **Memory Selection**
Colossians 3:10

◀ **Devotional Reading**
1 Corinthians 12:12-26

◀ **Background Scripture**
Colossians 3

◀ **Printed Scripture**
Colossians 3:1-17

LIFE IN CHRIST

Teacher's Target

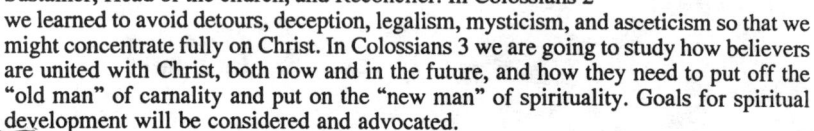

In Colossians 1 we learned about the superiorities of Christ as Redeemer, Representative of God the Father, Creator, Sustainer, Head of the church, and Reconciler. In Colossians 2 we learned to avoid detours, deception, legalism, mysticism, and asceticism so that we might concentrate fully on Christ. In Colossians 3 we are going to study how believers are united with Christ, both now and in the future, and how they need to put off the "old man" of carnality and put on the "new man" of spirituality. Goals for spiritual development will be considered and advocated.

Help your students to analyze the doctrinal content of our text and then to make it as personally applicable to themselves as possible. Be thoroughly prepared to serve as their human teacher. Pray that the Holy Spirit will serve as their divine instructor. This lesson should make a difference in their lives if they seriously seek to show how a position in Christ can be implemented in practice.

Lesson Introduction

Christians are sometimes accused of waiting for "pie in the sky" and not paying enough attention to improving their lot here on the earth. Some of that criticism may be justified, but there is much comfort and encouragement to be found in realizing what union with Christ means to believers. They are positionally fixed in Him, and He is in heaven at the right hand of God. Their hope is set on things above more than on earthly things. They are dead to themselves but alive unto God because of being hidden in Christ. When He comes again, they will share in His glory.

In the meantime, they have many things to do. They are to mortify (put to death) their sinful attitudes and deeds. They are to develop those Christian virtues which edify themselves and others, such as mercy, kindness, humility, meekness, patience, forbearance, forgiveness, and love. The peace of God is to rule in their hearts. The word of Christ is to dwell in them until whatever they do can be done in His holy name.

Teaching Outline

I. What to Seek: Col. 3:1-4
  A. Affection: 1-2
  B. Appearance: 3-4
II. What to Mortify: Col. 3:5-11
  A. Put off old man: 5-9
  B. Put on new man: 10-11
III. What to Pursue: Col. 3:12-17
  A. Way of Christ: 12-15
  B. Word of Christ: 16-17

Daily Bible Readings

Mon. Put on the New Nature in Christ
Col. 3:1-11
Tue. Let Christ's Word Dwell in You
Col. 3:12-17
Wed. Serve the Lord Christ
Col. 3:18-25
Thu. Be Steadfast in Prayer
Col. 4:1-6
Fri. Encourage One Another in Christ
Col. 4:7-11
Sat. Know and Do God's Will
Col. 4:12-18
Sun. A Great Variety, but One God
I Cor. 12:1-11

July 18, 1993

VERSE BY VERSE

I. What to Seek: Col. 3:1-11

A. Affection: 1-2

1. If ye then be risen with Christ, seek those things which are above, where Christ sitteth on the right hand of God.

If believers are alive when Christ comes again, they will be taken up to heaven without dying, being buried, and being resurrected. However, most will have died and been buried before He comes, and they will need to be resurrected. All will be taken by Him up to heaven (I Thess. 4:13-18).

In the meantime, believers were urged by Paul to consider themselves to be dead and buried to selfish attitudes and actions and resurrected to newness of life in Him. Their natural inclination should be to strive toward heavenly things, knowing that Christ even now sits there at the right hand of God the Father.

2. Set your affection on things above, not on things on the earth.

Paul realized that strong emotion is what drives most people in what they think, say, and do. He wanted Christians to set their affection on heavenly things rather than on earthly things. He knew the value of the eternal over the temporal. A parallel thought may be found in Christ's sermon on the mount—"Lay not up for yourselves treasures upon earth, . . .but lay up for yourselves treasures in heaven, . . .for where your treasure is there will your heart be also" (Matt. 6:19-21) Think of contrasts between earthly treasures and spiritual heavenly treasures.

B. Appearance: 3-4

3. For ye are dead, and your life is hid with Christ in God.

Let us see this in other words. "For (as far as this world is concerned) you have died, and your (new, real) life is hid with Christ in God" (Amplified Bible). "You should have as little desire for this world as a dead person does. Your real life is in heaven with Christ and God" (Living Bible).

Paul believed that Christians died to the bondage of sin at their conversion. As spiritual development took place, their selfish, carnal drives could be tempered and weakened. They would increasingly realize that their lives were absorbed into union with Christ and God, Who, by the Holy Spirit, would live within then. Divine wisdom and strength would replace human ignorance and frailty.

4. When Christ, who is our life, shall appear, then shall ye also appear with him in glory.

Christ is the Source of our physical life because of His role in creation. He is the Source of our spiritual life because of His role in our rebirth. He is going to reappear at the end of the age of grace by coming from heaven to the earth's atmosphere. All believers will thus share in His glory. Even now they may have a sure hope of becoming like Him, and that hope helps them to keep pure. "Beloved, now are we the sons of God, and it doth not yet appear what we shall be: but we know that, when he shall appear, we shall be like him; for we shall see him as he is. And every man that hath this hope in him purifieth himself, even as he is pure" (1 John 3:2-3).

II. What to Mortify: Col. 3:5-11

A. Put off old man: 5-9

5. Mortify therefore your members which are upon the earth; fornication, uncleanness, inordinate affection, evil concupiscence, and covetousness, which is idolatry:

These verses deal with "the old man" (sinful human nature) which Christians are supposed to put off. The word "mortify" means to deaden carnal desires by discipline. Leaning on the Holy Spirit, believers are to deal harshly with various sins such as those mentioned in Colossians 3:5, 8, and 9. Verse 5 lists tendencies inherent in the members (body parts) which can cause trouble. These are: fornication, uncleanness, inordinate affection, concupiscence and covetousness. Covetousness is labeled idolatry here, perhaps because it leads to craving people or things to displace devotion to God.

6. For which things' sake the wrath of God cometh on the children of disobedience:

7. In the which ye also walked some time, when ye lived in them.

It was because of the prevalence of such evil tendencies that the wrath of God came down on sinners. Paul reminded the Colossian believers that it was not long ago that they had walked beside sinners, living as they lived. Similar wording may be found in Ephesians 2:2-3— "In time past ye walked according to the course of this world, according to the prince of the power of the air, the spirit that worketh in the children of disobedience: now among whom also we all had our conversation [conduct, behavior] in times past in the lusts of our flesh, fulfilling the desires of the flesh and of the mind; and were by nature the children of wrath, even as others."

8. But now ye also put off all these; anger, wrath, malice, blasphemy, filthy communication out of your mouth.

9. Lie not one to another, seeing that ye have put off the old man with his deeds;

Paul concentrated here on sins of expression, much as he did in Ephesians 4:31—"Let all bitterness, and wrath, and anger, and clamour, and evil speaking, be put away from you with all malice." In Colossians 3:8-9 he condemned anger, wrath, malice, blasphemy, filthy communication out of your mouth and lying. These unacceptable forms of expression should have been laid aside with other sins when conversion took place. If they persisted, they should be dealt with at the present time. The "old man" must not be allowed to dominate believers and cause spiritual growth to decline or stop altogether.

B. Put on new man: 10-11

10. And have put the new man, which is renewed in knowledge after the image that created him:

Another rendering is "You are living a brand new kind of life that is continually learning more and more of what is right, and trying constantly to be more and more like Christ who created this new life within you" (Living Bible). Other versions translate "new man" as "new self." In another place, Paul urged believers to "put on the new man, which after God is created in righteousness and true holiness" (Eph. 4:24). The old sinful self cannot be made over or improved. The new righteous self must be formed within believers by the Holy Spirit (Gal. 2:20; 4:19; Col. 1:27). Believers may not be able to recapture the original innocence enjoyed by Adam and Eve before they fell, but they can show that they were made in the image of God by living holy lives and becoming increasingly like Christ.

11. Where there is neither Greek nor Jew, circumcision nor uncircumcision, Barbarian, Scythian, bond nor free: but Christ is all, and in all.

Those who live in Christ form the church, and in that body there should be no distinctions on the basis of being Greek, Jew, circumcised, uncircumcised, Barbarian, Scythian, bond, or free. No matter what a person's background might be, he was to be considered equal, for Christ was Lord over all.

III. What to Pursue: Col. 3:12-17

A. Way of Christ: 12-15

12. Put on therefore, as the elect of God, holy and beloved, bowels of mercies, kindness, humbleness of mind, meekness, longsuffering;

Those who had the new spiritual self formed within them were to develop certain Christian virtues, Having been elected by God, they were holy through partaking of Christ's righteousness and thus loved by God. Paul urged them to put on bowels of mercies and kindness (hearts producing sympathy and kind acts). He urged them to be humble and meek. He urged them to be longsuffering (patient, enduring).

13. Forbearing one another, and forgiving one another, if any man have a quarrel against any: even as Christ forgave you, so also do ye.

In the first part of this verse, Paul urged believers to practice forbearance. He then urged them to practice forgiveness, no doubt toward the repentant. These were the Christian ways to deal with quarreling if it happened. In the latter part of the verse, Paul used the forgiving action of Christ as the standard to follow. Since He had graciously forgiven them their sins, they should be ready to forgive others who offended them if they repented (Luke 17:3). Ephesians 4:32 is a parallel verse—"Be ye kind one to another, tenderhearted, forgiving one another, even as God for Christ's sake hath forgiven you."

14. And above all these things put on charity, which is the bond of perfectness.

Picture love here as the outer garment wrapped about the other virtues and holding them in place. This goes along well with 1 Corinthians 13.

15. And let the peace of God rule in your hearts, to the which also ye are called in one body; and be ye thankful.

Paul said that the peace of God could serve as an umpire in the hearts of believers, molding them into the one body of Christ. They were urged to develop a thankful spirit toward God and each other.

B. Word of Christ: 16-17

16a. Let the word of Christ dwell in you richly and in all wisdom; . . .

The word of Christ evidently referred to all the truth about Him. Paul wanted believers to study it and know the richness and wisdom of it. This was to be acquired not only through intellect but also by experience as they applied it in their lives.

16b. . . . teaching and admonishing one another in psalms and hymns and spiritual songs, singing with grace in your hearts to the Lord.

Paul expected the spiritual gifts of teaching and admonishing to be used by believers as they sought to spread the truth about Christ. One way in which they could do this was to sing with grace in their hearts to the Lord. We are not sure if the terms "psalms and hymns and spiritual songs" referred to different kinds of music, or if they were synonyms. We know that Hebrew psalms were set to music and sung. Unbelievers who heard them must have been favorably impressed.

17. And whatsoever ye do in word or deed, do all in the name of the Lord Jesus, giving thanks to God the Father by him.

In this summary statement, Paul said that believers in Colosse should govern their speech and actions by whether or not they brought credit or discredit to the name of the Lord Jesus. He obviously wanted them to say or do only what glorified the Savior. This was the way to thank God the Father for what He had done for them through Christ.

LIFE IN CHRIST

Evangelistic Emphasis

Today's reading can help us with what most people call "sins of the flesh." How can one ever win over the selfish desire to have it all, to run it all, to enjoy center stage? Is there really any way these deep needs can be controlled so that one can have peace and be a blessing to others? This teaching is important for evangelism in that people should be converted not only to Christ but to a Christian lifestyle.

In the gospels Jesus called disciples to follow Him. Not just in thought, but to follow Him in the way He lived. He taught them to care for the needy, to serve one another, to speak the truth even when it was expensive to do so. He took time with children, with older people and with outcasts of society. He claimed no extravagant dress or housing or transportation.

The Christian's de-emphasis on wealth and conspicuous consumption is not a denial of the earth's goodness or the goodness of creation. Nor does conversion always mean giving all of one's goods away to the poor. But conversion always means that all we own is used in service to God and for the benefit of others. We should help the inquirer to see that the answer for a constructive lifestyle is not to be found in a long list of rules, but in a change of heart. One's life is not reformed by a list of "dos" and "don'ts." What changes behavior is focusing on and absorbing into ourselves who Jesus is and what He calls us to be. It all comes down to trust, whether we believe Him and launch out with Him in His way of life. Many will not understand our new orientation. "Our lives are hid with Christ in God."

❖❖❖❖❖❖

Memory Selection

"And have put on the new man, which is renewed in knowledge after the image of him that created him:"
Colossians 3:10

When a candidate graduates from a police academy he or she is issued the official uniform. That uniform is more than clothing, it is a new identity, a new life and responsibility. The one who wears the uniform is given to understand that he or she represents a duly constituted authority, that the new identity is a trust and an honor. One is not allowed to launch his private police force according to his own rules and conducted for his own purposes. Nor is one allowed to abuse the uniform, to wear it dirty or in a slovenly fashion. The officer knows he represents those who have commissioned him in either a positive or negative manner. Not in all ways, but in some ways, becoming a Christian is like that. One is given a new coat to wear. Its label reads: "The Righteousness of God" and it was made at Golgotha. One receives it as a trust and a gift. It belongs to Another. Because God bestows it upon the believer in Christ the Christian is given a new identity. Christians no longer stand only in their own clothing, a new coat of honor has been issued. Paul urges the Colossians to "put on the new man," to claim their new identity, to wear the new coat with grateful pride and to have it renewed day by day in association with Jesus Christ.

July 18, 1993

Weekday Problems

Harold, Cynthia, and Ray work for the same advertising firm. They are all just out of school and in their first full-time jobs. Even though they were reared in three different Christian denominations, they share strong common beliefs about ethics. Almost immediately after reporting for work their supervisor asked them to twist the data slightly to sell products, to advance phoney claims, and to tell half-truths to clients.

The three talked about their dilemma in after hour discussions. "Well, I was reared in a sheltered, Protestant environment with hundreds of rules and regulations. But this is the real world, the rules are different now. I guess we'll just have to adjust," said Harold. Cynthia disagreed with feeling. "If we do not make a stand who will? The only way the top brass will ever reconsider its policies is to be challenged at some point. We will have to choose our time and place and we'll need to be respectful of their positions and ours, but we will have to raise the objections. Besides, what kind of witness will we have with others in the firm if they know we are Christians and we are willing to do anything unbelievers do?" Ray was not sure what to think. Both of his friends had good points to consider.

*What would you tell Ray?
*If Christian ethics are not driven by rules and regulations, then by what?

◆◆◆◆◆◆

Superintendent's Sermonette

A third-party politician once remarked that there was not "a dime's worth of difference" between the Republicans and the Democrats in the United States, and, therefore, people should vote for him, instead. He did get about ten million votes in the election. As we look at the world today, we may sometimes wonder if the distinctions between believers and unbelievers have become too blurred. The tendency seems to be for born-again Christians to become more and more like their worldly counterparts. We can be with some for quite awhile before knowing their true identity, and sometimes it may escape us.

The Apostle Paul believed in Christians being distinctive, and he urged this upon them in his letters. He called on the Colossian believers to get their affection off earthly things and place them on heavenly things. He urged them to put sinful tendencies to death. He urged them to clothe themselves with the righteousness and holiness of God. He encouraged them to become one in Christ and maintain a good testimony to an unbelieving world. What he wanted for them is what we should want for ourselves, as well. We cannot win the world through compromise. We must show that we are different, and then bring others to the One Who makes that difference.

LIFE IN CHRIST

This Lesson In Your Life

In every age and place Christians who have taken discipleship seriously have been considered a bit odd. In the early centuries ascetics made themselves different by wearing camel's hair shirts that irritated the skin, by sitting atop pillars or living in caves year after year to remove themselves from the contamination of society. Often believers have been different in other ways, not always by extremes in dress, diet and religious practice. They often seem peculiar because they are different. At the same time when some Christians were making spectacles of themselves by their odd behavior other Christians were different in other ways. Friends, relations, business associates noticed a change. Nothing so superficial as the texture of clothing, these people changed their values, their attitudes, their behavior toward others. Often dramatic turnarounds happened in a believer's goals and ambitions for life. They had a new attitude toward creation and all living things. Their values, world view, and ambitions were different.

The main point is that all Christians in every age march to a different drummer. It was so from the beginning. Peter addressed his first epistles to people who were "strangers and exiles" living abroad in the Roman Empire. They were "sojourners" not only physically but spiritually. A part of God's call to His people has always included the admonition: "Come out and be separate." The separation was not for exclusiveness but in order to be God's carefully fashioned mission to all mankind.

But often Christians have become proud, pious and superior about their different views and lifestyles. Many are the plays, songs, novels and movies written to puncture the ballooning hypocrisy of "holier than thou" Christianity. Like arrogant and superior Americans living abroad who earned the "ugly American" label, they continue on their merry way oblivious to the damage they do the cause of Christ. Always at the same time many quiet servants of Christ continue living day by day in imitation of their Master. They resent the high-profile, low-integrity Christians who give the faith a bad name. Their lives are salt and light to a world decaying in the darkness. Not salt and light in the eyes of others. The difference visible in their lives shows the way to life and peace.

Paul was not encouraging spiritual pride. In fact, he warned the Colossians that a faith full of "dos" and "don'ts" has an appearance of wisdom in imposing self imposed piety, humility and severe treatment of the body. But it is of no value in checking self-indulgence. Pride takes many forms: pride of possessions, pride of class and appearances, pride of knowledge, pride of power. But no form of pride is more odious to the unbeliever, more destructive to the life of the Christian than spiritual pride. An arrogant Christian who is spiritually proud does the Lord's cause more harm than a dozen raging atheists. In other words, hyper-pious legalistic Christianity or hyper-sophisticated liberated Christianity produce Christians just as self-centered in their own way as the world's hedonists are in theirs.

But Paul is not suggesting that, in reaction to strutting piety, one disappear into the world without a trace. He is urging Christians to recall that Jesus delivers them from the prison of self-centeredness by his death on the cross. The Christian now looks to Jesus Christ crucified and raised. Life is no longer about self, it is about God in Christ. One begins to see others about him or her, their needs and how they may be served in Christ's name. The Christian is different not by calculated peculiarity but by the change of heart, a re-direction of the affections and the will.

Seed Thoughts

1. Are rules destructive, should we do away with them?
No. Rules are necessary. But the Christian's life is not about rules.

2. Are not self-righteous Christians proof of the phoniness of Christianity?
No more than contaminated food proves that all food is bad.

3. Will the Christian lifestyle produce happiness?
In a profound and eternal, but not necessarily in a superficial and temporal way.

4. Does "honesty is the best policy" guarantee success and wealth?
No, many honest people struggle to survive while many dishonest ones "make it big."

5. How do I plan my program of moral self-improvement?
You don't; God changes you through His Son and the Spirit in your life.

(PLEASE TURN PAGE)

---

1. Are rules destructive, should we do away with them?

2. Are not self-righteous Christians proof of the phoniness of Christianity?

3. Will the Christian lifestyle produce happiness?

4. Does "honesty is the best policy" guarantee success and wealth?

5. How do I plan my program of moral self-improvement?

6. Is there nothing I can do to facilitate moral improvement?

7. How do I know when I have improved enough to receive God's love and approval?

8. Why should a church rite like baptism matter?

9. How can we who are so different come to love one another?

10. Can people really change?

(SEED THOUGHTS--Cont'd)

No. Rules are necessary. But the Christian's life is not about rules.

No more than contaminated food proves that all food is bad.

In a profound and eternal, but not necessarily in a superficial and temporal way.

No, many honest people struggle to survive while many dishonest ones "make it big."

You don't; God changes you through His Son and the Spirit in your life.

Yes, you can focus on Christ daily and let Him change you.

God's love for you has already been eternally expressed at Golgotha.

It is not a church rite; Jesus designated it as the place to meet Him to receive His gift from Calvary.

By confessing our common need and gratefully receiving common salvation In Christ.

Yes, inevitably. The only question is in what direction.

6. Is there nothing I can do to facilitate moral improvement?
Yes, you can focus on Christ daily and let Him change you.

7. How do I know when I have improved enough to receive God's love and approval?
God's love for you has already been eternally expressed at Golgotha.

8. Why should a church rite like baptism matter?
It is not a church rite; Jesus designated it as the place to meet Him to receive His gift from Calvary.

9. How can we who are so different come to love one another?
By confessing our common need and gratefully receiving common salvation In Christ.

10. Can people really change?
Yes, inevitably. The only question is in what direction.

July 25, 1993

Christ Unites

Philemon

4. I thank my God, making mention of thee always in my prayers,

5. Hearing of thy love and faith, which thou hast toward the Lord Jesus, and toward all saints;

6. That the communication of thy faith may become effectual by the acknowledging of every good thing which is in you in Christ Jesus.

7. For we have great joy and consolation in thy love, because the bowels of the saints are refreshed by thee, brother.

8. Wherefore, though I might be much bold in Christ to enjoin thee that which is convenient,

9. Yet for love's sake I rather beseech thee, being such an one as Paul the aged, and now also a prisoner of Jesus Christ.

10. I beseech thee for my son O-nes'-i-mus, whom I have begotten in my bonds:

11. Which in time past was to thee unprofitable, but now profitable to thee and to me:

12. Whom I have sent again: thou therefore receive him, that is, mine own bowels:

13. Whom I would have retained with me, that in thy stead he might have ministered unto me in the bonds of the gospel:

14. But without thy mind would I do nothing; that thy benefit shouldest be as it were of necessity, but willingly.

15. For perhaps he therefore departed for a season, that thou shouldest receive him for ever;

16. Not now as a servant, but above a servant, a brother beloved, specially to me, but how much more unto *thee*, both in the flesh, and in the Lord?

17. If thou count me therefore a partner, receive him as myself.

18. If he hath wronged thee, or oweth thee ought, put that on mine account;

19. I Paul have written it with mine own hand, I will repay *it:* albeit I do not say to thee how thou owest unto me even thine own self besides.

20. Yea, brother, let me have joy of thee in the Lord: refresh my bowels in the Lord.

21. Having confidence in thy obedience I wrote unto thee, knowing that thou wilt also do more than I say.

◆◆◆◆◆◆

◀ **Memory Selection**
Philemon 17

◀ **Devotional Reading**
I Peter 2:4-10

◀ **Background Scripture**
Philemon

◀ **Printed Scripture**
Philemon 4-21

CHRIST UNITES

Teacher's Target

We have heard people say, "Business is business!" That seems to excuse them from being concerned or responsible for personal considerations in interpersonal relationships. They want to hide behind that saying while protecting their own self-interests. Philemon, a member of the Colossian church, was master to a slave named Onesimus. His natural inclination would have been to demand that his "property" be returned to him, and he might have dealt harshly with Onesimus. Paul sought to put a different light on the situation.

Paul's letter to Philemon was an example of third-party advocacy at work. It often takes this in order to resolve a problem, and Paul did it in a gracious manner. At the same time, Paul taught Christian doctrine and its application. He showed that the union of all members in the body of Christ makes them brothers. It also fosters forgiveness and reconciliation. We need these positive forces in operation in society today.

Lesson Introduction

Although we act toward it with revulsion, slavery as a socially-accepted institution has existed from ancient times to the present. Philemon, master of Onesimus, was not the only slaveholder in the church at Colosse. In Colossians 4:1 Paul wrote, "Masters, give unto your servants [slaves] that which is just and equal; knowing that ye also have a Master in heaven." The church did not try to abolish slavery, but it did attempt to make it more humane. It also taught that equality in Christ took much of the sting out of it (Col. 3:11).

In the case of Onesimus, this slave had wronged his master by running away to Rome. He may have stolen from Philemon in order to finance the trip. While in Rome, Onesimus met Paul and was converted to Christ. Paul would have liked to keep him there to help him, but he would not do this without permission from Philemon. In the briefest of his letters, Paul explained the facts to Philemon and requested that he forgive his slave and accept him as a brother in Christ.

Teaching Outline

I. Report: Philemon 4-7
  A. Virtues: 4-5
  B. Vindication: 6-7
II. Request: Philemon 8-14
  A. Consideration: 8-9
  B. Choice: 10-14
III. Reception: Philemon 15-17
  A. Possibility: 15-16
  B. Partner: 17
IV. Repayment: Philemon 18-21
  A. Offer: 18-19
  B. Obedience: 20-21

Daily Bible Readings

Mon. Christ Refreshes Others through Faithful Servants - *Philemon 1-7*
Tue. Christ Frees and Unites *Philemon 8-14*
Wed. Christ Transforms Relationships *Philemon 15-25*
Thu. We Are One Fellowship in Christ *I Cor. 1:1-9*
Fri. Christ above All *I Cor. 1:10-17*
Sat. God's New People in Christ *7 Pet. 2:4-10*
Sun. Gladly Share Your Blessings *II Cor 9:1-15*

July 25, 1993

VERSE BY VERSE

I. Report: Philemon 4-7

A. Virtues: 4-5

4. I thank God, making mention of thee always in my prayers.

Paul had opened his letter to Philemon by calling himself "a prisoner of Jesus Christ," although he was literally a Roman prisoner. He referred to Timothy as his "brother" in Christ. He sent greetings to Philemon as "our dearly beloved" and a "fellowlabourer." He also sent greetings to "beloved Apphia," probably Philemon's wife, and to "Archippus our fellowsoldier," perhaps Philemon and Apphia's son, as well as to members of "the church in thy house." To all of these was wished grace and peace from God the Father and the Lord Jesus Christ (Philemon 1-3). Archippus evidently needed urging from Paul. He told believers in Colosse to "say to Archippus, Take heed to the ministry which thou hast received in the Lord, that thou fulfil it" (Col. 4:17).

Paul said that he thanked God for Philemon, mentioning him often in his prayers. This clearly implied that Paul had received a good report on him.

5. Hearing of thy love and faith, which thou hast toward the Lord Jesus, and toward all saints;

It appears that Philemon had the crowning virtue of love which binds all virtues together. He also had a strong faith. These caused him to relate well to the Lord Jesus and to other saints (believers). In this general commendation, Paul was laying the groundwork for his later request that Philemon accept Onesimus as a brother in Christ.

B. Vindication: 6-7

6. That the communication of thy faith may become effectual by the acknowledging of every good thing which is in you in Christ Jesus.

Paul wanted Philemon to share his faith in order that he might "have a full understanding of every good thing we have in Christ" (New International Version). Paul said that faith was communicated by recognizing that the love in believers should produce acts of love toward others. Here, again, we see the direction in which Paul was headed as far as Onesimus was concerned. Paul wanted what he had heard about Philemon to be vindicated by his actions in this situation.

7. For we have great joy and consolation in thy love, because the bowels of the saints are refreshed by thee, brother.

The "we" here probably referred to Paul, Timothy, Epaphras, Marcus (Mark), Aristarchus, Demas, Lucas (Luke), and other unnamed companions (Philemon 1, 23-24). They rejoiced and were comforted by hearing about love displayed by Philemon. The hearts of those who made the report to Paul regarding Philemon had been refreshed by this man in Colosse.

II. Request: Philemon 8-14

A. Consideration: 8-9

8. Wherefore, though I might be much bold in Christ to enjoin thee that which is convenient,

9. Yet for love's sake I rather beseech thee, being such an one as Paul the aged, and now also a prisoner of Jesus Christ.

Having given consideration to the situation, Paul concluded that he could have used his apostolic authority to com-

463

mand Philemon to grant a request. However, he decided to appeal to Philemon on the basis of Christian love to grant the request. Paul poignantly referred to himself as aging and as a prisoner of Jesus Christ (for the second time, cf. vs.1), as if these facts warranted special treatment by Philemon. We will look at another factor when we study verse 19.

B. Choice: 10-14

10. I beseech thee for my son Onesimus, whom I have begotten in my bonds:

We might wonder if effort had been made while Onesimus worked for Philemon in Colosse to convert him to Christ. Whatever the case, he had run away to Rome and had been led to Christ by Paul in spite of his bonds. This was the basic element in the reasoning pursued by Paul in subsequent verses. Philemon had to reckon with the fact that Paul now considered Onesimus a "spiritual son" of his.

11. Which in time past was to thee unprofitable, but now profitable to thee and to me:

Onesimus meant "useful," but we do not know if it was his original name or one given to him by Paul. Paul realized that Onesimus had once been unprofitable to Philemon. Perhaps he had not been a good worker in Colosse. He had run away and had thus stolen time and usefulness from his master, and he may have stolen money to finance his trip to Rome several hundred miles away. Paul now felt that Onesimus was truly profitable, for he was willing to work for either Philemon or for Paul.

12. Whom I have sent again: thou therefore receive him, that is, mine own bowels:

Paul's letter made it clear that he had sent Onesimus back home to Colosse. He hoped that Philemon would receive his slave as a special person who was dear to the apostle. In other words, Paul hoped that Philemon would love Onesimus as he himself did.

13. Whom I would have retained with me, that in thy stead he might have ministered unto me in the bonds of the gospel:

Paul was very bold here. He stated that he would have liked to keep Onesimus in Rome to help him while he was a prisoner. Onesimus could thus have taken Philemon's place in ministering to Paul, implying that Paul could have ordered Philemon himself to come to Rome and help him.

14. But without thy mind would I do nothing; that thy benefit should not be as it were of necessity, but willingly.

Rather than using his apostolic authority to demand that Onesimus stay with him in Rome, Paul had chosen to send him back to Philemon in Colosse. He wanted any favor Philemon did for him to be voluntary instead of forced. We do not hear of Philemon sending Onesimus back to Rome to be with Paul, but circumstances may have changed in the meantime.

III. Reception: Philemon 15-17

A. Possibility: 15-16

15. For perhaps he therefore departed for a season, that thou shouldest receive him for ever;

Philemon may have been highly irritated to lose the services of Onesimus between the time of his departure and his return. Paul saw this matter in a different way. Knowing the sovereignty of God, he realized that the Lord could have allowed Onesimus to leave Colosse for Rome in order that he might meet Paul and be saved. Now that Onesimus was a Christian, Philemon could look at the possibility of retaining him for the remainder of his earthly life and also being with him for eternity in heaven.

16. Not now as a servant, but above a servant, a brother beloved, specially to me, but how much more unto thee, both in the flesh, and in the Lord?

Paul did not want Philemon to take Onesimus back merely as a returned slave who could be beaten, sold, or even slain. He wanted him to see Onesimus as a loved brother in Christ. Although Paul thought of Onesimus as a special brother, he felt that Philemon should think of him in an even more special way, both as a person useful to him and as a brother in the Lord. The relationship between Philemon and Onesimus had lasted longer than the one between Paul and Onesimus. It had been strained before, but now it had the promise of rich development as master and slave walked together with the Lord.

B. Partner: 17

17. If thou count me therefore a partner, receive him as myself.

Partners in the gospel were expected to honor one another's requests. It was on this basis that Paul urged Philemon to accept Onesimus as if he were accepting himself. Philemon could not help but be impressed with Paul's opinion of Onesimus, seeing that he went this far in his defense.

IV. Repayment: Philemon 18-21

A. Offer: 18-19

18. If he hath wronged thee, or oweth thee ought, put that on my account;
19a. ... I Paul have written it with mine own hand, I will repay it: ...

Pressing on with his argument in favor of Onesimus, Paul offered to pay whatever loss Philemon might have suffered because of Onesimus' negligence in running away or perhaps because of Onesimus' stealing anything. Paul may have sent a promissory note along with the letter, written in his own hand, even though his eyesight was bad and he usually used a scribe to do his writing. We might wonder how Paul, as a missionary, could have a financial account from which to pay anyone anything. We know that he sometimes did manual labor as a tentmaker while pioneering new churches. His family back in Tarsus of Cilicia may have had ample funds and allowed him to draw on them. He hired a place in Rome for two years while under house-arrest. He could have been given funds by churches and individuals interested in his ministries. We would hardly expect him to make his offer to Philemon unless he had the means to back it up.

19b. ...albeit I do not say to thee how thou owest unto me even thine own self besides.

This obviously referred to spiritual rather than literal debt. Paul was reminding Philemon that he had led him to Christ and thus secured for him eternal life. No money value could be placed on this but there were other ways in which Philemon could try to repay what he owed Paul for this blessing. Acceptance of Onesimus was one way.

B. Obedience: 20-21

20. Yea, brother, let me have joy of thee in the Lord: refresh my bowels in the Lord.

Paul referred to Philemon in this letter as "our dearly beloved" and "fellowlabourer" (vs. l), as "brother" (vss. 7, 20), and as "partner" (vs. 17). Note similarities between verses 7 and 20, both of which refer to joy and refreshment. Paul urged Philemon to respond to him in such a way that he would rejoice over him in the Lord and have his heart cheered in the Lord.

21. Having confidence in thy obedience I wrote unto thee, knowing that thou wilt also do more than I say.

Paul fully expected Philemon to comply with his request regarding Onesimus. His confidence was apparently based on past and current knowledge of how Philemon acted. Paul may also have had some spiritual discernment which would let him know how Philemon was going to respond.

There is no other reference to Philemon in the Bible. Onesimus is mentioned by Paul in Colossians 4:7-9—"All my state shall Tychicus declare unto you [in Colosse], ...whom I have sent unto you for the same purpose, that he might know your estate, and comfort your hearts; with Onesimus, a faithful and beloved brother, who is one of you. They shall make known unto you all things which are done here [in Rome]." It is believed that Paul's letters to the Ephesians, Colossians, and Philemon were sent at the same time, being carried personally by Tychicus and Onesimus. In his letter to Philemon, Paul asked that lodging might be prepared for him, because he hoped to be able to come to Colosse himself soon afterward (Philemon 22) He closed the letter by passing on greetings from several companions (vss. 23-24) and a simple benediction—"The grace of our Lord Jesus Christ be with your spirit. Amen" (vs. 25).

Evangelistic Emphasis

We do not know how Philemon came to wealth. Perhaps he inherited it, or he may have been an enterprising entrepreneur who rose from rags to riches. But from Colossians and Philemon we surmise that he was a man of means. He had a house large enough for the church to use as a meeting place. He owned slaves. Other wealthy citizens must have thought Philemon strange for getting involved with the sect called Nazarenes. Why would anyone with so much to lose open his heart and spend a fortune on a group like those who assembled regularly at his address?

Whatever his vocation, we are sure that Philemon was not a minister or an evangelist. And, yet, by his generosity and care for people of all classes his life must have been a powerful witness. Especially if he granted Paul's request to release his runaway slave, Onesimus. In any case, Philemon's generosity issued not so much from his own initiative as from God's initiative in Jesus Christ. Philemon had met the One who divested Himself of the wealth of heaven to become poor so that: we might become rich in Him. The real mainspring of all true Christian generosity is God's generosity to us. One should not ask how much he should do for God but how much God has done for him. Even a few like Philemon in any church give God's kingdom a powerful evangelistic outreach. The wealthy among us should not be browbeaten for having money. They should not spend their lives feeling guilty for the blessings they have received. On the other hand, from whom much is given much is expected. Those who are especially gifted can be a mighty force for good in God's kingdom. The way they use their means can be as strong an evangelistic appeal as any sermon could ever be.

Memory Selection

"If thou count me therefore a partner, receive him as myself."
Philemon 17

On what basis did Paul urge Philemon to treat Onesimus kindly? What was the basis of their partnership? It was a lifelong friendship. The two men grew up in cities far apart and met when they were both adults. It was not race. Paul was a Jew and Philemon a Gentile. It was not comradeship at school, a college fraternity. Paul had attended school in Jerusalem where he was steeped in the Law while Philemon probably had a classical Roman education a world away from Paul's. Nor did they share membership in the same class or station in life. Philemon was wealthy, Paul had only the clothes on his back, a few tools for making tents, and some manuscripts he treasured. Paul carried all his possessions on his back and was scorned by the best people in town as a wandering prophet. So what accounts for the bond Paul obviously felt in writing to Philemon as his "partner"

It was not what they had in common, it was Who they had in common. Both had met Jesus Christ. He had ransomed each of these men from his own particular kind of slavery. Philemon held Paul in highest esteem because through him he had met Jesus. All three of the key players in this story shared life in Christ.

July 25, 1993

Weekday Problems

When Patrick finished medical school and residency he came to work at the same hospital where John had worked for two years. They had a great deal in common: they both grew up in Minnesota, they both grew up in Christian homes and professed faith in Jesus as their Lord, they had attended college at the university and even ended up at the same medical school. In fact, it was John's recommendation to the hospital staff which brought Patrick's resume to the top of the stack. Not long after Patrick signed on he discovered a problem.

It became apparent that John's workaholism was more than dedication to medicine. He and his wife were having serious problems and John found it more convenient to spend every waking hour at the hospital. Patrick noticed that John had a close friendship with an attractive intern at the hospital named Sally. As weeks became months the two were seen together constantly both at work and away. It became apparent to everyone at the hospital that they were having an affair. Everyone seemed to know except John's wife.

*What is Patrick's responsibility in this case?
*Should he decide to speak to John about the situation? Upon what basis should he approach him?

♦♦♦♦♦♦

Superintendent's Sermonette

The world has its ways of trying to uphold what it defines as justice, but no government can hope to write laws to cover every situation, and those which are written can be abused. Unscrupulous lawyers are universally scorned for allowing evil individuals and corporations to use existing laws to their own advantage. Special-interest groups are notorious for using various pressure tactics or bribes to get what they want. Some man-made laws are ill-conceived or not properly applied. Justice systems often make a mockery of true justice. We need faith in God and His higher, infallible justice in order to face life's challenges.

The incident described in today's text shows how a supernatural approach can bring what is fair and acceptable to a situation. Philemon was a slave-holder and a member of the church in Colosse. Paul was a prisoner in Rome and the means for the conversion of Onesimus, Philemon's runaway slave. Paul wrote a letter to Philemon to send home with Onesimus, explaining why Philemon's legal rights regarding Onesimus should be set aside in favor of receiving him as a brother in Christ. As in Paul's case, we should always look for the supernatural, loving, biblical way to resolve earthly problems.

This Lesson For Your Life

We can learn several important lessons from the small letter to Philemon. First, Paul did not "pull rank" on Philemon and order him to release Onesimus. He addressed him as a "partner" in the gospel. In one sense Philemon owed everything to Paul. Had it not been for Paul he would never have heard of Jesus Christ, never have known the love of God, would never have been a Christian. In another sense no Christian ever owes anything to another. Not in view of what the Lord has done for them both. Because of the cross of Christ believers who receive God's grace also assume certain fellowship responsibilities.

In making covenant with their Lord, Christians make covenant with one another. From that point on the quality of life in the community is judged and corrected by that covenant. Despite all that Philemon owed to Paul, the apostle appealed to him on the basis of the covenant they shared in Christ, he called him "partner." It is on that basis that we are to relate to one another in the Lord. Sometimes we must call one another to honesty and repentance about our lives. At other times, as with Paul and Philemon, we should point out opportunities for Christian service or the duty of our calling. That God's covenant is the context of our relationship means there are limits to our responsibilities one to another. None has total responsibility for another brother or sister. It is not ours to command another, to take charge of another's life, to claim success or failure for another's actions. We relate to one another "in Christ." That means we encourage one another and that each of us has a primary relationship to Christ. We are responsible ultimately only to Him.

Another lesson can be learned from Paul's tact in dealing with Philemon. Sometimes he could be blunt as with his reprimand of the Galatians. In Philippians 3 he was especially harsh with the legalistic teachers who insisted on circumcision for salvation. On the other hand, Paul could be tender as we see in I Thessalonians where he deals with the young Christians as a nurse with her children. As a rule, he was harsh only when circumstances dictated that he break through the willful pride and arrogance of his readers. From this we can learn that prayerful study of each situation should guide us in our approach to any person and any problem. Church leaders should learn from Paul the sensitivity to deal with each individual as the case dictates. Paul encouraged Philemon, not only by words, but by his own example. He had given up Onesimus who was a great encouragement and help to him up in service to Paul.

Perhaps our longer view of this episode from almost twenty centuries later can teach us something about faith and trust in the Lord to work His way in His own time. Abraham Lincoln is quoted as saying he would not own a slave because he would not be another's slave. Why didn't Paul say something like that? Perhaps it may not have occurred to Paul as many of the social ills of our own society do not appear evil to us. Or, perhaps, Paul knew the realities of the situation. The slave revolt of Spartacus tells us what happened to slaves who tried to throw off their chains. They were brutally put down, many crucified. Jesus started the revolution when He taught the Golden Rule, when He treated every person with respect as created in the image of God. Perhaps Paul's letter to Philemon pointing up the fact that slave and master were brothers in the Lord was also a part of the beginnings of that revolution. The issue would not be resolved in most places until the nineteenth century. But the seeds had been planted centuries before.

Seed Thoughts

1. Whose idea was Christian fellowship anyway?
It was Jesus' idea, he died to break down walls and unite all kinds of people.

2. What is unique about the unity we have in Christ?
It is not based on natural affinity but upon God's love in Christ.

3. What prayer for unity among his followers did Jesus pray the night before his crucifixion?
That they would all be one as He and the Father were one.

4 What is the greatest spiritual barrier to unity among believers?
The basis of all sin, human pride.

5. What right did Paul have to get involved with Philemon and Onesimus' problem?
His unique relation to each and his responsibility to the Lord.

(PLEASE TURN PAGE)

---

1. Whose idea was Christian fellowship anyway?

2. What is unique about the unity we have in Christ?

3. What prayer for unity among his followers did Jesus pray the night before his crucifixion?

4 What is the greatest spiritual barrier to unity among believers?

5. What right did Paul have to get involved with Philemon and Onesimus' problem?

6. What principle of Christian diplomacy seems obvious in the letter to Philemon?

7. Why did Paul not call for the abolition of slavery itself?

8. When should we get involved in other Christians' business?

9. Did Onesimus have a "right" to mercy from Philemon?

10. What is our responsibility when another Christian comes to us as Paul did to Philemon?

(SEED THOUGHTS--Cont'd)

It was Jesus' idea, he died to break down walls and unite all kinds of people.

It is not based on natural affinity but upon God's love in Christ.

That they would all be one as He and the Father were one.

The basis of all sin, human pride.

His unique relation to each and his responsibility to the Lord.

Respect for the other person's right to decision and action.

Evidently, the time was not right in God's plan.

When the Golden Rule makes involvement necessary.

No, according to Paul, the slave was wrong in those circumstances to run away.

To hear him out, pray and consider his words.

6. What principle of Christian diplomacy seems obvious in the letter to Philemon?
Respect for the other person's right to decision and action.

7. Why did Paul not call for the abolition of slavery itself?
Evidently, the time was not right in God's plan.

8. When should we get involved in other Christians' business?
When the Golden Rule makes involvement necessary.

9. Did Onesimus have a "right" to mercy from Philemon?
No, according to Paul, the slave was wrong in those circumstances to run away.

10. What is our responsibility when another Christian comes to us as Paul did to Philemon?
To hear him out, pray and consider his words.

August 1, 1993

New Life

Ephesians 2

AND you *hath he quickened*, who were dead in trespasses and sins;

2. Wherein in time past ye walked according to the course of this world, according to the prince of the power of the air, the spirit that now worketh in the children of disobedience:

3. Among whom also we all had our conversation in times past in the lusts of our flesh, fulfilling the desires of the flesh and of the mind; and were by nature the children of wrath, even as others.

4. But God, who is rich in mercy, for his great love wherewith he loved us,

5. Even when we were dead in sins, hath quickened us together with Christ, (by grace ye are saved;)

6. And hath raised *us* up together, and made us sit together in heavenly *places* in Christ Jesus:

7. That in the ages to come he might shew the exceeding riches of his grace in *his* kindness toward us through Christ Jesus.

8. For by grace are ye saved through faith; and that not of yourselves: *it is* the gift of God:

9. Not of works, lest any man should boast.

10. For we are his workmanship, created in Christ Jesus unto good works, which God hath before ordained that we should walk in them.

Ephesians 3

14. For this cause I bow my knees unto the Father of our Lord Jesus Christ,

15. Of whom the whole family in heaven and earth is named,

16. That he would grant you, according to the riches of his glory, to be strengthened with might by his Spirit in the inner man;

17. That Christ may dwell in your hearts by faith; that ye, being rooted and grounded in love,

18. May be able to comprehend with all saints what *is* the breadth, and length, and depth, and height;

19. And to know the love of Christ, which passeth knowledge, that ye might be filled with all the fulness of God.

◆◆◆◆◆◆

◀ **Memory Selection**
Ephesians 2:8

◀ **Devotional Reading**
Ephesians 1:3-14

◀ **Background Scripture**
Ephesians 1:15-2:10; 3:14-19

◀ **Printed Scripture**
Ephesians 2:1-10
Ephesians 3:14-19

NEW LIFE

Teacher's Target

We have heard some amazing things about people in recent years. Many have told of their near-death or after-death experiences before being revived. The zombies of voodism have fascinated us as we wonder how to explain the "walking dead." The actions of bizarre psychotics and drug-addicts have appalled us. The most amazing fact about the earth's five billion people, however, is that most of them are spiritually dead. The God-conscious part of them is inoperative. No matter how lively they may appear to be in their physical, mental, emotional, and social behavior, they are spiritually helpless and lost.

Sinners are dead in their trespasses and sins until they are made alive through faith in Christ and accept His saving grace. This is a free gift from God. Works have nothing to do with being saved, but being saved should produce good works. New life in Christ can become as full as we allow it to be.

Lesson Introduction

We can progress physically, materially, intellectually, emotionally, and socially but still be hampered, twisted, and ultimately destroyed by sin. Jesus said, "Wide is the gate, and broad is the way, that leadeth to destruction, and many there be which go in thereat: because strait is the gate, and narrow is the way, which leadeth unto life, and few there be that find it" (Matt. 7:13-14).

Paul explained that spiritual deadness caused people to walk according to the course of this sinful world-system, led by the prince of the power of the air (Satan). These children of wrath became redeemed children of God through faith in Christ, and they were appointed by God to do good works. He prayed that they might be filled with all the fulness of God. We need this today, too.

Teaching Outline

I. Wakening: Eph. 2:1-7
  A. Past condition: 1-3
  B. Present condition: 4-6
  C. Predicted condition: 7
II. Working: Eph. 2:8-10
  A. Salvation: 8-9
  B. Service: 10
III. Wishing: Eph. 3:14-19
  A. Cause: 14-15
  B. Concerns: 16-19

Daily Bible Readings

Mon. Life Apart from Christ
Eph. 2:1-5
Tue. Saved by Grace
Eph. 2:6-10
Wed. The Source of New Life
John 15:1-9
Thu. Bear Fruit of the New Life
John 15:10-17
Fri. Renewed by God's Power
Isa. 40:28-31
Sat. The Blessings of Newness
Eph. 3:13-19
Sun. A New Me
Gal. 6:11-16

August 1, 1993

VERSE BY VERSE

I. Wakening: Eph. 2:1-7

A. Past condition: 1-3

1. And you hath he quickened, who were dead in trespasses and sins:

This would appear to be a general statement by Paul presenting the positive and negative aspects of the human condition. However, note that the phrase "hath he quickened" is in italics, which means that it was not in the original manuscripts and was thus added by manuscript copiers at a later time. The phrase may have been borrowed from verse 5. Paul actually began the passage by concentrating on people as they were when they were spiritually dead in their trespasses and sins, and he elaborated on this in verses 2 and 3.

2. Wherein in time past ye walked according to the course of this world, according to the prince of the power of the air, the spirit that now worketh in the children of disobedience:

Paul's description of Gentile believers' past life pictured them as walking in lockstep with the sinful world-system. They were led by Satan, the prince of the power in the air.

Paul realized that no one was free from control. Every person is either under Satan's control or under God's control. Sinners who loudly demand their right to freedom seldom understand this until it is too late.

3. Among whom also we all had our conversation in times past in the lusts of our flesh, fulfilling. the desires of the flesh and of the mind; and were by nature the children of wrath, even as others.

Paul admitted that even he, as a Jew, along with his companions were once behaving under the motivation of their carnal passions, fulfilling cravings of their fleshly natures and sinful minds. Therefore, they were also objects of divine wrath. These harsh terms showed that Paul had a very low view of people apart from God. Left to themselves, they moved steadily downward to moral degradation and ultimate destruction. The false sense of freedom fostered by Satan and his evil hosts would eventually be revealed as enslavement. People needed salvation, and Paul knew where it could be found.

B. Present condition: 4-6

4. But God, who is rich in mercy, for his great love wherewith he loved us,

This is a transitional verse. Having described the negative condition of believers prior to their conversion, he now said that God made all of the difference in their positive present condition. He described God as having great love and as being rich in mercy. Without these two divine attributes, sinners would have been lost forever.

5. Even when we were dead in sins, hath quickened us together with Christ, (by grace ye are saved;)

Paul said that God had taken those who were spiritually dead in their sins and had quickened them. Even as He had literally raised Christ from the dead, so it was that He spiritually raised repentant sinners from their deadness. He did not do this because they paid him to do it or because they worked hard to attain it. It was His grace (unmerited favor) which made their salvation possible.

6. And hath raised us up together, and made us sit together in heavenly places in Christ Jesus:

This agrees with Ephesians 1:3—

473

"Blessed be the God and Father of our Lord Jesus Christ, who hath blessed us with all spiritual blessings in heavenly places in Christ." Jesus Christ is located in heaven at His Father's right hand. Believers who belong to Him by faith are fixed or positioned in Him there. Their potential for becoming like Him is tremendous, and during their lifetime this ought to be their goal. Realistically speaking, there is always a gap in this life between a believer's position in Christ and his practice of the Christian way. There is always room for growth and development of a Christlike character.

C. Predicted condition: 7

7. That in the ages to come he might show the exceeding riches of his grace in his kindness toward us through Christ Jesus.

When the sons of God meet Christ at His second coming, they will become like Him (I John 3:2). As the ages of eternity unfold, God will be able to point to redeemed believers as trophies of divine grace and kindness. The atoning death and shed blood of His beloved Son will have played a crucial role in making this everlasting blessing possible. Christians alone have this prospect.

II. Working: Eph. 2:8-10

A. Salvation: 8-9

8. For by grace are ye saved through faith; and that not of yourselves: it is the gift of God:
9. Not of works, lest any man should boast.

The first and last parts of verse 8 go together, and its second part goes with verse 9. It is by God's grace alone that sinners are saved when they place their faith in Jesus Christ as Savior, thus identifying themselves with Him and being justified through His atoning blood shed at Calvary. Jesus said, "I am the way, the truth, and the life: no man cometh unto the Father, but by me" (John 14:6). Salvation is a free gift from God because Jesus paid the price. "Ye were not redeemed with corruptible things, as silver and gold, . . . but with the precious blood of Christ" (1 Pet. 1:18-19).

Coming back to Ephesians 2:8-9, Paul said that salvation was not of or by individuals, nor by any works they could do. This included works associated with the law of Moses. In another place Paul wrote, "Where is boasting then? It is excluded. By what law? of works? Nay: but by the law of faith. Therefore we conclude that a man is justified by faith without the deeds of the law" (Rom. 3:27-28).

B. Service: 10

10a. For we are his workmanship, created in Christ Jesus . . .

According to Ephesians 4:24, a believer should "put on the new man, which after God is created in righteousness and true holiness." Paul claimed that believers are God's "workmanship," meaning that they are His handiwork or formation. He recreated them or regenerated them by placing them into the body of Christ. He is the Head of the body, and they are functioning members of it (I Cor. 12:12-27; Col 1:18).

10b. . . .unto good works, which God hath before ordained that we should walk in them.

God did not provide salvation in Christ for believers simply to get them into heaven. He did it in order that they might perform good works while they are still on this earth. Works do not bring them salvation, but salvation should produce good works within them. Note that God has foreordained that these works should be done by them. This raises an interesting question. If a believer fails to do the works ordained for him, will they be left undone or will God cause some other believer to do them?

Paul pictured the good works of believers as providing boundaries to guide them in their Christian walk. Perhaps the first good works new converts should perform are acts of restitution for past evil acts wherever that is possible. This will help them and those whom they have offended. In addition to these remedial deeds, they should look for ways to help others both inside and outside of the body of believers. "As we have therefore opportunity, let us do good unto all men, especially unto them who are of the household of faith" (Gal. 6:10). This promotes loving concern to those within the church and maintains a good testimony to those outside of the church.

III. Wishing: Eph. 3: 14-19

A. Cause: 14-15

14. For this cause I bow my knees unto the Father of our Lord Jesus Christ,

15. Of whom the whole family in heaven and earth is named,

Paul had previously stated that both Jewish and Gentile believers were of the household of God, being built on the foundation of the apostles and prophets, Jesus Christ being the chief cornerstone, and forming a building which grew into a holy temple in the Lord, a habitation of God through the Holy Spirit (Eph. 2:19-22). Chapter 3 began with Paul saying that it was for this cause, and then he digressed in verses 2-13 to comment on the dispensation of grace and his part in it. He now returns to this theme in verse 14 by saying that it was for this cause (believers growing into the household of God) that he prayed for them. He said that he bowed his knees in prayer to the Father of our Lord Jesus Christ.

15. Of whom the whole farmily in heaven and earth is named.

Some explain this as meaning that every family in heaven and earth is named after God the Father, thus showing that the concept of fatherhood comes from Him. Others explain this as meaning that the whole family of God, whether in heaven or on earth, is in view here. In other words, the redeemed who have passed on and who are still alive identify themselves with God, the Father of Jesus Christ.

B. Concerns: 16-19

16. That he would grant you, according to the riches of his glory, to be strengthened with light by his Spirit in the inner man;

Paul asked God to give the Ephesian believers strength out of His abundance of glory, so that they would be strengthened by the Holy Spirit in their inner man.

17. That Christ may dwell in your hearts by faith; that ye, being rooted and grounded in love,

18. May be able to comprehend with all saints what is the breadth, and length, and depth, and height;

19a And to know the love of Christ, which passeth knowledge, . . .

It was saving faith which had brought believers into the family of God. Now Paul wanted sustaining faith to help them develop their new lives in Christ. Note the use of mixed metaphors here. He mentioned being rooted as a plant in soil, and he mentioned being grounded as something that is built. In both cases, believers were to be established in love given from above. If this was true, they could comprehend the dimensions of the unfathomable love of Christ. If this seems to be a contradiction in terms, keep in mind that development of this comprehension is a continuing and lifelong process.

19b. . . .that ye might be filled with all the fulness of God.

The concept here seems to be that beleivers who seek to know the dimensions of God's love to them in Christ will be filled with His power and glory up to their capacity at any given point in their spiritual development. Here is an attainable goal toward which to strive, and the Holy Spirit stands ready to help us reach it today.

NEW LIFE

Evangelistic Emphasis

"Nothing is certain but death and taxes," the old saying goes. While that is true we live over the one and not the other. We spend much of our lives trying to postpone death. At the top of our list of priorities as a people is to look good and feel good. We are the most health-conscious generation the world has ever known, focusing enormous amounts of energy, time and attention on diets, exercise programs, and so on. The irony of the situation is that so many who stress fitness of body completely ignore fitness of the soul.

We may feel more alive than ever outside and more dead than ever inside. Our physical fitness craze has stimulated the Narcissus in many of us. We have lost the ability to love anyone else, to believe in anything outside ourselves, to hope great hopes for the future. The future is our enemy since it will inevitably bring physical decline and death. We try to ignore the fact that we have no hope except to grow old and infirm and to die. To our generation the gospel is truly good news. We are told that God came here, not to preserve His physical existence, but to provide for our spiritual life. His whole life was lived, not for the present, but for the future. Our future. He died for others and was raised in a new body victorious over death. To believe in Him, to know Him is to live life to the fullest, right through the declining years and to the end. Eternal life with Him is waiting beyond that.

♦♦♦♦♦♦

Memory Selection

"For by grace are ye saved through faith; and that not of yourselves; it is the gift of God."
Ephesians 2;8

Many Christians grow up in a legalistic atmosphere. They grow up believing that God's love is distributed to human beings with an eyedropper as a reward for faithful church attendance, tithing and good works. One is driven by the fear that he has never done enough to merit God's love. Then, as one subtracts credits for the sins of omission and commission, the picture becomes impossibly bleak. On the other hand, if one expends extraordinary effort the temptation comes to feel spiritually superior to all who have not done as much.

The memory verse reminds us upon what basis we are loved and accepted by God. All of the Christian faith, in fact all of life itself, is a gift from God. He gave us life in the beginning. Paul wrote the Ephesians that God had chosen them from before the beginning of creation and had plans for them to be at home with Him after creation passed away. He redeemed them from spiritual death, gave them the Christian fellowship, granted them every spiritual blessing in Christ Jesus. Good works were the natural and appropriate reaction of gratitude for God's love. We work, not to win God's love, but to celebrate it and share it with others.

August 1, 1993

Weekday Problems

When she was very small Christine was told that God loves "good" little girls. The clear implication was that He does not love "bad" little girls. Christine thought God's love for her came and went day by day, hour by hour. The moral was very clear: be good so God will love you. All through her childhood, grade school, high school and college years she attempted to do enough good things to outweigh the failures and sins in her life.

At college she earned the nickname of "Christine Do-gooder." She was deeply hurt and could not understand why she was so brutally treated for caring for others and giving herself in service projects. When she married, her husband soon tired of her obsessive tears and compulsive good works. He complained that she could *never relax, enjoy time with him, get off the merry*-go-round of PTA meetings, church activities and volunteer activities at the hospital. She found little joy in all the good she did; her life seemed to be driven by some deep fear she could never shake. Christine always felt breathless, drained, inadequate, defeated. She was also hurt deeply by any criticism of her good works and became extremely defensive.

*How can Christine find peace and joy in her Christian life?
*On what principle should she set about trying to find new balance in her life?

♦♦♦♦♦♦

Superintendent's Sermonette

The Bible is composed of narrative, poetic, doctrinal, and prophetic books. The narrative sections are of four types—problems to be solved, journeys to be completed, searches to be made, and character changes to take place. Even doctrinal sections may lend themselves to this kind of analysis. Our lesson texts are taken from Paul's letter to the Ephesians, and yet they tell a story. The problem of deadness in trespasses and sins needs to be solved. A journey from deadness to fulness of life needs to be completed. A search for the meaning of life needs to be made. A character change needs to take place. Paul writes about all four.

He began right where all sinners are found. They are spiritually dead and held fast by Satan in a lifestyle which will lead them to eternal perdition. Then God comes on the scene to quicken (make alive) those who believe in His Son as their Savior and who accept salvation as a free gift through faith. Believers who do the good works God has ordained for them and who are increasingly strengthened by God's power will be filled with His fulness up to their capacity at any given point. How is the story of your life being developed? Make sure that you follow the plot which God has laid out for you.

NEW LIFE

This Lesson for Your Life

One never feels so powerless as when standing beside the casket of a loved one or friend. Touching the cold, lifeless hand sends chills down the spine. If one does it once she will probably never do it again. Whatever life was with that person is all over. There may have been years of opportunity to change the relationship but no more. No human being can reverse the events; this is the end of the story. We grieve, not only for the loss we feel, but for ourselves. Despite all our posturing to the contrary, we sense that we are powerless when it comes to the most important issues of our lives. It's the same whether one is a pauper or President of the United States. Our power is limited.

Almost as difficult is the problem of human alienation. When a marriage breaks down the two involved may come to a point where reconciliation seems impossible and the relationship seems as cold and lifeless as the body in a casket. Sometimes church fights reach the same unfortunate impasse. Members who have been in fellowship for decades may find it impossible to continue working and worshipping together. In all such cases we human beings are thrown back hard against our limitations. We feel powerless.

Ephesians is a letter full of power. Its message is powerful. Again and again it speaks of a power beyond human strength. God chose the Christians before the beginning of time, redeemed them in the blood of His Son, and had a plan He would accomplish at the end of all things. That plan was "to unite all things in Jesus Christ." He had sealed Christians in His Spirit as His own possession. By His awesome power He raised Jews from spiritual death and gave them new life in Christ. By His mighty power He resurrected Gentiles from spiritual death and made them alive in Christ. They had all been dead, cold, lifeless. Their spiritual death was what they had in common. Because of God's awesome power they now had spiritual life in common. God broke down the walls between them by the body of His Son on the cross. All of this was done to show God's love and dominion.

It is no mystery, then, that Paul would pray for the Ephesians that they would come more and more to know God's awesome power. The same power which raised Jesus from the dead and made Him head over all things to the church. Paul ended the first half of the letter, that portion which explains the great gifts of God's grace, in words of praise and worship. "Now unto Him that is able to do exceeding abundantly above all that we ask or think, according to the power that worketh in us, unto Him be glory in the church by Christ Jesus through all ages, world without end. Amen."

"Unto Him be glory in the church" is an arresting statement. We see God's power in creation. We believe we will see it in the resurrection. But how do we see it in the church here and now. Many today are down on the church. "Give me Jesus, you can have the church" is not an uncommon sentiment even among believers But Paul was high on the church. He did not see it as a human organization run by human power for human ends. He was high on the church as an instrument of God's power and glory in the world. The churches at Ephesus and surrounding towns who would read this letter were not large and impressive. Yet Paul told them they were elected of God before the creation and would be reunited with God as the bride of Christ after creation passed away. It would be "From God to God." Meanwhile the church would be God's showcase in the world. In a world spiritually dead, there would be eternal life in the community of believers. In a world of alienation there would be a fellowship of unlikes. In a self-interested and self-serving world this group would love and give of themselves to others. In a hopeless world theirs would be a grand and certain hope. None of this would bring glory to the church itself. The glory is God's who by His power brought it all to pass.

Seed Thoughts

1. What is the biggest obstacle to salvation by grace?
   Human pride of self-salvation.

2. What does it mean to be spiritually dead?
   To be separated from God, the only Giver of life.

3. How can inquirers know that God can give life?
   He has already given them the life they now have.

4. What is the inspiration for believers to expect new birth?
   God raised Jesus from the dead.

5. Have others actually experienced the joy of spiritual rebirth?
   The Scriptures and church history are full of examples.

(PLEASE TURN PAGE)

---

1. What is the biggest obstacle to salvation by grace?

2. What does it mean to be spiritually dead?

3. How can inquirers know that God can give life?

4. What is the inspiration for believers to expect new birth?

5. Have others actually experienced the joy of spiritual rebirth?

6. What is the only channel through which we can accept the grace of God?

7. Does salvation by grace mean Christians can forget about good works?

8. How can one dead spiritually ever hope to be born again and to be fruitful in good works?

9. Why do all "Twelve Step Programs" begin by admission of inadequacy and asking help from the "Higher Power"?

10. What is God's great cosmic plan for all of us and for all of creation?

(SEED THOUGHTS--Cont'd)

Human pride of self-salvation.

To be separated from God, the only Giver of life.

He has already given them the life they now have.

God raised Jesus from the dead.

The Scriptures and church history are full of examples.

Trusting and obedient faith in His word and promises.

No, we are created by grace precisely for good works.

Only by God's power He promises to us.

Because men and women have found they are powerless on their own.

"To unite all things in Jesus Christ."

6. What is the only channel through which we can accept the grace of God?
Trusting and obedient faith in His word and promises.

7. Does salvation by grace mean Christians can forget about good works?
No, we are created by grace precisely for good works.

8. How can one dead spiritually ever hope to be born again and to be fruitful in good works?
Only by God's power He promises to us.

9. Why do all "Twelve Step Programs" begin by admission of inadequacy and asking help from the "Higher Power"?
Because men and women have found they are powerless on their own.

10. What is God's great cosmic plan for all of us and for all of creation?
"To unite all things in Jesus Christ."

August 8, 1993

New Fellowship

Ephesians 2
11. Wherefore remember, that ye *being* in time past Gentiles in the flesh, who are called Uncircumcision by that which is called the Circumcision in the flesh made by hands;
12. That at that time ye were without Christ, being aliens from the commonwealth of Israel, and strangers from the covenants of promise, having no hope, and without God in the world:
13. But now in Christ Jesus ye who sometimes were far off are made nigh by the blood of Christ.
14. For he is our peace, who hath made both one, and hath broken down the middle wall of partiton *between* us;
15. Having abolished in his flesh the enmity, *even* the law of commandments contained in ordinances; for to make in himself of twain one new man, so making peace;
16. And that he might reconcile both unto God in one body by the cross, having slain the enmity thereby:
17. And came and preached peace to you which were afar off, and to them that were nigh.
18. For through him we both have access by one Spirit unto the Father.
19. Now therefore ye are no more strangers and foreigners, but fellow citizens with the saints, and of the household of God;
20. And are built upon the foundation of the apostles and prophets, Jesus Christ himself being the chief corner stone;
21. In whom all the building fitly framed together groweth unto an holy temple in the Lord:
22. In whom ye also are builded together for an habitation of God through the Spirit.

◆◆◆◆◆◆

◀ **Memory Selection**
Ephesians 2:19

◀ **Devotional Reading**
Hebrews 13:1-7

◀ **Background Scripture**
Ephesians 2:11-3:6

◀ **Printed Scripture**
Ephesians 2:11-22

NEW FELLOWSHIP

Teacher's Target

The Israelites who came out of bondage in Egypt were the products of long years of humiliation. It was in the wilderness that God gave them His law and formed them into an independent nation. It was in Canaan that they grew in numbers and resources. It was in Assyria and Babylon that they were humiliated again. It was back in Canaan that the rebuilding of national life surged ahead, although under foreign domination. By the time Christ came, a mixture of humiliation and nationalism prevailed. Perhaps both contributed to Jewish alienation of all who stood outside of their race and religion. Help your students to see how that alienation of Gentiles was broken down when Jesus Christ died at Calvary to redeem all men who would believe on Him. Reconciliation of Jews and Gentiles to God prefaced reconciliation of believers from both sides to one another. This new fellowship was founded on Christ, the apostles, and New Testament prophets. Paul compared it to a building growing into a holy temple.

Lesson Introduction

Judaism has not been known for being an expanding, missionary-minded religion. Jews knew that God had made them a chosen, privileged people when He offered them the law at Mount Sinai. "Now therefore, if ye will obey my voice indeed, and keep my covenant, then ye shall be a peculiar treasure unto me above all people: ...and ye shall be unto me a kingdom of priests, and an holy nation" (Exod. 19:5-6).

Over the centuries, Jews allowed themselves to become proud and arrogant regarding their law and traditions. They admitted few proselytes (adherents) to share their divine oracles and worship, but they limited the number. They appeared to overlook such references as Isaiah 42:6, 49:6, and 60:3, which predicted the light of truth shining out to draw in Gentiles from all of the nations. Many found it difficult or impossible to embrace Christ's universal appeal to all men, but a few learned to welcome it.

Teaching Outline

I. Aliens: Eph. 2:11-12
 A. Gentile: 11
 B. Godless: 12
II. Allies: Eph. 2:13-18
 A. Approach: 13-17
 B. Access: 18
III. Additions: Eph. 2:19-22
 A. Fellowcitizens: 19
 B. Foundation: 20
 C. Frame: 21-22

Daily Bible Readings

Mon. Man's Hopeless Condition
Eph. 2:11-16
Tue. Together in the Household of God
Eph. 2:17-22
Wed. Dead to Sin
Rom. 6:1-74
Thu. The Inward Struggle
Rom. 7:14-25
Fri. Controlled by the Spirit
Rom. 8:1-10
Sat. Inseparable
Rom. 8:35-39
Sun. Justified by Faith
Gal. 2:16-21

August 8, 1993

VERSE BY VERSE

I. Aliens: Eph. 2:11-12

A. Gentile: 11

11. Wherefore remember, that ye being in time past Gentiles in the flesh, who are called Uncircumcision by that which is called the Circumcision in the flesh made by hands:

Paul told his Gentile readers to remember when they, as Gentiles in the physical sense, had also been strangers from God in the spiritual sense. Jews who had been literally circumcised had called them "uncircumcised" as an epithet of disdain. God had required all Jewish males from the time of Abraham, their progenitor, to have their foreskins excised as a symbol that they belonged to Jehovah. This was usually done on the eighth day after birth. It was supposed to represent Jewish separation from sin, but it was carried on long after its spiritual significance was abandoned, thus leading to hypocrisy. The difference between Jews and Gentiles on moral and spiritual levels became blurred, although Jews did not like to admit it.

B. Godless: 12

12. That at that time ye were without Christ, being aliens from the commonwealth of Israel, and strangers from the covenants of promise, having no hope, and without God in the world:

In time past (vs. 11), the Ephesian Gentiles had been without a knowledge of Christ. Those who were not proselytes to Judaism were alienated from the commonwealth of Israel, and they were strangers from the covenants of promise, which the Amplified Bible calls "the sacred compacts of the promise." Therefore, they had no hope or promise, and they were without God in this world. They were spiritually helpless and lost. This is the way Gentiles had remained until about the middle of the first century of the Christian era, but then there was a dramatic change for those who heard and accepted the gospel of Jesus Christ.

II. Allies: Eph. 2:13-18

A. Approach: 13-17

13. But now in Christ Jesus ye who sometimes were far off are made nigh by the blood of Christ.

Here is the basic statement of change, followed by several verses of elaboration. Those who had been alienated and afar off could be brought close by means of the blood Jesus shed to atone for sins while on the cross at Calvary. This served as a covering for the sins of those who put their trust in Christ. God looked at them, saw the covering, and counted them righteous in Him. This is the doctrine of justification by faith. It is the *only* acceptable approach which sinners can make to a holy God.

14. For he is our peace, who hath made both one, and hath broken down the middle wall of partition between us;

Note the recurrent use of the term "peace" in this passage. Jesus Christ *is* our peace, He *made* peace, and He *preached* peace (vss. 14, 15, 17). The initiative in bringing peace to the two antagonistic groups, Jews and Gentiles, came from Christ. He became peace personified, the divine instrument for creating it. There had been a hostile barrier, called here "the middle wall of partition," dividing them for many centuries. Even in the temple complex in Jerusalem, there had been a wall literally separating Jews from non-Jewish proselytes in the court of the Gentiles. Confined there, Gentiles could not participate in the most sacred ceremonies of Judaism. It is interesting to realize that that wall was destroyed when the Romans sacked Jerusalem in A.D. 70, but it is more important to realize that the "wall of hostility" between Jewish and Gentile Christians was eliminated before then.

15. Having abolished in his flesh the enmity, even the law of commandments contained in ordinances; for to make in himself of twain one new man, so making peace;

There is similar wording in Hebrews 10: 19-20—[We have] therfore, brethren, boldness to enter into the holiest by the blood of Jesus, by a new a living way which he hath consecrated for us, through the veil, that is to say, his flesh.

Paul said that Jesus abolished the enmity which separated sinful men from a holy God by sacrificing His flesh (body) at Calvary. The law of commandments contained in divine ordinances was annulled when He brought Jewish and Gentile believers together into one new man (people), thus creating peace between them through union in Himself. Colossians 1:20 is a parallel verse—"God made peace through his Son's death on the cross and so brought back to himself all things" (Today's English Version), Union is found only in God and Christ.

16. And that he might reconcile both unto God in one body by the cross, having slain the enmity thereby:

What Colossians 1:20 says that God did, Ephesians 2:16 says that Christ also did, thus showing the united action of Father and Son. Verse 15 states that Christ abolished the enmity which had existed, while verse 16 states that He slew it. Verse 15 states that Christ did this in his flesh, while verse 16 states that He did this reconciling work in His body on the cross. The truth of what happened is strengthened by the repetition of concepts using different terms.

17. And came and preached peace to you which were afar off, and to them that were nigh.

Jesus came to preach the gospel to all men. He confined Himself primarily to the Jews who were close to Him in His own country. His followers were given a commission by Him to take it to all the world, referring to those afar off. Isaiah the prophet called Him "The Prince of Peace" (Isa. 9:6). The angels announced His birth by wishing "on earth peace, good will toward men" (Luke 2:14), Jesus promised peace to His followers (John 14:27). He offered inner peace, even in times of trouble, and He offered eternal peace with Himself in heaven. No distinction was made between Jewish and Gentile followers in these things.

B. Access: 18

18. For through him we both have access by one Spirit unto the Father.

In another place, Paul wrote, "Being justified by faith, we have peace with God through our Lord Jesus Christ: by whom also we have access by faith into this grace wherein we stand" (Rom. 5:1-2). He added, "The love of God is shed abroad in our hearts by the Holy Ghost which is given unto us" (Rom, 5:1). In still another place, he wrote, "By one Spirit are we all baptized into one body, whether we be Jews or Gentiles, whether we be bond or free; and have been all made to drink into one Spirit" (1 Cor, 12:13). Ephesians 2:18 is an abbreviated version of these truths regarding the ministry played by the Holy Spirit in bringing believers to God the Father through Christ the Son.

III. Additions: Eph. 2:19-22

A. Fellow citizens: 19

19. Now therefore ye are no more strangers and foreigners, but fellowcitizens with the saints, and of the household of God;

This is a transition verse, moving from consideration of the union of Jewish and Gentiles believers in Christ to the building of the household of God, The wording in this and subsequent verses obviously does not refer to a literal building but to a spiritual building. All who came to Christ from either a sinful Jewish background or Gentile background became fellowcitizens (full members) with the saints (born-again believers).

B. Foundation: 20

20a. And are built upon the foundation of the apostles and prophets, ...

This is an interesting description. Paul said that the household of God, later called a holy temple and a habitation of God, was built on a foundation composed in part of the apostles and prophets. We know who the apostles were, for they were listed for us in a passage such as Mark 3:16-19, We know that Judas Iscariot committed suicide and was replace by Matthias (Acts 1:16-26). We know that others, such as Paul and Barnabas, were also called apostles.

Prophets are those who bear a message from God to the people. It often is a message contrary to popular prejudice and frequently involves a judgement. It is, on occasion, predictive but this is usually in the form of warning of consequences of disobedience.

20b. ... Jesus Christ himself being the chief corner stone;

The truth about Christ being the Son of the living God was the rock on which His church is built (Matt. 16:16-18). Paul wrote, "Other foundation can no man lay than that is laid, which is Jesus Christ" (1 Cor. 3:11). Ephesians 2:20 and 1 Peter 2:6 identify Jesus Christ as the chief cornerstone. It was not only what Jesus said, but what He did, which qualified Him to be the main component in the foundation of the household of God.

C. Frame: 21-22

21. In whom all the building fitly framed together groweth unto an holy temple in the Lord:

A complete building has to have not only a good foundation but a well-built superstructure. That is where individual believers find their places and their functions. When comparing the church to a body, Paul said, "Now hath God set the members every one of them in the body, as it pleased him" (1 Cor. 12:18). He went on to describe various members of that body and what they did. In Ephesians 2:21-22 the metaphor changes to parts in a building's superstructure, but the concept is the same. God places believers into His building so that they might serve as "lively stones" (1 Pet. 2:5). He expects each one to help develop it into a holy temple revealing His presence to all. In another place, Paul asked, "Know ye not that ye are the temple of God, and that the Spirit of God dwelleth in you?" (1 Cor. 3:16).

22. In whom ye also are builded together for an habitation of God through the Spirit.

We know that stones taken from a quarry have to undergo several steps in their prepartion for being used in a building. They have to be cut to size, ground down, and perhaps polished. Since they are inanimate, they feel nothing. The same is not true of "living stones" being prepared to fit into God's habitation New converts have many rough edges which have to be ground down and polished in order for them to function properly in God's living temple. However, it is through the comforting and enabling ministry of the Holy Spirit that this work goes on through the lifetime of each Christian. Someday the last addition to this building will be made, and Christ will come again to take the saints home to heaven.

NEW FELLOWSHIP

Evangelistic Emphasis

Not all the homeless of our land live under bridges or sleep on the streets. In fact, the vast majority have plenty of food, fine clothing, no problem with shelter or transportation. They are not jobless, many of them are consumed with well-paying, pressurized jobs. They are, nevertheless, homeless. "Sometimes you want to go where everybody knows your name," says the lead-in of a popular TV situation comedy about a bar in Boston. It's true, people frequent the local watering holes, not for the liquor, but for the fellowship. They feel homeless, alone, forsaken. If for a few minutes at the end of the day they can find friendship, someone to talk to, a common understanding of the day's battles they'll come back again and again.

It's clear that many of today's homeless are Christians in need of a church home. When one of these homeless persons, believer or unbeliever, enters a community of Christian faith he or she should feel something like the fellowship at the corner bar, only much better. The church is to be a place where everybody knows your name, where everyone owns up to being the same, where love and loyalty are the rules. This should be the place where anyone can find a group, a friend. Long before one of these homeless ones hears the sermon or reads the words in the hymnal he or she should feel the warmth of acceptance and love.

Memory Selection

"Now therefore you are no more strangers and foreigners, but fellow citizens with the saints, and of the household of God; . . ."
Ephesians 2:19

The most serious problem in the early church was the Jew-Gentile problem. Jesus' disciples thought it odd that he would talk with Roman centurions or visit with a woman of Samaria. They could not understand why he kept crossing the Sea of Galilee to touch, heal and teach people who spoke a different language, looked different, even smelled different. Peter had problems with the Gentile question all his life. Even after Jesus' death, resurrection and ascension when the disciples had received the commission to go into all the world to preach the gospel, Peter balked at going to Cornelius. Later, for fear of brotherhood disapproval, Peter withdrew from the table of the Gentiles when certain Jews were coming from Jerusalem.

Even Paul never got over the wonder that God loved the Gentiles and included them in his kingdom. For him it was the mystery of mysteries. The book of Ephesians sets out God's plan of all creation and all the ages: to unite all things in Jesus Christ. (1:10) For Jewish and Gentile Christians to work and fellowship together they had to see their small enterprize in the context of God's eternal plan. The Gentiles should remember that they had once been far away, strangers to God's covenant of Abraham. Because of God's amazing grace in Christ they were now full citizens in the kingdom, full heirs in the family

August 8, 1993

Weekday Problems

Cecil was a problem in the Finance Ministry at church. He was gifted in money management, committed to the fellowship, 100 percent involved. That was just his problem. He was so intense that others found it hard to work with him. He was convinced that the church's first priority should be on outreach programs. "If we are not using the Lord's money to reach out to others we have no right to exist as a church," he often said.

Cecil had no patience for emphasis and expenditure on in-house ministries: elementary education, teen programs, family enrichment, concerns for the elderly. He came from a non-church background. The only time he ever heard God's name used when he was growing up was when his father used it in vain. He spent six years in the Marines, pursuing "wine, women, and song." After the service he entered college where he met his wife-to-be. He was ready to make some changes in his life. She introduced him to the Lord and he made his confession and became a Christian. Ever since then Cecil was completely devoted to the outreach programs at church. He continually told his story as proof that outreach was the only really important concern of the church.

*What do you think is Cecil's problem?
*How should others try to help him'?

◆◆◆◆◆◆

Superintendent's Sermonette

Today's lesson is based on Paul's teaching that Gentiles were once alienated from the commonwealth of Israel, strangers to the covenants of promise, and without God or hope. Then Jesus Christ came to die on the cross, shed His blood, and make atonement for all men. Both Jewish and Gentile believers were welcomed into the redeemed family of God. There they found their places and their functions in becoming a holy temple in which the Lord's presence could be known. Let us ask God to shape and mold us into His holy habitation.

NEW FELLOWSHIP

This Lesson for Your Life

In the first century there were many clubs and associations to which people belonged. Trade guilds were something like our trade unions. Philosophical societies lived in major centers of learning for the exploration of truth. Burial clubs were formed in which members pooled their resources and pledged to one another that they would see to it that a proper burial was provided when members died. Then there were various religious groups. Across the Roman Empire Jews met in synagogues which served as community centers, schools, and places of worship. Temples to various pagan gods drew people together for worship, often for revelry and to buy off the capricious deities. People had a need to belong, to be a part of something larger than themselves. The yearning for fellowship was very strong.

The same is true today. We have garden clubs, book clubs, fishing and hunting associations. Our political energies can be channelled into any of a number of party organizations or candidates campaigns. Professional and trade associations abound. Special interest groups exist to protect the environment, prevent gun control, and rid the highways of drunken drivers. Religious organizations come in the thousands. Eastern and Western religions vie for devotees. As in the first century world, people need to belong.

The letter of Paul to the Ephesians gives the most exalted view of the church found in Scripture. From this book we should ask what the church is, what its aims are, and what makes it unique as a fellowship. What is there about the Lord's church which claims our loyalty and involvement beyond service organizations like the Rotary Club and the Junior League?

To begin with the church was God's idea, not the idea of any group of human beings. Paul told the Ephesians they were chosen from before the foundation of the world. They were to be a redeemed body of people, gifted with the finest treasures of heaven, called to participate in the world's greatest mission. In Ephesians 1:10 Paul explains what the great cosmic plan of God is in all time and creation. After all is said and done, God will "unite all things in Christ Jesus." Set in the context of the biblical narrative, this aim refers to the fall of mankind in the beginning. Man's grasping determination not to be limited in any way, to have it all, to be as God, brought alienation and fragmentation. The Creator and His creatures were alienated. Adam and Eve knew tension between them for the first time. The result of their pride and estrangement was an atmosphere in which one of their sons murdered the other. Even creation itself was splintered and set askew. Who would repair the damage? "All the king's horses and all the king's men could not put Humpty Dumpty together again." The loving Father Who created human beings was determined to redeem them, make them whole once again, bring them back home to Himself and into fellowship with one another. His plan was "to unite all things in Christ Jesus."

The church is not unique because the people in it are sinless saints. It is not different because those who comprise it are free of pride, ignorance and lust for power. The church is unique because God planned it as a showcase for the world to show that He could put things back together which seemed hopeless beyond repair. If one visited one of those little churches Paul established he could see a miracle. Jew and Gentile, slave and master, men and women, young and old, educated and illiterate met together around the Lord's Table to recite His words, recall His life of service, remember His death and resurrection. It was He who they had in common.

Seed Thoughts

1. On what basis should any believer feel a sense of belonging in a Christian community?
On the basis of what God did on Golgotha.

2. Does Christianity begin with a shared negative or a shared positive?
A shared negative, we are all in need and not adequate in ourselves.

3. What is the shared positive that bonds us together in the Lord?
His wisdom, love and power which breaks down the walls and makes us alive together.

4. Why do some Christians feel like outsiders all their lives?
There are many possible reasons, perhaps they do not feel good enough to associate with other Christians.

5. What can we do to make the Christian who feels unwanted feel wanted?
We might first check to see if our fellowship is centered in the cross of Christ.

(PLEASE TURN PAGE)

---

1. On what basis should any believer feel a sense of belonging in a Christian community?

2. Does Christianity begin with a shared negative or a shared positive?

3. What is the shared positive that bonds us together in the Lord?

4. Why do some Christians feel like outsiders all their lives?

5. What can we do to make the Christian who feels unwanted feel wanted?

6. What kinds of persons qualify for membership in the Lord's church?

7. What was Paul's program for bringing peace between races and classes of people?

8. What is the most insidious form of prejudice common among Christians and churches?

9. Name some of the natural ties which bind other groups together.

10. Is the church to be a perfect example of God's reconciling power in Christ?

(SEED THOUGHTS--Cont'd)

On the basis of what God did on Golgotha.

A shared negative, we are all in need and not adequate in ourselves.

His wisdom, love and power which breaks down the walls and makes us alive together.

There are many possible reasons, perhaps they do not feel good enough to associate with other Christians.

We might first check to see if our fellowship is centered in the cross of Christ.

Those who are sinners like the rest of us.

Speaking of Christ he said: "He is our peace."

Moral prejudice, the illusion that we are too far above the unwashed to accept them.

Race, poltical philosophy, special interests, professional interests, quest for pleasure.

No, nothing involving human beings is ever perfect. But here and there, now and again God's hand is seen reconciling Christians in profound ways.

6. What kinds of persons qualify for membership in the Lord's church?
Those who are sinners like the rest of us.

7. What was Paul's program for bringing peace between races and classes of people?
Speaking of Christ he said: "He is our peace."

8. What is the most insidious form of prejudice common among Christians and churches?
Moral prejudice, the illusion that we are too far above the unwashed to accept them.

9. Name some of the natural ties which bind other groups together.
Race, poltical philosophy, special interests, professional interests, quest for pleasure.

10. Is the church to be a perfect example of God's reconciling power in Christ?
No, nothing involving human beings is ever perfect. But here and there, now and again God's hand is seen reconciling Christians in profound ways.

August 15, 1993

WHERE THERE'S NO LOVE IS NO PEACE

New Behavior

Ephesians 5
Be ye therefore followers of God, as dear children;
2. And walk in love as Christ also hath loved us, and hath given himself for us an offering and a sacrifice to God for a sweet smelling savour.
3. But fornication, and all uncleanness, or covetousness, let it not be once named among you, as becometh saints;
4. Neither filthiness, nor foolish talking, nor jesting which are not convenient: but rather giving of thanks.
5. For this ye know, that no whoremonger, nor unclean person, nor covetous man, who is an idolater, hath any inheritance in the kingdom of Christ and of God.
6. Let no man deceive you with vain words: for because of these things cometh the wrath of God upon the children of disobedience.
7. Be not ye therefore partakers with them.
8. For ye were sometimes darkness, but now are ye light in the Lord: walk as children of light:
9. (For the fruit of the Spirit is in all goodness and righteousness and truth;)
10. Proving what is acceptable unto the Lord.
11. And have no fellowship with the unfruitful works of darkness, but rather reprove them.
12. For it is a shame even to speak of those things which are done of them in secret.
13. But all things that are reproved are made manifest by the light: for whatsoever doth make manifest is light.
14. Wherefore he saith, AWAKE THOU THAT SLEEPEST, AND ARISE FROM THE DEAD, AND CHRIST SHALL GIVE THEE LIGHT.
15. See then that ye walk circumspectly, not as fools, but as wise,
16. Redeeming the time, because the days are evil.
17. Wherefore be ye not unwise, but understanding what the will of the Lord is.
18. And be not drunk with wine, wherein is excess; but be filled with the Spirit
19. Speaking to yourselves in psalms and hymns and spiritual songs, singing and making melody in your heart to the Lord;
20. Giving thanks always for all things unto God and the Father in the name of our Lord Jesus Christ

◆◆◆◆◆◆

◀ **Memory Selection**
Ephesians 5:1-2

◀ **Devotional Reading**
Ephesians 4:25-32

◀ **Background Scripture**
Ephesians 5:1-20

◀ **Printed Scripture**
Ephesians 5:1-20

NEW BEHAVIOR

Teacher's Target

It is one thing to believe in great Christian truths, but it is something else to walk in them. In his letter to the Ephesian believers, Paul urged them to "walk in love" (Eph. 5:2), to "walk as children of light" (Eph. 5:8), and to "walk circumspectly, not as fools, but as wise" (Eph. 5:15). Throughout this lesson's text we note contrasts between following these directives and behaving in sinful ways. The light of truth stands out more clearly when shown against the blackness of evil.

Help your students to realize that their testimony must go beyond doctrinal statements and find application in everyday living. First-century Christians had to stand in stark contrast to the raw paganism of their time. Twentieth-century Christians have to do the same. Paul's comments on Godly living have relevance for us today. Science and technology have made sweeping changes in our lives, but human nature remains the same, and we need time-tested principles to guide us.

Lesson Introduction

Those of us who have had the benefits of over nineteen centuries of Christian heritage may feel shocked when we study the lesson's text, because we may wonder if Paul seriously anticipated believers indulging in such evils as fornication, covetousness, filthiness, foolish talking, jesting, whoremongering, idolatry, and drunkenness. Did he mention such things because Ephesian believers had recently come out of degraded heathenism and might be tempted to return to it? Was his concern dated for his period of history and therefore obsolete in today's Christendom?

Let us not be naive. Every sin mentioned by Paul, plus many more, can tempt Christians today and contribute to their fall. Scandalous behavior on the part of believers is not hard to find. That is why it is vitally important that continual emphasis be placed on the kind of Godly walk which will keep Christians on the straight and narrow path and help them avoid sinful detours and pitfalls.

Teaching Outline

I. Walk in Love: Eph. 5:1-7
  A. Examples: 1-2
  B. Evils: 3-4
  C. Evildoers: 5-7
II. Walk in Light: Eph. 5:8-17
  A. Children of light: 8-10
  B. Conduct in light: 11-17
III. Walk in the Spirit:
   Eph. 5:18-20
  A. Expectation: 18
  B. Expression: 19-20

Daily Bible Readings

Mon. Servants of Righteousness
Rom. 6:15-23
Tue. Obedience
I John 2:3-11
Wed. You Cannot Serve God and Mammon - *Luke 16:9-13*
Thu. Duties of the Christian Life
Eph. 5:15-21
Fri. Integrity Marks the Christian
Luke 11:33-42
Sat. Walk in New Life
Eph. 5:4-11
Sun. The Surrendered Life
Rom. 12:1-8

August 15, 1993

VERSE BY VERSE

I. Walk in Love: Eph. 5:1-7

A. Examples: 1-2

1. Be ye therefore followers of God, as dear children;

What did Paul mean when he said that believers should imitate God as dearly-beloved children love their earthly fathers? An example from the Old Testament may be found in Leviticus 19:2—"Ye shall be holy: for I the Lord your God am holy." A New Testament example may be found in Matthew 5:48—"Be ye therefore perfect even as your Father which is in heaven is perfect." Believers cannot be divine, but they can take on divine characteristics. God Himself provides an example to follow.

2. And walk in love, as Christ also hath loved us, and hath given himself for us an offering and a sacrifice to God for a sweetsmelling savour.

It was love which caused God to send His beloved Son to die so that He might provide atonement for sinners (John 3:16). It was love which motivated Jesus to submit to this humiliation at Calvary. The crucifixion was hideous, but it was for such a wonderful cause that it was wafted to heaven as a sweet aroma acceptable to God. For thousands of years He had received the sacrificial animal offerings presented by the Jews, but they were but forerunners and types of the perfect sacrifice of His Son as He died on the cross. Jesus provided an example of love to be followed.

B. Evils: 3-4

3. But fornication, and all uncleanness, or covetousness, let it not be once named among you, as becometh saints;

Paul listed three evils which saints should avoid entirely. They are fornication uncleanness, and covetousness. All three are manifestations of a selfish attitude.

4. Neither filthiness, nor foolish talking, nor jesting, which are not convenient: but rather giving of thanks.

The New International Version puts it this way—"Nor should there be obscenity, foolish talk, or coarse joking, which are out of place, but rather thanksgiving." If we spend time each day with unbelievers out in the world, we know how prevalent their evil expressions are. Christians are supposed to avoid vulgarity and speak graciously.

C. Evildoers: 5-7

5. For this ye know, that no whoremonger nor unclean person, nor covetous man, who is an idolater, hath any inheritance in the kingdom of Christ and of God.

The Living Bible puts it this way—"You can be sure of this: The kingdom of Christ and of God will never belong to anyone who is impure or greedy, for a greedy person is really an idol worshiper—he loves and worships the good things of this life more than God." Paul was referring here not just to evils but to evildoers. First-century Christians could look around them and see such people. Whatever they acquired had to be found in this life, for they had no prospect of entering the future kingdom of Christ and of God, and that contributed to their covetousness.

6. Let no man deceive you with vain words: for because of these things cometh the wrath of God upon the children of disobedience.

7. Be not ye therefore partakers with them.

Paul warned believers not to be fooled by empty words by those who promoted various evils. They stood under the threat of divine judgment reserved for "the children of disobedience" (cf. Eph. 2:2). Although Paul had previously said that believers had in time past walked according to the course of this sinful world-system, he now spoke as if they were still being fellow partakers of evil things, and he wanted them to stop it. Two things seem apparent here. First, he was using his apostolic authority. Second, he was using moral persuasion. In these first seven verses of Ephesians 5, we see the contrast between love which originated with God and evil which originated with Satan.

II. Walk in light: Eph. 5:8-17

A. Children of light: 8-10

8. For ye were sometimes darkness, but now are ye light in the Lord: walk as children of light:

Paul reminded believers in Ephesus that their life in darkness was supposed to be left behind. They had entered the kingdom of light (Col. 1:12-13). Light in the Bible often refers to truth and/or holiness based on divine truth. It describes a whole way of life. Believers are expected to walk in light on the path laid out for them, because they are now known as "children of light."

9. (For the fruit of the Spirit is in all righteousness and truth;)

Some manuscripts substitute "the Spirit" for "the fruit." The Amplified Bible reads—"For the fruit—the effect, the product—of the Light, the Spirit (consists) in every form of kindly goodness, uprightness of heart and trueness of life." A parallel reference is Galatians 5:22-23, which lists nine fruits of the Spirit as being love, joy, peace, longsuffering, gentleness, goodness, faith (or faithfulness), meekness, and temperance (or discipline). These express goodness, righteousness, and truth or holiness of life.

10. Proving what is acceptable unto the Lord.

This finishes the thought begun in the latter part of verse 8—"Walk as children of light: . . .proving what is acceptable unto the Lord." Christians are to learn what pleases the Lord through their everyday experiences. They will be guided by the light of divine truths revealed to them.

B. Conduct in light: 11-17

11. And have no fellowship with the unfruitful works of darkness, but rather reprove them.

Here again, as in verse 7, the wording suggests that believers in Ephesus were associating with evildoers to some extent. Paul wanted them to cut themselves off from close contact with those who walked in spiritual darkness. They were, in fact, urged to reprove them, although we do not know if this involved verbal rebuke or simply rebuke by the testimony of a Godly life.

12. For it is a shame even to speak of those things which are done of then in secret.

It is suggested that what Paul was saying here was that it was shameful for believers to speak of the evils done by sinners without at the same time reproving them (vs.11). However, verse 13 could be seen as describing a Godly testimony exposing shameful things done by sinners and thus avoiding the use of verbal rebuke.

13. But all things that are reproved are made manifest by the light: for whatsoever doth make manifest is light.

Consistent holy living by believers causes Satan, his demons, and sinful people to be uncomfortable. They do not like their works of darkness to be exposed to the light of divine truth. This will be truth whether they are laid bare through Christians' verbal rebukes or through their testimonies.

14. Wherefore he saith, Awake thou that sleepest, and arise from the dead, and Christ shall give thee light.

We are not sure of the derivation of this statement. It may have been combined from different sources. One might be, "Awake and sing, ye that dwell in dust: for thy dew is as the dew of herbs, and the earth shall cast out the dead" (Isa. 26:19). Another might be, "Arise, shine; for thy light is come, and the glory of the Lord is risen upon thee" (Isa. 60:1). Paul obviously added the last part about Christ giving light to those who heed the call to awaken from spiritual deadness.

15. See then that ye walk circumspectly, not as fools, but as wise,

16. Redeeming the time, because the days are evil.

In addition to walking in love (vs. 2) and walking in light (vs. 8), Paul urged believers to walk circumspectly (carefully). In contrast to sinners, who were foolish, believers were to be wise. They were to redeem the time, meaning that they were to buy up every opportunity for doing good, because the days in which they lived were evil. We could say the same about our modern times. Christians can keep on the right track only as they study, believe, and act upon the divine principles laid down in God's Holy Word.

17. Wherefore be ye not unwise, but understanding what the will of the Lord is.

This is a summary statement, showing Paul's concern that believers avoid foolishness by embracing the will of the Lord as revealed in His Word. They will always act wisely, if they are governed by it.

III. Walk in the Spirit: Eph. 5:18-20

A. Expectation: 18

18a. And be not drunk with wine, wherein is excess; . . .

The Bible contains many warnings against drunkenness attributed to an excessive imbibing of wine. The record of Bible-believing Christians has added beer, liquor, and illicit drugs to the list. Those who allow themselves to come under the domination of these ingested substances create difficulties for themselves and for many other people.

18b. . . but be filled with the Spirit;

In contrast to domination by harmful substances, Paul urged believers to be filled and controlled by the Holy Spirit.

The wording here suggests that this is to be a continual infilling. New challenges would demand new infillings for believers. Believers should be open to the Holy Spirit for daily infilling and guidance.

B. Expression: 19-20

19. Speaking to yourselves in psalms and hymns and spiritual songs, singing and making melody in your heart to the Lord;

You may recall that we touched on this same subject in Lesson 7 earlier this quarter when we studied Colossians 3:16, Paul said that Christians should teach and admonish one another with psalms, hymns, and spiritual songs, singing with grace in their hearts to the Lord. Ephesians 5:19 says essentially the same thing. Psalms set to music and sung by the Israelites were common. They were used in the early Christian church—"When ye come together, every one of you hath a psalm" (1 Cor. 14: 26)—"Is any among you afflicted? let him pray. Is any merry? let him sing psalms" (Jas. 5:13). Hymns may have been specially designed to give God praise, such as the "praises" sung to God by Paul and Silas in the Philippian jail (Acts 16:25). We are uncertain about spiritual songs, but they may have contained exhortations and prophecies.

20. Giving thanks always for all things unto God and the Father in the name of our Lord Jesus Christ.

Colossians 3:17 is quite similar— "And whatsoever ye do in word or deed, do all in the name of the Lord Jesus, giving thanks to God and the Father by him." Once again, we note that it is by expressing ourselves in music that we send our gratitude heavenward for all that the Lord Jesus Christ has done and is doing for us. This kind of worship pleases God the Father. It also is enjoyed by believers who participate in it, and this helps to explain the importance music has played in Christian worship from the first century onward. Someday they will join the heavenly chorus (Rev. 19:5-6).

NEW BEHAVIOR

Evangelistic Emphasis

"I don't need Christianity or the church. That church down there is full of hypocrites!" We may want to get defensive and reply: "No, it's not full, we have room for one more. Come on in." It is true that unbelievers often use the imperfections of Christians as a shield against God's moving in their lives.; We want to show them that the church is composed of sinners redeemed and being redeemed by the blood of Christ. The pretension that we have arrived will turn people away from the Lord. So we should confess openly that we all fall short of the glory of God and stand before Him, not in our own goodness, but in His.

On the other hand, the world has a right to observe how we live and compare our words and our lives. Paul admonished the Romans to present themselves body and soul to the Lord to be "transformed by the renewing of their minds . . ." Outsiders who see no observable growth in Christians over the years have a right to ask questions. Said positively, a church composed of Christians taking their discipleship seriously, submitting themselves to the teaching and Lordship of Jesus, adjusting their lives accordingly is a power tool for evangelistic outreach. The synagogue of Paul's day was attractive to the pagans because of its high moral teachings and practice. Nowhere else in the world of the time could one find such lofty ethical standards taught as those contained in the covenant theology of Israel and the Ten Commandments. The church inherited that moral seriousness and won many converts because of its values and lifestyle. This truth presents us a painful diagnostic question about the church when we do not see people coming to the Lord.

◆◆◆◆◆◆

Memory Selection

"Be ye therefore followers of God, as dear children; And walk in love, as Christ also hath loved us and hath given himself for our offering."
Ephesians 5:1,2

"Be imitators of God, as beloved children. And walk in love, as Christ loved us and gave himself up for us,..." is how the RSV translates this passage. There is something beautiful about children playing dress-up in their parents' clothes. Struggling to keep the shoes on, the hat down over the ears, the little one parades proudly for all to see. Responsible parents enjoy the game and contemplate the task of being a role model. The admiration of mom or dad is obvious.

Paul puts the moral claims of the faith in these terms. Christians are to be serious about their morality, not out of fear, but out of love for their Father.

How do they know their Father and what He is like? Jesus told the twelve in John 1:3: "if you have seen me you have seen the Father." In I John the apostle says the Christian personality and lifestyle is not something one produces from scratch by his or her own design. Since Christians have life in them from the Father, they show a family likeness. The common characteristic most noticeable is love. Not a sentimental, bargain-basement love which is all words and no action. The kind of love which moved God to send His Son here for us. The kind of love which took Jesus to the cross where he "gave himself up for us."

August 15, 1993

Weekday Problems

Sinclair came into the minister's study with a thick folder of materials. He had for several years been on the road as the lead singer for a band. His eleven-by-fourteen promotional glossies pictured him as, indeed, a very handsome young man. He had almost made the big time, just one step away from a record contract in Nashville. When that fell through the group decided to disband. He settled in a major city and began working various jobs. He was especially good as a salesman.

Despite the good money, his life was incomplete. He started attending church, looking for a Christian girl to marry. He attended a weekend singles' retreat and met an attractive, committed Christian woman. She had been divorced and was struggling to feed her two little children. Before two months were up they decided to get married. She moved from a small town to the city. No sooner had she moved in than both were disillusioned. He seemed always to be gone. She was miserable in the metropolis. "When we first met she assured me that she could have children. Now she told me that she could not; normal sexual relations were out. She hated my two expensive dogs. One cold winter night she put them out on the patio. When I came home we had an enormous fight. The next day she packed up and left and we got a divorce. Do you think I have a scriptural right to marry again?"

*What would you think from this brief description were the problems in this marriage?
*Where would you start in counseling Sinclair?

♦♦♦♦♦♦

Superintendent's Sermonette

Non-Christians are sometimes shocked when they come into contact with real Christians. They are surprised at differences in the way believers think, speak, and act. That is the way it should be. Nominal Christians, who seem to be almost identical with the sinful world system, are not likely to surprise anyone. We may criticize them, but, if we are not careful, we can gradually drift in their direction and become like them. If we do, we shall soon lose our distinctiveness and our testimony as we merge into the crowd.

Our lesson today shows us that it is important for us to get onto the path of righteousness and stay there. Paul urged believers in Ephesus to walk in love, walk in light, and walk circumspectly (Eph. 5:2, 8, and 15). He also urged them to be filled with the Holy Spirit and to express their devotion through music.

If we want to be outstanding Christians, we must know the will of God shown through the Word of God and be determined to live by it. This will not be easy, and we may suffer scorn from the world, but the rewards will be great. Are you ready to consecrate yourself fully to Christ and make your whole life an offering of praise to God for Him?

NEW BEHAVIOR

This Lesson for Your Life

"I therefore, the prisoner of the Lord, beg you to lead a life worthy of the calling to which you have been called." with these words Paul begins the ethical section of Ephesians. In the last three chapters there are many imperatives. "Be angry and do not sin; do not let the sun go down on your anger . . ." "Let no evil talk come out of your mouths . . ." "Put away from you all bitterness and wrath and anger and wrangling and slander, together with all malice and be kind to one another . . ." "But fornication and impurity of any kind, or greed, must not even be mentioned among you, . . .," "Be subject to one another . . ." "Be strong in the Lord . . .

Imperatives turn many people off. Many believers were reared in legalistic homes where Christianity was full of rules, regulations and imperatives. They went to church and heard the preacher shout commands week after week. They were almost tempted to give up the faith when they were saved by hearing for the first time someone teaching grace. It was sunshine and fresh air after life in a dark, dank cellar. To discover that "you were saved by grace and that not of yourselves, it is the qift of God" was a wonderful new lease on spiritual life. After striving for perfection what wonderful good news it is to learn that God does not demand perfection of us, He sent His only Son to do it perfectly. "Therefore, since we are justified by faith, we have peace with God through our Lord Jesus Christ..." That's the truth of the gospel Luther discovered in Romans and It redeemed his life from anguished self-salvation. It is the core gospel about which John Newton wrote in his immortal hymn, "Amazing Grace."

Other Christians and unbelievers turn away from passages like Ephesians 4 through 6 because it sounds childishly simplistic to tell people to be good. A religion full of moralisms has no power except to insult the intelligence of all who have any understanding of human nature. "Be good," "Be sweet," "Be kind," have some place in a kindergarten classroom. But adults are not helped out of moral dilemmas by such simplistic admonitions.

Perhaps we should look once again at the ethical teachings in Scripture. Take the Ten Commandments, for example. Lifted out of the exodus story they sound like any other list of imperatives or moralisms. But as a part of the story they are anything but arbitrary commands. God saw and heard the suffering of the Hebrews in Egyptian slavery. He determined to deliver them and make covenant with them as His chosen people. Patiently he dealt with Pharaoh and Moses until the people finally were liberated. Their peaceful exodus was deceptive. Soon Pharaoh realized that he had lost a large part of his slave work force. He sent his army after them. God led the people across the sea on dry land and the Egyptians perished. He led them across the desert to the place of covenant-making. They complained all along the way. The rigors of life on the road made slavery in Egypt look good to them.

Finally, at Sinai this Redeemer and Provider God offered to make covenant with the people and waited for an answer. They answered in the affirmative. He wanted them to understand what being His people would mean. Identifying Himself as the One who rescued them from Egypt, He stated the ten commandments, The ten words of life. They described who God is and what a healthy covenant community would look like. They were sure they wanted to make covenant. But when Moses was delayed on the mountain they made a golden calf and worshipped it. The story goes on. But the point for us is that the moral guidelines arose out of the goodness and grace of God. Because he loved them, God wanted them to know who He was and how to live together in peace and harmony.

498

Seed Thoughts

1. **What is the difference in moralism and ethics flowing from grace?**
Moralisms depend for action on the hearer's power; biblical ethics depend on God's power in us.

2. **From what situation in his own life did Paul plead for ethical behavior?**
He was, himself, a prisoner for the Lord at the time.

3. **Were Christians and Jews the only people who had lists of ethical standards by which to live?**
No, most philosophers and religious teachers had similar lists.

4. **Why do most people today resist an ethic of giving one's self up for others?**
We live in a world in which the rights, interests and pleasure of "No. 1" come first.

5. **Do grown people need models by which to pattern their lives'?**
Most of us have someone in our own specialized world whom we admire and from whom we learn.

(PLEASE TURN PAGE)

---

1. What is the difference in moralism and ethics flowing from grace?

2. From what situation in his own life did Paul plead for ethical behavior?

3. Were Christians and Jews the only people who had lists of ethical standards by which to live?

4. Why do most people today resist an ethic of giving one's self up for others?

5. Do grown people need models by which to pattern their lives'?

6. Do ethical standards change?

7. What limits should I feel on the exertion of my own rights?

8. Can a person maintain a healthy relationship with God and ignore His calls to ethical behavior?

9. What should we adults say to our teenagers about the dangers of following the crowd?

10. Why does this section of Ephesians end with words about worship and praise in song?

(SEED THOUGHTS--Cont'd)

Moralisms depend for action on the hearer's power; biblical ethics depend on God's power in us.

He was, himself, a prisoner for the Lord at the time.

No, most philosophers and religious teachers had similar lists.

We live in a world in which the rights, interests and pleasure of "No. 1" come first.

Most of us have someone in our own specialized world whom we admire and from whom we learn.

Cultural norms change from year to year, from place to place. The nature of God, however, remains the same forever.

The good of others, the good of the community, the calling of God to help Him with his mission in the world.

No. His calls teach us how to live in a healthy relationship with him.

That we, also, have great peer pressures and can "follow a crowd to do evil."

Because one of the strongest safeguards for ethical living is giving joyful praise appropriate to God.

6. Do ethical standards change?
Cultural norms change from year to year, from place to place. The nature of God, however, remains the same forever.

7. What limits should I feel on the exertion of my own rights?
The good of others, the good of the community, the calling of God to help Him with his mission in the world.

8. Can a person maintain a healthy relationship with God and ignore His calls to ethical behavior?
No. His calls teach us how to live in a healthy relationship with him.

9. What should we adults say to our teenagers about the dangers of following the crowd?
That we, also, have great peer pressures and can "follow a crowd to do evil."

10. Why does this section of Ephesians end with words about worship and praise in song?
Because one of the strongest safeguards for ethical living is giving joyful praise appropriate to God.

August 22, 1993

New Family Order

Ephesians 5
21 Submitting yourselves one to another in the fear of God.
22 Wives, submit yourselves unto your own husbands, as unto the Lord.
23 For the husband is the head of the wife, even as Christ is the head of the church: and he is the saviour of the body.
24 Therefore as the church is subject unto Christ, so let the wives *be* to their own husbands in every thing.
25 Husbands, love your wives, even as Christ also loved the church, and gave himself for it;
26 That he might sanctify and cleanse it with the washing of water by the word,
27 That he might present it to himself a glorious church, not having spot, or wrinkle, or any such thing; but that it should be holy and without blemish.
28 So ought men to love their wives as their own bodies. He that loveth his wife loveth himself.
29 For no man ever yet hated his own flesh; but nourisheth and cherisheth it, even as the Lord the church:
30 For we are members of his body, of his flesh, and of his bones.
31 For this cause shall a man leave his father and mother, and shall be joined unto his wife, and they two shall be one flesh.
32 This is a great mystery: but I speak concerning Christ and the church.
33 Nevertheless let every one of you in particular so love his wife even as himself; and the wife *see* that she reverence *her* husband.

Ephesians 6
CHILDREN, obey your parents in the Lord: for this is right.
2 Honour thy father and mother; which is the first commandment with promise;
3 That it may be well with thee, and thou mayest live long on the earth.
4 And, ye fathers, provoke not your children to wrath: but bring them up in the nurture and admonition of the Lord.

◆◆◆◆◆◆

◀ **Memory Selection**
Ephesians 5:21

◀ **Devotional Reading**
Colossians 3:12-21

◀ **Background Scripture**
Ephesians 5:21-6:4

◀ **Printed Scripture**
Ephesians 5:21-6:4

NEW FAMILY ORDER

Teacher's Target

We live in an age when individual rights and freedoms are strenuously defended. Therefore, it is customary for people to reject the concepts of submission and obedience. Family structure is so loose or missing in some situations that everyone is moving off in his or her own direction. As families weaken, society weakens. This provides a breeding ground for all kinds of social ills.

Help your students to see what Paul taught regarding family unity and mutual support. He called for the operation of both authority and love. Authority was needed to preserve the chain of command from God to father, mother, and children. Love was needed to provide the cohesion of family members. The model to follow was the mysterious relationship binding Christ to His church. What happens there can, with God's help, be repeated in individual Christian families.

Lesson Introduction

It is natural for worldly-minded people to turn to professionals when they are assailed by problems they do not know how to handle. There seems to be an inherent respect for those who have spent long years training in schools of higher education, who have had to secure governmental licenses, and who are set up in impressive offices. Troubled individuals flow to seek the advice of psychiatrists, psychologists, sociologists, criminologists, and other types of counselors. The advice they receive may be helpful, but it may also be useless or even harmful in some cases.

There is a much higher authority than professional counselors, and that is God Himself. Following the principles He laid down long ago, and being led by the Holy Spirit, believers can find help for family living which is unsurpassed. Those principles may raise some people's hackles at first, but once they are understood and applied, they work. Our text today supplies those principles.

Teaching Outline

I. Submission: Eph. 5:21-24
 A. In general: 21
 B. In particular: 22-24
II. Support: Eph. 5:25-33
 A. Announcement: 25a
 B. Analogy: 25b-32
 C. Amalgamation: 33
III. Sensitivity: Eph. 6:1-4
 A. Promise: 1-3
 B. Program: 4

Daily Bible Readings

Mon. The Family before the Curse
Gen. 2:18-25
Tue. The Duties of the Wife
I Pet. 3:1-6
Wed. Submission Exemplified
Phil. 2:1-8
Thu. Marital Mutuality
I Cor. 7:1-8
Fri. The Duties of the Husband
Eph. 5:25-33
Sat. The Duties of Children
Prov. 23:15-25
Sun. The Duties of Parents
Deut. 6:1-9

August 22, 1993

VERSE BY VERSE

I. Submission: Eph. 5: 21-24

A. In general: 21

21. Submitting yourselves one to another in the fear of God.

Begin with Paul's admonition in the latter part of Ephesians 5:18 and then add the subordinate instructions to it— "Be filled with the Spirit; speaking to yourselves in psalms and hymns and spiritual songs, singing and making melody in your heart to the Lord; giving thanks always for all things unto God... submitting yourselves one to another in the fear of God" (Eph. 5:18-21). Submission in general, then, becomes an outgrowth of submission first to the Holy Spirit. It also involves fear of God (or Christ, as many old manuscripts translate it). One paraphrase puts it very simply— "Honor Christ by submitting to each other" (Living Bible). Submission requires believers to be sensitive toward the feelings of others, rather than loudly demanding their rights.

B. In particular: 22-24

22. Wives, submit yourselves unto your own husbands, as unto the Lord.

Throughout Paul's treatment of family relationships, remember that he was describing the ideal. Then, as now, situations might not always be ideal. The husband was supposed to take the lead, and the wife was supposed to follow it. If he was incapable or unwilling to do this, the wife might have to make necessary adjustments. Where the ideal prevailed, the wife could take comfort in knowing that she submitted to her husband because God wanted her to do this.

23. For the husband is the head of the wife, even as Christ is the head of the church: and he is the saviour of the body.

We now come to the model to follow. Even as Christ is the Head of the church and is its Savior, so the Christian husband is to be the head of his wife and give himself for her protection and maintenance. This sets aside any idea that a husband has the right to tyrannize his wife in order to gratify his desires. As we shall see, a study of the whole text provides no support for domination.

24. Therefore as the church is subject unto Christ, so let the wives be to their own husbands in every thing.

Keep in mind that Paul referred to the ideal couple here. Christ wants only the best for His bride the church. A Christian husband should want only the best for his wife. However, suppose that a husband fails God and his wife by asking her to do something sinful. In that case, the wife would be justified in obeying God and refusing to do it. The principal involved is found in Acts 5:29— "We ought to obey God rather than men." In this situation, the woman would have to take the consequences of her brave action and trust God to supply sustaining grace until deliverence comes. Hopefully, it would not take long for the husband to repent of his sin and be restored to his leadership position.

II. Support: Eph. 5:25-33

A. Announcement: 25a.

25a. Husbands, love your wives...

Here is Paul's advice to Christian husbands. It is concise but powerful. He simply tells them to love their wives. This prevents tyranny. It provides protection, praise, and preservation. Emotions can be deceptive, and there may even be situations in which love seems to die or be misplaced. In spite of these threatening possibilities, love from God can be generated to solve these problems.

B. Analogy: 25b-32

25b. ...even as Christ also loved the Church and gave himself up for it;

It was divine love which motivated Christ to love the church and give His life for it. He went to Calvary to shed His precious blood as an atonement for the sins of men. We cannot fathom that love, for it involved One Who was sinless, holy, and enjoying heaven's glory, and yet He was willing to come to earth and humble Himself to death by crucifixion (Phil. 2:5-8). It is this giving quality which Paul said Christian husbands should have for their wives.

26. That he might sanctify and cleanse it with the washing of water by the word,

To sanctify is to set apart from sin and set apart to righteousness. Cleansing through the word finds explanation in a couple of places in John's gospel. Jesus told His disciples, "Now ye are clean through the word which I have spoken unto you," meaning that He had cleansed them of misunderstandings and errors by giving them divine truth (John 15:3) In His high-priestly prayer, Jesus said to His heavenly Father, "Sanctify them through thy truth: thy word is truth" (John 17:17).

27. That he might present it to himself a glorious church, not having spot, or wrinkle, or any such thing; but that it should be holy and without blemish.

Paul knew that the church was not perfect, but he hoped for it to make spiritual progress toward maturity in Christ. In his benediction, Jude described what Christ is doing with His church during this age of grace —"Now unto him that is able to keep you from falling, and to present you faultless before the presence of his glory with exceeding joy, to the only wise God our Saviour, be glory and majesty, dominion and power, both now and ever. Amen." (Jude 24-25). Following the judgment seat of Christ and in marriage of the Lamb to His bride, believers will be clothed in fine, white linen, a symbol of righteousness having no spot, wrinkle, or blemish of any kind (Rom. 14:10-12; Rev. 19:7-9).

28. So ought men to love their wives as their own bodies, He that loveth his wife loveth himself.

Genesis 2:24 and Mark 10:6-9 make it clear that God considers a husband and wife to be one flesh. Therefore, to love one's wife is to love one's own self, and this should guard against exploitation of the wife by the husband.

29. For no man ever yet hated his own flesh; but nourisheth and cherisheth it, even as the Lord the church:

30. For we are members of his body, of his flesh, and of his bones.

God created people with the instinct to survive, and this causes them to take care of their bodies through adequate nourishment and protection whenever possible. Self-abuse and suicide, for example, are aberrations. The same should hold true for a husband's treatment of his wife, for she and he are one. Once again, the model to follow is that of Christ and His church. Verse 30 refers to this as a body, flesh and bones, but Paul was obviously describing the spiritual union which believers have with Christ.

31. For this cause shall a man leave his father and mother, and shall be joined unto his wife, and they two shall be one flesh.

This is a practical observation by Paul. It states that it is natural for a man to leave his father and mother and create a new home with his wife as they face life together.

32. This is a great mystery; but I speak concerning Christ and the church.

The Song of Solomon in the Old Testament described the romance which would come between Christ and His church, but this symbolic meaning was a hidden mystery until it was revealed in New Testament times. We know now that individual members have been continuously added to the bride of Christ since the first century until now, and they will continue to be added during this age of grace until Christ comes again to claim His bride.

C. Amalgamation: 33

33. Nevertheless let every one of you in particular so love his wife even as himself; and the wife see that she

reverence her husband.

The analogy was now over, and in this summary verse Paul reminded his readers on the personal level that a Christian husband and wife should be bound together by mutual love and respect.

III. Sensitivity: Eph. 6:1-4

A. Promise: 1-3

1. Children, obey your parents in the Lord: for this is right.

The emphasis now shifts to the relationship between parents and children in the Christian home. Children were told by Paul to obey their parents "in the Lord," meaning that parents were God's representatives on the earth in this matter. Therefore, obedience to parents was right and just, because God demanded it. There may also be the concept that children should obey their parents when those parents are doing God's will. Little children, of course, have hardly any choice but to do what their parents say. Older children and adolescents may sometimes have to resist obeying a parental order, if it involves sinning. In such cases, the principle of Acts 5:29 would again come into play— "We ought to obey God rather than men it may be that some Christian adult, such as a teacher or the pastor, will have to be consulted in determining how to handle this type of problem.

2. Honour thy father and mother, which is the first commandment with promise;

3. That it may be well with thee, and thou mayest live long on the earth.

Paul's advice to children in a Christian home was that they show honor to their father and mother. This was not only right in God's sight, but it carried a promise with it. In the fifth of the ten commandments it was stated, "Honour thy father and thy mother: that thy days may be long upon the land which the Lord thy God giveth thee" (Exod. 20:12). The "land" was no doubt Canaan, which the Israelites hoped to conquer and settle. Paul changed "land" to "the earth" in Ephesians 6:3 and thus made it applicable to converted Jews and Gentiles everywhere. Obedience to parents produces a sense of wellbeing and holds the promise of long life. Even if a person dies young, he can look forward to eternal life reserved for believers.

B. Program: 4

4a. And ye fathers, provoke not your children to wrath:...

Although children are supposed to obey both parents, the primary responsibility for family discipline and development rests with the father. Paul urged a father to avoid provoking his children to the point of anger on their part. They will become rebellious enough on their own, and he should refrain from irritating and exasperating them by demanding foolish or unreasonable things from them. Smoldering resentment on the part of children can only lead to problems which may become unsolvable.

4b. ...but bring them up in the nurture and admonition of the Lord.

In addition to caring for the physical, material, mental, emotional, and social needs of children, a father should be concerned about the spiritual development they need. He should nourish and admonish them with the principles of God's holy Word, for He is their ultimate Authority.

Evangelistic Emphasis

Nothing is a bigger challenge to us today than the establishment and growth of a good home. Over half the marriages performed end in divorce.

Broken homes result in broken people, at least for a while. Many are permanently scarred. Children are the innocent victims. We have more singles living alone today than ever before, our society and the church have yet to learn their challenges and to integrate them fully.

The "graying of America" is the latest challenge to confront us on the home front. More and more of us ask how we are to deal with aging parents. We have more senior citizens than ever before and the number continues to grow rapidly. Many ask today: "What does Christianity say to me, do for me as I try to make a happy, peaceful, healthy life at home?"

What should the unbeliever see in the Christian home that is not present in other homes? Today almost all well-intentioned people are committed to the development and dignity of every person in the family unit. So what is distinctive about the Christian home? Perhaps the secret, more than anything else, is the approach, method, and power believers have for making the home what it ought to be. Nothing is more distinctive than the key verse of today's lesson: "Be subject to one another out of reverence for Christ." It is precisely because this sentence sounds so foreign to today's reader that we need to look at it closely to find what is distinctive about the Christian home. That distinctiveness will be a powerful magnet to draw the unbeliever to a closer examination of the faith.

◆◆◆◆◆◆

Memory Selection

Submitting yourselves one to another in the fear of God.
Ephesians 5:21

The RSV renders our verse more accurately: "Be subject to one another out of reverence for Christ." This admonition represents what is unique about the Christian home. First, the idea of being subject to another is abhorrent to most people in our society. Kings and Queens have subjects; not husbands and wives. Many will protest strongly that they are subject to no one, they are free as Americans and as Christians. That is not literally true. They are subject to the boss at work, to the rulings of the IRS, even to the policeman who stops them for speeding. The truth is society cannot function without the principle of subjection. The real question is not whether subjection is a fact of life. The real question is how the principle applies in the home.

When Paul wrote these words they were revolutionary to the ears of the first hearers. Not because they resisted the principle of subjection. That principle was self-evident. But because Paul added the phrase "to one another." Wives were always to be subject to husbands, children to parents, slaves to their masters. No one had ever suggested that husbands should be subject in some sense to wives, parents in some way to children, masters to slaves. That idea was unheard of. The principle of reciprocity was founded on reverence for Christ. Somehow Who He was, what He had done, had turned the accepted order of things upside down.

August 22, 1993

Weekday Problems

Don and Judy had problems almost from the first of their marriage. They both grew up in Christian homes and were devoted to the dream of making Christ the center of their lives. Within the first six months they had problems with roles and expectations. Judy was reared in a home where the chores were almost interchangeable between husband and wife. Both her parents could cook and each did prepare evening meals from time to time. Both changed diapers, prepared formula and got up with fussy babies in the middle of the night. She was seen mowing the yard and helping paint the trim on the house. They were professional people. Long before the women's liberation movement these two agreed to share almost every role.

On the other hand, Don came from a farming family where the roles were strictly defined. His father worked from sunup to sunset in the fields. When he came in his dinner was on the table. His mother delighted in making her hard-working man comfortable at the end of the day. Don's father would not have heard of his wife working in the fields, tending the stock, or even doing the heavy yard work. Their roles were clearly defined and they were happy with them. It was predictable that Don and Judy would have some adjustments. They just didn't really know until they got married how deep-rooted their ideas about roles really were.

*Which orientation toward roles is the true, Christian view?
*What would you say to Don? To Judy?

♦♦♦♦♦♦

Superintendent's Sermonette

The modern family is under attack. wife abuse, sexual molestation, and incest are rampant. Alcoholism and drug-addiction are tearing families apart. Domestic quarreling is epidemic.

What role can the Christian family play in the midst of this chaos? Paul's advice, given over nineteen centuries ago, is relevant for us today. He said that every member of a family must take God into account. A good relationship with Him is required in order to develop good relationships with other family members. Wives are to submit to their husbands in the Lord. Husbands are to love their wives as Christ loved the church. Children are to obey their parents in the Lord. Fathers are to bring up their children in the nurture and admonition of the Lord. Christian families need to give the world good examples of how to live for God.

This Lesson For Your Life

We begin with the concept of reciprocity. Why would Paul instruct the Ephesians to "be subject to one another"? First, because he understood that individuals cannot grow and become all they can be while oblivious to others, never bending to the needs of others, never knowing the nurture of others. One distinguished Old Testament scholar observed that God called the people out of Egypt as a large group because "the desert is no place for an isolated individual." Our deserts are not made of sand, they are made of impersonal relationships. Too often we become merely numbers at school, at work, even at church. Psychologists have discovered the paradoxical biblical truth about human development: individuality is only developed out of a strong sense of belonging to a group.

The Christian home is not a place where each one fends for himself or herself. It is not a place where one member is expected to care for and serve another who accepts service but is not willing to serve. Neither vocational demands nor role orientation can excuse self-centeredness on the husband's part. Neither vocational demands nor role orientation can excuse self-centeredness on the wife's part. In the last few decades many Christians have developed a "rights" orientation which has become license for gross selfishness. Christianity is profoundly rights oriented. Paul exhorted the Philippians "do not think only of your own things, but also about the things of others." It is legitimate to think about one's own things; even mandatory.

The unique feature of Christian teaching is that each party is to be jealous for the rights of the other. When each is concerned beyond his or her own rights that the other is respected and loved and cared for, the rights of each are protected far better than if each, thinks only of his or her own things.

The key to reciprocal love is the phrase, "out of reverence for Christ." Perhaps the best place to discover what the spirit of the home should be is one of the gospel stories of Jesus' life. Take, for example, the gospel of Mark. Mark began by saying it was the "beginning of the gospel of the Son of God." One would expect a figure of regal power and glory. In the first half of the book that expectation is rewarded. Jesus came up from the waters of baptism and was pronounced the Son of God. He went into the desert and resisted the devil's temptations. He healed the sick, cast out demons, even calmed the sea. On one occasion he even brought a little girl back from the dead! Crowds were building. The disciples must have been ecstatic about their candidate!

Just then he began to say strange things about going up to Jerusalem to die. Peter rebuked him and was rebuked for presuming to know the plan. Jesus called all who would follow him to take up their crosses. Those who would try to save their lives would lose them. On a mountain top he appeared with Moses and Elijah and something within him shone with incredible brightness, another pronouncement was made from above and for a moment it was clear Who He was. Peter and the others liked that experience and wanted to stay. Jesus took them back down to serve. On down the path toward Jerusalem twice more He told them He was headed for a cross and resurrection. After the last time James and John asked if they could be his Secretary of State and Secretary of Defense. That's how much they comprehended His mission. He explained His life and mission. His kingdom would not be like others where power and prestige were the name of the game. He came full of authority and stayed to save by serving. His story is the backdrop for every Christian marriage. Out of reverence for Him husbands and wives think not only of themselves but of each other.

Seed Thoughts

1. What is the difference between "subjection" and "subjugation"?
Subjugation is being put down, subjection in the biblical sense is refusing to play God, the Center of the universe.

2. How is the husband's role to be compared to Christ's relationship to the church?
He gives himself in relationship to his wife, concerned for her welfare.

3. How can a couple in marriage know intimacy and retain their identity as persons?
Each is made in God's image, in Christ they can be one and remain two.

4. Why would Paul in an exalted letter on the church and God's cosmic plan take time to teach about the home?
Because exalted truth is meant to bless everyday relationships.

5. Whose responsibility is it to nuture up the children in the Lord, according to Paul?
The fathers role is to teach the faith and nuture up the children.

(PLEASE TURN PAGE)

---

1. What is the difference between "subjection" and "subjugation"?

2. How is the husband's role to be compared to Christ's relationship to the church?

3. How can a couple in marriage know intimacy and retain their identity as persons?

4. Why would Paul in an exalted letter on the church and God's cosmic plan take time to teach about the home?

5. Whose responsibility is it to nuture up the children in the Lord, according to Paul?

6. What part are the children to play in the Christian family?

7. Is Paul teaching an unrealistic ideal in this passage on the home?

8. What safeguards the lives of children in this teaching?

9 Where can one find the self-worth to give without giving it all away?

10. What is the relationship between roles in a home and the dignity of the individuals involved?

(SEED THOUGHTS--Cont'd)

Subjugation is being put down, subjection in the biblical sense is refusing to play God, the Center of the universe.

He gives himself in relationship to his wife, concerned for her welfare.

Each is made in God's image, in Christ they can be one and remain two.

Because exalted truth is meant to bless everyday relationships.

The fathers role is to teach the faith and nuture up the children.

They are to obey their parents in the Lord.

No, he is not calling flawed human beings to be Christ, he is calling them to live out of reverence for Christ.

That same motive which is to guide the marriage, reverence for Christ, recalling how he treated little ones.

The biblical bases of self-worth are: made in God's image and redeemed at the cross.

Our self-worth should not be defined by roles. Irksome tasks should be shared by all.

6. What part are the children to play in the Christian family?
They are to obey their parents in the Lord.

7. Is Paul teaching an unrealistic ideal in this passage on the home?
No, he is not calling flawed human beings to be Christ, he is calling them to live out of reverence for Christ.

8. What safeguards the lives of children in this teaching?
That same motive which is to guide the marriage, reverence for Christ, recalling how he treated little ones.

9 Where can one find the self-worth to give without giving it all away?
The biblical bases of self-worth are: made in God's image and redeemed at the cross.

10. What is the relationship between roles in a home and the dignity of the individuals involved?
Our self-worth should not be defined by roles. Irksome tasks should be shared by all.

August 29, 1993

"YE SHALL RECEIVE POWER..."

New Strength

Ephesians 6
10 Finally, my brethren, be strong in the Lord, and in the power of his might.
11 Put on the whole armour of God, that ye may be able to stand against the wiles of the devil.
12 For we wrestle not against flesh and blood, but against principalities against powers, against the rulers of the darkness of this world, against spiritual wickedness in high *places*.
13 Wherefore take unto you the whole armour of God, that ye may be able to withstand in the evil day, and having done all, to stand.
14 Stand therefore, having your loins girt about with truth, and having on the breast-plate of righteousness;
15 And your feet shod with the preparation of the gospel of peace;
16 Above all, taking the shield of faith, wherewith ye shall be able to quench all the fiery darts of the wicked.
17 And take the helmet of salvation, and the sword of the spirit, which is the word of God:
18 Praying always with all prayer and supplication in the Spirit, and watching thereunto with all perseverance and supplication for all saints;
19 And for me, that utterance may be given unto me, that I may open my mouth boldly, to make known the mystery of the gospel,
20 For which I am an ambassador in bonds: that therein I may speak boldly, as I ought to speak.

◆◆◆◆◆◆

◀ **Memory Selection**
Ephesians 6:10

◀ **Background Scripture**
Ephesians 6:10-20

◀ **Devotional Reading**
II Timothy 2:1-13

◀ **Printed Scripture**
Ephesians 6:10-20

NEW STRENGTH

Teacher's Target

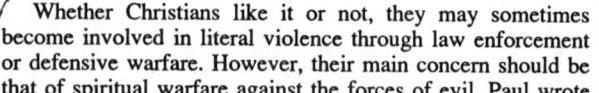

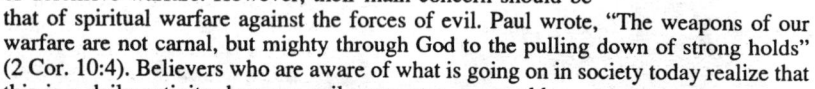

Whether Christians like it or not, they may sometimes become involved in literal violence through law enforcement or defensive warfare. However, their main concern should be that of spiritual warfare against the forces of evil. Paul wrote, "The weapons of our warfare are not carnal, but mighty through God to the pulling down of strong holds" (2 Cor. 10:4). Believers who are aware of what is going on in society today realize that this is a daily activity, because evil permeates our world.

Help your students to know how to be strong in the Lord and to be familiar with both the defensive armor and offensive weapon needed for spiritual warfare. Never underestimate the enemy and his hosts nor treat them in a frivolous manner. Unseen powers are more dangerous than visible ones. Use of the spiritual armor and weapon available must be accompanied by the resource of prayer in the Spirit for ourselves and for other believers. Confidence comes through knowing we are on the winning side.

Lesson Introduction

The Apostle Paul absorbed a tremendous amount of punishment for Christ's sake during his years of ministry. His remarkable record is found in II Corinthians 11:23-28. He did hard manual labor. He bore innumerable stripes from beatings. He was imprisoned. His life was often threatened. He was stoned. He suffered shipwreck, including a night and day in the deep. He was imperiled in his many travels by floods, robbers, savages, Jewish antagonists, and false brethren. He endured weariness, pain, sleepless nights, hunger, thirst, cold, and nakedness. He was burdened by care for all of the churches he founded and nourished spiritually.

Through it all we have no reference to Paul striking back with literal blows, although he did speak up for what was right. He was not a coward or wimp, but his responses were spiritual and had the power of God behind them. He and his companions survived their challenges through daily renewal of their inner selves (II Cor. 4:16). Here is the model for believers to follow today.

Teaching Outline

I. Admonition: Eph. 6:10-12
   A. Resource: 10-11a
   B. Reason: 11b-12
II. Armor: Eph. 6:13-17
   A. Completeness: 13
   B. Components: 14-17
III. Ambassador: Eph. 6:18-20
   A. Prayer for others: 18
   B. Prayer for Paul: 19-20

Daily Bible Readings

Mon. Our Enemy
Matt. 4:1-11
Tue. Our Position
Eph. 1:1-6
Wed. Our Power
Eph. 1:9-23
Thu. Our Weapon
II Cor. 10:1-6
Fri. Our Consecration
II Tim. 2:1-5
Sat. Our Security
Eph. 6:13-17
Sun. Our Victory
Heb. 2:9-15

VERSE BY VERSE

I. Admonition: Eph. 6:10-12

A. Resource: 10-11a

10. Finally, my brethren, be strong in the Lord, and in the power of his might.
Paul was ready to conclude his letter to believers in Ephesus, and there was one final subject on his mind, namely that of spiritual warfare. He urged his readers to be strong in the Lord and in the power of His unlimited might, not in their own limited strength. His emphasis was first placed on the power of God and then on the power of Satan and his hosts (vs. 12). It was obvious that Paul felt believers could tap into God's divine power in order to deal with the forces of evil. This was to be done by daily dependence on the indwelling Holy Spirit (Acts 1:8; Rom. 15:13).

11a. Put on the whole armour of God,...
Paul made it clear that there was spiritual armor available to believers, and it was their privilege and responsibility to put it on by an act of faith. That armor is described in detail in verses 14-17 and will be studied later in this lesson. It was sufficient at this point to know that the armor was from God Himself. Now we come to the reason for putting on the armor.

B. Reason: 11b-12

11b. . . that ye may be able to stand against the wiles of the devil,
Opinions regarding Satan are wide-ranging. Some refuse to believe he exists. Some think of him as merely a symbol to suggest evil, perhaps viewing him as a red-skinned, evil-eyed monster, with a pitchfork and a forked tail. Some worship him. Some are possessed by him or by other demons. He is known to oppress and obsess others. The Bible states that he and his hosts pose a dire threat to all people, whether they are saved or unsaved, and he must be resisted by those whom he influences (Jas. 4:7). Contrary to cartoon representation of him, Satan can transform himself into "an angel of light" (II Cor. 11:14). Paul warned believers to stand firmly against his wiles directed at them in the spiritual realm. They were warned not to become vulnerable to his subtle ways.

12. For we wrestle not against flesh and blood, but against principalities, aginst powers, against the rulers of the darkness of this world, against spiritual wickedness in high places.
Paul knew about hostile human enemies of flesh and blood, but he was more concerned about hostile spiritual enemies who could not be seen. He referred to Satan and other demons as principalities, powers, rulers of this world's darkness, and spiritual wickedness in high places. It is interesting that there is a current surge of attention being paid to them. Discussion of the occult is no longer considered taboo, and some people are busy promoting it to the general public.

Caution your students to avoid dabbling in these things, even for the sake of curiosity or research. They can *study* about them, but they ought not to experiment personally *in* them, for they can become confused or perhaps even committed.

II. Armor: Eph. 6:13-17

A. Completeness: 13

13. Wherefore take unto you the whole armour of God, that ye may be able to withstand in the evil day, and

having done all, to stand.

Having warned believers against Satan and his demons, Paul now returned to his reference to the armor of God which should be put on by believers (vs. 11). He made the point here that it was the whole armor which should be put on, rather than only certain parts of it. This advice had to be heeded if believers hoped to be able to hold their ground against Satan and his demons on any day in which they might bring evil against them. If they did as they were told, they would be left standing when the dust of spiritual battle settled.

B. Components: 14-17

14a. Stand therefore, having your loins girt about with truth,...

The first part of the armor mentioned was truth. The literal symbol for it was a belt or sash into which a soldier's outer garment might be tucked as he prepared for battle. Lies and errors were to be warded off by truth. Peter wrote, "Gird up the loins of your mind, be sober, and hope to the end for the grace that is to be brought unto you at the revelation of Jesus Christ" (I Pet. 1:13). Believers gird up their minds by studying the Holy Scriptures and learning how to apply it in all kinds of circumstances.

14b. ... and having on the breastplate of righteousness; The second part of the armor was righteousness.

The symbol for it was a breastplate covering the soldier's heart, normally thought of as the center of emotion. Proverbs 4:23 says, "Keep thy heart with all diligence; for out of it are the issues of life." Righteousness has to be internal, imparted by God, and then it can work its way out to deal with evils attacking it. Only a person with a righteous testimony can have a positive influence on the sinful world-system.

15. And your feet shod with the preparation of the gospel of peace;

The third part of the armor was a readiness to spread the gospel. The symbol for it was a pair of shoes worn by the soldier. It is likely that Paul was thinking of Isaiah 52:7 here— "How beautiful upon the mountains are the feet of him that bringeth good tidings, that publisheth peace; that bringeth good tidings of good, that publisheth salvation; that saith unto Zion, Thy God reigneth!" Paul would adapt this to imply that those who bear the gospel give it to all the world.

16. Above all, taking the shield of faith, wherewith ye shall be able to quench all the fiery darts of the wicked.

The fourth part of the armor was faith. The symbol for it was a shield, an instrument of protection held up to stop penetration of enemy darts or arrows toward any part of the body. The term "above all" referred to this function of covering whatever part was exposed. Faith was to be used to defeat Satan's attempts to discourage or frustrate a believer's determination to serve God.

17a. And take the helmet of salvation,...

The fifth part of the armor was salvation. The symbol for it was a helmet. Elsewhere, Paul called a helmet "the hope of salvation" (1 Thess. 5:8). This is a sure hope for the Christian soldier, and it helps protect him from spiritual attacks by the enemy. Ideas contrary to the gospel will be deflected by it.

17b. .. and the sword of the Spirit, which is the word of God:

The sixth part of the armor was the word of God. The literal symbol for it was a sword. Note that all the other parts were defensive, whereas this one was offensive, although it could also be defensive. There might be room for making prayer offensive, as well, with the sword being "of the Spirit" and prayer being "in the Spirit" (vs. 18) Christians in the first century had the Old Testament to use in their warfare and could follow the skillful example of Jesus when He used it to defeat Satan's temptations in the wilderness (Matt. 4:1-11; Luke 4:1-13). They were also gaining use of the New Testament which was then in the process of being formed. Both the Old and New Testaments are in the completed revelation of God's Word and are available for us to use today. The Holy Spirit inspired the formation of the whole Bible, and He guides Christian soldiers in understanding it, believing it, and applying it.

III. Ambassador: Eph. 6:18-20

A. Prayer for others: 18

18a. Praying always with all prayer and supplication in the Spirit,...

Paul saw spiritual armor as a divine resource for believers to use on a regular basis in their warfare against Satan and wicked men. He also saw prayer as a divine resource for believers to use on a continual basis. The term "prayer" referred to prayer in general. The term "supplication" referred to petition. Praying "in the Spirit" was necessary in order that believers might adhere to the will of God (Rom. 8:26-27; 1 John 5:14-15), thus assuring them of positive responses.

18b. ... and watching thereunto with all perseverance and supplication for all saints;

The "watching" here referred to alertness on the part of believers. They were to persevere in knowing the needs of others, and in praying (petitioning) God to meet those needs.

B. Prayer for Paul: 19-20

19. And for me, that utterance may be given unto me, that I may open my mouth boldly, to to make known the mystery of the gospel,

While they prayed for others, Paul requested the Ephesian believers to pray for him, too. He was anxious to testify about Jesus Christ. He wanted his mouth to be filled with the right words, presented in the right tone, and characterized by holy boldness. His message was to be "the mystery of the gospel," meaning it was divine truth once withheld but now revealed for all to hear. Paul knew that the boldness he wanted could come only from the Holy Spirit. For examples of this, see Acts 2:4, 4:8, and 4:31.

20. For which I am an ambassador in bonds: that therein I may speak boldly, as I ought to speak.

Although Paul was a prisoner in Rome for Christ's sake, he did not count this as a liability. He saw in this situation an opportunity which he might not have otherwise had. He used this terminology in 2 Corinthians 5:20— "Now then we are ambassadors for Christ, as though God did beseech you by us: we pray you in Christ's stead, be ye reconciled to God." Those who went out to spread the gospel had to realize that they might not be treated with the diplomatic immunity enjoyed by earthly ambassadors, but their eternal rewards would be greater. Paul wanted to do his work well so that he could be commended by God when his earthly ministry ended and he moved on to his heavenly reward.

NEW STRENGTH

Evangelistic Emphasis

There is something powerfully attractive about a person who survives and wins over evil in this mixed-up world. That is especially true if that person has no odor of arrogance about him or her. Whatever the secret, the person does not seem to take credit, sometimes does not even seem aware of the achievement. This person does not win by his or her own wit and strength alone. There seems to be an invisible source of power. All people, whether religious or not, wrestle with moral decisions. Their moral dilemmas are defined by their codes of ethics and may not be the same as we have, but they face struggles just the same.

All of us lose battles from time to time and suffer the consequences. Yet, there are some who endure the storms "with no visible means of support." They do not look different from anyone else. They are not shielded from the "slings and arrows of outrageous fortune." These people can hurt and bleed, suffer and cry out like anyone else. Yet they come back, almost as if resurrected. They make mistakes in judgment, errors in calculation, have moral failures and suffer the consequences like the rest of humanity. But they have something which keeps them from sinking into the depths of despair. Through it all they have an abiding sense of their own worth; not based in themselves but somewhere else. They seem to know of a resource others have not found, a fountain of living waters others do not know. Their answers are not in themselves but come from outside. Consequently, there is no pride or arrogance, only gratitude. The sweet disposition and lack of posturing is a powerful witness to unbelievers. They are "strong in the Lord and in the strength of his might."

Memory Selection

"Finally, my brethren, be strong in the Lord, and the power of His might."
Ephesians 6:10

Paul was evidently not a strong person physically. He had some kind of "thorn in the flesh" which continually irritated him and made his work more difficult. Nor was he a paragon of mental health who always had everything in perspective. He got low and depressed like the rest of us. However, through it all, he learned the secret of a victorious spiritual life. He learned how to have much and how to have little, how to be up and to be down without losing his faith or failing his opportunities to serve others.

We would all do well to study this subject in Scripture to find the answer for our limitations in facing life. Three Bible characters show us the alternatives concerning self-confidence. Moses resisted God's call to deliver the people because he did not feel equal to the task. God explained that He never intended to send Moses alone to do the job. Peter pledged his undying loyalty to Jesus. The others might forsake him, but Peter knew he had what it took to remain faithful. Then he denied the Lord three times before the night was over. Moses said: "I can't." Peter said: "I can." Both were wrong. By painful experience Paul found the answer: "I can do all things through Christ who strengthens me." So he was speaking from his own experience when he admonished the Ephesians: "Be strong in the Lord and in the strength of His might."

August 29, 1993

Weekday Problems

From morning till night Linda never stopped. She had a highly pressurized job in a legal firm as secretary to the most productive lawyer in the firm. He billed the most hours, won the most cases, and made the most money for the firm. By definition, whatever he wanted everyone scurried to provide. She liked him personally, he was good to her and amply rewarded her for her work.

Yet there was a problem. Another reason for his productivity and winning record was his lack of moral sense. His motto was: "Whatever it takes to win." He would distort evidence, hold back vital information from opposing lawyers, bill for hours he did not really spend on cases. All of this involved Linda. She was there to do whatever he asked of her. The problem is that she had a conscience developed in a Christian home. Day by day she worried more and more about her involvement and her responsibility to speak to him about his practices. She thought about the problem, talked to others who shared her value system, lost nights of sleep tossing and turning. No matter how disturbing his activities she found no strength to take action. She could neither resign nor speak to him about his ways of doing business.

*Where could Linda find the strength to face up to her situation?
*What practical daily steps might she take to gain strength for coping?

♦♦♦♦♦♦

Superintendent's Sermonette

We live in an age when war is denounced as stupid, brutal, wasteful, and wrong. Peace movements proliferate. Efforts to stave off hostilities include frantic diplomatic missions, threats of economic sanctions, and regional military maneuvers. Alliances are formed between nations.

The United Nations organization goes into emergency sessions and produces its resolutions. Clashes seem inevitable, however, and confrontations are going on around the world continually. Political realignments proceed at a dizzying pace.

It is against this background in world events that Christians must define their objectives and the means to be used in achieving them. They do want to conquer the world for Christ, but they know that this is not to be done with carnal weapons. A tremendous war is being waged for the souls of people everywhere, and it demands the best that soldiers of the cross can bring to it.

Let us not be lulled into thinking that we can ever sit back and relax when it comes to spiritual warfare. We must fight Satan's temptations personally, and we must strive to get the gospel out to the ends of the earth. None of this will be easy, but divine protection and power is available.

This Lesson For Your Life

A professor of ethics who attended public grade school in the southern United States told of his early education. His classmates came from a variety of denominations: Catholic, Protestant and Jewish. He remarked that it might have been called a public parochial school. The reason was that, despite differences of religious tradition, there was a broad and deep consensus about matters of morality. Everyone knew what was right and what was wrong. All the students knew and most accepted the rules. Parents did not hesitate to correct the child of another family because they would expect the same from them. He went on to say that such is hardly the case today. We live in a pluralistic society with no broad and deep consensus on ethical standards.

When Christians who are now forty or more were in Sunday School Paul's words about "putting on the whole armor of God" may have sounded strange. What did we need armor for? We were not embattled. It is so today. One knowledgeable professor of church history has observed that we are living in an atmosphere closer to the situation of the first century church than any culture of any century since. When one reads daily of drug abuse, drug-related killings, joy killings, corruption in high places, the deterioration of the home, organized crime, gang wars and all the rest he begins to wonder if the "whole armor of God" would not be appropriate for survival.

In our context Paul's words seem to take on new and powerful meaning: "For our struggle is not against enemies of blood and flesh, but against the rulers, against the authorities, against the cosmic power of this present darkness, against the spiritual forces of evil in the heavenly places."

Our children experience more of the dark side of life before they are out of junior high than we experienced all the way through college. At the same time the work place is not what it was just a few years ago. From professional people, business people, people in education one hears it repeatedly, "You just can't take anyone at his word anymore. He may have some agenda he considers more important than the truth." Most disturbing of all, sometimes we get the uneasy feeling that years of exposure to the secular culture may have eroded some of our own deepest convictions. Without knowing it we may have bought too deeply into the "what works is good" ethos of modern culture.

From the text in Ephesians we ask what the medicine is for our growing infection. It's not unfamiliar. All of it comes under Paul's familiar prescription: faith, hope, and love. He admonishes us to take the whole armor of God so that "having done everything," "when the smoke clears" we will still be standing. Truth is our belt, perhaps we should think of those broad strong belts the weight lifters use. It is there for support and to hold us together. The breastplate of righteousness protects our vital organs. We are protected, not by our own righteousness, but by God's goodness given to us at Golgotha. Because of what Christ has done we need not shrink back from anyone. The gospel protects our feet from the rough road and gives us peace. The shield of faith, trusting always in God and not in ourselves, protects us against the accusations of the Evil One that we are unworthy. Salvation, security in Christ, protects our heads like a helmet. The only weapon which is offensive is the word of God. We use it not to slay sinners but to help rescue them from the Evil One. We are given all we need to survive and help others to survive the darkness of this world.

Seed Thoughts

1. Is strength a Christian virtue or does faith in Christ mean disavowing strength?
As with our physical existence, without strength we cannot stand up and function.

2. Is there really a force of evil in the world or just the absence of good like cold is the absence of heat?
According to Scripture, there is a real force who would destroy us.

3. Are the force of evil and the Force for good in the world equal in power?
The Bible assures us that God is greater than Satan in power.

4. Is the battle between good and evil still undecided?
No, on Good Friday and Easter Sunday the decisive battle was won and we know how the story ends.

5. How is it, then, that Christians sometimes go down in defeat to the Evil One?
Because they try to take him on in their own strength and not in the Lord's might.

(PLEASE TURN PAGE)

---

1. Is strength a Christian virtue or does faith in Christ mean disavowing strength?

2. Is there really a force of evil in the world or just the absence of good like cold is the absence of heat?

3. Are the force of evil and the Force for good in the world equal in power?

4. Is the battle between good and evil still undecided?

5. How is it, then, that Christians sometimes go down in defeat to the Evil One?

6. Can one always tell from the suffering of a Christian whether he is winning or losing?

7. What is the main purpose for the armor of God explained in Ephesians six?

8. What place has prayer in the battle raging in and around us?

9. What is probably the main reason we Christians fail to arm ourselves for battle and to rescue others?

10. What can safeguard us from becoming crazed, trigger-happy warriors for God?

(SEED THOUGHTS--Cont'd)

As with our physical existence, without strength we cannot stand up and function.

According to Scripture, there is a real force who would destroy us.

The Bible assures us that God is greater than Satan in power.

No, on Good Friday and Easter Sunday the decisive battle was won and we know how the story ends.

Because they try to take him on in their own strength and not in the Lord's might.

No, ours is a resurrection faith; not even death is the last word with God.

The armor is given to preserve God's children in the battle and to arm them for rescuing others.

Paul encouraged the Ephesians to pray for all the saints, especially those who witness in difficult and dangerous situations.

Most likely it is our ignorance that a battle is raging above our heads.

A confidence that the decisive battle is won, we are privileged to be a part of the "mopping up" action.

6. Can one always tell from the suffering of a Christian whether he is winning or losing?
No, ours is a resurrection faith; not even death is the last word with God.

7. What is the main purpose for the armor of God explained in Ephesians six?
The armor is given to preserve God's children in the battle and to arm them for rescuing others.

8. What place has prayer in the battle raging in and around us?
Paul encouraged the Ephesians to pray for all the saints, especially those who witness in difficult and dangerous situations.

9. What is probably the main reason we Christians fail to arm ourselves for battle and to rescue others?
Most likely it is our ignorance that a battle is raging above our heads.

10. What can safeguard us from becoming crazed, trigger-happy warriors for God?
A confidence that the decisive battle is won, we are privileged to be a part of the "mopping up" action.